KT-442-339

INDIAN OCEAN

Andasibe-Mantadia National Park
page 257

Ranomafana National Park
page 190

Antananarivo (Tana)
page 139

Avenue des Baobabs
page 397

Isalo National Park
page 206

Toliara (Tulear)
page 211

Berenty Reserve
page 240

KEY
■ Capital city
● Main town
○ Other town/village
Main road
Railway
Road in poor condition
National Park (NP),
Special Reserve (SR) or
other protected area
● Other site

20°S
25°S
45°E
50°E

Tropic of Capricorn

Brickaville (Ampasimanolotra)
Ambilo-Lematso
Vatomandry
Mahanoro
RN2
Ambatolampy
Mananjary
Jalatsara Lemur Forest Camp
Manakara
Ranomafana NP
RN45
RN12
Vohipeno
Farafangana
Vangaindrano
(TANA) Moramanga
Lemurs' Park
Miarinarivo
Tsiroanomandidy
RN1
Tsirafovona 2643m
Betafo
Ansirabe
RN34
RN7
Ambositra
Ambohimahasoa
Fianarantsoa (Fianar)
Ambalavao
Andringitra NP
Imarivolanitra (Boby) 2658m
Ivohibe
Manombo SR
Midongy Atsimo
Midongy du Sud NP
Manantenina
Bekopaka
Mandrivazo
Andranomena SR
RN35
Malaimbandy
Ambatofinandrahana
Ihosy
Betroka
Mandena Conservation Zone
Taolagnaro (Fort Dauphin)
RN13
Lac Anony Site of Biological Interest
Belo sur Tsiribihina
Kirindy Reserve
Mahabo
Kirindy-Mitea NP
Mandabe
Beroroha
RN7
Ranohira
Isalo NP
Zombitse-Vohibasia NP
Berenty Reserve
Ambovombe
Avenue des Baobabs
Belo sur Mer
Morondava
Manja
Mongoky
Beza-Mahafaly SR
Bezaha
Beraketa
Ejeda
Andohahela NP
Morombe
Mitsinjoriaka 1348m
Sakaraha
RN7
Betioky
RN10
Ampanihy
Cap Sainte Marie SR
Tsiombe
Cap Sainte Marie
Ifaty
Toliara (Tulear)
Anakao
Lake Tsimanampetsotsa NP
Itampolo

Madagascar
Don't
miss...

Rainforests
Montagne d'Ambre
National Park is a fine
example of montane
rainforest
(DA) page 334

Avenue des Baobabs
These majestic trees make
for a curious landscape
(DA) page 397

Madagascar

the Bradt Travel Guide

Hilary Bradt

Updated by
Daniel Austin

edition
10

www.bradtguides.com

Bradt Travel Guides Ltd, UK
The Globe Pequot Press Inc, USA

45°E
50°E
15°S
15°S
N
Bradt
0 100km
0 100 miles
INDIAN
OCEAN
Mozambique
Channel
Montagne d'Ambre National Park
page 334
Nosy Be
page 349
Anjajavy
page 381
Masoala National Park & Nosy Mangabe
pages 296–301
Ile Sainte Marie
page 315
Cap Ambre
Antsiranana
(Diego Suarez)
Montagne d'Ambre NP
Montagne d'Ambre
1475m
Analamera SR
Ankarana NP
Daraina
Ambilobe
Nosy Be
Andoany
(Hell-Ville)
RN6
Iharana
(Vohemar)
Ambanja
Maromokotro
2876m
RN5a
Maromandia
Sambava
Doany
Marojejy NP
Anjanaharibe-Sud SR
Andapa
Analalava
Antsohihy
Antalaha
Anjajavy Reserve
Cap Est
RN6
Maroantsetra
Mahalevona
Mahajanga
(Majunga)
Nosy Mangabe SR
Masoala NP
Baie de Baly NP
Rantabe
Antongil Bay
Mandritsara
Soalala
Marovoay
Ankarafantsika NP
Aye-Aye Island
Ankofa
1301m
Mananara
Mananara-Nord NP
RN4
Besalampy
Manompana
Soanierana-Ivongo
Ile Sainte Marie (Nosy Boraha)
Maevatanana
Ambodifotatra
RN5
Lac Alaotra Site of
Biological Interest
Fénérive (Fenoarivo Atsinanana)
Zahamena NP
Andriamena
Ikopa
Parc Ivoloina
RN4
Maintirano

Lemurs
Coquerel's sifaka is one of more than a hundred varieties of lemur, all endemic to Madagascar
(DA) page 59

Beaches
Glorious tourist-free sandy beaches are easy to find
(DA) page 82

The chance to give something back
Responsible tourism and volunteering opportunities mean you can do your bit through numerous community and conservation projects
(HB) page 132

left RN5: even many 'main' roads are verging on impassable! (DA) page 94

below left The train from Fianarantsoa to Manakara passes through tiny villages amid stunning scenery (DA) page 190

below right *Taxi-brousses* offer an affordable means of travelling long distances (DA) page 94

bottom The rubber-tyred Micheline railcar is the only one in the world still running a regular service (DW) page 252

right   Rice paddies: the Malagasy eat more rice per head than anyone else (DA) page 184

below left   Zebu are used as beasts of burden throughout the country (DA) page 196

below right   Sakalava burial, northwest. The boat-shaped coffin was broken open in a cyclone (HB) page 18

bottom   Market in a remote village (DA)

above   Sorting cloves to ensure they are export quality. Up to 16,000 tonnes are exported each year (DA)

left   Traditional Antaimoro paper is decorated with flowers (DA) page 195

bottom   Tea pickers on Sahambavy Tea Estate. Most of the tea produced is exported to Kenya (DA) page 189

AUTHOR

Hilary Bradt's career as an occupational therapist ended when potential employers noticed that the time taken off for travel exceeded the periods of employment. With her former husband George, she self-published her first guidebook in 1974 during an extended journey through South America. As well as running Bradt Travel Guides, Hilary worked for 25 years as a tour leader in Madagascar. Her in-depth knowledge of the country has brought her lecture engagements at the Royal Geographical Society, the Smithsonian Institution and on board expedition cruise ships, as well as numerous commissions for travel  articles. She now lives in semi-retirement in Devon and is delighted to hand over the hard graft of researching this new edition to Daniel Austin.

UPDATER

Daniel Austin was fascinated by Madagascar before he even realised it. He developed a deep interest in flora and fauna from a young age, so it was only a matter of time before he noticed one name occurring particularly frequently in connection with the most bizarre lifeforms. Thus his love affair with the island began, and a voyage of discovery revealed Madagascar's curiosities to extend beyond botanical and zoological wonders to geological, historical, linguistic and cultural surprises too.

Over the past five years, Daniel has spent more than twelve months exploring and photographing Madagascar, and feels privileged to have been entrusted with the responsibility of writing the updated version of this award-winning guidebook. Daniel is also founder of the Madagascar Library project (*www.madagascar-library.com*), a committee member of the Anglo-Malagasy Society, and editor of Bradt's *Madagascar Wildlife* guide (see ad after page 408).

Tenth edition March 2011
First published 1988

Bradt Travel Guides Ltd, 23 High Street, Chalfont St Peter, Bucks SL9 9QE, England
www.bradtguides.com
Published in the USA by The Globe Pequot Press Inc, PO Box 480, Guilford, Connecticut
06437-0480

ISBN-13: 978 1 84162 341 2
British Library Cataloguing in Publication Data
A catalogue record for this book is available from the British Library

Photographs Daniel Austin (DA); Hilary Bradt (HB); Nick Garbutt: NHPA
(NG/NHPA), Nature Picture Library (NG/NPL); Piotr Naskrecki/FLPA (PN/FLPA);
Donald Wilson (DW)
Front cover Black-and-white ruffed lemur, *Varecia variegata* (DA)
Back cover Boy carrying bananas from market (DA), *Furcifer lateralis* chameleon (DA)
Title page Diademed sifaka, Vakôna, Andasibe (DA), A baobab (DA), Tomato frog (DA)

Illustrations Janet Robinson, Carole Vincer (baobabs)
Maps Alan Whitaker

Typeset from the author's disc by Wakewing
Production managed by Jellyfish Print Solutions; printed in India

Acknowledgements

Throughout this guidebook, 'boxes' written by specialists give the reader background information on a host of subjects. We owe a huge debt of gratitude to these experts for their invaluable contributions. Zoological material was provided by Nick Garbutt (mammals), Alison Jolly, Kara Moses (both lemurs), Frances Kerridge (carnivores), Richard Jenkins (bats), Duncan Murrell (whales), Jonathan Ekstrom (parrots), Bill Love (reptiles), Len de Beer and John Roff (invertebrates). Clare and Johan Hermans, and Gavin Hart enthused on the wonders of Malagasy flora. Conservation issues were covered by Jamie Spencer, Joanna Durbin, Alasdair Harris and Lennart Pyritz. The expertise of Tim Ireland enriched the sections on geology and gemstones. Special thanks go to Dr Jane Wilson-Howarth and Dr Felicity Nicholson for the health and safety chapter; Ailie Tam, Samantha Cameron and Chris Howles provided further medical background. Insights into history and politics came from John Grehan, Matthew Hatchwell and Richard Cowper, as well as Sir Mervyn Brown who has lent his expertise since the very first edition. Specialists in traditional customs, crafts and social issues included Seraphine Tierney Ramanantsoa, Joseph Radoccia, Carrie Antal, Camilla Backhouse, Christina Corbett, Peter Jourdier, Theresa Haine and Ruth Rosselson. Musicologist Paddy Bush offered his expertise with Derek Schuurman, who also authored sections on such diverse subjects as birds, fish, illegal logging and mangosteens. Janice Booth added her helpful tips on getting to grips with the Malagasy language. Specialist advice to mountain bikers was provided by Lex Cumber, Bill French and Julian Cooke. Divers will benefit from the input of Tim Healy, Liz Bomford and Rob Conway. Gordon Rattray added advice on travel for people with disabilities. Entertaining travellers' tales came from Nigel Vardy, Donald Wilson, Rupert Parker, Marko Petrovic, Colin Palmer, Kathryn Goodenough, Kelly Green and Lee Miller.

Many kind people living or working in Madagascar have helpfully provided updates or logistical support. Thanks in this regard go to Franco Andreone, Olivier Behra, An Bollen, Edward Tucker Brown, Len and Sonja de Beer, Daniel De Witt-Peters, Ann Ferrier and Richard Cowper, Neil Cullen, Michel Desclaux, Rainer Dolch, Remi Doomernik, Stuart Edgill, Tiana Maminjanahary Faraniaina, Barry Ferguson, Karen Freeman, Jolijn Geels, Ken and Lorna Gillespie, Chris Inman, Harriet Joao, Gareth Kett, Kyle and Monika Lussier, Paul Racey, Kimberly Baldwin and Colin Radford, Ony Rakotoarivelo, Rakotovazaha, Harrison Rasolomandimby, John Segeritz, Miguel Vences, Rojo Harinala and Mike Wilson, River William Wilson, Laetitia Wittock and Zanarison Zephyrin.

A small army of travellers have written in to share their experiences. Many took the time to write tremendously detailed trip reports for which we are extremely grateful. This book would not be as rich in detail without the eyes and ears of so many helpful readers. Thank you to: Sonja Aebersold, Wendy Applequist, Anne Axel, Freda Barwell, Max Battle, Mike Bertram, Naomi Billingsley, Bart Blaauw,

Bert Blontrock, Valentina Carrabino, Jeremy Carter, Dave Clegg, Eurico Covas, Benjamin de Ridder, Yves Deluz, D-J Demolin, Michel Desclaux, Rosie Dewick, Esther Lutz Donaldson, Klaas Druiter, Carol du Toit, Lynda Duffett, Alex Dunkel, Devin Edmonds, Marie-Noëlle Epars, Emily Ewins, Tony and Stacey Frallicciardi, Charlotte Gill, Rory Graham, Eileen Synnott and Paul Gurn, Sunniva Gylver, Sacha Hannah, E Hanratty, Lynette Hartley, Max Helfer, Lauren Leigh Hinthorne, Freytag Horthy, Danny Hutley, Kate Jackson, Harriet Joao, David Jones, Lucy Kemp, Silvie Koanda, Wara Kocher, Paul and Inbal Kolodziejski, Alice Koski, Hannah Larkin, Sara LeHoullier, Nicole Loi, Lut Maertens, Kathy Majerus, Martin Mamett, Rachele Mariani, Patrick Marks, Laszlo Mate, Marshall McCormick, Callista Meeusen, Heidi and David Mundy, Colm O Driscoll, Susan Opie, Trevor Perry, Paola Petrolati, Alexander Post, Becky and Gareth Rees, P Rennison, Wybe Rood, Oren Salzman, Andrew Satow, Giovanna Savarese, Rogier Schuch, Graham Sherbut, Ian Skelton, Tim Smith, Julia and Kaspar Spörri, Valda Stanley, Nikki Stevens, Susan Stokes, Itziar and Pablo Strubell, Richard Swatman, Rosa Diez Tagarro, Philip Trangmar, Rosanne Turner, Aina Ulvmoen, Miebet van der Poel, Inge and Ron van Oudenallen, Arie van Wjingaarden, Marije Veenstra, Steve Venton, Laszlo Wagner, Jenny Whitehead and Frances Wolferstan.
Misoatra (thank you) to you all!

LIST OF MAPS

Contents

NOTE ABOUT MAPS

Several maps use grid lines to allow easy location of sites. Map grid references are listed in square brackets after listings in the text, with page number followed by grid number, eg: [146 C3].

Introduction

Hilary Bradt

In 1975 I attended a slide show in Cape Town given by a zoo collector who had just returned from a country called Madagascar. By the end of the evening I knew I had to go there. It wasn't just the lemurs; it was the utter otherness of this little-known island that entranced me. So I went, and I fell in love, and I've been returning ever since.

Madagascar has brought me the best of times and the worst of times. I have exalted at the discovery of some of the strangest creatures in the world, laughed at the dancing sifakas and gushed over baby lemurs; I have snorkelled over multicoloured coral and watched a lobster make its cautious way over the seabed; I have made the only footprints on a deserted beach overhung with coconut palms and swum in the sand-warmed sea in the moonlight. I have also endured the misery of 14-hour *taxi-brousse* journeys, the exhausting heat of the lowlands and the unexpectedly cold nights in the highlands. And I have been lost in the rainforest for four days and eaten roasted insects. I have also been robbed on several occasions. Yet all I remember are the good times. Even the insects – treehoppers belonging to the Fulgoridae family if you must know – were tasty! A few years ago someone wrote to me: 'I went for the lemurs, but in the end it's the people I'll remember.' Me too. This is one of the poorest countries in the world, yet the overriding impression is of joy and laughter.

I can hardly remember a time when I wasn't writing this biennial guide. Although the first edition was published in 1988, it was preceded in 1984 by a stapled booklet, *A Glance at Madagascar*, written for the handful of tour operators venturing to send visitors to this woefully haphazard country, then the *No Frills Guide to Madagascar* in 1986.

I never imagined that I would find someone to hand over to, but in 2006 I received 19 pages of impeccable update information along with six newly drawn maps from Daniel Austin following a six-month exploration of Madagascar. He became my 'leading contributor' for the ninth edition of this guide, and has twice returned to Madagascar to update this edition and add to his extensive collection of photographs. Daniel's dedication to the job is illustrated by an email that began: 'Once more the arrival of the postman heralds the dawning of my bedtime.'

Thus the 'I' in this book may be Daniel but mostly it is me. His update is so seamless that even we don't always know where I end and he begins. That's how it should be.

GETTING UPDATED INFORMATION BETWEEN EDITIONS

Madagascar is always changing. Tourist sites open and close; restaurants get new names; hotels are extended, renovated, or even – on occasion – flattened by cyclones. So to keep you up to date with the very latest developments we have created a companion website for this guidebook, where you can find out what's new. Log on to updates.bradtguides.com/madagascar for the most recent Madagascar news.

Part One

GENERAL INFORMATION

GEOGRAPHY

Full name Republic of Madagascar (Repoblikan'i Madagasikara)
Motto Tanindrazana, Fahafahana, Fandrosoana (Fatherland, Liberty, Progress)
Area 587,041km² (world's fourth largest island; 2½ times size of UK)
Capital city Antananarivo (Tana; Tananarive)
Major towns Fianarantsoa, Antsirabe, Toliara (Tulear), Taolagnaro (Fort Dauphin), Toamasina (Tamatave), Mahajanga (Majunga), Antsiranana (Diego Suarez)
Main international airport Ivato Airport, Antananarivo (TNR)
Other main airports Antsiranana (DIE), Mahajanga (MJN), Morondava (MOQ), Nosy Be (NOS), Sambava (SVB), Toamasina (TMM), Taolagnaro (FTU), Toliara (TLE)
Transport 7,617km paved roads; 854km railways; 432km navigable waterways

PRACTICALITIES

Public holidays 1 Jan, 29 Mar, Easter (movable), 1 May, Ascension Day (movable), Whit Monday (movable), 26 Jun, 15 Aug, 1 Nov, 25 Dec, 30 Dec
Time zone 3 hours ahead of GMT (no daylight savings time observed)
Electricity 220 volts, European-style round-pin sockets
Currency Ariary (Ar; MGA)
International dialling code +261 (followed by 20 when calling landlines)
Internet domain extension .mg
Driving side Right
Visa Required by all tourists; available on arrival; max 90 days; prices on page 87

HUMAN STATISTICS

Population 22 million (2011 est); growing at 3% per year
Age structure 0–14yrs 44% of population; 15–64 yrs 53%; 65yrs and over 3%
Life expectancy Male 61 years; female 65 years
Poverty 68% of population live on less than US$1/day; 90% on less than US$2/day
Literacy 69% of over-15s can read and write
Official languages Malagasy, French, English
Religions Indigenous beliefs (52%), Christian (41%), Muslim (7%)

POLITICS AND ECONOMY

Leader Andry Rajoelina (self-appointed president of High Transitional Authority)
Head of government Prime Minister Albert Camille Vital
GDP US$20bn (PPP); US$8.6bn (official exchange rate); US$1,000 (per capita PPP)
Main agriculture Rice, coffee, vanilla, sugarcane, cloves, cocoa, cassava (tapioca), beans, bananas, peanuts, livestock products
Main exports Vanilla, prawns, coffee, sugarcane, cloves, cocoa, pepper, peanuts
Main import partners China (13%), Thailand (12%), Bahrain (7%), France (6%)
Flag Horizontal bands of red and green alongside a vertical white band (the red represents sovereignty, the green stands for hope, and the white for purity)
Independence 26 June 1960 (from France)
National anthem (Translation) Oh our beloved fatherland / Oh good Madagascar / Our love for you will not leave / For you, for you for ever / Bless you, oh creator / This island of our ancestors / To live in peace and joy / Hey! We are truly blessed / Oh our beloved fatherland / We wish to serve you with / The body and heart, spirit that is ours / You are precious and truly deserving / Oh our beloved fatherland / We wish that you will be blessed / So this world's creator / Will be the foundation of your laws.

The Country

GEOGRAPHY

A chain of mountains runs like a spine down the east-centre of the island descending sharply to the Indian Ocean, leaving only a narrow coastal plain. These eastern mountain slopes bear the remains of the dense rainforest which once covered all of the eastern section of the island. The western plain is wider and the climate drier, supporting forests of deciduous trees and acres of savanna grassland. Madagascar's highest mountain is Maromokotro, part of the Tsaratanana Massif, in the north of the island. In the south is the spiny forest.

CLIMATE

Madagascar has a tropical climate: November to March (summer/wet season) is hot with variable rainfall; April to October (winter/dry season) is mainly dry and mild. That said, global climate change is making Madagascar's weather patterns less predictable.

Typically, southwest trade winds drop their moisture on the eastern mountain slopes and blow hot and dry in the west. North and northwest 'monsoon' air currents bring heavy rain in summer, decreasing southward so that the rainfall in Taolagnaro is half that of Toamasina. There are also considerable variations of temperature dictated by altitude and latitude. On the summer solstice of 22 December the sun is directly over the Tropic of Capricorn, and the weather is very warm. June is the coolest month.

Average midday temperatures in the dry season are 25°C (77°F) in the highlands and 30°C (86°F) on the coast. These statistics are misleading, however, since in June the night-time temperature can drop to near freezing in the highlands and it is cool in the south. The winter daytime

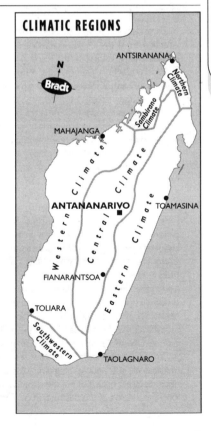

CLIMATIC REGIONS

N

Bradt

ANTSIRANANA

Northern Climate

Sambirano Climate

MAHAJANGA

Western Climate

Central Climate

Eastern Climate

ANTANANARIVO

TOAMASINA

FIANARANTSOA

TOLIARA

Southwestern Climate

TAOLAGNARO

temperatures are very pleasant, and the hot summer season is usually tempered by cool breezes on the coast.

Madagascar frequently suffers from cyclones, especially during February and March, and primarily down the east coast (see the box below).

The map and chart in this section give easy reference to the driest and wettest months and regions, but remember: even in the rainiest months there will be sunny intervals, and in the driest there may be heavy showers. For more advice on the best months to visit Madagascar see *When to visit, Chapter 4*.

CLIMATIC REGIONS

West Rainfall decreases from north to south, with day/night temperatures more variable in the south. The zone is usually quite dry from May to mid-December. Annual rainfall ranges from 36cm in Toliara to 152cm in Mahajanga.

Central Both temperature and rainfall are influenced by altitude. Day/night temperatures in Antananarivo vary by 14°C. The major rainy season usually starts at the end of November. Antsirabe has the highest average annual rainfall (140cm) in this zone.

East In the northeast and central areas rarely does a week pass without rain; but drier, more settled weather prevails in the southeast. Reasonably dry months:

CYCLONES   *Daniel Austin*

Madagascar has always suffered from cyclones, which generally receive scant attention from the English-speaking media. In the decade to 2010 a total of 23 cyclones made landfall on the island, with varying levels of destruction.

In May 2003 a late cyclone, **Manou**, destroyed almost all the buildings in Vatomandry and Brickaville, claiming 89 lives. The following year **Elita** struck in the northwest then crossed the country twice, killing 33, then barely a month later Madagascar was struck near Antalaha by **Gafilo**, the most intense cyclone to form in the Indian Ocean since records began. Its 160mph winds resulted in at least 363 deaths, over 250,000 left homeless, and damage estimated at US$250 million. In 2005 cyclones **Ernest** and **Felapi** hit the Toliara region within five days of one another. The combined death toll was 233. **Indlala** was the next major cyclone, resulting in 276 dead or missing after it struck the northeast coast in March 2007. Then in 2008, **Ivan** caused devastation around Toamasina and Ile Sainte Marie, resulting in 93 fatalities and rendering some 190,000 homeless.

It is often said that Madagascar's cyclone season is January to March and its cyclone region is the east coast. In truth, although the east does suffer worst, cyclones strike all parts of Madagascar and can hit anytime from October to May.

But the risk to tourists is much less than you might imagine. Bear in mind that the majority of lives claimed by Madagascar's cyclones are lost at sea (109 of Gafilo's victims died in the sinking of a single ferry) and almost all of the buildings destroyed are huts constructed from natural materials rather than sturdy brick hotels. There is usually several hours' or days' warning of a cyclone's arrival. Never embark on a boat journey if a cyclone may be approaching. In the unlikely event of being caught up in a severe cyclone, take shelter inside a strong building well away from the sea or any large trees.

To put the numbers of fatalities into perspective, for every cyclone death in Madagascar, 300 people die from malaria. The real threat from a major cyclone is not in its direct casualties but the many thousands who will suffer in the months that follow as a result of the destruction of crops and infrastructure.

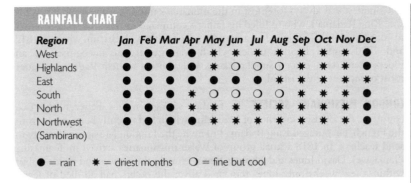

RAINFALL CHART

Region	Jan	Feb	Mar	Apr	May	Jun	Jul	Aug	Sep	Oct	Nov	Dec
West	●	●	●	●	✳	✳	✳	✳	✳	✳	✳	●
Highlands	●	●	●	●	✳	○	○	○	✳	✳	✳	●
East	●	●	●	●	●	●	●	✳	✳	✳	✳	✳
South	●	●	●	✳	○	○	○	○	✳	✳	✳	●
North	●	●	●	✳	✳	✳	✳	✳	✳	✳	✳	●
Northwest (Sambirano)	●	●	●	●	✳	✳	✳	✳	✳	✳	✳	●

● = rain   ✳ = driest months   ○ = fine but cool

May and September–November. April, December and January are also good times to visit. The risk of torrential rain and cyclones is highest in February and March. Annual rainfall ranges from 152cm in Taolagnaro to 410cm in Maroantsetra.

Southwest The driest part of Madagascar. The extreme west may receive only 5cm of rain a year, increasing to around 34cm in the east.

North This is similar to the east zone except for the dry climate of the Antsiranana region, which gets only 92cm of rain, with a long and fairly reliable dry season.

Northwest (Sambirano) Dominated by the Tsaratanana Massif, this region includes the island of Nosy Be and has a micro-climate with frequent heavy rain alternating with sunshine.

A BRIEF HISTORY

THE FIRST EUROPEANS The first Europeans to sight Madagascar were the Portuguese in 1500, although there is evidence of earlier Arab settlements on the coast. There were unsuccessful attempts to establish French and British settlements during the next couple of centuries but these failed due to disease and hostile local people. Hence a remarkably homogeneous and united country was able to develop under its own rulers.

By the early 1700s, the island had become a haven for pirates and slave-traders, who both traded with and fought the local kings of the east and west coast clans.

THE RISE OF THE MERINA KINGDOM The powerful Merina Kingdom was forged by Andrianampoinimerina (be thankful that this was a *shortened* version of his full name: Andrianampoinimerinandriantsimitoviaminandriampanjaka!).

Succeeding to the tiny kingdom of Ambohimanga in 1787, by 1808 he had united the various Merina kingdoms and conquered the other highland tribes. In many ways the Merina Kingdom at this time paralleled that of the Inca Empire in Peru: Andrianampoinimerina was considered to have almost divine powers and his obedient subjects were well provided for. Each subject was given enough land for his family's rice needs, with some left over to pay a rice tribute to the king, and community projects such as the building of irrigation canals were imposed through forced labour (though with bonuses for the most productive workers). The burning of forests was forbidden.

Conquest was always foremost in the monarch's mind, however, and it was his son, King Radama I, who fulfilled his father's command to 'Take the sea as frontier to your kingdom'. This king had a friendly relationship with Britain, which in 1817 and 1820 signed treaties under which Madagascar was recognised as an independent state. Britain supplied arms and advisers to help Radama conquer most of the rest of the island.

LONDON MISSIONARY SOCIETY To further strengthen ties between the two countries, the British Governor of Mauritius, which had recently been seized from the French, encouraged King Radama I to invite the London Missionary Society to send teachers. In 1818 a small group of Welsh missionaries arrived in Toamasina (Tamatave). David Jones and Thomas Bevan brought their wives and children, but within a few weeks only Jones remained alive; the others had all died of fever. Jones retreated to Mauritius, but returned to Madagascar in 1820, along with equally dedicated missionary teachers and artisans, to devote the rest of his life to its people. The British influence was established and a written language introduced for the first time (apart from some ancient Arabic texts) using the Roman alphabet.

ROBERT DRURY   *Hilary Bradt*

The most intriguing insight into 18th-century Madagascar was provided by the diary of Robert Drury, who was shipwrecked off the island in 1701 and spent over 16 years there, much of the time as a slave to the Antandroy or Sakalava chiefs.

Drury was only 15 when his boat foundered off the southern tip of Madagascar (he had been permitted by his father back in Britain to go to India with trade goods). The shipwreck survivors were treated well by the local king but kept prisoners for reasons of status. After a few days they made a bid for freedom by seizing the king and some of his courtiers as hostages and marching east. They were followed by hundreds of warriors who watched for any relaxation in the guard; they were without water for three days as they crossed the burning hot desert and just as they came in sight of the River Mandrare (having released the hostages) they were attacked and many were speared to death.

For ten years Drury was a slave of the Antandroy royal family. He worked with cattle and eventually was appointed royal butcher, the task of slaughtering a cow for ritual purposes being supposedly that of someone of royal blood – and lighter skin. Drury was a useful substitute. He also acquired a wife.

Wars with the neighbouring Mahafaly gave him the opportunity to escape north across the desert to St Augustine's Bay, some 250 miles away. Here he hoped to find a ship to England, but his luck turned and he again became a slave, this time to the Sakalava. When a ship did come in, his master refused to consider selling him to the captain, and Drury's desperate effort to get word to the ship through a message written on a leaf came to nothing when the messenger lost the leaf and substituted another less meaningful one. Two more years of relative freedom followed, and he finally got away in 1717, nearly 17 years after his shipwreck.

Ever quick to put his experience to good use, he later returned to Madagascar as a slave trader!

Some consider his diary to be a work of fiction, although Robert Drury is known to have existed. The places and events described correlate so well with reality, however, that it is almost certainly a genuine, if embellished, account. A ghost-writer is thought to have been involved in preparing the diary for publication, and many scholars believe that to have been none other than Daniel Defoe. See *Further information* (on page 415) for more on Robert Drury.

'THE WICKED QUEEN' AND HER SUCCESSORS Radama's widow and successor, Queen Ranavalona I, was determined to rid the land of Christianity and European influence, and reigned long enough (33 years) to largely achieve her aim. These were repressive times for Malagasy as well as foreigners. One way of dealing with people suspected of witchcraft or other evil practices was the 'Ordeal of Tangena' (see box on page 410).

It was during Queen Ranavalona's reign that an extraordinary Frenchman arrived in Madagascar: Jean Laborde. Building on the work of the British missionaries he introduced the island to many aspects of Western technology. He remained in the queen's favour until 1857 – much longer than the other Europeans (see box on page 168).

The queen drove the missionaries out of Madagascar and many Malagasy Christians were martyred. However, the missionaries and European influence returned in greater strength after the queen's death and in 1869 Christianity became the official religion of the Merina Kingdom.

After Queen Ranavalona I came King Radama II, a peace-loving and pro-European monarch who was assassinated after a two-year reign in 1863. There is a widely held belief, however, that he survived strangulation with a silk cord (it was taboo to shed royal blood) and lived in hiding in the northwest for many years (see box on page 371).

After the death of Radama II, his widow Queen Rasoherina came to the throne, but the monarchy was now in decline and power shifted to the prime minister who shrewdly married the queen. He was overthrown by a brother, Rainilaiarivony, who continued the tradition by marrying three successive queens and exercising all the power. During this period, 1863–96, the monarchs (in title only) were Queen Rasoherina, Queen Ranavalona II and lastly Queen Ranavalona III.

THE FRENCH CONQUEST Even during the period of British influence the French maintained a long-standing claim to Madagascar and in 1883 they attacked and occupied the main ports. The Franco-Malagasy War lasted 30 months, and was concluded by a harsh treaty making Madagascar a form of French protectorate. Prime Minister Rainilaiarivony, hoping for British support, managed to evade full acceptance of this status but the British government signed away its interest in the Convention of Zanzibar in 1890. The French finally imposed their rule by invasion in 1895. For a year the country was a full protectorate and in 1896 Madagascar became a French colony. A year later Queen Ranavalona III was exiled to Algeria and the monarchy abolished.

The first French Governor-General of Madagascar, Joseph Simon Gallieni, was an able and relatively benign administrator. He set out to break the power of the Merina aristocracy and remove the British influence by banning the teaching of English. French became the official language.

BRITISH MILITARY TRAINING AND THE TWO WORLD WARS Britain has played an important part in the military history of Madagascar. During the wars which preceded colonisation British mercenaries trained the Malagasy army to fight the French. During World War I 46,000 Malagasy were recruited for the Allies and over 2,000 killed. In 1942, when Madagascar was under the control of the Vichy French, the British invaded Madagascar to forestall the possibility of the Japanese Navy making use of the great harbour of Diego Suarez (see box on page 332).

In 1943 Madagascar was handed back to France under a Free French Government. A Malagasy uprising against the French in 1947 was bloodily repressed (some 80,000 are said to have died) but the spirit of nationalism lived on and in 1960 the country achieved full independence.

During the latter years of the 1930s, German Nazis, as well as many anti-Semites across Europe, wanted to rid the continent of all Jews. Their solution to the 'Jewish Question' was the wholesale deportation of European Jews to Madagascar. What became known as 'The Madagascar Plan' was first discussed as early as November 1938, a year before the outbreak of World War II. (As Madagascar was a French colony one can only wonder at what degree of collusion there was between the French and German governments over this proposal at that time.)

The annexation of Poland in 1939 brought yet more Jews under German administration. This led to a revival of The Madagascar Plan and prompted the President of the Academy of German Law – Hans Franc – to suggest that as many as three million Jews should be shipped to Madagascar. This would have meant the German occupation of the island and this was certainly discussed in 1940 within days of the fall of France. Indeed, Franz Rademacher of the German Foreign Office drew up firm arrangements for installing the Jews in Madagascar in September 1940, and he planned to visit the island to 'map out' the details.

It was intended that the island would be under the authority of Heinrich Himmler though largely administered by the Jews themselves. Franc, in a speech in July 1940, even claimed that Jewish leaders had accepted The Madagascar Plan. But the Jews had been deceived if they thought that Madagascar had been chosen as the place for a sustainable Jewish homeland. Madagascar was to be a vast 'reservation' in which, because of the harsh climatic and agricultural conditions, the Jews would slowly die out. Some have gone even further and suggested that Madagascar was to be the place where the mass extermination of the Jews – with the gas chambers, ovens and all the associated paraphernalia of the death camps – would take place. Certainly the remoteness of Madagascar would have provided the Germans with the privacy they wanted for conducting such atrocities.

Until well into 1941 The Madagascar Plan was Germany's stated 'Final Solution'. It was only when such a policy became impractical, and it was the Royal Navy's mastery of the seas which made the plan impractical, that exportation gave way to extermination and another, and more terrible, Final Solution to the Jewish Problem took its place.

John Grehan is the author of The Forgotten Invasion *(see Further information).*

THE FIRST 40 YEARS OF INDEPENDENCE The first president, Philibert Tsiranana, was 'pro-France' but in 1972 he stepped down in the face of increasing unrest and student demonstrations against French neo-colonialism. An interim government headed by General Ramanantsoa ended France's special position and introduced a more nationalistic foreign and economic policy.

In 1975, after a period of turmoil, a military directorate handed power to a naval officer, Didier Ratsiraka, who had served as Foreign Minister under Ramanantsoa. Ratsiraka established the Second Republic, changing the country's name from The Malagasy Republic to The Democratic Republic of Madagascar. He introduced his own brand of 'Christian-Marxism' and his manifesto, set out in a 'little red book', was approved by referendum. Socialist policies such as the nationalisation of banks followed. Within a few years the economy had collapsed and has remained in severe difficulties ever since. Ratsiraka was nevertheless twice re-elected, though there were claims of ballot rigging and intimidation.

Albert Zafy defeated Ratsiraka in elections in 1993, but his Third Republic was to be short-lived. The constitution was revised but Zafy refused to accept the limitations on his presidential role and continued breaches of the constitution led to his impeachment in 1996. In the ensuing election former president Ratsiraka emerged the winner, and he promptly piloted through major amendments to the constitution restoring most of the dictatorial powers he had formerly enjoyed.

POLITICAL CRISIS 2002 The official results of 2001 elections showed the mayor of Antananarivo (Tana), Marc Ravalomanana, leading with 46% so that a second round would be necessary. Results collected by observer groups indicating Ravalomanana was actually the outright winner with 52% were rejected by the incumbent president Ratsiraka. Both men declared victory. Ravalomanana installed his own ministers in government offices and Ratsiraka retreated with his government to his hometown of Toamasina.

The world looked on as the farcical situation of one country with two presidents and two capital cities descended into stalemate. In an attempt to gain the upper hand, Ratsiraka's supporters isolated Tana by dynamiting the bridges on the main transport routes into the city. The people of Tana faced a tenfold increase in the price of fuel, and basic staples such as rice, sugar and salt disappeared from the shops. Flights were grounded. As the months passed, the blockade caused malnutrition and death to the vulnerable in Tana and hardship to all. Many businesses faced bankruptcy.

Eventually the balance of power slowly shifted and Ratsiraka finally fled to France. The USA, Norway and Switzerland were the first nations to recognise Ravalomanana as rightful president. France, which had prolonged the crisis by delaying recognition because of its close links with Ratsiraka, was finally compelled to go along with this, followed by most European countries, which had been awaiting a lead from France. However most African presidents, who had supported Ratsiraka as a fellow member of their dictators' club, continued to reject Ravalomanana's legitimacy and it was nearly a year before Madagascar was re-admitted to the African Union.

SIX YEARS OF PROGRESS Once safely in power, Ravalomanana set about rebuilding the infrastructure, launching an ambitious road-building programme, and putting in motion his Durban Vision (see page 70) with the aim of conserving the environment by tripling the protected areas. He is also credited with significant improvements in education, health and the reduction of corruption.

As a successful businessman, Ravalomanana understood well the importance of promoting foreign trade and investment. But his business approach to politics was also to contribute heavily to his eventual downfall.

POLITICAL CRISIS 2009 Well into Ravalomanana's second term in office, the young mayor of Tana, Andry Rajoelina, made an unexpected challenge to his presidency. Accusing Ravalomanana of undemocratic behaviour and abuse of his position, Rajoelina mustered sufficient military and popular support to stage a successful coup d'état. Ravalomanana fled to mainland Africa when the self-appointed High Transitional Authority vowed to capture and imprison him. See the box on page 10 for a first-hand description of how the coup unfolded.

GOVERNMENT AND POLITICS

Madagascar is governed by a presidential system, but the powers of the president have varied under the different constitutions adopted over the last 40 years. At independence the constitution was based closely on the French, with the president head of the government as well as head of state. Under the 'socialist revolution' (1975–91) Ratsiraka had virtually dictatorial powers, supported by large majorities for his party AREMA in the National Assembly. The strength of older left-wing parties prevented him from establishing a formal one-party state, but the constitution provided that only socialist parties could compete in elections. After his overthrow in 1991 the pendulum swung to a parliamentary constitution similar to the German or the British, with a largely ceremonial president and power vested in a prime minister elected by the National Assembly. But this was effectively destroyed by Zafy's refusal to accept the constitutional limits on his power and when Ratsiraka subsequently returned to power he essentially reverted the constitution to its previous form.

Since colonial times the country has been divided for purposes of local government into six provinces, each consisting of hundreds of communes or municipalities with governors and prefects appointed by the central government.

An important factor in politics has been the coastal people's mistrust of the Merina who conquered them in the 19th century. The numerical superiority of the

MADAGASCAR'S SPRING COUP
Richard Cowper

It was a very Malagasy coup, achieved with a traditional mixture of chaos, plots, charm and relatively little bloodshed.

The latest unconstitutional power switch – from the elected government of President Marc Ravalomanana to the regime of Andry Rajoelina – took place in spring 2009 after months of speeches and looting had left much of the country bewildered and most heavyweight members of the international community powerless to influence events.

Andry Rajoelina the coup-maker, a handsome and youthful advertising executive, had started his working life as a disc jockey before going on to become mayor of Antananarivo in December 2007. He was made furious by the president's refusal to allow him to effect change in the city and by the closure of his radio station. He was quick to use his powerful political and French connections to buy off sections of the Malagasy army and to pay demonstrators to destabilise the government.

The personal animosity between the two men was rumoured to have deepened because of a failed love match between the mayor and one of the president's daughters, though this was never publicly admitted by either side. Rajoelina was nicknamed TGV after the French express train for his desire to take over the country as speedily as possible, and his organisation Tanora malaGasy Vonona (Determined Malagasy Youth).

In a dramatic series of events in February and March 2009 the presidential palace was stormed by hardened Rajoelina supporters, the Central Bank's coffers were raided by armoured military vehicles and at a crucial moment the French embassy in Tana gave shelter to Rajoelina when it looked as if he might be arrested for fomenting violence and riot. Finally on 21 March 2009 in a huge ceremony in the capital Rajoelina declared himself president.

Many who had been shocked at Ravalomanana's inability to act decisively during the crisis breathed a sigh of relief that the country might now get back to normal. But it was not to be. More than a year after he declared himself president Rajoelina was still not recognised as the legitimate leader of Madagascar by most of the world, including the US and the EU, even though he had been running the country day-to-day as the head of the so-called High Transitional Authority. His takeover led western countries to freeze aid and resulted in Madagascar's suspension from the African Union and the Southern African Development Community.

This lack of legitimacy has helped to make impoverished Malagasy even poorer. Growth in economic output has declined to less than 1%, new foreign investment has

coastal people has ensured their dominance of parliament and government. When Ratsiraka was in trouble in 1991, and again in 2002, he stirred up coastal hostility to the Merina. However, the emergence of Ravalomanana as the first Merina elected president indicates that the coastal/plateau divide is now less significant. Rajoelina, who seized control in 2009, is also from Merina roots.

ECONOMY

Over the past 40 years Madagascar has declined from being modestly prosperous to becoming one of the poorest countries in the world. Around 90% of the population lives on less than US$2 a day. Under Tsiranana's post-independence government, a combination of careful management and political stability produced a steady growth in GNP and an improvement in living standards. However, from the late '70s Ratsiraka's unwise policies of nationalisation and centralisation, coupled with a worsening of the terms of trade following successive oil-price shocks, led to the collapse of the economy. For 25 years the average GNP growth

slowed to a trickle, tourist income has fallen sharply and most non-humanitarian aid has ground to a halt.

At risk is Madagascar's privileged access to the world's biggest trade bloc under the Cotonou Agreement, a 2000 deal that provides the framework for European aid to African, Caribbean and Pacific nations. Under the accord, Madagascar was due to receive assistance of €600 million between 2008 and 2013.

The decline in aid has serious implications for government spending and development. The International Monetary Fund estimates that in 2008 donor assistance accounted for about 50% of Madagascar's budget and 75% of government investment.

During much of 2009 the international community, led by South Africa, attempted unsuccessfully to broker a deal between the former president and Rajoelina, but enmity between the two ran too deep. Ravalomanana was a self-made man who had come to power in controversial circumstances in February 2002 and was re-elected in 2006 with a 62% majority. He had been determined to move away from old-style crony socialism and catapult his country out of poverty with the aid of big business and help from the World Bank, the IMF and a group of western nations led by the US. But he paid scant heed to the Francophone Malagasy political old guard and contrived to alienate important sections of the army.

His political naivety and a growing public feeling that he was using his position as president to rapidly expand his own business empire at the expense of others was brought to a head when he attempted to allow the leasing of a huge tract of Malagasy land to a South Korean company for agricultural purposes and also ordered a second jet airliner, believed to be mostly for his personal use.

But protestations by the 35-year-old Rajoelina that he represented a new moral democratic force were never wholly believed by the public, who noted that over 100 people died in the coup he instigated. For the most part only very small numbers attended his demonstrations. Nor were most Malagasy surprised when Rajoelina refused to hold early elections and in June 2009, three months after he seized power, the constitution was changed to allow candidates aged 30 and over to stand for president. The previous constitution had stipulated a lower age limit of 40 for the position.

Economist and foreign policy expert Richard Cowper was living in Madagascar at the time of the coup.

was zero so that, with the population doubling, living standards were halved. Reluctant recourse to the IMF and its policies of austerity and liberalisation led to some improvement in the late '80s but the disruptions of successive political crises checked and sometimes reversed this recovery.

Madagascar has always had an adverse balance of trade, but in the post-independence days the deficit was modest and covered by various payments from France. The economic collapse under the Second Republic greatly increased the deficit, and the country has since been dependent on massive support from the IMF, World Bank, EU and various bilateral donors led by France and the USA.

The local currency, the *franc malgache*, was maintained in parity with the French franc long after its real value had declined. In 2003 the franc was replaced by the ariary. Ravalomanana's abolition of a wide range of import taxes, designed to stimulate the economy, led in the short term to a rapid increase of imports without a corresponding rise in exports. The consequent increase in the trade gap caused a spectacular collapse of the currency in the first half of 2004, with the ariary losing over half its value.

The economy has always been based on agriculture, with rice by far the largest crop, providing enough to feed the population and leave some over for export. However, under the Second Republic the severe decline in the road infrastructure isolated many rice-growers from the markets, while the low official price paid to the growers discouraged them from growing a surplus for sale and led them to revert to a subsistence economy. Rice production accordingly failed to keep pace with the growing population so that the country now has to import some 30% of its needs, at considerable expense in foreign exchange. The main cash crops for export have been vanilla, of which Madagascar is the world's largest producer, and coffee; but while vanilla has remained a leading export earner, coffee production has declined and the sector seems unlikely to recover. In the last decade prawns, either fished or farmed along the west coast, have become a major export item.

Much hope has been invested in tourism, and with the doubling of visitor figures in seven years things were looking promising until the 2009 coup decimated the industry. Only time will tell how quickly it can recover.

The hitherto small mining sector (semi-precious stones, mica and chromite) has recently expanded with the discovery of large deposits of sapphire but, partly because of government corruption, nearly all the gems have been exported illegally so that the economy has not benefited. Several major mining projects, principally for ilmenite, nickel and cobalt, have made headway over the past five years and are already responsible for a considerable part of the country's export earnings. Plans to exploit deposits of copper, bauxite, platinum and gold are also being looked at. There are known to be substantial reserves of oil and gas, which were hitherto uneconomic to extract when the oil price was low. The rise in global prices has caused a revival of interest.

The 2009 coup had a devastating effect on the country's economy. A World Bank report one year on noted a modest recovery getting underway, but emphasised that uncertainty has become the main feature of the economy, exacerbated by a lack of consistency in policy decisions.

2

People and Culture

ORIGINS

Archaeologists believe that the first people arrived in Madagascar from Indonesia/Malaya about 2,000 years ago. A journey in a reconstructed boat of those times has proved that the direct crossing of the Indian Ocean – 6,400km – was possible, though most experts agree that it is much more likely that the immigrants came in their outrigger canoes via Southern India and East Africa, where they established small Indonesian colonies. The strong African element in the coastal populations probably derived from later migrations from these colonies since their language is also essentially Malayo-Polynesian with only slightly more Bantu-Swahili words than elsewhere in the island. The Merina people of the highlands retain remarkably Indonesian characteristics and may have arrived as recently as 500–600 years ago.

Later arrivals, mainly on the east coast, from Arabia and elsewhere in the Indian Ocean, were also absorbed into the Malagasy-speaking population, while leaving their mark in certain local customs clearly derived from Islam. The two-continent origin of the Malagasy is easily observed, from the highland tribes who most resemble Indonesians, to the African type characterised by the Bara or Makoa in the south. In between are the elements of both races which make the Malagasy so varied and attractive in appearance. Thus there is racial diversity but cultural uniformity.

BELIEFS AND CUSTOMS

The Afro-Asian origin of the Malagasy has produced a people with complicated and fascinating beliefs and customs. Despite the various tribes or clans, the country shares not only a common language but a belief in the power of dead ancestors – *razana*. This cult of the dead, far from being a morbid preoccupation, is a celebration of life since the dead ancestors are considered to be potent forces that continue to share in family life. If the *razana* are remembered by the living, the Malagasy believe, they thrive in the spirit world and can be relied on to look after their descendants in a host of different ways. These ancestors wield considerable

> **DID YOU KNOW?**
> - Earthquakes mean that whales are bathing their children.
> - If a woman maintains a bending posture when arranging eggs in a nest, the chickens will have crooked necks.
> - If the walls of a house incline towards the south, the wife will be the stronger one; if they incline towards the north it will be the husband.
> - Burning a knot on a piece of string causes the knees to grow big.

power, their 'wishes' dictating the behaviour of the family or community. Their property is respected, so a great-grandfather's field may not be sold or changed to a different crop. Calamities are usually blamed on the anger of *razana*, and a zebu bull may be sacrificed in appeasement. Large herds of zebu cattle are kept as a 'bank' of potential sacrificial offerings.

Belief in tradition, in the accumulated wisdom of the ancestors, has shaped the Malagasy culture. Respect for their elders and courtesy to all fellow humans is part of the tradition. But so is resistance to change.

SPIRITUAL BELIEFS At the beginning of time the Creator was Zanahary or Andriananahary. Now the Malagasy worship one god, Andriamanitra, who is neither male nor female.

Many rural people believe in 'secondary gods' or nature spirits, which may be male or female, and which inhabit certain trees, rocks (known as *ody*) or rivers. People seeking help from the spirit world may visit one of these sites for prayer. Spirits are also thought to possess humans who fall into a trance-like state, called *tromba* by the Sakalava and *bilo* by the Antandroy. Some clans or communities believe that spirits can also possess animals, particularly crocodiles.

The Malagasy equivalent of the soul is *ambiroa*. When a person is in a dream state it can temporarily separate from the body, and at death it becomes an immortal *razana*. Death, therefore, is merely a change and not an end. A special ceremony usually marks this rite of passage, with feasting and the sacrifice of zebu. The mood of the participants alternates between sorrow and joy.

Fady The dictates of the *razana* are obeyed in a complicated network of *fady*. Although *fady* is usually translated as 'taboo' this does not truly convey the meaning: these are beliefs related to actions, food, or days of the week when it is 'dangerous to...'. *Fady* vary from family to family and community to community, and even from person to person.

FADY AND THEIR ORIGINS

THE INTRUDERS AND THE GEESE During the rule of King Andrianampoinimerina, thieves once attempted a raid on the village of Ambohimanga. The residents, however, kept geese which caused a commotion when the intruders entered the compound, thus alerting the people who could take action. Geese are therefore not eaten in this part of Madagascar.

THE BABY AND THE DRONGO Centuries ago the communities of the east coast were persecuted by pirates who made incursions to the hills to pillage and take captives. At the warning that a pirate band was on its way the villagers would flee into the jungle. When pirates approached the village of Ambinanetelo the women with young children could not keep up with the others so hid in a thicket. Just as the pirates were passing them a baby wailed. The men turned to seek the source of the cry. It came again, but this time from the top of a tree: it was a drongo. Believing themselves duped by a bird the pirates gave up and returned to their boats. Ever since then it has been *fady* to kill a drongo in Ambinanetelo.

THE TORTOISE AND THE POT A Tandroy man put a tortoise in a clay pot of boiling water to cook it, but the tortoise kicked so hard that the pot shattered to smithereens. The man declared that his descendants would never again eat tortoise because it broke his pot.

The following are some examples related to actions and food among the Merina: it may be *fady* to sing while you are eating (violators will develop elongated teeth); it is also *fady* to hand an egg directly to another person – it must first be put on the ground; for the people of Andranoro it is *fady* to ask for salt directly, so one has to request 'that which flavours the food'. A *fady* connected with objects is that the spade used to dig a grave should have a loose handle since it is dangerous to have too firm a connection between the living and the dead.

Social *fady*, like *vintana* (see below), often involve the days of the week. For example, among the Merina it is *fady* to hold a funeral on a Tuesday, or there will be another death. Among the Tsimihety it is *fady* to work the land on Tuesdays; Thursday is also a *fady* day for some people, both for funerals and for farming.

A *fady* is not intended to restrict the freedom of the Malagasy but to ensure happiness and an improved quality of life. That said, however, there are some cruel *fady* which Christian missionaries have been trying, over the centuries, to eliminate. One is the taboo against twins among the Antaisaka people of Mananjary. Historically twins were killed or abandoned in the forest after birth. Today this is against the law but still persists and twins may not be buried in a tomb. Catholic missionaries have established an orphanage in the area for the twins born to mothers torn between social tradition and maternal love. Many mothers who would otherwise have to suffer the murder or abandonment of their babies can give them to the care of the Church.

Many *fady* benefit conservation. For instance the killing of certain animals is often prohibited, and the area around a tomb must be left undisturbed. Within these pockets of sacred forest, *ala masina*, it is strictly forbidden to cut trees or even to burn deadwood or leaf litter. In southeast Madagascar there are *alam-bevehivavy* (sacred women's forests) along a stretch of river where only women may bathe. Again, no vegetation may be cleared or damaged in such localities.

For an in-depth study of the subject get hold of a copy of *Taboo* (see page 416).

Vintana Along with *fady* goes a complex sense of destiny called *vintana*. Broadly speaking, *vintana* is to do with time – hours of the day, days of the week etc – and *fady* usually involve actions or behaviour. Each day has its own *vintana* which tends to make it good or bad for certain festivals or activities. Sunday is God's day; work undertaken will succeed. Monday is a hard day, not a good day for work although projects undertaken (such as building a house) will last; Tuesday is an easy day – too easy for death so no burials take place – but all right for *famadihana* (exhumation) and light work; Wednesday is usually the day for funerals or *famadihana*; Thursday is suitable for weddings and is generally a 'good' day; Friday, *zoma*, is a 'fat' day, set aside for enjoyment, but is also the best day for funerals; Saturday, a 'noble' day, is suitable for weddings but also for purification.

As an added complication, each day has its own colour. For example Monday is a black day. A black chicken may have to be sacrificed to avoid calamity, dark-coloured food should not be eaten and people may avoid black objects. Tuesday is multicoloured, Wednesday brown, Thursday black, Friday red, Saturday blue, and Sunday white.

Tsiny and tody A third force shapes Malagasy morality. In addition to *fady* and *vintana*, there is *tody* and its partner *tsiny*. *Tody* is somewhat similar to the Hindu/Buddhist karma. The word means 'return' or 'retribution' and indicates that for any action there is a reaction. *Tsiny* means 'fault', usually a breach of the rules laid down by the ancestors.

A recent reprint of a 1957 book (in French) – *Le Tsiny et le Tody* – is easily found in Tana's bookshops.

After death Burial, exhumation and second burial are the focus of Malagasy beliefs and culture. To the Malagasy, death is the most important part of life, when a person abandons his mortal form to become a much more powerful and significant ancestor. Since a tomb is for ever whilst a house is only a temporary dwelling, it follows that tombs should be more solidly constructed than houses.

Burial practices differ among the various tribes but all over Madagascar a ritual known as *sasa* is practised immediately after a death. The family of the deceased go to a fast-flowing river and wash all their clothes to remove the contamination of death.

Funeral practices vary from clan to clan. The Antankarana (in the north) and Antandroy (south) have 'happy' funerals during which they may run, with the

FAMADIHANA DIARY
Seraphine Tierney Ramanantsoa

I travelled across the seas to be here today. This day was long awaited; I would soon be in contact with my mother again. She had died seven years previously and I had not been able to be at her funeral. Tradition had always been so important to her so I knew she would be happy that I have come for her *famadihana*.

The meeting point is at 06.00 outside Cinema Soa in Antananarivo. My household woke up at 04.00 to pack the food that had been prepared during the previous week. Drinks and cutlery are all piled into the car. A great number of people are expected as it is also the *famadihana* of the other members of my mother's family.

Fourteen cars and a big *taxi-brousse* carrying in all about 50 people, squashed one on top of the other, turn up. Everybody is excited. It is really great to see faces I haven't seen since my childhood. Everybody greets each other and exchanges news.

At 8am we all set off. We are heading towards Ifalimanjaka (meaning 'Joy Reigns Here'), in the *fivondronana* of Manjakandriana. Driving through villages with funny names like Ambohitrabiby (the 'Town of Animals') brings me back to the time when such names were familiar. We make one stop at Talatan'ny Volonondry for a breakfast of rice cakes and sausages: another opportunity to reacquaint myself with long-lost cousins with whom I spent the long summer holidays as a child. We used to run around together playing games like catching grasshoppers and then finding carnivorous plants to drop the insect in.

At 10am we reach the tombs. Faces are bright, full of expectancy. I ask what the day means to them. They all agree that it's a day for family togetherness; a day for joy, for remembrance. We are in front of my mother's tomb. It is made out of stone and marble: very elegant. The family will have spent more money on keeping that tomb nice and well maintained than on their own house.

Everybody stands around in front of the tomb waiting for the main event: the opening of the tomb door. We have to wait for the president of the *fokontany* (local authority) to give permission. Although it had been arranged beforehand he cannot be found anywhere. This wait, after such anticipation, is taken patiently by all – just one of those things.

Mats are laid on the ground on one side of the tomb. The atmosphere of joy is so tangible! Music is blaring out. Permission is finally granted to enter the tomb. The *ray aman-dreny* (elders) are the first to enter.

The inside of my mother's tomb looks very comfortable with bunk beds made out of stone. It is very clean. There are names on the side of the beds. The national flag is hoisted on top of the tomb as a sign of respect. The conversation goes on happily on the little veranda outside the tomb's door, people chatting about the event and what they have been doing in the last few days.

They start to take the bodies out. Voices could be heard above the happy murmur: 'Who is this one? This is your ma! This one your aunt! Here is your uncle! Just carry them

coffin, into the sea. An unusual ritual, *tranondonaky*, is practised by the Antaisaka of the southeast. Here the corpse is first taken to a special house where, after a signal, the women all start crying. Abruptly, after a second signal, they dance. While this is happening the men are gathered in the hut of the local chief from where, one by one, they go to the house where the corpse is lying and attach money to it with a special oil. The children dance through the night, to the beat of drums, and in the morning the adults wrap the corpse in a shroud and take it to the *kibory*. These tombs are concealed in a patch of forest known as *ala fady* which only men may enter, and where they deliver their last messages to the deceased. These messages can be surprisingly fierce: 'You are now at your place so don't disturb us any more' or 'You are now with the children of the dead, but we are the children of the living.'

around!' The closest relations carry the body but others could touch and say hello. When carrying them, they make sure that the feet go first and the head behind. Everybody carries their loved ones out of the tomb in a line, crying but happy.

When all the bodies are out, they are put on the ground on the front side of the tomb, the head facing east, with their immediate family seated around their loved one. This is a very important moment of the *famadihana*: the wrapping of the body. The old shroud in which the body was buried is left on and the new silk shroud put on top, following the mummified shape and using baby safety pins to keep it in place. There are three new silk shrouds for my mother which have been donated in remembrance and gratitude. The belief is that she won't be cold and the top shroud befits her, being of top quality silk with beautiful, delicate embroidery. This is the time to touch her, give her something, talk to her. Her best friend is there, making sure that my mother is properly wrapped, as the ritual has to follow certain rules. Lots of touching as silent conversation goes on, giving her the latest news or family gossip, and asking for her blessing. Perfume is sprinkled on her and wishes made at the same time.

The music plays on, everyone happily sitting around the mummified bodies. Flowers are placed on the bodies. The feeling of togetherness and love is so strong. This occasion is not just for the immediate family, but for cousins, and cousins of cousins, uncles and aunts and everybody meeting, bonded by the same ties, belonging to one unique extended family.

Photographs of the dead person are now put on top of each body. There is a photograph of a couple on top of one body: they were husband and wife and are now together for ever in the same silk shroud. Food is served in the forest area just next to the tombs. The huge feast and celebration begins.

Back to the bodies. We lift them, carrying them on our shoulders. We sing old rhymes and songs and dance in a line, circling the tomb seven times, moving the body on our shoulder and making it dance with us.

The last dance ends. The bodies have to be back inside the tombs by a precise time and the tomb is immediately closed after a last ritual cleaning. This moment of goodbye is very emotional. When next the tomb is opened it will not be for happiness but grief because it will be for a burial. *Famadihana* happens only once every seven or ten years.

Everybody returns to the cars and drives to my uncle's, where a huge party finishes the day. Everyone is happy at having done their duty, *Vita ny adidy!*

It has been a very special day for me. My mother was extremely traditional, spending endless energy and money during her lifetime to keep the traditions. It all makes sense now because this *famadihana* brought so much joy, a strong sense of belonging and identity, and give a spiritual feeling that death is not an end but an extension into another life, linked somehow with this one. *Misaotra ry neny* ('Thank you Mum').

More disturbing, however, is the procedure following the death of a noble of the Menabe Sakalava people. The body may be placed on a wooden bench in the hot sun until it begins to decompose. The bodily fluids which drip out are collected in receptacles and drunk by the relatives in the belief that they will then take on the qualities of the deceased.

It is after the first burial, however, that the Malagasy generally honour and communicate with their dead, not only to show respect but to avoid the anger of the *razana* who dwell in the tombs. The best-known ceremony in Madagascar is the *famadihana* ('turning of the bones') by the Merina and Betsileo people. This is a joyful occasion which occurs about every seven years after the first burial, and provides the opportunity to communicate with and remember a loved one. The remains of the selected relative are taken from the tomb, rewrapped in a new burial shroud (*lambamena*) and carried around the tomb a few times before being

TOMB ARCHITECTURE AND FUNERARY ART   *Hilary Bradt*

In Madagascar the style and structure of tombs define the different clans or tribes better than any other visible feature, and also indicate the wealth and status of the family concerned. Below is a description of the tombs.

MERINA In early times burial sites were near valleys or in marshes. The body would be placed in a hollowed-out tree trunk and sunk into the mud at the bottom of a marsh. These *fasam-bazimba* marshes were sacred. Later the Merina began constructing rectangular wooden tombs, mostly under the ground but with a visible structure above. In the 19th century the arrival of the Frenchman Jean Laborde had a profound effect on tomb architecture: tombs were built with bricks and stone, no longer just from wood. It was Laborde's influence which led to the elaborate structure of modern tombs, which are often painted with geometric designs. Sometimes the interior is lavishly decorated.

SAKALAVA During the Vazimba period, the Sakalava tombs were simple piles of stones. As with the Merina the change occurred with the introduction of cement and a step design was added. At a later stage, wooden stelae, *aloalo*, were placed on the tombs, positioned to face east. These were topped with carvings, often of a most erotic nature. Since Sakalava tombs are for individuals and not families, there is no attempt at maintaining the stelae as it is believed that only when the wood decays will the soul of the buried person be released.

Tomb construction commences only after the person's death and can take up to six weeks, the body meanwhile being kept in a house. While a tomb is under construction, many zebu are sacrificed to the ancestors. The Sakalava call their tombs *izarana*, 'the place where we are separated'.

ANTANDROY AND MAHAFALY The local name of these tombs is *fanesy* which means 'your eternal place'. Zebu horns are scattered on the tomb as a symbol of wealth (on Sakalava tombs, zebu horns are only a decoration, not an indication of status). The Antandroy and Mahafaly tombs have much the same architecture as those of the Sakalava, but are more artistically decorated. The Mahafaly *aloalo* bear figures depicting scenes from the person's life, and the entire length is often carved with intricate designs. These tombs are carefully maintained, and it is probably the Mahafaly tombs in the southern interior which are the most colourful and striking symbols of Malagasy culture. Antandroy tomb paintings tend to be merely decorative and do not represent scenes from the deceased person's life.

replaced. Meanwhile the corpse is spoken to and informed of all the latest events in the family and village. The celebrants are not supposed to show any grief. Generous quantities of alcohol are consumed amid a festive atmosphere with much dancing and music. Women who are trying to conceive take small pieces of the old burial shroud and keep these under their mattresses to induce fertility.

By law a *famadihana* may take place only in the dry season (June–September). It can last up to a week and involves the family in considerable expense, as befits the most important celebration for any family. In the *hauts plateaux* the practice of *famadihana* is embraced by rich and poor, urban and rural, and visitors fortunate enough to be invited to one will find it a strange but very moving occasion; it's an opportunity to examine our own beliefs and rituals associated with death. For an account of what *famadihana* means to a sophisticated London-based Merina woman, see box on page 16.

Variations of *famadihana* are practised by other tribes. The Menabe Sakalava, for example, hold a *fitampoha* every ten years. This is a royal *famadihana* in which the remains of deceased monarchs are taken from their tomb and washed in a river. A similar ritual, the *fanampoambe*, is performed by the Boina Sakalava further north.

HEALERS, SORCERERS AND SOOTHSAYERS The 'Wise Men' in Malagasy society are the ***ombiasy***; the name derives from *olona-be-hasina* meaning 'person of much virtue'. Traditionally they were from the Antaimoro clan and were the advisors of royalty: Antaimoro *ombiasy* came to Antananarivo to advise King Andrianampoinimerina and to teach him Arabic writing.

The astrologers, ***mpanandro*** ('those who make the day'), work on predictions of *vintana*. There is a Malagasy proverb, 'Man can do nothing to alter his destiny'; but the *mpanandro* will advise on the best day to build a house, or hold a wedding or *famadihana*. Though nowadays *mpanandro* do not have official recognition, they are present in all levels of society. A man (or woman) is considered to have the powers of an *mpanandro* when he has some grey hair – a sign that he is wise enough to interpret *vintana*. Antandroy soothsayers are known as *mpisoro*.

The Malagasy have a deep knowledge of herbal medicine and all markets display a variety of medicinal plants, amulets and talismans. The Malagasy names associated with these are *ody* and *fanafody*. Broadly speaking, *ody* refers to fetishes such as sacred objects in nature, and *fanafody* to herbal remedies (nowadays it is used for medicine of all kinds, as in the word for a pharmacy: *fivarotam-panafody*, literally 'medicine shop'). Travellers will sometimes come across conspicuous *ody* in the form of stones or trees which are sacred for a whole village, not just for an individual. Such trees are called *hazomanga* ('good tree') and are presided over by the *mpisoro*, the senior man of the oldest family in the village. Another type of *ody* is the talisman, *aoly*, worn for protection if someone has transgressed a *fady* or broken a promise. *Aoly* are sometimes kept in the house or buried. *Ody fitia* are used to gain love (white magic) but sorcerers also sell other forms of *ody* for black magic and are paid by clients with either money, zebu or poultry (a red rooster being preferred).

Mpamonka are witch doctors with an intimate knowledge of poison and *mpisikidy* are sorcerers who use amulets, stones, and beads (known as *hasina*) for their cures. Sorcerers who use these in a destructive way are called ***mpamosavy***.

On their death, sorcerers are not buried in tombs but are dumped to the west of their villages, barely covered with soil so that feral dogs and other creatures can eat their bodies. Their necks are twisted to face south.

THE WAY IT IS... Visitors from the West often find the beliefs and customs of the Malagasy merely bizarre. It takes time and effort to understand and respect the

The *lamba* is the most distinctive item of traditional Malagasy clothing, and among one of the island's most vibrant forms of artistic expression. There are many types of *lamba*, each with its own role in Malagasy culture. The Merina highlanders have a long tradition of handweaving; *lamba* are the fruit of this tradition. However, the variety most often encountered is not handwoven, but rather the machine-manufactured *lamba hoany*.

This, the category designated for everyday use, is a large decoratively printed rectangular cotton cloth. Some feature brilliantly hued patterns surrounding a central medallion; others, printed in two or three colours, depict a rural or coastal scene within an ornate border. You may also find some with images of Malagasy landmarks, the annual calendar, or historic events. A consistent feature of the various styles of *lamba hoany* is one essential recurring element that makes each unique: in a narrow box along the bottom you will find a Malagasy proverb or words of wisdom. For this reason the *lamba hoany* are often referred to as 'proverb cloths'.

As you travel the island you will discover that this seemingly simple wraparound cloth is adapted for many purposes. It is an invaluable essential for almost every citizen of rural Madagascar. As clothing, it is worn in coastal regions as a sarong, while in the highlands *lamba* are draped around shoulders as shawls for added warmth in the evening chill. Everywhere the *lamba hoany* is employed as a sling to carry a child on a mother's back or rolled up to cushion the weight when carrying a large basket on one's head. You may also encounter a *lamba* used as a light blanket, curtains in a window or door, and on occasion as a wall-hanging or tablecloth.

You can purchase a *lamba* at almost any market. The souvenir vendors usually carry a few, but you will find a much wider selection and better prices with the textile merchants. The widest choice is to be found at the fabric stores just north of the Analakely market pavilions in Antananarivo. Here hanging from the ceiling in each shop is row after row of gorgeously coloured *lamba*. Point one out and the merchant will spread it out for your perusal. Be sure to look at a few, because each one is a unique piece of art. Take your new purchase to one of the tailors in the market to have the edges hemmed for a small fee.

Also noteworthy is the *lambamena* (literally 'red cloth', although not necessarily red in colour). These are handwoven from the silk of an indigenous Malagasy silkworm and used primarily as burial shrouds in funerary ceremonies. If you prefer a traditional handwoven *lamba*, a nice colourful selection can be found at the Anosy flower market in Tana.

Joseph Radoccia is an artist and Malagasy art enthusiast who visits Madagascar frequently to paint. His lamba-inspired paintings can be viewed at www.radoccia.com.

richness of tradition that underpins Malagasy society, but it is an effort well worth making.

Leonard Fox, author of *Hainteny*, sums it up perfectly:

Whoever has witnessed the silent radiance of those who come to pray... at the house of Andrianampoinimerina in Ambohimanga and has experienced the nobility, modesty, unobsequious courtesy, and balanced wholeness of the poorest Merina who has remained faithful to his heritage can have no doubt as to the deep integrative value of the Malagasy spiritual tradition.

MARRIAGE AND CHILDREN The Malagasy have a strong sense of community which influences their way of life. Just as the ancestors are laid in a communal tomb, so their descendants share a communal way of life, and even children are almost considered common property within their extended family. Children are seldom disciplined but learn by example.

Marriage is a fairly relaxed union and divorce is common. There is no formal dowry arrangement or bride price, but a present of zebu cattle will often be made. In rural communities the man should bring his new wife home to his village (not vice versa) or he will lose face. You often see young men walking to market wearing a comb in their hair; they are advertising their quest for a wife.

Most Malagasy (and all Christians) have only one wife, but there are exceptions. There is a well-known man living in Antalaha, who has 11 wives and 120 children. This arrangement seems to work surprisingly well, with each wife working to support her own children, and a head wife to whom the others defer. The man is wealthy enough to provide housing for all his family.

THE VILLAGE COMMUNITY Malagasy society is a structured hierarchy with two fundamental rules: respect for the other person and knowing one's place. Within a village, the community is based on the traditional *fokonolona*. This concept was introduced by King Andrianampoinimerina when these councils of village elders were given responsibility for, among other things, law and order and the collection of taxes. Day-to-day decisions are still made by the *fokonolona*.

Rural Malagasy houses are always aligned north–south and generally have only one room. Furniture is composed of mats, *tsihy*, often beautifully woven. These are used for sitting and sleeping, and sometimes food is served on them. There are often *fady* attached to *tsihy*. For example you should not step over a mat, particularly one on which meals are eaten.

Part of the Malagasy culture is the art of oratory, **kabary**. Originally *kabary* were the huge meetings where King Andrianampoinimerina proclaimed his plans, but the word has now evolved to mean the elaborate form of speech used to inspire and control the crowds at such gatherings. Even rural leaders can speak for hours, using highly ornate language and many proverbs; a necessary skill in a society that reached a high degree of sophistication without a written language.

The market plays a central role in the life of rural people, who will often walk as far as 20km to market with no intention of selling or buying, but simply to catch up on the gossip or continue the conversation broken off the previous week. You will see well-dressed groups of young people happily making their way to this social centre. Often there is a homemade tombola, and other outlets for gambling.

FESTIVALS AND CEREMONIES Malagasy Christians celebrate the usual holy days, but most tribes or clans have their own special festivals.

Ala volon-jaza This is the occasion when a baby's hair is cut for the first time. With the Antambahoka people in the south the haircut is performed by the grandparents. The child is placed in a basin filled with water, and afterwards bathed. Among the Merina the ceremony is similar but only a man whose parents are still alive may cut a baby's hair. The family then have a meal of rice, zebu, milk and honey. Coins are placed in the bowl of rice and the older children compete to get as many as possible.

Circumcision Boys are usually circumcised at the age of about two; a baby who dies before this operation has been performed may not be buried in the family tomb.

During my year working in Madagascar I was particularly struck by the wonderful array of different hats worn there. Market stalls were piled high with hats of all shapes, colours and sizes.

Little had been noted about Malagasy headwear until the missionaries came in the early 19th century. At that time, few hats were worn as a person's hairstyle was regarded as more important and a sign of beauty. People from each region of Madagascar had different ways of plaiting their hair and they would often incorporate shells, coins or jewels. Oils and perfumes were massaged into the hair – the richer people used *tseroka*, a type of castor oil mixed with the powdered leaf of *Ravintsara*, which produced a nutmeg scent, while the poorest population were satisfied with zebu fat.

The chiefs wore simple headdresses but it was not until the Europeans came that hats became more popular. Although plaiting and the art of weaving were already very well established, there was little evidence of woven hats. The cutting of hair was introduced in 1822 which may have changed the Malagasy attitudes – to cover an unplaited head certainly would not be any detriment to their beauty. Initially hats were worn by the wealthy. Chiefs could be seen wearing caps made of neatly woven rushes or coarse grass and the people of Tana began to wear hats of more costly and durable material (often imported from overseas). It was Jean Laborde in the 1850s who started the industry of hat-making and helped to increase production.

In each region the hats vary: they use different plant fibres depending on what grows locally, different weaves and occasionally dyes. The colours used are not the vegetable or plant dyes I had imagined but imported from China. The fibres are usually from palms (raffia, *badika*, *manarana*, *dara*), reeds (*penjy*, *harefo*) or straw. Some of the best regions that I came across for seeing weaving were near Lake Tritriva (straw), Maroantsetra (raffia), Mananjary (*penjy*, *dara*), Mahsoabe near Fianarantsoa (*badika*) and Vohipeno (*harefo*).

The ways of preparing the fibres for weaving differ, but in general they are dried, flattened and then, if necessary, stripped into thin fibres using a sharp knife. Some are woven into strips which are eventually machined together, while other regions use a continuous weave method to make the entire hat. The latter can be extremely complicated and is an amazing art to watch. The weaver will place their foot on the central part of the woven circle and gradually intertwine hundreds of different fibres into position. One of my lasting memories was spending time in Maroantsetra where they make the most beautiful crochet-style raffia hats. Women sit on palm mats outside their houses weaving, while children play, plait hair or busily prepare food for the next meal. Occasionally the hats are blocked (shaping a crown or brim over a wooden block). There are places in Tana where they heat steel blocks on a fire and then press the woven hat into a trilby style for example. This was a fascinating sight to see as normally these blocks are electrically heated.

The variety of hats is astounding. It can take a day for a woman to weave a hat, and this can be a main source of family income. If you are interested in getting a Malagasy hat, it is worthwhile getting to know a weaver so they may be able to make one large enough for the *vazaha* head!

The operation itself is often done surgically, but in some rural areas it may still be performed with a sharpened piece of bamboo. The foreskin is not always simply discarded. In the region of the Antambahoka it may be eaten by the grandparents, and in Antandroy country it could be shot from the barrel of a gun!

Different clans have their own circumcision ceremonies. Among the Antandroy, uncles dance with their nephews on their shoulders. But the most famous ceremony is *sambatra*, which takes place every seven years in Mananjary.

Tsangatsaine This is a ceremony performed by the Antankarana. Two tall trees growing side by side near the house of a noble family are tied together to symbolise the unification of the tribe, as well as the tying together of the past and present, the living and the dead.

Fandroana This was the royal bath ceremony which marked the Malagasy New Year. These celebrations used to take place in March, with much feasting. While the monarch was ritually bathed, the best zebu was slaughtered and the choicest rump steak presented to the village nobles. The day was the equivalent of the Malagasy National Day, but the French moved this to 14 July, the date of the establishment of the French Protectorate. This caused major resentment among the Malagasy as effectively their traditional New Year was taken from them. After independence the date was changed to 26 June to coincide with Independence Day. These days, because of the cost of zebu meat and the value attached to the animals, the traditional meat has been replaced by chicken, choice portions again being given to the respected members of the community. In the absence of royalty there is, of course, no longer a royal bath ceremony.

ETHNIC GROUPS

The different clans of Madagascar are based more upon old kingdoms than upon ethnic grouping. Traditions are changing: the descriptions below reflect the tribes at the time of independence, rather than in the more fluid society of today. The groups may differ but a Malagasy proverb shows their feeling of unity: *Ny olombelona toy ny molo-bilany, ka iray mihodidina ihany*; 'Men are like the lip of the cooking pot which forms just one circle'.

For English-language anthropological books about the Malagasy, see page 415.

ANTAIFASY (PEOPLE-OF-THE-SANDS) Living in the southeast around Farafangana, they cultivate rice, and fish in the lakes and rivers. Divided into three clans, each with its own 'king', they generally have stricter moral codes than other tribes. They have large collective burial houses known as *kibory*, built of wood or stone and generally hidden in the forest.

ANTAIMORO (PEOPLE-OF-THE-COAST) These are among the most recent arrivals and live in the southeast around Vohipeno and Manakara. They guard Islamic tradition and Arab influence and still use a form of Arab writing known as *sorabe*. They use verses of the Koran as amulets.

ANTAISAKA Centred south of Farafangana on the southeast coast but now fairly widely spread throughout the island, they are an off-shoot of the Sakalava tribe. They cultivate coffee, bananas and rice – but only the women harvest the rice. There are strong marriage taboos amongst them. Often the houses may have a second door on the east side which is used only for taking out a corpse. They use the *kibory*, communal burial house, the corpse usually being dried out for two or three years before finally being put there.

ANTANKARANA (THOSE-OF-THE-ROCKS) Living in the north around Antsiranana (Diego Suarez) they are fishermen or cattle raisers whose rulers came from the

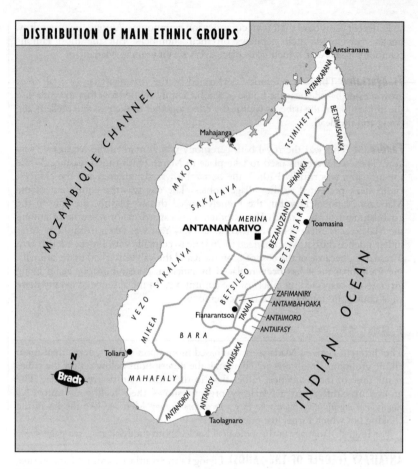

DISTRIBUTION OF MAIN ETHNIC GROUPS

Sakalava dynasty. Their houses are usually raised on stilts. Numerous *fady* exist amongst them governing relations between the sexes in the family; for example a girl may not wash her brother's clothes. The legs of a fowl are the father's portion, whereas amongst the Merina, for instance, they are given to the children.

ANTAMBAHOAKA (THOSE-OF-THE-PEOPLE) The smallest tribe, of the same origin as the Antaimoro and living around Mananjary on the southeast coast. They have some Arab traits and amulets are used. They bury in a *kibory*. Mass circumcision ceremonies are carried out every seven years.

ANTANDROY (PEOPLE-OF-THE-THORNS) Traditionally nomadic, they live in the arid south around Ambovombe. A dark-skinned people, they wear little clothing and are said to be frank and open, easily roused to either joy or anger. Their women occupy an inferior position, and it is *fady* for a woman to milk a cow. The villages are often surrounded by a hedge of cactus plants. Until recently they ate little rice, their staples being maize, cassava and sweet potatoes. They believe in the *kokolampo*, a spirit of either good or bad influence. Their tombs are similar to those of the Mahafaly tribe. Sometimes it is *fady* among them for a child to say his father's name, or to refer by name to parts of his father's body. Thus he may say 'what he moves with' for his feet or 'the top of him' for his head.

ANTANOSY (PEOPLE-OF-THE-ISLAND) The island is a small one in the Fanjahira River. They live in the southeast, principally around Taolagnaro (Fort Dauphin). Their social structure is based on clans with a 'king' holding great authority over each one. There are strict *fady* governing relationships in the family. For example, a brother may not sit on or step over his sister's mat. As with many other tribes there are numerous *fady* regarding pregnancy: a pregnant woman should not sit in the doorway of the house; she should not eat brains; she should not converse with men; people who have no children should not stay in her house overnight. Other *fady* are that relatives should not eat meat at a funeral and the diggers opening a tomb should not wear clothes. When digging holes for the corner posts of a new house it may be *fady* to stand up so the job must be performed sitting down.

BARA Originally in the southwest near Toliara, these nomadic cattle raisers now live in the south-central area around Ihosy and Betroka. Their name has no special meaning but it is reputed to derive from an African (Bantu) word. They may be polygamous and women occupy an inferior position in their society. They attach importance to the *fatidra* or 'blood pact'. Cattle-stealing is regarded as proof of manhood and courage, without which a man cannot expect to get a wife. They are dancers and sculptors, a unique feature of their carved wooden figures being eyelashes of real hair set into the wood. They believe in the *helo*, a spirit that manifests itself at the foot of trees. In the past a whole village would move after somebody died owing to the fear of ghosts. They use caves in the mountains for burial. It is the custom to shave the head on the death of a near relative.

BETSILEO (THE-MANY-INVINCIBLES) They are centred in the south of the *hauts plateaux* around Fianarantsoa but about 150,000 also live in the Betsiboka region. They are energetic and expert rice-producers, their irrigated, terraced rice-fields being a feature of the landscape. *Famadihana* was introduced to their culture by the Merina at the time of Queen Ranavalona I. It is *fady* for the husband of a pregnant woman to wear a *lamba* thrown over his shoulder. It may be *fady* for the family to eat until the father is present or for anyone to pick up his fork until the most honourable person present has started to eat.

BETSIMISARAKA (THE-MANY-INSEPARABLES) They are the second largest tribe and live on the east coast in the region between Nosy Varika and Antalaha. Their culture has been influenced by Europeans, particularly pirates. They cultivate rice and work on vanilla, coffee and lychee plantations. Their clothes are sometimes made from locally woven raffia. Originally their society included numerous local chiefs. The *tangalamena* is the local official for religious rites and customs. The Betsimisaraka have many superstitious beliefs: *angatra* (ghosts), *zazavavy an-drano* (mermaids), and *kalamoro*, little wild men of the woods, about 65cm high with long flowing hair, who like to slip into houses and steal rice from the cooking pot. In the north coffins are generally placed under a shelter, in the south in tombs. It may be *fady* for a brother to shake hands with his sister, or for a young man to wear shoes while his father is still alive.

BEZANOZANO (MANY-SMALL-PLAITS) The name refers to the way in which they do their hair. They were probably one of the first tribes to become established in Madagascar and now live in an area between the Betsimisaraka lowlands and the Merina highlands. Like the Merina, they practise *famadihana*. As with most of the coastal tribes their funeral celebrations involve the consumption of considerable quantities of *toaka* (rum).

MAHAFALY (THOSE-WHO-MAKE-TABOOS OR THOSE-WHO-MAKE-HAPPY) The etymology of the word is sometimes disputed but the former meaning is generally regarded as being correct. They probably arrived around the 12th century and live in the southwest desert area around Ampanihy and Ejeda. They are farmers, with maize, sorghum and sweet potatoes as their chief crops; cattle-rearing occupies a secondary place. They kept their independence under their own local chiefs until the French occupation and still keep the bones of some of their old chiefs – this is the *jiny* cult. Their villages usually have a sacrificial post, the *hazomanga*, on the east side where sacrifices are made. Some of the blood is generally put on the foreheads of the people attending.

The tombs of the Mahafaly attract a great deal of interest. They are big rectangular constructions of uncut stone rising a metre above the ground and decorated with *aloalo* (sculpted wooden posts) and the horns of the cattle slain at the funeral feast. The tomb of the Mahafaly king Tsiampody bears the horns of 700 zebu. The *aloalo* are set upright on the tomb, often depicting scenes from the person's life. The burial customs include waiting for the decomposition of the body before it is placed in the tomb. It is the practice for a person to be given a new name after death.

The divorce rate is very high and it is not at all uncommon for a man to remarry six or seven times. It is often *fady* for children to sleep in the same house as their parents. Their *rombo* (similar to the *tromba* of the Sakalava) is the practice of contacting various spirits for healing purposes. Amongst the spirits believed in are the *raza* who are not real ancestors and in some cases are even supposed to include *vazaha* (white foreigners), and the *vorom-be* which is the spirit of a big bird.

MAKOA The Makoa are descended from slaves taken from the Makua people of Mozambique, and although sometimes classified as Vezo, they maintain a separate identity. Typically of larger stature than most Malagasy, Makoa men were often employed by the French as policemen and soldiers, thus reinforcing their distinction from other Malagasy.

MERINA (PEOPLE-OF-THE-HIGHLANDS) They live on the *hauts plateaux*, the most developed area of the country, the capital being 95% Merina. They are of Malayo-Polynesian origin and vary widely in skin colour, with straight hair. They used to be divided into three castes: the Andriana (nobles), the Hova (freemen) and the Andevo (serfs); but legally these divisions no longer exist. Most Merina houses are built of brick or mud; some are two-storey buildings with slender pillars, where the people live mainly upstairs. Most villages of any size have a church – probably two: Catholic and Protestant. There is much irrigated rice cultivation, and the Merina were the first tribe to have any skill in architecture and metallurgy. *Famadihana* is essentially a Merina custom.

MIKEA The term refers not so much to a tribe as to a lifestyle. They subsist by foraging in the dry forests of the west and southwest. Various groups of people along the west coast are called Mikea, although their main area is the Mikea Forest between Morombe and Toliara. The Mikea are Malagasy of various origins, having adopted their particular lifestyle (almost unique in Madagascar) for several reasons, including fleeing from oppression and taxation exerted on them by various powers.

HAINTENY   *Hilary Bradt*

The Merina have a rich and complex spiritual life. Perhaps the shortest route to the soul of any society is through its poetry, and we are fortunate that there is a book of the traditional Malagasy poetry: *Hainteny*. Broadly speaking, *hainteny* are poems about love: love between parent and child, between man and woman, the love of nature, the appreciation of good versus evil, the acceptance of death. Through the sensitive translations of Leonard Fox, the spiritual and emotional life of the Merina is made available to the reader who cannot fail to be impressed by these remarkable people. As Leonard Fox says: 'On the most basic level, *hainteny* give us an incomparable insight into a society characterised by exceptional refinement and subtlety, deep appreciation of beauty, delight in sensual enjoyment, and profound respect for the spiritual realities of life.' Here are two examples.

What is the matter, Raivonjaza,
That you remain silent?
Have you been paid or hired and your mouth tied,
That you do not speak with us, who are your parents?
– I have not been paid or hired
and my mouth has not been tied,
but I am going home to my husband
and am leaving my parents,
my child, and my friends,
so I am distressed,
speaking little.
Here is my child, dear Mother and Father.
If he is stubborn, be strict, but do not beat him;
and if you hit him, do not use a stick.
And do not act as though you do not see him
when he is under your eyes, saying:
'Has this child eaten?'
Do not give him too much,
Do not give him the remains of a meal,
and do not give him what is half-cooked,
for I will be far and will long for him.

———

Do not love me, Andriamatoa, as one loves
the banana tree exposed to the wind,
overcome and in danger from cold.
Do not love me as one loves a door:
It is loved, but constantly pushed.
Love me as one loves a little crab:
even its claws are eaten.

Tantely tapa-bata ka ny foko no entiko mameno azy.
This is only half a pot of honey but my heart fills it up.

Mahavoa roa toy ny dakam-boriky.
Hit two things at once like the kick of a donkey.

Tsy midera vady tsy herintaona.
Don't praise your wife before a year.

Ny omby singorana amin' ny tandrony, ary ny olona kosa amin' ny vavany.
Oxen are trapped by their horns and men by their words.

Tondro tokana tsy mahazo hao.
You can't catch a louse with one finger.

Ny alina mitondra fisainana.
The night brings wisdom.

Aza manao herim-boantay.
If you are just a dung beetle don't try to move mountains.

Aza midera harena, fa niter-day.
Do not boast about your wealth if you are a father.

Ny teny toy ny fonosana, ka izay mamono no mamaha.
Words are like a parcel: if you tie lots of knots you will have to undo them.

SAKALAVA (PEOPLE-OF-THE-LONG-VALLEYS) They live in the west between Toliara and Mahajanga and are dark-skinned with Polynesian features and short curly hair. They were at one time the largest and most powerful tribe, though disunited, and were ruled by their own kings and queens. Certain royal relics remain – typically being kept in the northeast corner of a house. The Sakalava are cattle raisers, and riches are reckoned by the number of zebu owned. There is a record of human sacrifice amongst them up to the year 1850 at special occasions such as the death of a king. The *tromba* (trance state) is quite common. It is *fady* for pregnant women to eat fish or to sit in a doorway. Women hold a more important place amongst them than in most other tribes.

SIHANAKA (PEOPLE-OF-THE-SWAMPS) Their home is the northeast of the old kingdom of Imerina around Lake Alaotra and they have much in common with the Merina. They are fishermen, rice growers and poultry raisers. Swamps have been drained to make vast rice-fields cultivated with modern machinery and methods. They have a special rotation of *fady* days.

ST MARIANS The population of Ile Sainte Marie is mixed. Although Indonesian in origin there has been influence from both Arabs and European pirates.

TANALA (PEOPLE-OF-THE-FOREST) These are traditionally forest-dwellers, living inland from Manakara, and are rice and coffee growers. Their houses are usually built on stilts. The Tanala are divided into two groups: the Ikongo in the south and the Menabe in the north. The Ikongo are an independent people who never submitted to Merina domination, in contrast to the Menabe. Burial customs include keeping the corpse for up to a month. Coffins are made from large trees to which sacrifices are sometimes made when they are cut down. The Ikongo usually bury their dead in the forest and may mark a tree to show the spot.

Some recent authorities dispute that the Tanala exist as a separate ethnic group.

TSIMIHETY (THOSE-WHO-DO-NOT-CUT-THEIR-HAIR) The refusal to cut their hair (to show mourning on the death of a Sakalava king) was to demonstrate their independence. They are an energetic and vigorous people in the north-central area and are spreading west. The oldest maternal uncle occupies an important position.

MALAGASY WITHOUT (TOO MANY) TEARS   *Janice Booth*

Once you've thrown out the idea that you must speak a foreign language correctly or not at all, and that you must use complete sentences, you can have fun with only a few words of Malagasy. Basic French is understood almost everywhere, but the people warm instantly to any attempts to speak 'their own' language.

If you learn only three words, choose *misaotra* (thank you), pronounced 'misowtr'; *veloma* (goodbye), pronounced 'veloom'; and *manao ahoana* (pronounced roughly 'manna owner'), which is an all-purpose greeting. If you can squeeze in another three, go for *tsara* (good); *azafady* (please); and *be* (pronounced 'beh'), which can be used – sometimes ungrammatically, but who cares! – to mean big, very or much. Thus *tsara be* means very good; and *misaotra be* means a big thank you. Finally, when talking to an older person, it's polite to add *tompoko*. This is equivalent to Madame or Monsieur in French. If your memory's poor, write the vocabulary on a postcard and carry it round with you.

In a forest one evening, at dusk, I was standing inside the trunk and intertwining roots of a huge banyan tree, looking up through the branches at the fading sky and a few early stars. It was very peaceful, very silent. Suddenly a small man appeared from the shadows, holding a rough wooden dish. Old and poorly dressed, probably a cattle herder, he stood uncertainly, not wanting to disturb me. I said '*manao ahoana*' and he replied. I touched the bark of the tree gently and said '*tsara*'. '*Tsara*,' he agreed, smiling. Then he said a sentence in which I recognised *tantely* (honey). I pointed questioningly to a wild bees' nest high in the tree. '*Tantely*,' he repeated quietly, pleased. I pointed to his dish – '*Tantely sakafo?*' Yes, he was collecting wild honey for food. '*Tsara. Veloma, tompoko.*' I moved off into the twilight. '*Veloma*,' he called softly after me. So few words said.

Another day, in Tana, a teenage girl was pestering me for money. She didn't seem very deserving but wouldn't give up. Then I asked her in Malagasy, 'What's your name?' She looked astonished, eyes suddenly meeting mine instead of sliding furtively. 'Noro.' So I asked, very politely, 'Please, Noro, go away. Goodbye.' Nonplussed, she stared at me briefly before moving off, the cringing attitude quite gone. By using her name, I'd given her dignity. You can find that vocabulary in the language appendix on page 411.

'What's your name?' is probably the phrase I most enjoy using. Say it to a child and their eyes grow wider, as a timid little voice answers you. Then you can say '*manao ahoana*', using the name, and you've forged a link. Now learn how to say 'My name is...' – and you're into real conversation!

When I'm in Madagascar I still carry a copy of the language appendix in my bag. It's dog-eared now, and scribbled on. But it's my passport to a special kind of contact with friendly, gentle and fascinating people.

VEZO (FISHING PEOPLE) They are not generally recognised as a separate tribe but as a clan of the Sakalava. They live on the coast in the region of Morondava in the west to Faux Cap in the south. They use dugout canoes fitted with one outrigger pole and a small rectangular sail. In these frail but stable craft they go far out to sea. The Vezo are also noted for their tombs, which are graves dug into the ground surrounded by wooden palisades, the main posts of which are crowned by erotic wooden carved figures.

ZAFIMANIRY A clan of some 15,000 people distributed in about 100 villages in the forests between the Betsileo and Tanala areas southeast of Ambositra. They are known for their woodcarvings and sculpture, and are descended from people from the *hauts plateaux* who established themselves there early in the 19th century. The Zafimaniry are thus interesting to historians as they continue the forms of housing and decoration of past centuries. Their houses, which are made from vegetable fibres and wood with bamboo walls and roofs, have no nails and can be taken down and moved from one village to another.

LANGUAGE

The Indonesian origin of the Malagasy people shows strongly in their language which is spoken, with regional variations of dialect, throughout the island. (Words for domestic animals, however, are derived from Kiswahili, indicating that the early settlers, sensibly enough, did not bring animals with them in their outrigger canoes.) Malagasy is a remarkably rich language, full of images, metaphors and proverbs. Literal translations of Malagasy words and phrases are often very poetic. 'Dusk' is *maizim-bava vilany*, 'darken the mouth of the cooking pot'; the very early hours of the morning are referred to as *misafo helika ny kary*, 'when the wild cat washes itself'. The richness of the language means that there are few English words that can be translated into a single word in Malagasy, and vice versa. An example given by Leonard Fox in his book on the poetry of Madagascar, *Hainteny*, is *miala mandry*. *Miala* means 'go out/go away' and *mandry* means 'lie down/go to sleep'. Together, however, they mean 'to spend the night away from home, and yet be back in the early morning as if never having been away'!

Learning, or even using, the Malagasy language may seem a challenging prospect to the first-time visitor. Place names may be very long (because they usually have a literal meaning, such as Ranomafana: 'hot water'), with seemingly erratic syllable stress. However, as a courtesy to the Malagasy people you should learn a few Malagasy words. There is a Malagasy vocabulary on page 411 and a recommended phrase book in *Appendix 3*.

3

Natural History

Daniel Austin & Kelly Green

INTRODUCTION

Isolated for 65 million years, Madagascar is the oldest island on earth. As a result its natural history is unique. There are over 200,000 species on the island, living in habitats ranging from rainforests to deserts and from mountain tops to mangrove swamps. The residents are as unique as they are diverse – a list of Malagasy species reads like a hurried appendix tagged onto the end of a catalogue of the world's wildlife. Eight whole plant families exist only on Madagascar, as do close to 1,000 orchid species, many thousands of succulents, countless insects, at least 350 species of frog, around 370 kinds of reptile, five families of birds and approaching 200 different mammals, including an entire branch of the primate family tree, the order to which we ourselves belong.

This magnificent menagerie is the product of a spectacular geological past. About 167 million years ago Madagascar was a land-locked plateau at the centre of the largest continent the Earth has ever seen: Gondwana. This was during the age of the reptiles at about the time when flowering plants were beginning to blossom and primitive mammals and birds were finding a niche among their giant dinosaur cohabitants. With a combination of sea-level rises and plate movements Gondwana subsequently broke apart. Madagascar, still attached to present-day India, drifted away from Africa. Then, around the time of the mass dinosaur extinction,

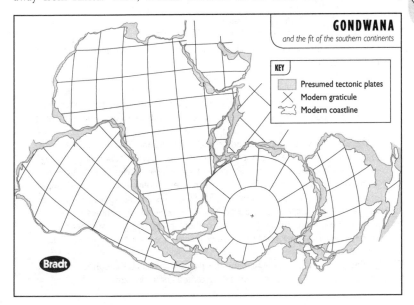

GONDWANA
and the fit of the southern continents

KEY
- Presumed tectonic plates
- ✕ Modern graticule
- Modern coastline

Bradt

Madagascar broke completely free, setting itself adrift as one of the earth's great experiments in evolution.

Some of the plants and animals present on the island today are the results of adaptation from the original, marooned Gondwana stock. Ancient groups such as the ferns, cycads, palms and screw pines, and primitive reptiles such as the boas and iguanids, are descendants of this relic community. Yet the magic of Madagascar is that a select band of species has enriched the community by arriving *since* the break-up. Flying, swimming, journeying as seeds or riding the floodwaters of the east African rivers in hollow trunks, wave after wave of more recent plants and animals came from over the horizon during a period of 100 million years, bringing with them the latest adaptations from the big world beyond. Colonisers, such as the lemurs and carnivores, may have had a helping hand from a partial land-bridge which is thought to have appeared from beneath the waves of the Mozambique Channel about 40 million years ago.

Yet, whatever their mode of transport, upon landfall each species spread outwards in every direction, through the tremendous range of habitats, changing subtly as they encountered new environments, frequently to the extent that new species were formed. This evolutionary process is termed 'adaptive radiation' and it results in the creation of an array of new species found nowhere else.

The patterns in the island's diversity tell us something of the timing of these colonisations. A large number of unique succulent plants indicates an early arrival from Africa in the dry west, followed by a radiation eastwards ending in the rainforests. On the other hand, the two Malagasy pitcher plants found in the east probably arrived at about the same time as people, and from the same direction.

From this great evolutionary melting pot has emerged the bewildering array of animals and plants that bless Madagascar today; most are unique to the island and countless still await discovery.

BIODIVERSITY In recognition of its massive wealth of endemic flora and fauna, Madagascar has been designated a Biodiversity Hotspot by Conservation International – and as hotspots go, Madagascar is considered one of the hottest.

SCIENTIFIC CLASSIFICATION *Daniel Austin*

Hundreds of thousands of animals and plants are known to science but most do not have common names. Those that do may have many common names, or the same name could be used for multiple plants or animals. To avoid confusion, scientists use scientific names (sometimes called 'Latin names'). These are unambiguous and universal across languages, which is why we have often used them in this book. For those who are not familiar with the system, here is a brief explanation.

All life is divided into kingdoms including Plantae (plants) and Animalia (animals). Each of these groups is divided, then further subdivided, through several levels of classification, right down to individual species. The bottom two levels (genus and species) together form the scientific name. For example, mankind belongs to the genus *Homo* and the species *sapiens*. Our species can be written as *Homo sapiens* (or abbreviated to *H. sapiens*). Sometimes species are further divided into subspecies. Modern humans belong to a subspecies (also called *sapiens*) so if we want to be really specific, we refer to ourselves as *Homo sapiens sapiens*.

You will encounter scientific names for plants and animals throughout this book, especially where there is no universally accepted common name.

Madagascar is famed for its bizarre and unique wildlife today, but many of the island's most fascinating animal inhabitants have long since disappeared.

Recently a truly remarkable discovery was made in southern Madagascar. Scientists unearthed two prosauropods (herbivorous dinosaurs) that dated back 230 million years, making them not only the earliest fossils ever to be found in Madagascar, but also probably the oldest in the world.

Another unusual find was of a very strange blunt-snouted, herbivorous crocodile in northwest Madagascar, dating from the late Cretaceous (97–65 million years ago). Prior to the discovery of this beast (*Simosuchus clarki*) experts had believed ancient crocodiles to resemble more closely those alive today.

In 2001 a new species of dinosaur was found and is thought to be the first animal to take its name from a pop star. Palaeontologists named *Masiakasaurus knopfleri* after the lead guitarist of Dire Straits because whenever they played his music they struck lucky finding fossils! *M. knopfleri* was a ferocious little bipedal carnivore (the genus name comes from the Malagasy for 'violent') whose larger cousin *Majungatholus atopus* was discovered by the same team from the State University of New York, Stony Brook. This lived around 70–65 million years ago and is believed to have been cannibalistic. An examination of distinctive marks on the fossilised bones suggests that they could only have been caused by the teeth of the same species, though it is still a matter of debate whether the victim was alive at the time. (Cannibalism has been documented in only one other species of dinosaur.)

Until very recently, Madagascar had a flourishing megafauna (a word used to refer to all large animals). When humans first settled on the island less than 2,000 years ago, they would have been greeted with great forests populated by huge tortoises, dwarf hippos and lemurs the size of gorillas. Around 16 species of lemur are known to have been bigger than the indri, the largest alive today, but all are now extinct as a result of the arrival of man.

Perhaps the most amazing of Madagascar's extinct animals is still fresh in Malagasy folklore. Tales of this creature were passed along to Marco Polo who wrote extravagantly of an awesome bird, the giant roc, capable of carrying off an elephant. This majestic animal was, in fact, the flightless elephant bird or Aepyornis.

Standing over 3m tall, it would have made an ostrich seem like a goose. The largest, *Aepyornis maximus*, weighed in at more than 500kg and is thought to have been the largest bird ever to have lived. Sadly, like the famous dodo of neighbouring Mauritius, it was driven to extinction by humans in the last few centuries.

The roc as visualised by an artist in 1598

Biodiversity Hotspots cover less than 1% of the earth's surface, yet are home to well over half of its plant and animal species. Although it is not entirely understood why Madagascar has so many species, two factors have helped: it is near to the Equator and it contains an astonishing array of habitats. The tropical climate is a perfect host to the processes of life – far more living things survive within the tropics than in cooler regions – and the habitat variety provides greater opportunity for animal and plant variation.

Natural History   INTRODUCTION

3

The story of Madagascar's astonishing natural history begins millions of years ago. The island's geology raises plenty of interesting questions – many still unanswered – and attracts geologists and mining companies from around the world. Madagascar comprises three main geological terranes: a **crystalline core** comprising the central highlands, a **sedimentary shelf** that flanks this core on the west, and dispersed **volcanic edifices**.

The **crystalline core** dates to the Late Proterozoic, 900–550mya (million years ago), a period long before the evolution of complex life, and before the assembly of the continents as we know them. Yet these rocks contain tiny crystals of zircon which testify to a far greater antiquity (2,600mya). It is thought that this zircon records the formation of a continent that would later become part of Gondwana. Other continental masses also existed, several that would later become the northern continents, and one that would split and become South America and Africa.

Two of these (South America-Africa and Australia-Antarctica-India-Madagascar) had been drifting slowly closer together until they collided 690mya, just as the first large multicellular marine creatures were beginning to evolve. During such collisions the edges of the continents crumple and sheets several kilometres thick are thrust over each other forming mountain ranges. The so-called Mozambique Belt of mountains was immense, extending 7,000km from present-day Kenya down to Antarctica, with Madagascar right at the centre.

The rocks buried during mountain-building are recrystallised and partially melted under the intense pressure and heat. The central highlands of Madagascar are just a small part of the exhumed roots of this vast and ancient mountain belt, consisting of recrystallised rocks such as gneisses, granulites, migmatites and granites. The ramparts of the Mozambique Belt then stood sentinel, slowly eroding but largely unchanged, for several hundred million years, while soft-bodied life in the oceans experimented with the idea of greater progression.

The **sedimentary shelf** began to form early in the Palaeozoic (500mya), as macroscopic organisms with external skeletons evolved and diversified explosively. The old mountain belt had been eroded down near to sea level, and the waning of an ice age caused flooding of the land. Across the world, life evolved dramatically towards a climax of plant productivity in the Carboniferous (320mya) and then shivered through its most severe ice age and most catastrophic extinction only 30 million years later (96% of marine species vanished). That ice age scraped all evidence of the preceding sedimentation from Madagascar and the geological record there is reset, beginning with gravel and boulder deposits laid down as the glaciers retreated. In the middle Permian (270mya) the southern continents were still assembled as one supercontinent – Gondwana – in which Madagascar was a central part without identity, bound on the west by present-day Africa, the east by India and the south by Antarctica.

Gondwana began to split apart soon after, towards the modern continental distribution. As a continent divides, rifts form, gradually becoming seas, then oceans. The rocks of the sedimentary shelf record 100 million years of deposition spanning that cycle for the rift separating Madagascar from Africa. The earliest sediments are mixed glacial, river and lake deposits that contain a fossil flora common to all the modern southern continents. Later, the land was inundated and marine carbonates were deposited in this new shallow sea preserving the remains of some primitive fish. During the Triassic (240–210mya) the landscape was uplifted and terrestrial gravels and sands were deposited, including those exposed in Isalo National Park. A major rise in sea level followed, and from this time until after the demise of the dinosaurs (63mya) fossil-bearing limestone sedimentation dominated in the growing Mozambique Channel. These sediments today make up the Bemaraha Plateau and the *tsingy* landscapes of western Madagascar. The shallow marine ecosystems were characterised by a great abundance of ammonites, and today the sedimentary carbonates of west Madagascar are an incredible repository of these fossils. Uplifting occurred again 50–30mya as a major eastern rift developed between India and Madagascar, ending sedimentation on the shelf.

The **volcanic edifices** of Madagascar are less obvious than the volcanoes responsible for the islands of the Comoros, Réunion and Mauritius. They are widespread in the north and along the east coast, and inland they make up the Ankaratra Massif, Itasy highlands and Montagne d'Ambre. Underwater volcanic activity began during the Cretaceous (120mya) and has persisted off the north coast up to the present day. The lavas and intrusive rocks produced have a bizarre and unique chemistry. The most recent major volcanic activity occurred less than 2mya, giving rise to Nosy Be, where modern hot springs testify to the island's relative youth. There are suggestions that the volcanic focus is moving southeast towards Madagascar; the volcanic record in the island is potentially far from over.

Significant **landscape evolution** has occurred over the last 40 million years. Since India began to head northeast, the rift between Africa and Madagascar stabilised and mountains were regenerated by activity on major NNE- and NNW-oriented faults. These orientations can be recognised across the country bounding smaller sedimentary basins and mountain ranges, and most noticeably control the strikingly linear geometry of the east coast. The centre and east were uplifted more than the west, providing the basis for the modern shape of the island. Completely emergent for the first time for several hundred million years, land plants and animals proliferated and evolved towards the island's present flora and fauna. Local lake and river deposits developed in the lowlands and erosion cut back the highlands. In the centre and east, the entire marine record was stripped away, revealing the crystalline core and resulting in undulating dome-like mountains, such as Pic d'Imarivolanitra. In the west the sedimentary rock was eroded flat to near sea level. Tectonic activity in the last million years has again uplifted the Malagasy terrain, and this ancient erosional surface now defines the plateaux of the west, including Bemaraha.

HUMAN COLONISATION The final chapter starts just 2,000 years ago, when skilled Malay boatmen found their way to then-uninhabited Madagascar and began a dramatic demonstration of how humans can affect geological processes. Reduction in primary forest since the colonisation of Madagascar has indisputably influenced the shape of the land. Soils once stabilised by deep root systems became susceptible to erosion, and the sediment load in the rivers increased. In the 50 years to 1945, 40m of clay was deposited in the delta of the Betsiboka River at Mahajanga, immensely more than the underlying sedimentary record suggests was usual prior to deforestation. Ubiquitous hillside scars (called *lavaka*) are the inland testimony to this accelerated redistribution of material from highlands to coast, an inexorable environmental response to deforestation that is sending the Malagasy highlands towards eventual peneplanation (flattening) at an incredible rate. Even with an average annual erosion of 1mm taking place continuously, Madagascar will be reduced to near sea level in a geologically short three million years.

FLORA

Madagascar and its adjacent islands harbour some 13,000 species of flowering plants of which a staggering 89% are endemic. Although some other regions of the world (such as the Tropical Andes, Indonesia and Brazil) have more plant species, they have substantially lower rates of endemism, typically below 50%. Madagascar

Clare & Johan Hermans

Like so many other living things on the island, the orchids of Madagascar are extremely varied; and well over three-quarters are endemic. More than 950 different species have been recorded so far and new ones are still being discovered. The orchids have adapted to every possible habitat, including the spiny forest and the cool highland mountain ranges, but their highest density is in the wet forests of the east. Whilst orchid habitats are becoming scarcer, one or other of them can be seen in flower at most times of the year; the best season for flowers is the rainy season from January to March.

Some of the most memorable orchids are to be found in the eastern coastal area, which is the habitat of large *Angraecums, Eulophiellas* and *Cymbidiellas*. Many are epiphytes living on tree branches or trunks; anchored by their roots they scramble over their host collecting moisture and nutrients, but they are not parasites.

Angraecum eburneum can be seen in flower from September to May, its thick leathery leaves forming a half-metre-wide fan shape; the flower stems reach above the leaves carrying a number of large greenish-white fragrant flowers. Like many Malagasy orchids the blooms are strongly scented and white in colour to attract pollinating moths at night.

The comet orchid, *A. sesquipedale*, is one of the most striking. It flowers from June to November and the plants are similar to *A. eburneum* but are slightly more compact. Individual flowers can be 26cm across and over 30cm long including the lengthy nectary spur, characteristic for the angraecoid orchids, at the back of the flower. The flower was described by Charles Darwin at the end of the 19th century when he predicted that there would be a moth with a very long tongue that could reach down to the nectar at the bottom of the spur. This idea was ridiculed by his contemporaries, but in 1903 – more than two decades after his death – he was proved right: a hawk moth with a proboscis of over 30cm (*Xanthopan morganii praedicta*) was discovered, and it has recently been caught on film pollinating this orchid.

Aeranthes plants look similar to *Angraecum*. Their spider-like greenish flowers are suspended from long thin stems, gently nodding in the breeze.

Eulophiella roempleriana, which can reach almost 2m tall, is now very rare. One of the few remaining plants can be seen on Ile aux Nattes, off Ile Sainte Marie. The large, deep

is the world's number one floral hotspot for an area its size. The fortuitous break from Africa and Asia at a time when the flowering plants were just beginning to diversify allowed many groups to develop their own lineage, supplemented occasionally by the later colonisations of more advanced forms.

FERNS AND CYCADS Ferns were in their heyday before Gondwana was even formed. Their best efforts were the impressive **tree ferns**, which had large spreading fronds sprouting from a tall, scaly stem. These structures created vast forests in all warm, humid areas during the Carboniferous, 350 million years ago. Although they eventually lost ground to seed-bearing plants during the age of the dinosaurs, it is a credit to their design that they are still abundant and successful. Indeed the soft, symmetrical foliage of ferns very much epitomises the lushness of hot, wet places. It's true that they have been relegated to a life in the shade of more recently evolved plants, but here they excel, out-competing all others.

Although some species are present in dry habitats, the vast majority of Madagascar's ferns decorate the branches and trunks of the eastern rainforests. One eye-catching species is the huge **bird's nest fern** (*Asplenium nidus*) which adorns many large trunks with luxuriant balconies of leaves. The ancient tree ferns

pink flowers are well worth the pirogue trip to the island. A few more of these plants survive in the reserves around Andasibe. They normally flower from October onwards.

Cymbidiella orchids are also very striking; they flower from October to January. *C. pardalina*, with its huge crimson lip, cohabits with a staghorn fern, while *C. falcigera*, with black-spotted yellow flowers, prefers the exclusive company of the raffia palm.

The highlands, with their cooler and more seasonal climate, are inhabited by numerous terrestrial orchids, growing in soil or leaf litter; underground tubers produce deciduous leaves and flower stems – not dissimilar to temperate orchids.

Eulophia plantaginea is a relatively common roadside plant; large colonies can sometimes be found, especially in boggy areas. *Cynorkis* can also be seen along the roads. Many are terrestrials, others grow on wet rock or in swamps. Epiphytes like *Angraecum* and *Aeranthes* can still be found in the few remaining pockets of forest in the highlands.

Aerangis plants are instantly recognisable by their shiny, dark green foliage. The flowers superficially resemble those of *Angraecum* but they are often much smaller, carried on elegant racemes, and their scent is exquisite. The plants are commonly seen in the wet shade of the rainforest reserves of Andasibe and Ranomafana. *Jumellea* are again similar but have a narrower, folded-back single flower on a thin stem.

Bulbophyllum orchids are easily missed by the untrained eye; their rounded, plump pseudo-bulbs are often seen on moss-covered trees. They are always worthwhile to investigate: small gem-like blooms may be nestled amongst the foliage.

Oeonia with its huge white lip and two red dots on its throat can be found rambling amongst the undergrowth. The apparently bare higher peaks of the *hauts plateaux* also contain a very specialised community of orchids. The thick-leaved, sun-loving angraecoids and *Bulbophyllums*, known as lithophytes, share the rock faces with succulents.

One of the best and easiest places to see orchids – including *Angraecum*, *Cymbidiella* and *Gastrorchis* – is in the grounds of hotels and private gardens, but one must be aware that these domestic collections may contain the odd foreign interloper. Orchids from the Orient and South America are brought in as pot plants, the flowers often being bigger and brighter than the natives'.

Note that export permits are required to transport orchids out of Madagascar.

(*Cyathea* spp) that once supplied the forest canopy are still present on its floor, contributing to the prehistoric atmosphere of the forest.

Often mistaken for a tree fern, the **cycad** (*Cycas* spp) is in fact one of the original seed-bearing plants. The evolution of seed propagation eventually led to the flowering plants that currently dominate all of the world's habitats, marking the end of the ferns' reign on earth. Resembling a tree fern with palm-like leaves, the single Malagasy representative of the genus, *Cycas thouarsii*, is found only in the eastern rainforests. Look closely at its cone: it holds seeds which, 30 million years ago, became the most significant single plant adaptation in the history of life.

PITCHER PLANTS There are only two species of insect-eating pitcher plant (*Nepenthes* spp) in Madagascar, but they are spectacular enough to deserve a mention. In wetlands in the south they poke out of the marsh beds like triffids planning an ambush. One of their leaves wraps upon itself to create a fly trap, which then serves up trace elements, from the flies' remains, unobtainable from the mud below. The rest of the family live thousands of miles away in southeast Asia, and it is thought that the arrival of Madagascar's two species stemmed from a fortuitous migration along the same path that originally brought the first people – perhaps they inadvertently shared the boats.

SUCCULENTS *With information from Gavin Hart*

In Madagascar, wherever rainfall is below about 40cm a year, succulents reign. The entire southwest of the island is dominated by their swollen forms. Further north they decorate the natural rock gardens of Isalo, Itremo and the countless outcrops on the central plateau. They also appear within the sparse dry forests of the west, among the stony chaos of the *tsingy* (see box on page 389), and even venture onto the grasslands and into the rainforests. About 150 succulent species occur in Madagascar, distributed widely across the island.

Euphorbia is one of the largest genera of flowering plants with over 2,000 species worldwide. Almost 500 are succulent species occurring predominantly in Africa and Madagascar. They have diversified into countless different forms, from bushes resembling strings of sausages, and trees sprouting smooth leafless green branches, to spiny stalks emerging from swollen underground tubers. Many species shed their leaves at the start of the dry season, but when present they are swollen with water and shining with wax. To replace the leaves they often yield wonderful flowers and in so doing brighten up the landscape.

E. *oncoclada* is sometimes called the sausage bush because of the regular constrictions along its cylindrical green stems, giving a string-of-sausages appearance. E. *stenoclada* is a large shrub with flattened spiny branches. By contrast there are dwarf prostrate species, such as E. *decaryi* and E. *ambovombensis*, often with swollen underground roots

The E. *milii* complex (a group of closely related forms) is undoubtedly the most prominent euphorbia in Madagascar, lining the streets of many towns. These are small shrubby plants with spiny stems (hence the common name: crown of thorns) and a few terminal leaves. The most dominant feature, however, is the bright red bracts surrounding the flowers which produce a blaze of colour from the mass plantings. All euphorbias have white milky sap which is toxic on skin contact, and can cause temporary blindness, so caution is urged in handling these plants.

Pachypodium is a genus of five species from southern Africa and about 20 from Madagascar. The Malagasy pachypodiums have an unusual flower structure in that the stamens are covered by a segmented cone which must be penetrated to achieve pollination. They vary from tree-like species to caudiciforms (stem succulents) with white, red or yellow flowers. They are mostly quite spiny when young but tend to lose their spines as they mature.

The bizarrely compressed P. *brevicaule*, which has been likened to a sack of potatoes, has most of its large mass beneath the ground. P. *lamerei* – widespread in the southwest – is the most common species in cultivation, often sold under the name Madagascar palm. P. *rutenbergianum* is widely distributed from the mid-west coast to the north and is the largest of the pachypodiums, reaching up to 15m tall with a heavily branched crown.

Didiereaceae of the arid southwest are the most intriguing plants in Madagascar, for they are an entire family of bizarre plants found nowhere else on earth. They look similar to cacti, but their tiny deciduous leaves – and the immense thorns that protect them – indicate that they are not (cacti don't have thorns; their spines are modified leaves). Of this family's four genera, **Alluaudia** contains six species, **Alluaudiopsis** and **Didierea** each contain two species and **Decaryia** is monotypic.

The octopus trees (*Didierea* spp) are the most famous members of this group. Species vary greatly in form and flower colouration within the family. *Alluaudia ascendens* is the largest, growing initially as a single stem, but then branching from the base forming massive V-shaped plants 10–15m tall with white to reddish

Unlike animals, plants cannot escape harsh environments. The plants of Madagascar's dry southwest have therefore had to adapt to tolerate strong sunlight, high temperatures and – most restrictive of all – desiccation. These high demands have produced unusual-looking and fascinating plant species called **xerophytes**.

All xerophytes have deep root systems to acquire what little water there is available. Their leaves are usually small and covered in hairs, and much of their photosynthesis is done by the green stems. This design lowers the surface area of the plant and traps still air adjacent to the leaf, reducing water loss – the key aim. In addition to desiccation, overheating is as much a problem for plants as it is for animals. Xerophytes have therefore evolved various techniques to minimise heating: usually they have their narrowest edge facing the sun and they often add grey pigments to their leaves to deflect the harsh rays of midday.

The most extreme adaptations for a dry life are to be seen in the **succulents**. This general term describes all xerophytes which store water in their waxy leaves, roots or stems. Water is a valuable commodity in a dry habitat, and one that must be protected from thirsty grazers, so succulents usually employ toxins or spines as a defence. This is evident in many of the island's spectacular plants, not least the octopus trees (*Didierea*) of the spiny forest.

flowers. *Alluaudia comosa* also branches from the base, but forms a wide, flat-topped shrub 2–6m tall. The spines are up to 2cm long and white flowers cover the ends of its shoots. The beautiful *Alluaudiopsis marnieriana* grows to 4m and has the most colourful flowers of the whole family – up to 3cm across and bright crimson.

Aloe is a genus containing about 450 species occurring in southern and eastern Africa and Madagascar. Over a hundred are recognised in Madagascar but there are distinct differences between African and Malagasy species. Madagascar does not have any grass aloes or spotted aloes, but has numerous species which differ markedly from those growing elsewhere. Even though aloes are known as low-growing plants, some species have stems to raise their broad foliage above the ground. The largest aloes have stocky 3m stems covered in untidy dead scales which sport huge succulent leaves and, in June and July, a large red inflorescence. *A. divaricata* is a fast-growing species common in the southwest. Its single or branched stems are 2–6m long with narrow blue-grey leaves and red-brown marginal teeth, scattered along the whole length. Highly branched inflorescences of up to 1m bear coral-red flowers. *A. suzannae* is unique among aloes in being a night-bloomer; flowers open before midnight and close the following morning. Flowers (which only appear on plants at least ten years old) are pollinated by the souimanga sunbird and Madagascar white-eye as well as by bats and mouse lemurs.

Kalanchoe contains 143 species of succulent perennials distributed through Africa, Madagascar, Arabia and Asia – with 63 occurring in Madagascar. The most well known is the panda plant (*Kalanchoe tomentosa*), a shrub with dense rosettes. The species are highly variable in form (from low leafy succulents to tall tree-like plants), leaf shape, size and colour. *Kalanchoe* flowers have parts in multiples of four – four connected petals forming a tube, four sepals, four carpals and eight stamens – whereas most other Crassulaceae flowers have parts in multiples of five. In Madagascar the largest species (eg: *K. arborescens*, *K. beharensis*, *K. grandidieri*) tend to be restricted to the semi-arid regions of the south and southwest, while the smaller species occur mostly in the more humid areas up to 2,000m.

Adenia is a genus of about 150 species in the passionflower family. Most are deciduous vines, climbing with the aid of tendrils, extending from a swollen stem base. They are usually dioecious (either male or female) with inconspicuous creamy greenish flowers and fruit that's often vividly coloured when ripe.

Uncarina is an endemic genus of 13 species in the Pedialaceae family. The plants are deciduous shrubs or small trees up to 8m tall with a substantial underground tuber. Flowers may be yellow, white, pink or violet, and the fruits are large capsules covered with numerous, ferociously hooked thorns, which aid dissemination by attaching to the hairy coats of animals.

Cyphostemma (family Vitaceae) is a genus with over 300 species (a minority of which are succulent). Twenty-four occur in Madagascar. *Cyphostemma sakalavense* is bottle-shaped with a stem up to 3m tall. It can be found on the limestone rocks of the *tsingy* in northwest Madagascar.

Senecio is a genus of leaf succulents, existing essentially as a collection of swollen leaves sprouting from the earth. The leaves are often ornamental, tinged with terracotta and bearing harsh spines, but also display showy red flowers during times of drought.

PALMS Madagascar is home to one of the world's richest palm floras. There are around 170 species – three times more than in the rest of Africa put together – and 165 of these are found nowhere else.

A lack of large herbivores in Madagascar has left its palms – with no need for defences – spineless and without poisons. Pollination is mostly by bees and flies, but some have tiny flowers to entice unknown insect guests. For seed dispersal lemurs are often employed. Ring-tailed, black, red ruffed and brown lemurs all assist in scattering the seeds. The bright colours of some fruits serve to attract birds and forest pigs, while the handful of African palms, which normally use elephants as dispersers, presumably make do with zebu.

The dominance of species with Asian relatives betrays the fact that Madagascar severed with India millions of years *after* it broke away from African shores.

The species present range from the famous to the recently discovered, from dwarf to giant, and almost all have intriguing characteristics. One palm has led to a Malagasy word entering the English language – the **raffia palm** (*Raphia ruffia*). The fibres from its leaves are woven into hats, baskets and mats. Of the 50 new palm species discovered in the last decade, one is worth particular attention: *Ravenea musicalis*, the world's only water palm. It starts life underwater in only one of Madagascar's southeastern rivers. As it grows, it surfaces, eventually bears fruit, and then seeds. Its discoverer named it *R. musicalis* after being charmed by the chimes of its seedpods as they hit the water below. There are other riverside palms in Madagascar adapted to tolerate the recurrent floods of the island's lowland rainforest, but none as perfectly as the musical water palm.

Another unusual group is the **litter-trapping palms**. The crown of their leaves is arranged like an upturned shuttlecock, sprouting at first from the forest floor, and then gaining height as the stem grows from below. Its watertight crown catches leaves falling from the canopy, perhaps to obtain trace minerals, but no one knows for sure. A strange consequence of this growth is that the roots of other plants, which originally grew through the soil into the crown by mistake, later dangle down from its heights as alabaster-white zigzags.

Although the vast majority of palms live among the hardwoods of the lowland rainforests, there are species which brave the more arid environments, notably the feather palms (*Chrysalidocarpus* spp) which nestle in the canyons of Isalo National Park and stand alone amongst the secondary grasslands of the west.

Looking like a messy cross between a palm and a pine tree, **pandan palms** or screw pines (*Pandanus* spp) are different from those above, but equally fond of Madagascar. Their foliage consists of untidy grass-like mops which awkwardly adorn rough branches periodically emerging from their straight trunks. Common in both rainforests and dry forests there are 75 species, only one of which is found elsewhere, placing the country alongside Borneo in the pandan diversity stakes.

Note: The word palm is often used rather liberally. The **traveller's palm** (*Ravenala madagascariensis*), symbolic of Madagascar, is not a palm at all (see *Trees* overleaf). In fact it is in the same family as the bird of paradise flower (Strelitziaceae). A second 'false palm' is the **Madagascar palm**, which is actually a spiny succulent *Pachypodium lamerei* (see page 38).

TAVY
Jamie Spencer

Slash-and-burn farming, *tavy* in Malagasy, is blamed for the permanent destruction of the rainforest. Even those practising *tavy* agree with this. They also respect the forest and they can see that *tavy* greatly jeopardises the future for the next generations. So why destroy what you love and need?

One answer to a very complex question is the practical need. In Madagascar poverty is extreme and there are few options. Life's priority is to feed your family and children. Rice, the food staple, is grown both on the flat ground in sustainable paddy fields, and on the steep slopes of slashed and burned forest. Cyclones often wash away much of the paddy rice crop and wipe out the earth dams and irrigation waterways built at great cost and effort. Some farmers have invested a lifetime's savings employing labour for their construction. So if floods strike, people rely on the hill rice. Fertility in these fields is not replenished as in paddies where nutrients are carried in the water. The soil quickly becomes unproductive so new slopes must be cut after a few years.

The cultural explanation for *tavy* is less obvious. The people of 'my' village, Sandrakely, are Tanala (meaning 'people of the forest'). The forest is their world and to survive in this surprisingly harsh environment they clear the land with fire – the ancient agricultural technique brought by the original immigrants from Indonesia perhaps 2,000 years ago. In more recent history the Tanala were forced into the forest by warring neighbours and colonial occupants of more fertile areas.

As the traditional means of survival and provision, *tavy* can be seen as central to society's make-up and culture. The calendar revolves around it, land ownership and hierarchies are determined by its practice, and politics are centred on it. It is the pivot and subject of rituals and ceremonies. The forest is the domain of the ancestors and site of tombs and religious standing stones. *Tavy* is an activity carried out between the living and the dead: the ancestors are consulted and permit its execution to provide for the living. The word *tavy* also means 'fatness', with all the associations of health, wealth and beauty.

If they have the choice, many are happy to pursue sustainable agricultural alternatives, so Feedback Madagascar is ready to help them. But the practical and cultural context must always be respected. The alternatives must be rock solid when people's lives are at stake and to be truly enduring they must be accommodated within the culture by the people themselves. It is they who understand the problems and know the solutions that are acceptable. They must not be forced.

Jamie Spencer is the founder of the charity Feedback Madagascar; see page 133.

TREES Until the arrival of humans, Madagascar is thought to have been largely cloaked in forest. There remain examples of each of the original forests, but vast areas have become treeless as a result of *tavy* (slash-and-burn agriculture; see box on page 41) and soil erosion.

Most of the remaining **evergreen trees** form the superstructure of the rainforest. They are typically 30m high, with buttressed roots, solid hardwood trunks and vast canopies. There can be up to 250 species of tree in a single hectare of lowland rainforest, but from the ground they all look very similar. To identify a species, botanists must often wait for flowering, an event that is not only extremely difficult to predict, but also one that takes place 30m high, out of sight.

One notable and obvious tree is the **strangler fig** (*Ficus* spp), which germinates up in the canopy on a branch of its victim, grows down to the floor to root, and then encircles and constricts its host leaving a hollow knotted trunk. The Malagasy prize the forest hardwoods; one canopy tree is called the 'kingswood' because its wood is so hard that, at one time, any specimens found were automatically the property of the local king.

The only evergreen species to be found outside the rainforest are the **tapia tree** (*Uapaca bojei*), the nine species of **mangrove tree** and some of the **succulent trees** in the extreme southwest where sea mists provide water year-round. In tolerating the conditions of west Madagascar, these evergreens have borne their own unusual communities.

The rest of Madagascar's trees are **deciduous**, ie: they lose their leaves during the dry season. The taller dry forests of the west are dappled with the shadows of **leguminous trees** such as *Dalbergia* and *Cassia*, characterised by their long seedpods and symbiotic relationships with bacteria which provide fertilisers within their roots. Sprawling **banyan figs** (*Ficus* spp) and huge **tamarind trees** (*Tamarindus indica*) create gallery forest along the rivers of the west and south, yielding pungent fruit popular with lemurs. In drier woodland areas Madagascar's most celebrated trees, the **baobabs** (*Adansonia* spp), dominate.

One last species deserves a mention. The **traveller's palm** (*Ravenala madagascariensis*) is one of Madagascar's most spectacular plants. It is thought to have earned its name from the relief it affords thirsty travellers: water is stored in the base of its leaves and can be released with a swift blow from a machete. Its elegant fronds are arranged in a dramatic vertical fan, which is decorative enough to have earned it a role as Air Madagascar's logo. Its large, bulbous flowers sprout from the leaf axils and, during the 24 hours that they are receptive, are visited by unusual pollinators – ruffed lemurs. The lemurs locate flowers which have just opened, and literally pull them apart to get at the large nectary inside. Keeping a lemur fed puts quite a demand on the tree, but it produces flowers day after day for several months, and during this time the lemurs eat little else. The traveller's palm is perhaps the only native species to have benefited from *tavy* agriculture – it dominates areas of secondary vegetation on the central plateau and east coast.

This secondary rainforest that grows back after *tavy* is called *savoka*. Aside from the traveller's palm, these areas of *savoka* are sadly dominated by foreign tree species which will eventually infest all returning forest, changing Madagascar's rainforest communities forever. A handful of native plants have managed to compete with these exotics but relatively few animals live in this vegetation.

BAOBABS *With information from Jim Bond*

The baobab – a freak among trees with its massively swollen trunk and sparse stubby branches – is emblematic of Madagascar. This is the motherland of baobabs. Of the eight species found worldwide, six grow exclusively in Madagascar. The others (one in Australia and one across Africa) are believed to have originated from seedpods that were swept away from Malagasy shores around 10mya and survived the ocean crossings. Even the African species can be seen in Madagascar today, for it was introduced by Arab traders as street planting in towns.

The reason for the baobab's extraordinary girth – sometimes exceeding 30m – is that it is well adapted to inhospitably dry conditions. It is capable of taking up and storing water from sporadic downpours very efficiently, its porous wood acting like a huge sponge. No doubt inspired by the great size of some specimens, claims have been made that these giants can live for many thousands of years. In fact, recent studies suggest that few are older than 500, but it is difficult to be certain because unlike other trees baobabs do not produce growth rings.

Floral groups The six Malagasy species can be divided into two groups based on floral characteristics: the Brevitubae (short-tubed) and Longitubae (long-tubed). Baobabs have large, showy flowers – up to 30cm long – that open at dusk and are receptive for one night only.

Brevitubae This group comprises *Adansonia grandidieri* in the south and *A. suarezensis* in the north. They typically have flat-topped crowns of predominantly horizontal branches, emerging just above the canopy of the surrounding forest. This arrangement is thought to assist their favoured pollinator, a fruit bat, in hopping between flowers. The cream-coloured flowers, which are held erect rather like a cup and saucer, and have a foul carrion-like smell, are also visited by fork-marked lemurs, giant mouse lemurs, sunbirds and bees.

Longitubae The remaining Malagasy species, *A. za* and *A. rubrostipa* in the south, and *A. perrieri* and *A. madagascariensis* in the north, have long floral parts, which in contrast to the Brevitubae are red and yellow and have a sweetly fragrant scent. They dangle downwards concealing the nectar at the end of an elongated tube. Only the long tongues of certain hawk moths – commonly reaching 25cm unfurled – can reach it. These trees tend to be smaller than the Brevitubae because, being pollinated by hawk moths, they have less need to emerge above the canopy.

Species of baobab Even to the expert eye, individual species can be tough to identify. Their form is highly dependent on environmental factors meaning there can be massive variation within one species. Grandidier's baobabs near Morondava, for example, are smooth, columnar giants up to 30m tall. But in the spiny scrub at Andavadoaka, mature trees of the same species are quite knobbly and almost spherical, often reaching no more than 3m in height. Nevertheless, the following descriptions should help you to determine which are which.

Adansonia grandidieri These, the most majestic and famous of the Malagasy baobabs, were named in honour of French naturalist Alfred Grandidier.  They may reach 30m in height and 7.5m in diameter, with some large hollow ones reportedly having been used as houses. The best-known specimens form the Avenue des Baobabs near Morondava (one of the most photographed sights in Madagascar). The isolated trees in this area would once have been surrounded by dense forest; but today their silhouettes can be seen for miles

A. grandidieri Morondava

A. grandidieri Andavadoaka

across the flat, featureless rice fields. Better examples (being in relatively intact forest) can be seen in the Mangoky Valley. Grandidier's baobabs tend to be found on flood plains or near rivers. Malagasy names: *renala, reniala* (literally 'mother of the forest'); flowers: May–August; distribution: Manambolo lakes system down to Mikea Forest.

Adansonia za Typically with a tall, straight trunk and grey bark around the crown, this is the most widespread species. It is found further inland than the others, most notably around Zombitse. This is probably because it is more tolerant of the cooler climate. The fruits are ovoid rather than round and have peculiarly swollen stalks. Malagasy names: *za, boringy, ringy, bojy, bozy, bozybe*; flowers: November–January; distribution: west of Taolagnaro (Fort Dauphin) up to Analalava.

Adansonia rubrostipa (formerly A. fony) Preferring sandy soil, this is the smallest of the baobabs. In the spiny forest they assume a bottle shape, but at Kirindy they are taller and more slender. The fruits are rather thin-walled and do not carry far without breaking open. This may explain why clusters of *A. rubrostipa* are often found growing in relatively high concentrations. Identifying features include serrated leaf edges and bark that tends to have a reddish tinge. Malagasy names: *fony, zamena, boringy, ringy*; flowers: February–March; distribution: along the west coast from Itampolo to Soalala.

Adansonia suarezensis Restricted to a few sites in the extreme north of Madagascar, this is the world's second rarest baobab. It is closely related to *A. grandidieri* but specimens tend to be somewhat smaller. It is characterised by its horizontal branches and smooth red bark. Malagasy names: *bojy, bozy*; flowers: May–July; distribution: areas near Antsiranana and the forests of Mahory and Analamera.

Adansonia perrieri Some people call this the 'rainforest species' for it shuns the drier habitats where its siblings thrive. It occupies a specialised niche on the sheltered banks of small streams running down from Montagne d'Ambre. It is the largest of the three northern baobabs, and with just a few dozen specimens remaining it is also one of the rarest trees in the world. One of the best sites to see it in its full glory is by the stream that runs down from the Grande Cascade in the National Park. You will need to set aside a half-day, but the sight of these tall trees rising majestically from the steep valley floor is well worth the walk. Malagasy names: *bojy, bozy*; flowers: November–December; distribution: a few very small populations near Montagne d'Ambre.

Adansonia madagascariensis This is the most variable and consequently the most difficult to identify of the baobabs. Given favourable soil and water conditions, such as at the east entrance to Ankarana, it may reach an imposing 20m in height, while on the nearby karst the same species is squat and pear-shaped. The bark is pale grey and the flowers are dark red. The fruits are smaller, rounder, less furry, and narrower-stalked than in most species. Malagasy names: *zabe, renida, bojy, bozy*; flowers: March–April; distribution: Ankarana plateau northwards.

Adansonia digitata Although an introduced species, the African baobab has become naturalised in several parts of Madagascar. The best known specimen grows in the middle of a road at the western side of Mahajanga, where it has a role as a traffic island! This is the fattest tree in Madagascar with a circumference of 22m. In Africa

Many Malagasy plants crop up in garden centres throughout Europe. Familiar to horticulturalists are the dragon tree (*Dracaena marginata*), the crown of thorns (*Euphorbia millii*), the Areca palm, the flamboyant tree (*Delonix regia*) and the Madagascar jasmine (*Stephanotis floribunda*) of bridal bouquet fame. Other natives are valued for their uses rather than their aesthetic qualities. Recent interest has grown in Madagascar's various wild coffees (Rubiaceae family). Many are naturally caffeine-free and hybrids with tastier coffees are currently being produced to exploit this trait. (Naturally caffeine-free coffees are highly desirable because artificial decaffeination processes tend to leave toxic residues in the finished product.)

The Madagascar rosy periwinkle (*Catharanthus roseus*) is a champion of those who campaign to conserve natural habitats. The plant has a long history of medicinal use the world over. In India, wasp stings were treated with juice from the leaves; in Europe, it was long used as a folk remedy for diabetes; in Hawaii, the plant was boiled to make a poultice to stop bleeding; in China, it was considered a cough remedy; in Central and South America, it has also been used in homemade cold remedies to ease lung congestion, inflammation and sore throats; and in the Caribbean, an extract of the flower was used to treat eye infections. Most importantly, however, it is now used in chemotherapy. Substances called vinblastine and vincristine extracted from the rosy periwinkle have proved effective in the treatment of leukaemia and Hodgkin's disease.

There are certainly many other plants with equally life-saving chemical properties yet to be found, but the rate of forest destruction may be driving these to extinction before we have a chance to appreciate them or even discover the species at all.

it grows in 31 countries. Malagasy names: *sefo*, *bontona*, *vontona*; flowers: November–December.

Uses and conservation Baobabs provide a number of resources for humans. The seeds are eaten and used for cooking oil; the bark is used to make rope and roofing materials; and the leaves are fed to cattle, as is the wood in times of drought. Baobab wood is neither strong enough for building nor particularly good for burning, so the trees tend to be left standing when the surrounding forest is cleared. Removal of the bark does little damage since baobabs possess the rare ability to regenerate it. Mature trees are even quite resistant to fire and so rarely succumb to the regular burning of undergrowth carried out to stimulate new grazing.

Nevertheless, the outlook for the Malagasy baobabs is bleak. Half of the species are listed as endangered and all are recognised as threatened by habitat loss. The main problem is that there is virtually no new growth. Deprived of the protection afforded by the surrounding forest, those seedlings that escape burning are promptly devoured by zebu. Furthermore, two species (*A. grandidieri* and *A. suarezensis*) are thought to depend on animals to disperse their seeds. But since no living Malagasy creature is known to eat the fruit of the baobab, it can only be assumed that these seed dispersers are now extinct – very bad news indeed for the future of these species.

If these trees were allowed to die out it would be a terribly sad loss. But the impact penetrates much deeper than that. Baobabs provide food, support and homes for a plethora of creatures, both directly and indirectly, including: lemurs, bats, birds, insects, geckos, humans and even other plants and fungi. Treat these majestic giants with respect and remember that many are honoured as *faly* (sacred) – so try to ask permission before you take photos.

FOREIGN INVADERS In common with many islands around the globe, Madagascar has suffered from accidental and intended introductions of alien species. Sometimes referred to as weeds, because they do not really belong there, they can cause havoc when they arrive.

Out-competing native species, sharp tropical grasses from South America permanently deface the burnt woodlands of the west. And their populations explode because zebu do not find these exotic species appetising. Where thick forest is cleared, fast-growing *Eucalyptus* and *Psidium* trees step in. The trumpet lily (*Datura* spp) is now rampant in localised areas. Another growing problem is the rubber bush (*Calotropis procera*), which is native to tropical Africa and Asia; this has become the dominant plant in some areas around Antsiranana. They either suffocate competitors with their dense growth or poison the soil with their toxins. In drier areas, superbly adapted and profoundly damaging *Opuntia* cacti spread from the nearby sisal plantations and flourish where there was once spiny forest.

Needless to say, the native animal populations, unable to adapt to these invaders, also suffer – and this, perhaps even more than the endangerment of plant species, has prompted action from conservation bodies.

FAUNA

Compared with the breathtaking ecosystems of mainland Africa, Madagascar's fauna has far more subtle qualities. A combination of ancient Gondwana stock and 165 million years of isolated evolution has created a haven for a plethora of strange and unusual creatures. Here are a seemingly random collection of animal groups that had the opportunity to prove themselves in the absence of large predators and herbivores. The resulting 180,000 species, existing in habitats from rainforests to coral reefs, bring human opportunity too: for numerous truly unique wildlife encounters.

INVERTEBRATES There are well over 150,000 species of invertebrate in Madagascar, the majority in the eastern rainforests. To spot them turn over leaves and logs on the forest floor, peer very closely at the foliage or switch on a bright light after dark. Although perhaps creepy, and undeniably crawly, they do contribute substantially to the experience of wild areas on the island and – provided you can suppress the spine shivers – your mini-safaris will be hugely rewarding.

It is a difficult task to pick out the most impressive invertebrates, but notable are the hugely oversized **pill millipedes** (*Sphaerotherium* spp) which roll up when threatened to resemble a stripy brown or green golf ball. Among the forest foliage are superbly camouflaged **praying mantises**, **net-throwing spiders** that cast their silk nets at fliers-by, and **nymphs** and bugs of all shapes, colours and adornments. Among the leaf litter there are spectacular striped and horned **flatworms**, the otherworldly **ant lions** (see boxes on pages 48 and 395) and vast numbers of wonderful **weevils**, the most spectacular being the bright red giraffe-necked weevil (most easily seen at Ranomafana National Park). The species gets its name from the male whose tremendously long neck is almost three times the length of his body!

One invertebrate whose presence will not be welcomed by most visitors is the **leech**, but it is a more fascinating creature than you might at first imagine; turn to the box on page 311 to discover why.

There are around 300 species of **butterfly** in Madagascar, 211 of which are endemic to the island. The most eye-catching are the heavily-patterned swallowtails, and the nymphalids with their dominant blue and orange liveries. Madagascar's **moths** are significantly older in origin and are probably descendants

Len de Beer & John Roff

LOOKING LIKE... You're walking through a patch of forest and stop to photograph an unusual flower, when you notice some thoughtless bird has relieved itself on a leaf you were about to lean on. You're about to wipe it off when you have a hunch that you should look closer. What looked like a bird dropping turns out to be a fine specimen of *Phrynarachne* – a specialised crab spider that spends its time sitting on top of a leaf looking like poo. Some even emulate the scent of urine and faeces.

Why? Flies delight in landing on faeces and other choice decomposing substances; bird droppings are a fine source of nutrition for forest flies. Bird-dung crab spiders like *Phrynarachne* take full advantage of this, waiting on leaves or other prominent surfaces for hungry flies to come and investigate the latest tempting blob of excrement. Once the fly is within reach, the spider seizes it with lightning speed and administers a deadly bite.

A FREAK BACK FROM THE DEAD In 1881 a spider hunter with the charming moniker of Octavius Pickard-Cambridge was staring at a 'fossil' that had come crawling out of the substrate as if to proclaim: 'Hah! You thought I had gone!' in much the same way that Prof J L B Smith would later stare at the resurrected coelacanth as it received instant worldwide recognition as a living fossil.

The archaea – or pelican spider – has languished in obscurity, a victim of its small size, northern hemisphere bias and irrational arachnophobia. The archaeid spiders with their giraffe necks and cannibalistic natures were first described from Baltic amber in 1854. Imagine Octavius's rapture when 27 years later, on an expedition to the dripping escarpments of the red isle, archaea tiptoed back into the list of species with which humans are privileged to share the earth.

'Bizarre' seems too mild an adjective for an arachnid that does not build a web, has massively elongated, spiked jaws that can extend outward at right angles, and stilt-like legs that enable it to hover over its prey. The fact that the victims are exclusively other spiders just adds to the archaea's mystique. Living archaeids have only been found on the southern landmasses of Madagascar, Africa and Australia, yet more evidence that these places were once a continuous continent. Is it a coincidence that both archaea and the coelacanth are associated with an island renowned for the freakier designer labels of creation that so fascinate us?

SPIDER-WATCHING Madagascar's spiders are well worth a closer look. You never know what you may find. They show an incredible range of design and diversity. Keep an eye out for the iridescent jumping spiders, the giant orb-web weavers and the multi-coloured lynx spiders. Who knows – you could even find a new species.

Spider-watching in Madagascar is particularly enjoyable because you can do it anywhere. Even most hotels have at least one tree or bush in the garden where you can find extraordinary spiders easily before you even get to the national parks.

Natural History **FAUNA**

3

of the Gondwana insects marooned on the island. This explains the diversity – 4,000 species – including many groups active during the day, filling niches that elsewhere are the realm of butterflies. Most dramatic is the huge yellow comet moth (*Argema mittrei*) with a wingspan of up to 25cm, and the elaborate urania moths (*Chrysiridia* spp), which look just like swallowtails decorated with emeralds. A very close relative is found in the Amazon rainforest.

There's one impressive invertebrate which you will encounter almost everywhere you go; all you need do is look up. The huge **golden orb-web**

John Roff & Len de Beer

A couple of fascinating stories have recently emerged from Madagascar concerning the relationship between bugs and drugs – and both involve lemurs too.

The first relates to lemur hygiene. In 1996 black lemurs (*Eulemur macaco*) were being studied at Lokobe on Nosy Be as part of research into seed dispersal. A mature female was observed to grab a millipede (*Charactopygus* sp), bite it and rub the juices of its wounded body vigorously over her underside and tail. While enacting this strange ritual she half closed her eyes and salivated profusely with a silly grimace on her primate face. She was seen to do this a second time and it is speculated that the toxins in the millipede serve to protect her against parasites such as mosquitoes. Or maybe she just needed a fix?

In a relationship that goes the other way, the golden bamboo lemur – a species unknown to science until 1984 – has developed a startling specialism. These furry honey-coloured characters avoid competition with other resident species of lemur at Ranomafana by feeding exclusively on the shoots of *Cephalostachyum viguieri* – a giant bamboo that contains about 150mg of cyanide per kilogramme of fresh shoots. In so doing each individual consumes 12 times the theoretical lethal dose for a primate of it's size per day – that's enough cyanide to kill three grown men. High concentrations of this deadly chemical are found in its dung and it turns out that this is the exclusive food source of a very specialised rainforest dung beetle. It is currently not known how either creature manages to survive this poisonous diet, but one thing is fairly certain: were the golden bamboo lemur to become extinct, the fascinating beetle that relies on its toxic excrement would follow suit.

spiders (*Nephila madagascariensis*) string together massive webs often extending between trees and telephone wires. Along Fianar's telegraph cables hundreds of *Nephilas* string their webs together forming an impressively huge net several hundred metres long! Their silk is so strong that it was once woven into a fabric; Queen Victoria even had a pair of *Nephila* silk stockings. For more spider oddities see the box on page 47.

Other arachnids in Madagascar include **scorpions** and **tarantulas**, though neither is frequently encountered.

Angus McCrae

Should you come across little conical craters up to 5cm across in dry, sandy places, you are looking at traps built by ant lions. Out of sight at the bottom of each pit lurks a strange and ravenous larva, buried but for the tips of its needle-sharp mandibles. Should an unwary ant or other small prey stray over the brink, a blur of action may suddenly erupt: showers of sand are hurled back by the ant lion's jerking head and the resultant landslide carries the intruder helplessly down into the waiting jaws.

Seen close up, the larval ant lion is a termite-like alien with a flattened head attached, apparently upside down, to its hunched body. It has eyes arranged in groups either side of the head, and thin whiskers sprout from around its sickle-like jaws. Its mouth is permanently sealed, so it feeds through a narrow groove along each mandible. It is thus incapable of chewing or taking in anything but liquid. (With no solids to be excreted the stomach ends blindly, disconnected from the hind-gut.)

The adults, which superficially resemble clumsy dragonflies, are seldom noticed by non-specialists as most are drab and nocturnal. About 20 ant lion species are known from Madagascar, but probably many more remain undescribed.

FISH *With information from Derek Schuurman*

Freshwater species The inhabitants of Madagascar's abundant lakes, marshes, estuaries, rivers and mountain brooks have been as much isolated by history as those of the land. The most interesting species are the **cichlids** (known locally as *damba*) with their huge variety, colourful coats and endearing habits of childcare – they protect their young by offering their mouths as a retreat in times of danger. Other Malagasy species demonstrate the parental instinct, a feature rare in fish. Some of the island's **catfish** are also mouth-brooders, and male **mudskippers** in the mangroves defend their nest burrows with the vigour of a proud father.

Another major group is the **killifish**, which resemble the gouramis found in pet shops. Specialised **eels** live high up in mountain brooks, and blind **cave fish** are to be found in the underground rivers of western Madagascar, in some cases surviving entirely on the rich pickings of bat guano. The one problem with the island's fish is that they are not big and tasty. Consequently many exotic species have been introduced into the rivers and are regularly on display in the nation's markets. These new species naturally put pressure on the native stock and, as is so often the story, the less-vigorous Malagasy species have been all but wiped out. The main culprit seems to be the Asian snakehead (*Channa* spp). North Koreans farmed them in Madagascar in the 1980s, but following the first floods they spread and are now present in all the major lakes of Madagascar. The snakehead is a voracious predator and has severely reduced populations of endemic fish wherever it occurs. The other predatory fish which has decimated indigenous species is the largemouth bass, *Micropterus salmoides*.

Marine species More robust are the marine species to be found swimming off the island's 4,000km of coastline. Madagascar is legendary for its **shark** populations and a quick dip off the east coast should be considered carefully. On the opposite side, the Mozambique channel is the most shark-infested stretch of water in the world, both in terms of number of species and number of individuals. However, swimming on this west coast is generally safe because the inshore waters are mostly shallow and protected by fringing **coral reefs**. Much of this reef is in good condition and bursting with life, outdoing even the Red Sea for fish diversity. The reefs are host to a typical Indo-Pacific community of clownfish, angelfish, butterflyfish, damselfish, tangs, surgeonfish, triggerfish, wrasse, groupers, batfish, blennies, gobies, boxfish, lionfish, moray eels, flutefish, porcupinefish, pufferfish, squirrelfish, sweetlips and the moorish idol.

Scuba-diving in Madagascar can therefore be very rewarding; see pages 80–3 for practical information.

FROGS Madagascar is home to a staggering 266 recorded frog species, but it seems that is just the tip of the iceberg. Only very recently have thorough investigations of the island's amphibian population got under way, and well over 100 further species are already awaiting formal description!

The box on page 51 describes a selection of Madagascar's most interesting ranine inhabitants.

REPTILES The unique evolutionary history of Madagascar is typified by its reptiles. There are around 365 endemic species, representing 96% of the island's reptilian population. Some are derived from ancient Gondwana stock, many of which are more closely related to South American or Asian reptiles than to African ones. There are also large groups of closely related species marking the radiations that stemmed from African immigrations in more recent times. This is illustrated most dramatically by the **chameleons**. Madagascar is home to about half the world's chameleon species including the smallest and the largest. With impressive adaptive dexterity, they have dispersed throughout the habitats of the island to occupy every conceivable niche.

Similar in their success have been the **geckoes**. The hundred or so gecko species in Madagascar seem to be split between those that make every effort imaginable to camouflage themselves and those that go out of their way to stick out like a sore thumb. The spectacular **day gecko** (*Phelsuma madagascariensis*) and its relatives can be seen by passing motorists from some distance. Their dazzling emerald coats emblazoned with Day-Glo orange blotches are intended for the attentions of the opposite sex and competitors. Once in their sights they bob their heads and wave their tails as if an extra guarantee of visibility is needed. In contrast a magnificently camouflaged **leaf-tailed gecko** (*Uroplatus* spp) could easily be resting on a tree trunk right under your nose without being noticed. With its flattened body, splayed tail, speckled eyes, colour-change tactics and complete lack of shadow, you may remain ignorant of its presence unless it gets nervous and gapes its large, red tongue in your direction.

A quiet scuttle on the floor of a western forest may well be a **skink**, while louder rustlings are likely to be one of the handsome **plated lizards**. However, the most significant disturbances, both in the forest and the academic world, are made by the **iguanids**. This group of mostly large lizards is primarily found in the Americas but no evidence of their presence has ever been discovered in Africa. The question of how some came to be in Madagascar has not yet been answered convincingly.

Madagascar's three **boas** are in the same boat. They exist only as fossils in Africa, supplanted by the more stealthy pythons, but they do have distant relatives in South America. Most often seen is the Madagascar tree boa (*Sanzinia madagascariensis*), which although decorated in the same marbled glaze, varies in colour from orange or green (when juvenile) to grey and black, brilliant green or brown and blue, depending on the location. Its larger relative the ground boa (*Acrantophis madagascariensis*) is also often spied at the edge of waterways in the humid east and north. Of the remaining species of snake, the metre-long **hog-nosed snake** (*Leioheterodon madagascariensis*), in its dazzling checkerboard of black and yellow, is one of the most frequently encountered, usually gliding across a carpet of leaves on the lookout for frogs.

Despite the fact that none of the island's snakes poses a danger to humans, the Malagasy are particularly wary of some species. The blood-red tail of one harmless tree snake (*Ithycyphus perineti*), known to the Malagasy as *fandrefiala*, is believed to have powers of possession. It is said to hypnotise cattle from up high, then drop down tail-first to impale its victim. Similar paranormal attributes are bestowed on other Malagasy reptiles. The chameleons, for example, are generally feared by the Malagasy, and when fascinated *vazaha* go to pick one up, this is often met with surprised gasps from the locals. Another reptile deeply embedded in the folklore is the **Nile crocodile** (*Crocodilus niloticus*) which, although threatened throughout the island, takes on spiritual roles in some areas (see *Lake Antanavo*, page 338).

Stop and listen to the sounds of the rainforest. You may think those mysterious chirps, squeaks and clicks are birds and insects, but in most cases you would be wrong. Unlike the stereotypical Amazon jungle, where birdcalls permeate the air, the dominant sound in the Malagasy rainforest is the frog chorus. Yet these remarkable creatures are largely overlooked by tourists.

Frogs are the only amphibians in Madagascar – no toads, newts, or salamanders here – but with over 260 described species, and countless more in the pipeline, they outnumber Madagascar's lemurs, chameleons and snakes combined. Compare this to Britain with just one native frog (plus three introduced by man).

All but two of Madagascar's frogs (99%) are endemic. These frogs come in all colours and sizes: from tiny *Stumpffia pygmaea* measuring just 1cm fully grown to the giant *Hoplobatrachus tigerinus* reportedly reaching 17cm in length. In their struggle for survival Malagasy frogs have evolved numerous ingenious forms of protection. In Masoala we stumbled across *Mantidactylus webbi*, looking for all the world like a tuft of moss – the perfect camouflage amongst the damp green rocks of its habitat. In contrast, the eye-catching mantellas are anything but camouflaged. Their dramatic colours warn predators that they contain alkaloid toxins, making them a rather unpleasant snack. Another frog it would be wise to avoid eating is the aptly named tomato frog. When attacked these obese, bright red frogs gum up the predator's mouth with a thick gluey substance secreted from their skin. The unfortunate attacker is forced to release its prey and cannot eat for some days after.

Each December, for just three or four days, *Aglyptodactylus* frogs gather in huge numbers to mate. Males and females alike turn a bright canary yellow for the occasion. With hundreds of thousands of individuals gathered in a single marshy pool the noise of their croaking is deafening. This bizarre sound, coupled with the carpet of garishly coloured pairs of mating frogs stretching off into the distance in every direction, makes for a truly bewildering spectacle. After this colourful orgy each female will produce a clutch of up to 4,130 eggs. At the other end of the spectrum, green climbing mantellas lay just one egg at a time. A male will defend his waterlogged bamboo stump which he hopes will attract a female. If successful the female will lay her egg and leave it in his care. This can be risky as the egg may not be alone – on Nosy Mangabe we saw many males defending their wells, only to discover that the egg had been eaten by another tadpole (probably from the same male) or by other predators.

Frogs here also have a widely varied diet. They are well-known to eat flies, ants, slugs and other small invertebrates, but scientists have discovered that some Malagasy frogs will even eat scorpions, young chameleons, tadpoles and occasionally other frogs. Most surprising, however, are the reports from Malagasy farmers that *Hoplobatrachus tigerinus* – apparently introduced to control the rat population around Mahajanga – can even eat snakes and birds!

New frog species are constantly being discovered in Madagascar, with at least 60 described in the last decade. But for many it is a race against extinction. More than 50 of Madagascar's frog species are considered vulnerable or endangered (nine critically so) and over a quarter have yet to be assessed. Despite this, until recently only three species were protected by international law. However, in 2000, restrictions on the trade of mantellas were imposed, bringing the total number of protected Malagasy frogs to 19.

Natural History FAUNA

3

Everybody thinks they know one thing about chameleons: that they change colour to match their background. *Wrong!* You have only to observe the striking Parson's chameleon (*Calumma parsonii*), commonly seen at Andasibe, staying stubbornly green while transferred from boy's hand to tree trunk to leafy branch, to see that in some species at least this is a myth. Most chameleons are cryptically coloured to match their preferred resting place (there are branch-coloured chameleons, for instance, and leaf-coloured ones) and some do respond to a change of surroundings, but their abilities are mainly reserved for expressing emotion. An anxious chameleon will darken and grow stripes and an angry chameleon, faced with a territorial intruder, will change his colours dramatically. The most impressive displays, however, are reserved for sexual encounters. Chameleons say it with colours. Enthusiastic males explode into a riot of spots, stripes and contrasting colours, whilst the female usually responds by donning a black cloak of disapproval. Only on the rare occasions that she is feeling receptive will she present a brighter appearance.

Chameleons use body language more than colour to deter enemies. If you spot a chameleon on a branch you will note that his first reaction to being seen is to put the branch between you and him and flatten his body laterally so that he is barely visible. If you try to catch him, he will blow himself up, expand his throat, raise his helmet (if he has one) and hiss. His next action will be to bite, jump, or try to run away. Fortunately they must be the slowest of all lizards, are easily caught, and pose for the camera with gloomy resignation (who can resist an animal that has a constantly down-turned mouth like a Victorian headmistress?). This slowness is another aspect of the chameleon's defence: when he walks, he moves like a leaf in the wind. This is fine when the danger is an animal predator, but less effective when it is a car. In a tree, his best protection is to keep completely still. He can do this by having feet shaped like pliers and a prehensile tail so he can effortlessly grasp a branch, and eyes shaped like gun-turrets which can swivel 180 degrees independently of each other, enabling him to view the world from front and back without moving his head. This is the chameleon's true camouflage.

The family Chamaeleonidae is represented by three genera, the true chameleons –

A number of Madagascar's **tortoises** are severely threatened with extinction. Captive breeding programmes at Ankarafantsika are currently successfully rearing the ploughshare (*Astrochelys yniphora*) and flat-tailed tortoises (*Pyxis planicauda*) and further south, the Beza-Mahafaly reserve is protecting the handsome radiated tortoise (*Astrochelys radiata*). Four species of freshwater **turtle** inhabit the western waterways, the only endemic species being the big-headed or side-necked turtle (*Erymnochelys madagascariensis*), now also being bred at Ankarafantsika. Beyond, in the Mozambique Channel, there are **sea turtles** (hawksbill, loggerhead, Olive Ridley, leatherback and green turtles) which periodically risk the pot as they visit their nesting beaches.

BIRDS *With information from Derek Schuurman*

Madagascar's score sheet of birds is surprisingly short: of 283 species recorded there, only 209 regularly breed on the island. However 51% of these are endemic, including five endemic families and 37 endemic genera – rendering Madagascar one of Africa's top birding hotspots.

Key endemics include the three rail-like **mesites** – the brown mesite (*Mesitornis unicolor*) in the rainforests, the white-breasted mesite (*M. variegata*) in the western dry woods and the subdesert mesite (*Monias benschi*) in the southwestern spiny

Calumma and *Furcifer* – and the little stump-tailed chameleons, *Brookesia*. Unlike the true chameleons, the *Brookesia*'s short tail is not prehensile.

In chameleons there is often a striking colour difference between males and females. Many males have horns (occasionally used for fighting) or other nasal protuberances. Where the two sexes look the same you can recognise the male by the bulge of the scrotal sac beneath the tail, and a spur on the hind feet.

It is interesting to know how the chameleon achieves its colour change. It has a transparent epidermis, then three layers of cells – the top ones are yellow and red, the middle layer reflects blue light, and the bottom layer consists of black pigment cells with tentacles or fingers that can protrude up through the other layers. The cells are under control of the autonomic nervous system, expanding and contracting according to a range of stimuli. Change of colour occurs when one layer is more stimulated than others, and patterning when one group of cells receives maximum stimulation.

In the early 17th century there was the firm conviction that chameleons subsisted without food. A German author, describing Madagascar in 1609, mentions the chameleon living 'entirely on air and dew' and Shakespeare refers several times to the chameleon's supposed diet: 'The chameleon... can feed on air' (*Two Gentlemen of Verona*) and 'of the chameleon's dish: I eat the air promise-crammed' (*Hamlet*). Possibly at that time no-one had witnessed the tongue flash out through the bars of its cage to trap a passing insect. This tongue is as remarkable as any other feature of this extraordinary reptile. It was formerly thought that the club-shaped tip was sticky, allowing the chameleon to catch flies, but researchers discovered that captive chameleons had been catching much larger prey – lizards, intended to coexist as cage-mates. These animals were far too heavy to be captured simply with a sticky tongue, so a high-speed video camera was brought into use. This showed that a chameleon is able to use a pair of muscles at the tip of its tongue to form a suction cup milliseconds before it hits its prey. The whole manoeuvre, from aim to mouthful, takes about half a second.

The name apparently comes from Greek for 'dwarf lion'. I suppose a hissing, open-mouthed reptile could remind one of a lion, but to most visitors they are one of the most appealing and bizarre of the 'strange and marvellous forms' on show.

bush. A similar allocation of habitats is more generously employed by the ten species of **coua**, which brighten forests with their blue-masked faces. Six species are ground-dwellers, occupying roles filled elsewhere by pheasants and roadrunners. Difficult to see are the **ground-rollers**, which quietly patrol the rainforest floor in their pretty uniforms. One member of the family, the long-tailed ground-roller (*Uratelornis chimaera*), inhabits the southwestern spiny bush. The two **asities** (*Philepitta* spp) resemble squat broadbills, to which they are related. In the eastern rainforests, the **sunbird-asities** (*Neodrepanis* spp) appear as flashes of blue and green in the canopy, their down-turned beaks designed for the nectaries of canopy flowers.

Beak variation is remarkable among Madagascar's most celebrated endemic family, the **vangas**. All species have perfected their own craft of insect capture, filling the niches of various absent African bird groups, which they may resemble superficially. Vangas often flock together or with other forest birds, presenting a formidable offensive for local invertebrates. Most prominent is the sickle-billed vanga (*Falculea palliata*) which parallels the tree-probing habits of Africa's wood hoopoes. The heavily carnivorous diet of shrikes is adopted by – among others – the hook-billed vanga (*Vanga curvirostris*) and the dramatic, blue-billed helmet vanga (*Euryceros prevostii*) which resembles a small hornbill. Other vangas mimic nuthatches, flycatchers and tits. In short, if *The Beagle* had been caught by the West Wind Drift and Darwin had arrived in Madagascar instead of the Galapagos, the vangas would certainly have ensured that his train of thought went uninterrupted.

Malagasy representatives of families found elsewhere make up the bulk of the remaining birdlife. Herons, ibises, grebes, ducks and rails take up their usual positions in wetlands, including endemics such as the endangered Madagascar teal (*Anas bernieri*) of some western mangroves, and the colourful Madagascar malachite kingfisher (*Alcedo vintsioides*). Game birds include the attractive Madagascar partridge and Madagascar sandgrouse. The impressive Madagascar crested ibis (*Lophotibis cristata*), Madagascar blue and green pigeons and tuneful vasa parrots (*Coracopsis* spp) occupy the various strata of vegetation. More colourful birds include the grey-headed lovebird (*Agapornis cana*); the Madagascar bee-eater (*Merops superciliosus*); the Madagascar paradise flycatcher (*Terpsiphone mutata*); the Madagascar hoopoe (*Upupa marginata*); the Madagascar red fody (*Foudia madagascariensis*) dressed in scarlet during the breeding season (October to March); souimanga and long-billed green sunbirds; and the crested drongo (*Dicrurus forficatus*), with its black plumage, forked tail and silly crest. The four **rock thrushes** (*Monticola* spp) look like European robins in morning suits. The

BIRDING IN MADAGASCAR
Derek Schuurman

To see a fair spectrum of Madagascar's endemic birds, visit at least one site in each of the island's three chief climatic/floristic zones: eastern rainforest, southern spiny forest and western dry deciduous forests. Each holds its own complement of regional endemics. In addition, a select band of birds is dependent on the dwindling wetlands, so include these in your itinerary. The transition forest of Zombitse should definitely be visited. During a stay of two or three weeks and armed with field guides (see page 417) you should be able to tick off most of the island's sought-after 'lifers'. The standard birding route is as follows:

EASTERN RAINFOREST Rainforest birding is best in spring and early summer (mid-September to January).

Andasibe-Mantadia (Périnet) and surrounds At Andasibe you can see most of the broadly distributed rainforest endemics. Specials include collared nightjar, red-fronted coua, Rand's warbler, coral-billed nuthatch vanga and Tylas vanga. In rank herbaceous growth, look for Madagascar wood-rail, white-throated rail and Madagascar flufftail.

In Mantadia, the pitta-like, scaly (rare) and short-legged ground-rollers occur, as do velvet asity, common sunbird asity and brown emutail. Two wetlands nearby, the Torotorofotsy Marsh (a four-hour walk) and the more accessible Ampasipotsy Marsh, hold Madagascar rail, Madagascar snipe, grey emutail and Madagascar swamp warbler.

Ranomafana Above all, Ranomafana is known for its ground-rollers (pitta-like and rufous-headed especially). Other 'megaticks' include brown mesite, yellow-browed oxylabes, Crossley's babbler, grey-crowned tetraka (greenbul), forest rock-thrush and Pollen's vanga. Velvet and common sunbird asities are plentiful. On high ridges, look for yellow-bellied sunbird asity, brown emutail and cryptic warbler.

Masoala Birding in this lowland rainforest is exceptional. Aside from nearly all the broadly distributed rainforest endemics, specials include brown mesite, red-breasted coua, scaly ground-roller and the helmet and Bernier's vangas. The extremely rare Madagascar serpent eagle and Madagascar red owl have a stronghold here but seeing them is extremely difficult: both are highly elusive.

confiding endemic Madagascar magpie robin (*Copsychus albospecularis*) sports black-and-white attire and flirts fearlessly with humans.

The Madagascar kestrel (*Falco newtoni*) is joined by other **raptors** such as the banded kestrel (*Falco zoniventris*), the exceptionally handsome Madagascar harrier-hawk (*Polyboroides radiatus*), Frances's sparrow-hawk (*Accipiter francesii*), Madagascar buzzard (*Buteo brachypterus*), Madagascar cuckoo-hawk (*Aviceda madagascariensis*) and seven species of owl. The two endemic eagles – the critically endangered Madagascar fish eagle (*Haliaeetus vociferoides*) of the west coast and the Madagascar serpent eagle (*Eutriorchis astur*) of the northeastern rainforests – are among the world's rarest raptors. Like the Madagascar red owl (*Tyto soumagnei*), the serpent eagle had managed to escape detection for several decades and was feared extinct, until both species were found thriving discretely in various rainforest sites. The ultra-rare Sakalava rail (*Amaurornis olivieri*) was also recently rediscovered in the Mahavavy Delta, which holds a small breeding population. But the most sensational avian news to emerge from Madagascar in recent years was the discovery, in November 2006, of 13 **Madagascar pochards** (*Aythya innotata*) living on a remote northern lake. This diving duck, previously thought to have been confined to Lake Alaotra, had not been seen alive since 1992 and was thought likely to be extinct.

TROPICAL DRY DECIDUOUS FORESTS (WESTERN REGION)
Ankarafantsika (Ampijoroa) An outstanding birding locality year-round, this forest holds most of the specials of western Madagascar. They include white-breasted mesite, Coquerel's coua, Schlegel's asity and Van Dam's vanga. Several other vangas (sickle-billed, rufous, Chabert's, white-headed, blue and rufous) abound. Raptors include the critically endangered Madagascar fish eagle, Madagascar harrier-hawk and Madagascar sparrow-hawk. Other sought-after species often seen include Madagascar crested ibis and Madagascar pygmy kingfisher. In the Betsiboka Delta (Mahajanga) look for Humblot's heron, Madagascar teal, Madagascar white ibis and Madagascar jacana.

TRANSITION FOREST
Zombitse-Vohibasia A serious 'OOE' (Orgasmic Ornithological Experience) year-round and included in all birding itineraries for its 'megatick': the Appert's tetraka. Zombitse also holds an impressive variety of other endemics, like giant and crested couas. Look out for Madagascar partridge, Madagascar buttonquail, Madagascar sandgrouse, greater and lesser vasa parrots, grey-headed lovebird, Madagascar green pigeon, Madagascar hoopoe, Thamnornis warbler, common newtonia, common jery, long-billed green sunbird, white-headed and blue vangas, and Sakalava weaver.

Spiny forest Excellent birding year-round; start just before daybreak.

Ifaty/Mangily (The protected portion of the PK 32 spiny bush parcel.) Ifaty's bizarre *Euphorbia*-Didiereaceae bush holds some extremely localised birds, notably sub-desert mesite, long-tailed ground-roller, Lafresnaye's vanga and Archbold's newtonia. Look for running coua and subdesert brush-warbler. Excellent for banded kestrel and Madagascar nightjar too.

St Augustine's Bay and Anakao The coral ragg scrub here is lower than Ifaty's spiny bush and holds Verreaux's coua, littoral rock thrush and the recently described red-shouldered vanga (La Table is a good site for these birds). At puddles along the road look for Madagascar plover.

MAMMALS Madagascar's mammals are the prize exhibit in the island's incredible menagerie. They exist as an obscure assortment of primates, insectivores, carnivores, bats and rodents, representing the descendants of parties of individuals who, curled up in hollow trunks or skipping across temporary islands, accidentally completed the perilous journey from eastern Africa to the island beyond the horizon at different times over the last 100 million years. Once established, they gradually spread through the diverse habitats of their paradise island, all the time evolving and creating new species.

Biologists often refer to Madagascar as a museum housing living fossils. This is because almost all the mammals on the island today closely resemble groups that once shone elsewhere but have since been replaced by more advanced species. Although evolution has certainly occurred on the island, it seems to have plodded on with less momentum than back in Africa. Hence, while their cousins on the mainland were subjected to extreme competition with the species that were to develop subsequently, the Malagasy mammals were able to stick more rigidly to their original physiques and behaviours.

The word 'cousins' is especially poignant when applied to the lemurs, for across Africa primate evolution was eventually to lead to the ascent of humankind. How opportune then for an understanding of our own natural history that one of our direct ancestors managed to end up on this island sanctuary and remain, sheltered from the pressures of life elsewhere, relatively true to its original form for us to appreciate 35 million years later.

Lemurs Lemurs are to a biologist what the old masters are to an art critic: they may not be contemporary, but historically they are very important and they are beautiful to look at. Lemurs belong to a group of primates called the prosimians, a word which means 'before monkeys'. Their basic body design evolved about 40 to 50 million years ago. With stereoscopic colour vision, hands that could grasp branches, a brain capable of processing complex, learned information, extended parental care and an integrated social system incorporating a wide range of sound and scent signals, the lemurs were the latest model in evolution's comprehensive range of arboreal (tree-living) mammals. Their reign lasted until about 35 million years ago, when a new model – the monkey – evolved. Monkeys were superior in a number of ways: they were faster, could think more quickly, used their vision more effectively and were highly dextrous. Their success rapidly drove the less adaptable prosimians to extinction across most of the world. A few stowaways managed to take refuge in Madagascar, a corner of the world never reached by more advanced primates (until the recent arrival of humans). Today we see the results of 35 million years of leisurely evolution. The single ancestral species has adapted into around 100 recognised varieties and instead of gazing at inanimate rocks we have the luxury of being able to watch, hear and smell the genuine article.

Smell is an extremely important aspect of lemur lives. Through scents, lemurs communicate a wide range of information, such as who's in charge, who is fertile, who is related to whom and who lives where. They supplement this language with a vocal one. Chirps, barks and cries reinforce hierarchies in lemur societies, help to defend territories against other groups and warn of danger. Socially the lemurs show a great variety of organisational skills and the strategy used by each species is largely dependent on the nature of their diet. The small, quick-moving, insectivorous lemurs such as the mouse lemurs and dwarf lemurs are nocturnal and largely solitary except during the mating season when they pair up with a member of the opposite sex. Literally surrounded by their insect food, they require only small territories, hence they never cover large distances and spend their entire lives in the trees. A different way of life is led by the larger leaf-eating species such

THE AYE-AYE   *Hilary Bradt*

The strangest lemur is the aye-aye, *Daubentonia madagascariensis*. It took a while for scientists to decide that it was a lemur at all: for years it was thought to be a peculiar type of squirrel. Now it is classified in a family of its own, Daubentoniidae. The aye-aye seems to have been assembled from the leftover parts of a variety of animals. It has the teeth of a rodent (they never stop growing), the ears of a bat, the tail of a fox and the hands of no living creature, since the middle finger is like that of a skeleton. It's this finger which so intrigues scientists, as it shows the aye-aye's adaptation to its way of life. In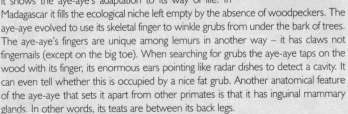
Madagascar it fills the ecological niche left empty by the absence of woodpeckers. The aye-aye evolved to use its skeletal finger to winkle grubs from under the bark of trees. The aye-aye's fingers are unique among lemurs in another way – it has claws not fingernails (except on the big toe). When searching for grubs the aye-aye taps on the wood with its finger, its enormous ears pointing like radar dishes to detect a cavity. It can even tell whether this is occupied by a nice fat grub. Another anatomical feature of the aye-aye that sets it apart from other primates is that it has inguinal mammary glands. In other words, its teats are between its back legs.

This fascinating animal was long considered to be on the verge of extinction, but recently there have been encouraging signs that it is more widespread than previously supposed. Although destruction of habitat is the chief threat to its survival, it is also at risk because of its supposedly evil powers. Rural people believe the aye-aye to be the herald of death. If one is seen near a settlement it must be killed, and even then the only salvation may be to burn down the village.

'I WANT TO SEE AN AYE-AYE' A glimpse of Madagascar's weirdest lemur is a goal for many visitors. And many go away disappointed. When weighing up whether to try to see one in the wild or to settle for a captive animal, you should bear in mind that the aye-aye is a rare, nocturnal and largely solitary animal. Most of its waking hours are spent foraging for food in the upper canopy; only occasionally does it descend to the ground. So even in the reserve of Nosy Mangabe, which was created for aye-ayes, your chance of seeing more than two distant shining eyes in the beam of your torch is very small. I know of more than one visitor who spent a week on Nosy Mangabe and never saw this animal.

That leaves the choice between the semi-wild aye-aye on the eponymous island at Mananara or those caged in the two Malagasy zoos: Tsimbazaza in Tana and Ivoloina near Toamasina. Mananara seems to satisfy most people, providing they know what to expect. The animals are 'wild' in that they live free and find some of their food in their environment, but they are thoroughly accustomed to people so are easy to approach and photograph. Don't assume, however, that aye-aye sightings are guaranteed here. Some visitors are unlucky and see nothing.

Of the two zoos, Ivoloina is my choice because there are fewer visitors, which means the animals are less stressed. At the time of writing they have just one female. You can arrange to see the aye-aye at dusk as it starts to become active. Tsimbazaza now has a day-to-night house, allowing you to see the creatures awake.

Outside Madagascar, an increasing number of zoos have night-reversed aye-aye cages. The best are London, Bristol and Jersey (the late Gerald Durrell's zoo) in the UK and Duke University Primate Center in the USA.

Diurnal (day-active) lemurs are the largest and easiest to identify. They are usually found in groups of between three and 12 individuals. In many of the island's renowned wildlife locations two or more species can been seen relatively easily.

RING-TAILED LEMUR (*Lemur catta*) Instantly recognisable by its banded tail. More terrestrial than other lemurs and lives in troops of up to 20 animals in the south and southwest, notably in Isalo, Andohahela and Andringitra National Parks, and Berenty Reserve.

RUFFED LEMURS (genus *Varecia*) Large lemurs commonly found in zoos but difficult to see in the wild. There are two species and both live in eastern rainforests: black-and-white ruffed lemur is found sporadically in pristine areas and can sometimes be seen in Mantadia and Ranomafana National Parks, and on Nosy Mangabe, while the red ruffed lemur is restricted to Masoala.

Ring-tailed lemur

Black-and-white ruffed lemur

TRUE LEMURS (genus *Eulemur*) All roughly cat-sized, with long noses, and live in trees. A confusing characteristic is that males and females of most species have somewhat different markings and coat colours. The well-known black lemur (*E. macaco*; called *maki* by the Malagasy), from northwest Madagascar, notably Nosy Komba and Lokobe, is perhaps the best example. Only males are black; females are chestnut brown. Visitors to Ranomafana and Mantadia often see red-bellied lemurs; males have white tear-drop face-markings, while females have creamy-white bellies. In far northern reserves crowned lemurs (*E. coronatus*) are common: males are sandy-brown, females are grey.

The six species of brown lemur present the ultimate challenge, but fortunately their ranges do not overlap, so locality helps identification. In most cases males are more distinctively marked and look quite different from females which tend to be uniformly brown. Two neighbouring male brown lemurs have beautiful cream or white ear-tufts and side whiskers: Sanford's brown lemur (*E. sanfordi*) is found in far northern reserves, while the white-fronted brown lemur (*E. albifrons*) occurs in the northeast and males have bushy white heads and Santa-Claus-like side whiskers.

Collared brown lemur

Further south you will find common brown lemur (*E. fulvus*) in both the east (eg: Andasibe-Mantadia National Park) and also the northwest (eg: Ankarafantsika). Red-fronted brown lemurs (*E. rufus*) live in the southeast and southwest. The males of the two variations of collared brown lemur (*E. collaris* and *E. cinereiceps*) unsurprisingly have distinctive tufty fur collars and both occur in far southeastern areas, but the grey-headed brown lemur (*E. cinereiceps*) has an extremely restricted range and is very rare.

BAMBOO LEMURS (genera *Hapalemur* and *Prolemur*) Smaller than the true lemurs, with short muzzles and round faces. They occur in smaller groups (one to four animals), cling to vertical branches, and feed mainly on bamboo. You may see the commonest species, grey bamboo lemur (*Hapalemur griseus*), in several eastern parks including Marojejy, Andasibe-Mantadia and Ranomafana. The very much rarer golden bamboo lemur (*H. aureus*) and greater bamboo lemur (*Prolemur simus*) are, realistically, only seen at Ranomafana.

Grey
bamboo
lemur

INDRI (*Indri indri*) The largest lemur and the only one with virtually no tail. This black-and-white teddy-bear lemur is unmistakable, having a characteristic eerie wailing song. It is seen in Andasibe-Mantadia National Park.

Indri

SIFAKAS (genus *Propithecus*) Sifakas belong to the same family as the indri, and have characteristic long back legs. Some sifakas (pronounced *sheefahk*) are the famous dancing lemurs that bound upright over the ground and leap spectacularly from tree to tree. The commonest sifakas are white or mainly white and are quite unmistakable. Verreaux's sifaka (*P. verreauxi*) shares its southern habitat with the ring-tailed lemur, while its cousin the Coquerel's sifaka (*P. coquereli*), which has chestnut-maroon arms and legs, is seen at Ankarafantsika in the northwest. You may also see the stunningly beautiful diademed sifaka (*P. diadema*) in Mantadia and the rich chocolate-coloured Milne-Edwards' sifaka (*P. edwardsi*) at Ranomafana.

Verreaux's sifaka

Because they are generally smaller than the diurnal lemurs (sometimes *very* tiny) and active primarily after dark, the various types of nocturnal lemur are often more challenging to identify. However, night walks in Madagascar's forests are safe and very exciting as you can never really be sure what you might discover. Two types of nocturnal lemur – sportive lemurs and woolly lemurs – often helpfully sleep or doze in the open during the day so are regularly seen by tourists.

Brown mouse lemur

MOUSE LEMURS (genus *Microcebus*) This group are the smallest of all primates: the most minuscule is Madame Berthe's mouse lemur (*M. berthae*) which could sit in an egg cup and weighs 30g. As a group these are the most abundant type of lemur and are generally common in virtually all native forests types, they even survive in some forest fragments where other lemurs have disappeared. There are now a number of species (18 at the last count), which makes accurate identification confusing and difficult. The easiest places to see them are Andasibe-Mantadia and Ranomafana National Parks in the east and Ankarafantsika, Ankarana and Berenty Reserves in drier areas.

DWARF LEMURS (genera *Cheirogaleus*, *Mirza* and *Allocebus*) Dwarf lemurs are mostly squirrel-sized and run along branches in a similar fashion. Some, like the fat-tailed dwarf lemur (*Cheirogaleus medius*), become dormant during the winter, sleeping in tree holes and surviving on reserves of fat stored in their tails. Dwarf lemurs from the genus *Cheirogaleus* have distinctive dark spectacle-like rings around their eyes which helps

Greater dwarf lemur

identification. Giant dwarf lemurs (genus *Mirza*) are unusual as they are sometimes predatory and eat baby birds, frogs, lizards and even small snakes. For a long time it was through the hairy-eared dwarf lemur (*Allocebus trichotis*) was exceedingly rare, it now turns out to have been overlooked and is actually quite widespread; it can even be seen in Andasibe-Mantadia National Park. It is about the size of a large mouse lemur, but look out for its distinctive ear-tufts.

Eastern fork-marked dwarf lemur

FORK-MARKED LEMURS (genus *Phaner*) These lemurs prefer to live high in the canopy so are often rather difficult to see and identify. Their distribution is also somewhat sporadic. Perhaps the best places to look are the dry western forests like Kirindy and Zombitse. The dark fork markings on the face are highly distinctive.

SPORTIVE LEMURS (genus *Lepilemur*) Sportive lemurs mostly spend the day in tree-holes from which they peer drowsily. Their name is something of a misnomer as they are rarely particularly energetic, even at night. They cling vertically to tree trunks and, after dark, their high pitched calls are often a feature of the forests they inhabit. Recently scientists have described many new species (the genus now contains 25 species) and in appearance they are often very similar. The best guide for identification is locality.

WOOLLY LEMURS (genus *Avahi*) Woolly lemurs also adopt a vertical posture and are similar in size to sportive lemurs, but have round, owl-like faces and conspicuous white thighs. They often sleep in the tangled branches of trees. Many park guides use 'woolly lemur' and 'avahi' interchangeably as the common name. One

Western woolly lemur

Small-toothed sportive lemur

recently described species is named after British comic actor John Cleese: Cleese's woolly lemur (*Avahi cleesei*) is currently known only from Tsingy de Bemaraha National Park.

AYE-AYE (*Daubentonia madagascariensis*) This gargoyle of a lemur is Madagascar's most bizarre mammal. Many people think aye-ayes are small, but in fact they are larger than a domestic cat and have huge bushy tails. However, it is their face and hands that make them unique; with teeth like a rabbit's, ears like a bat's and fingers like Edward Scissorhands' there is nothing else to compare. Once thought to be on the brink of extinction but now known to be quite widespread (though still rare), it is theoretically possible to see one in many reserves. The chances are extremely slight but you could get lucky.

Aye-aye

as the indri. In a rainforest there is no shortage of leaves; however, as a food source leaves are poor in nutrients, so each lemur needs to consume a large amount. Leaf-eaters therefore tend to collect in small groups, together defending their territory of foliage with scents and often loud calls which in the dense forests are the best forms of communication.

Their sex lives vary, but most of these species have family groups in which a single male dominates. The most social lemurs on the island are those with a more varied diet concentrating on fruit, but also including seeds, buds and eaves. These include the ring-tailed lemur, ruffed lemur and true lemurs. The diet of these species requires active foraging over large areas during the day, so in order to defend their expansive territory, and to protect themselves in daylight, these lemurs form troops. The societies are run by matriarchs, who organise the troop's movement, courtship and defence. But there are also whole groups of males, which often separate for week-long excursions away from the home base. Usually operating in more open country, these lemurs use a wide range of visual signals to accompany their scents and sounds, making them particularly entertaining to watch.

THE BATS OF MADAGASCAR
Richard Jenkins, Madagasikara Voakajy

DIVERSITY Bats make a significant contribution to tropical diversity but in Madagascar they have only recently received the concerted attention of biologists. New species of Malagasy bat continue to be discovered. Five new endemic bats have been described since 2004, bringing the total to at least 37 species (24 of which are thought to be endemic) with a further six currently in the process of being formally described. The megachiropterans (fruit bats) are represented by three endemic species (*Pteropus rufus*, *Eidolon dupreanum* and *Rousettus madagascariensis*); they feed on flowers, fruits and leaves. Six families of insectivorous microchiropterans (*ramanavy*, *kinakina* or *kananavy* in Malagasy) are also found in Madagascar, including the endemic family of sucker-footed bats (genus *Myzopoda*).

CONSERVATION Bats are threatened in Madagascar from habitat loss, persecution (as fruit crop pests and unwanted house guests), hunting (bushmeat) and roost site disturbance. Bats are not protected under Malagasy law and only populations inside reserves or at sacred sites receive any protection. Many species are gregarious and roost in cavities (eg: caves, tree-holes, roofs) or on vegetation.

BAT-WATCHING The Madagascar flying fox *P. rufus* (*fanihy* in Malagasy) is large (wingspan 1.2m) and forms colonies of up to 5,000 individuals. It makes short flights during the day and excellent viewing rewards patient observers. Good tourist sites to see them include Berenty Reserve, Nosy Tanikely, Nosy Mangabe, the mangroves near Anjajavy and independent travellers can visit other sites, such as near Moramanga. The Madagascar straw-coloured bat *E. dupreanum* (*angavo*) is best seen in the Grotte des Chauve-souris at Ankarana or flying around rock overhangs at Cap Sainte Marie.

The smallest Malagasy fruit bat *R. madagascariensis* (*matavikely*) lives in caves and a large colony is resident at the aforementioned Ankarana cave. These bats betray their presence by noisy chattering and reflective orange eye-shine. The best time to view fruit bats is during June and July when the kapok trees are flowering in western Madagascar. All three species flock to these trees at night to feed on nectar and can be observed in torchlight at close quarters.

The circuits at Tsingy de Bemaraha offer the chance of seeing some roosting microchiropterans. Other reserves with bat caves include Ankarana, Tsingy de Namoroka and Tsimanampetsotsa. House-roosting bats can be seen at dusk as they emerge to feed;

Perhaps the most entertaining of all is the ring-tailed lemur. Among lemurs it forms the largest and liveliest troops. Each troop typically stirs at dawn, warms up with a period of sunbathing and then, guided by the matriarchs, heads off to forage, breaking at noon for a siesta. The troop moves along the ground, each individual using its distinctive tail to maintain visual contact with the others. If out of eyesight, the troop members use the cat-like mews that prompted their scientific name. By dusk they return to the sleeping trees which they use for three or four days before moving on. In the April breeding season the males become less tolerant of each other and engage in stink fights where, after charging their tails with scent from glands on their wrists, they waft them antagonistically at opponents. Similar aggressive interactions occur when two troops of ring-tails meet, sometimes leading to serious injury or death, but usually one side backs down before it reaches this stage.

Identifying species Even for a keen naturalist, sorting out Madagascar's 105-plus varieties (species and subspecies) of lemur can be challenging. The two illustrated layman's guides on pages 58–61 should help you put names to faces. The first box covers diurnal (day-active) species; the second describes the nocturnal ones more

a good site to watch this is at the post office in Andasibe. There are interpretation boards located around the post office to raise the awareness of tourists and local people to bats. Mauritian tomb bats can be seen in a rock crevice on the Manambolo circuit at Tsingy de Bemaraha and also roosting on tree trunks in the camp site at Ankarafantsika.

Bats are sensitive to disturbance whilst roosting. Always ask advice from your guide and use common sense: avoid handling bats, avoid shining bright lights at roosting bats, keep quiet at roosts and don't try to provoke resting bats into flight.

Bats are key species in Madagascar's fragile environment; they disperse seeds over vast distances and pollinate trees such as baobabs. They don't have it easy. They tend to be vilified by most people, eaten by some and ignored by the rest. By showing a genuine interest in bats when you visits protected areas you can help Madagasikara Voakajy and its partners to raise bats onto the conservation agenda.

MADAGASIKARA VOAKAJY This Malagasy conservation organisation is dedicated to conserving the island's bats and their habitats. Our Malagasy bat experts study all aspects of bat ecology and operate a conservation awareness campaign. There are many bat roosts in Madagascar that remain unknown to conservationists and we would very much like to hear from anyone who finds a bat cave or tree roost that is not mentioned in this article (e *voakajy@moov.mg; www.madagasikara-voakajy.org*).

SPECIFIC SITES
Cap Sainte Marie There is a roost site of *E. dupreanum* that can be seen from one of the tourist trails as it passes a deep valley. The bats are sometimes active in the day and can be seen flying between different rock overhangs.

Mananara-Nord There is a *P. rufus* roost reported from Nosy Atafana, an offshore island in the marine reserve.

Moramanga A Malagasy NGO called ACCE, based in Moramanga, is conserving a number of Madagascar flying fox roosts in the Mangoro Valley. Visits to their sites often allow excellent views of roosting bats (4x4 or motorcycle required). Arrangements can be made through Ndriana at their office (m *033 05 017 89;* e *ACCE@isuisse.com*).

likely encountered on a night walk. Serious naturalists should consider purchasing a field guide (see page 417).

Tenrecs Employing one of the most primitive mammalian body plans, the tenrecs have been able to fill the vacancies created by an absence of shrews, moles and hedgehogs, and in doing so have diversified into about 27 different species. Five of these are called the spiny tenrecs, most looking just like hedgehogs, some with yellow and black stripes. However, the largest, the tailless common tenrec (*Tenrec ecaudatus*), has lost the majority of its spines. Not only is this species the largest insectivore in the world at 1.5kg, but it can also give birth to enormous litters which the mother feeds with up to 24 nipples. The 19 species of furred tenrecs are mostly shrew-like in stature, although three species look and act more like moles, and one has become aquatic, capturing small fish and freshwater shrimps in the fast-flowing streams of the *hauts plateaux*.

Rodents Highly successful elsewhere, rodents have made little impression on Madagascar. There are 20 species, most of which are nocturnal. The easiest to see is the red forest rat (*Nesomys rufus*) which is active during the day. The most unusual are the rabbit-like giant jumping rat (*Hypogeomys antimena*) from the western forests and the two tree-dwelling *Brachytarsomys* species which have prehensile tails.

Civets and mongooses The island's nine carnivores belong to the civets and mongooses, Viverridae, which evolved 40 million years ago at about the same time as the cats. The largest, the fossa (*Cryptoprocta ferox*), is very cat-like with an extremely long tail which assists balance during canopy-based lemur hunts. This extremely shy creature is quite widespread but rarely seen – except in November, see pages 391–2. The size of a chubby cat, the striped civet (*Fossa fossana*) hunts in the eastern rainforests for rodents, and a third, very secretive animal, the *falanouc* (*Eupleres goudotii*) inhabits the northeastern rainforests where it lives almost entirely on earthworms. Each of Madagascar's forest types plays host to mongooses. There are six species in all (one only just discovered near Lake Alaotra as this book went to press), the most commonly seen being the ring-tailed mongoose (*Galidia elegans*) which varies in colour but is typically a handsome, rusty red.

Bats Possessing, among mammals, the unique gift of flight, it is not surprising that most of Madagascar's bats are also found on mainland Africa or Asia. There are

SEX AND THE FOREST   *Hilary Bradt*

It's a jungle out there! I don't know what it is about Madagascar, but when it comes to male equipment the animals seem to be more interestingly and excitingly endowed here than anywhere else in the world. For starters there's the parrot that does it with a golf-ball (see page 382), but the fossa puts even that eye-watering performance in the shade. For a few days each year the females are penetrated by the largest penis in proportion to its size of any mammal. This impressive member is supported by a baculum, or penis bone, which enables the lucky fellow to perform for up to six hours at a time. To the female, size definitely does matter, and if her fellow isn't up to scratch she'll disengage and try someone else.

While size is everything to the parrot and fossa, reptiles such as chameleons go one better. One and one makes two, or a hemipenis. The two penes (yes, that really is the plural) are like a key: they only fit the female of the species, thus avoiding the risk of trying to get off with the wrong lady.

three species of fruit bat which are active during the day, very noisy, large and unfortunately often on the Malagasy menu. If the fruit bats look like flying foxes (their alternative name), then the remaining 30 or so species are not unlike flying mice. These are nocturnal, prefer moths to figs and find them by echolocation. They tend to have shell-like ears and distorted noses. It is known that some moths outwit these bats by chirping back at them in mid-flight, scrambling the echo and sending the aggressor off into the night.

Marine mammals Antongil Bay marks the northern extent of **humpback whale** migrations. The whales calve just beyond the coral reefs in July and August, and after this period migrate south as far as the Antarctic coast to feed. **Dugongs** (sea cows) are extremely rare. The Vezo of the west coast share their fishing grounds with an abundance of **dolphins**, and regard them as kin. If a dolphin is discovered dead they wrap it in shrouds and bury it with their ancestors.

MADAGASCAR'S ECOSYSTEMS

Madagascar's amazing array of habitats is the result of the effects of ocean currents, prevailing winds and geological forces. Rain is heaviest in the north and east, and lightest in the south and west. Rainfall is the single most significant factor in creating habitat characteristics, so a complex spectrum of habitat types has resulted within Madagascar's relatively small area. Madagascar's geology brings further variety by creating undulating coastlines, broad riverbeds and estuaries, shallow ocean shelves for coral reefs, high mountainous slopes and plateaux, a wealth of soil types and even bizarre limestone 'forests' riddled with caves. These various habitats house a wealth of ecosystems, the most important of which are described below.

RAINFORESTS The spine of mountains which border the central plateau forces the saturated air arriving from over the Indian Ocean to drop its moisture onto the east coast of the island. Madagascar's rainforests therefore form in a distinct band adjacent to the east coast where the continuous rainfall is high enough to sustain the evergreen canopy trees. Known as the Madagascar Sylva, this band of forest – now seriously fragmented by deforestation – extends inland only as far as the mountain range, so it is broadest in the northeast. The southern end of the range near Taolagnaro forms a unique but fragile divide between the evergreen rainforest to the east and the arid spiny forest beyond.

Littoral rainforest (sea level) Very little of Madagascar's unique coastal, or littoral, rainforest remains. Rooted in sand, washed with salty air, battered by cyclones and bordering lagoons and marshes, coastal forests harbour a very unusual community. The architecture of the forest is similar to the more widespread lowland forest, but the plants are different: they are salt-tolerant and highly efficient at extracting water and nutrients from the shallow, porous sand beneath. *Good example: Tampolo Forestry Station.*

Lowland rainforest (0–800m) Most of the rainforest in Madagascar is lowland, that is, below around 800m. This type of forest is hot and sticky, with humidity at 100% and annual rainfall of up to 5,000mm. The forest canopy is 30m above the ground, with few trees emerging beyond this level. Butterflies flutter as monstrous beetles and myriad ants and termites patrol the forest floor.

Lemurs skip among the branches and lianas which serve as highways between the forest floor and the world above. Preying on the lemurs, the fossa is at home among the canopy branches, while above the leaves birds of prey and fruit bats patrol. Tenrecs and forest birds rummage through the leaf litter, and the Madagascar striped civet and mongooses wait to pick off any unsuspecting prey. *Good examples: Masoala, Nosy Mangabe and the lower parts of Marojejy.*

Montane rainforest (800–1,300m) As altitude increases and air temperature drops, the tree species of the lowland rainforests give way to those more able to tolerate the cooler conditions. These species have lower canopies and are the foundation of the montane rainforest. The change from lowland to montane forest is a gradual one influenced by a number of factors. In southern Madagascar, montane forest occurs lower down; in the warmer north lowland forest may continue up to around 900m.

Once in true montane forest the landscape is very different. Not only is the canopy lower and the temperature much cooler, the understorey is far more dense. Tree ferns and bamboos litter the forest floor and there is a tight tangle of trunks, roots and woody lianas, all sporting furry lichens and lines of bright fungi.

Montane reserves are excellent places to spot mammals and birds, including many lemur species. *Good examples: Ranomafana, Andasibe-Mantadia, Montagne d'Ambre and parts of Marojejy.*

Cloudforest (above 1,300m) The forest beyond 1,300m has an even lower canopy and is characteristically thick with ferns and mosses. It is properly called high-altitude montane rainforest, but because it is often cloaked in mists it is also known as cloudforest. The low temperatures slow down decomposition, creating waterlogged peaty soils in valleys. Termites cannot live at these altitudes, so large earthworms and beetles take their place as detritivores. The canopy can be as low as 10m, and in places the understorey gives way to a thicket of shrubs. Mosses, lichens and ferns inhabit every branch and stone, and cover the floor along with forest succulents and *Bulbophyllum* orchids. *Good examples: Marojejy and Andringitra.*

DRY DECIDUOUS FOREST The magnificent dry forests of the west once covered the vast lowland plain west of the *hauts plateaux*. Now only a few patches remain, sharing the coast with the mangroves, bordering the largest rivers of the south and dotted about the plains near Isalo and inland from Mahajanga. The forest supports far fewer species than the eastern rainforests but has higher levels of endemism. The trees are less densely arranged and the canopy is typically 12–20m high.

The canopy leaves are shed during the seven or eight months of the dry season and a carpet of leaves begins to accumulate on the forest floor shortly after the rains stop in May. These decompose creating a thick humus layer in the soil. During this dry period much of the wildlife goes to ground, quite literally: amphibians and insects bury themselves in the soil to await the return of the rains.

Sifakas, sportive lemurs, brown lemurs and the ubiquitous mouse lemurs are particularly in evidence. Vangas live in the canopy and tuneful vasa parrots make territories in the understorey. The deep litter layer is home to tenrecs, tortoises, boas and hog-nosed snakes. Fossas and mongooses regularly run along their patrol trails, sometimes pursuing their prey up into the canopy. *Good examples: Kirindy, Ankarafantsika and Berenty.*

INSELBERG AND *TSINGY* COMMUNITIES In the west, where the underlying rocks are exposed, localised communities of specialised plants and animals develop. Since rain simply drains off, or through, the rocks, all the residents must be tolerant of desiccation. Magnificent *Euphorbias*, *Aloes*, *Kalanchoes* and *Pachypodiums* grip on to tiny crevices, bringing foliage and flowers to the rock face. The insects, birds and lemurs rely on these for sustenance, only retreating in the heat of the day to rest beneath the trees in nearby canyons.

Plants and animals are also to be found among the knife-edge pinnacles of the spectacular limestone karst massifs known as *tsingy* (see page 389). These bizarre eroded landscapes enable a complex mosaic of communities to live side-by-side. The towering pinnacles which sport the succulents are in fact the ornate roofs of extensive cave systems below. These caves are inhabited by bats and rodents, with millions of insects and arachnids feeding on the bat guano and each other. Blind cave fish share these dark subterranean rivers with lurking cave crocodiles.

This diverse habitat supports numerous birds and mammals. It has even been claimed that Ankarana has the highest density of primates on earth. *Good examples: Isalo, Ankarana, Bemaraha and Namoroka.*

SPINY FOREST Whenever photographers wish to startle people with the uniqueness of Madagascar they head for the spiny forest. Its mass of tangled, prickly branches and swollen succulent trunks creates a habitat variously described by naturalists as 'a nightmare' and 'the eighth wonder of the world'. Stretching in a band around the southwest coast from Morombe to Taolagnaro, the spiny forest is the only primary community able to resist the extremely arid environment. All the plants here are beautifully adapted to survive on the sporadic rainfall, sometimes going without water for more than a year. The unworldly landscape of this community is a result of the dramatic and striking forms of tall *Aloes*, broad-leaved *Kalanchoe* 'trees', octopus trees, *Pachypodium*, *Euphorbia*, endemic orchids and palms – all extremely specialised to withstand the harsh dry conditions.

The most evident animal life, aside from reptiles and desert arthropods, are the groups of sifakas which somehow avoid the vicious spines of the *Didierea* as they leap from one trunk to another. *Good examples: Berenty, Ifaty, Beza-Mahafaly and along the road from Taolagnaro to Ambovombe.*

WETLANDS Wetlands everywhere are regarded as important habitats. The plants here are terrestrial species adapted to tolerate waterlogging. Lakes, swamps and marshes all over the island are popular with birds, attracted by the shelter and materials of the reeds and rushes, and the sustenance to be gained from the insect life. On open water and lagoons near the coast, large flocks of flamingoes gather, accompanied in their feeding by various waders.

But in Madagascar it is not only birds that make their homes among the reeds. In the reed beds of Lake Alaotra, a rare species of bamboo lemur, *Hapalemur alaotrensis*, has given up bamboo for papyrus to become the world's only reed-dwelling primate. Lakes and waterways also play host to sometimes-sacred populations of crocodiles. *Good examples: Tsimanampetsotsa, Lake Alaotra, Lake Ampitabe, Lake Ravelobe and Ankarafantsika.*

MANGROVES Where trees dominate the wetlands instead of grasses, there are swamps. The most important of these are the mangrove swamps. Madagascar possesses the largest area of mangroves in the western Indian Ocean – about 330,000ha. The aerial roots of their characteristic salt-tolerant trees are alternately submerged and exposed twice daily with the tide. Some of the trees get a head start in life by germinating their seeds whilst still on the parent tree.

Mangroves are important and rich ecosystems. They support a wealth of bird species, which feast on the swarms of insects above the water and shoals of fish below. Many marine fish and crustaceans use mangroves as a nursery, coming in from the open sea to mate, breed and rear their young in relative safety. However, mangroves are now under threat in Madagascar. *Good examples: Mangoro (south of Anakao), Katsepy, Marovoay and Morombe.*

CORAL REEFS Madagascar has about 1,000km of coral reefs. Most of the species they support come from a community of globetrotting fish, corals and invertebrates, which crop up wherever the environment is just right.

The 1,600km difference in latitude between north and south Madagascar results in a subtle temperature gradient. The slightly cooler waters of the south are dominated by different corals and other species from those found in the north.

The continental shelf surrounding Madagascar also contributes to diversity. A sharp drop-off on the east coast limits fringing reef growth, while the west coast's vast and shallow shelf – spreading out under the Mozambique Channel and warmed by the Agulhas Current – is much better suited to coral reef development. Along this coast there are fringing and barrier reefs sporting remote cays and a wealth of fish and invertebrates. Loggerhead, green and hawksbill turtles cruise the underwater meadows between reefs and nesting beaches, and from July to September migrating humpback whales use the warm waters of eastern Madagascar for breeding. *Good examples: Ile Sainte Marie, islands off Nosy Be, Ifaty, Anakao and Lokaro.*

CONSERVATION *With information from Joanna Durbin*

AN AGE-OLD PROBLEM When people first settled in Madagascar, the culture they brought with them depended on rice and zebu cattle. Rice was the staple diet and zebu the spiritual staple, the link with the ancestors. Rice and zebu cannot be raised in dense forest, so the trees were felled and the undergrowth burned.

Two hundred or so years ago King Andrianampoinimerina punished those of his subjects who wilfully deforested areas. The practice continued, however. In 1883,

DURRELL WILDLIFE CONSERVATION TRUST IN MADAGASCAR

Joanna Durbin, Madagascar Programme Director

Durrell Wildlife Conservation Trust is an international conservation organisation with its headquarters in Jersey, Channel Islands. It was established by the visionary conservationist and renowned author Gerald Durrell in 1963. The organisation, with the mission 'to save species from extinction', has pre-eminent expertise in hands-on management of endangered species and a global reputation for its work through its field conservation projects, captive breeding, re-introduction and research (in the wild and under conservation care). Durrell currently has 40 conservation projects in 18 countries, as well as an extensive programme of research, training, conservation and breeding of endangered species. Our largest programme is in Madagascar, where we have been working for over 20 years in a range of different locations and habitats. Our current efforts are concentrated on eight sites in western dry forests, wetlands and fragmented lowland rainforest – fragile and poorly studied ecosystems with their own complement of Madagascar's endemic species, which have often been neglected by other conservation programmes.

The Menabe forests near Morondava on the west coast contain a remarkable cluster of locally endemic, endangered species including the giant jumping rat, the flat-tailed tortoise and the narrow-striped mongoose. They are threatened by slash-and-burn maize cultivation, which has created vast holes in the forest, and by unsustainable logging operations that damage the forest's structure and open up trails that lead to increased hunting and other extractive uses. Our work has been focused on raising awareness of the locally endemic species by defining their conservation status and threats; on working with local communities using traditional laws called *dina* to agree on limits to cultivated areas in exchange for rights to cultivate on illegally deforested land; and working with government and NGO partners to create a new protected area to ensure the survival of Menabe's forests and species. Durrell's partnership approach is starting to show success

a century later, the missionary James Sibree commented: 'Again we noticed the destruction of the forest and the wanton waste of trees.' The first efforts at legal protection came as long ago as 1927 when ten reserves were set aside by the French colonial government, which also tried to put a stop to the burning. Successive governments have tried – and failed – to halt this devastation.

Since independence in 1960, Madagascar's population has quadrupled to 22 million and the remaining forest has been reduced by half. Only about 10% of the original cover remains and an estimated 2,000km² is destroyed annually – not by timber companies (although there have been some culprits) but by impoverished peasants clearing the land by the traditional method of *tavy*, slash-and-burn (see box on page 41), and cutting trees for fuel or to make charcoal. However, Madagascar is not overpopulated; the population density averages only 37 people per square kilometre (compared to 254 in the UK). The pressure on the forests is because so much of the country is sterile grassland. Unlike in neighbouring Africa, this savanna is lifeless because Malagasy animals evolved to live in forests; they are not adapted to this new environment.

Change in Madagascar's vegetation is by no means recent. Scientists have identified that the climate became much drier about 5,000 years ago. Humans have just catalysed the process.

THE RACE AGAINST TIME Madagascar has more endangered species of mammal than any other country in the world. The authorities are well aware of this environmental crisis: as long ago as 1970 the Director of Scientific Research made this comment in a speech during an international symposium on conservation: 'The people in this room

with a halt to deforestation in this area since 2003. The Malagasy government decided to legally protect the Menabe forests in March 2006.

The Durrell Madagascar programme has been working to conserve endemic wetland species through two projects. The Western Wetland Project concentrates on species such as Madagascar teal, side-necked turtle and sacred ibis, while the Eastern Wetland Project includes action for the Lac Alaotra gentle lemur, Meller's duck and 19 endemic species of fish found in the Nosivolo River near Marolambo. In addition to their biodiversity importance, wetlands are highly productive and sustain large human populations through fisheries and agriculture. Our wetland conservation campaign at Lake Alaotra has also been a success (see page 255).

The ploughshare tortoise is a prime example of an extremely rare species – occurring only at a single site – that is vulnerable to a variety of pressures such as uncontrolled bush fires and collection for international trade. Our conservation action for this species, in Baie de Baly National Park, which includes all remaining tortoise habitat, demonstrates how concentrating on a single species can provide multiple benefits for the conservation of a range of endangered species typical of the highly threatened western dry forest and coastal habitats. In particular, we have helped to revive a traditional fire management technique based on burning firebreaks at the start of the dry season. We also run a captive breeding centre for the ploughshare tortoise, the flat-tailed tortoise and the side-necked turtle at Ampijoroa forestry station in Ankarafantsika National Park. Captive-bred juveniles are being returned to the wild to reinforce the depleted populations.

We have extended our conservation actions to Manombo Special Reserve in southeastern Madagascar, a lowland rainforest patch which is home to the southernmost population of black-and-white ruffed lemurs and is the only protected site for the critically endangered grey-headed lemur.

know that Malagasy nature is a world heritage. We are not sure that others realise that it is *our* heritage.' Resentment at having outsiders make decisions on the future of their heritage without proper consultation with the Malagasy was one of the reasons there was little effective conservation in the 1970s and early 1980s. This was a time when Madagascar was demonstrating its independence from Western influences. Things changed in 1985, when Madagascar hosted a major international conference on conservation for development. The Ministry of Animal Production, Waters and Forests, which administered the protected areas, went into partnership with the World Wide Fund for Nature (WWF). Their plan was to evaluate all protected areas in the country, then numbering 37 (2% of the island), and in their strategy for the future to provide people living near the reserves with economically viable alternatives. They have largely achieved their aims. All the protected areas have been evaluated and recommendations for their management are being implemented. These original protected areas are now the responsibility of Madagascar National Parks (formerly ANGAP) which was established under the auspices of the Environmental Action Plan (EAP) sponsored by the World Bank working together with many other donors. Among their successes has been the establishment of a number of new national parks and several Debt for Nature swaps, in which international debts are cancelled in return for some of Madagascar's repayments going into conservation projects.

Numerous projects in Madagascar are funded by many conservation NGOs and other agencies including WWF, Durrell Wildlife Conservation Trust (UK), German Primate Centre – DPZ, Conservation International, Missouri Botanical Garden, Duke University Primate Center, Wildlife Conservation Society, Madagascar Fauna Group and The Peregrine Fund; also USAID (US Agency for International Development), Cooperation Francaise, GTZ and KfW (German government), UNDP (United Nations Development Programme) and UNESCO. One of the most active Malagasy NGOs is FANAMBY.

THE DURBAN VISION In a dramatic announcement in 2003, then president Marc Ravalomanana promised to triple the area of Madagascar's protected reserves within five years. Deforestation, the president said, has taken its toll on the island, reducing the country's forest by nearly half over the last 20 years. 'We can no longer afford to sit back and watch our forests go up in flames. This is not just Madagascar's biodiversity; it is the world's biodiversity. We have the firm political will to stop this degradation.'

A programme was launched to identify areas in need of protection, and to create wildlife corridors connecting existing parks (see box on page 263). The new and existing protected areas are now grouped into the new System of Protected Areas of Madagascar (SAPM) which has three major objectives: to conserve Madagascar's unique biodiversity; to conserve its cultural heritage; and to enable sustainable use to contribute to help alleviate poverty.

Unfortunately, since the collapse of the Ravalomanana government, the incoming regime has not shown the same dedication to conservation (see box on page 302) so the future is unclear.

PROTECTED AREAS

CATEGORIES The main types of protected area are those managed by Madagascar National Parks, still often referred to by its former title of ANGAP. These are: national parks, special reserves and strict nature reserves. The first two categories are generally open to tourism.

At the time of writing there are 19 national parks: Montagne d'Ambre, Ankarana, Marojejy, Masoala, Mananara-Nord, Zahamena, Andasibe-Mantadia, Andringitra,

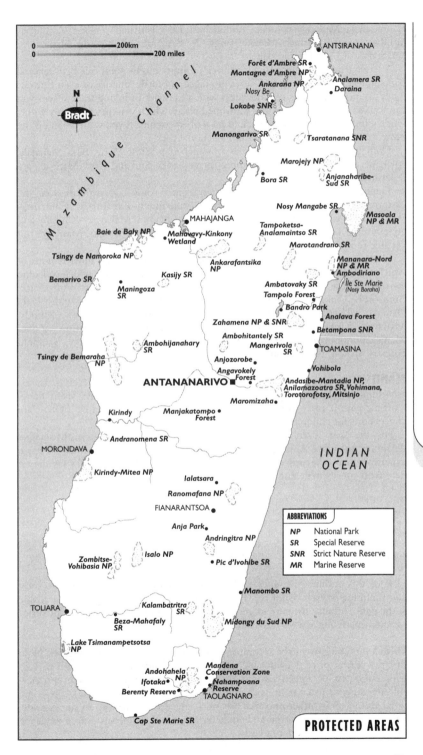

ABBREVIATIONS

NP	National Park
SR	Special Reserve
SNR	Strict Nature Reserve
MR	Marine Reserve

PROTECTED AREAS

Ranomafana, Midongy Befotaka, Andohahela, Lake Tsimanampetsotsa, Zombitse-Vohibasia, Isalo, Kirindy-Mitea, Tsingy de Bemaraha, Tsingy de Namoroka, Ankarafantsika and Baie de Baly.

A letter from an American adventurer prompts me to point out that national parks in Madagascar are very different to those in North America or even Europe. They are not huge areas of wilderness with a network of hiking trails where you can wander at will, but carefully controlled places which you may visit only with a guide who will require you to stick to prescribed circuits. If you want to get off the beaten track, don't try to do it within a national park.

There are 20 or so special reserves, of which Cap Sainte Marie, Beza-Mahafaly, Analamera, Andranomena, Manombo, Anjanaharibe-Sud and Nosy Mangabe are described in this book.

The new areas coming under protection include some vast corridors along the eastern rainforest belt such as Makira, Ankeniheny-Zahamena, Fandriana-Vondrozo, as well as important wetlands at Lake Alaotra, Mahavavy-Kinkony and a plethora of other sites conserving important species and habitats. Many are not yet able to accept visiting tourists.

There are also an increasing number of private reserves, the most famous of which are Berenty and Anjajavy, and the NGO-run protected areas which welcome tourists. These include Ambodiriana Reserve, Analalava Forest, Anja Park, Anjozorobe, Ankafobe, Mitsinjo's Analamazaotra and Torotorofotsy, Bandro Park, Daraina, Ialatsara Lemur Forest Camp, Ifotaka Community Forest, Kirindy, Mahavavy-Kinkony Wetland Complex, Mandena Conservation Zone, Manjakatompo Forestry Station, Maromizaha, Nahampoana Reserve, Tampolo Forestry Station, Vohibola and Vohimana.

PERMITS The cost of permits to visit the national parks and reserves varies, according to which one you are visiting and the number of days spent there. Current permit prices for adult foreign tourists are shown below. (There are concessions for children, residents, nationals and researchers.)

For the 'big seven' – Isalo, Andasibe-Mantadia, Ranomafana, Montagne d'Ambre, Ankarana, Ankarafantsika and Tsingy de Bemaraha – the rates are more expensive than other reserves managed by Madagascar National Parks (as shown here with approximate euro equivalents):

	Main Parks	Others
1 day	25,000Ar (€10)	10,000Ar (€4)
2 days	37,000Ar (€14)	15,000Ar (€6)
3 days	40,000Ar (€16)	20,000Ar (€8)
4 days or more	50,000Ar (€20)	25,000Ar (€10)

Half of this entrance fee goes to Madagascar National Parks and half to local communities, so each visitor is playing his or her part. Permits are always available at the park entrance (be sure to get a receipt) but you may wish to visit the office in Antananarivo or www.parcs-madagascar.com.

GUIDES It is obligatory to be accompanied by a guide in all parks and reserves. Note that the permit price does not include their fee. Guide prices vary from park to park but a list of agreed rates is normally on display at each park entrance. Additionally it is usual to tip your guide for good service (see page 93).

Reserves run by other organisations normally also require you to take a guide, although the entrance permit and guide fee are usually combined into a single fee often charged on a per-circuit basis.

4

Practical Information

WHEN TO VISIT

Read the section on climate (page 3) before deciding when to travel. Broadly speaking, the dry months are in the winter between April and September, but rainfall varies enormously in different areas. The months you may want to avoid are August and during the Christmas holidays, when popular places are crowded, and February and March (the cyclone season) when it will probably rain – and worse. However, the off-peak season can be rewarding, with cheaper international airfares and accommodation and fewer other tourists. September is nice, but frequently windy in the south. April and May often have lovely weather, and the countryside is green after the rainy season.

Keen naturalists have their own requirements: botanists will want to go in February when many of the orchids are in flower, and herpetologists will also prefer the spring/summer because reptiles are more active – and brightly coloured – during those months. Bear in mind that giant jumping rats, dwarf lemurs, tenrecs and some reptiles are less active and so harder to see during the cool dry months of June to September. Alasdair Harris reported, after a January visit: 'I just returned from a research trip in the southwest where there has been some very heavy rain recently. It was quite extraordinary to see the spiny forest looking so lush and wet. The scenery changed completely, and within hours of the first rains arriving took on a deep leafy green, resonating at night time to the deafening chorus of relieved amphibians.'

My favourite months to visit Madagascar are October and November, when the weather is usually fine but not too hot, the jacarandas are in flower, the lemurs have babies, and lychees are sold from roadside stalls in the east.

CHOOSING A TRIP TO SUIT YOU

Over the years I've come to believe that everyone *can* enjoy Madagascar but not everyone does because they do not take sufficient care in matching the trip to their personality. When planning a holiday most people consider only their interests and how much they are prepared to spend. I feel that a vital component has been missed out.

WHAT SORT OF PERSON ARE YOU? The Catch-22 of tourism in Madagascar is that the type of person who can afford the trip is often the type least suited to cope with the Malagasy way of life. In our culture assertiveness, a strong sense of right and wrong, and organisational skills are the personality traits which lead to success in business, and thus the income to finance exotic travel. But these A-type personalities often find Madagascar unbearably inefficient and frustrating. By having control over their itinerary through a tailor-made tour, or by renting a vehicle and driver, such people are more likely to get the most out of their trip. A group tour, where they must go with the flow, may be the least successful option.

Conversely, the happiest travellers are often either those who choose to travel on a low budget (providing they're not obsessed with being ripped off) or those who can adopt the attitude of one elderly woman on a group tour who said 'I'm going to give up thinking; it doesn't work in Madagascar.' It doesn't, and she had a great time!

These days there is a trip to suit everyone in this extraordinary country. It won't be a cheap holiday, but it will be one you never forget, so choose wisely.

Below are the main options, in descending order of price and comfort.

The luxury package Four-star hotels are no longer unusual in Madagascar, and luxury seekers will have no problem planning their tour around the new upmarket 'boutique' hotels. These include Nosy Iranja and Tsarabanjina (Nosy Be), Anjajavy (north of Mahajanga), Jardin du Roy (Isalo) and Domaine de Fontenay (Joffreville, near Antsiranana), but this is by no means the complete list. The fly-in hotels even shield you from the realities of Madagascar by whisking you off to their resort by private plane.

Expedition cruising On a ship you know that you will sleep in a comfortable bed each night and eat familiar food. It is thus ideal for the adventurous at heart who are no longer able to take the rigours of land travel. It is also sometimes the only way of getting to remote offshore islands. In the UK try Noble Caledonia (\ 020 7752 0000; www.noble-caledonia.co.uk), and in the US Zegrahm Expeditions (\ 1 800 628 8747 or 206 285 4000; www.zeco.com) is recommended.

Tailor-made tours This is the ideal option for a couple or small group who are not restricted financially. It is also the best choice for people with special interests or who like things to run as smoothly as possible. You will be the decision-maker and will choose where you want to go and your preferred level of comfort, but the logistics will be taken care of.

You can organise your tailor-made trip through a tour operator in your home country, in which case you will have the benefit of legal protection if things go wrong, or use email to contact some Malagasy tour operators. Let the tour operator know your interests, the level of comfort you expect, and whether you want to cram in as much as possible or concentrate on just a few centres.

Tour operators which specialise in tailor-made tours in Madagascar are listed later in this chapter.

Group travel Group travel is usually a lot of fun, ideal for single people who do not wish to travel alone, and if you choose the tour company and itinerary carefully you will see a great deal of the country, gain an understanding of its complicated culture and unique wildlife, and generally have a great time without the need to make decisions (but you need to be able to relinquish the decision-making; not everyone can do this).

Semi-independent travel You can save money by dealing directly with a tour operator in Madagascar by email. Many are listed later in this chapter (see page 86). Now tourism is established in Madagascar, local operators have a clear understanding of tourists' needs and are impressively efficient. The downside to using a local operator is that they won't be bonded, so if things go wrong you will not get a refund nor be able to sue the company.

Perhaps the ideal do-it-yourself trip is to hire a local driver/guide and vehicle when you arrive in Tana. This way you are wonderfully free to stop when you please and stay where you wish. There are some drivers listed in *Chapter 7*.

Independent travel Truly independent travellers usually have a rough idea of where they want to go and how they will travel but are open to changes of plan dictated by local conditions, whim and serendipity. Independent travellers are not necessarily budget travellers: those who can afford to fly to major towns, then rent a vehicle and driver, can eliminate a large amount of hassle and see everything they set out to see – providing they set a realistic programme for themselves. What they may miss out on is contact with the local people, and some of the smells, sounds and otherness of Madagascar.

The majority of independent travellers use public transport and stay in middle-range or budget hotels. They are exposed to all Madagascar's joys and frustrations and most seem to love it. The key here is not to try to do too much, and to speak at least some French. Pages 94–5 tell you about the trials and tribulations of travelling by *taxi-brousse*: no problem providing you allow time for delays.

Independent travellers can save money and help Madagascar by avoiding the few most popular national parks in favour of the less well known and less expensive (but often equally rewarding) ones – see page 72.

The seriously adventurous Madagascar must be one of the very few countries left in the world where large areas are not yet detailed in a guidebook. A study of the standard 1:2,000,000 map of Madagascar reveals some mouth-watering possibilities, and a look at the more detailed 1:500,000 maps confirms the opportunities for people who are willing to walk or cycle. Or drive. Two of my most adventurous correspondents, Valerie and John Middleton, have travelled all over Madagascar by 4x4 vehicle. Asked why they keep coming back, they replied: 'We have had a passion for worldwide cave and karst exploration for well over 40 years and for plants, and in particular their adaptation to extreme conditions.' Having a focus helps, especially when explaining your presence to bemused locals.

Serious adventurers will need to plan their trip beforehand with the FTM regional maps. The Middletons tell me: 'It is possible to obtain photocopies of the 1:100,000 maps that cover Madagascar, plus a few of the 1:25,000 that cover only a small area, in person only from The Institut Geographique Nationale, 2–4 Avenue Pasteur, 94165 Saint-Mande, Paris.' If you don't live within reach of Paris you will have to purchase the maps in Tana; see page 158.

Valerie and John also support my theory that the seriously adventurous are often 'pensioners'. Not that the youngsters don't do their bit for exploring Madagascar's uncharted areas. Throughout this book there are quotes from people who did just that, sometimes after a lot of preparation and sometimes on a whim.

Not everyone is courageous enough to step or pedal into the unknown like this, but in fact it's one of the safest ways to travel: the Malagasy that you meet will, once they have got over the shock of seeing you, invariably be welcoming and hospitable. It's how I first saw Madagascar and why I fell in love with the place.

Travelling alone To travel alone may be a matter of choice or necessity. The trick is to make the necessity into choice by revelling in the opportunity to get close to the local people and to immerse yourself in their culture.

Lone travellers need to be prepared for the long evenings. Robert Bowker found nights at national parks particularly lonely: 'Dinner is early, and after that nothing to do but go to your bungalow. Take a powerful torch and lots to read. I got through a fair number of crossword puzzles. Also take music...' For budding writers evenings alone are the perfect time to develop your diary skills.

Another problem which needs to be borne in mind when planning a solo trip is that national parks and reserves will be expensive unless you team up with other travellers, because guide fees are usually the same for one person as for a group of

4

four. The same goes for trips involving hire of a 4x4 or boat. Conversely, one person can squeeze into any *taxi-brousse*.

Solo travellers should consider avoiding the usual tourist routes where the local people will be less friendly and the prices higher. The real rewards come when you travel off the beaten track; here you'll meet genuinely hospitable locals still leading traditional lives. For more on solo female and solo male travel, see pages 122–4.

Family travel It is becoming more practical to travel in Madagascar with children. For specific advice on this refer to page 123.

Disabled travel With careful planning and help from a local tour operator, even wheelchair users can see something of the landscape and wildlife. See box on page 121.

Working holidays and volunteering There is a growing interest in paying to be a volunteer in a scientific or community project in Madagascar. This is an excellent way of 'giving something back' while enjoying a learning experience which will

AKANY AVOKO THROUGH THE EYES OF A VOLUNTEER

Peter Jourdier

Akany Avoko was originally set up as a refuge for young girls 'who would otherwise be in prison, awaiting trial to prove their innocence against allegations of petty crime'. That was 40 years ago. Now most of the children either have no family or are separated from what family they have by poverty or domestic problems. Despite this, it is an amazingly happy place. At the moment the centre is near full capacity with about 140 children up to 18 years old.

The thought of bio-gas loos and outdoor showers did not excite me too much, but when I arrived I was pleasantly surprised. The place was clean, bright and everyone was incredibly friendly.

It took a while for me to get used to the life. They get up extremely early and go to bed at around 18.00 when the sun goes down, but I soon found my feet and saw that there were plenty of things I could do to help. Before going out to Madagascar I had been sent rather a worrying email saying 'we are thrilled to read you have carpentry skills, there is much to do in the way of fixing and making items around Akany Avoko' ...and there was. Many of the windows had warped so much that they couldn't shut, furniture needed to be made, doors repaired, leaking pipes fixed. I had done some woodwork at school, but was certainly not a plumber, carpenter, electrician or cabinetmaker when I arrived – and I'm still not now. However, this was a large part of what I did during my stay there. The windows now close, some furniture is made, most of the doors now lock and the pipe still leaks (I did try!).

I also gave computer lessons to some of the children in the evenings, when the electricity was strong enough to keep the computer going. Here there was a great difference in the levels of the children, depending on their background. To make matters a little more interesting, it was generally the ones with less education who couldn't use a computer, meaning they also spoke little or no French, and I didn't speak Malagasy.

Overall I had a fantastic three months there, as well as (I hope) being useful to them. I would strongly recommend Akany Avoko, or simply Madagascar, to anyone. The country is incredibly beautiful (as are the beaches), the people are so friendly and they need – and are very grateful for – all the help we can offer.

stay with you much longer than the normal holiday memories. There are also some opportunities of working as a volunteer for local charities or NGOs. These volunteers still need to pay for their air fare and basic living costs, and are sometimes only accepted if they have a particular skill.

Many of the organisations listed below are covered in more detail in Bradt's *Wildlife and Conservation Volunteering* by Peter Lynch.

Akany Avoko \ 22 441 58; e akany.avoko@ moov.mg; www.akanyavoko.com. This wonderful children's organisation welcomes volunteers with suitable skills. See page 164 & boxes on pages 76 & 128.

Arboretum d'Antsokay m 032 02 600 15; e andry.petignat@caramail.com. This splendid arboretum near Toliara (see page 216) welcomes botanist volunteers.

Azafady London, UK; \ 020 8960 6629; f 020 8962 0126; e info@azafady.org; www.madagascar.co.uk. This charity/NGO works in southeast Madagascar to tackle human poverty & suffering, & protect unique environments. Volunteers work in village communities helping to develop sustainable livelihoods, set up health & education infrastructure, & carry out habitat conservation.

Blue Ventures \ 020 7359 0770; e madagascar@ blueventures.org; www.blueventures.org. This award-winning organisation, based in Andavadoaka, is setting up the largest community-run protected area in Madagascar with great success so far. Their work includes marine monitoring (scuba training included) & wide-ranging community projects from education to family planning schemes. See boxes on pages 135, 399 & 400.

Earthwatch Oxford, UK & Maynard, MA, USA; \ 01865 318838 (UK), 1 800 776 0188 (USA); e info@ earthwatch.org; www.earthwatch.org. Pioneers in upmarket scientific research trips. In Madagascar you can work with Dr Alison Jolly on lemur research in Berenty.

Frontier London, UK; \ 020 7613 2422; www.frontierprojects.ac.uk. Also works in marine conservation, taking paying volunteers for their marine research programmes.

Hope for Madagascar 3150 Iris Av, Ste 210, Boulder, CO USA; e hopeformadagascar@comcast.net; www.hopeformadagascar.org. This US charity seeks volunteers with previous experience of living abroad & teaching English. Besides providing English lessons, they build schools, distribute school supplies & run village development projects.**Mada Clinics** e info@madaclinics.org; www.madaclinics.org. Operates clinics in the north. Welcomes volunteers, especially those with some medical experience.

People & Places \ 01795 535 718; e madagascar@travel-peopleandplaces.co.uk; www.travel-peopleandplaces.co.uk. With their team of local people, this company offers community-led volunteering placements.

The Dodwell Trust \ 020 8740 6302; e dodwell@ madagascar.freeserve.co.uk; www.dodwell-trust.org. Volunteers spend 1–6 months living in a community. They may teach English, work at the zoo or botanical gardens, hold events, run tree nurseries, make radio shows & more. No skills required & weekends are free. Conservation & biology research work is available to graduates.

World Challenge Expeditions London, UK; \ 020 8728 7200; e welcome@world-challenge.co.uk; www.world-challenge.co.uk. This organisation is aimed mainly at students.

WWF www.wwf.mg. A new Youth Volunteer Programme for ages 19–27 currently operates 10 projects ranging from coral reef & wetland management to various forest & community projects.

SPECIAL INTERESTS

Trekking It's a misnomer to call it trekking because Madagascar is not like the Himalayas or Andes where your gear is carried by porters or pack animals to a different campsite each night. Two national parks are specifically set up for hiking: Andringitra and Isalo. I count Andringitra as one of my best hiking trips anywhere (see page 197) and Marojejy (page 309) is one of the most exciting mountains I have (nearly) climbed. There are a growing number of national parks and reserves that offer good treks – but you must always be accompanied by a guide.

Hiking My advice to people wanting to strike out on their own is to bear in mind that many of Madagascar's 'roads' are overgrown tracks, and ideal for hiking. There

Lex Cumber with additional recommendations from Bill French & Julian Cooke

If you are thinking of taking a bike to Madagascar, do it; you'll love it. On most of the roads you will be more comfortable than anyone in motorised transport. The simplicity and strength of the humble bike will get you virtually anywhere, bring you closer to the wonderful people of the island and allow you to see things that you would miss if you travelled any other way.

If you intend to cycle between the major centres and in the more developed parts of the island, then you can plan as for touring but in tough conditions. You will need a mountain bike as the tarred roads can be broken, especially after rains, and there are many unmade roads. You should carry a good supply of spares and tools, some food and plenty of container capacity for water, though you probably will find enough to eat and drink in most areas, as well as places to stay. If you plan to go into more remote areas and to tackle the smaller roads, then here are some tips.

THE BIKE What you need to think is simplicity, strength and self sufficiency. Don't take it if it can't be fixed with the tools you carry yourself, or with a hammer by a Malagasy mechanic. Fit a new chain and block, carry spare spokes, brake blocks, cables, inner-tubes and take plenty of oil (the dust is unbelievable). Go with the strongest wheels you can afford, and the fattest tyres you can fit (1.95 minimum). You can pick up cheap bike parts in the larger towns. Bill adds: 'Take at least two dozen patches for punctures, a chain riveter, a few dozen plastic cable ties plus ten jubilee clips.'

ON THE BIKE Lex: 'Forget panniers unless you are staying on good roads. A 20–35-litre backpack held away from your back with mesh for ventilation is ideal: it's more flexible, stays with you at all times, and you do get used to it. A rear rack with a rack bag is a good addition, and allows you to carry heavy tools/food/water away from your back.' Bill: 'Only front panniers break off, they tend not to survive Malagasy roads. Sturdy back panniers are necessary – tie them together so you don't lose them on bumpy roads; a backpack makes you more tired.'

CLOTHING You need two sets, one for cycling and one for socialising/resting. If you are going to explore the deserts, I advise the 'Beau Geste' style of hat with peak on front, and flap on back. General purpose shorts, with cycling short inners underneath (two pairs minimum) are ideal. Also take leather cycling gloves (artificial materials disintegrate with the sweat and the heat); footwear of the trainer/walking boot variety is ideal, again go for natural materials; lightweight socks, with a clean set of underwear spare at all times. I find an Arabic scarf a fantastic all-purpose bit of kit: sleep under it, dry yourself with it, use it as a picnic blanket or head covering for dust-storms etc. Bandannas are a useful addition and keep the sweat out of your eyes. Just think tough kit for your contact points on the bike, and breathable kit everywhere else. The rule to apply for your clothing is 'one set wet, one set dry'. At night consider a clean T-shirt/vest with a cotton or similar shirt, and lightweight trousers. Your appearance is always worth considering, as you never know who you are going to meet! Finally, take a lightweight fleece as it can get cold at night, and some sort of wind breaker/waterproof shell.

PERSONAL HYGIENE Take a good first-aid kit, and Savlon for your backside. My colleague on our 3,000km Madagascar adventure had golf-ball sized boils on his behind for 3–4 weeks as a result of a) lots of saddle time b) sweat c) lack of 'arse discipline' (as we called it). Apply Savlon liberally, and if you get the chance to wash, take your time and be particular down below. Anti-fungal creams are a good idea as well. Take rehydration salts, Imodium type pills and laxatives. Your body will not know what's hit it, and you never know how it will react. Salt pills are useful as well. Remember to drink as much as you can at night. Take water purifiers.

REMOTE TOWNS When pulling into a town/village, think of riding right the way through it first, to select your likely bar/bunkhouse, and then cycle back to it. You don't want to miss the heavenly spot 500m up the road because you pulled over early. If in doubt look for a village elder. If you are really remote, the locals will often run away, but just wait and the relevant person will find you. You may not always be able to buy food. If you do buy food in remote villages make sure you give the women-folk the money, not the men. Bear in mind villagers will often offer you food, and as result go without themselves.

RIDE ROUTINE Be moving before sunrise if you're in the desert: 05.00 is about right. If you can finish your riding for the day by 11.00–12.00, that's perfect, but be realistic. Don't ride in the middle hours of the day unless you really have to. Just find or make some shade and rest. You'll probably be exhausted by then anyway, but after a short while you should be able to put in 6–8 hours' riding per day. Rest days are vital, and give you the benefit of time in great places.

FOOD Carry two days' rations if you can, because you just never know when you may have to spend a night out. Try peanuts, raisins, dates, processed cheese, salt, couscous, muesli with powdered milk and boiled sweets. Take some with you or pick it up in Tana or the larger towns. This food stash will supplement your basic rice diet, which soon becomes boring, and lacks the calories required for hard riding. Otherwise, watch where the locals eat and don't be afraid of the road-side stands; they are fantastic. Carry a lightweight stove that does not rely on gas.

CAMPING Strangely in Madagascar there is a totally different attitude to camping. It is viewed as suspicious behaviour by many rural communities. Where possible avoid it. However, you need to carry a sleeping bag and mat anyway, so a poncho or tent will allow you the flexibility to camp out should you need to, or just take a mozzie net if in the dry season. Best advice: try not to be too obvious or you will attract a lot of unwanted attention.

SECURITY As a rule Madagascar is a very safe place, but on a bike you are exposed. Your best defence is learning some of the language, using humour and keeping some small denomination notes handy. Note that outside the four or five main towns you will not find banks that know what a credit card is, so you will have to carry cash – though your costs will be low. Spread it around, hide some in your bike etc. Have photocopies of documentation on you, as well as originals. Leave details in Tana, and inform your national consulate or someone of an approximate return date. If in trouble, don't raise your voice, and negotiate calmly with the head man, be patient, and keep smiling.

NAVIGATION Even the best maps available in Madagascar are inaccurate. Rely on local knowledge when navigating the minor roads. If you are travelling cross country, good compass work and the ability to read the terrain is essential. Again local knowledge and the ability to stay calm when lost, are essential.

Biking in Madagascar is breathtaking in every sense of the word. It's not easy, but you don't go to Madagascar to be pampered! I can promise you will see the country at its best, and the desert sunrises are worth the journey alone. Go for it!

are a couple of well-known routes, the **Smugglers' Path** and the **Trans-Masoala Trail**, but these do not appeal to me nearly as much as the huge regions that have seen few foreigners.

Hiking in the south is fascinating from a cultural perspective but you will need to carry a lot of water. Conversely, if hiking in the east you will get very wet but never be short of a drink! Read the advice on page 130 on the cultural aspects of travelling off the beaten path safely and enjoyably.

Climbing The centre for rock-climbing is Andringitra (page 197). There is also a rock-climbing centre based in Antsiranana (page 330). Those interested in tree-climbing should see pages 262 and 331.

Mountain biking Madagascar is becoming increasingly popular for travelling using your own muscle-power. The advantages are obvious: bad roads and broken-down vehicles do not delay you, con-men will not overcharge you and – most important – by passing slowly through Madagascar's small villages and communities you will experience the Malagasy culture in an unforced way. These advantages far outweigh the security risks; you are much more likely to be overwhelmed by hospitality than robbed.

Bill and Nina French, who have made two trips in Madagascar by bicycle, recommend the following routes: Manompana–Mananara (52km with some very difficult stretches), the Masoala Peninsula, Ambalavao–Fianarantsoa, Manakara–Sahasinaka, Ranomafana–Fianarantsoa, Fianarantsoa–Soatanana–RN42, Lac Tritriva–Marinanpona and Ambatolampy–Antananarivo.

For more information see the box on page78.

Caving Madagascar has some fabulous caves, and several expeditions have been mounted to explore them. Caving is not a popular Malagasy pursuit, however, so cavers should take particular care to explain what they are doing and get the necessary permits for exploring protected areas. An experienced local tour operator will help with the red tape.

The best karst areas are in the north and west: **Ankarana** (the best explored and mapped area, with more than 100km of subterranean caves), **Narinda** (where the longest cave is over 5km), **Bemaraha**, the **Mikoboka Plateau** (north of Toliara, with pits to a depth of 165m) and the **Mahafaly Plateau** (south of Toliara).

Diving Liz Bomford, an experienced diver who has been visiting Madagascar for 25 years, provided the following information.

'By far the best and most exciting diving is around Nosy Be and its galaxy of islands and reefs. The biodiversity in this area is outstanding. Coral bleaching caused by global warming has not affected the reefs to any great degree and you can find almost every hard coral species known in the western Indian Ocean. You may see humpback whales as well as dolphins from the boat. Underwater you could get lucky and find whale sharks. Nosy Be is extraordinarily good for nudibranchs so there's something for everyone. The diving operators in Nosy Be work with local fishermen to protect the environment with the aim of providing good diving conditions for tourists. You won't be disappointed.

'At Ile Sainte Marie, off the east coast, there are several good dive sites, and the dive operators are a responsible bunch. However, visibility is often limited due to heavy rainfall in this area.

'The west coast around Toliara used to offer very good diving (I first dived there in 1976) but these days over-fishing has taken its toll and the diving is a shadow of what it used to be.

'The water is colder in August and September (take a hood or a sweat) but the rest of the year a 3mm or 5mm suit will do. Men will have no trouble hiring a suit but if you're a woman, consider taking your own wetsuit – otherwise you may have trouble finding one to fit.'

If you are considering diving in Madagascar, read the box on page 82 and *Diving safety* on page 116.

River trips Madagascar has some splendid rivers, particularly in the west. Some offer the perfect means to pass through otherwise inaccessible areas of the country. The range includes extended calm water floats to exciting white-water sections. See page 402 for a description of the western rivers. Close to Tana there are some great white-water trips on the highland rivers coming off the plateau. Many of these offer medium and extreme white-water runs to challenge rafters and kayakers of all skill levels. Gondwana Explorer is one tour operator that offers white-water excursions.

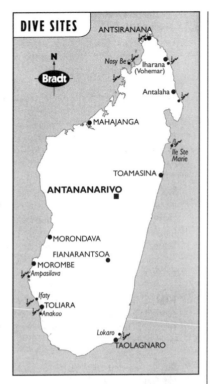

Birdwatching There are several tour operators that specialise in birding trips. 'Twitchers' travel with such a different focus from other wildlife viewers that it's well worth going with a like-minded group and an expert tour-leader. See page 54 for full details on the best birding places.

HIGHLIGHTS AND ITINERARIES

Having sorted out the 'whats' and 'hows' of travelling in Madagascar, you must turn your attention to the all-important subject of 'where'. One of the hardest decisions facing the first-time visitor to a country as large and diverse as Madagascar is where to go. Even a couple of months is too short to see everything, so itineraries must be planned according to interests and the level of comfort wanted.

HIGHLIGHTS

Wildlife The following well-established reserves and national parks have comfortable accommodation nearby, easy access and experienced guides (starting from the north and going clockwise): Montagne d'Ambre, Nosy Mangabe, Andasibe-Mantadia, Ranomafana, Berenty, Isalo and Ankarafantsika. Others, with more difficult access and simple accommodation or camping, include Daraina, Marojejy, Masoala, Andohahela, Beza-Mahafaly, Kirindy and Ankarana.

Scenery Most recommended for views are the central highlands between Fianarantsoa and Ambalavao, Andringitra, Isalo and Andohahela national parks, Avenue of the Baobabs (near Morondava), Tsingy de Bemaraha, Ankarana, Montagne d'Ambre and the Andapa region.

The coast and islands of Madagascar can be divided into key regions based on the principal marine ecosystems and the presence of important species of fish, birds, turtles and marine mammals.

NORTH Composed principally of coral reefs, lagoons, mangroves and an abundance of small islands. One of the richest in marine life of all the regions in Madagascar. Important species seen in this area include whale sharks, turtles and manta rays. Due to the variety of sites and beauty of this region, tourism is well established and is supported by several hotels and dive centres which offer diving and snorkelling excursions.

Sites *Islands and coral reefs:* Archipelago of Nosy Mitsio including llots des Quatres Frères, Nosy Hara, Nosy Be, Nosy Manitse and Nosimborona, Nosy Ratafanika, Nosy Iranja, Nosy Haramy and Nosy Milomboka, Nosy Faho, Nosy Mangabe, Nosy Tanikely (unofficially protected area), islands of the Baie d'Emeraude (Nosy Antaly-Be, Nosy Suarez, Nosy Lava), Nosy Lowry, and Nosy Ankao. Continental shelf from Nosy Be to Antsiranana (sites with specific coral and topographic formations). *Mangroves and estuaries:* Ambanja and Antsiranana.

WEST Characterised by extensive beaches, several rocky rivers and large estuaries supporting extended mangroves. Most of this region's small islands and coral reefs are seldom visited. Its coast offers enormous potential for quality dive tourism. Hotels and dive centres are limited.

Sites *Islands and coral reefs:* Kirindy-Mitea coast and small islands, and Nosy Barren (several small islands). *Mangroves and estuaries:* Tsiribihina, Betsiboka, Mahajamba, Manambolomaty, and Mahavavy estuary.

SOUTHWEST Composed of a variety of habitats including large areas of mangroves and vast lagoons lined with endless beaches. Some of the most notable sites are located within one of the largest coral reef systems in the world stretching over 150km from the coastal town of Toliara northwards. Tourism is well developed in this region, where access to various marine sites is assured.

Beaches and watersports Madagascar's best beaches are on the west coast, but some people are disappointed because of the shallow water (it is often impossible to swim at low tide). The beautiful beaches of the east coast offer better swimming but the weather is uncertain and strong currents and sharks are occasionally a danger. The very best beaches are in remote areas such as Anjajavy, the islands around Nosy Be, Ile Sainte Marie and south of Toliara.

Diving is covered on page 80. Surfing is a growing sport in the southwest, kitesurfing in the north, and sport fishing can be organised from Nosy Be.

Nightlife The people of southern Madagascar are the most outgoing on the island, with good discos in Taolagnaro and Toliara, but Nosy Be (and specifically Ambataloaka) is undoubtedly where the action is for tourists.

Museums Madagascar has only a few good museums. The best by a long way is the Museum of the Antandroy in Berenty Reserve. Toliara has a good ethnological museum and a marine museum, and Museum Akiba in Mahajanga

Sites *Islands and coral reefs:* Mikea coastal reef, islands and lagoons, Toliara's Grand Récif (frontal reef wall and pools), Nosy Ve and reefs, and Nosy Manitse. Continental shelf from Toliara to Morombe (sites with specific coral and topographic formations).

SOUTHEAST Composed of principally rocky shoreline with some isolated coral reefs supporting Madagascar's largest lobster fishery. There are a few dive good sites which benefit from both a diverse and picturesque coastline. Tourism is being developed, offering opportunities for diving.

Sites *Coral and rocky reefs:* between Lokara and St Luce. *Offshore:* migrating humpback whales.

EAST Composed of long beaches divided by rivers running down from the rainforest. There are some patches of coastal forest and a natural river network known as the Pangalanes. Diving opportunities are limited along this coast, which is well known for its spices and rainforest.

Sites *Islands:* Nosy Fonga and Dombola, and Nosy Faho. *Wetland:* Pangalanes Canal and coastal forest.

NORTHEAST Composed of a diverse range of habitats from rocky shores to long sandy beaches and impressive coral reefs circling several small islands. This is an important area for the breeding of humpback whales during Madagascar's winter months. Equally, this area's coastline is located near some of Madagascar's most impressive rainforests.

Sites *Islands, wrecks and reef:* Ile Ste Marie (coastal wrecks and reef), Nosy Atafana (attached to Mananara–Nord National Park), Masoala Marine Reserve (three small islands) and Cap Est reef. *Offshore:* breeding humpback whales (Ile Ste Marie and Antongil Bay).

Tim Healy is an environmental consultant, regular radio broadcaster for the BBC and a keen diver based in Madagascar for over 10 years. He is compiling information for a dive and snorkelling guide with WWF. This is his overview of places where you can definitely snorkel, whilst at other sites you have to either organise trips with the nearest dive centre or take along your own kit. For more information: e *aquater@moov.mg.*

showcases cultural history. Moramanga has a unique and fascinating police museum.

People and tombs Your tour operator may be able to organise a visit to a *famadihana* (only in the highlands and only between June and September) – an unforgettable experience. Merina tombs can be seen easily between Antananarivo and Antsirabe, but the most intriguing and interesting tombs are those of the Mahafaly in the Toliara region. Many are well off the beaten track and make this a particularly interesting area to explore by mountain bike.

Finally... Remember that you are in Madagascar to enjoy yourself. Here's a comment from a traveller who spent eight days in Ranomafana: 'Now I will make my confession: I never actually went into the park itself! I'm not that keen on lemurs anyway – they look like half monkeys and half cat, and I don't much like either animal. I absolutely love the thermal baths, though!' Good for Sarah for knowing what she wants and doesn't want to do!

ITINERARIES The information above should enable you to plan your itinerary with a degree of confidence. Beware of trying to cram too much into your visit – this is a huge island and it can take a while to get from place to place. Bear in mind also that tour operators usually divide the country into north and south (with Tana at the centre) because there are no connecting domestic flights linking the two halves. You often have to spend a night in Tana. If your time is limited you should choose either the north or the south.

TOUR OPERATORS

UK The internet is the ideal way of finding out the best tour operator for your purposes. ATTA (African Travel and Tourism Association; *www.atta.co.uk*) has a comprehensive listing for Madagascar, separated into different interests. Safaribookers (*www.safaribookers.com*) has a listing of Madagascar specialists. The organisation Responsibletravel.com promotes ethical tour operators.

The listings below are the specialists.

Gane & Marshall \ 01822 600 600; e holidays@
ganeandmarshall.co.uk; www.ganeandmarshall.com
Naturetrek \ 01962 733051; f 01962 736426;
e info@naturetrek.co.uk; www.naturetrek.co.uk.
Special focus: birds & mammals.
Okavango Tours & Safaris \ 020 8347 4030; f 020
8347 4031; e info@okavango.com;
www.okavango.com. Long-established specialists in
Africa & Indian Ocean. See ad on page 169.
Papyrus Tours \ 01405 785 211; f 01405 785 232;
e info@papyrustours.co.uk; www.papyrustours.co.uk.
Wildlife tours led by Nick Garbutt.
Pulse Africa \ 020 8995 5909; e pulseafricauk@
easynet.co.uk; www.pulseafrica.com. Beaches & lemurs
galore!
Rainbow Tours \ 020 7226 1004; f 020 7226
2621; e info@rainbowtours.co.uk;
www.rainbowtours.co.uk. Madagascar experts offering
tailor-made trips for individuals & small groups, with
an emphasis on wildlife, birding, culture &
community tourism. Also expert-led wildlife & birding
tours. See ad on inside back cover.
Reef & Rainforest Tours \ 01803 866965; f 01803
865916; e mail@reefandrainforest.co.uk;
www.reefandrainforest.co.uk. A wide variety of tours,
including family itineraries. See ad on page 106.

Safari Consultants \ 01787 888590; f 01787
228096; e bill@safariconsultantuk.com; www.safari-
consultants.co.uk. Private holidays in the south. See
ad on page 313.
Steppes Discovery \ 01285 643333; e enquiry@
steppesdiscovery.co.uk; www.steppesdiscovery.co.uk.
Tailor-made holidays to Madagascar.
Sunbird \ 01767 262522; f 01767 262916;
e sunbird@sunbirdtours.co.uk; www.sunbirdtours.co.uk
The Ultimate Travel Company \ 020 7386 4646;
e enquiry@theultimatetravelcompany.co.uk;
www.theultimatetravelcompany.co.uk. Upmarket, tailor-
made tours with experts.
Wildlife Worldwide \ 0845 130 6982; f 0845 130
6984; e sales@wildlifeworldwide.com;
www.wildlifeworldwide.com. Tailor-made wildlife tours
with expert naturalists.
World Odyssey \ 01905 731373; f 01905 726872;
e info@world-odyssey.com; www.world-odyssey.com.
Private, tailor-made, guided tours.
World Primate Safaris \ 1866 357 6569 (USA), or
01273 774 347 (UK); e sales@
worldprimatesafaris.com; www.worldprimatesafaris.com.
Specialist operating tailor-made trips to see lemurs.
A percentage of profits goes towards primate
conservation. See ad on page 406.

USA The website for the Madagascar embassy has a selection of US tour operators:
www.embassy.org/Madagascar/tours.html. Below are specialists I know and trust.

Blue Chameleon Ventures \ +239 697 4414;
e bill@bluechameleon.org; www.bluechameleon.org.
Herping trips with an expert.
Cortez Travel \ 858 755 5136 or 1 800 854 1029; f 1
858 481 7474; e info@cortez.usa.com; www.cortez-
usa.com. The specialist Madagascar operator in the US,
with decades of experience. See ad on page 170.

Field Guides \ 512 327 4953/800 728 4953;
e fieldguides@fieldguides.com; www.fieldguides.com.
Birding tours.
Remote River Expeditions \ 95 52347; m 032 47
326 70; e info@remoterivers.com;
www.remoterivers.com. Specialising in river journeys,
birding & wildlife tours. See ad on page 406.

AUSTRALIA
Adventure Associates \ 61 2 8916 3000; f 02 8916
3090; e mail@adventureassociates.com;
www.adventureassociates.com
Heritage Destinations \ 61 2 9267 0129; f 61 2
9267 2899; e heritagedest@bigpond.com

Wildlife Safari \ 61 8 9388 9900; f 61 08 9388
9232; e info@wildlife-safari.com.au;
www.wildlife-safari.com.au

SOUTH AFRICA
Birding Africa 21 Newlands Rd, Claremont 7708;
\ 021 531 9148; e info@birdingafrica.com;
www.birdingafrica.com. Specialist for birding trips.
Extraordinary Expeditions PO Box 67126, Bryanston
2021; \/f 011 706 5959; e ellie@ex-ex.co.za or
Conrad@ex-ex.co.za; www.ex-ex.co.za. Luxury tailored
trips. See ad after page 408.

Jenman Island Safaris \ 021 683 7826;
e madagascar@jenmanafricansafaris.com;
www.travel2madagascar.com. Island-hopping trips by
dhow in the Nosy Be region. Tailor-made &
scheduled travel. See ad on page 106.
Pulse Africa \ 011 325 2290; e info@pulseafrica.com;
www.pulseafrica.com. Beaches & lemurs.

Unusual Destinations PO Box 97508, Petervale 2151, Johannesburg; \ 011 706 1991; f 011 463 1469; e info@unusualdestinations.com; www.unusualdestinations.com. The SA experts in Madagascar. Very helpful & knowledgeable. Regular group departures & specialist natural history trips. See ad on page 124.

MADAGASCAR
There are many tour operators in Madagascar. This is by no means a complete list, just a selection of those that I can recommend. See page 105 for an explanation of phoning Malagasy numbers from abroad.

Boogie Pilgrim \ 22 530 70; f 22 530 69; e contact@boogiepilgrim-madagascar.com; www.boogiepilgrim-madagascar.com. One of the leading tour operators in Madagascar, organising tours of every sort including by helicopter. Own lodges & some private reserves. Recommended.

Cortez Expeditions \ 22 219 74; f 22 213 40; e cortezexpeditions@simicro.mg; www.air-mad.com. One of the most experienced tour operators in Madagascar & owner of Relais du Masoala in Maroantsetra & Satrana Lodge in Isalo. See ad on page 170.

Cristal Tours \ 24 531 19; m 032 02 157 08/033 03 045 04; e cristaltours@netclub.mg. Tailor-made trips & travel advice.

Evasion Sans Frontière \ 22 616 69; m 032 11 000 96; e esf@moov.mg. Specialists for the north & Nosy Be.

Gondwana Explorer \ 22 296 96; e cecile@gondwanaexplorer.com; www.gondwanaexplorer.com. One of Madagascar's oldest tour operators. Highly praised by several readers.

Mad Caméléon \ 22 630 86; f 22 344 20; e madcam@dts.mg; www.madcameleon.com. Specialised in river trips.

Madagascar Airtours \ 22 241 92/22 627 99; f 22 641 90; e office@airtours.mg or airtours@moov.mg; http://takelaka.dts.mg/airtours. Many specialist tours.

Madagascar Discovery \ 22 351 65; f 22 351 67; e mda@mda.mg; www.madagascar-discovery.com. Booking agent for several lodges.

Madagascar Expedition Agency \ 22 261 14; e mea@moov.mg; www.tourmadagascar.com. Agents for Masoala Forest Lodge. See ad after page 408.

Madagascar Green Tours m 032 04 364 27; e info@madagascar-green-tours.com; www.madagascar-green-tours.com. Antsirabe-based; offers tailored & standard tours, including birding & river trips. See ad on page 106.

Madagascar Ortour m 032 07 704 64/034 05 704 64; e ortour@gmail.com; www.madagascar-ortour.com or www.ortour.com. Reliable operator of package & tailor-made trips since 1996. See ad on page 277.

Madagascar Tour Guide m 032 52 503 65; e info@madagascar-tour-guide.com; www.madagascar-tour-guide.com. Enthusiastic operator for camping, trekking & other tours. See ad on page 405.

Madamax \ 22 351 01; m 032 02 216 15; www.madamax.com. Specialise in 'high-adrenaline adventures' including climbing & white-water rafting.

Malagasy Tours \ 22 627 24/22 356 07; f 22 622 13; e malagasytours@blueline.mg; www.malagasy-tours.com. Specialised itineraries for ethnobotany, amongst other things, with local guides. Good for off-the-beaten-track exploration. See ad on page 169.

PRIORI \ 22 625 27; e priori@moov.mg; www.priori.ch. Recommended Swiss-owned, Malagasy-run agency.

Remote River Expeditions \ 95 523 47; e info@remoterivers.com; www.remoterivers.com. See ad on page 406.

SETAM Madagascar \ 22 324 31/33; e setam@moov.mg; www.setam-madagascar.com

Visit Mada Tours m 033 11 319 24; e visitmadatours@gmail.com; www.madagascar-tour.com. Tours, car rental, canoeing, trekking etc. See ad on page 406.

Za Tour \ 24 253 08/22 424 22/24 253 07; m 032 40 376 44; f 22 422 86; e zatour@iris.mg; www.zatours-madagascar.com. One of the most experienced & conscientious operators in Madagascar. Highly recommended.

RED TAPE

VISAS A visa is required by all foreign tourists and is easy to obtain at the airport on arrival, although if you prefer you can get it in advance of your trip at the Malagasy embassy in your country (this option may be more expensive).

Visas are normally issued for the exact duration of your intended stay, up to a maximum of 90 days. The cost for visas issued at the airport is €65, US$90, or 140,000Ar for 61–90 days, or 100,000Ar for 31–60 days. At the time of writing visa fees are waived for stays of less than 30 days, but it is unclear whether this initiative to encourage tourism will be extended beyond 2011.

Extension of a 90-day visa is possible in theory, but it can be much less hassle to make a brief departure from Madagascar (to Mauritius or Réunion) in order to get a new 90-day visa on your return.

Ⓔ EMBASSIES AND CONSULATES

Australia 3rd level, 100 Clarence St, Sydney, NSW 2000; ✆ 02 9299 2290; f 02 9299 2242; e tonyknox@ozemail.com.au; ⏱ 09.00–13.00

Austria Pötzleindorferstr 94, A-1184 Wien; ✆ 47 91 273; f 47 91 2734

Belgium 276 Av de Tervueren, 1150 Bruxelles; ✆ 770 1726 & 770 1774; f 722 3731; e ambassade.madagascar@skynet.be

Canada 649 Blair Rd, Gloucester, Ontario K1J 7M4; ✆ 613 744 7995; f 613 744 2530; e ambmgnet@inexpres.net

France 4 Av Raphael, 75016 Paris; ✆ 1 45 04 62 11; f 1 45 03 31 75

Germany Seepromenade 92, D-14612 Falkensee; ✆ 03322 23 140; f 03322 23 14 29

Italy Via Riccardo Zandonai 84/A, Roma 400194; ✆ 36 30 77 97; f 396 329 43 06

Kenya 1st floor, Hilton Hotel (PO Box 41723), Nairobi; ✆ 225 286; f 252 347

Mauritius Av Queen Mary, Port Louis; ✆ 686 3956; f 686 7040

Réunion 73 Rue Juliette Dodu, 97461 Saint-Denis; ✆ 21 05 21/21 65 58

South Africa 13 6th St, Houghton Estate, Johannesburg; ✆ 442 3322; f 442 6660; e consul@infodoor.co.za; www.madagascarconsulate.org.za

Spain Lluria 85 pal 2a, 08009, Barcelona; ✆ 93 272 2125

Switzerland 2 Theaterplatz, 3011 Bern; ✆ 311 3111; f 311 0871; e Hocomad@datacomm.ch

UK 33 Stadium St, London SW10 0PU; ✆ 020 7751 4410; e contact@embassy-madagascar-uk.com; www.embassy-madagascar-uk.com

USA 2374 Massachusetts Av NW, Washington DC 20008; ✆ 202 265 5525; e malagasy@embassy.org; www.madagascar-embassy.org

Other countries Refer to www.madagascar-consulate.org.

GETTING THERE

✈ **BY AIR** If you are planning to take several domestic flights during your stay, choose Air Madagascar as your international carrier. This gives you a 50% discount on domestic flights booked before the trip. For full up-to-date rules governing this offer, check www.airmadagascar.com.

From Europe It is often cheaper to book through an agency such as Trailfinders (✆ 020 7938 3366), WEXAS (✆ 020 7581 8768), STA (✆ 020 7361 6262), or the Flight Centre (✆ 01892 530030) rather than phoning the airline direct.

At the time of writing there are no direct flights to Madagascar from the UK, but Kenya Airways flies from London via Nairobi, and Air France goes via Paris.

Air Madagascar (*www.airmadagascar.com*; see ad after page 408) flies direct between Paris and Antananarivo most days, taking 10½ hours. Schedules and promotions are updated regularly, so keep an eye on their website. Air Mad is represented in the UK by Aviareps (*www.aviareps.com*). For information on domestic flights see page 96.

Air France (*www.airfrance.com*) fly from London Heathrow via Paris most days. The advantage of Air France is that you book your luggage straight through from London. The disadvantage, apart from the inferior service, is that you must pay in full within a week of booking the ticket.

From the UK, **Kenya Airways** (*www.kenya-airways.com*; see ad after page 408) is not only the cheapest option (for travellers not wishing to take advantage of the half-price domestic Air Mad flights) but also has the most generous baggage allowance. Currently there are flights between Nairobi and Antananarivo on Thursday and Saturday, and connecting flights between Nairobi and London daily.

Corsairfly (*www.corsairfly.com*) connects Paris with Antananarivo four times a week and is usually cheaper than Air France, but they don't operate any connecting flights to the UK.

From other Indian Ocean islands You can fly with **Air Madagascar** from Mauritius, Réunion, and the Comoro Islands. **Air Austral** (*www.air-austral.com*) connects Madagascar with Mayotte and Réunion. **Air Mauritius** (*www.airmauritius.com*) also flies to Antananarivo from Mauritius.

From Africa Air Madagascar flies twice a week to/from Johannesburg and once a week to/from Nairobi. Kenya Airways also connects to Nairobi (see above).

From the USA Madagascar is about as far from California as it is possible to be. Understandably, therefore, fares from the USA are expensive. Air France is probably the best carrier, or via United or Delta to Paris to connect with an Air Madagascar flight. From California you can travel west via Bangkok (from where there are Air Madagascar flights).

From Australia Air Madagascar has an office in the same building as the Sydney consulate. Flights are usually routed via Hong Kong or Bangkok. Alternatively you can go from Melbourne or Perth to Mauritius to connect with an Air Madagascar flight to Antananarivo, or fly from Perth via Johannesburg.

BY SEA

From other Indian Ocean islands Passenger ferries run fortnightly between Réunion/Mauritius and Toamasina in Madagascar, but the price is no cheaper than flying. See www.croisiere-madagascar.com for details or contact Mauritius Shipping direct (e *passagers@scoam.fr; www.mauritiusshipping.intnet.mu*).

From South Africa There are no passenger boats crossing the Mozambique Channel to Madagascar, but many people sail their own yachts from Durban.

Yacht clubs
Royal Natal Yacht Club PO Box 2946, Durban 4000; \ 031 301 5425; f 031 307 2590
Point Yacht Club PO Box 2224, Durban 4000; \ 031 301 4787; f 031 305 1234
Zululand Yacht Club PO Box 10387, Meer'en'see 3901; \ 035 788 0256; f 035 788 0254
Royal Cape Yacht Club PO Box 777, Cape Town 8000; \ 021 421 1354; f 021 421 6028

Many yachts sail from Natal to Madagascar. It takes six or seven days to sail to Anakao, south of Toliara. Most stop *en route* at Europa Island, where a French garrison will advise on the next stage. Experienced sailors and divers will want to reach the atoll of Bassas da India which offers superb diving but has been responsible for the shipwreck of numerous vessels.

Because of the increasing number of yachts visiting the northwest of Madagascar, I give information for 'yachties' in the *Nosy Be* chapter.

EXPORT RESTRICTIONS The long-standing 100g limit on vanilla pods for passengers departing Madagascar has been raised to 2kg. Other allowances are 400,000Ar in local currency, 1kg of gemstones, 1kg of coffee, 1kg of pepper and, bizarrely, 1kg of onions – onion-smugglers, you have been warned!

Certificates are required to take out of the country any precious woods, precious stones, precious metals, or animal or vegetable material. If unsure, enquire at the mining, forestry, veterinary and phytosanitary kiosks inside Antananarivo airport.

WHAT TO TAKE

LUGGAGE A soft bag or backpack is more practical than a hard suitcase (and you may not be allowed to take a suitcase on a Twin Otter plane). Backpackers should consider buying a rucksack with a zipped compartment to enclose the straps when using them on airlines. Or bring a lightweight rucksack bag, which protects the straps, gives added security, and may also double as a rain cover.

CLOTHES Before deciding what clothes to pack, take a look at the *Climate* section (page 3). There is quite a difference between summer and winter temperatures, particularly in the highlands and the south where it is distinctly cold at night between May and September. A fibre-pile jacket or a body-warmer is useful in addition to a light sweater. In June and July a scarf can give much-needed extra warmth. At any time of the year it will be hot during the day in low-lying areas, and very hot between October and March. Layers of clothing – T-shirt, sweatshirt, light sweater – are warm and versatile, and take less room than a heavy sweater. Don't bring jeans, they are too heavy and too hot. Lightweight cotton or cotton mix trousers are much more suitable. At any time of year you will need a light shower-proof jacket, and during the wet season, or if spending time in the rainforest, appropriate raingear and perhaps a small umbrella. A light cotton jacket is always useful for breezy evenings by the coast. Don't forget a sunhat.

For footwear, trainers and sandals are usually all you need. Sports sandals which strap securely to the feet are better than flip-flops. Hiking boots are necessary for Marojejy and may be required in places like Ankarana, Andringitra and Isalo but are not necessary for the main tourist circuits.

Give some thought to beachwear if you enjoy snorkelling. You may need an old pair of trainers or some diving booties to protect your feet from coral and sea urchins, and a T-shirt and shorts to wear while in the water to prevent sunburn.

TOILETRIES Although you can buy just about everything in Madagascar, imported goods can be very expensive.

Bring moist wipes for freshening up, and antibacterial hand gel. When used regularly, especially after shaking hands or handling money, this is a real help in preventing traveller's diarrhoea. Some toilet articles have several uses: dental floss is excellent for repairs as well as for teeth, and a nail brush gets clothes clean too.

Don't take up valuable space with a bath towel; almost all hotels provide towels. If you want to bring your own, then pack a sarong (or buy a *lamba* on arrival). It is more absorbent than you'd think, very lightweight, incredibly fast-drying (which can be really useful), and more multi-purpose than a towel: you can lie on it on the beach, sleep under it, use it for shade, hang it up for a bit of privacy to change behind, or wear it like a skirt.

PROTECTION AGAINST MOSQUITOES

Repellents With malaria on the increase, it is vital to be properly protected (see page 110). DEET-based repellents are recommended but need to be at least 20% concentration (ideally 50%) to be effective and can damage synthetic fabrics and plastics. For hotel rooms, pyrethrum coils which burn slowly are available cheaply all over Madagascar. They really do work. Plug-in repellents which work in a similar way are also effective.

Mosquito nets Most upper- and mid-range hotels either have effective screening or provide mosquito nets, but if you are staying in budget hotels you should consider bringing one. Most hotels do not have anything to hang a net from, so a free-standing net is more practical (though a lot more expensive). A couple of bungee cords with hooked ends can be useful for rigging up a normal net.

BACKPACKING EQUIPMENT
Basic camping gear gives you the freedom to travel adventurously and can add a considerable degree of comfort to overland journeys.

The most important item is your backpack. Protect it from oil, dirt and the effluent of young/furry/feathered passengers with a cover. You can buy a commercially-made one or use a rice sack from a Madagascar market.

In winter (June to August) a lightweight sleeping bag will keep you warm in cheap hotels with inadequate bedding. A sheet sleeping bag plus a light blanket (buy it in Tana) are ideal for the summer months (October to May).

An air-mattress or pillow pads your bum on hard seats as well as your hips when sleeping out. One of those horseshoe-shaped travel pillows lets you sleep sitting up (which you'll need to do on *taxi-brousses*).

A lightweight tent allows you to strike out on your own and stay in national parks and on deserted beaches. It will need to be well ventilated. Tent designs that can be erected without pegs are best, as many sheltered tent pitches at campsites have wooden floors which pegs cannot be driven into.

Most people forgo a stove in order to cut down on weight, but if you will be camping extensively bring a petrol/paraffin stove. Gas camp stoves are not recommended owing to the difficulty of sourcing gas canisters in Madagascar.

There are always fresh vegetables for sale in the smallest village so bring some stock cubes to make vegetable stew. Take your own mug and spoon (and carry them with you always). That way you can enjoy roadside coffee without the risk of a cup rinsed in filthy water, and market yoghurt without someone else's germs on the spoon. Milk powder tastes (to most people) better in tea or coffee than the widely available condensed milk. You can buy it locally, or bring it from home. Don't forget a water-bottle and water-purifiers.

Give some thought to ways of interacting with the locals. A Malagasy phrase-book (see page 415) provides lots of amusement as you practise your skills on fellow-passengers, and playing-cards are universally understood.

A good book allows you to retreat from interaction for a while. Bring enough with you – English-language books are not easy to find. If you want to read at night, a small clip-on reading light would be useful.

MISCELLANEOUS ITEMS FOR BUDGET TRAVELLERS
Bring a roll of insulating tape or gaffer tape which can be used for all manner of things, including patching up the inevitable holes in the mozzie nets provided by cheaper hotels. Blu-Tack is equally versatile; bring enough to make a plug for your sink, to stop doors banging or to hold them open. A torch and penknife are essential, a rubber wedge will secure your hotel door at night, and a combination lock has many uses. A light tarpaulin and a length of strong cord both have multiple uses too.

Earplugs are just about essential, to block out not only the sounds of the towns but those of enthusiastic nocturnal animals when camping in reserves! (Personally I think it's worth being kept awake by these, but it can pall after several nights.) A large handkerchief or bandanna has many uses, from mopping your streaming face to protecting your neck from the sun or your hair and lungs from dust.

ELECTRICAL EQUIPMENT
The voltage in Madagascar is 220V. Outlets are European-style two-pin round plugs.

PHOTOGRAPHIC EQUIPMENT These days most people use digital cameras. Apart from the obvious advantages it is great to be able to show local people their photo. Most travellers just show the image on their cameras, but Derek Antonio Serra writes: 'I bought a portable printer that prints colour postcards directly from your camera in 90 seconds. I'd take a stroll and ask one or two people if I could photograph them, then rush back to my hotel to print their photos. Imagine their amazement when I returned minutes later and presented them with these valued gifts. From then on I had no problems finding subjects to photograph.'

Batteries AA batteries, although sold everywhere, are almost universally of poor quality, which will not be a problem for low-drain applications like alarm clocks or small torches, but will work for barely five minutes in a digital camera. Bring good rechargeable batteries from home. It may be useful to bring a solar charger as well as a plug-in one.

CHECKLIST
- Small torch (flashlight) with spare batteries/bulb, headlamp (for nocturnal animal hunts)
- Sewing kit, scissors, tweezers, safety pins
- Insulating tape or Sellotape (Scotch tape), string
- Permanent marker pen, notebook and pens
- Plastic bags (Zip-loc are particularly useful)
- Universal plug for baths and sinks, elastic clothes line or cord and pegs, concentrated detergent
- Ear plugs
- Insect repellent
- Sunscreen, lipsalve
- Spare glasses or contact lenses, sunglasses
- Medical and dental kit (see *Chapter 5*), dental floss
- Water bottle, water purifying tablets or other sterilising agent
- Compact binoculars, camera and film
- Travel alarm clock
- Books, miniature playing cards or other travel games
- French dictionary, Malagasy phrasebook
- Star chart for the southern hemisphere

GOODS FOR PRESENTS, SALE OR TRADE This is a difficult area. In the past tourists have handed out presents to children and created the tiresome little beggars you will encounter in the popular areas (if you don't now know the French for 'pen' or 'sweets', you soon will). They have also handed T-shirts to adults with similar consequences. For more on this subject see *Chapter 6*. There are, however, plenty of occasions when a gift is appropriate. Giving money in return for services is entirely acceptable so in rural areas it's best to pay cash and refrain from introducing a new consumer awareness.

In urban areas or with the more sophisticated Malagasy people, presents are a very good way of showing your appreciation for kindness or extra good service. If you want to contribute something a little more intellectually satisfying, here is a suggestion from Dr Philip Jones of Money for Madagascar: 'I was asked several times for an English Grammar, so any such books would be valued gifts. If visitors take a French–English dictionary, why not leave it in Madagascar?'

The most deserving of your gifts are the hard-pressed charities who work with the very poor. So check www.stuffyourrucksack.com to see if there are any urgently needed goods you can take to the organisations they support.

It is easy to find places to exchange **foreign cash** (euros or US dollars). The ideal denomination is around €50/US$50, because high-value notes are sometimes not accepted (owing to the large number of counterfeits in circulation) but there is sometimes a worse exchange rate for low-value notes.

It is more difficult to find somewhere to cash **travellers' cheques** than to exchange foreign currency, but it is the safest option. Bring only euro or US dollar travellers' cheques, as it can be quite a challenge to find a bank that will change sterling ones.

Most of the large hotels now accept **credit cards**, but only Visa is in widespread use. The rate of exchange/charges can be exorbitant, however. Credit and debit cards may be used to draw cash at most banks. Branches of BFV bank only accept Visa, BOA only MasterCard, and BNI now takes both. American Express is rarely accepted anywhere. Almost all banks in Antananarivo and the major towns now have **ATMs**. BNI machines dispense a maximum of 385,000Ar per withdrawal; for BFV the limit is 300,000Ar.

If you need cash in a hurry there are **Western Union** offices at most banks and post offices across Madagascar. Money can be transferred from home in a few hours, or in minutes if your nearest and dearest are willing to go to a Western Union office with cash (*www.westernunion.com*).

THE CURRENCY Madagascar's currency has always been difficult to cope with. Here is an extract from an account written over a hundred years ago: 'The French five-franc piece is now the standard of coinage in Madagascar; for small change it is cut up into bits of all sizes. The traveller has to carry a pair of scales about with him, and whenever he makes a purchase the specified quantity of this most inconvenient money is weighed out with the greatest exactness, first on his own scales, and then on those of the suspicious native of whom he is buying.'

So it is perhaps not surprising that, in keeping with this tradition of confusing foreigners, and its own people, the currency was changed in 2003. The franc malgache (FMG) was replaced by the ariary. Only larger towns and tourist centres have fully adapted to the 'new' currency; in rural areas the locals still quote prices in the old FMG. One ariary is equal to 5FMG.

Banknotes in circulation range from 100Ar to 10,000Ar. Smaller denomination coins exist down to 1Ar, although tourists rarely encounter these.

EXCHANGE RATE AND HARD CURRENCIES The ariary floats against hard currencies and the exchange rate changes frequently. For this reason many upper-range hotels quote their prices in euros.

Exchange rates in November 2010:

£1	= 3,200Ar
€1	= 2,750Ar
US$1	= 2,000Ar

HOW MUCH WILL IT COST? The airfare is the most expensive part of your trip. Once there, you will find Madagascar a relatively cheap country. Travel by *taxi-brousse*, and eat and sleep like the locals, and you can keep your costs down to about £15/€20/US$30 per day for a couple. Note that couples can travel almost as cheaply as singles, since most budget and mid-range hotels charge by the room (with double bed).

However, fuel is expensive in Madagascar, with petrol prices equivalent to those in Europe, so car hire is costly, especially since you normally have to hire a driver as part of the deal. Costs also mount up if you are visiting many national parks or reserves, where you have the park permit fee plus the cost of a guide.

The easiest way to save money on a day-to-day basis is to be sensible about where you buy bottled water: a bottle of Eau Vive may cost 5,000Ar or more in smart hotels, but 1,000Ar in a shop (likewise for beer). Use a water bottle and purification tablets (bring herbal tea bags to make it taste nicer) to avoid this expense entirely (but unfortunately there's no similar solution for beer!).

TIPPING I (and even *vazaha* residents) find this an impossible subject on which to give coherent advice. Yet it is the one that consistently causes anxiety in travellers. The problem is you have to balance up the expectation of the tip recipient – who may be used to generous tippers – and the knowledge of local wages. A policeman, school teacher or junior doctor will earn around US$100 a month, while an experienced doctor or a university professor might get US$200. At the other end of the scale, although the minimum wage is around US$125, many manual workers are paid far less in the private sector; a waiter or labourer would be lucky to be paid US$15 and some girls working as maids receive no payment at all, just board and lodging. Near Toamasina is a small community where everyone breaks rocks for road-building. They are paid US$1 for ten buckets of gravel. No wonder everyone in Madagascar dreams of finding a job in tourism.

Some tipping is relatively simple: if a service charge is added to the restaurant bill, tipping is not strictly necessary. About 10% is ample; a Malagasy would tip far less. Taxi drivers should not expect a tip, though you may want to add something for exceptional service.

The most manipulative are baggage handlers, because they usually catch you before you are wised up to Madagascar, and are masters at the disappointment act.

The hardest tipping question is how much to pay guides, drivers... people who have spent several days with you and given excellent service. I do try to ensure that the people who work behind the scenes, such as cooks and cleaners, also get tipped. Guides know, and accept, that independent travellers often cannot afford to tip much, or at all. Generally speaking, 5,000–10,000Ar per day is a sensible starting point. Keep in mind that it costs around 4,000Ar to feed a family of five for a day in rural areas, and adjust your tip accordingly.

Where it is essential not to over-tip is when travelling off the beaten track, where you could be setting a dangerous precedent. It can cause problems for *vazaha* that follow, who are perhaps doing research or conservation work and who cannot afford to live up to these new expectations.

Finally, pay and tip guides in ariary rather than foreign currency.

GETTING AROUND

PUBLIC TRANSPORT You can get around Madagascar by road, air, water and rail. Whatever your transport, you'd better learn the meaning of *en panne* – broken down. During these *en panne* sessions one can't help feeling a certain nostalgia for the pre-mechanised days when Europeans travelled by *filanzana* (palanquin). These litters were carried by four cheerful porters who, by all accounts, were so busy swapping gossip and telling stories that they sometimes dropped their unfortunate *vazaha* in a river. The average distance travelled per day was 45km – not much slower than a *taxi-brousse* today! The *filanzana* was used for high officials as recently as the 1940s. To get around town the locals depended on an earlier version of the *pousse-pousse*. The *mono-pousse* was a chair slung over a bicycle wheel.

One man pulled and another pushed. The more affluent Malagasy possessed a *bœuf-cheval*: a zebu trained to be ridden. (I've seen a photo; the animal looks rather smug in its saddle and bridle.)

🚗 **BY ROAD** 'If I make roads, the white man will only come and take my country. I have two allies: *hazo* [forest] and *tazo* [fever],' declared King Radama I.

Coping with the 'roads' used to be one of the great travel challenges in Madagascar. It's not that the royal decree has lasted 200 years but there's a third ally that the king didn't mention – the weather. Torrential rain and cyclones destroy roads as fast as they are constructed.

Taxi-brousse is the generic name for public transport in Madagascar. *Car-brousse*, *camion-brousse*, *taxi-be* and *kat-kat* are also used, but they all refer to the 'bush-taxis' which run along every road in the country. These have improved a lot in recent years, especially along tourist routes.

Red-and-white 'milestones' mark out one-kilometre intervals along main roads. These markers, known as Points Kilométriques, are numbered starting from a major town (usually Tana). PK numbers are given throughout this book to specify points on major routes.

Taxi-brousse *Taxi-brousses* are generally minibuses, or sometimes Renault vans with seats facing each other (also known as *kat-kat*). A *baché* is a small van with a canvas top. More comfortable are the Peugeot 404s or 504s designed to take nine people, but often packed with 14 or more. A *car-brousse* is usually a Tata sturdy enough to cope with bad roads. *Kat-kat* is also used in the northeast for the 4x4 vehicles which are needed to cope with the atrocious roads. The back is covered with a tarpaulin and there are no seats: you sit on your luggage. For even worse conditions, you may find a *tracteur-brousse*!

Vehicles leave from the *gare routière* (bus station) on the side of town closest to their destination. You should try to go there a day or two ahead of your planned departure to check times and prices, and for long journeys you should buy a ticket in advance. Buy from the kiosk, not a middleman, and make sure you get a receipt. You should only have to pay about half the fare as a deposit.

Arriving at a big *taxi-brousse* station can be a scary experience. You are likely to get mobbed by touts demanding to know where you are going. Some may even jump into your moving taxi with you before you reach the station. Keep an eye on your luggage; it's not likely to be stolen, but touts often take bags hostage by loading them onto their preferred vehicle before you've even decided which company you want to travel with. Just head determinedly for one of the kiosks before starting discussions with the official at the desk.

It is something of a lottery when choosing which company to use. Mami and Kofmad are two that readers regularly recommend. Most offices display a board showing the official prices to each destination.

Come prepared for a long wait. *Taxi-brousses* do sometimes leave on time, but as they never depart until they are full it can be hours before you set off.

If you want to reserve a particular seat, check they write your name on their seat plan when you book. Choose your seat carefully. The two seats up front may be the most comfy, but sitting next to the driver you'll be punched in the leg each time he changes gear (no good if you want to sleep) and these seats can get hot as they are above the engine. The row directly behind the driver has the best leg room.

Tourists are occasionally charged for luggage that is strapped on to the roof, but you are entitled to 20kg or so for free, so refuse politely. If you have a very large quantity of luggage then a fee is reasonable, but you should only pay about 5,000Ar per 50kg of extra stuff.

Every visitor has a *taxi-brousse* story or two. Here are a few sent in by readers. There are more *taxi-brousse* stories in the boxes on pages 264 and 345.

At about 10 o'clock the two of us went to the *taxi-brousse* station. 'Yes, yes, there is a car. It is here, ready to go.' We paid our money. 'When will it go?' 'When it has nine passengers.' 'How many has it got now?' 'Wait a minute.' A long look at notebooks, then a detailed calculation. 'Two.' 'As well as us?' 'No, no, including you.' It finally left at about 7 o'clock. (Chris Ballance)

After several hours we picked up four more people. We couldn't believe it – the driver had to sit on someone's lap! (Stephen Cartledge)

I was jammed in behind a very sick soldier, who spent most of the journey with his head out of the window spewing lurid green bile like something from a horror-movie. After 20 minutes we had to stop at a roadside stall to buy mangoes. Since I was now on the sunny side of the vehicle the temperature of my shirt rose to what, had it been made of polyester, would have been melting point. Our next stop was Antsirabe where we were surrounded by apple vendors. All and sundry went absolutely berserk. I hadn't seen so many apples since... since we left Ambositra. At about 5pm the radio was turned on so we could listen to two men shouting at each other at a volume which would have caused bleeding of the eardrums in Wembley Stadium. At about 6pm it started to get decidedly brisk, and since the ailing squaddie in front of me showed no sign of having rid himself of toxic enzymes I now had to endure an icy blast in my face. Our next stop was for grapes. We now had enough fruit on board to start a wholesale business in Covent Garden, and I was a bit tetchy. (Robert Stewart)

We eventually made it after an eventful four-hour *taxi-brousse* journey which entailed the obligatory trawl around town for more passengers, selling the spare tyre shortly after setting off, a 30-minute wait outside the doctor's as the driver wasn't feeling very well, and all of us having to bump-start the vehicle every time we stopped to pick anyone up. (H & M Kendrick)

I woke up nice and early to get my *taxi-brousse* to Mahamasina from Diego. I clambered onto a nice new minibus, eager to hit the open road. There was one other passenger. We cruised around for three hours, frequently changing drivers, trying to get more customers. In this time our driver got into three fights, one lasting half an hour. There was even a painful-looking tug-of-war with passengers to persuade them to use their *taxi-brousse*. (Ben Tapley)

Our journey from Morondava to Antsirabe began with nine sweaty hours of east-coast heat, then rapidly became teeth-chatteringly cold as we climbed up to the *hauts plateaux* in the middle of the night. Sat alongside the driver we wondered why he kept leaning across us to fiddle with the seal around the windscreen. We understood when, after bumping across miles of potholes, the window worked its way loose and eventually slipped out of its frame entirely. Unable to push it back into place, the driver attempted to tie it with rope. This was unsuccessful, so it fell to me to hold the windscreen in place for the rest of the journey! We barely raised an eyebrow when later in the journey the side door fell off. (Daniel Austin)

On one memorable trip from Fianar to Tana the back three seats were stacked high with crates of chicks which chirped noisily for the full ten hours. In addition to the breakdowns we've come to expect, we drove through a fire, came close to colliding with at least one oncoming vehicle, dodged an exploding tyre from the truck in front, and a chicken lost its life under our wheels. (Kelly Green)

On overnight journeys, come prepared for cold even if it's sweltering at the time of departure. On the winding roads of the highlands, motion sickness can be a problem, so take medication if you are susceptible to this, and keep plastic bags and tissues to hand. Drivers stop to eat, but usually drive all night. If they do stop during the night most passengers stay in the vehicle or sleep on the road outside.

If you're prepared for the realities, an overland journey can be very enjoyable and gives you a chance to get to know the Malagasy.

✈ **BY AIR** Air Madagascar started its life in 1962 as Madair but understandably changed its name after a few years of jokes. Most people now call it Air Mad.

See the map opposite for the current domestic routes. At the time of writing the cost of flying from Tana to Toliara, Taolagnaro or Nosy Be (one way) was €205 (but remember you can get 50% off domestic flights if you chose Air Mad as your international carrier).

Air Madagascar has a Boeing 767 for international routes, two 130-seat Boeing 737s for flights to the larger cities and Nosy Be, smaller ATR 49-seater turbo props, and the little 19-seater Twin Otters for the more rural airstrips.

Often flights which are said to be fully booked in Antananarivo are found to have empty seats when you reapply at the town of departure. Because you are still allowed to make a reservation without payment, flights always appear full. The trick is to go to the airport two hours in advance and put your ticket on the counter. The *liste d'attente* works on a first-come-first-served basis and half an hour before the flight is due to leave they start filling the empty seats, taking the tickets in order of arrival. Conversely, passengers with booked seats who check in late will find their seats sold to waiting-list passengers. Always arrive at least an hour before the scheduled departure, and add your ticket to the 'queue' of tickets on the counter.

Hand luggage should weigh no more than 5kg. Passengers should not be surprised if they are weighed *themselves* before a Twin Otter flight. It's not that there's a tax on fat people; they're just gathering data for take-off calculations.

There are no numbered seats on internal flights, and no toilets in a Twin Otter! Although no longer a requirement, you are recommended to reconfirm a day before departure. Air Madagascar schedules are reviewed twice-yearly, in March and October, but are subject to change at any time and without notice. Their website is regularly updated (*www.airmadagascar.com*).

Planes are not infrequently delayed or cancelled, but usually not without good reason. Air Mad are exceptionally efficient at making arrangements for those stranded by a cancelled flight. They will quickly arrange taxis, hotels and meals at their expense, and a replacement flight will usually be planned for very early the following morning.

⛴ **BY BOAT** The Malagasy are traditionally a seafaring people (remember that 6,000km journey from Indonesia) and in the absence of roads, their stable outrigger canoes are used to cover quite long sea distances. Pirogues without outriggers are used extensively on the rivers and canals of the watery east. Quite a few adventurous travellers use pirogues for sections of their journeys. Romantic though it may be to sail in an outrigger canoe, it can be both uncomfortable and, at times, dangerous.

Ferries and cargo boats travel to the larger islands and down the west coast (see box on page 384). River journeys are becoming increasingly popular as a different way of seeing the country.

🚂 **BY RAIL** After years of deterioration, Madagascar's rail system has seen improvement over the past decade. Passenger services now run a few times a week

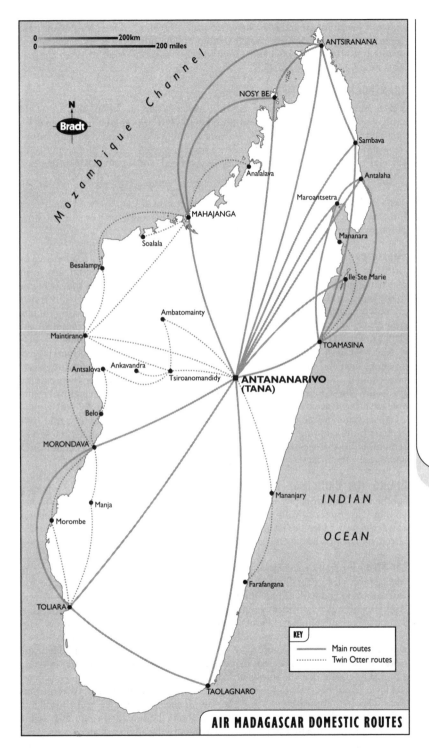

AIR MADAGASCAR DOMESTIC ROUTES

KEY
Main routes
Twin Otter routes

between Fianarantsoa and Manakara (see page 190) and between Moramanga and Toamasina (page 251). Even more excitingly, being now unique to Madagascar, a restored rubber-tyred Micheline train makes weekend trips to Andasibe and Antsirabe (see box on page 252).

TRANSPORT WITHIN CITIES

Buses Most cities have cheap buses but few travellers use them because of the difficulty in understanding the route system. No reason not to give it a try, however. Andrew Shimmin says: 'I would strongly recommend travelling around Tana and Antsirabe by bus – an absolute bargain, people smiley, and really seeing the real city.' Ask the locals which service you need... or for a real adventure, pick one, hop on, and see where you end up!

Taxis Taxi rates have gone up in recent years because of a sharp rise in fuel prices, but they are still reasonable. Taxis have no meters, so you must agree on the price before you get in. In some places there are official set rates.

Pousse-pousses **(rickshaws)** *Pousse-pousses* were introduced into Madagascar by British missionaries who wanted to replace the traditional palanquin due to its association with slavery. The name is said to originate from the time they operated in the capital and needed an additional man behind to push up the steep hills. They are now a Madagascar speciality and are mostly pulled by a running man, although *cyclo-pousses* (pedal rickshaws) have been introduced to Toamasina. Most of the flatter towns have *pousse-pousses*, but not the hilly towns of the highlands.

Many Western visitors are reluctant to sit in comfort behind a running, ragged, sweating man and no-one with a heart can fail to feel compassion for the *pousse-pousse* pullers. However, this is a case of needing to abandon our own cultural hang-ups. These men want work. Bargain hard (before you get in) and make sure you have the exact money. A medium-length journey will generally cost around 2,000Ar. *Pousse-pousse* pullers love carrying soft-hearted tourists and some have become quite cunning – and tiresome – in their dealings with *vazaha*. However, remember how desperately these men need a little luck – and an innocent tourist could make their day!

HIRING (OR BRINGING) YOUR OWN TRANSPORT Reader Tim Ireland puts it
succinctly: 'The great pity is watching so many magnificent landscapes tear past your eyes as you strain your neck trying to get a better view past 15 other occupants of a *taxi-brousse*.' He goes on to recommend a mountain bike as the perfect means of transport, but a hired vehicle will achieve the same flexibility.

Car hire You really need to be a competent mechanic to hire a self-drive car in Madagascar, and generally cars come with chauffeurs (providing a local person with a job and you with a guide/interpreter). A few days on Madagascar's roads will cure you of any regret that you are not driving yourself. Night-time driving is particularly challenging: headlights often don't work or are not switched on. Your driver will know that the single light bearing down on you is more likely to be a wide truck than a narrow motorbike and react accordingly. The Merina Highway Code (informal version) decrees that drivers must honk their horns after crossing a bridge to ensure that the spirits are out of the way.

Having said that, a few agencies do rent vehicles without drivers. Adventurous souls who are tempted by this must be sure to check the vehicle over thoroughly before departure, get as much information about the intended route as possible (including where the fuel stops are), and avoid driving after dark at all costs.

A British driving licence is valid in Madagascar, but to be safe you may prefer to get an International Driving Licence. These are available in the UK from the AA and RAC for £5.

Reader Paul Kolodziejski has this questionable advice for self-drivers: 'Stopping at police checkpoints seems to be optional. There are a lot and I did stop at one but it was a big waste of time. So from then on whenever I was waved to stop, I just waved back pretending I was replying in greeting. I never had any problems.'

There are car-hire outfits in most towns. The regional tourist offices have information on these (or ask your hotel) and local tour operators can organise vehicles too. For a saloon car, €65 per day including fuel and driver seems about average. Taxi drivers will often agree to a full-day hire for around €45.

Bicycle The French for mountain bike is VTT. Bikes can be hired in most major towns. Alternatively, you can bring your own bike (see page 78) or buy one there.

 ## ACCOMMODATION

In recent years upper- and mid-range hotels have been brought up to international standard, and visitors looking for comfort should not be disappointed.

Rates are normally quoted *per room* in Madagascar, with the notable exceptions of the two main tourist areas – Nosy Be and Ile Sainte Marie – where the more expensive hotels tend to quote prices *per person*. Breakfast is rarely included in the room price, and when it is it is usually just bread and coffee. There is a tourist tax, *vignette touristique*, of between 600Ar and 3,000Ar per room per night. This is sometimes absorbed into the price, but is often additional to prices quoted.

Outside the towns, accommodation is usually in bungalows which are often constructed of local materials and are quiet, atmospheric and comfortable.

Note that *hotely* usually means a restaurant/snack bar rather than accommodation, but some also have rooms.

Most mid-range and budget hotels will do your washing for you at a very reasonable price. This gives employment to local people and is an important element of responsible travel. In upper-range and top-end hotels laundry can be disproportionately expensive!

HOTEL CATEGORIES: WHAT YOU GET FOR YOUR MONEY

Luxury The top hotels and lodges are truly luxurious. They are, without exception, foreign-owned, but most show a good sensitivity to the needs of the local people. One such French owner explained that as foreigners their conscience dictates that they do not appear as neo-colonials and so they go out of their way to contribute to community-based projects.

Top end These are either a cut above the average upper-range hotel or are in an expensive part of Madagascar, such as Nosy Be, where all prices are higher.

Upper range These are very comfortable hotels which can be found in all major towns and tourist centres. They have all the trappings that upmarket tourists expect: TV, minibar, and perhaps a business centre with internet connections. They will have en-suite bathrooms and restaurants with good food. The larger ones are popular with groups, so check the listed number of rooms if you're looking for a more intimate atmosphere.

Mid-range These are often just as clean and comfortable, and most have at least some en-suite rooms. There will be no TV beaming CNN into your bedroom, but you should have comfortable beds. The hotels are often family-run and very friendly.

Budget and penny-pincher In early editions I described these as 'exhilaratingly dreadful at times' until a reader wrote: 'We were rather disappointed by the quality of these hotels... We found almost all the beds comfortable, generally acceptably clean, and not one rat. We felt luxuriously cheated!' However, the following description from Rupert Parker of a hotel in Brickaville should gladden the masochistic heart: 'It is a conglomeration of shacks directly beneath the road bridge. The rooms are partitioned-off spaces, just large enough to hold a bed, in a larger wooden building – the partitions don't reach to the ceiling and there is only one light bulb for all the rooms – the hotel manageress controls the switch. Not only can you hear everyone's conversation and what they're up to, but when there is a new arrival, at whatever time of the night, the light comes on and wakes everyone up – that is if you've managed to ignore the rumbling and revving of trucks as they cross the bridge above you, or the banging on the gate announcing the new arrival. Suffice to say the toilet and washing facilities are non-existent.' It would be rather a shame if they've improved it in the intervening years!

Such hotels certainly give the flavour of how Madagascar used to be, and in remote areas you will still find the occasional sagging double bed and stinking hole toilet. Most of the budget hotels in this book are clean, friendly and excellent value. In an out-of-the-way place you will pay as little as £0.60/€0.70/US$0.90 for the most basic room. For this you get a bed, candle, mozzie coil, and ripped mozzie net. In small towns about £3/€3.60/US$4.40 would be average for a room with a shared toilet – of sorts.

CAMPING Until a decade ago Madagascar had no official campsites, although backpackers with their own tent were often allowed to camp in hotel gardens. Now there are many, especially in national parks. Such camping is usually on a wooden platform with a thatched roof above. If you have your own tent, make sure it is self-standing since you can't drive tent pegs into the platform.

Self-sufficient backpackers will know the wonderful sense of freedom that comes with carrying their own tent – there is all of Madagascar to explore!

✗ EATING AND DRINKING

FOOD Eating well is one of the delights of Madagascar, and even the fussiest tourists are usually happy with the food. International hotels serve international food, usually with a French bias, and often do special Malagasy dishes. Lodges and smaller hotels serve local food which is almost always excellent, particularly on the coast where lobster (crayfish), shellfish and other seafood predominates. Meat lovers will enjoy the zebu steaks, although they are sometimes tougher than we are used to (free-range meat usually is). In remoter areas, hotels tend to offer a set menu. This can cost as little as £0.90/€1.10/US$1.30. At the upper end you can expect to pay around £10/€12/US$15 for that special treat. There is generally not much variation in price between typical tourist restaurants.

The national dish in Madagascar is *romazava* (pronounced 'roomazav'), a meat and vegetable stew, spiced with ginger and containing *brèdes mafana* ('bred mafana') – tasty, tongue-tingling greens. Another good local dish is *ravitoto* ('ravtoot'), shredded manioc leaves with fried beef and coconut. Volker Dorheim adds: 'if you like your food really spicy ask for *pimente verde*; if this isn't hot enough ask for *pimente malgache*'.

Independent travellers on a tight budget will find Chinese restaurants in nearly every town; these are almost always good and reasonably priced. *Soupe Chinoise* is available nearly everywhere, and is filling, tasty and cheap. The Malagasy eat a lot of rice, but most restaurants cater to foreign tastes by providing fries. Away from the tourist routes, however, most dishes are accompanied by a sticky mound of rice (sometimes embellished with small stones, so chew with caution!)

Local dishes For a real Malagasy meal, eat at a *hotely*. These are often open-sided shacks where the menu is chalked up on a blackboard: *henan-omby* (beef), *henan-borona/hen'akoho* (chicken), *henan-kisoa* (pork), *trondro* or *henan-drano/hazan-drano* (fish), all served with *vary* (rice). Other dishes include: *tsaramaso* (rice with beans and pork), *vary sosoa* (rice pudding/porridge), *mofo boule* or *mofogasy* (doughnut-like bread rolls made from rice), and *koba* (rice ground with peanuts and banana, wrapped in a banana leaf and served in slices). For a more detailed rundown of Malagasy cuisine, see the box on page 313.

Along with the meat or fish and inevitable mound of rice comes a bowl of stock. This is spooned over the rice or drunk as a soup.

Thirst is quenched with *ranovola* obtained by boiling water in the pan in which the rice was cooked. It has a slight flavour of burnt rice, and since it has been boiled for several minutes it is safe to drink.

For do-it-yourself meals there is a great variety of fruit and vegetables, even in the smallest market. A selection of fruit is served in most restaurants, along with raw vegetables or *crudités*. From June to August the fruit is mostly limited to citrus and bananas, but from September there are also strawberries, mangoes, lychees, pineapples and loquats. As an extra special treat you may come across mangosteen (see box on page 266). Slices of coconut are sold everywhere, but especially on the coast where coconut milk is a popular and safe drink, and toffee-coconut nibbles are sold on the street, often wrapped in paper from school exercise books.

There are some good, locally produced cheeses and Malagasy yoghurt is excellent and available in even the smallest shops. Chocaholics should keep their eyes peeled for Chocolate Robert – available in several varieties.

Vegetarian food Madagascar is becoming more accustomed to *vazaha* vegetarians. With patience you can usually order meatless dishes anywhere, even at small *hotelys*. The problem tends to be communicating what you do and don't eat; once this is clear, most kitchens can offer some vegetarian options. *Tsy misy hena* means 'without meat' and *tsy oman-kena aho* means 'I don't eat meat'.

DRINK The most popular drink, Three Horses Beer, known universally as THB (*www.star-thb.com*), is wonderful on a hot day. I think it's wonderful on a cold day, too. It has 5.4% alcohol, but there are some new varieties: THB Special (6.2%), THB Bex (5%) and THB Lite (1%) – created to circumvent new laws restricting advertising of stronger alcoholic beverages. Another low-alcohol option is THB Fresh, a light shandy produced, like those above, by Star Brewery.

Madagascar produces its own wine in the Fianarantsoa region, and some is very good. Lazan'i Betsileo (see page 189) is recommended. A pleasant aperitif is Maromby (the name means 'many zebu') and Litchel, made from lychees, is good. Rum, *toaka gasy*, is very cheap and plentiful, especially in sugar-growing areas such as Nosy Be; and fermented sugar cane juice, *betsabetsa* (east coast), or fermented coconut milk, *trembo* (north), make a change. *Rhum arrangé* – fruit slices soaked in rum – is found in most locally run hotels. The best cocktail is *punch coco*, with a coconut-milk base, a speciality of the coastal areas. Yummy!

The most popular mineral water is called Eau Vive, but other brands are now available. Coca-Cola, Sprite and Fanta are also available (produced under licence by Star Brewery). The locally produced *limonady* sadly bears no resemblance to lemons, and I think Bonbon Anglais is revolting, though not every *anglais* agrees (it is not dissimilar to Irn-Bru, but without the lurid orange colourant).

Malagasy coffee is OK – just – if taken black, but often only condensed milk is available. I find that one quickly regresses to childhood and surreptitiously spoons the condensed milk not into the coffee but into the mouth. If you prefer unsweetened white coffee it might be better to bring your own powdered milk. Caffeine-addicts who don't get along with the local coffee can find Nescafé sachets in the local supermarkets.

The locally grown tea is weak, the best quality being reserved for export. A nice alternative is *thé citronelle*, lemongrass tea, which is widely available.

☞ **WARNINGS!** If you are travelling on a prepaid packaged tour, you may be disconcerted to find that you are charged for coffee and tea along with drinks. These beverages count as 'extras' in Madagascar. The Malagasy are enthusiastic smokers and non-smoking restaurants, or sections in restaurants, are a rarity.

PUBLIC HOLIDAYS

The Malagasy take their holidays seriously. In every town and village there will be a parade with speeches and an air of festivity. Readers Bryan and Eve Pinches report: 'New Year was celebrated throughout the night and on New Year's Day everyone paraded their new clothes through the streets in a Malagasy version of an Easter Parade. New Year parties were held by every conceivable organisation during the next two months.'

OFFICIAL HOLIDAYS

1 January	New Year's Day
29 March	Commemoration of 1947 rebellion
(movable)	Easter Monday
1 May	Labour Day
(movable)	Ascension Day
(movable)	Whit Monday
26 June	Independence Day
15 August	Feast of the Assumption
1 November	All Saints' Day
25 December	Christmas Day
30 December	Republic Day

When these holidays fall on a Thursday, Friday will be tacked onto the weekend. Banks and other businesses often take a half-day holiday on the preceding day.

⚜ SHOPPING

You can buy almost anything in the handicrafts line in Madagascar. Most typical of the country are woodcarvings, raffia work (in amazing variety), crocheted and embroidered table-cloths and clothes, leather goods, carved zebu horn, Antaimoro paper (with embedded dried flowers), marquetry and so on. The choice is almost limitless, and it can all be seen in the handicrafts markets and shops in Antananarivo and throughout the country. In the south you can buy attractive heavy silver bracelets that are traditionally worn by men. In Tana, and the east and north (including Nosy Be), you will be offered vanilla pods, peppercorns, cloves and other spices, and honey. Almost anywhere you can find shops selling *lambas*.

Do not buy products from endangered species. That includes tortoise/turtle shell, snake skins (but crocodiles are farmed commercially so their skins may be sold legally), shells, coral and, of course, live animals. Butterflies are farmed commercially so buying mounted specimens is permitted. Also prohibited are endemic plants, most fossils (including elephant bird eggshells, which may not be taken out of the country) and any genuine article of funerary art. To tell turtle shell from zebu horn, hold it up to the light: turtle shell is semi-transparent.

To help stamp out the sale of endangered animal products, tourists should make their feelings – and the law – known. If, for instance, you are offered tortoise or turtle shell, tell the vendor it is *interdit*; and to push the point home you could explain it is *fady* for you to buy such a thing.

Be sure to obtain receipts for wood and stone items and anything expensive; you may need to show them on departure.

BARGAINING It always seems strange to me that people who think nothing of slipping a dollar to the doorman who heaves their bags from the pavement to the hotel lobby will spend five minutes trying to cut the same amount off a beautifully crafted woodcarving that may have taken its maker weeks to complete. In my early days of travelling on a tight budget I too bargained hard. I had no option. Now, if I think the price is fair, I'm quite happy to pay it. If it's really true that you lose the respect of the vendor if you don't bargain – well, I can cope with that; there'll be plenty of Real Travellers boasting about how they beat him down to less than half to balance my foolishness.

SEMI-PRECIOUS STONES Madagascar is a rewarding place for gem hunters, with citrine, tourmaline and beryl inexpensive and easy to find. The solitaire sets using these stones are typical and most attractive. The centre for gems is traditionally Antsirabe but they are for sale in many highland towns, and now Ilakaka, the town that has sprung up at the centre of the sapphire rush, is the main hub. If you buy uncut stones bear in mind the cost of having them cut at home. Better to have it done in Tana, if you have time.

☺ ARTS AND ENTERTAINMENT

MUSIC Malagasy music is distinctive and justly famous. See box on page 104. Finding good local music is a hit and miss affair when travelling. Often your best bet is to look out for posters advertising concerts, regularly put up near the *gare routière*.

CINEMA Films are dubbed into French; Bruce Lee is one of the most popular stars.

TELEVISION Posh hotels have CNN but some local stations show BBC World Service news at 09.00. Most of the output on local channels comprises Malagasy music videos.

Derek Schuurman & Paddy Bush

Like everything else in Madagascar, the island's music portrays characteristics from other parts of the world but the end result is uniquely Malagasy.

Justin Vali (Justin Rakotondrasoa) – a Merina from the *hauts plateaux* – is today the country's best-known Malagasy musician outside of his country. Apart from Vali, other Malagasy musicians who have enjoyed success abroad include D'Gary, who has a huge following in Canada and USA; Regis Gizavo; Jojoby, the King of Salegy, who is once again performing after a near-fatal car accident; the band Tarika, which was highly rated in an international *Time Magazine* poll a few years ago; and Mahaleo, the Malagasy version of the Beatles, who have been going strong since the 1970s and whose songs contain profound lyrical content.

Many western instruments have found their way into Malagasy music. It is not uncommon to see accordions in particular, but also clarinets and certain brass instruments, being played at the colourful *hira gasy* events. On the other hand, visit a vibrant nightclub and you'll very likely see contemporary musicians belting out thumping dance tracks using modern electric and bass guitars and synthesisers.

The national instrument is the *valiha*, which belongs to the family of tube and box zithers. This fascinating instrument goes back generations in Justin Vali's family, who both make and play it. The original or 'ancestral' form of *valiha* is constructed from certain rare species of bamboo, known as *volo* ('hair from the ground' – a wonderful way to describe bamboo!). *Valiha* are of great spiritual significance and have been played for centuries in ceremonies sacred to the *razana* (ancestors).

The *valiha* is thought to have arrived some 2,000 years ago from southeast Asia, where various forms of the instrument are still to be found in the Borneo and Philippines region. In these areas it is also an instrument of the spiritual world, being used in ceremonies to appease animistic forest spirits.

The bamboo from which the *valiha* is made must be cut during the three-day period during a full moon, which is when the plants are apparently free of certain insects – otherwise months later they will emerge from eggs laid inside and destroy the instrument. (I have seen this happen when a friend tried to import a huge consignment of *valiha*, only to have them ruined by the insects; we were forced to make an enormous bonfire consisting of hundreds of contaminated *valiha*!)

The *valiha* has a royal heritage: according to Justin Vali, King Radama II was a superb composer. During his reign Queen Victoria gave him a piano, which resulted in the standardising of *valiha*-tuning into diatonic form – called *lalandava* ('straight road') – corresponding to the white notes on a keyboard. One of the most legendary players of the instrument, the late Rakotozafy, built himself a *marovany*-like *valiha* out of sheet iron, and today his music is still widely played on the island's radio stations.

The *marovany*, unlike the tube *valiha*, appears to have African origins. It is tuned in a very different way and is played in the coastal regions where the African influence is more apparent than in the highlands. If you happen to be in the right places in Madagascar, searching for recordings of Malagasy music, and you want to hear phenomenal *marovany* players, ask for Madame Masy, Bekamby, Daniel Tomo or Albi, to name a few of the best.

In recent years, there has been an explosion of CDs of Malagasy music; good websites on which to find these include: www.discovermadagascar.co.uk (from which you can order, among others, *The Sunshine Within*, a beautiful album by Justin Vali), www.madagate.com, and www.frootsmag.com/content/madagascar/cdography.

Paddy Bush is a musicologist. He is one of very few westerners to have mastered playing the marovany and valiha, and has performed in the UK with Justin Vali.

COMMUNICATIONS

TELEPHONES

Making calls The seven-digit phone numbers given in this guide (marked with a \ symbol) are landline numbers. The ten-digit numbers are mobile/cellphone numbers, which all begin 03 and are indicated by a m symbol in this book.

The international dialling code for Madagascar is +261. When calling a **landline**, you must also add 20. Thus to phone Air Madagascar (\ *22 510 00*) from abroad, you would dial +261 20 22 510 00. To call a **mobile number** from abroad, simply replace the initial 0 with +261.

When making an international call out of Madagascar, the international prefix (represented by +) is 00, as in most other countries.

Mobile phones Mobiles/cellphones are very popular in Madagascar. Nowadays network coverage is good, reaching almost everywhere that most tourists are likely to go. You can buy a SIM card at the airport (or in any town) for next to nothing and call rates are reasonable too, so if you're going to be in Madagascar for more than a week or so it would probably be worth getting one (especially considering that making/receiving calls using a foreign mobile in Madagascar is typically many times more expensive).

There are three operators: **Orange** (numbers starting with 032), **Zain** (formerly Madacom/Celtel, 033) and **Telma** (034). Calls to phones with the same operator are much cheaper than to a different network, so if you envisage mainly communicating with one or two specific people then pick the same network as them. For general use, I recommend Orange as this is the most commonly encountered, and they also have some good deals for cheap international calls to the USA and Canada.

Top-up cards are available in shops everywhere. Values range from 1,000Ar to 100,000Ar (but you will have to go to an Orange/Zain/Telma shop for recharge cards over 20,000Ar).

Emergency numbers The emergency telephone number for **police** is \ 17 or \ 117. For the **fire service**, the emergency number is \ 18 or \ 118. There is no general emergency number for medical assistance, but you will find numbers for local hospitals and medical services throughout this guide.

POST The mail service is unpredictable: more often than not it is quite efficient, with letters taking about two weeks to reach Europe and a little longer to North America. Stamps are quite expensive. There are post offices (*www.paositra.mg*) even in small towns, with some 220 branches around the country.

Courier services Colis Express (*www.colis-express.net*) has some 70 branches around Madagascar and is an efficient way of sending domestic parcels. Internationally they hook up with DHL, which also has its own offices in major towns, and there is a FedEx office in Tana (see page 159).

INTERNET Cybercafés or internet offices are established in all major towns and tourist centres, with broadband increasingly available. The prices vary a lot, depending on the competition. Be warned that the keyboards are usually French, not English-qwerty, which is intensely frustrating if you are normally a fast typist. Also the offices in coastal towns are often stiflingly hot; I drip steadily over the keyboard while searching for the elusive y that forms part of my name.

Practical Information COMMUNICATIONS

4

Most businesses open 08.00–12.00 and 14.00–18.00. Banks are normally open 08.00–16.00 and closed at weekends, though the largest towns generally have one bank that opens Saturday morning.

5

Health and Safety

Dr Jane Wilson-Howarth and Dr Felicity Nicholson

BEFORE YOU GO

MALARIA PREVENTION Take advice from a travel clinic, your GP or the website www.fitfortravel.nhs.uk. Malaria (including cerebral malaria) is a risk in Madagascar, including in the *hauts plateaux*, and it is crucial to protect yourself by **avoiding bites** especially between dusk and dawn and also by taking tablets. There is chloroquine resistance so it is important to take one of the prescribed kinds of **antimalarial tablets**. Seek current advice on the best antimalarials to take: usually mefloquine, Malarone or doxycycline. If mefloquine (Lariam) is suggested, start this two-and-a-half weeks (three doses) before departure to check that it suits you; stop it immediately if it seems to cause depression or anxiety, visual or hearing disturbances, severe headaches, fits or changes in heart rhythm. Side effects such as nightmares or dizziness are not medical reasons for stopping unless they are sufficiently debilitating or annoying. Anyone who has been treated for depression or psychiatric problems, has diabetes controlled by oral therapy, or who is epileptic (or who has suffered fits in the past), or has a close blood relative who is epileptic, should probably avoid mefloquine.

In the past doctors were nervous about prescribing mefloquine to pregnant women, but experience has shown that it is relatively safe and certainly safer than the risk of malaria. That said, there are other issues to be aware of, so if you are travelling to Madagascar whilst pregnant, seek expert advice before departure.

Malarone (proguanil and atovaquone) is as effective as mefloquine. It has the advantage of having few side effects and need only be continued for one week after returning. However, it is expensive and because of this tends to be reserved for shorter trips. Malarone may not be suitable for everybody, so advice should be taken from a doctor. The licence in the UK has been extended for up to three months' use and a paediatric form of tablet is also available, prescribed on a weight basis.

Another alternative is the antibiotic doxycycline (100mg daily). Like Malarone it can be started one day before arrival. Unlike mefloquine, it may also be used in travellers with epilepsy, although certain anti-epileptic medication may make it less effective. In perhaps 1–3% of people there is the possibility of allergic skin reactions developing in sunlight; the drug should be stopped if this happens. Women using the oral contraceptive should use an additional method of protection for the first four weeks when using doxycycline. It is also unsuitable in pregnancy or for children under 12 years.

Chloroquine and proguanil are no longer considered to be effective enough for Madagascar but may be considered as a last resort if nothing else is deemed suitable.

All tablets should be taken with or after the evening meal, washed down with plenty of fluid and, with the exception of Malarone (see above), continued for four weeks after leaving.

Any prolonged immobility including travel by land or air can result in deep vein thrombosis (DVT) with the risk of embolus to the lungs. Certain factors can increase the risk and these include:

- Previous clot or close relative with a history
- People over 40 but greater risk for those aged over 80
- Recent major operation or varicose veins surgery
- Cancer
- Stroke
- Heart disease
- Obesity
- Pregnancy
- Hormone therapy
- Heavy smokers
- Severe varicose veins
- People who are very tall (over 6ft/1.8m) or short (under 5ft/1.5m)

A deep vein thrombosis (DVT) causes painful swelling and redness of the calf or sometimes the thigh. It is only dangerous if a clot travels to the lungs (pulmonary embolus). Symptoms of a pulmonary embolus include chest pain, shortness of breath, and sometimes coughing up small amounts of blood and commonly start three to ten days after a long flight. Anyone who thinks that they might have a DVT needs to see a doctor immediately.

PREVENTION OF DVT
- Keep mobile before and during the flight; move around every couple of hours
- Drink plenty of fluids during the flight
- Avoid taking sleeping pills and excessive tea, coffee and alcohol
- Consider wearing flight socks or support stockings (see www.legshealth.com)

If you think you are at increased risk of a clot, ask your doctor if it is safe to travel.

Some travellers like to carry tablets for the emergency treatment of malaria; if you choose to do this make sure you understand when and how to take them, and carry a digital thermometer.

Take plenty of **insect repellent**; 50% DEET-based repellents are best. Loose-fitting outfits with long-sleeved shirts and long trousers will allow you to cover up at dusk; for additional protection you can spray your evening clothes with permethrin (eg: Bug Proof from Nomad). Consider carrying a **mosquito net** (see page 90). Bed-nets are most effective if treated with permethrin or a similar contact insecticide. Such treatment remains effective for six months; kits are sold at many travel clinics.

IMMUNISATIONS Preparations to ensure a healthy trip to Madagascar require checks on your immunisation status: it is wise to be up to date on tetanus, polio and diphtheria (now given as an all-in-one vaccine, Revaxis, that lasts for ten years), and hepatitis A. Immunisations against rabies may also be recommended. Proof of vaccination against yellow fever is required from travellers coming from yellow fever areas, but there is no risk from this disease in Madagascar itself. Immunisation against cholera is no longer required for Madagscar but it may be suggested if there has been a recent outbreak.

Hepatitis A vaccine (Havrix Monodose or Avaxim) comprises two injections given about a year apart. The course costs about £100, but may be available on the NHS; it protects for 25 years and can be administered even close to the time of departure. Hepatitis B vaccination should be considered for longer trips (two months or more) or for those working with children or in situations where contact with blood is likely. Three injections are needed for the best protection and can be given over a three-week period if time is short for those aged 16 or over. Longer schedules give more sustained protection and are therefore preferred if time allows. Hepatitis A vaccine can also be given as a combination with hepatitis B as 'Twinrix', though two doses are needed at least seven days apart to be effective for the hepatitis A component, and three doses are needed for the hepatitis B. Again this schedule is only suitable for those aged 16 or over.

The newer injectable typhoid vaccines (eg: Typhim Vi) last for three years and are about 85% effective. Oral capsules (Vivotif) may also be available for those aged six and over. Three capsules over five days lasts for approximately three years but may be less effective than the injectable forms. They should be encouraged unless the traveller is leaving within a few days for a trip of a week or less, when the vaccine would not be effective in time. Vaccinations for rabies are ideally advised for everyone, but are especially important for travellers visiting more remote areas, particularly if you are more than 24 hours from medical help and definitely if you will be working with animals (see *Rabies* page 112). The disease is a problem in Madagascar because of the half-wild dogs found in many parts of the island; there is also a theoretical risk of rabies after lemur bites (see box on page 113).

Experts differ over whether a BCG vaccination against tuberculosis (TB) is useful in adults: discuss this with your travel clinic.

In addition to the various vaccinations recommended above, it is important that travellers should be properly protected against malaria. For detailed advice, see page 110.

Ideally you should visit your own doctor or a specialist travel clinic (see page 117) to discuss your requirements at least eight weeks before you plan to travel.

TEETH If travelling off the beaten track, have a dental check-up before you go and if you have a lot of fillings and crowns carry a dental emergency kit.

INSURANCE Make sure you have insurance covering the cost of helicopter evacuation and treatment in Réunion or Nairobi, which offer more sophisticated medical facilities than are available in Madagascar. Europe Assistance International, which has an office in Antananarivo, gives cover for scuba-diving. Divers Alert Network (DAN; *www.diversalertnetwork.org*) is the best insurance available for scuba-diving. With all insurance make sure that you tell them about any pre-existing problems when applying.

WATER STERILISATION Most traveller's diarrhoea comes from inadequately cooked, or reheated, contaminated food – salads, ice, ice cream etc – rather than from water. Even so it is best to take care with what you drink. Bringing water to the boil kills all microbes that are likely to make you ill so tea, coffee or *ranovola* (rice water) are safe. Mineral water, although widely available, causes a litter problem and can be quite expensive. Chemical sterilisation methods do not render water as safe as by boiling, but it is good enough for most purposes. The cheapest and most effective sterilising agent is chlorine dioxide. To make treated water more palatable, add vitamin C after the sterilisation time is complete or bring packets of powdered drink. Silver-based sterilising tablets (sold in Britain under the trade name Micropur) are tasteless and have a long shelf life but are less effective than chlorine dioxide. An alternative is a water filter such as the Pur system or Aquapure Traveller, which provide safe water with no unpleasant flavour; they are expensive, however, and – like any filter – are prone to blockage. Cheaper and more versatile is a plug-in immersion heater, so that you can have a nice hot cuppa.

SOME TRAVELLERS' DISEASES

MALARIA AND INSECT-BORNE DISEASES Tablets do not give complete protection from malaria (though it will give you time to get treatment if it does break through) and there are other insect-borne diseases in Madagascar so it is important to protect yourself from being bitten. The *Anopheles* mosquitoes that spread malaria usually bite in the evening (from about 17.30) and throughout the night, so it is wise to dress in long trousers and long-sleeved shirts, and to cover exposed skin with insect repellent. These mosquitoes generally hunt at ankle level, and tend to bite the first piece of exposed flesh they encounter, so applying an effective repellent (DEET is best) to feet and ankles is important in reducing bites. In most countries, malaria transmission is rare in urban environments, but it does occur around Antananarivo because rice fields are so close to the city. Most hotels have screened windows or provide mosquito nets. Bring your own freshly impregnated net if staying in cheap hotels. Burning mosquito coils reduces but does not eliminate the risk of bites.

Be sure to take your malaria tablets meticulously for the requisite time after you get home. Even if you have been taking your malaria prophylaxis carefully, there is still a slight chance of contracting malaria. The symptoms are fevers, chills, joint pain, headache and sometimes diarrhoea – in other words the symptoms of many illnesses including flu. Malaria can take as little as seven days to develop. Consult a doctor if you develop a flu-like illness within a year of leaving a malarial region. The life-threatening cerebral malaria will become apparent within three months and can kill within 24 hours of the first symptoms.

Mosquitoes pass on not only malaria but also Rift Valley fever, elephantiasis, dengue and other serious viral fevers. By avoiding mosquito bites you also avoid illness, as well as those itching lumps which so easily become infected. Once you've been bitten, tiger balm or calamine lotion will help stop the itching.

TRAVELLER'S DIARRHOEA Diarrhoea is very common in visitors to Madagascar, and you are more likely to suffer from this if you are new to tropical travel. The new oral Dukoral cholera vaccine may give partial protection against traveller's diarrhoea. Tourists tend to be obsessed with water sterilisation but, contrary to popular belief, traveller's diarrhoea usually comes from contaminated food not water. Ice cream, sadly, is risky, especially if it is homemade and even factory-made ice creams can be bad news if they are stored badly. So, particularly if you have a sensitive stomach or haven't travelled much before, you should avoid ice cream, and also ice, salads, fruit with lots of crevices such as strawberries, uncooked foods and cooked food that has been hanging around or has been inadequately reheated. Sizzling hot street food is likely to be far safer than the food offered in buffets in expensive hotels, however gourmet the latter may look. Yoghurt is usually safe, as are sorbets. Remember: *peel it, boil it, cook it or forget it!*

The way to the quickest recovery from traveller's diarrhoea is to reduce your normal meals to a few light or high carbohydrate items, avoid milk and alcohol and drink lots of clear fluids. You need to replace the fluids lost down the toilet, and drinks containing sugar and/or salt are most easily absorbed. Add a little sugar to a salty drink, such as Marmite (available in Tana!) or Oxo, or salt to a sugary drink like non-diet Coca-Cola. Sachets of rehydration mixtures are available

With less than a week left until the end of my seven months in Madagascar I fell ill with a serious infection. About a fortnight earlier, I had scratched a mozzie bite on my ankle just a bit too vigorously and it had turned septic. I treated it with antiseptic powder and covered it with plasters and it almost healed. So I went out with it uncovered and while I was engaged in conversation the infernal flies found the minute spot and had a feast.

Next day I found I could hardly walk because the infection had spread to the muscle. I obtained some antibiotics and had a good dressing put on it. By evening the whole foot had ballooned and looked quite frightening. The next two days I spent mainly in bed because even sitting put me in great discomfort. I had high fever and couldn't eat. But with my visa running out and my flight back booked I had to get to Tana. The two-day road journey from Vangaindrano was out of the question so I flew from Farafangana via Taolagnaro to Tana. The Air Mad steward helpfully folded down the seat in front so I could keep my leg up. I was very impressed with how quickly I was provided with a wheelchair at both Taolagnaro and Ivato without even having asked.

My flight back to Paris was the following evening but an 11-hour flight in a sitting position was completely out of the question and, having no insurance, I didn't want to pay for extra seats. So I decided to stay in Madagascar for treatment. The infection was already creeping up the leg and an enormous sausage-like blood blister now spanned the whole length of the foot. The first doctor that saw me at the clinic where I was taken was so fascinated by the sight that the first thing he did was to take out his mobile phone to take pictures! I was given a bed in a room on my own. Everything was wonderfully clean and new. The following day an old, greying doctor performed an operation under local anaesthetic to remove the worst infected tissue. He told me that he'd studied neo-natal surgery at Great Ormond Street Hospital.

Despite large doses of intravenous antibiotics the infection spread up as far as my knee and it was four or five days before it showed signs of receding. Meanwhile the big blood blister had burst, dried and formed a large scab which the doctor now wanted to remove (under general anaesthetic) because it was sealing in the infected tissue underneath. I became scared, both about having an open wound covering half my foot, as well as the expense of the operation, and decided to risk the flight back to Paris. I had spent a week in hospital, at the end of which the infection had been successfully driven down and confined to the foot and my body temperature was brought down to normal. I paid only about £200.

The people looking after me all this time were a Slovenian missionary priest, a French nun who took care of my expiring visa and I'm especially grateful to the parishioners of another Slovenian missionary, Père Pedro, who took me to this hospital and provided me with a *guarde* (a personal carer, as is normal practice in Malagasy hospitals). The parishioners visited me every day with food and drink. Unfortunately I couldn't eat anything, not even the hospital dinners which looked wonderful. The nurses, in an effort to get me to eat, were even so kind as to ask me what I liked and, being fed up with rice, I said mashed potatoes. I felt ashamed when I couldn't eat them. I think the doctors and nurses were rather disappointed that I decided to go. Before I was discharged the nurses took pains over my dressing saying: 'We don't want people to think we're under-developed'! The awful treatment I was later to get from the *vazahas* at Charles de Gaulle airport where I waited three hours for a wheelchair made me wonder who was the more developed.

At the end the parishioners took me to the airport in their Land Rover ambulance. I lay on the stretcher in the back and there were children on both sides singing all the way there. It had been worth staying in Madagascar just for that experience!

commercially but you can make your own by mixing a rounded dessertspoon (four teaspoons) of sugar with a quarter-teaspoon of salt and adding it to a glass of boiled and cooled water. Drink two glasses of this every time you open your bowels – more often if you are thirsty. Substituting glucose for sugar will make you feel even better. If you are in a rural area drink young coconut water or *ranovola* (rice water).

Hot drinks and iced drinks cause a reflex emptying of the bowel and cause belly-ache, so take drinks tepid or at room-temperature while the diarrhoea is at its worst. Once the bowel has ejected the toxic material causing the diarrhoea, the symptoms will settle quite quickly and you should begin to feel better again after 24–36 hours. Should the diarrhoea be associated with passing blood or slime, it is important to seek medical advice as soon as possible as this is likely to be a form of dysentery which will need antibiotics to treat it.

Holiday schedules often make it impossible to follow the 'sit it out' advice. When a long bus journey or flight is anticipated you may wish to take a blocker such as Imodium, but if you are tempted to do that it is better to take an antibiotic with it. 'Blockers' are dangerous if you have dysentery and work best if combined with an antibiotic such as Ciprofloxacin (500mg twice daily for at least three days). The three-day course used to be highly effective but resistance is developing. It is probably best, therefore, to take local advice and try to find a clinic rather than treating yourself. Drink lots whatever treatment you are taking and if you are worried or feel very ill, find a local medic. Keep well hydrated and the symptoms will usually settle.

CHOLERA Although it has a fearsome reputation, cholera doesn't usually make healthy people ill. It takes the debilitated, poor and half-starved of famine or conflict zones, or it is present along with other gastro-intestinal infections. Cholera is avoided in the same way as other 'filth-to-mouth' diseases and – if there are symptoms – it can be treated with the usual oral rehydration fluids that all wise travellers know about (see above). However, for those who prefer to prevent the disease in the first place, an oral cholera vaccine, Dukoral, can be taken. This vaccine is suitable from two years and older but the doses vary so allow at least three to four weeks before travel.

OTHER HITCHHIKERS There is a high prevalence of tapeworm in zebu, so eat your steaks well done. If you do pass a worm, this is alarming but treatment can wait.

BILHARZIA (SCHISTOSOMIASIS) This is a nasty, debilitating disease which is a problem in much of lowland Madagascar. The parasite is carried by pond snails and is caught by people who swim or paddle in clean, still or slow-moving water (not fast-flowing rivers) where an infected person has defecated or urinated. The parasite causes 'swimmer's itch' when it penetrates the skin. Since it takes at least ten minutes for the tiny worm to work its way through your skin, a quick wade across a river, preferably followed by vigorous towelling off, should not put you at risk. Bilharzia is cured with a single dose of Praziquantel. If you think you may have been exposed to the disease, ask your doctor to arrange a blood test when you get home. This should be done more than six weeks after the last exposure.

SEXUALLY TRANSMITTED INFECTIONS These are common in Madagascar and AIDS is on the increase. If you enjoy nightlife, male or female condoms will make encounters less risky.

RABIES (*LA RAGE*) Rabies is a disease that is feared wherever it occurs – and it occurs on Madagascar. However there are highly effective vaccines that give absolute protection.

The rabies virus can be carried by any mammal, and the commonest route of infection is from a dog bite. It is likely that lemurs could pass on rabies, and bats can certainly carry the disease. Unfortunately, most rabid animals do not look mad or froth at the mouth so it is important to assume that any mammal bite could be dangerous. It is not safe to wait and see because once the symptoms of hydrophobia become apparent, the victim is doomed and the mode of death is terrible.

After any animal bite, scratch or a lick over broken skin it is wise to administer good first aid to prevent infection. Vigorously clean the wound with plenty of soap under running water (from a tap or poured from a water bottle) for at least five minutes – timed with a watch. After the cleaning process, the wound should be flooded with any strong antiseptic solution or alcohol. Next the victim should get the wound dressed – but not stitched – and post-bite jabs need to be arranged. Tetanus jabs, and sometimes antibiotics, may be needed to treat wound infection.

If rabies virus enters the body, it slowly progresses along the nerves until it gets to the brain at which point it causes encephalitis and hydrophobia – fear of water, including one's own saliva. The incubation period for rabies depends upon the severity of the bite and also the distance from the brain. If a toddler gets savaged on the face the child can become ill in as little as four days.

LEMURS AND RABIES   *Hilary Bradt*

When I was leading a trip in Madagascar a few years ago one of my group was bitten on the forearm by a female ring-tailed lemur. The animal was carrying a baby and was startled. It bit in self-defence. The skin was broken and there was a small amount of bleeding. In the days that followed, Susanne and I agonised about the possibility of rabies and what to do about it.

We asked advice from a local hotel manager who reassured her that there was almost no possibility of the lemur being rabid. I felt the same way so Susanne decided to wait until she returned to Germany, but the uncertainty spoiled the rest of her trip. Even the tiniest chance of catching rabies is too terrible to contemplate – and she couldn't stop contemplating it.

She saw her doctor 18 days after the bite and was started on a course of injections. Rather than being reassuring, her doctors told her that she'd left it much too late, and that she would not know for three months whether or not she would get rabies – and die. Of course she is fine now, but what *should* we have done?

I've talked to several people about this dilemma. What is the likelihood of an infected animal surviving long enough to bite a human? Lemurs tame enough to bite a tourist are found only in private reserves where dogs are excluded. Even if a rabid dog did get into the reserve would it be able to catch a lemur? And if it did catch one, would it inflict a bite which infected the animal but didn't kill it? The likelihood seems very small.

Alison Jolly, who has been studying lemurs for 50 years, says: 'I have never heard of anyone catching rabies from a lemur. I think that the chances are so small that I wouldn't dream of getting rabies shots after a lemur bite – except in one circumstance. If the lemur was hand-raised, either a current pet or a pet released into the wild, it may attack a human without provocation. In that case you get a deep bite with no warning. It probably is just misguided "normal" behaviour, treating you as one of its own species, but you can't be sure, so I would get shots. A bite in self-defence, though, isn't worth bothering about.'

Dr Jane comments: 'I have now been involved in quite a number of cases of tourists who have been bitten overseas and then are badly scared by the prospect of the disease and finding clinical services abroad. Increasingly I encourage travellers to pay out for the jabs before they travel.'

If you have not had pre-exposure rabies vaccine then you need to get rabies immunoglobulin and five doses of a modern rabies vaccine. This may not be easy to get in Madagascar, even in Tana, so the advice would be to evacuate to South Africa. If you have had all three doses of pre-exposure vaccine then you should only need two more given on day zero and three days later. Ensure that the vaccine being given is either Verocell, HDCV or PCEC. The old brain-derived vaccines are not safe to have and should be avoided. You should also take your own syringes and needles to ensure that sterile equipment is being used. If you are unsure then again you may need to evacuate.

Reputable travel health insurers should be able to advise where the nearest source of safe vaccine and immune globulin might be. Sometimes embassies can help with such information.

INFECTION AND TRIVIAL BREAKS IN THE SKIN The skin is very prone to infection in hot, moist climates: even the smallest nick or graze allows bacteria to enter and cause problems. Mosquito bites – especially if you scratch them – are a common route of infection, so apply a cream to reduce the itching. White toothpaste helps if you are stuck for anything better. Cover any wounds, especially oozing ones, so that flies don't snack on them. Antiseptic creams are not advised, since they keep the wounds moist and this encourages further infection. A powerful antiseptic, which also dries out moist wounds, is potassium permanganate crystals dissolved in water. Another alternative is diluted tincture of iodine or povidone-iodine. Large bottles of the latter are available at a reasonable price in the many pharmacies in Madagascar or can be bought in spray form as Betadine or Savlon Dry before arrival. Bathe the wound twice a day, more often if you can, by dabbing with cotton

---

GETTING JIGGY ON MY BIRTHDAY   *Kara Moses, primatologist*

My 26th birthday was one I'll never forget. Friends at Durrell threw me a very Malagasy party: much local food, music, dancing and of course rum.

The next morning, my actual birthday, I blearily awoke in the sweltering heat with a pounding head and searing pain in my right foot. Washing away the dirt revealed three large white lumps, each with a black dot at the centre: the dreaded *parasy* (jiggers) that I'd been having nightmares about. These parasitic fleas burrow beneath the skin, periodically laying and releasing eggs through a hole.

Fidy volunteered to dig them out and gathered a disturbing array of equipment: sewing needles, scissors, candles and, to my bewilderment, a bottle of brake fluid. Miles from the nearest town, this was the best antiseptic available. I swallowed hard and prepared myself for the ordeal, wondering if there was any rum left over.

Closer inspection revealed my foot to have, in fact, five new residents. My stomach churned. For what seemed like an eternity, Fidy hacked at my foot, gleefully singing *Happy Birthday to You*, while I fought back tears and vomit. They were the biggest one's he'd ever seen, Fidy announced, adding that they must have been there at least a month, hidden under the permafilth covering my feet. With number three out, I took a breather, consoling myself we were over half way. Then he discovered yet another two.

Once they were all finally removed (and burnt on the candle with a satisfying pop), the seven sore, gaping holes were steeped in brake fluid. I spent the rest of my birthday dousing the entire camp with insecticide. From then on I religiously washed and inspected my feet daily, deferring for a second opinion at the slightest mark, much to the amusement of all. '*Parasy?*' I'd ask fearfully. '*Tsy misy parasy*' they'd laugh, and I'd breathe a sigh of relief.

wool dipped in dilute potassium permanganate, or iodine solution. Bathing in sulphur springs cures too.

SUNBURN Light-skinned people, particularly those with freckles, burn remarkably quickly near the Equator, especially when snorkelling. Wearing a shirt, preferably one with a collar, protects the neck and back, and long shorts can also be worn. Use a sunscreen with a high protection factor (at least SPF25) on the back of the neck, calves and other exposed parts.

PRICKLY HEAT A fine pimply rash on the trunk is likely to be heat rash; cool showers, dabbing (not rubbing) dry and talc will help relieve it. Treat the problem by slowing down to a relaxed schedule, wearing only loose, baggy 100% cotton clothes and sleeping naked under a fan; if it is bad, check into an air-conditioned hotel room for a while.

FOOT PROTECTION Wearing shoes or sandals even on the beach will protect the feet from injury and from parasites. Old trainers (running shoes) worn when you are in the sea will help you avoid getting coral or urchin spines in the soles of your feet and give some protection against venomous fish spines. Booties, which can be bought for about £25, will protect from coral but not venomous fish. See page 222 for first aid advice following encounters with marine nasties.

THE NASTY SIDE OF NATURE

Animals Malagasy terrestrial **snakes** are back-fanged, and so are effectively non-venomous. **Sea-snakes**, although venomous, are easy to see and are rarely aggressive. However, if you are bitten then seek immediate medical treatment; try to keep the bitten part as still and as low as possible to slow the spread of venom. Large **spiders** can be dangerous, and the black widow, an innocuous-looking small spider, is found in Madagascar. Navy digger **wasps** have an unpleasant sting, but it is only **scorpions** that commonly cause problems because they favour hiding places where one might plunge a hand without looking. If you sleep on the ground, isolate yourself from these creatures with a mat, a hammock or a tent with a sewn-in ground sheet.

Scorpion and **centipede** stings are very unpleasant and worth avoiding. Scorpions often come out after rain. They are nocturnal but they like hiding in small crevices during the day. People camping in the desert or the dry forest often find that a scorpion has crept into the pocket of a rucksack – despite taking the sensible precaution of suspending their luggage from a tree. Scorpion stings are very painful for about 24 hours. After a sting on the finger, I had an excruciatingly painful hand and arm for several days. The pain was only eased with morphine. My finger had no feeling for a month, and over 20 years later it still has a slightly abnormal sensation.

Leeches can be a nuisance in the rainforest, but are only revolting, not dangerous (AIDS is not spread via leeches). They are best avoided by covering up, tucking trousers into socks and applying insect repellent (even on shoes – but beware, DEET dissolves plastics). Once leeches have become attached they should not be forcibly removed or their mouthparts may remain causing the bite to itch for a long time. Either wait until they have finished feeding (when they will fall off) or encourage them to let go by applying a lit cigarette, a bit of tobacco, chilli, salt or insect repellent. A film canister is a convenient salt container. The wound left by a leech bleeds a great deal and easily becomes infected if not kept clean. For more on leeches see the box on page 311.

Beware of strolling barefoot on damp, sandy riverbeds and areas of beach where locals defecate. This is the way to pick up **jiggers** (and geography worms). Jiggers

Liz Bomford with additional information by Rob Conway

Madagascar has some truly wonderful underwater opportunities but divers need to be cautious. There is no hyperbaric chamber in the country; diving casualties must be evacuated overseas by air. The nearest recompression facilities are in Kenya, South Africa, Réunion and Mauritius. As flying exacerbates decompression sickness, this is not an ideal situation so you need to keep risks to the minimum. Divers Aware Network (DAN) offers comprehensive diving insurance for evacuation from Madagascar and has experience in doing this.

If you are going to dive in Madagascar you should be an experienced diver, taking responsibility for your own dives. Madagascar is not suitable for newly qualified PADI open-water divers. It is essential to dive within guidelines and take your own computer so you do not depend blindly on the local dive leaders. Do not dive with any outfit that does not carry oxygen on the boat. Make sure you ask about this; your life may depend on it.

There are no regulations in Madagascar and dive operators are not obliged to provide good quality octopus rigs, or to service equipment regularly, or indeed to carry out any of the 'housekeeping' that is required to provide safe diving. If you can manage it, bring your own equipment. Also make sure that you are conservative with your dive profiles and take an extra long safety stop on ascending.

Don't be afraid to ask about safety issues. You are not being a wimp. I had a 'bend' in Madagascar in 2003. If my instructor had not been equipped with oxygen, I would be dead. As it was, he didn't have enough and I now have mild but permanent neurological injuries. Don't let them tell you 'there are no accidents in Madagascar'. I was that statistic and I feel sure I'm not the only one.

are female sand fleas, which resemble maggots and burrow into your toes to incubate their eggs. Remove them, using a sterilised needle, by picking the top off the boil they make and teasing them out (this requires some skill, so it is best to ask a local person to help). Disinfect the wound thoroughly to avoid infection.

Plants Madagascar has quite a few plants which cause skin irritation. The worst one I have encountered is a climbing legume with pea-pod-like fruits that look furry. This 'fur' penetrates the skin as thousands of tiny needles, which must be painstakingly extracted with tweezers. Prickly pear fruits have the same defence. Relief from the secretions of other irritating plants is obtained by bathing. Sometimes it is best to wash your clothes as well, and immersion fully clothed may be the last resort!

MEDICAL KIT

Apart from personal medication taken on a regular basis, it is unnecessary to weigh yourself down with a comprehensive medical kit, as many of your requirements will be met by the Malagasy pharmacies.

Expeditions or very adventurous travellers should contact a travel clinic (see opposite)

PERSONAL FIRST-AID KIT A minimal kit contains:
- A good drying antiseptic (eg: iodine or potassium permanganate), don't take antiseptic cream
- A few small dressings (Band-Aids)
- Suncream

- Insect repellent; anti-malarial tablets; impregnated bed-net or permethrin spray
- Aspirin or paracetamol
- Antifungal cream (eg: Canesten)
- Ciprofloxacin or norfloxacin, for severe diarrhoea
- Tinidazole for giardia or amoebic dysentery (see page 112 for regime)
- Antibiotic eye drops, for sore, 'gritty', stuck-together eyes (conjunctivitis)
- A pair of fine pointed tweezers (to remove caterpillar hairs, thorns, splinters, coral etc)
- Alcohol-based hand rub or bar of soap in plastic box
- Condoms or femidoms
- Travel sickness pills

TRAVEL CLINICS AND HEALTH INFORMATION

A comprehensive list of current travel clinic websites worldwide is available on www.istm.org. For other journey preparation information, consult www.tripprep.com. Information about various medications may be found on www.emedicine.com.

UK
Berkeley Travel Clinic 32 Berkeley St, London W1J 8EL; ✎ 020 7629 6233

Cambridge Travel Clinic 48a Mill Rd, Cambridge CB1 2AS; ✎ 01223 367362; e enquiries@ travelcliniccambridge.co.uk; www.travelcliniccambridge.co.uk

Edinburgh Travel Clinic Regional Infectious Diseases Unit, Ward 41 OPD, Western General Hospital, Crewe Rd South, Edinburgh EH4 2UX; ✎ 0131 537 2822. Travel helpline (✎ 0906 589 0380) Mon–Fri mornings.

Fleet Street Travel Clinic 29 Fleet St, London EC4Y 1AA; ✎ 020 7353 5678; www.fleetstreetclinic.com

Hospital for Tropical Diseases Travel Clinic, Mortimer Market Bldg, Capper St, London WC1E 6AU; ✎ 020 7388 9600; www.thehtd.org. Healthline (✎ 0906 133 7733) for country-specific information.

Interhealth Worldwide 111 Westminster Bridge Rd, London SE1 7HR; ✎ 020 7902 9000; www.interhealth.org.uk. Profits go to providing health care for overseas workers on Christian projects.

MASTA (Medical Advisory Service for Travellers Abroad) Moorfield Rd, Yeadon LS19 7BN; ✎ 0870 606 2782; www.masta-travel-health.com. Provides travel health advice, anti-malarials & vaccinations. There are over 50 MASTA travel clinics.

NHS www.fitfortravel.nhs.uk. Online country-by-country advice.

Nomad ✎ 0906 863 3414; e sales@ nomadtravel.co.uk; www.nomadtravel.co.uk. Clinics in London (✎ 020 7833 4114), Bristol (✎ 01179 226 567), Southampton (✎ 023 8023 4920), Manchester (✎ 0161 832 2134) & Bishops Stortford (✎ 01279 653 694).

Trailfinders 194 Kensington High St, London W8 7RG; ✎ 020 7938 3999; www.trailfinders.com/travelessentials/travelclinic.htm

Travelpharm ✎ 01159 512 092; www.travelpharm.com. Advice & online pharmacy.

IRISH REPUBLIC
Tropical Medical Bureau Grafton Street Medical Centre, Grafton Bldgs, 34 Grafton St, Dublin 2; ✎ 1 671 9200; www.tmb.ie. A useful website specific to tropical destinations. Check website for other bureaux locations throughout Ireland.

USA AND CANADA
Centers for Disease Control 1600 Clifton Rd, Atlanta, GA 30333; ✎ 800 311 3435; travellers' health hotline ✎ 888 232 3299; www.cdc.gov/travel. *Health Information for International Travel* is published annually by their Division of Quarantine.

Connaught Laboratories PO Box 187, Swiftwater, PA 18370; ✎ 800 822 2463. They will send a free list of specialist tropical-medicine physicians in your state.

International Medicine Center 920 Frostwood Drive, Suite 670, Houston, TX 77024; ✎ 713 550 2000; www.traveldoc.com

IAMAT (International Association for Medical Assistance to Travelers) 1623 Military Rd, 279

Samantha Cameron

Faced with environmental degradation and increasing exposure to Western medicine, there are many people who fear for the future of ethnobotanical knowledge. However, recent research in rural southeast Madagascar found that traditional healing practices continue to be widespread and that, although older people generally have more faith in them, the younger generation are also very knowledgeable about traditional remedies.

Many people consult both healers and the hospital, the decision depending on the type of illness they are suffering from and, to a lesser extent, the cost of treatment. Often healers are seen when people have an illness that they believe Western medicine cannot cure. The two are also used in combination, or people resort to one having found the other ineffective. If symptoms of a disease are recognised, treatment is often self-administered. Some health problems of a sensitive nature, such as gynaecological problems and sexually transmitted diseases, are commonly treated by healers; women being afraid or too embarrassed to go to the hospital. Other conditions are often of a more psychological or supernatural nature, such as phobias and spirit possessions.

Healers commonly first receive their powers on the death of another healer, usually their parent or grandparent, and often through a dream. Many practise clairvoyance, using cards or mirrors in order to communicate with their ancestors so as to diagnose illness and treatment. Sometimes, even if the disease is known, treatment varies according to what is identified as the cause. Some healers update treatments annually, on the advice of their ancestors, and many are blessed with healing hands; so the medicinal plants they use would not be as effective if self-administered.

Despite deforestation, people living near the forest do not suggest any dramatic change in the abundance of medicinal plants, only stating that they have to go slightly further afield to find them. Some medicinal plants originating from secondary vegetation have even increased in abundance as a result of environmental degradation.

Although use of forest plants is generally higher in villages near the forest, some healers living near the forest use exclusively savanna-originating medicinal plants, and some living far from the forest use forest plants. Such patterns of medicinal-plant use can result from the method of plant collection; some healers have plants come to them overnight by a supernatural force, some send people to harvest them, and some buy in the market or elsewhere. Many healers also conserve plants by drying them, thus making frequent collection unnecessary. Migration is another factor, some healers originating from forested areas and later moving away but continuing to use the forest plants that tradition passed onto them. Medicinal plant knowledge therefore changes more according to the speciality of the healer, and the healer's origin, as opposed to their proximity to the forest.

Although traditional healing does not appear to be dying out and Western medicine does not seem to pose a real threat, perhaps its greatest threat is from religion. Common belief has it that traditional healing is the devil's work as it comes from the power of the ancestors rather than the power of God. The risk is that young people may resist the healing power they inherit. Recording traditional medicine practices enhances understanding of the context in which it is used in Madagascar, by distributing the results to local communities, authorities and scientists. It is also necessary to increase appreciation and valuation of these secondary forest products, with the aim of conservation and sustainable natural resource management.

Samantha Cameron is co-ordinator of Feedback Madagascar's health programme in the Fianarantsoa region. She led an RGS-supported expedition researching ethnobotany.

Niagara Falls, NY14304-1745; ☎ 716 754 4883;
e info@iamat.org; www.iamat.org. Provides lists of
English-speaking doctors abroad.
IAMAT Canada Suite 1, 1287 St Clair Av W, Toronto,
Ontario M6E 1B8; ☎ 416 652 0137

TMVC Suite 314, 1030 W Georgia St, Vancouver BC
V6E 2Y3; ☎ 1 888 288 8682; www.tmvc.com. Private
clinic with several branches in Canada.

AUSTRALIA AND NEW ZEALAND
IAMAT 206 Papanui Rd, Christchurch 5, New Zealand;
www.iamat.org
TMVC ☎ 1300 65 88 44; www.tmvc.com.au. Clinics
in Australia, New Zealand & Singapore, including:
Canterbury Arcade, 170 Queen St, Auckland (☎ 9

373 3531); 6th floor, 247 Adelaide St, Brisbane, QLD
4000 (☎ 7 3221 9066); 393 Little Bourke St, 2nd
floor, Melbourne, VIC 3000 (☎ 3 9602 5788);
Dymocks Bldg, 7th floor, 428 George St, Sydney, NSW
2000 (☎ 2 9221 7133).

SOUTH AFRICA
SAA-Netcare Travel Clinics P Bag X34, Benmore 2010;
www.travelclinic.co.za. Clinics throughout South Africa.

SAFETY

Before launching into a discussion on crime, it's worth reminding readers that by far the most common cause of death or injury while on holiday is the same as at home: road accidents. No one seems to worry about this, however, preferring to focus their anxieties on crime. I have been taken to task by some readers for over-emphasising the danger of robbery, and certainly it is true that most visitors to Madagascar return home after a crime-free trip. However, this is one area where being forewarned is forearmed: there are positive steps that you can take to keep yourself and your possessions safe, so you might as well know about them, while knowing also that the vast majority of Malagasy are touchingly honest. Every traveller can think of a time when his innocence could have been exploited – and wasn't. In my experience, hotel employees are, by and large, trustworthy. So try to keep a sense of proportion. Like health, safety is often a question of common sense. Keep your valuables hidden and keep alert in potentially dangerous situations.

Bear in mind that thieves have to learn their profession so theft is common only where there are plenty of tourists to prey on. In little-visited areas you can relax and enjoy the genuine friendliness of the people.

BEFORE YOU GO You can enjoy peace of mind by giving some time to making your luggage and person as hard to rob as possible before you leave home. Also make three photocopies of all your important documents: passport (information page and visa), airline ticket (including proof of purchase), travellers' cheques (sales advice slip), credit cards, emergency phone number for stolen credit cards, emergency phone number of travel insurance company and insurance documents. Leave one copy with a friend or relative at home, one in your main luggage and one in your handbag or hand luggage. A simpler alternative is to have a web-based email account and send yourself scans of all these documents to access if necessary.

Leave your valuable-looking jewellery at home. You do not need it in Madagascar. Likewise your fancy watch; buy a cheap one. Lock your bag when travelling by plane or *taxi-brousse*; combination locks are more secure than small padlocks. Make or buy a lockable cover for your backpack (some of these double as handy rain covers).

CRIME PREVENTION Violent crime is still relatively rare in Madagascar, and even in Antananarivo you are probably safer than in a large American city. The response to a potentially violent attack is the same in Madagascar as anywhere: if you are outnumbered or the thief is armed, it is sensible to hand over what they want.

You are *far* more likely to be robbed by subterfuge. Razor-slashing is very popular (with the thieves) and is particularly irritating since your clothes or bag are ruined, maybe just for the sake of the used tissue that caused the tempting-looking bulge. When visiting crowded places avoid bringing a bag (even a daypack carried in front of your body is vulnerable, as is a bum-bag); bring your money and passport or ID in a moneybelt under your clothes, or in a neck pouch. Women have advantages here: the neck pouch can be hooked over their bra so no cord shows at the neck and a moneybelt beneath a skirt is safe since it needs an unusually brazen thief to reach for it! If you must have a bag, make sure it is difficult to cut, and that it can be carried across your body so it cannot be snatched. Passengers in taxis may be the victims of robbery: the thief reaches through the open window and grabs your bag. Keep it on the floor by your feet.

Having escorted scores of first-timers through Madagascar, I've learned the mistakes the unprepared can make. The most common is wearing jewellery ('But I always wear this gold chain'), carelessness with money etc ('I just put my bag down while I tried on that blouse'), and expecting thieves to look shabby ('But he was such a well-dressed young man').

PASSPORTS AND IDS If you prefer to leave your passport in a safe place in your hotel room when you go out, carrying a photocopy is no longer sufficient for ID purposes, unless it is an authorised copy, with red stamps all over it, available either from the police or from the office of the mayor. You must provide your passport (photo page and visa page) and as many photocopies of it as you think you might need. This authorised copy is then valid for the police, for banks, for Western Union, or anyone else who might demand your ID. This is all quite a hassle, but losing your passport is worse. I've never been stopped in all my trips to Madagascar, but have had plenty of reports of people (mostly young) who have.

TIPS FOR AVOIDING ROBBERY

- Remember that most theft occurs in the street not in hotels; leave your valuables hidden in a locked bag in your room or in the hotel safe.
- If you use a hotel safe at reception, make sure your money is in a sealed envelope that cannot be opened without detection. There have been cases of the key being accessible to all hotel employees, with predictable results.
- If staying in budget hotels bring a rubber wedge to keep your door closed at night. If you can't secure the window put something on the sill which will fall with a clatter if someone tries to enter.
- Pay particular attention to the security of your passport.
- Carry your cash in a moneybelt, neck pouch or deep pocket. Wear loose trousers that have zipped pockets. Keep emergency cash (dollars or euros) in a Very Safe Place. Keep a small but reasonable amount of cash in a wallet that you can give away if threatened.
- Divide up travellers' cheques so they are not all in one place. Keep photocopies of important documents in your luggage.
- Remember, what the thief would most like to get hold of is money. Do not leave it around (in coat pockets hanging in your room, in your hand while you concentrate on something else, in an accessible pocket while strolling.
- In a restaurant never hang your bag on the back of a chair or lay it by your feet (unless you put your chair leg over the strap). When travelling in a taxi, put your bag on the floor by your feet.

Gordon Rattray, www.able-travel.com

Madagascar can be a physical challenge for any traveller, yet with some effort even those less fleet of foot can also appreciate much of what this unique country has to offer.

PLANNING AND BOOKING As yet, no UK operator runs specialised trips to Madagascar for disabled people, and although many travel companies will listen to your needs and try to create a suitable itinerary, independent travellers can just as easily plan their trip by contacting local operators and establishments by email.

ACCOMMODATION In general, it is not easy to find disabled-friendly accommodation; only top-of-the-range lodges and hotels have 'accessible' rooms, and I've yet to hear of anywhere with grab-handles, roll-under sinks and a roll-in shower. Occasionally bathrooms are wheelchair accessible, but where this is not the case, you should be prepared to be lifted, or do your ablutions in the bedroom. Many toilets in out-of-the-way places are of the squat variety, so if this is a problem for you then ask your tour organiser to have an easily transportable commode frame made, or do this yourself.

TRANSPORT Regardless of how much help you need, there will always be assistance at **airports**, although it is not guaranteed to be as slick or efficient as you may be used to. This is especially true of smaller provincial terminals where, if you cannot walk at all, you may need to be manhandled (without an aisle chair) to and from the aircraft. But Air Mad are often very efficient in this respect (see box on page 111).

There is no effective legislation in Madagascar to facilitate disabled travellers' journeys by **public transport**, so if you cannot walk at all, then both of these options are going to be difficult. You will need to ask for help from fellow passengers to lift you to your seat, it will often be crowded and there will be no accessible toilet.

Most **hire cars** come with a driver. 4x4 vehicles are often higher than normal cars which makes transfers more difficult and although drivers and guides are always willing to help, they are not trained in this skill. You must therefore explain your needs thoroughly and always stay in control. Distances are great and roads often bumpy, so if you are prone to skin damage you need to take extra care. Place your own pressure-relieving cushion on top of (or instead of) the original seat and, if necessary, pad around knees and elbows.

ACTIVITIES Although the majority of Madagascar's wildlife highlights are not disabled-friendly, there are two outstanding exceptions. The luxurious Anjajavy resort has villas, of which one is officially accessible (see page 381), and Berenty (page 240) has broad, smooth, well-maintained forest paths. Although the latter has no designated disability rooms, there will always be plenty of willing hands to help lift you over obstacles.

The ideal route for a disabled traveller would be RN7 from Tana to Toliara by hired car and driver – worth it for scenery alone. For lemurs try Lemurs Park (page 166).

HEALTH AND INSURANCE Doctors will know about 'everyday' illnesses, but you must be able to explain your own particular medical requirements. Rural hospitals and pharmacies are often basic, so take all essential medication and equipment with you; it is advisable to pack this in your hand luggage in case your main luggage gets lost. If heat is a problem for you then try to book accommodation with air-conditioning.

Travel insurance can be purchased from Age Concern (\ 0845 601 2234; www.ageconcern.org.uk), who have no upper age limit, and Free Spirit (\ 0845 230 5000; www.free-spirit.com), who cater for people with pre-existing medical conditions.

Health and Safety SAFETY

5

- For thieves, the next best thing after money is clothes. Avoid leaving them on the beach while you go swimming (in tourist areas) and never leave swimsuits or washing to dry outside your room near a public area.
- Bear in mind that it's impossible to run carrying a large piece of luggage. Items hidden at the bottom of your heaviest bag will be safe from a grab-and-run thief. Pass a piece of cord through the handles of multiple bags to make them one unstealable unit when waiting at an airport or *taxi-brousse* station.
- Avoid misunderstandings – genuine or contrived – by agreeing on the price of a service before you set out.
- But above all, enjoy yourself. It's preferable to lose a few unimportant things and see the best of Madagascar than to mistrust everyone and ruin your trip!

A WOMAN TRAVELLING ALONE   FRB

I had a fantastic time travelling alone for a few weeks in rural Madagascar! Making a journey between S-Ivongo and Maroantsetra I'd expected to be left with overwhelming impressions of beautiful coastlines, an extraordinary ecosystem, improbable fauna and near-impossible transport conditions. I wasn't disappointed! Just as special though were the warmth and hospitality of the Malagasy people.

I'd landed in Tana with the doubtful benefit of four months' (poorly) self-taught French and only the vaguest idea of an itinerary, having booked the flight on a whim to satisfy a long-standing but uninformed curiosity about the island. In an almost *vazaha*-free area I must have been quite a novelty but I learnt a few words of Malagasy and tried to take an interest in everything – although after attempting to de-husk rice grains with a giant (6ft) pestle and mortar, I decided that this was best left to the experts!

Travelling alone is perhaps nobody's ideal but I really wouldn't have missed the experience for the world, at least in this part of the world; I was constantly touched by the friendship and companionship extended by local people. My limited linguistic skills were no bar to laughter and camaraderie in the back of a *camion*, as our lurching vehicle threw us among the sacks of rice, flour and sugar, the cooking pots and tomatoes, whilst the beer crates crashed alarmingly on shelves just above our heads... although it was sometimes difficult to see each other through the diesel fumes! My (all male) companions on this journey were unfailingly charming, lowering a plank which I used to enter and exit more easily as we made the numerous stops required to rebuild bridges and take on/offload people, poultry and produce... and I found this pattern of courtesy and kindness repeated again and again in so many situations as I progressed via 4x4s and ferries, pirogues, on foot, by boat and even, briefly, on the back of a motorbike.

I should have at least one cautionary tale to tell of an intimidating experience – but I haven't! I enjoyed myself far more than I'd anticipated and am left humbled by the simple humanity of the people who made this possible. I never felt unsafe and while eating in *hotelys* or having bread and coffee from a roadside stall would generally find people willing to chat.

Having said that, it was a relief to speak English when happy chance found me a travelling companion. Perhaps the solo experience might have been more uncomfortable among the groups of *vazaha* present in the more touristy areas. But if you're thinking of seeing Madagascar alone – do it! I found that the rural Malagasy respond with relief to someone who trusts them and will make you welcome. If you're in a tourist area, try to find a like-minded *vazaha* to enjoy it with – and don't forget to exchange email addresses; sharing the memories afterwards is as important as living them.

The Malagasy people are very child-friendly although facilities typically are not. Travelling with children in Madagascar should not be undertaken lightly, but with the right preparation it can be a fun and rewarding experience.

Family travel needn't break the bank. Under-5s travel free on *taxi-brousses*. On domestic flights, under-2s go free and under-12s get a 33% discount. Many places offer discounts for children and most hotels have family-size rooms costing not much more than a double.

Highchairs and cots are generally only found in top-end establishments and not commonly outside of Tana. But you will always find staff to be accommodating – offering to store baby formula in the chef's fridge or helping to organise a babysitter.

Imported supplies such as baby food, nappies (diapers) and wipes are available in supermarkets in Tana. Jumbo Score also stocks baby carriers, bottles, clothing and other accessories, but they are generally rather poor quality. Don't rely on finding any of these goods outside Tana.

Ex-pats Len and Sonja de Beer, who live in Tana with their three youngsters, advise stocking up well on snacks before a trip (although safe bottled water is available everywhere) and point out that kids often get car sick on the winding roads of the highlands – so bring travel sickness tablets and keep plastic bags to hand.

If you'll be walking in national parks, it is useful to have some means of carrying young children when they get tired. 'Even in towns, strollers are almost entirely useless – much better to invest in a good kid carrier/backpack to tote your little one around the island. And if you plan to travel by car, you will want to bring a car seat' (Kyle & Monika Lussier).

Always take care to protect children adequately from the sun, keep them hydrated, use mosquito repellent, and bring a mozzie net for night time (those provided by hotels are often snagged or ripped) especially if your infant is too young to take malaria prophylaxis. Hotels will help you find a doctor if you need one, but for serious emergencies keep in mind that you may need to return to Tana to find reliable medical care.

Finally, Len and Sonja note that their children do not enjoy being called *vazaha*: 'you need to prep kids on the fact that they will look different and be stared at'.

...AND WHAT TO DO IF YOU ARE ROBBED Have a little cry and then go to the police. They will write down all the details then send you to the chief of police for a signature. It takes the best part of a day, and will remind you what a manual typewriter looks like, but you will need the certificate for your insurance. If you are in a rural area, the local authorities will do a declaration of loss.

WOMEN TRAVELLERS Things have changed a lot in Madagascar. During my travels in the 1980s my only experience of sexual harassment (if it could be called that) was when a small man sidled up to me in Nosy Be and asked: 'Have you ever tasted Malagasy man?'

Sadly, with the increase of tourism comes the increase of men who think they may be on to a good thing. A firm 'no' is usually sufficient; try not to be too offended: think of the image of Western women that the average Malagasy male is shown via the cinema or TV. A woman Peace Corps volunteer gave me the following advice for women travelling alone on *taxi-brousses*: 'Try to sit in the cab, but not next to the driver; if possible sit with another woman; if in the main body of the vehicle, establish contact with an older person, man or woman, who will

Health and Safety **SAFETY**

5

then tend to look after you.' Common advice is to wear a ring and say you are married, but some readers report that this is not effective in Madagascar.

Lone travellers, both male and female, seem to have a better time well off the beaten track. My correspondent FRB (see box on page 122) is not alone in saying that the true warmth of ordinary Malagasy is more likely to be found away from tourist areas.

MEN TRAVELLERS To the Malagasy, a man travelling alone is in need of one thing: a woman. In tourist spots, particularly in beach resorts, lone male travellers may find themselves pursued or harassed. Prostitutes are ubiquitous and very beautiful, but venereal disease is common, and prostitutes have been known to drug a tourist's drink to render him unconscious then rob his possessions.

The government is clamping down hard on sex tourism. Considering the risks you would be foolish to succumb to temptation.

6

Madagascar and You

Tsihy be lambanana ny ambanilantra
All who live under the sky are woven together like one big mat.

Malagasy saying

YOUR CARBON FOOTPRINT

The question I'm most often asked by journalists is how do I deal with the dilemma of encouraging people to fly halfway across the world while knowing that this contributes to carbon emissions and global warming? I reply that to me it's no dilemma...

Not long ago, I was the lecturer on board a cruise ship. Yes, a long flight then a ship which also contributed its share of CO_2, so thumbs down. But in my lectures I described the work done by the Ivoloina Zoo and the charity HELP in Toamasina, and invited passengers to see the work for themselves. Afterwards some told me it was one of the highlights of the trip, and the outcome was a combined on-the-spot donation of about US$1,500. In my experience this sort of generosity is not unusual once people can see for themselves the work done in Madagascar in conservation and educating the next generation.

The budget travellers' contribution is equally valuable because they bring goodwill and an enthusiasm for breaking down cultural barriers. The backpackers who contribute their stories and philosophies to this book may be the politicians or businessmen and women of the future. Their experiences in Madagascar will help inform the decisions they make as leaders.

And even those visitors who simply enjoy Madagascar, relaxing on the beaches, visiting the national parks, buying handicrafts and gaining a little understanding of what makes the average Malagasy tick, have made a contribution to the economy of the country.

So, although I admire those conscientious people who are prepared to make the sacrifice of not flying, I think they're wrong. The best way to save Madagascar is to

ANGLO-MALAGASY SOCIETY

If you live in the UK and have fallen in love with Madagascar, or indeed are involved with the country in any way – whether through family, charity, NGO or business connections – consider joining the Anglo-Malagasy Society.

A detailed quarterly newsletter keeps members informed of news and developments from the island. The AMS holds meetings in London four times a year with speakers on a diverse range of Malagasy topics, followed by a delicious Malagasy buffet. See www.anglo-malagasysociety.co.uk for more information and a membership form.

go there – and that means taking a plane. If you want to offset your carbon emissions do it by contributing to one of the reforestation programmes in Madagascar. See pages 261, 269 and 381 for details of some.

RESPONSIBLE TOURISM

In recent years there has been a welcome shift of attitude among visitors to developing countries from 'What can I get out of this trip?' to 'How can I give something back?' This chapter addresses those issues, and suggests ways in which you can help this marvellous, but sometimes tragic, country.

THEY DO THINGS DIFFERENTLY THERE I once caught our Malagasy guide scowling at himself in the mirror. When I teased him he said: 'As a Malagasy man I smile a lot. I can see that if I want to work with tourists I must learn to frown.' He knew that the group considered him insufficiently assertive. Tolerance and the fear of causing offence is an integral part of Malagasy social relationships. So if a tourist expresses anger in a way that is entirely appropriate in his or her own culture, it may be counter-productive in Madagascar. Deeply unsettled, the person at the receiving end may giggle in response, thus exacerbating the situation. If you are patient, pleasant and keep your temper, your problem will be solved more quickly.

Avoid being too dogmatic in conversation (you do not have exclusivity of the truth). Make use of 'perhaps' and 'maybe'. Be excessive in your thanks. The Malagasy are very polite; we miss the nuances by not understanding the language. Body language, however, is easier to learn. For instance, 'Excuse me, may I come through?' is indicated by a stooping posture and an arm extended forward. Note how often it is used.

Part of responsible tourism is relinquishing some of our normal comforts. Consider this: fuelwood demand in Madagascar has far outstripped supply. Wood and charcoal are the main sources of energy, and the chief users are city dwellers. In rural areas, tourist establishments may be the main consumers. Do you still feel that hot water is essential in your hotel? Another source of energy is hydroelectric power, so drought – as is common in these times of climate change – causes electricity cuts. So think again before leaving the air-conditioning and lights on when absent from your room.

One of the keys to responsible tourism is ensuring that as much as possible of the money you spend on your holiday remains in Madagascar. Independent travellers should try, whenever possible, to stay at small hotels run by Malagasy. Madagascar now has a homestay programme – see page 197. Tourists on an organised tour will probably find themselves in a foreign-owned hotel, but can do their bit by buying handicrafts and perhaps donating to local charities.

Madagascar's shortcomings can be infuriating. Sometimes a little reflection reveals the reasons behind the failure to produce the expected service, but sometimes you just have to tell yourself 'Well, that's the way it is'. After all, you are not going to be able to change Madagascar, but Madagascar may change you.

TOURIST POWER I recently learned that a hotel which used to keep caged lemurs as an attraction has now released them after some customers complained (although release is not that straightforward; see page 226). We can sometimes be too cautious about making our feelings felt because so often the hotel management is only trying to please us. So, if your chambermaid leaves the lights or air-conditioning on in your room, it's worth explaining to the manager that you would rather save Madagascar's precious resources. If a smart new hotel has proudly stated that they use the valuable – and highly endangered – hardwoods such as rosewood or palisander for their furniture or – worse – their floors, you could get into a conversation about sustainability.

There is, of course, a big difference between complaining about bad service and informing the management about a shift in tourist values. Even your disapproval of caged lemurs should be expressed tactfully, and your views about sustainable tourism need even more care. Your green views won't be shared by all tourists and it's not a conversation you can have in a hurry when paying your bill. Take some time to discuss it over a drink.

PHOTOGRAPHY Lack of consideration when taking photos is perhaps the most common example of irresponsible tourist behaviour – one that each of us has probably been guilty of at some time. It is so easy to take a sneaky photo without first establishing contact with the person, so easy to say we'll send a print of the picture and then not get round to it, so easy to stroll into a market or village

---

'PLEASE SEND ME A PHOTO'   *Hilary Bradt*

It is not always easy to keep a promise. Of course we intend to send a print after someone posed cheerfully for the photo, but after we get home there are so many other things to do, so many addresses on scraps of paper. I now honour my promises. Here's why.

I was checking my group in to a Nosy Be hotel when the bellboy asked if he could speak to me. He looked nervous, so suspecting a problem with the bookings I asked him to wait until everyone was in their rooms. When we were alone he cleared his throat and recited what was obviously a carefully prepared speech: 'You are Mrs Hilary Bradt. Ten years ago you gave your business card to the lady at Sambava Voyages and she gave it to a schoolboy who wrote to you. But you were away so your mother answered the letter. She wrote many letters. My name is Murille and I am that boy. And now I want to talk to you about Janet Cross and Brian Cross and Andrew and...' There followed a list of every member of my family. As I listened, incredulous, I remembered the original letter. 'We love England strongly,' he wrote, 'especially London, Buckingham, Grantham, Dover...' I remembered passing it to my mother saying I was too busy for such a correspondence but maybe she'd like to write. She kept it up for several years, answering questions such as 'How often does Mrs Hilary go to Grantham and Dover?' and she sent a photo of the family gathering at Christmas, naming every member on the back of the photo.

This brought an indignant letter from a cousin. 'I have seen your photo. It is a very nice one. I asked Murille if he would lend it for one day only because we all study English so we must have photo of English people more to improve this language, but he refused me strongly because they are only his friends not mine...'

Murille brought out the treasured photo. It had suffered from the constant handling and tropical heat and was peeling at the edges. He wanted to trim it, he explained, 'but if I do I will have to cut off a bit of your mother's beautiful chair and I can't do that.'

Later that year I sent Murille a photo album filled with family photos. I never heard from him again – that's the way it is in Madagascar – but the story has a twist to its tail. I returned to Sambava 12 years after the original visit, and found myself addressing a classroom of eager adult students of English and their local teacher. Searching for something interesting to say, I told them about the time I was last in their town and the series of letters between Murille and my mother. And I told them about the cousin who also wrote to her. 'I think his name was Patrice,' I said. The teacher looked up. 'I'm Patrice. Yes, I remember writing to Janet Cross...'

thinking what a wonderful photo it will make and forgetting that you are there to experience it.

The rules are not to take people's photos without permission, and to respect an answer of 'no'. Give consideration to the offence caused by photographing the destitute. Be cautious about paying your way to a good photo; often a smile or a joke will work as well, and sets no precedent. People love to see pictures of themselves, and in these days of digital photography you can show them immediately. Or you can go further, as one reader did (see page 91) and bring a small photo printer so you can hand out prints. Otherwise be sure to write down the addresses of people in your photos and honour your promise to send copies.

Philip Thomas writes: 'A Malagasy, for whom a photograph will be a highly treasured souvenir, will remember the taking of the photograph and your promise to send them a copy, a lot longer than you might. Their disappointment in those who say one thing and do another is great, so if you think you might not get it together to send the photograph then do not say that you will.'

A responsible attitude to photography is so much more fun! And it results in better pictures. It involves taking some time getting to know the subject of your photo: making a purchase, perhaps, or practising your Malagasy greetings.

THE EFFECTS OF TOURISM ON LOCALS The impact of foreigners on the Malagasy was noted as long ago as 1669 when a visitor commented that formerly the natives were deeply respectful of white men but were changed 'by the bad examples which the Europeans have had, who glory in the sin of luxury in this country...'.

AKANY AVOKO   *Hilary Bradt*

Akany Avoko is a Children's Home caring for around 120 abandoned and impoverished children. For over 40 years Akany Avoko has fed, clothed, educated and given a secure home to orphans, street kids, children from broken families, young people with disabilities, teenage girls on remand and teenage mums with their babies. It is sustained solely by charitable donations and income-generating projects within the centre itself.

As well as providing food, shelter, schooling and primary healthcare to the children who live there, Akany Avoko works to ensure that the children are capable of supporting themselves in the future and also to provide environmental education, enabling future generations of Malagasy people to help both themselves and Madagascar's precious environment.

Akany Avoko's 'green' projects are an inspiration: they use solar cooking and water-heating, organic food production, and sustainable water and waste management. Biogas and compost toilets provide methane for cooking as well as fertiliser. Carbonised pine-needles are mixed with clay for fuel.

In addition to the academic education offered to its children, vocational training includes cookery, hairdressing, dressmaking, hospitality, woodwork, IT and gardening. Traditional dance, sports, games and fun are also very much part of the centre's weekly routine.

The cost of caring for the orphans and abandoned children who end up at Akany Avoko is very high and the centre is always short of money. They are always delighted to welcome visitors who can take a tour of the centre before visiting the on-site shop or café. Please phone or email ahead to arrange a visit – you won't regret it.

BP29 Ambohidratrimo 105, Madagascar; ☎ 22 441 58. Ken and Lorna Gillespie: e akany.avoko@moov.mg; blog: http://akany-avoko.blogspot.com; www.akanyavoko.com

In developing countries tourism has had profound effects on the inhabitants, some good, some bad. Madagascar seems to me to be a special case – more than any other country I've visited it inspires a particular devotion and an awareness of its fragility, both environmental and cultural. Wildlife is definitely profiting from the attention given it and from the emphasis on ecotourism. For the people, however, the blessings may be very mixed: some able Malagasy have found jobs in the tourist industry, but for others the impact of tourism has meant that their cultural identity has been eroded, along with some of their dignity and integrity. Village antagonisms are heightened when one or two people gain the lion's share of tourist revenue and gifts, leading in at least one case to murder, and hitherto honest folk have lapsed into corruption, alcoholism or thievery.

BEGGARS Whether or not to give to professional beggars (but not children) is up to you. My policy is to give to the elderly and, on an extended trip, I also single out 'beggar days' when I fill my pockets with small change and give to every beggar who looks needy and over school age. And if I make some trickster's day, so be it.

It is important to make up your mind about beggars before you hit the streets so you can avoid standing there riffling through a conspicuously fat wallet for a low-denomination bill.

DEALING WITH CHILD BEGGARS The unintentional effect of giving sweets, pens, money or whatever to children can be seen in any popular resort. Kids trail after you, grabbing your hands and beseeching you for gifts. Many tourists are simply worn down by their persistence and give in, thus perpetuating the problem. Bill French who, with his wife Nina has made two long trips by bicycle in Madagascar, offers the following advice: 'Just don't give anything. Ignore their begging and change the subject, eg: do *cinque, cinque* (fist to fist), amuse them – sing, play, do tricks or just chatter away. These are skills you have to work on. Just don't give to anybody. Salve your conscience by giving a larger lump of money to an organised charity that will distribute more fairly and where needed.'

GIVING PRESENTS This is a subject often discussed among experienced travellers who cannot agree on when, if ever, a present is appropriate. Most feel that giving presents is appropriate only when it is in exchange for a service.

My repeat visits to Madagascar over the course of 39 years have shaped my own view: that giving is usually done for self-gratification rather than generosity, and that one thoughtless act can change a village irreparably. I have seen the shyly inquisitive children of small communities turn into tiresome beggars; I have seen the warm interaction between visitor and local turn into mutual hostility; I have seen intelligent, ambitious young men turn into scoundrels. What I haven't sorted out in my mind is how much this matters. Thieves and scoundrels make a good living and are probably happier than they were in their earlier state of dire poverty. Should we be imposing our cultural views on the Malagasy? I don't know.

But giving does not have to be in the form of material gifts. We should never underestimate our value as sheer entertainment in an otherwise routine life. We can give a smile, or a greeting in Malagasy. And we can learn from people who in so many ways are richer than us.

MORE AND MORE... Visitors who have spent some time in Madagascar and have befriended a particular family often find themselves in the 'more and more and more' trap. The foreigner begins by expressing appreciation of the friendship and hospitality he or she received by sending a gift to the family. A request for a more expensive gift follows. And another one, until the luckless *vazaha* feels that she is seen as a bottomless cornucopia of goodies. The reaction is a mixture of guilt and resentment.

Understanding the Malagasy viewpoint may help you to come to terms with these requests. You may be considered as part of the extended family, and family members often help support those who are less well-off. You will almost certainly be thought of as fabulously wealthy, so it is worth dispelling this myth by giving some prices for familiar foodstuffs at home – a kilo of rice, for instance, or a mango. Explain that you don't have servants, that you pay so much for rent, and that you have a family of your own that needs your help. Don't be afraid to say 'no'.

It is sensible to be cautious about giving your name and address to local people with whom you have only a passing acquaintance. Women may be surprised – and possibly delighted – to receive a letter declaring undying love, but it's just possible that this comes with a few strings attached.

...AND THE MOST I know two couples, one in America and the other in Australia, who have translated their wish to help the Malagasy into airfares to their home country. This is not to be undertaken lightly – the red tape from both governments is horrendous – but is hugely rewarding for all concerned.

OFF THE BEATEN PATH Travellers venturing well off the beaten path will want to do their utmost to avoid offending the local people, who are usually extremely warm and hospitable.

Unfortunately, with the many *fady* prohibitions and beliefs varying from area to area and village to village, it is impossible to know exactly how to behave, although outsiders are exempt from the consequences of infringing a local *fady*.

Sometimes, in very remote areas, Malagasy will react in sheer terror at the sight of a white person. This probably stems from their belief in *mpakafo*, the 'stealer of hearts'. These pale-faced beings are said to wander around at night ripping out people's hearts. So it is not surprising that rural Malagasy often do not like going out after dark – and it's a problem if you are looking for a guide. In the southeast it is the *mpangalak'aty*, the 'taker of the liver', who is feared. The adventurous *vazaha* is not helped by the fact that mothers still threaten that 'If you don't go to bed, the *vazaha* will get you' to gain the obedience of their children.

Villages are governed by the *fokonolona*, or People's Assembly. On arrival at a village you should ask for the *président du fokontany*. Although traditionally this was the village elder, these days it is more likely to be someone who speaks French – perhaps the schoolteacher. He will show you where you can sleep (sometimes a hut is kept free for guests, sometimes someone will be moved out for you). You will usually be provided with a meal. Now travellers have penetrated most rural areas, you may be expected to pay. Certainly you should offer, and if the answer is vague, make a donation of an appropriate amount. Philip Thomas, a social anthropologist who has conducted research in the rural southeast, points out several ways that tourists may unwittingly cause offence. 'People should adopt the common courtesy of greeting the Malagasy in their own language. *Salama, mana hoana* and *veloma* are no more difficult to say than their French equivalents.

'*Vazaha* sometimes refuse food and hospitality, putting up tents and cooking their own food. But in offering you a place to sleep and food to eat the Malagasy are showing you the kindness they extend to any visitor or stranger, and to refuse is a rejection of their hospitality and sense of humanity. You may think you are inconveniencing them, and this is true, but they would prefer that than if you keep to yourselves as though you were not people (in the widest sense) like them. It may annoy you that it is virtually impossible to get a moment away from the gaze of the Malagasy, but you are there to look at them and their activities anyway, so why

Alasdair Harris, Blue Ventures

Madagascar's coastal environments comprise some of the most ecologically sensitive areas of the country. Visitors should be aware of the intrinsic effect that their presence and activities will have on local habitats and plan their holiday in a way that minimises impact on the environment.

When trekking, try to avoid sensitive habitats and vegetation types, reducing the impact of your movement and access to and from campsites. All waste should be sorted and disposed of sensibly. In arid environments such as the southwest, keep freshwater use to a minimum.

Swimmers, snorkellers and divers should avoid all physical contact with corals and other marine life. Divers should take care to avoid damaging reefs by maintaining good buoyancy control to avoid accidental contact or stirring up sediment.

In coastal hotels and restaurants, seafood is commonly caught to order, regardless of the sustainability of the catch. In some tourist areas it is not uncommon to see critically endangered species such as the humphead or Napoleon wrasse served up in a restaurant kitchen. Shellfish should not be bought out of season, since this can have devastating consequences on populations.

The marine curios trade is equally driven by tourism and visitors must refrain from purchasing shells. In Toliara alone, almost 150 species of gastropods are exploited for the ornamental shell trade. Several of these – notably the magnificent helmet shell and the cowries – are now threatened with extinction. Similarly, the exploitation of sea turtles is increasingly focused at the tourist market, turtle shells now fetching staggering prices in markets and *bijouteries*.

should there not be a mutual exchange? Besides, you are far more fascinating to them than they are to you, for their view of the world is not one shaped by mass education and access to international images supplied by television.

'It is perfectly acceptable to give a gift of money in return for help. Gifts of cash are not seen by the Malagasy as purchases and they themselves frequently give them. Rather, you give as a sign of your appreciation and respect. But beware of those who may try to take advantage of your position as a foreigner (and you may find these in even the remotest spot), those who play on your lack of knowledge of language and custom, and their perception of you as extremely wealthy (as of course you are by their standards).'

Valerie and John Middleton, who have travelled more adventurously and successfully in Madagascar than anyone else I know, add this advice: 'In three long visits to Madagascar we have never had a bad experience. We have, however, noted several people who have not fared so well and feel that we could pass on some advice for anyone wanting to go off the beaten path.

'To prevent misunderstanding always take a guide with you at least for communication as many isolated peoples speak only Malagasy. Always introduce yourself to the local *président* and explain why you are in his village or passing through; you will never cease to be amazed at how helpful they wish to be once your purpose is understood and perhaps even more importantly the authority of his backing confers a considerable degree of protection. Always defer to his advice. And find out about local *fady* before doing anything.'

Waste disposal Madagascar has no mechanised recycling plants. Instead, the poorest of the poor scavenge the rubbish dumps in the larger towns. Clothes, containers and suchlike will be found and reused. In rural areas rubbish is simply dumped on the beach or on wasteland. Therefore whenever possible take your rubbish home with you, or at least back to the city. The exception is plastic bottles: rural people in Madagascar need all the containers they can get for carrying or storing water or other liquids, so whenever possible, give your empty water bottles to villagers.

HOW YOU CAN HELP

There are several ways in which you can make a positive contribution. By making a donation to a local project you can help the people – and the wildlife – without creating new problems.

My initiation to the concept of 'giving something back' was 15 years ago when I met a couple of English teachers, Jill and Charlie Hadfield, who told me how they had started The Streetkids Project. Visiting a charity run by the Sisters of the Good Shepherd in Tana, they could see where a little money could go a long way and they started raising money for the Centre Fihavanana (see page 164). The nuns run – amongst other things – a preparatory school for the very poor. When the children are ready to go on to state school, however, the parents can't afford the £15 a year they must pay for registration, uniform and books, so the children are condemned to return to the streets as beggars. The Streetkids Project raises money to continue their education. It is surprising how often tourists are so affected by what they experience in Madagascar that they team up with local people to found a charity.

CENTRE FIHAVANANA (STREETKIDS CENTRE)   *Hilary Bradt*

Run by the Sisters of the Good Shepherd, their activities are aimed mainly at women and children. About 300 children aged 3–12 are taught in four classes and many do well enough to get into state primary school. Undernourished babies are fed and their destitute mothers given training in childcare. Teenagers come to the centre to learn basic skills and handicrafts. Elderly people come twice a month for a little food, company and care. Food is taken weekly to over 300 women, teenagers and children in prison. At the centre 82 children are being helped by the Child Sponsor Programme, but there is a growing number still needing sponsors. The Centre also has a scheme called Wheels4Life which provides bicycles for young men who need them to earn a living. There are photos of these boys beaming from ear to ear on their shiny new bikes. Finally, a group of 86 women do beautiful embroidery at home while caring for their families, which provides an income both for them and for the centre.

A recent project is housing for needy women and their children; simple houses have been built on donated land on the outskirts of Tana and this is now a thriving community with its own livestock and kitchen gardens. Added to this is the new Fanilo Crisis Home for girls and women who have been battered, abandoned or sexually abused.

The challenges of working with the destitute were brought home to me on a recent visit, when Sister Jeanette (who speaks English) told that women enrolling in the embroidery programme have first to be shown how to hold a pen, and then how to take measurements, before they can even begin to be taught how to sew. They also need to be 'paid' in food during their training to compensate for loss of earnings as beggars. Hard to believe when you see the exquisite work done by these former street-women.

Centre Fihavanana (Sœurs du Bon Pasteur), 58 Lalana Stephani, Antananarivo; ⤡ 22 299 81; e *bpfihavanana@moov.mg*

One example is the Dutch/Malagasy organisation Fitiavana in Ambositra (see box on page 179). Anything is possible if you care enough.

The organisations and charities listed below are all working with the people of Madagascar, and, by extension, habitat conservation. Most of them are very small, run by dedicated volunteers who would welcome even modest donations. Other charities work specifically for wildlife. What better way to channel your empathy for Madagascar and its problems?

UK AND US CHARITIES ASSISTING MADAGASCAR
People

Andrew Lees Trust ☎ 020 7424 9256; www.andrewleestrust.org. Set up in 1995, this charity helped to launch & support training at the Libanona Ecology Centre. Named after the international environmental campaigner Andrew Lees, the Trust develops social & environmental education projects in the south, specifically to increase access to information & education that empowers local populations to improve food security, reduce poverty & manage natural resources more sustainably. Project Radio, shortlisted for the UNESCO international prize for rural development communications, works with a network of 58 local partners & 38 radio stations across the south to produce & broadcast vital information & educational radio programmes to isolated rural communities. A sister programme, Project Energy, trained women in the south to build 37,000 wood-efficient stoves that reduce domestic fuel consumption by over 50% & help reduce pressure on forest resources. Tree planting follows the stove trainings & over 3,500 trees are already growing in a drought area.

Azafady Studio 7, 1a Beethoven St, London W10 4LG; ☎ 020 8960 6629; e info@azafady.org; www.madagascar.co.uk. Works mainly in the southeast of Madagascar, aiming to break the cycle of poverty & environmental degradation so apparent in that area. Projects include tree planting & facilitation of small enterprises such as village market gardens, beekeeping, basket making & fruit drying. They fund a Health & Sanitation Programme to improve access to clean drinking water & basic healthcare; also HIV prevention. Conservation projects include studies of the remaining littoral forest in southeast Madagascar & of endangered loggerhead turtle populations. They also run the Pioneer scheme for volunteers (see page 77).

The Dodwell Trust 16 Lanark Mansions, Pennard Rd, London W12 8DT; ☎ 020 8740 6302; e dodwell@madagascar.freeserve.co.uk; www.dodwell-trust.org. A British-registered charity founded by Christina Dodwell, running a radio project designed to help rural villagers, through the production & broadcast of a drama & magazine radio series for family health,

AIDS prevention, poverty issues, & environment. The Trust has set up 1,000 listener-groups with donated wind-up/solar radios, to send back useful information & take part in programmes. In collaboration with the Ministry of Education, the Trust also sends any donated computers from the UK to Madagascar & assists with the twinning of schools in the UK. There is also a volunteer programme (see page 77).

Feedback Madagascar 5 Lyndale Av, London NW2 2QD; ☎/f 020 7431 7853; e info@feedbackmadagascar.org; www.feedbackmadagascar.org. Head office in Madagascar: 1er étage, Lot IB 65 Bis Isoraka, 6 Rue Raveloary, Antananarivo 101; ☎/f 22 638 11; e eugenie@feedbackmadagascar.org. A small, but highly effective Scottish charity that has worked to alleviate poverty & environmental degradation in Madagascar for nearly 20 years. Projects focus on improving primary healthcare & education, & promoting natural resource management & income-generating schemes. They are currently working with the Malagasy organisation Ny Tanintsika on revitalising the silk industry & other traditional crafts, community forest management & beekeeping, social action & awareness campaigns through adult literacy programmes, & capacity-building of communities on health, agriculture, environment & good governance.

Mad Imports 262 Court St, Suite 3, Brooklyn, NY 11231; ☎ 718 802 9757; e laurel@madimports.org; www.madimports.org. A socially responsible company that imports & sells handmade art & accessories from Madagascar. The sale of these products supports community & economic development in Malagasy communities including Akany Avoko. They work with individual & collective groups of artists to import fine quality handmade art & accessories for sale in the US. This enables families to gain economic independence.

Mission Aviation Fellowship Ivato Airport, Antananarivo; ☎/f 22 453 22; e mafm-mad@iris.mg; www.maf-madagascar.org. MAF provides transport by light aircraft & various logistical services to support people & organisations. See box on page 134.

Money for Madagascar Llwyncelyn Isaf, Llangadog SA19 9BY; e info@moneyformadagascar.org; www.moneyformadagascar.org. This long-established & well-run Welsh charity funds rural health & agricultural projects & supports deprived groups in urban areas. It also provides funds for cyclone relief & other natural disasters. MfM sends funds on a regular basis to The Streetkids Project (page 132) & Akany Avoko (page 128), both of which run child sponsorship schemes. As with MOSS (see below), the staff are all volunteers & they don't even have an office, so the overheads are very low. Thus you can be confident that almost all the money you give will go directly to the project you want to support. If you are singling out the Streetkids Project or Akany Avoko, write the cheque to Money for Madagascar but enclose a note saying where you want it to be sent and address the envelope simply to 'Madagascar' at the above address.

MOSS c/o Oliver Backhouse, Denby Hse, Minskip, York, North Yorkshire YO51 9JF; e obackhouse@doctors.org.uk. MOSS (Madagascan Organisation for Saving Sight) was set up in 1993, following a year's work by ophthalmologist Oliver Backhouse & his wife. Approximately 250,000 people in Madagascar are blind. Research undertaken by MOSS has shown that 70% of adult blindness is treatable & 90% of childhood blindness is preventable. MOSS is currently involved in a Childhood Refraction project in Fianarantsoa & an Outreach Cataract programme, delivering ophthalmic services in remoter areas. A recent similar project in Antsirabe was very successful: of the 65,000 children & teachers screened, 3,000 required spectacle correction.

Population Concern Studio 325, Highgate Studios, 53–79 Highgate Rd, London NW5 1TL; \ 020 7241 8500; f 020 7267 6788; e info@populationconcern.org.uk; www.populationconcern.org.uk. This organisation is working in Toliara & Antsiranana on a variety of initiatives to improve the sexual health of young people. They also aim to reduce the incidence of teenage pregnancies. Doing similar work in Madagascar since 1988 is Population Services International (www.psi.org).

Water Aid e wateraidmg@dts.mg; www.wateraid.org. A UK-based NGO, which works to help poor communities gain access to drinking water, safe sanitation & good hygiene. In Madagascar, where the majority of the population has none of these vital services, they have been working since 1999 with local partner organisations & the national government. In the highlands they support programmes in rural parts of Antananarivo & Fianarantsoa provinces, as well as parts of Toliara & Toamasina.

FLYING (AND DIGGING) FOR LIFE

John Segeritz, MAF yieldmaster

We'd already cleared 450 metres of the Ampasinambo runway there was still 100 metres to go. If only there would not be that enormous hill in the way! Digging and levelling were on the schedule. But within six weeks of labouring, with support from local workers and two excavators, we finished the 15-metre-wide airstrip.

It was not just a period of work, but also an unforgettable experience to camp out in the bush, take showers in a giant waterfall and be woken up before sunrise by roosters.

Mission Aviation Fellowship is a Christian organisation whose mission is to fly light aircraft in isolated areas to bring hope and help to people in need. The construction of airstrips is just one branch of MAF's many services for Madagascar's population.

Beside that, MAF, whose motto is 'flying for life', enables the work of many missions in their outreach by offering them charter flights for example, or the SMS service (assisting those in remote areas to know when and where a MAF plane is landing).

Whether it is the repair and maintenance of a car or a special machine, help in acquiring Malagasy papers or the storage of freight or medicines, MAF is not just busy in the air. Among its partners, MAF counts local churches, governments and NGOs as well as mission organisations.

Most visitors to Madagascar will quickly notice just how many children there are. With an average of around six children per family, it's clear that population growth is a huge challenge for a country already struggling to conserve its natural resources. In 2007, Blue Ventures recognised that there was a need to address population growth for its own conservation goals to have any chance of success.

Instigated by British-based GP, Vik Mohan, the family planning service began by conducting initial research in the village of Andavadoaka. This found that girls were having their first sexual experience as young as eight, with many having their first pregnancy soon after puberty. Some families had up to 16 children, with parents not always able to provide for such large families. The research also flagged up the difficulty for women who wanted to access family planning clinics as the nearest service was 50km away. Awareness of sexually transmissible infections was also low, despite high levels of gonorrhoea and syphilis. The survey discovered that women wished to be better informed and wanted better access to contraception. There clearly was a huge unmet need for family planning services in Andavadoaka.

In August 2007, Mohan flew out to Madagascar to launch the clinic with the help of the Blue Ventures medic. Initial meetings to raise awareness were set up with the women, men and teenage girls separately. The response was overwhelmingly positive and large numbers of women took up the service when it was first launched. Mohan felt that from the beginning, it was clear that the facility was important in emancipating the women of the village who hadn't had control over their fertility and who were, largely, coping with men who didn't want to use condoms.

In January 2008, the new medic, Rebecca Hill, took over the running of the weekly clinic which offered advice and access to a range of contraception. As well as condoms, which were promoted for safe sex and contraception, the clinic offered Depo-Provera injections, the combined contraceptive pill, and the progesterone only pill. The clinic also offered advice to the women so that they could choose which type of contraception was right for them. Hill believed that the service could be reaching more women and was shocked at the high level of ignorance about sexual health matters. Hill held more meetings with different sections of the community, hoping to dispel some of the misconceptions. She also persuaded Blue Ventures volunteers to wear T-shirts embroidered with slogans promoting condom use. 'There aren't billboards here,' she reasoned, 'so I thought that volunteers could be walking posters instead'. She also wanted to tackle the myth that 'only white people wear condoms'. A play about STIs was performed using humour and recognisable local stereotypes to make the play entertaining and relevant. The play, 'Captain Kapoty' (Condom) was performed again a month later to a packed audience on the beach. Another advertisement was created – a huge pirogue sail emblazoned with Captain Kapoty – and posters about the benefits of family planning placed in highly visible locations. A competition was also held, getting members of the community to devise and perform their own plays about STIs and family planning. The message was getting across.

'When I started here in January, no one would take condoms' said Rebecca. 'But just before I left in August, most women would take a supply. I regularly had boys knocking on the door to my room asking for them.'

Much more still needs to be done. The future challenge is to understand what is stopping more people from using the service, what the barriers to using contraception are, and to keep the momentum going. There are plans for satellite clinics in other villages with the hope of reaching the coastal community of 10,000 people who cannot get to Andavadoaka, and for more education and awareness work, including a tour of the play.

My last trip was unforgettable! I once again contacted 'my' little school in Ankify to arrange a cultural visit for my group. We visited the two-room school and M Farajao, a teacher, helped us exchange questions and answers about life in the USA and Madagascar. Everyone with me had packed half their suitcase with school supplies, sports gear, and toys and games to donate. These went a long way, even among the 160+ school kids ranging from six to 15 years old.

As a special treat this year I also brought in a six-foot-long ground boa, the largest kind of snake found in Madagascar. Our guide had found it the previous evening and knew I'd want to show the kids. I kept it hidden, saving it for the grand finale of a live Show & Tell style 'biology lesson'.

The kids went wild when I suddenly lifted the four-inch-thick snake out of a box on the floor. Some ran for the door; others leaped out of windows. But soon the whole class was back crowding around to touch the tail end of the huge boa. Malagasy boas are usually very mellow, but just to be safe, I held its head up and out of reach in case the commotion upset it. That proved to be wise because the snake quickly tired of the handling, sunk its teeth into my armpit, and held on. I shielded the bite from view and tried not to wince as I continued to smile and allow everyone to quench their curiosity. I don't think anyone realised what was actually happening, which is good because I certainly didn't want to give anyone a bad impression of this beautiful and essentially harmless local snake that was only reacting to the hundreds of hands touching it.

I've made visiting L'Ecole Primaire Publique d'Ankify an annual event since I always return to this magical area with my tours. Besides Madagascar's unique animals, the people are a true treasure that I proudly include in interactions as often as possible as we rove the countryside seeing and photographing nature.

Bill Love is a photographer, writer, and tour operator (www.bluechameleon.org) who regularly runs eco-tours to Madagascar.

Wildlife

Conservation International (USA) 1015 18th St NW, Washington DC, 20003; www.conservation.org. One of the most active conservation organisations in Madagascar.

Durrell Wildlife Conservation Trust Les Augres Manor, Trinity, Jersey JE3 5BP, Channel Islands, British Isles; ℡ 01534 860000; f 01534 860001; www.durrell.org

Wildlife Conservation Society e membership@wcs.org; www.wcs.org. A US-based organisation at the Bronx Zoo in New York City which supports a wide range of conservation projects in Madagascar.

WWF *Switzerland* Av du Mont-blanc, 1196 Gland, (International Office); *UK* Panda Hse, Weyside Park, Godalming, Surrey GU7 IXR; *USA* 1250 24th St NW, Washington DC 20037-1175; *Madagascar* Aires Protégées, BP738, Antananarivo 101; www.wwf.org

above   Girls at Mahasoa on RN7 (DA)

above right   A banana seller near Manakara (DA)

right   Malagasy woman on market day (DA)

bottom   Children carrying sacks of newly fired bricks for a new house (DA)

above The *rova* (queen's palace) in Tana was destroyed by fire in 1995 but the stone shell still stands and is undergoing renovations (DA) page 162

left House near Moramanga (DA) page 254

below Settlement alongside Pangalanes Canal (DA) page 267

top left   **Angraecum humbertii orchid, Zombitse-Vohibasia National Park** (DA) page 210

top right   **Baobabs growing on coastal rocks in the northwest. Madagascar has six endemic species of baobab** (DA) page 42

above left   **Insect-eating pitcher plant, Ankanin'ny Nofy** (DA) page 269

above right   **The spiny forest near Anakao** (DA) page 67

left   **Impatiens tuberosa flower, Montagne d'Ambre National Park** (DA) page 334

above — Madagascar is home to some 1,000 different orchid species (DA) page 36

right — Octopus trees, *Didierea*, of the southwest. This semi-desert area is known for its endemic desert-adapted flora (DA) page 38

below — *Pachypodium*, Isalo National Park (DA) page 38

left Cascade d'Antomboka, Montagne d'Ambre National Park (DA) page 337

below A stream in Ranomafana National Park (DA) page 192

bottom left Isalo National Park is excellent for trekking (DA) page 206

bottom right Piscine Naturelle, Isalo National Park (DA) page 208

top & above	**A cave in the northwest (DA). Sub-fossil remains of extinct lemurs have been found in the caves of this region** (HB) pages 80 & 33
above	**Sub-fossil remains of extinct lemurs have been found in the caves of this region** (HB) page 33
above right	**The surreal and colourful Red Tsingy** (DA) page 338
right	**Tsingy Rary in Ankarana National Park** (DA) page 339

above   The luxury face of Madagascar: dining on the beach at Anjajavy (DA) page 381

left   Madagascar's oldest church, at Ambodifotatra on Ile Sainte Marie (DA) page 315

below   Small village along the route of the Fianarantsoa–Manakara railway (DA) page 190

Part Two

THE GUIDE

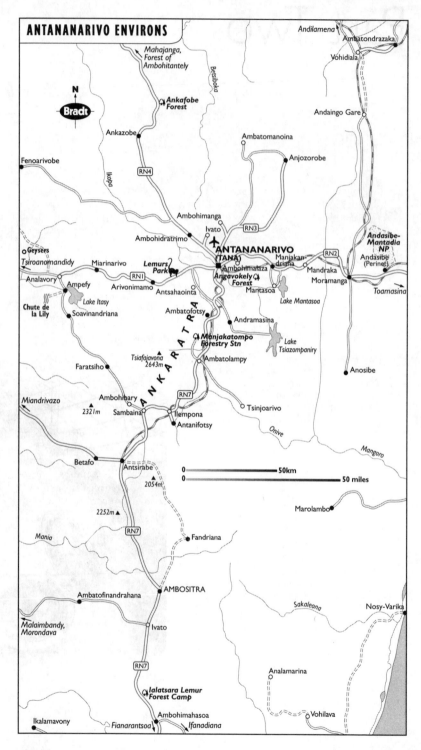

ANTANANARIVO ENVIRONS

N
Bradt

Mahajanga, Forest of Ambohitantely

Andilamena

Ambatondrazaka

Vohidiala

Betsiboka

Ankafobe Forest

Andaingo Gare

Ankazobe

Ambatomanoina

Fenoarivobe

RN4

Anjozorobe

Ikopa

Ambohimanga

Ivato

RN3

Andasibe-Mantadia NP

Geysers

Ambohidratrimo

ANTANANARIVO (TANA)

Andasibe (Perinet)

Tsiroanomandidy

Miarinarivo

Lemurs Park

Manjakan-driana

RN2

Mandraka

Analavory

Ampefy

RN1

Ambohimalaza

Angavokely Forest

Moramanga

Arivonimamo

Antsahaointa

Mantasoa

Toamasina

Lake Itasy

Chute de la Lily

Soavinandriana

Ambatofotsy

Andramasina

Lake Tsiazompaniry

A N K A R A T R A

Manjakatompo Forestry Stn

Faratsiho

Tsiafajavona 2643m

Ambatolampy

Anosibe

Ambohibary

2321m

Sambaina

RN7

Ilempona

Antanifotsy

Tsinjoarivo

Miandrivazo

Onive

Mangoro

Betafo

Antsirabe

0 50km

0 50 miles

2054m

2252m

Marolambo

Mania

RN7

Fandriana

Ambatofinandrahana

AMBOSITRA

Sakaleona

Nosy-Varika

Ivato

RN7

Analamarina

Ialatsara Lemur Forest Camp

Ikalamavony

Fianarantsoa

Ambohimahasoa

Ifanadiana

Vohilava

7

Antananarivo and Area

Looking down from the plane window as you approach Antananarivo you can see how excitingly different this country is. Clusters of red clay houses and steepled churches stand isolated on the hilltops overlooking a mosaic of green and brown paddy fields. Old defence ditches, *tamboho*, form circles around villages or estates, and dotted in the empty countryside are the white concrete Merina tombs from where the dead will be exhumed in *famadihana* ceremonies.

Most people stay only a day or so in Tana (as Antananarivo is often called), but there is plenty to see in the city and the surrounding *hauts plateaux*. A week would not be too long to experience the cultural, historical and natural sites which lie within a day's excursion from the capital. The kingdom of Imerina thrived for over a century before French colonisation, so it is here that the rich and fascinating history and culture of the Merina people are best appreciated.

HISTORY

At the end of the 16th century the Merina king Andrianjaka conquered a Vazimba town called Analamanga, built on a great rock thrusting above the surrounding plains. He renamed it Antananarivo and ordered his palace to be built on its highest point. With its surrounding marshland ideal for rice production, and the security afforded by its position, this was the perfect site for a Merina capital city.

In the 18th century there were two centres for the Merina kingdom: Antananarivo and Ambohimanga. The latter became the more important and around 1787 Ramboasalama was proclaimed king of Ambohimanga and took the name of Andrianampoinimerina. The name means 'the prince in the heart of Imerina' which was more than an idle boast: this king was the Malagasy counterpart of the great Peruvian Inca Tupac Yupanqui, expanding his empire as much by skilful organisation as by force, and doing it without the benefit of a written language. (History seems to demonstrate that orders in triplicate are not essential to efficiency.) By his death in 1810 the central plateau was firmly in control of the Merina and ably administered through a mixture of old customs and new. Each conquered territory was governed by local princes, answerable to the king, and the system of *fokonolona* (village communities) was established. From this firm foundation the new king, Radama I, was able to conquer most of the rest of the island.

Antananarivo means 'city of the thousand', supposedly because a thousand warriors protected it. By the end of the 18th century Andrianampoinimerina had taken Antananarivo from his rebellious kinsman and moved his base there from Ambohimanga. From that time until the French conquest in 1895 Madagascar's history centred around the royal palace or *rova*, the modest houses built for Andrianjaka and Andrianampoinimerina giving way to a splendid palace designed for Queen Ranavalona I by Jean Laborde and later clad in stone by James

139

Cameron. The rock cliffs near the palace became known as **Ampamarinana** (the place of hurling) as Christian martyrs met their fate at the command of the queen.

There was no reason for the French to move the capital elsewhere: its pleasant climate made it an agreeable place to live, and plenty of French money and planning went into the city we see today.

IVATO AIRPORT

The airport has been modernised, with the international and domestic sections separated by a long corridor. Each has its own restaurant. The main one, upstairs in the international section, is quite smart with waiter service and a self-service buffet for 20,000Ar. In the domestic area there is a simple café open from 06.00. As in all airports there are plenty of (expensive) souvenir shops and money-changing facilities. There are also booths for the three cellphone networks where you can buy a SIM card for your mobile phone for around €1 (see page 105).

ARRIVING In the good old days Ivato was like the cottage of a wicked witch, seducing innocent visitors through its beguiling doors. Once inside, only the good and the brave emerged unscathed. Now (sigh) it is much the same as other international airports in the developing world. On arrival the procedure is:

1 Fill in a landing card if you haven't already (usually these are handed out on the plane as part of a little booklet about Madagascar). The questions are straightforward, but be prepared to say where you'll be staying the first night.
2 If you already have your visa, join the left-hand immigration queue.
3 If you do not have a visa, head to the 'stamps for visa' kiosk and pay (see page 87 for prices). The official will stick receipt stamps inside your passport. Then proceed to the no-visa immigration queue, where your return flight tickets must be shown, and a visa will be issued for the exact duration of your stay (maximum 90 days). At the time of writing, in an effort to attract more tourism, visa fees are being waived for stays of up to 30 days.
4 Your luggage should shortly arrive on the baggage carousel (if not, see *Lost luggage* opposite).
5 There are trolleys to take your bags through customs. Show your passport to the official who will ask what is in your bags, but most tourists pass through without having to open them up for inspection. After one final passport check, you're free.

The porters at Ivato are quite aggressive. Be on your guard and, unless you need help, insist on carrying your own stuff. They are well aware that new arrivals are unlikely to have any small change and will often ask for euros, feigning disappointment on being given anything less than a small fortune. Remember even a single euro coin is five or ten times the usual porter's tip in Madagascar, so if you need their services try to have some low-value ariary currency to hand. If you are being met by a tour operator you won't need a porter, so be firm.

You may also be approached by freelance guides offering to organise trips. Some travellers have reported these 'guides' disappearing with their money, never to be heard from again. That's not to say they are all scammers, but do exercise caution and avoid handing over cash upfront to agents not working out of the office of a reputable tour agency.

CHANGING MONEY On arrival most people will need to change money at the airport to pay for a taxi into the city. There is a BNI bank (hours vary to coincide with major flights but the ATM is 24-hour) and SOCIMAD bureau de change (🕐 *24hr*) which tends to have more favourable exchange rates. Think carefully before changing a large amount of cash; just €300 will give you a thick wad of at least a hundred ariary banknotes. There are plenty of places to change money later in the city centre (see page 158).

LEAVING This has been streamlined and is now a normal procedure. You are no longer required to reconfirm for Air Madagascar flights, although you may wish to be on the safe side and also ask for a seat allocation.

You must exchange or spend any unwanted ariary before passing through security; the souvenir shops, bar and cybercafé in the international departure lounge accept only euros and dollars.

LOST LUGGAGE Sometimes your luggage doesn't arrive. These days there is a relatively efficient procedure: at the lost luggage kiosk near the baggage carousel, fill in a form and they'll phone your hotel when the bag arrives. To be on the safe side ask for their phone number so you can find out if your luggage has been traced yet. Depending on the policy of the airline you are travelling with, your bag may be delivered to your hotel once it materialises, or you may have to collect it from the airport yourself. Some airlines now use a system that allows you to track your bag's recovery online.

TRANSPORT TO THE CITY CENTRE (12KM) A comfortable new airport shuttle bus service run by ADEMA (m *032 07 062 56/032 07 063 02*) runs to the city centre after most flights for 10,000Ar, and will make request stops at any hotels *en route*.

Most mid- and upper-range hotels offer airport transfers. Otherwise official taxis should cost no more than 30,000Ar (you may be shown an 'official' price card indicating a higher rate but you can haggle), although outside the airport perimeter you can find taxis willing to take you for 20,000Ar. The trip can take up to an hour, although 20 minutes is possible when the roads are clear (late evenings and Sundays). Experienced travellers can take the local bus for a fraction of the price. It stops at the road junction about 100m from the airport, costs 600Ar, and you can pay for an extra seat for your luggage.

GETTING THERE AND AWAY BY ROAD

The *gares routières* (bus stations) for national *taxi-brousses* are sited on the outskirts of the city and should cost about 5,000Ar to reach by taxi from the centre. Although there is some overlap of destinations served by each station, the main three are **Ampasampito**, 4km east of the centre, the starting point for trips east (Moramanga and Toamasina); **Ambodivona**, just north of Andravoahangy craft market, where you will find services heading north (Mahajanga and Antsiranana) and also some east; and **Fasan'ny Karana** on RN4, 1km west of its junction with RN7, which serves the south of the country (Fianarantsoa and Toliara) and the west.

☞ *WARNING!* Numerous travellers have reported being cheated at **Fasan'ny Karana** station; so be on your guard against overcharging. A favourite scam is for them to draw your attention to Malagasy small print on your ticket that says '*ny zaza 5 taona...*', explaining that this means there is a €5 fee for bags, or there is a 5kg luggage limit. In reality the text states that kids under 5 travel free! This station is also notorious for sellers lying to customers (Malagasy and *vazaha* alike) about expected departure times and the number of empty seats remaining.

GETTING AROUND

Traffic jams and pollution are major problems in Tana. Traffic is often gridlocked on the narrow, hilly streets so it makes sense to avoid vehicular transport when possible. Get to know the city on foot during the day (but carry nothing of value); use taxis for long distances, unknown destinations and always at night.

Taxis are easily recognised by their cream colour. Tough bargainers will pay no more than 4,000Ar for a short trip but most *vazaha* end up paying around 5,000Ar. Prices are higher after dark. Taxis do not have meters so agree the price before you get in. The taxis that wait outside posh hotels like the Colbert are more expensive but also more reliable than those cruising the streets. Check the fare with the hotel receptionist if you think you are being ripped off. The cheaper option is to take one of the battered, old vehicles which wouldn't dare go near a hotel and you have the extra bonus of watching the street go by through the hole in the floor, or being pushed by helpful locals when it breaks down.

The advantage of having no meters is that if the driver gets lost (not unusual) you won't pay any more for the extra journey. Tana's taxi drivers are usually honest and helpful, and can be trusted to get you to your destination – eventually. They will also pick you up at an agreed time.

Local buses are much cheaper, but sorting out the destinations and districts can be a challenge. With some 70 lines operating, and no map of the routes available, your best bet is to ask helpful locals which bus number you need.

ANTANANARIVO (TANA) TODAY

From the right place, in the right light, Antananarivo is one of the most attractive capitals in the developing world. In the evening sunshine it has the quality of a child's picture book: brightly coloured houses stacked up the hillsides with mauve jacarandas and purple bougainvillea against the dark blue of the winter sky. Red crown-of-thorns euphorbias stand in rows against red clay walls, rice paddies are tended right up to the edge of the city, clothes are laid out on canal banks to dry, and zebu carts rumble along the roads on the outskirts of town. It's all deliciously foreign and can hardly fail to impress the first-time visitor as he or she drives in from the airport. Indeed, this drive is one of the most varied and interesting in the highlands. The good impression is helped by the climate: during the dry season the sun is hot but the air pleasantly cool (the altitude is between 1,245m and 1,469m).

Sadly, for many people this wonderful first impression does not survive a closer acquaintance. Tana can seem squalid and dangerous, with conspicuous poverty, persistent beggars and a worrying crime rate.

The geography of the city is both simple and confusing. It is built on two ridges which meet in a 'V'. On the highest hill, dominating all the viewpoints, is the queen's palace or *rova*. Down the central valley runs a broad boulevard, Avenue de l'Indépendance, which terminates at the railway station, now beautifully restored as a small shopping precinct. It narrows at the other end to become Rue du 26 Juin. To escape from this valley means climbing steps if you are on foot, or driving through a tunnel if you are in a vehicle.

It is convenient to divide Tana into the two main areas most often wandered by visitors: Avenue de l'Indépendance and the side streets to its southwest (districts Analakely and Tsaralalana, or the lower town) and the smarter area at the top of the steps leading up from Rue du 26 Juin (districts Antaninarenina and Isoraka, or the upper town). Of course there are lots of other districts but most tourists will take taxis to these rather than going on foot. This can be a challenging city to explore; streets are often unnamed, or change name several times within a few hundred

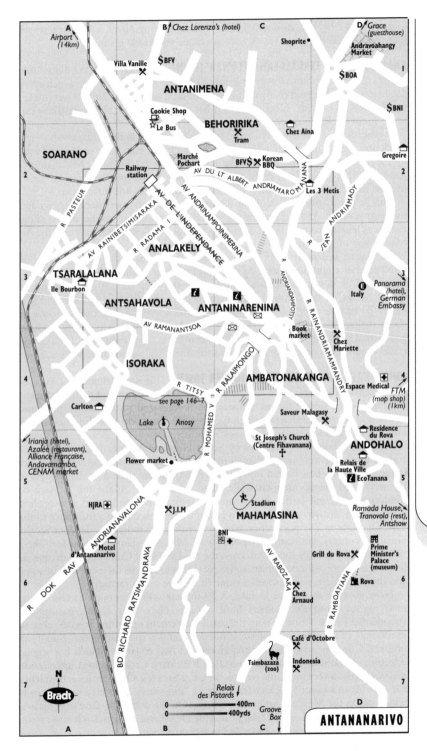

A

Airport
(14km)

B Chez Lorenzo's (hotel)

C

D Grace
(guesthouse)

Shoprite

Andravoahangy
Market

Villa Vanille

$ BFV

$ BOA

ANTANIMENA

$ BNI

Cookie Shop

Le Bus

BEHORIRIKA

Chez Aina

Tram

Gregoire

SOARANO

Marché
Pochart

BFV $ Korean
BBQ

Railway
station

AV DU LT ALBERT ANDRIAMARO

Les 3 Metis

AV ANDRINAMPOINIMERINA

AV DE L'INDEPENDANCE

R RAINIBETSIMISARAKA

R RADAMA I

ANALAKELY

R JEAN ANDRIAMADY

R PASTEUR

TSARALALANA

Panorama
(hotel),
German
Embassy

Ile Bourbon

E

Italy

ANTSAHAVOLA

ANTANINARENINA

AV RAMANANTSOA

Book
market

Chez
Mariette

ISORAKA

R TITSY

AMBATONAKANGA

Espace Medical

FTM
(map shop)
(1km)

Carlton

see page 146–7

Saveur Malagasy

Lake   Anosy

R MOHAMED V

R RALAIMONGO

Residence
du Rova

Flower market

St Joseph's Church
(Centre Fihavanana)

ANDOHALO

Relais de
la Haute Ville

EcoTanana

Irianja (hotel),
Azalée (restaurant),
Alliance Française,
Andavamamba,
CENAM market

HJRA

J.I.M

Stadium

Ramada House,
Tranovola (rest),
Antshow

BNI

MAHAMASINA

Prime
Minister's
Palace
(museum)

Motel
d'Antananarivo

AV RABOZAKA

Grill du Rova

Rova

BD RICHARD RATSIMANDRAVA

R RAMBOATIANA

R DOK RAV ANDRIANAVALONA

Chez
Arnaud

Café d'Octobre

N

Tsimbazaza
(zoo)

Indonesia

Bradt

Relais
des Pistards

0   400m

0   400yds

Groove
Box

ANTANANARIVO

A

B

C

D

metres, or go by two different names. When reading street names it's worth knowing that *lalana* means street, *arabe* is avenue and *kianja* is square.

ANALAKELY AND TSARALALANA (LOWER TOWN) Analakely (which means 'little forest') used to be famous for its large forest of white umbrellas, under which every product imaginable (and many unimaginable) used to be sold. Tana's *zoma* market was famous worldwide. Now most of it has gone and traffic and pedestrians can move more freely.

Avenue de l'Indépendance is a broad boulevard (grassed in the centre) with shops, snack bars, restaurants and hotels along each side. If you start at the station and walk up the right-hand side you will pass the Tana Plaza hotel, Librairie de Madagascar (a good bookshop) and Hôtel de France. Continuing south you reach one of Tana's liveliest bars, Le Glacier, and then you're at the steps up to Antaninarenina.

This is not a street for strolling – there are too many persistent beggars and souvenir vendors. And pickpockets, so walk briskly. Shopwise, the north side of the avenue is less interesting, but it does have several excellent snack bars, and the Air Madagascar office is here.

Tsaralalana is a more relaxing area of side streets to the south of Avenue de l'Indépendance (although maps do not indicate the steep climbs involved if you go too far). Walk down Rue Indira Gandhi, past the shoe shop Aigle d'Or and Le Grand Mellis, to the cumbersomely named Place du 19 Mai 1946. Beyond it is Hôtel Taj and the very popular Sakamanga hotel/restaurant. A couple of souvenir shops are here and, at the top of the road, is BioAroma, which sells beauty products and herbal remedies. But to avoid this steep (rather dull) climb to Isoraka you could double back on one of the parallel streets to Avenue de l'Indépendance.

ANTANINARENINA AND ISORAKA (UPPER TOWN) This is the Islington of Tana; or the Greenwich Village. Here are the jewellers, the art shops and craft boutiques, the atmospheric hotels, the inexpensive guesthouses and a little-known museum. There is also a rose garden where, in October, the jacaranda trees drip their nectar onto the heads below.

Start at the bottom of the steps by Select Hotel on Avenue de l'Indépendance and, as you climb up, marvel that so many men can make a living selling rubber stamps. Visit the Tana tourist office (ORTANA) on the right near the bottom of the steps, and check out their leaflets and information. At the top is Place de l'Indépendance, and Jardin Antaninarenina with its jacarandas and rose bushes. And benches. Nearby is Le Buffet du Jardin where you can sip a fruit juice in the sun. Opposite is the post office where, if you go through a side door to the philatelic counter, you can buy special-issue Malagasy stamps. If you feel like a coffee, yummy cake or ice cream, cross the road to Hôtel Colbert. The street-side bar/café is where conservationists and expats meet to discuss their latest challenges, and the patisserie is where tourists come to indulge their cravings.

Now it's time to explore Isoraka. A 30-minute walk is enough to take in the main sights. From the Colbert head towards Place Lars Dahle, passing the Presidential Palace. Pause to note the small monument opposite the gates, erected in memory of the 50 or so protesters shot dead on this spot during the coup d'état of 2009. Continue towards Radama Hotel and Arts & Jardin, which has a good selection of crafts, then turn left onto Rue Raveloary. Cross the next intersection and you'll pass a very nice little restaurant: Chez Sucett's. On a corner is Résidence Lapasoa. At this point look out for a bronze 'tree' hung with clay pots opposite which marks the Musée d'Art et Archéologie. On the way back, drop in at Galerie Yerden, one of Tana's best craft shops, on Rue Dr Villette, then pick whatever street you fancy to get you back to Place de l'Indépendance.

☞ **WARNING!** Sadly robbery is not uncommon in Tana. Leave your valuables in the hotel (preferably in a safe or locked in your bag) and carry as little as possible. Avenue de l'Indépendance has been a pickpocketing hotspot in the past but any busy area can be risky. If you feel yourself being pushed or shoved, this should arouse suspicion; the normally polite Malagasy are respectful of personal space even in crowded situations and unexpected firm bodily contact with a stranger is often a sign that something is amiss. Also be on your guard inside vehicles, especially taxis, when stuck in traffic. Recent years have seen an increase in thieves snatching valuables through open car windows or by opening unlocked doors.

If you can manage to carry nothing at all – no watch, no camera, no money – you will bring back the best souvenirs: memories. But few (myself included) heed this advice, so just be on your guard and never wander around with passports or a large amount of cash unless they are safe in a money belt.

WHERE TO STAY

New hotels and restaurants are opening all the time in Tana. This selection is by no means complete – be adventurous and find your own.

LUXURY ♛

⌂ **Carayon Suite** [147 F6] At the Colbert (see below). The only true luxury accommodation in Tana. Beautiful views & separate, comfy sitting rooms in the Senior Suite. The marble-dressed bathrooms are almost embarrassingly opulent, with his-'n'-hers washbasins, deep bathtubs & separate showers.

⌂ **Colbert** [147 F6] (124 rooms) Rue Ratsimamanga, Antaninarenina; ☎ 22 202 02; f 22 340 12/254 97; e colbert@moov.mg; www.hotel-luxe-madagascar.com. In a prime location in upper town, the main hotel has standard, comfortable accommodation (including suites with separate sitting room), plus indoor pool, sauna, gym, cybercafé, bar & 3 restaurants. Very French. Recommended for its central location, nice atmosphere, excellent food & decadent patisserie. Credit cards accepted.

⌂ **Carlton** [143 A4] (171 rooms) Rue Pierre Stibbe, Anosy; ☎ 22 260 60; f 22 260 51; e contact@carlton.mg; www.carlton-madagascar.com. 5-star ex-Hilton hotel near Lake Anosy. Skyscraper with lovely views. Its advantages are the on-site offices & shops, restaurants, cybercafé, ATM & swimming pool. Some way from the

town centre but the walk is enjoyable. Credit cards accepted. Airport transfers inc.

⌂ **Royal Palissandre** [147 G3] (36 rooms) 13 Rue Andriandahifotsy, Faravohitra; ☎ 22 605 60; f 22 326 24; e resapalissandretana@hotel-palissandre.com; www.hotel-palissandre.com. Recommended; popular with tourists & businesspeople. All comforts, good food, lovely views & pleasant location within walking distance of town centre. Bar, meeting room, massage, pool & fitness centre. B/fast inc.

⌂ **Tana Plaza** [146 C1] (71 rooms & 2 studios) 2 Av de l'Indépendance; ☎ 22 218 65; f 22 642 19; e contact@siceh-hotels.com; www.hotel-tanaplazza.com. Sgl, dbl & twin rooms with TV, minibar & AC. Studios have kitchenette. Cybercafé. Good restaurant. B/fast inc. Credit cards accepted.

⌂ **Hôtel de France** [146 D3] (30 rooms) 34 Av de l'Indépendance; ☎ 22 213 04; f 22 201 08; e contact@siceh-hotels.com; www.hotel-de-france-madagascar.com. Same ownership as Tana Plaza. Very pleasant with large rooms (some with terrace), convenient central location & very good food. Internet facilities. B/fast inc. Credit cards accepted.

TOP END €€€€€

⌂ **Louvre** [147 E6] (60 rooms) 4 Pl Philibert Tsiranana; ☎ 22 390 00; f 22 640 40; e reservation@hotel-du-louvre.com; www.hotel-du-louvre.com. Convenient, safe upper-town location. Comfortable & well-run, with very pleasant rooftop bar, good restaurant, free internet & massage room.

⌂ **Sunny Hotel** [147 E7] (16 rooms) Rue Ralaimongo (northeast of Lake Anosy); ☎ 22 263 04; f 22 290 78; e sunny@moov.mg. A good location (though not sunny!), handy for both lower & upper town; friendly staff; good food.

⌂ **Pavillon de l'Emyrne** [146 C7] (10 rooms) 12 Rue Rakotonirina; ☎ 22 259 45/46; m 033 02 566

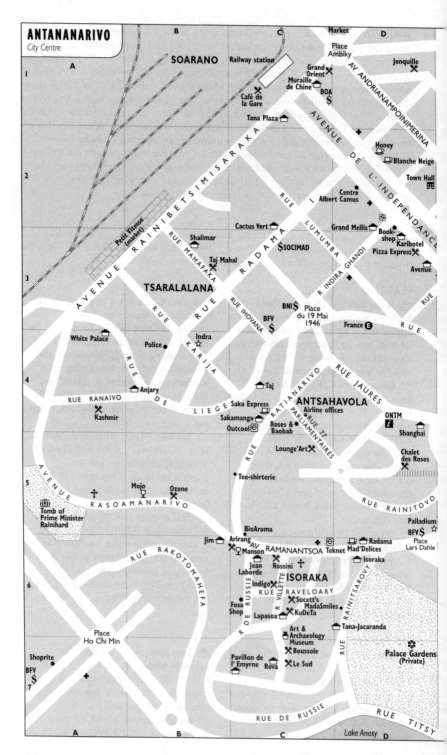

ANTANANARIVO
City Centre

SOARANO

Railway station

Market

Place Ambiky

Jonquille

AV ANDRIANAMPOINIMERINA

Grand Orient
Muraille de Chine
BOA $

Café de la Gare

Tana Plaza

AVENUE DE L'INDEPENDANCE

Honey
Blanche Neige

Town Hall

Centre Albert Camus

Cactus Vert

Grand Mellis

Book-shop
Karibotel
Pizza Express

Avenue

AVENUE RAINIBETSIMISARAKA

RUE MAHAFAKA

RUE RADAMA I

RUE LUMUMBA

R INDIRA GHANDI

Shalimar

Taj Mahal

$ SOCIMAD

TSARALALANA

RUE IHOVANA

BNI $ Place du 19 Mai 1946

BFV $

France E

White Palace

Police

Indra

RUE KARIJA

RUE DE LIEGE

Anjary

Kashmir

Taj

Saka Express

RUE RANAIVO

Sakamanga
Outcool

ANTSAHAVOLA
Airline offices

RUE JAURES

Roses & Baobab

Lounge'Art

ONTM

Shanghai

Chalet des Roses

Tee-shirterie

AVENUE RASOAMANARIVO

RUE RAINITOVO

Tomb of Prime Minister Rainihard

Mojo

Ozone

Palladium

BFV $

Place Lars Dahle

BioAroma

Jim

Arirang

AV RAMANANTSOA

Manson

Teknet

Radama
Mad'Delices

RUE RAKOTOMAHEFA

Jean Laborde

Rossini

Isoraka

Indigo

ISORAKA

RUE VILLETTE

RUE RAVELOARY

RUE DE RUSSIE

Fosa Shop

Lapasoa

Sucett's
MadaSmiles
KuDeTa

RUE RAINITSAROVY

Tana-Jacaranda

Place Ho Chi Min

Art & Archaeology Museum

Boussole

Palace Gardens
(Private)

Shoprite

BFV $

Pavillon de l'Emyrne

Rova

Le Sud

RUE DE RUSSIE

RUE TITSY

Lake Anosy

146

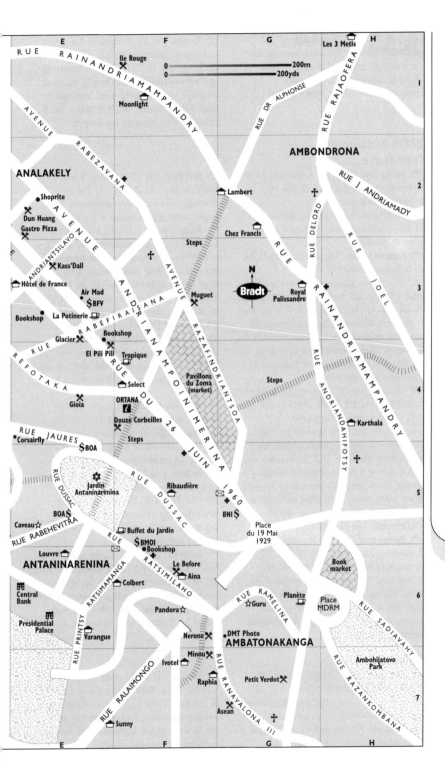

38/032 45 795 99; e reservation@
pavillondelemyrne.com; www.pavillondelemyrne.com.
This charmingly restored 1930s house is quiet
despite its central position; well located for
restaurants. Rooms have TV, minibar & Wi-Fi.

UPPER RANGE €€€€
Town centre

🏠 **Avenue** [146 D3] (7 apts & 8 studios) Av de
l'Indépendance; ☎ 22 228 18; f 22 356 24;
e bj-karim@malagasy.com or
kamoula@blueline.mg. Self-catering apartments with
TV. Long-stay discounts. Bar/restaurant & popular
cybercafé. B/fast inc.

🏠 **Résidence Lapasoa** [146 C6] (10 rooms) 15 Rue
de la Réunion, Isoraka; ☎ 22 611 40; m 032 07
611 40; e corossol@malagasy.com; www.lapasoa.com.
Small & friendly; ideal for lone travellers. Rooms with
TV, safe & Wi-Fi. 'I had a most comfortable stay here.
It is tastefully decorated & furnished, immaculately
clean, with simple elegance. A common room with free
internet encourages interaction with other guests.
Breakfast is in the equally pleasing downstairs
restaurant KuDeTa' (Lee Miller).

🏠 **Sakamanga** [146 C4] (32 rooms) Rue Ratianarivo;
☎ 22 358 09; m 032 02 668 34/033 11 769 27;
f 22 245 87; e saka@malagasy.com;
www.sakamanga.com. Lovely French-run hotel decorated
throughout with interesting historic artefacts. Rooms en
suite with fan, phone, safe, TV & free Wi-Fi. Also suite
with AC, balcony & minibar. Usually full so booking is
essential. The excellent, lively restaurant/bar is popular
& also heavily booked. Movies shown (in French) at
17.00 every Sun (for programme see website).
Cheapest rooms from 34,000Ar.

🏠 **Radama Hotel** [146 D6] (16 rooms) 22 Av
Ramanantsoa, Isoraka; ☎ 22 319 27; f 22 353 23;
e radama@moov.mg; www.radama-hotel.com.
A small hotel in a great location. Sgl, twin & dbl
rooms with hot water, TV, minibar & free Wi-Fi;
some with AC, balcony & view. **Tatao** restaurant
features rather indifferent Malagasy & international
cuisine. Credit cards accepted.

Outskirts

🏠 **Résidence du Rova** [143 D3] (9 rooms) Pl
Ratsimandrava, Ambohijatovo (nr rova); ☎ 22 341
46/49; f 22 239 12; e residence.rova@moov.mg;
www.residence-antananarivo.com. Self-catering
apartments with fully equipped kitchen, TV, phone &
small lounge. Secure parking. Visa accepted.

🏠 **Varangue** [147 E6] (9 rooms) 17 Rue
Ratsimamanga, Antaninarenina; ☎ 22 273 97/251 74;
m 032 05 273 97; f 22 552 30; e varangue@
moov.mg; www.tana-hotel.com. Charming, traditional,
Creole-style home; interesting décor. Comfortable
rooms with fan, heating, safe, TV & minibar. Secure
parking. Excellent restaurant. Visa accepted.

🏠 **Rova Hotel** [146 C7] (17 rooms) Rue Dr
Villette, Isoraka; ☎ 22 292 77; f 22 292 97;
e resa@rovahotel.com; www.rovahotel.com. Smart
en-suite rooms with TV, minibar & free Wi-Fi.

🏠 **Raphia** [147 F7] (11 rooms & 1 bungalow)
Rue Ranavalona III, Ambatonakanga; ☎ 22 253 13;
e hotelraphia@moov.mg; www.hotels-raphia.com.
Nice hotel with lovely views over Lake Anosy from
upper floors; bungalow in garden. Sgl, dbl & trpl
rooms. B/fast inc. Group tours organised to Ifaty in
the south. Restaurant with great Indian food.

🏠 **Les 3 Metis** [147 H1] (25 rooms) Antaninandro
(opposite Jovenna); ☎ 22 359 83/231 06; m 033
05 520 20; e infos@les-trois-metis.com; www.les-
trois-metis.com. En-suite rooms with minibar & safe.
Bar, free Wi-Fi, secure parking & vehicle hire. Visa
accepted.

🏠 **Ribaudière** [147 F5] (11 rooms) Rue Paul
Dussac, Analakely Sud; ☎ 24 215 25;
e laribaudiere@moov.mg. Centrally located hotel;
very comfortable with TV & impeccable bathrooms.
Pleasant, inexpensive restaurant; booking advised.

🏠 **Karibotel** [146 D2] (25 rooms) 26 Av de
l'Indépendance; ☎ 22 665 54/629 31; m 033 11
665 54; f 22 629 32; e karibotel@moov.mg;
www.karibotel.mg. Clean, comfortable rooms with
bath/shower; some with balcony. Lively folk music
every Fri night. Visa accepted.

🏠 **Cactus Vert (Indri)** [146 C2] (15 rooms) 15 Rue
Radama I, Tsaralalana; ☎ 22 209 22/624 41; f 22
624 40; e lecactusvert@moov.mg. Comfortable,
friendly, medium-sized hotel in a convenient location.
Rooms have TV & safe. Small craft shop & lively
cocktail bar. Restaurant serves Malagasy &
international cuisine.

🏠 **Panorama** [143 D3] (55 rooms) Rte d'Andrainarivo;
☎ 22 412 44/412 45/409 65; m 033 11 054 35/033
07 054 35; f 22 412 47; e panorama@moov.mg;
www.panoramatana.com. Spacious, comfortable rooms
with AC. Swimming pool & conference room. Good
quality but not conveniently located.

🛏 **Chez Lorenzo's** [143 B1] (5 rooms) Rte des Hydrocarbures; ☎ 22 427 76; **f** 22 421 71; **e** lorenzo@moov.mg. A peaceful place away from city bustle, 8km from town centre on road to Ivandry. TV. Good restaurant & pizzeria with international & Malagasy food. B/fast inc.

🛏 **Radama House (Aparthotel)** [143 D5] (4 rooms & 10 apts) Rte d'Ambohipo, Ambatoroka; ☎ 22 334 71/249 84; **f** 22 334 94; **e** radama.house@ moov.mg; www.tranovola.com. Caters mainly for business travellers with apartments & studios that can be taken by the week as well as hotel rooms. Excellent **Tranovola** restaurant (see page 152).

MID-RANGE €€€
Town centre
🛏 **Ivotel** [147 F7] (20 rooms) Rue Razafindratandra, Ambohidahy; ☎ 22 227 16; **f** 22 249 29; **e** sitivoltel@moov.mg. Sgl, dbl & twin rooms & suites, most with bath. Visa accepted.

🛏 **Muraille de Chine** [146 C1] (20 rooms) 1 Av de l'Indépendance; ☎ 22 230 13; **f** 22 628 82; **e** murchine@moov.mg. One of Tana's longest-established hotels. Clean, bright en-suite rooms with TV. Friendly staff. Chinese restaurant (☎ 22 281 41) & **Montana Voyage** travel agency on premises.

🛏 **White Palace** [146 A4] (75 rooms) 101 Rue de Liège, Tsaralalana; ☎ 22 664 59/669 98; **f** 22 602 98; **e** white_palace@sohofi.com; www.sohofi.com. Conveniently located in lower town. Sgl, dbl & trpl rooms in 3 categories: gold, silver (with bath) & bronze. B/fast inc.

🛏 **Grand Mellis** [146 D2] (50 rooms) 3 Rue Indira Gandhi; ☎ 22 234 35/625 35; **e** resa@ hotel-mellis.com; www.hotel-mellis.com. A perennial favourite in a good location with rooms from dbl to suite. Some with AC & balcony.

🛏 **Tana-Jacaranda** [146 D6] (7 Rooms) 24 Rue Rainitsarovy; ☎ 24 235 77/22 562 39; **m** 032 07 056 51; **e** tana-jacaranda@tana-jacaranda.com; www.tana-jacaranda.com. Simple clean sgl, dbl & twin rooms with shared bathroom. Guesthouse with very friendly owner & staff. Use of kitchen & dining room with wonderful views. Free Wi-Fi. Visa accepted.

🛏 **Shalimar** [146 B3] (23 rooms) 5 Rue Mahafaka, Tsaralalana; ☎ 22 640 03; **f** 22 689 93; **e** yascom@moov.mg. Dbl, twin & trpl rooms with AC & TV. Some with shower/bath. Its restaurant offers Indian & mixed cuisine.

🛏 **Chez Francis** [147 G2] (16 rooms) Rue Andriandahifotsy; ☎ 22 613 65; **f** 22 613 65; **e** francisvacheresse@yahoo.fr. Super little place in a good location; lovely views over Tana from back

🛏 **Antshow Madagascar** [143 D5] (5 rooms) Ambatolava, Morarano; ☎ 22 565 47; **e** info@ antshow.nu; www.antshow.nu. Not just a hotel but a complete Malagasy cultural experience (see page 163). Trpl rooms. Malagasy meals served with 24hrs' notice. Highly recommended.

🛏 **Gregoire** [143 D2] (30 rooms) Besarety; ☎ 22 222 66; **f** 22 292 71; **e** gregoir@moov.mg; www.hotel-gregoire.com. Near Andravoahangy craft market. Comfy rooms with AC, minibar, TV & safe.

rooms. Rooms en suite with TV. There is also an annexe with spacious rooms. But one recent visitor reported a bedbug problem.

🛏 **Taj** [146 C4] (23 rooms) 69 Rue de Liège, Tsaralalana; ☎ 22 624 09/10; **f** 22 331 34; **e** taj@moov.mg. Comfortable sgl & dbl rooms with hot water. Good restaurant. 6 floors & no lift, so choose your room wisely!

🛏 **Ile Bourbon** [143 A3] (9 rooms) 12 Rue Benyowski, Tsaralalana; ☎ 22 279 42; **f** 22 624 96; **e** hotelbourbon@freenet.mg. The owner is from Réunion. This Creole-style house has dbl & trpl rooms with TV.

🛏 **Aina** [147 F6] (12 rooms) 17 Rue Ratsimilaho; ☎ 22 630 51; **f** 22 212 71; **e** ainahotel@ gmail.com; www.ainahotel.com. Dbl & twin rooms with Wi-Fi. Visa accepted.

🛏 **Jean Laborde** [146 C6] (13 rooms) 3 Rue de Russie, Isoraka; ☎ 22 330 45; **m** 032 02 692 85/033 02 330 45; **f** 22 327 94; **e** labordehotel@hotmail.com. Very conveniently located with rooms ranging from en-suite ones with sitting area & balcony to basic ones with hot shower & basin but shared toilets. Rooms fronting the street can be noisy.

🛏 **Anjary** [146 B4] (133 rooms) 89 Rue de Liège, Tsaralalana; ☎ 22 279 58/244 09; **f** 22 234 18; **e** anjary-hotel@moov.mg; www.anjary-hotel.com. Clean, large, secure & friendly. Rooms with fan, AC, fridge & safe. Room service & lift. Rooms on 4th floor are best but avoid those facing the street. Spa & massage. Their 7th-floor **Terrasse Exotique** restaurant (**m** 033 11 358 29) offers Indian & Malagasy cuisine.

🛏 **Select** [147 F4] (20 rooms) 54 Av de l'Indépendance; ☎ 22 629 16; **m** 032 07 965 18. En-suite rooms with TV. An ugly, rather run-down tower block with little to commend it but its prime location.

⌂ **Shanghai** [146 D4] (19 rooms) 4 Rue Rainitovo, Antsahavola; \ 22 314 72/675 13; f 22 315 61; e shanghai@malagasy.com. Competitive rates.
⌂ **Karthala** [147 H4] (8 rooms) 48 Rue Andriandahifotsy; \ 22 248 95/272 67;

e le_karthala@yahoo.fr. A short walk from Av de l'Indépendance. A secluded enclave in central Tana, the traditional Malagasy home of Mme Rafalimanana. B/fast inc.

Outskirts

⌂ **Relais de la Haute Ville** [143 D5] (9 rooms) Rue Pierre Rapiera, Ambohijatovo; \ 22 604 58; m 033 11 755 42/033 11 776 20; e rhvl@moov.mg. An old colonial house on the way to the *rova*. Comfortable rooms with TV, internet & minibar. Restaurant with Malagasy & European food.
⌂ **Relais des Pistards** [143 C7] (7 rooms) Rue Fernand Kasanga (1km past Tsimbazaza zoo); \ 22 291 34; m 032 46 067 40/033 11 913 26; f 22 629 56; e pistards@freedsl.mg. A friendly, family-style hotel run by Florent & Jocelyn Colney. Sgl & dbl rooms, some en suite. Pleasant dining room & excellent cooking. Florent is an avid mountain biker, so a stay here is a must for those cycling in Madagascar.

⌂ **Grace Guest House** [143 D1] (4 rooms) Ambatobe (nr Lycée Français); \ 24 308 66; m 032 05 308 66; e akany_soa@yahoo.fr; www.grace-guesthouse.com. Comfortable & peaceful in a quiet residential area 10mins from town centre & 25mins from airport. Sgl, twin & family rooms, en suite with lounge, minibar & TV. Malagasy décor, beautiful garden & views from terrace.
⌂ **Motel d'Antananarivo** [143 A6] (32 rooms) Rue Andrianavalona, Anosy (opposite hospital); \ 22 250 40; m 032 05 185 50/033 12 318 31; f 22 358 20; e motelanosy@moov.mg. Rooms have phone & TV. Swimming pool & tennis court at extra cost. Good restaurant serving European/Malagasy cuisine & pizzas.

BUDGET €€

⌂ **Hôtel Isoraka** [146 D6] (7 rooms) 11 Av Ramanantsoa; \ 22 355 81. Simple well-located hotel owned by Sakamanga. Bright rooms with safe & fan; some en suite. Sgl & dbl available but the cheapest rooms are very small. Staff friendly & helpful.
⌂ **Lambert** [147 G2] (24 rooms) Ambondrona; \ 22 229 92; m 032 02 540 89; e hotellambert@yahoo.fr; www.hotellambert.tk. Basic but clean, convenient, good value & popular; be prepared to climb a lot of stairs! Free aperitifs on Sun for guests.

⌂ **Moonlight** [147 F1] (10 rooms) Rue Rainandriamampandry, Ambondrona; \ 22 268 70; e hasinaherizo@yahoo.fr. This old refurbished Malagasy house retains much of its former charm; recommended by several readers. Good for lone travellers (cheap sgl rooms & dorm beds).
⌂ **Jim** [146 B6] (4 rooms) Av Ramanantsoa; \ 26 281 97; m 033 12 277 47. Clean; balconies with sunset views. En-suite showers; shared toilet.

BED AND BREAKFAST Staying with a family, bed-and-breakfast style, is an excellent introduction to Madagascar.

⌂ **Country View** (5 rooms) RN4, Ambohidratrimo; \ 24 231 55; m 033 12 591 00; e cview@madxp.co.za. A spacious, comfortable South-African-owned guesthouse; quite far from Tana centre but only 7km from airport. Some rooms en suite, one with kitchen. €€€€
⌂ **Irianja Guest House** (5 rooms) Avarabohitra, Itaosy; m 033 11 546 56; e info@irianja.com; www.irianja.com. En-suite dbl & twin rooms in a large, comfortable home set in a splendid tranquil garden. Warm hospitality, traditional Malagasy cuisine, massage & botanical garden tours. B/fast inc & meals on order. €€€€
⌂ **Chez Aïna** [143 C2] (5 rooms & 1 apt) Ambatomitsangana; \ 22 641 86; e chezaina@moov.mg; www.chezaina-maison-hote.com; Skype:

chezaina. A traditional house set away from the street down a cobbled alley 15mins' walk from the city centre. €€€€
⌂ **Villa Soamahatony** (5 rooms & 2 studios) Nr Rte Digue, Ankadivory; \ 24 900 60/22 585 18; m 033 11 033 37; e reservations@soamahatony.com; www.soamahatony.com. A delightful villa set in 2ha of grounds with fantastic views over the rice paddies. Owned by a French-Malagasy couple who can arrange car rental for short excursions. Sgl & dbl rooms with shared facilities. €€€€
⌂ **Soamiandry** (7 rooms) Ankadivory, Talatamaty; m 033 11 861 41/034 19 464 15; e soamiandry@gmail.com. Family-run. Joshua & Fara go out of their way to help guests. Garden with pool. €€€

ACCOMMODATION NEAR THE AIRPORT At busy times it can take an hour to get to the airport from the centre of town, so staying nearby is a sensible option if you have an early flight.

🏠 **Relais des Plateaux** (42 rooms) Antanetibe, Ivato; 📞 22 441 18/22; m 032 05 678 93; f 22 444 76; e relaisdesplateaux@moov.mg; www.relais-desplateaux.com. Just 4km from airport in a quiet setting. Sgl & dbl rooms with AC, minibar, safe, TV & Wi-Fi. Children's playground, heated pool, large restaurant, craft boutique & minibus rental. Airport transfers inc. €€€€€–☕

🏠 **Orchid** (68 rooms) Mandrosoa; 📞 22 442 03/05; m 032 07 343 62; e orchid.hotel@blueline.mg; www.orchidhotel-antananarivo.com. New 3-star hotel 3mins from the airport. Restaurant **Vanilla** overlooks pool & nice view. €€€€–€€€€€

🏠 **Combava** (12 rooms) Ambohimanarina; 📞 23 252 49/584 94; m 033 15 584 95; f 23 252 59; e contact@hotel-combava.com; www.hotel-combava.com. Not only is each room named after a different spice or fragrance of Madagascar, but that product inspires the décor of each unique room. Spacious rooms & suites with AC, TV, Wi-Fi, kitchenette & some with terrace. Also excellent restaurant. €€€€

🏠 **IC Hotel** (16 rooms) Ivato; 📞 24 347 67; m 033 07 144 64. Excellent Malagasy-owned hotel with panoramic views & pool. Less than 5mins from the airport. Tours & vehicle rental. €€€€

🏠 **Mahavelo** (18 rooms) Fitroafana, Ivato; 📞 22 004 64; m 032 07 720 68; e hotelmahavelo@netclub.mg or hotelmahavelo@yahoo.fr. Quiet, comfortable, en-suite sgl, dbl & twin rooms with garden view. Restaurant **Alamanda** offers tropical & French dishes. €€€

🏠 **Les Flots Bleu** (14 rooms) Ambohibao; 📞 24 614 17; m 032 02 609 51/033 11 417 66; f 26 019 35; e flotsbleu@yahoo.fr; www.lesflotsbleutana.com. Spacious en-suite rooms with TV, 15mins from airport. Restaurant, bar, pizzeria, pool & Wi-Fi. €€€

🏠 **Sifaka Auberge** (8 rooms) Antanetibe, Antehiroka, Ivato; 📞 22 481 32; f 22 583 32; m 032 07 174 67; e sifaka.auberge@moov.mg. Peaceful, pleasant surroundings. Dbl & twin rooms, some en suite. Good restaurant **Clos Semillon**. €€€

🏠 **Tonga Soa** (4 rooms & 1 bungalow) Mandrosoa; 📞 22 442 88; m 032 02 181 11; f 24 254 50; e tongasoahotel@moov.mg. Pleasant place just 5mins from airport. Clean, nice rooms; excellent b/fast & meals. Also well known for its garden full of endemic plants, birds & jewel chameleons. Booking advised. €€€

🏠 **Hôtel Ivato** (26 rooms) Imotro, Ivato; 📞 22 445 10; f 22 586 93; e ivatotel@moov.mg. Only 900m from airport. Friendly, clean & comfortable. Dbl, twin & family rooms with hot showers. Restaurant specialises in Malagasy & Chinese food. Arrival airport transfer inc. €€€

🏠 **Farihy** (15 rooms & 5 bungalows) Mandrosoa, Ivato; 📞 22 580 76; m 032 40 263 31/032 04 586 73/033 12 727 31. Dbl & twin rooms & bungalows. Meals available. €€€

🏠 **Auberge du Cheval Blanc** (32 rooms) Ivato; 📞 22 446 46; e chevalblanc@moov.mg; www.chevalblanc-madagascar.com. This is one of Madagascar's longest-established hotels, just 1km from the airport. Sgl & dbl rooms set in a pleasant garden. TV lounge. Restaurant with live music nightly & buffet Sun eve. Airport transfers inc. €€€

🏠 **Manoir Rouge** (23 rooms) Ivato; 📞 24 576 96/22 441 04; f 22 482 44; m 032 40 260 97; e madatana@moov.mg; www.manoirrouge.com. A mere 600m from airport. Fairly basic rooms for 1–6 people, some en suite. Snack bar & takeaway food. Cybercafé & TV. Camping permitted. Airport transfers inc. €€–€€€€

🏠 **Raphia** (6 rooms) Mandrosoa; 📞 22 452 97; m 033 12 191 73; e hotelraphia@moov.mg; www.hotelsraphia.com. En-suite rooms colourfully refurbished. Tennis court & trampoline! Restaurant serves Indian & French food. €€–€€€

🏠 **Motel au Transit** (16 bungalows & 6 rooms) Antanetibe, Ivato; m 033 11 338 31. Near airport. Basic but good value. Meals available. €–€€€

✕ **WHERE TO EAT**

HOTEL RESTAURANTS Most of the better hotels serve good food. Expats and Malagasy professionals favour the **Colbert**. The all-you-can-eat Sunday buffet is good value (but beware of the health risks of eating cold buffets – see page 110). There are three restaurants at the Colbert: the smart **Taverne** specialises in French gastronomy; **La Fougère** with its outside terrace is great for lunch; and **Le Cellier** is a more intimate space for evening dining with good wine.

Tana Plaza has an excellent restaurant with live Malagasy music in the bar. On Avenue de l'Indépendance there is the popular **O! Poivre Vert** (\\ *22 213 04*), next to Hôtel de France, and a short walk away is the **Sakamanga** restaurant: crowded and lively, with excellent food, though almost exclusively European clientele. Book ahead (\\ *22 358 09*). Finally, **La Varangue** (see page 148) is rated by resident Lorna Gillespie as the best of all Tana's restaurants: 'sophisticated surrounds, exceptionally well-presented food, well-trained and professional staff'.

SPECIAL TREAT

✘ **Villa Vanille** [143 B1] Pl Antanimena; \\ 22 205 15; ⏲ 11.30–23.00. A fine century-old Tana house specialising in Creole food. Music (traditional Malagasy & jazz) every evening. 'Exceptional food, wine, service & music. The lady owner very much in evidence, talking to every guest & making sure that everything was A1' (Daniel Morgan).

✘ **Chez Mariette** [143 D4] 11 Rue George V, Faravohitra; \\ 22 216 02; f 22 277 19. Beautifully prepared Malagasy food, traditionally served. Described by one visitor as 'caught in a time warp' but I loved the elegant stylisation when I last ate there.

✘ **Tranovola** Rte d'Ambohipo, Ambatoroka; \\ 22 334 71/249 84; www.tranovola.com. This is the place to go for an end-of-trip treat. Superb & unusual Malagasy cooking & music. Manager Elyane

Rahonintsoa ensures an evening to remember. Malagasy buffet Sat eve with traditional *valiha* musicians; piano bar with happy hour Fri eve.

✘ **Grill du Rova** [143 D6] About 100m down from the *rova*; \\ 22 627 24; ⏲ Mon–Sat 10.00–22.00, Sun 10.00–18.00. Excellent food, eaten indoors or outside, with a view over the city. Traditional Malagasy music every Sun from 12.00 till sunset; piano bar Fri eve; music from 19.30 on 1st & 3rd Wed each month.

✘ **Au Bois Vert** Ivato \\ 22 447 25; m 032 05 593 70; e boisvert@moov.mg; www.auboisvert.com. Set in 3ha of pleasantly landscaped surroundings 5mins from the airport this new restaurant offers top-notch cuisine with both inside & outside dining. Also has bungalows & pool.

SERIOUS EATING AND MID-RANGE
Town centre

✘ **Rossini** [146 C6] Av Ramanantsoa, Isoraka; \\ 22 342 44. Upmarket French restaurant. Meat dishes particularly recommended.

✘ **Boussole** [146 C7] 21 Rue Dr Villette, Isoraka; \\ 22 358 10. Stylish French restaurant with excellent food, cosy bar & charming patio for outdoor dining. Especially lively Fri eve.

✘ **KuDeTa** [146 C6] 15 Rue de la Réunion, Isoraka; \\ 22 281 54. Opinions are divided on this upmarket restaurant. Several readers report that it is classy with beautifully presented food; others complain that it is 'dreadfully overpriced' & 'pompously French'. Wi-Fi.

✘ **Indigo** [146 C6] 5 Rue Raveloary, Isoraka; \\ 24 220 52; e fhorm@simicro.mg. Tex-Mex speciality restaurant with Algerian owner/chef. Fantastic food; vibrant & colourful décor; excellent service.

✘ **Ozone** [146 B5] Rue Rasoamanarivo, Isoraka; \\ 24 749 73; m 033 14 999 47; ⏲ 11.00–15.00 & 18.00–00.00. Recommended Thai restaurant with extensive menu & takeaway.

✘ **Nerone** [147 F6] 28 Rue Ratsimilaho, Ambatonakanga; \\ 22 231 18; e smietana@

moov.mg; ⏲ 10.00–14.00 & 18.00–23.00. Small, upmarket Italian restaurant offering a variety of à la carte dishes & Italian wines. Sometimes live music.

✘ **Le Sud** [146 C7] 23 Rue Dr Villette, Isoraka; \\ 22 310 22; ⏲ 12.00–14.30 & 18.00–23.00. Specialises in grills but also serves European food. W/end cabaret.

✘ **Chez Sucett's** [146 C6] 23 Rue Raveloary, Isoraka; \\ 22 261 00. Pleasant, small restaurant specialising in Creole food & often some unusual dishes. Universally praised; excellent service.

✘ **Le Before** [147 F6] 15 Rue Ratsimilaho (upstairs), Antaninarenina; m 034 16 852 89; ⏲ Mon–Sat 12.00–14.30 & 18.00–late, Sun closed. New place with modern black & silver décor. Good view over upper town.

✘ **Grand Orient** [146 C1] Pl Ambiky (nr Soarano railway station); \\ 22 202 88. One of Tana's longest-established restaurants. Chinese, fairly expensive but extensive menu, nice atmosphere & piano music at w/end.

✘ **Kashmir** [146 A4] 5 Rue Dr Ranaivo; \\ 22 328 42; m 032 04 009 19; ⏲ 07.30–21.00. Muslim-run, very good & reasonably priced. Malagasy, French & Indian cuisine.

✗ **Jonquille** [146 D1] 7 Rue Rabezavana, Soarano; ☎ 22 206 37. A small restaurant with imaginative menu, mainly Chinese; especially good seafood. Reasonable prices.

✗ **El Pili Pili** [147 F4] 39 Av de l'Indépendance; ☎ 22 556 14; ⏰ 09.00–00.00. Popular with locals. Low prices & good pizzas.

Outskirts

✗ **J.I.M** [143 B5] Bd Ratsimandrava, Soanierana; ☎ 22 655 15; m 032 07 788 88. Good, though rather overpriced Chinese food. Plush décor & casino.

✗ **Saveur Malagasy** [143 D4] 56 Rue Tsiombikibo, Ambatovinaky; ☎ 22 613 91; ⏰ Mon–Sat 10.00–22.30, Sun closed. About 10mins' walk from

BUDGET
Town centre

✗ **Chalet des Roses** [146 D5] 13 Rue Rabary, Antsahavola (upstairs); ☎ 22 642 33; www.chaletdesroses.com. Delicious pizzas & other dishes. Also has rooms.

✗ **Arirang** [146 C6] Av Ramanantsoa; ☎ 24 271 33. Popular authentic Korean restaurant with good prices.

✗ **Minou** [147 F7] Rue Ratsimilaho, Ambatonakanga; ☎ 22 288 62; ⏰ 08.00–late. Very good budget restaurant with inexpensive, tasty Malagasy, Chinese & European dishes.

✗ **Petit Verdot** [147 G7] 27 Rue Rahamefy; ☎ 22 392 34. Friendly & welcoming with great food at great prices.

✗ **Douze Corbeilles** [147 F4] On the steps up to Antaninarenina. Malagasy-run, non-smoking restaurant (a rarity!); excellent food at very reasonable prices.

✗ **Asean** [147 G7] Rue Ranavalona III, Ambatonakanga; ☎ 22 764 44. Japanese & Thai cuisine including takeaway sushi.

✗ **Lounge'Art** [146 C5] Rue des 77 Parlementaires; ☎ 22 612 42; e contact@lelounge.net; www.lelounge.net. Pub & restaurant. European food served in a nice open area. Free Wi-Fi. Credit cards accepted.

✗ **Dun Huang** [147 E2] 1 Rue Andriamisa, Analakely (nr Shoprite); ☎ 22 669 65; f 22 669 67; m 033 11 188 42. Good Chinese food; large portions.

✗ **Taj Mahal** [146 B3] 15 Rue Mahafaka, Tsaralalana; ☎ 22 309 02; ⏰ 08.00–22.00. Specialises in Indian but Malagasy & European dishes also served, including vegetarian.

✗ **Pizza Express** [146 D3] Galerie Kamoula, 26 Av de l'Indépendance, Analakely; ☎ 22 228 18/310 30;

✗ **Café de la Gare** [146 C1] 1 Av de l'Indépendance (at Soarano railway station); ☎ 22 611 12; www.cafetana.com; ⏰ Tue–Sat 07.00–23.00, Sun 11.00–22.00, Mon closed. Smart new place under same ownership as Princesse Bora on Ile Sainte Marie. Modest portions but quality food. Free Wi-Fi & parking.

✗ **Tram** [143 C2] Casino 2000 Bldg, Behoririka; ☎ 26 388 28; ⏰ Mon–Sat 12.00–15.00 & 18.30–22.00, Sun closed. New restaurant with bar.

upper town post office towards the *rova*. European & Malagasy food in a romantic setting.

✗ **Ocean Planet** PACOM compound, Andranomena; m 032 07 611 30. Mauritian-owned restaurant above BFV bank with stylish décor. Specialities: seafood (including oysters from Mahajanga) & vegetarian.

f 22 356 24. Good pizzas. Stays open late (usually until 02.00 at w/end).

✗ **Glacier** [147 E3] 46 Av de l'Indépendance; ☎ 22 202 60; e hotel.glacier@moov.mg; www.hotel-glacier.com. This old hotel has been a prostitutes' hang-out for years but is lively & fun, often with live music. The cheaper of the 2 restaurants is on the left. Good value & great Malagasy food.

✗ **Kass' Dall** [147 E3] 4 Rue Andriantsilavo, Analakely; ☎ 22 308 13; m 032 41 471 13. Specialises in French salads & sandwiches.

✗ **Gioia** [147 E4] 15 Rue de Liège, Ambatomena (upstairs); m 033 11 943 24; ⏰ Mon–Sat, Sun closed. Serves great cheap food. Good pasta. Owner Marie-Ange speaks English & is very friendly.

✗ **Muguet** [147 F3] Rue Razafindriantsoa. Cheap & cheerful Chinese restaurant at the bottom of the steps up to Hôtel Lambert.

✗ **Korean BBQ** [143 C2] Rue Ranarivelo, Behoririka; ☎ 22 681 88; m 033 07 033 07/033 12 666 88; ⏰ 10.00–14.00 & 17.00–20.00. Traditional Korean restaurant. Customers choose & grill their own food. Great for sushi & some unusual dishes too.

✗ **Ile Rouge** [147 F1] Ambondrona (opposite Moonlight Hotel); m 032 04 059 86/032 04 685 96. Small French-Malagasy restaurant with a good food at low prices.

✗ **Gastro Pizza** [147 E2] Av de l'Indépendance; ☎ 24 215 29; ⏰ Mon–Fri 09.00–00.00, w/end 09.00–02.00. Takeaway pizza & local delivery. Also ice cream & juice. See overleaf for other branches.

Outskirts

✗ **Café d'Octobre** [143 C7] Tsimbazaza (opposite zoo); ☏ 24 200 27; m 032 40 009 63/032 02 400 32; ⏱ 11.30–22.00. European & Malagasy cuisine.

✗ **Indonesia** [143 C7] 35 Rue Kasanga, Tsimbazaza (nr zoo); m 032 40 066 42/032 04 807 27; ⏱ 09.00–00.00. Surprisingly, given Madagascar's history, this is the country's only Indonesian restaurant. Serves seafood if pre-ordered. Evening karaoke.

✗ **Chez Arnaud** [143 C6] 21 Rue Rabozaka; ☏ 22 226 49; ⏱ Tue–Sun 11.30–14.30 & 18.00–22.00, Mon closed. Marvellous pizza & pasta dishes, but quite pricey.

✗ **Chaumière** Rte d'Ivato; ☏ 22 442 30; f 22 489 64. Well signposted on the left as you drive to the airport. Specialises in Réunionese cuisine. Delightful surroundings, good value meals. Very popular with locals & expats from Réunion.

✗ **Azalée** 67ha Sud (nr CENAM crafts market); m 033 12 167 10. A small budget restaurant with good food & fast service. All cuisines, but Chinese a speciality.

✗ **Gastro Pizza** [147 F3] (see previous page) also has branches at Ivato (☏ 22 488 80), Antanimora (☏ 24 571 85), Antanimena (☏ 22 567 73), Soanierana (☏ 22 558 26) & Mahamasina (m 032 53 178 53).

SNACK BARS Avenue de l'Indépendance has a number of eateries: **Tropique** (good pastries and ice cream; also Chinese food), **Honey** (very good for breakfast and ice cream; closed Tuesday), and **Blanche Neige** (for ice cream and pastries; closed Monday). Try **Shalimar** for tamarind juice and **La Potinerie** (near Air Mad). In the upper town **Patisserie Colbert** does excellent pastries and teas; the almond croissants are particularly exquisite.

🍽 **Buffet du Jardin** [147 F5] Pl de l'Indépendance. A convenient place for a fast-food lunch, beer or coffee. Pleasant outdoor tables ideal for people-watching & meeting other *vazaha*.

🍽 **Planète** [147 G6] Pl MDRM (nr book market). Good value fast food. Filling burgers, fries & sandwiches for hungry tourists.

🍽 **Pandora** [147 F6] 1 Rue Rabobalahy, Antaninarenina; ☏ 22 377 48; ⏱ 18.30–dawn. This nightclub serves pizzas, hamburgers & other fast food.

🍽 **Saka Express** [146 C4] ☏ 24 334 39; ⏱ Mon–Thu 11.00–22.00, Fri–Sun 11.00–23.00. Small but good. Pizzas, sandwiches & salads.

🍽 **Mad'Delices** [146 D6] 29 Av Ramanantsoa, Isoraka; ☏ 22 266 41; ⏱ 06.30–23.00. Intimate

eatery with mainly Malagasy menu, luscious pastries & ice cream. Friendly service; spotless restaurant! Really good b/fast.

🍽 **Cookie Shop** [143 B1] 14 Rue Rainizanabololona, Antanimena; m 032 07 142 99; ⏱ 08.00–19.00. American-style coffee, muffins, cookies & bagels for homesick *vazaha*. English spoken.

🍽 **Akany Avoko Café** ☏ 22 441 58. A meal at the café is a natural extension of a visit to this inspiring children's home (see page 164). The café showcases Malagasy cooking by the older girls undertaking vocational training, many of whom speak English. Vegetarians are especially catered for. It is essential to book at least a day in advance.

NIGHTLIFE

♀ **Mojo Bar** [146 B5] Rue Rasoamanarivo, Isoraka; ☏ 22 254 59; m 032 50 294 82; e mojo@ mojo.mg; ⏱ 18.00–late. Popular stylish bar; live music on Fri.

♀ **Manson Drink & Flower Lounge** [146 C6] Av Ramanantsoa, Isoraka; m 032 05 050 32; ⏱ 18.00–late. New bar; good cocktails.

♀ **Glacier** [147 E3] (see page 153). It's worth having a drink at this famous hangout to admire the wonderful 1930s décor & to observe the more disreputable side of Tana nightlife!

♀ **Outcool** [146 C4] Rue Ratianarivo; ☏ 22 553 77. This small internet café near Sakamanga is also a popular *vazaha* bar.

☆ **Le Bus** [143 B2] Av Rainizanabolone, Antanimena; ☏ 22 691 00; e lebus@moov.mg; http://lebus.blogparty.fr; entry 5,000Ar; ⏱ Thu from 19.00 & Fri/Sat from 22.30, but check website as special events regularly change the programme. Tana's best & largest club, attracting a young crowd; has good DJs & latest music.

☆ **Pandora** [147 F6] 1 Rue Rabobalahy, Antaninarenina; ☎ 22 377 48. Notable for surreal décor & UV lighting. Popular spot for clubbers, although unaccompanied men are likely to be hassled by prostitutes. Tends to get going quite late. Outdoor terrace & 3 separate bar areas; snacks served include pizza.

☆ **Palladium** [146 D5] Rue Rabehevitra; ☎ 24 317 76; e palladium.mcar@yahoo.fr; www.palladium-mcar.com; entry 5,000Ar with drink. Lounge bar & dance floor. Fewer *vazaha* here; a more Malagasy clientele. Recently changed name from **Buddha Club** after a complaint from the Thai consulate.

☆ **Caveau** [147 E5] Rue Rabehevitra; ☎ 22 343 93. Dating from 1949 this iconic underground club attracts all walks of life.

☆ **Guru Club** [147 G6] Rue Ramelina; ☎ 24 301 61. Cosy smaller club not far from Pandora.

☞ *WARNING!* Some male travellers have spent the night with prostitutes, only to wake up with a headache and minus their wallets and other possessions. Be cautious about accepting a drink; it may be drugged.

ENTERTAINMENT If you are in Tana for a while, buy a local newspaper to see what's on or keep an eye out for posters advertising special shows or events. Or drop into the Centre Albert Camus [146 D2] on Avenue de l'Indépendance to pick up a programme of concerts and films. Films are dubbed into French.

> ### HIRA GASY   Hilary Bradt
>
> A visit to a session of *hira gasy* (pronounced 'heera gash') provides a taste of genuine Malagasy folklore – performed for the locals, not for tourists.
>
> In the British magazine *Folk Roots*, Jo Shinner describes a *hira gasy*:
>
> > It is a very strange, very exciting affair: a mixture of opera, dance and Speaker's Corner bound together with a sense of competition.
> >
> > The performance takes place between two competing troupes of singers and musicians on a central square stage. It's an all-day event so the audience packs in early, tea and peanut vendors picking their way through the throng. Audience participation is an integral part – the best troupe is gauged by the crowd's response. Throughout the day performers come into the crowd to receive small coins offered in appreciation.
> >
> > The most immediate surprise is the costumes. The men enter wearing 19th-century French, red, military frock-coats and the women are clad in evening dress from the same period. Traditional *lamba* are carefully arranged around their shoulders, and the men wear straw Malagasy hats. The musicians play French military drums, fanfare trumpets, flutes, violins and clarinets. The effect is bizarre rather than beautiful.
> >
> > The *hira gasy* is in four parts. First there are the introductory speeches or *kabary*. Each troupe elects a speaker who is usually a respected elder. His skill is paramount to a troupe. He begins with a long, ferociously fast, convoluted speech excusing himself and his inadequacy before the audience, ancestors, his troupe, his mother, God, his oxen, his rice fields and so on – and on! Then follows another speech glorifying God, and then a greeting largely made up of proverbs.
> >
> > The *hira gasy* pivots around a tale of everyday life, such as the dire consequences of laziness or excessive drinking, is packed with wit, morals and proverbs and offers advice, criticism and possible solutions. The performers align themselves along two sides of the square at a time to address different parts of the audience. They sing in harsh harmony, illustrating their words with fluttering hand movements and expressive gestures, egged on by the uproarious crowd's appreciation. Then it is the dancers' turn. The tempo increases and becomes more rhythmic as two young boys take to the floor with a synchronised display of acrobatic dancing that nowadays often takes its influence from karate.

For a truly Malagasy experience go to a performance of *hira gasy* (see box on page 155). There are regular Sunday performances at Andavamamba, in the front yard of a three-storey grey concrete house set back from the street that goes past the Alliance Française. A few Malagasy flags fly above the high, red brick wall and the entrance is via an unsignposted footpath. It starts at 10.00 and finishes around 16.00. Tickets cost 800Ar. Part of the seating is under a tarpaulin canopy and the rest is in the open. It's an exciting and amusing day out. Have plenty of small-denomination notes ready to support the best performers. There are food stalls with drinks. Any entertainment that allows you to join a Malagasy audience will be worth the entrance fee.

SHOPPING

Note that bargaining is expected only in markets. It is neither customary nor appropriate to bargain in shops.

THE HANDICRAFTS MARKETS While traditional Malagasy handicrafts are available at boutiques across the city, you will find a wider selection and better prices at the artisan markets. Most noteworthy are the embroidery, basketry, woodcarving, minerals and leatherwork (stiff cowhide, not soft leather). Items made from raffia are common, as is carved zebu horn, and the unique Antaimoro paper embedded with pressed flowers.

The most centrally located handicrafts market is at **Marché Pochart** [146 D1], near Soarano railway station. A second one, accessible from Rue Ramananarivo in **Andravoahangy** [143 D1], has a particularly good selection of carved games, including solitaire, chess and the traditional Malagasy *fanorona* (sellers can provide a rule sheet). It is about 30 minutes' walk northeast of the centre. Heading out of the city towards the airport you cannot miss the roadside **Digue** market, which also has an impressive range of wares. And on the east side of Tana in District 67ha is the **CENAM** market with its 'artisan village'. There's also a **bamboo market** near the Carlton hotel.

OTHER MARKETS Most of the handicrafts markets above are parts of larger general markets, which are always intriguing to explore. You cannot walk far in Tana without coming upon a market – and indeed often the streets *in between* are filled with illicit street sellers, their wares laid out on a sheet.

In the centre **Marché Pochart**, and the **Pavillons du Zoma** [147 F4] at the other end of Avenue de l'Indépendance, are both particularly active on Fridays (*zoma* is Malagasy for 'Friday'). They sell everything from fruit and veg to chicken heads and frog legs, as well as non-food items like stationery and clothes. To the west of the station is **Petite Vitesse** [146 B2], where you will find a section selling medicinal plants. **Mahamasina** (market day Thursday) hosts another bustling

---

FANORONA: THE NATIONAL GAME   *Hilary Bradt*

Stroll around Tana – or anywhere in Madagascar – and you'll come across groups of men and boys clustered round a board marked with squares and criss-crosses. Usually the 'board' is scratched in the earth. They are playing a game unique to Madagascar: *fanorona*. It is a game of strategy; in its simplest version it has some similarities to draughts/chequers but for advanced players it is more like chess. In Tana the best place to watch a game in progress is the Esplanade de la Pergola. Carved *fanorona* boards can be purchased at the Andravoahangy craft market.

bazaar on the western side of the stadium [143 C5]. And a colourful **flower market** is held daily to the south of Lake Anosy [143 B5].

SERIOUS SHOPPING The best-quality goods are sold in specialist shops. There are numerous boutiques, particularly in the upper town. You'll find several **Baobab Company**, **Maki** and **Kameleon** franchises, which specialise in T-shirts.

High-quality handicrafts are produced and sold at the **Fihavanana** orphanage [143 C5] and **Akany Avoko** refuge; both places are highly recommended for a visit and buying your gifts here ensures your money goes to a good cause. Details of both organisations are on page 164.

Town centre

Fosa Shop [146 C6] Rue de Russie, Isoraka; ⊕ 09.30–18.30. Quality original T-shirts, including several bearing fossa parodies of the Puma logo.

Tee-shirterie [146 C5] Rue Ratianarivo. The largest selection of Madagascar-themed T-shirts in the city centre.

Galerie d'Art Malgache Yerden [146 C6] 9 Rue Dr Villette, Isoraka (opposite Japanese Embassy); ☏ 22 244 62; ⊕ Mon–Sat. Sells a huge variety of quality products.

Viva Home Galerie Zoom, Ankorondrano; ☏ 22 692 71. An excellent place for wood crafts.

Arts & Jardin [146 D6] 26 Av Ramanantsoa Isoraka (next to Radama Hotel); ☏ 22 295 13; m 033 05 041 74; e artetjardinmalgasy@yahoo.fr; ⊕ Mon–Sat from 08.30. Sells a good range of crafts.

Flamant Rose [147 E3] 45 Av de l'Indépendance; ☏ 22 557 76/24 268 04; m 032 02 354 19; e flamant.rose@simicro.mg; ⊕ 09.00–18.00. A good art gallery.

Roses & Baobab [146 C5] Rue des 77 Parlementaires; m 032 40 615 60; www.rosesetbaobab.com. Carvings, paintings & other work by local artists.

BioAroma [146 C5] 54 Av Ramanantsoa; ☏ 22 326 30; m 032 02 575 23; e bioaroma@simicro.mg; ⊕ Mon–Fri 08.00–18.00, Sat 09.00–17.00, Sun 09.00–12.00. At the top of the hill, this shop has a huge selection of their own brand of natural remedies, essential oils, cosmetics & beauty products. Also aromatherapy, manicure & massage available.

Soarano [146 C1] 1 Av de l'Indépendance. Shops inside the newly refurbished railway station: **Ivahona** sells natural products including soaps, candles, spices & scarves; **Galerie de la Gare** has pricey but top-quality artwork, mainly paintings, sculptures & marquetry.

Outskirts

Lisy Art Gallery Rte de Mausolée (nr Hôtel Panorama); ☏ 22 277 33; m 032 02 444 16/033 14 085 00; e lisy@moov.mg; ⊕ Mon–Fri 08.30–18.30, Sat 08.30–12.30 & 14.00–18.30. A delightful shop, very large & an excellent range of Malagasy products.

Vatosoa Boutique Ilanivato; ☏ 22 320 01. This is the place for exquisite *lamba*. In the same block is **Lambamena** boutique.

Galerie Le Bivouac Antsofinondry (on the road to Ambohimanga); ☏ 22 429 50; e bivouac@dts.mg. Beautiful painted silk items, woodcarvings & other handicrafts of a high quality.

Atelier Jacaranda Antsofinondry. This place specialises in batik. The quality here is excellent & the prices low. The Jacaranda workshop is next to Le Bivouac but sales are made from the gallery 1km down the road, on the other side of the canal.

Sataria Antaimoro paper made by 2 families from Ambalavao. Look for a small green building on the right on the way to the airport. Ask for Tsaramila or Rasoa. The other business is run by Mr Iarivo (m 033 11 386 58).

Le Village Ambohibao (nr airport); ☏ 22 451 97; e village@moov.mg; www.maquettesdebateaux.com; ⊕ Mon–Sat 07.30–17.00, Sun by appointment only. They make scale models of every type of ship imaginable including replicas of some famous ones. Prices €100–1,500. They can package & ship your purchase with DHL so no need to worry how to get it home in one piece. Visits to the workshop are interesting too.

Gasific Talatamaty; ☏ 22 444 24; e centcent@moov.mg; www.madagascar-handicraft.com; ⊕ Mon–Sat 09.30–18.00. More model boats to suit all budgets – over a thousand designs!

Ferronnerie d'Art Andranobevava; ⊕ Mon–Fri 08.00–12.00 & 13.30–17.30, Sat 08.00–13.00 & 14.30–17.30. Original products in metal, stone & zebu horn.

SUPERMARKETS Instead of buying the usual T-shirts and carvings, how about taking back some of the local consumables? If you have a sweet tooth, Robert chocolate is recommended. On my last visit I bought some very good tea (Sahambavy) which is also produced flavoured delicately with vanilla. Similarly flavoured coffee is also available. I always buy wine as well. Maybe it's not the most superior wine in the world, but it'll impress your guests.

The most central supermarket is **Shoprite** [147 E2] on a side street halfway along Avenue de l'Indépendance. Other branches are near the Carlton in a big glass building called Fiaro [146 A7], near Andravoahangy market [143 C1], in Talatamaty not far from the airport, and at Tana Waterfront north of the city centre. The last of these has a nice T-shirt shop and restaurant. **Leader Price** supermarkets in Tanjombato (on the way to Antsirabe) and Ankorondrano (*en route* to the airport) are well-stocked out-of-town stores, as are the **Jumbo Score** supermarkets (at Tanjombato, Ankorondrano and on the Digue road), which have the biggest selection of goods at the best prices.

BOOKS AND MAPS Good bookshops include **Librairie de Madagascar** [147 E3] and **Librairie Md Paoly** [146 D2] on Avenue de l'Indépendance, and the well-stocked **Librairie Mixte** [147 E3] opposite Le Glacier. Near Résidence Lapasoa in Isoraka, **CMPL** [146 C6] specialises in academic books but also has many books about Madagascar. For imported books (mainly French) try **Espace Loisirs** [147 F6] at 11 Rue Ratsimilaho, round the corner from the Colbert. Bibliophiles should also explore the secondhand **book market** [147 H6] at the top of Rue du 26 Juin 1960.

Assorted maps may be found at many of the above, but the best selection is undoubtedly at **FTM** (*Rte Circulaire, Ambanidia;* \ *22 229 35;* e *ftm@moov.mg; www.ftm.mg;* ⊕ *Mon–Fri 07.30–16.00*). They publish a series of 12 folded 1:500,000 maps, together covering Madagascar (10,000Ar each) as well as a broad range of other maps at different scales.

PHOTOGRAPHY Several **Fuji** and **Photorama** shops in Tana cater for digital camera users. Among other services they can transfer your photos to a CD. There is a convenient one just past Le Grand Mellis on Rue Indira Gandhi. Also recommended is **DMT Photo** [147 G6] in the upper town.

CAMPING AND OUTDOOR EQUIPMENT A new outdoor store, **CS Events** (*Rte du Mausolée, Andrainarivo;* \ *22 413 82/24 383 43;* m *032 02 143 79/033 12 576 11;* f *22 416 11;* e *csevents-madagascar@blueline.mg; www.csevents-madagascar.com;* ⊕ *Mon–Fri 08.00–18.00, Sat 08.00–13.00*), has opened on the eastern side of Tana selling camping, hiking and survival equipment: tents, sleeping bags, rucksacks, binoculars, GPS, torches, camp stoves, penknives, first-aid kits, hammocks, mosquito nets, walking poles, and lots else besides. It is not cheap, but they stock quality brands (Garmin, Petzl, Coleman etc) that you will not find elsewhere in Madagascar.

MONEY

Banks open Monday to Friday, and a few also on Saturdays. Most banks in Tana now have ATMs and will change **travellers' cheques** as well as cash (the best exchange rates are usually found at SOCIMAD). Visa is accepted at most banks and you can now use MasterCard at BNI and BOA. **Western Union** services are available at nearly all branches of BFV, BOA and post offices. Check www.bni.mg for the current ariary exchange rate.

$ **BFV** [147 E3] 33 Av de l'Indépendance; Mon—Fri 08.00—17.00 & Sat 09.00—17.00. Main branch. Stays open later than other banks & is the only bank open all day Sat.
$ **BFV** [146 C3] 2 Rue Ihovana, Tsaralalana; Mon—Fri 08.00—16.00
$ **BFV** [143 C2] 20 Rue Ranarivelo, Behoririka; Mon—Fri 08.00—16.00 & Sat 08.00—13.00
$ **BFV** [146 D5] 14 Rue Rabehevitra, Isoraka; Mon—Fri 08.00—16.00
$ **BFV** [146 A7] ARO Bldg (nr Carlton hotel); Mon—Fri 08.00—16.00
$ **BFV** [143 B1] 115 Rue Lénine Vladmir, Antanimena; Mon—Fri 08.00—16.00
$ **BMOI** [147 F5] Pl de l'Indépendance
$ **BMOI ATM** [143 A4] inside Carlton Hotel
$ **BNI** [146 C3] Pl du 19 Mai 1946

$ **BNI** [147 G5] 74 Rue du 26 Juin 1960
$ **BNI** [143 D1] Rue Boudry, Andravoahangy
$ **BNI ATM** [143 C6] Rue Andriba, Mahamasina
$ **BNI ATM** [146 D2] Rue Indira Ghandi (nr Hotel Mellis)
$ **BOA** [147 E5] 2 Pl de l'Indépendance; Mon—Fri 08.00—15.30. Main branch.
$ **BOA** [146 C1] 3 Avenue de l'Indépendance; Mon—Fri 08.00—15.30
$ **BOA** [147 E5] Rue Jean Jaures; Mon—Fri 08.00—15.30
$ **BOA** [143 D1] Rue Ramananarivo, Andravoahangy; Mon—Fri 08.00—15.30
$ **SOCIMAD** [146 C3] 14 Rue Radama I; Mon—Fri 08.00—11.45 & 14.00—16.45, Sat 08.00—11.00. Bureau de change.

COMMUNICATIONS

INTERNET For efficiency the best option is **Teknet** [146 C6] (*32 Av Ramanantsoa, Isoraka;* \ *22 313 59;* f *22 642 95; www.teknetgroup.com*). Internet access costs 9–30Ar/minute (depending on how many hours you prepay). They have many more computers than most cybercafés, including four with qwerty keyboards. They are even open Sunday (afternoon only) and the computers are fast. Teknet also has a small cybercafé in the departure lounge at Ivato airport.

There are good computers with smart flat screens in the cybercafé upstairs at the **Colbert** [147 F6], but it's expensive. The **Outcool Web Bar** [146 C4] (*nr Sakamanga;* Mon—Sat 09.00–23.00, Sun 15.30–21.00) has seven computers (50Ar/minute; cheaper if you prepay) plus additional sockets for laptops.

Nowadays many Tana hotels and some restaurants have Wi-Fi, usually free.

POST OFFICE [147 F6] (Mon—Sat 07.00–15.00) The main post office is opposite the Colbert. There is a separate philately section where you can buy attractive stamps. It is open non-stop to make phone calls – useful in an emergency and much cheaper than phoning from a hotel – and you can send faxes too. Internet facilities can be found here and at some other post offices (look for *cyberpaositra* signs) but the computers can be very slow.

COURIERS

Colis Express e colisexpress2 @ netclub.mg; www.colis-express.net. With 70 branches across Madagascar this is the option for sending parcels & documents nationally. Of a dozen offices in Tana the most central is at 11 Rue Ratianarivo (nr Sakamanga); \ 22 272 42.

DHL 13 Rue Lumumba; \/f 22 241 48; e mgweb @ dhl.com; www.dhl.com.mg; Mon—Fri 08.00—18.00, Sat 08.00—12.00. Also has branches in Ivandry & on Rte Circulaire.
FedEx New Havana Bldg, Ankorondrano; \ 22 321 16/548 00; f 22 607 23; www.fedex.com/mg

TRANSPORT AND TRIP PLANNING

AIRLINE OFFICES

✈ **Air Madagascar** [147 E3] 31 Av de l'Indépendance; \ 22 510 00; f 22 257 28; e commercial @

airmadagascar.com; www.airmadagascar.com; Mon—Fri 07.30—17.00, Sat 08.30—12.00

✈ **Air France** Tour Zital (2nd floor), Rte des Hydrocarbures, Ankorondrano; ✆ 23 230 01/23; f 23 230 41; e mail.tana@airfrance.fr; ⊕ Mon–Fri 08.30–17.00, Sat 08.30–12.30

✈ **Kenya Airways** [146 C4] Rue des 77 Parlementaires (nr Sakamanga); ✆ 22 359 90; m 032 05 359 90; e rajt@moov.mg; www.kenya-airways.com; ⊕ Mon–Fri 08.30–12.30 & 13.30–17.30, Sat 08.30–12.00

✈ **Interair** [143 A4] Carlton Hotel; ✆ 22 224 06; f 22 624 21; e interair@moov.mg;

www.interair.co.za; ⊕ Mon–Fri 08.00–17.00, Sat 08.30–12.30

✈ **Corsairfly** I Rue Rainitovo; ✆ 22 633 36; f 22 626 76; e corsair@moov.mg; www.corsairfly.com; ⊕ Mon–Fri 08.30–17.00, Sat 09.00–12.00

✈ **Air Mauritius** ✆ 22 309 71; e airmauritius@ariomad.com; www.airmauritius.com. Address/hours as Kenya Airways.

✈ **Air Austral** ✆ 22 309 97; e tananarive@air-austral.com; www.airaustral.com. Address/hours as Kenya Airways.

LAND TRANSPORT OFFICES

MadaRail [146 C1] Soarano railway station, 1 Av de l'Indépendance; ✆ 22 345 99; f 22 218 83; e tourisme@madarail.mg; www.madarail.mg. Operators of the line to Toamasina (see page 251).

GasyCarBus Rue Ampanjaka Toera, Antanimena; ✆ 26 317 54; m 032 53 745 07/033 11 417 15;

e tiana_rft@yahoo.fr. Bus services most days to Fianar, Toliara & Toamasina.

MadaSmiles [146 D6] Rue Rainitsarovy, Isoraka; ✆ 26 255 35; m 032 02 468 88/032 40 264 97; e madasmiles@yahoo.fr. Bus services to most major towns.

VEHICLE HIRE Full details on hiring a car or motorbike are given in *Chapter 4*. Large hotels usually also have car-hire agencies.

🚗 **Madarental** ✆ 24 144 95; m 032 47 600 45/033 07 103 50; e madarental@yahoo.com; www.madarental.com. Minibus & 4x4 with or without driver. Rental by the day, month or year.

🚗 **Hertz** SICAM Bldg, 17 Rue Rabefiraisana; ✆ 22 229 61; m 032 04 873 16. Quality vehicles for hire & airport transfers.

🚗 **Soa Car** m 032 50 151 44/032 41 542 93; e soacar.location@gmail.com. Car, 4x4 & minibus hire.

🚗 **Europcar** Rue Dr Raseta, Andraharo; ✆ 23 336 47; m 033 11 321 70; f 23 273 33; e europcar@moov.mg; www.europcar.com/car-MADAGASCAR.html. Various mainly VW vehicles. Online booking.

🚗 **Mad Malin** I Rue Raintovo, Ambatomena; ✆ 22 271 95; m 032 11 004 96; www.oceane-aventure.com. Car, 4x4 & minibus hire arm of tour operator Océane Aventure.

🚗 **Buzzy Bee Rental** Ambodimanga, Besarety; ✆ 22 569 35; m 032 02 371 95; f 22 279 82;

e optimus.group@yahoo.com. Citroën 2CV hire for those on a budget.

🚗 **Madagas-Car-Rental** ✆ 24 375 53; m 032 04 416 80; www.location-voiture-4x4-madagascar.com. Without-driver rentals of 4x4 & other vehicles.

🚗 **Tanalahorizon** m 032 07 545 29; e info@tanalahorizon.com. Tour operator with reliable vehicles & good rates. See ad after page 408.

🚗 **Justin Randrianarison** ✆ 22 472 46; m 032 07 532 19. Driver with Peugeot 505; recommended & speaks some English.

🚗 **Traces** Andraharo; ✆ 23 350 35; m 032 02 272 81; www.traces.mg. Experienced motorbike hire operation owned by a Réunionaise cross biking champion. Guided off-road tours.

🚗 **Madagascar on Bike** Mandrosoa; ✆ 22 484 29; m 033 11 381 36; e manfred@madagascar-on-bike.com; www.madagascar-on-bike.com; Skype: MannieLuft. German-owned motorbike rental & tours.

FIXERS A local guide/fixer can take a lot of hassle out of planning an independent trip, but bear in mind that anyone recommended here will charge more than newcomers whom you have found yourself!

Solofonirina Pierrot Patrick Ambohijatovo; ✆ 22 697 27; m 032 40 699 66. Pierrot often meets flights.

Henri Serge Razafison District 67ha; ✆ 22 341 90

Christophe Andriamampionona ✆ 22 445 08

Serge Razafison ✆ 22 341 90; m 032 02 811 80; e razafisonserge@yahoo.fr

Liva m 032 07 551 46. Recommended English-speaking guide & driver.

Andry \ 24 367 73; m 032 02 583 83;
e he_andry@yahoo.fr. Tailor-made tours of Tana.

INFORMATION AND PERMITS FOR NATURE RESERVES

Madagascar National Parks (formerly ANGAP)
Ambatobe (HQ); \ 22 415 38; f 22 425 39;
e contact@madagascar.national.parks.mg;
www.parcs-madagascar.com. There's a more central
office at Océane Aventures (22 *Rue Ratianarivo*;
\ 22 312 10; f 22 312 22; ⊕ *Mon–Fri*

08.00–12.00 & 14.00–18.00). Permits for the
national parks & reserves may be purchased here
(see page 72), although they are also available at
the local park offices.
WWF Rue Hugues Rabesahala, Antsakaviro; \ 22 348
85/88; www.wwf.mg

EMERGENCIES

The emergency phone numbers are \ 17 for police and \ 18 for the fire service.
Medical services are listed below. To find the current out-of-hours pharmacy rota
check local TV, newspapers or www.moov.mg/pharmacie.php. There is more
advice on health and safety in *Chapter 5*.

MEDICAL

✚ **Espace Medical** Ambodivona; \ 22 625 66/260
97; m 032 02 088 16; e esmed@moov.mg.
Complete medical service includes clinic, X-ray,
home/hotel visits, ambulance & helicopter evacuation.
✚ **Polyclinique d'Ilafy** \ 22 425 66/69/73. Modern
facilities & equipment, helpful staff, ambulance
service.
✚ **Medical Plus** Ankaditoho, Rte Circulaire; \ 22 567
58; f 22 629 71. Reliable 24hr home/hotel visits &
ambulance service.
✚ **Mpitsabo Mikambana** Rte de l'Université; \ 22
235 55; e mm24@moov.mg. Very good inexpensive
clinic.
✚ **Clinique des Sœurs Franciscains** Ankadifotsy; \ 22
235 54/695 20; f 22 230 95. Dr Louis Razafinarivo
speaks English.
✚ **Centre Hospitalier de Soavinandriana** \ 23 645
69/22 397 53. Military hospital with consultation,

dentistry, X-ray, surgery etc. Well set up for
emergencies.
✚ **Jean-Marc Chapuis** 13 Av de l'Indépendance; \ 22
208 88. Dentist.
✚ **Nadia Raboana Rabedasy** 9 Rue La Réunion,
Isoraka; \ 22 358 70. Dentist.
✚ **Leontine Ramambazafy Ralainony** 6 Rue de
Russie, Isoraka; \ 22 263 32. Dentist.
✚ **Pharmacie Métropole** [147 F6] Rue Ratsimilaho,
Ambatonakanga; \ 22 200 25. Well stocked.
✚ **Pharmacie Principale** Rte des Hydrocarbures,
Ankorondrano (opposite Digital bldg); \ 22 533
93/439 15; e pharm.s@dts.mg. The largest
pharmacy in the city.
✚ **Pharmacie d'Isoraka** [146 C6] Av Ramanantsoa;
\ 22 285 04
✚ **Pharmacie de la Croix du Sud** [146 D2] 9 Av de
l'Indépendance; \ 22 220 59

EMBASSIES AND CONSULATES

⊖ **UK** (consulate) Zoom, Ankorondrano; \ 24 521 80;
e ricana@moov.mg; http://ukinmadagascar.fco.gov.uk.
The Honorary Consul is Richard Hyde.
⊖ **USA** Nr Point PACOM; \ 22 212 57;
www.antananarivo.usembassy.gov. Huge new embassy
compound midway between city centre & airport.
⊖ **France** [146 D3] 3 Rue Andriantsilavo,
Ambatomena; \ 22 239 98; www.ambafrance-mada.org

⊖ **Germany** Rue Pasteur Rabeony, Ambodiroatra;
\ 22 238 02; www.antananarivo.diplo.de
⊖ **Switzerland** ARO Bldg, Ampefiloha; \ 22 629
97/98; www.eda.admin.ch/antananarivo
⊖ **Netherlands** (consulate) Galaxy Bldg, Andraharo;
\ 22 224 22
⊖ **South Africa** Zoom, Ankorondrano; \ 22 433 50

WHAT TO SEE AND DO

As if to emphasise how different it is from other capitals, Tana has relatively little
conventional sightseeing. However, there's quite enough to keep you occupied for
a few days.

ORTANA [147 F4] (regional tourist office) \ 24 304 84/22 270 51; e ortana2006@yahoo.fr; www.tourisme-antananarivo.com; ⊕ Mon–Fri 08.30–17.00, Sat 08.00–16.00. Helpful tourist office for Tana & surrounding area conveniently located near the bottom of the steps connecting the lower & upper towns. Good selection of tourist literature & maps. English spoken.

EcoTanana [143 D5] Pl Andohalo; m 032 71 472 65; e ecotanana@ecotanana.net; www.ecotanana.net; ⊕ 10.00–17.00. A network of guides, guesthouses & craftsmen supporting ecotourism in Tana. Visit the project's kiosk near Mahamasina.

ONTM [146 D4] (national tourist office) 3 Rue Elysée Ravelontsalama; \ 22 661 15/22 216 11; f 22 660 98; e ontm@moov.mg; www.madagascar-tourisme.com

ONTM Ivato. Located in the international section of the airport, this branch of the national tourist office has irregular opening hours to coincide with main flight arrivals.

ROVA [143 D5] The queen's palace, or *rova*, the spiritual centre of the Merina people, dominates the skyline of Tana. It was destroyed by fire in 1995, leaving only the stone shell – an act of arson unprecedented in Madagascar's history.

The palace has been closed for restoration since 2005. It may be open again by the time you read this, although at the time of writing work has stopped owing to lack of funds. In any case, it is worth the walk up to the palace for the view and to imagine its former grandeur.

PRIME MINISTER'S PALACE (PALAIS D'ANDAFIAVARATRA) [143 D5] (⊕ *Sat–Thu 10.00–17.00, Fri 10.00–12.00; entry 3,000Ar*) This former residence of Rainilaiarivony (he who married three queens) has been restored and now houses the few precious items that were saved from the *rova* fire, mostly gifts from foreign prime ministers and monarchs (including Queen Victoria). It was built in 1872 by the British architect William Pool. After independence it became in turn an army barracks, law courts, school of fine arts, the presidential palace and (again) the prime minister's palace. It was damaged by fire in 1975 but subsequently restored.

TSIMBAZAZA ZOO [143 D5] (\ 24 517 78/510 74; ⊕ *daily 09.00–17.00; entry 10,000Ar*) This comprises a museum, botanical garden and zoo exhibiting mainly Malagasy species.

The **zoo** at Tsimbazaza (pronounced 'tsimba*zazz*' and meaning 'where children are forbidden', dating from when it was a sacred site) has an extensive collection of animals so is worth a visit providing you don't expect it to measure up to Western standards. Locals love coming here, and put on their best clothes for the occasion. The chief attraction is the ostriches! And why not? An ostrich is a far more extraordinary animal to a Malagasy child than a lemur. An example of the difference between the Western and Malagasy views of animal management, and life in general, was the argument some years ago over a project to have a free-ranging group of lemurs in the park. All agreed on the visitor appeal of the idea, but there was conflict over the components of the group. The American co-ordinator insisted on single-sex lemurs ('we do not want babies when we have a surplus of lemurs') whilst the Malagasy were holding out for a proper family unit: mother, father and children – because that's what happiness is all about.

Among the animals at the zoo are four aye-ayes displayed in a day-to-night house. You can take a guided tour of the zoo (be sure to agree the fee first). This may discourage the sort of 'help' offered to a recent visitor: 'A zoo employee spotted us watching the sleeping fossa. He came over and began throwing stones at the animal to wake it up so that we could get a better photo. We were even more shocked when he insisted we pay for this service! (We didn't.)'

The **botanical garden** is spacious and well laid out, and its selection of Malagasy endemics is being improved with the help of advisers from Kew (UK)

and Missouri Botanical Garden (USA). There's an interesting palm garden and the botanical area provides a sanctuary for numerous birds including a huge colony of egrets. There are also some reproduction Sakalava graves.

The **Museum of Ethnology and Palaeontology** (closed for renovation at the time of writing) is excellent for gaining an understanding of Madagascar's prehistoric natural history as well as the traditions and way of life of its inhabitants. Skeletons of extinct animals, including several species of giant lemur and the famous elephant bird, provide a fascinating glimpse of the Malagasy fauna that the first humans helped to extinction. There are also displays of stuffed animals, but the efforts of the taxidermist have left little to likeness and a lot to the imagination. Do take a close look at the aye-aye to study its remarkable hands. An ethnological exhibit explains the customs and handicrafts of the different ethnic groups.

Tsimbazaza is 3km from the city centre (buses 115 and 125 go there from Avenue de l'Indépendance). There is a good souvenir shop and a couple of snack bars. It's also a fine place for a picnic or you can ask to have your ticket clipped so you can pop across the road to a restaurant.

TSARASAOTRA PARK (LAC D'ALAROBIA) (⊕ daily; entry 12,000Ar) This tranquil paradise of trees and birds, 4km north of the city centre, is owned and operated by Boogie Pilgrim (see page 86). Dominated by its lake, the 27ha park is a classified Ramsar site in recognition of its importance as a wetland habitat. A total of 27 water bird species and 36 other birds have been recorded there, including several herons, egrets and teals. Early morning visits are best for birdwatching. A variety of chameleons are found here too. Near the main lake an information centre has field guides for visitors' use.

CROC FARM (↘ 22 030 71/007 15; f 22 070 49; e info@reptel-mada.com; www.reptel-mada.com; ⊕ daily 09.00–17.00 inc gift shop & restaurant; entry 10,000Ar, under-8s free) Situated ten minutes from the airport, this French-owned place is worth a visit. As its name suggests, it is a working farm, raising crocodiles for leather, meat and other products. But the 3ha park is also a zoo, home to some 80 animal species. Crocs of every size are top of the bill with many hundreds in residence. Visit during feeding time (around 13.00 on Wednesday, Friday and Sunday) to see the most activity. Croc Farm also informs visitors about the threats faced by the few wild crocs left in Madagascar and local superstitions surrounding them. For an unusual culinary experience, try grilled crocodile in vanilla sauce – or cooked some other way – at the restaurant **Coco d'Iles Taverne** (non-croc dishes also available) overlooking the main lake. Other animals on display include lemurs, fossa, chameleons, tortoises and parrots.

MUSEUM OF ART AND ARCHAEOLOGY [146 C6] (17 Rue Dr Villette, Isoraka; e musedar@syfed.refer.mg; ⊕ Tue–Fri 12.00–17.00, Sat–Mon closed) This lovely little museum in Isoraka is supported by the University of Antananarivo and has changing exhibitions of archaeology and ethnology, as well as art.

ANTSHOW (Androndra, about 20mins southeast of city centre; ↘ 22 565 47; m 033 11 258 68; e info@antshow.nu; www.antshow.nu) This Malagasy cultural arts centre is the brainchild of Hanitrarivo Rasoanaivo, the lead singer of Tarika (she also founded the charity Valiha High to promote the teaching of the valiha – see page 104). It comprises a large exhibition space, a performance area, the first professional music studio in Madagascar, and a restaurant serving Malagasy food. Five rooms provide luxury accommodation (see hotel listings). Live music, dance workshops, poetry readings and craft shows contribute to the rich cultural experience of Antshow.

AKANY AVOKO (\ *22 441 58;* e *akanymail@moov.mg; www.akanyavoko.com*) A visit to this heart-warming halfway house and orphanage offers an insight into the tremendous work being put into helping the disadvantaged girls and women of Tana. Akany Avoko is not far from the airport, so why not schedule a visit on your last day to donate your leftover ariary, clothes or medical supplies? Various handicrafts are produced and sold here, including screen-printed T-shirts. And you can also give something back by having a meal at the café. Make sure you allow time for a tour as well as for lunch and shopping; this visit could be one of the highlights of your trip to Madagascar. Seriously! Book at least a day ahead.

Akany Avoko is located about 1km past Ambohidratimo, the last suburb on RN4 towards Mahajanga, about 15km from Tana centre (look for the sign on the left with the small waving hands logo). For more on their work see page 128.

CENTRE FIHAVANANA [143 C5] (\ *22 271 59;* e *bpfihavanana@moov.mg*) Run by the Sisters of the Good Shepherd, Centre Fihavanana has a similar mission to Akany Avoko. Sited near Mahamasina stadium, the centre is set back from the road, just to the right of the orange-painted St Joseph's church. The women here work to a very high standard, producing beautiful embroidery and greeting cards. Judith Cadigan writes: 'We are so glad you suggested visiting the Sœurs du Bon Pasteur. We bought lots of embroidered linens and were shown around the school, shook hands with what felt like most of the 200 children, were serenaded by one of the classes, and were altogether greatly impressed by what the nuns are doing. We took along unused antibiotics and they were glad to have them.' Find out more on page 132.

GOLF CLUB INTERNATIONAL DU ROVA (\ *24 310 55;* m *032 04 210 99/032 41 368 11;* e *golfdurova@moov.mg; www.golf-du-rova.com*) There is a good golf course at Ambohidratimo, ten minutes from the airport. Designed in the 1950s, this 18-hole 72-par 6,670-yard course also has a swimming pool and clubhouse restaurant. Inexpensive lessons and caddy services are available.

HORSERIDING (*Villa Fahafinaretana, Ambodisaha;* m *032 07 039 04/033 08 765 68;* e *fedrova@gmail.com*) The **Ferme Equestre du Rova** at Ambohidratimo offers horseriding around the northern outskirts of Tana, including the Rova d'Ambohidratimo.

POVERTY IN TANA – WHAT'S BEING DONE?   *Hilary Bradt*

The very poor of Tana are known as '*les quatre mis*' ('the four mis') after the Malagasy words *miloka* (gambling), *mifoka* (smoking), *misotro* (drinking) and *mijangajanga* (prostitution). Some 10% of Madagascar's population of 22 million is estimated to live in and around the capital, over half of them below poverty level. And it can be grim. However, encouragingly, more and more local organisations are targeting specific sectors. Two that I know personally are **Akany Avoko** and the **Centre Fihavanana**. Both places welcome visitors, sell an excellent range of handicrafts, and are guaranteed to give anyone's spirits a lift. See page 157.

Another highly effective charity in Tana is the **Frères Missionnaires de la Charité** (*85 Rue Andriamaromanana, Tsiazotafo*) on the hills above the railway station. This is a Charity of Mother Theresa. The brothers take care of orphans and feral street kids, run classes and a hospital, feed handicapped and deprived people and the poor. The sisters of this order are based on the outskirts of Tana where they run an orphanage for about 120 babies and young children up to school age.

AMBOHIMANGA (🕐 *daily 09.00–17.00; entry 7,000Ar*) Lying 21km northeast of Antananarivo, accessed by RN3, Ambohimanga ('blue hill') was for a long time forbidden to Europeans. From here began the line of kings and queens who were to unite Madagascar into one country, and it was here that they returned for rest and relaxation among the forested slopes of this hill-top village. These days tourists find the same tranquillity and spirit of reverence and this World Heritage Site is highly recommended as an easy day trip. The journey takes about 30 minutes on a good road by taxi or *taxi-brousse*.

Ambohimanga has seven gates, though some are all but lost among the thick vegetation. By the main entrance gate is an enormous stone disc which was formerly rolled in front of the gateway each night. A few small shops selling drinks and snacks are just inside. Climb up the stairs to the ceremonial courtyard shaded by two giant fig trees. Ambohimanga still retains its spiritual significance for the Malagasy people. On the slope to the left of the entrance to the compound is a sacrificial stone. Melted candle wax and traces of blood show that it is still used for offerings, particularly in cases of infertility. Rituals involving the placing of seven small stones in the 'male' or 'female' hole will ensure the birth of a baby boy or girl.

Inside the compound The centrepiece here is the wooden house of the great king Andrianampoinimerina, who reigned from 1787 to 1810. This simple one-room building is interesting for the insight it gives into royal daily life of that era. There is a display of cooking utensils (and the stones that surrounded the cooking fire), weapons, and the two beds – the upper one for the king and the lower for one of his 12 wives. The roof is supported by a 10m rosewood pole. A visit here can be full of surprises, as Alistair Marshall recounts: 'Remember this is not a museum, it is the king's palace: he is there. On all my visits there were always several people asking the king for favours. On one memorable occasion I entered his hut to find what seemed like a party in full flow. A man had been possessed by the spirit of a king from the south and he had come to the palace to greet, and be greeted by, King Andrianampoinimerina. The man had gone into a trance and a group of mediums were assisting him. They had found an accordion player and the man was dancing to get the king's attention. We were spellbound by all this, but the Malagasy visitors totally ignored what was going on and continued to look round the hut as though nothing was happening!'

With British help Andrianampoinimerina's son, Radama, went a long way to achieving his father's ambition to expand his kingdom to the sea. His wife succeeded him as Queen Ranavalona. Three more queens followed and, although the capital had by that time been moved to Antananarivo, they built themselves elegant summerhouses next to Andrianampoinimerina's simple royal home. These have been renovated and provide a fascinating glimpse of the strong British influence during those times, with very European décor and several gifts sent to the monarchs by Queen Victoria. French influence is evident too: there are two cannons forged in Jean Laborde's Mantasoa iron foundry. Here also is the small summerhouse of Prime Minister Rainilaiarivony. Understandably cautious about being overheard (he wielded more power than the queens he married) he chose an open design with glazed windows so that spies could be spied first.

Also within the compound is a mundane-looking concrete pool (the concrete is a recent addition) which was used by the queens for ritual bathing and had to be filled, so they say, by 70 virgins, and a corral where zebu were sacrificed. An enclosing wall built in 1787, and faced with a rock-hard mixture of sand and egg, completes the tour.

From a high point above the bath you can get a superb view of the *hauts plateaux* and Tana in the distance, and on an adjacent hill the white mausoleum of the king's *ombiasy* (witchdoctor).

Ambohimanga is an ideal place for a picnic. There is no longer a restaurant here, although a *hotely* by the car park serves Malagasy food. Visitors with their own transport could try **Relais du Rova**, situated 5km away at the main turn-off.

LEMURS PARK (✆ 22 234 36; m 033 11 728 90; e *lemurspark@moov.mg*; *www.lemurspark.com*; ⊕ 09.00–16.30; *in Jan–Mar restaurant is closed Mon; entry inc guide: adults 15,000Ar, under-12s 8,000Ar*) This free-range 'zoo' makes a good day trip, particularly for those on a quick visit who are not able to see lemurs in the wild. Bordered by the dramatic River Katsaoka, the 5ha park is divided into areas planted with endemic flora of Madagascar's different climate zones. Nine species of lemur live free; many are confiscated pets, and this is the first step towards rehabilitation. Feeding times are 10.00, 12.00, 14.00 and 16.00. A few nocturnal species are kept in rather small cages. The park is 22km west of Tana on RN1, clearly signposted on the right-hand side. A shuttle bus to the park runs from outside Le Glacier in central Tana at 09.00 and 14.00 daily.

OVERNIGHT EXCURSIONS

In recent years the region around Tana has been developed for tourism. Travel-worn visitors with some time to spare at the end of their trip should consider spending a day or two winding down in one of the lake hotels at Itasy or Mantasoa.

MANTASOA Some 65km east of Antananarivo is Mantasoa, on the western shore of a large artificial lake, where in the 19th century Madagascar had its first taste of industrialisation. Indeed, industrial output was greater then than at any time during the colonial period. Thanks to Jean Laborde a whole range of industries were started, including an iron foundry which enabled Madagascar to become more or less self-sufficient in weaponry, thereby increasing the power of central government. Laborde was soon highly influential at court and he built a country residence for the queen at Mantasoa.

Many of the buildings remain, and although a one-day visit to Mantasoa is rewarding, a stay of a few days would be even better. Mantasoa can be reached by direct *taxi-brousse* from Tana in about three hours. With your own transport, turn off RN2 near PK 48 or PK 59 and head south about 10km. The village and its attractions are quite spread out, but it is a pleasant area for walking.

🏠 Where to stay and eat

🏠 **Domaine de l'Ermitage** (31 rooms) ✆ 42 660 54. The rooms are so-so but the meals & old-fashioned atmosphere make it well worth a stay. The Sunday buffet is excellent value with a small band playing 1950s songs. It is set up as a country club & offers recreational activities including riding, tennis, boating, country walks etc. €€€–€€€€

🏠 **Riverside** (12 bungalows) ✆ 42 660 85; m 033 12 640 21; e *riversidehotel@moov.mg*. A resort-style hotel with an outdoor eating area overlooking the lake; the hotel of choice in Mantasoa. Pool, ping-pong, bowling, jet ski, canoeing & bike hire. €€€–€€€€

🏠 **Chalet Suisse** (8 bungalows) ✆ 42 660 95. Still Swiss-owned but now managed by Mme Lala Razanadraibe. 'There's a lovely Swiss restaurant serving cheese fondue & raclette – funny place to find it, but delicious.' Meals must be eaten there. The walk here from the *taxi-brousse* drop-off point is a pleasant 1½hrs. €€–€€€

What to see Beside the school playing field is a chimney, once part of the china factory. The cannon factory still stands (part of it is lived in) and the large furnace of the foundry remains. All are signposted and fascinating to see; you can just imagine the effort that was required to build them.

Laborde's tomb is in the cemetery outside the village, along with 12 French soldiers. There is an imposing mausoleum with a strikingly phallic monument. The very active Amis de Jean Laborde (\ *42 402 97;* e *topoi@dts.mg*) are developing the area for tourism. The first project was to restore Laborde's house. It is now a very interesting museum set in a lovely garden. All the labels are in French but a guide may be available to translate. It is worth making the effort to follow Laborde's remarkable story and achievements (see box on page 168).

Boat trips on Lake Mantasoa offer further relaxation in this tranquil area.

ANJOZOROBE This FANAMBY-run reserve on the northeast of Tana is reached via RN3. It comprises 2,500ha of the Anjozorobe–Angavo Forest Corridor, one of the last vestiges of dense forest in the central plateau of Madagascar. Established as a protected area in 2005, the corridor covers an area of 52,200ha, and stretches for over 80km. Nine species of lemur are found here including indri and diademed sifaka. It is also rich in birdlife (82 recorded species) and has 550 species of plant. The reserve itself has a variety of hiking trails and a mountain-bike track.

Nearby **Mananara Lodge** (\ *22 530 70;* e *mananaralodge@boogiepilgrim-madagascar.com; www.mananaralodge-madagascar.com;* €€€€€) is 10km from RN3, a beautiful drive through typical highland villages. Five luxurious en-suite igloo tents with large beds, mounted on a wooden platform, stand under a thatched roof. The food is good – served in a tented dining and lounge area. It is managed by Boogie Pilgrim – see page 86 .

AMPEFY AND THE LAKE ITASY AREA Approximately 2½–3 hours' drive west of the capital, this region offers much of interest as well as a chance to relax in one of the comfortable hotel complexes. Great strides have been made to make Lake Itasy tourist-friendly. There are now comfortable resort-style hotels and the roads have been improved. The drive there along RN1 is interesting, as Derek Schuurman reports: 'One of the first things I noticed on the western outskirts of Tana are some marvellous Merina tombs. About 40km further on, we stopped at the Thursday farmers' market at **Mangatary**, where the local farmers sell produce from colourful zebu-drawn wagons. Another notable feature of this part of the highlands is the groves of tapia trees.'

In addition to the hotels listed below, the Dodwell Trust (see page 77) has clean, budget accommodation with part-time volunteer activities (advance booking essential).

Where to stay and eat

Kavitaha (21 rooms) Ampefy; \ 48 840 04; m 033 09 325 99; e bicrakotomavo@moov.mg; www.hotelkavitaha.com. The hotel offers a range of activities: pedalos, kayaks, pirogues, ping-pong, fishing etc. Ideal for families. €€€

La Terrasse (10 bungalows) Ampefy; \ 48 840 28; m 032 07 167 80; e laterrasse.ampefy@moov.mg; www.ampefy.com. This resort-style hotel is on the right as you drive through Ampefy. Run by Mash (from Tana) & Claude (from France), it has simple en-suite bungalows in a garden & on the lake shore. Activities range from hiking to river-rafting. Highly praised by all. €€€

Relais de la Vierge (6 rooms & 7 bungalows) Ilot Boisé Antanimarina, Ampefy (on the way to Soavinandriana); m 032 02 796 20/032 41 085 29. Ping-pong, tennis, billiards etc; also children's activities. A relaxing & enjoyable place. €€€

Lake Itasy Once you've had your fill of watersports you can do some walking: 'From Ampefy continue south and 1km from the hotel is a turn-off (to the left) to a peninsula. A 5km-long route takes you along the edge of the lake with beautiful

Technology was largely introduced to Madagascar by two remarkable Europeans: James Cameron, a Scot, and Jean Laborde, a Frenchman.

JAMES CAMERON arrived in Madagascar in 1826 during the country's 'British phase' when the London Missionary Society (LMS) had attempted to set up local craftsmen to produce goods in wood, metal, leather and cotton. Cameron was only 26 when he came to Madagascar but was already skilled as a carpenter and weaver, with a broad knowledge of other subjects which he was later to put to use in his adopted land: physics, chemistry, mathematics, architecture and astronomy. Cameron seemed able to turn his hand to almost anything mechanical. Among his achievements were the successful installation and running of Madagascar's first printing press (by studying the manual, since the printer sent out with the press had died with unseemly haste), a reservoir (now Lake Anosy), an aqueduct, and the production of bricks.

Cameron's success in making soap from local materials ensured his royal favour after King Radama died and the xenophobic Queen Ranavalona came to power. But when Christian practice and teaching were forbidden in 1835, Cameron left with the other missionaries and went to work in South Africa.

He returned in 1863, when the missionaries were once more welcome in Madagascar, to oversee the building of stone churches, a hospital, and the stone exterior to the original wooden *rova* or queen's palace built by Jean Laborde in Antananarivo in 1839.

JEAN LABORDE was even more of a renaissance man. The son of a blacksmith, Laborde was shipwrecked off the east coast of Madagascar in 1831. Queen Ranavalona, no doubt pleased to find a less godly European, asked him to manufacture muskets and gunpowder, and he soon filled the gap left by the departure of Cameron and the other artisan-missionaries. Laborde's initiative and inventiveness were amazing: in a huge industrial complex built by forced labour, he produced munitions and arms, bricks and tiles, pottery, glass and porcelain, silk, soap, candles, cement, dyes, sugar, rum... in fact just about everything a thriving country in the 19th century needed. He ran a farm which experimented with suitable crops and animals, and a country estate for the Merina royalty and aristocracy to enjoy such novelties as firework displays.

So successful was Laborde in making Madagascar self-sufficient that foreign trade was discontinued and foreigners – with the exception of Laborde – expelled. He remained in the queen's favour until 1857 when he too was expelled because of involvement in a plot to replace the queen by her son. The 1,200 workmen who had laboured without pay in the foundries of Mantasoa rose up and destroyed everything – tools, machinery and buildings. The factories were never rebuilt, and Madagascar's Industrial Revolution came to an abrupt end.

He returned in 1861 and became French consul, dying in 1878. A dispute over his inheritance was one of the pretexts used by the French to justify the 1883–85 war.

views. But the best view is on top of the hill of the peninsula, where a shrine of the Virgin Mary overlooks the lake' (R Mulder & P Janssen).

Chute de la Lily This large waterfall is 7km from Ampefy. It can be reached by *taxi-brousse* if you don't have your own vehicle. Guides are available but not really necessary. Going towards Tana turn left along the river before crossing it. Keep going till you reach the falls. There is a second large and lovely waterfall about 20 minutes downstream. The landscape here is geologically interesting with hexagonal basalt columns.

Geysers of Andranomandraotra To get here head 4km west from Analavory, then at the sign turn right and continue 8km on a dirt road. You can take a *taxi-brousse* this far. You must pay a small fee to pass this point, from which it is a mere 1¼km walk. The colourful clay formations created by the geysers are most surreal.

TSIROANOMANDIDY Lying 222km to the west of Tana, on a surfaced road (four hours), this town is a pleasant and attractive place to spend a day or two. Its main attraction is the large **cattle market** (Wednesday 12.00 to Thursday 12.00). The Bara people of the south drive huge herds through the Bongolava Plateau to sell at the market.

Of the two basic hotels, **Chez Marcelline** (north of the market, near the airport) seems to be the better.

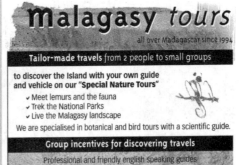

8

The Highlands South of Tana

Many visitors drive the full length of Route Nationale 7 (RN7) to Toliara, either by hired car or by public transport. It is a delightful journey, providing an excellent overview of the *hauts plateaux* and Merina and Betsileo culture, as well as spectacular scenery, especially around Fianarantsoa. More and more excursions off this main route are opening up, ideal for cyclists or backpackers.

FROM TANA TO ANTSIRABE

It takes about three hours to drive to Antsirabe non stop, but there are numerous suggested pauses and diversions so most people take the best part of a day to do the 169km. The photo opportunities are terrific: all along this stretch of road you will see Merina tombs, and can watch the labour-intensive cultivation of rice paddies.

About 15km from Tana look for the huge, white replica of the *rova* (as it was before it burned) across the paddy fields on the right. This was ex-president Didier Ratsiraka's palace, funded by North Korea.

AMBATOFOTSY (PK 21) An interesting diversion for those with their own vehicle is this lakeside resort just over 20km south of Tana. There's a small nature park here with around 160 plant species, a few lemurs and one or two snakes and other reptiles. There is also a museum and a couple of places to stay.

Some 20km further on is the village of **Behenjy** (PK 43), which has been a centre for production of *foie gras* since independence.

AMBATOLAMPY (PK 68) Some two hours from Tana, Ambatolampy and its surrounding villages are famous for their metalwork – mainly cooking pots and kitchen utensils. Cast aluminium souvenirs are often for sale along the main road. The town has a colourful Thursday market and on Sundays there is horseracing at the nearby hippodrome. This is also the starting point for excursions to Tsinjoarivo, with its summer *rova*, and the forestry station of Manjakatompo.

DISTANCES IN KILOMETRES			
Antananarivo–Ambatolampy	68km	Antsirabe–Miandrivazo	246km
Antananarivo–Antsirabe	169km	Antsirabe–Ihosy	449km
Antananarivo–Ambositra	259km	Ambositra–Ranomafana	138km
Antananarivo–Fianarantsoa	412km	Fianarantsoa–Mananjary	197km
Antsirabe–Ambositra	90km	Fianarantsoa–Manakara	254km
Antsirabe–Fianarantsoa	243km	Fianarantsoa–Ihosy	206km

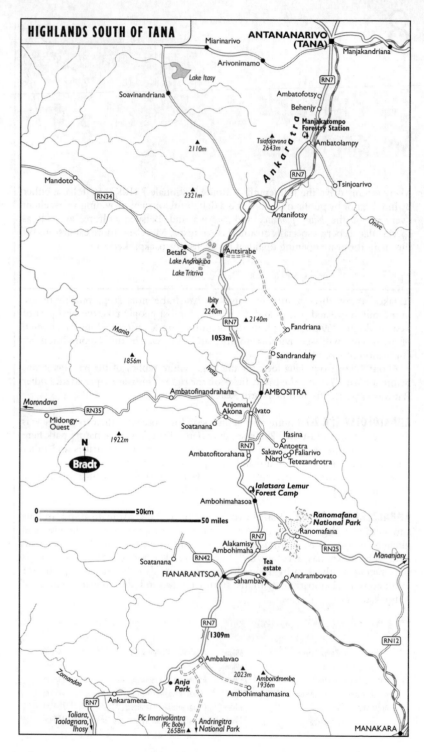

HIGHLANDS SOUTH OF TANA

Miarinarivo

ANTANANARIVO (TANA)

Manjakandriana

Arivonimamo

RN7

Lake Itasy

Ambatofotsy

Soavinandriana

Behenjy

Manjakatompo Forestry Station

2110m

Tsiafajavona 2643m

Ambatolampy

Mandoto

RN34

2321m

RN7

Tsinjoarivo

Onive

Antanifotsy

Mania

Betafo

Antsirabe

Lake Andraikiba

Lake Tritriva

Ibity 2240m

RN7

2140m

Fandriana

1053m

Sandrandahy

1856m

Ivato

Ambatofinandrahana

AMBOSITRA

Morondava

RN35

Anjoman' Akona

Ivato

Midongy-Ouest

1922m

Soatanana

Ifasina

Antoetra

Sakavo Nord

Faliarivo

Ambatofitorahana

RN7

Tetezandrotra

N

Bradt

Ialatsara Lemur Forest Camp

Ambohimahasoa

Ranomafana National Park

0 ———— 50km

0 ———— 50 miles

RN7

Ranomafana

Alakamisy Ambohimaha

RN25

Mananjary

Soatanana

RN42

FIANARANTSOA

Tea estate

Sahambavy

Andrambovato

RN7

1309m

RN12

Ambalavao

2023m

Ambondrombe 1936m

Anja Park

Ambohimahamasina

Zomandao

Ankaramena

RN7

Pic Imarivolanitra (Pic Boby) 2658m

Andringitra National Park

Toliara, Taolagnaro, Ihosy

MANAKARA

Where to stay and eat

🏠 **Antsaha** (27 bungalows) ✆ 44 050 02; m 032 40 564 69/033 12 220 46; e antsaha@ freenet.mg. Off RN7 near **Tombotsoa**, this is a relaxing place to get away from the city. Numerous activities: tennis, ping-pong, badminton, bowling, bikes, swimming pool etc. €€€–€€€€

🏠 **Rendez-vous des Pêcheurs** (7 rooms) ✆ 42 492 04. Renowned for its large restaurant which caters to tour buses (can get crowded at lunch). Rooms are simple but comfortable, mostly with shared bathrooms (with a big bathtub) & a few en suite. €€

🏠 **Manja Ranch** Lot B 153, Mandrevondry; m 033 11 993 70/032 04 648 57; e bijouxline@yahoo.fr. About 2km south of town. Owned by an American-Malagasy couple. Rooms & bungalows. Camping permitted. Bike hire. B/fast inc. €€

🏠 **Njara** The cheapest place in Ambatolampy, close to the market. €

TSINJOARIVO *ROVA* From Ambatolampy a road leads southeast to Tsinjoarivo. Johan and Clare Hermans write: 'Check conditions before setting out; although only about 50km it takes a good three to four hours by car and is not an all-weather road (an alternative road on higher ground bypasses some of the boggiest stretches). The journey is worthwhile for the series of waterfalls and the *rova* of Queen Rasoherina; in her time it took three days from Tana by palanquin. There is a guardian who will show you round the buildings: one for the queen with the remains of some fine wooden carving from her bed, and others for the prime minister, chancellor and guard. Situated on a promontory overlooking the falls, the site has spectacular views.'

MANJAKATOMPO FORESTRY STATION A road leads west and then north from Ambatolampy to Manjakatompo, an hour's drive (17km). The road passes through aluminium smelting villages – worth a stop to watch them at work. Entry to the forest costs 5,000Ar and guides are not obligatory. Walks are well signposted and there was even a handy guide booklet published in 1995, with a good map of the trails, still available from some bookshops in Antsirabe and Tana.

It is possible to get there by *taxi-brousse*, but they don't run every day. Local hotels should be able to find a driver to take you there for around 20,000Ar.

MUSÉE DE LA NATURE (⊕ 08.00–17.00; entry 5,000Ar) Near to Manja Ranch is a small museum with an extensive collection of over 6,000 butterflies, moths and other insects (mainly Malagasy and some French) set in a labelled botanic garden. It is signposted from RN7.

MERINA TOMBS About 15 minutes beyond Ambatolampy are some fine painted Merina tombs. These are on both sides of the road, but the most accessible are on the right.

ANTSIRABE (PK 169)

Antsirabe lies 1,500m above sea level. It was founded in 1872 by Norwegian missionaries attracted by the cool climate and the healing properties of the thermal springs. The name means 'place of much salt'.

For Madagascar, this is an elegant city. A broad avenue links the handsome railway station with Hôtel des Thermes, an amazing building in both size and architectural style, but sadly recently closed down. At the station end is a monolith depicting Madagascar's 18 main ethnic groups.

Antsirabe is the agricultural and industrial centre of Madagascar. It is also the centre for beer: you can smell the Star Brewery as you enter the town. The cool climate allows it to produce apples, pears, plums and other temperate fruit. Indeed it can get so cold that you will need a sweater in the evening if you are travelling between May and September.

GETTING THERE AND AWAY Antsirabe is about three hours from Tana and 5½ hours from Fianarantsoa. Onward travel by *taxi-brousse* costs 7,000Ar to Ambositra and 15,000Ar to Fianar. Heading west costs 15,000Ar as far as Miandrivazo or 35,000Ar all the way to Morondava.

There is currently no regular passenger service by rail from Tana to Antsirabe, but the Trans-Lemurie Express and Micheline trains run some weekends and are now available on this route on a private-hire basis for groups (see page 252).

GETTING AROUND This is the *pousse-pousse* capital of Madagascar. There are hundreds, perhaps thousands of them. The drivers are insistent that you avail yourself of a ride, and why not? But be very firm about the price and be cautious if they want to take you to a different hotel from the one you request: at least one disreputable hotel in town pays *pousse-pousse* drivers a commission for bringing new customers, so they can be quite persistent.

WHERE TO STAY A special feature of Antsirabe is the private guesthouses. These offer a friendly and economical alternative to hotels. Particularly recommended is **Résidence Madalief**, where all profits go to support orphans and homeless women.

Upper range €€€€

🏠 **Arotel** [175 C5] (41 rooms & 4 suites) Rue Ralaimongo; ✆ 44 481 20/485 73/485 74; f 44 491 49; e arotel.inn@moov.mg. Well-situated; comfy rooms with TV, minibar & luxurious bathtubs. Secluded garden with pool (non-guests 2,000Ar).

Mid-range €€€

🏠 **Résidence Madalief** (11 rooms) m 034 08 521 03/034 18 999 54; e residence@madalief.nl; www.madalief.nl. En-suite trpl rooms in wonderful new guesthouse; all profits go directly to social projects of Madalief (see box on page 179). 7km south of Antsirabe (take Ambohimanga turn for 1.5km). Transfers into town arranged.

🏠 **Camélia** [175 C4] (10 rooms) North of Grande Av; ✆ 44 488 44; e camelia@simicro.mg; www.laresidencecamelia.com. A converted villa set in lovely gardens in the French part of town. Rooms in the main house are small, with shared bathrooms; there's an annexe with 2 spacious en-suite rooms with verandas.

🏠 **Avana** [175 B1] (25 rooms) Mahafaly; ✆ 44 492 99; e malalatianadisaine@yahoo.fr. A large hotel near the north *taxi-brousse* station. Rooms have TV, lounge & bath. B/fast inc.

🏠 **Imperial** [175 C5] (32 rooms) Grande Av; ✆ 44 483 33/493 33. Plain hotel with dingy en-suite rooms, some with TV & balcony.

🏠 **Retrait** [174 B4] (22 rooms) Rte d'Andranomadio; ✆ 44 050 29. Down a small path opposite the Total filling station. Comfy en-suite rooms with TV.

🏠 **Trianon** [175 C4] (7 rooms) Rue Foch; ✆ 44 051 40; m 032 05 051 40; e letrianon@ moov.mg; http://letrianon.hautetfort.com. Comfortable en-suite rooms for 1–5 people; TV, safe & free Wi-Fi.

🏠 **Villa Nirina** [175 B3] (5 rooms) Rte d'Andranobe; ✆ 44 485 97/486 69; e bbvillanirina@hotmail.fr. Cosy B&B with dbl & family rooms.

🏠 **Hasina** [175 A3] (31 rooms) Rue Jean Ralaimongo (same building as Courts); ✆ 44 485 56; f 44 483 55; e hotelhasina@moov.mg. Dbl, twin & trpl rooms with en-suite shower; some also with private toilet.

🏠 **Prima** [175 B2] (4 rooms) RN7; ✆ 44 493 02; m 033 19 767 25; e rest.manambina@yahoo.fr. B&B; en-suite rooms with TV. Internet.

🏠 **Villa Salemako** [175 B3] (8 rooms) RN7; ✆ 44 495 88; e salemakojulia@yahoo.fr. A good-value private home; dbl, twin & trpl rooms, some en suite. Spacious lounge & beautiful garden.

🏠 **Diamant** [175 B3] (53 rooms) Rte d'Andranobe; ✆ 44 488 40/494 40; e diamant@madawel.com; www.madawel.com/hd. Big selection of heated rooms, many with fridge & TV. Good-price 'VIP suite'. Cybercafé & nightclub.

🏠 **Bouzou (Shanti)** [175 B1] (8 rooms) Mahafaly, Vatofotsy; ✆ 44 932 44; m 033 03 044 57. Indian hotel; en-suite dbl & trpl rooms. TV for 5,000Ar.

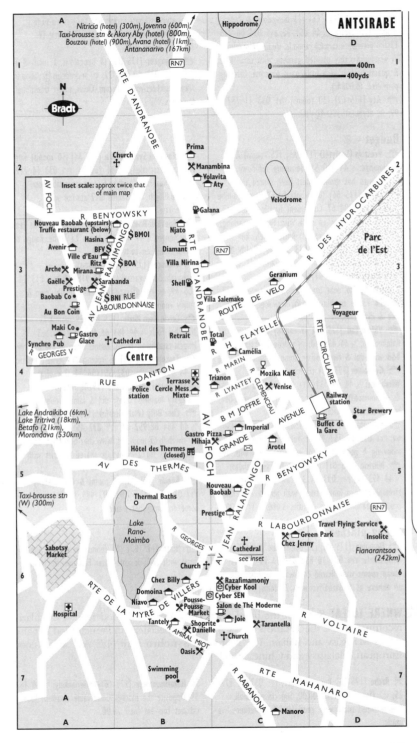

ANTSIRABE

A | **B** | **C** | **D**

Nitricia (hotel) (300m), Jovenna (600m),
Taxi-brousse stn & Akory Aby (hotel) (800m),
Bouzou (hotel) (900m), Avana (hotel) (1km),
Antananarivo (167km)

Hippodrome

RN7

0 — 400m
0 — 400yds

N

Bradt

RTE D'ANDRANOBE

AV FOCH

Church

Prima
Manambina
Volavita
Aty

Velodrome

Galana

Inset scale: approx twice that
of main map

R BENYOWSKY
Nouveau Baobab (upstairs)
Truffe restaurant (below)
Hasina
Avenir
Ville d'Eau
Ritz
Arche
Mirana
Gaëlle
Prestige
Baobab Co
Au Bon Coin
BFV
Sarabanda
BMOI
BOA
BNI

AV JEAN RALAIMONGO

RUE LABOURDONNAISE

Maki Co
Synchro Pub
Gastro Glace
Cathedral

R GEORGES V

Centre

Njato
Diamant
Villa Nirina

Villa Salemako

Retrait

Total

Shell

Geranium
Voyager

RTE DES HYDROCARBURES

Parc
de l'Est

ROUTE DE VELO

R DES HYDROCARBURES

RTE CIRCULAIRE

RUE DANTON

Lake Andraikiba (6km),
Lake Tritriva (18km),
Betafo (21km),
Morondava (530km)

R H FLAYELLE
Camélia
Trianon
Terrasse
Cercle Mess
Mixte
Police
station

R MARIN
R LYANTEY
Mozika Kafé
Venise
B M JOFFRE

AV FOCH

R CLEMENCEAU

GRANDE AVENUE

R BENYOWSKY

Railway
station
Star Brewery
Buffet de
la Gare

Gastro Pizza
Mihaja
Imperial
Arotel

AV DES THERMES

Taxi-brousse stn
(W) (300m)

Thermal Baths

Lake
Rano-
Maimbo

Nouveau
Baobab
Prestige

R JEAN RALAIMONGO

R LABOURDONNAISE
Travel Flying Service
Green Park
Chez Jenny
Insolite

RN7

Fianarantsoa
(242km)

Sabotsy
Market

RTE DE LA MYRE DE VILLERS

R GEORGES V

AV FOCH

Cathedral
see inset

Church

Hospital

Chez Billy
Domoina
Niavo
Tantely
Razafimamonjy
Cyber Kool
Cyber SEN
Pousse-
Pousse
Market
Salon de Thé Moderne
Joie
Shoprite
Danielle
Church
Tarantella

R AMIRAL MIOT

Oasis

Swimming
pool

R VOLTAIRE

RTE MAHANARO

R RABANONA

Manoro

🛏 **Green Park** [175 C6] (13 bungalows & 2 rooms) Tsarasaotra; \ 44 051 90; m 034 08 725 13; e greenparktsara@yahoo.fr. Quaint bungalows in wonderful richly planted gardens with small lake & quaint bridges – a little oasis paradise. Camping permitted (6,000Ar).

🛏 **Aty** [175 C2] (20 rooms) m 033 11 757 99; e atyguesthouse@yahoo.fr;

www.atyguesthouse.mcnyh.org. Various en-suite rooms under same ownership as Volavita; TV 3,000Ar. B/fast inc.

🛏 **Voyageur** [175 D3] (8 bungalows, 1 room & 1 villa) m 032 40 866 22; e androdenis@yahoo.fr; www.chambres-voyageur.com. Clean, smart traditional buildings.

Budget €€

🛏 **Prestige (Soafytel)** [175 A3] (15 rooms) Av Ralaimongo; \ 44 480 55. Becoming run-down. Rooms with hot shower; most have shared toilet.

🛏 **Niavo** [175 B6] (8 rooms) Rue Rakotondrainibe Daniel; \ 44 484 67. Convenient location close to market. Some rooms en suite with TV. Safe parking.

🛏 **Joie** [175 C6] (5 rooms) Antsenankely, Rue Duplex; \ 44 962 47; m 033 37 440 97. Dbl & family rooms, mostly with shared facilities. TV 4,000Ar.

🛏 **Akory Aby** [175 B1] (5 rooms) Miaramasoandro, near *taxi-brousse* station; m 032 40 878 73; e mialifitiavana@moov.mg. B&B. Car hire & cybercafé.

🛏 **Ville d'Eau** [175 A3] (9 rooms) Rue Ralaimongo; \ 44 499 70; e villedeau@simicro.mg. B&B with dbl & twin rooms, some en suite.

🛏 **Geranium** [175 C3] (8 rooms) Rte du Vélodrome; \ 44 497 31; m 033 12 218 66; e geranium@moov.mg. A pleasant guesthouse. Dbl rooms, some en suite.

🛏 **Volavita** [175 B2] (27 rooms) RN7; \ 44 488 64; m 033 11 757 99; e volavita.hotel@moov.mg. A good variety of en-suite rooms with TV.

🛏 **Nitricia** [175 B1] (7 rooms) Miaramasoandro; \ 44 493 02; m 033 14 349 20. Friendly, relaxing atmosphere in a family home with terrace near *taxi-brousse* station. Cooking facilities 3,000Ar; TV 3,000Ar.

🛏 **Nouveau Synchro Pub** [175 A4] (10 rooms) Rue Pasteur Antsenakely; \ 44 962 24; m 033 14 212 09; e souveram@yahoo.fr; www.antsirabe-hotel-synchro.blog.fr. Dbl rooms & 2 studios with kitchenette, fridge & TV.

🛏 **Nouveau Baobab** [175 B5] (12 rooms) Rue Jean Ralaimongo; \ 44 483 93. Above La Truffe. Range of rooms, some en suite with TV.

🛏 **Manoro** [175 C7] (10 rooms) Ambavahadimangatsiaka; \ 44 918 24; m 033 14 905 69; e edm@moov.mg. En-suite dbl, twin & family rooms.

🛏 **Cercle Mess Mixte** [175 B4] (29 rooms) Av Maréchal Foch; \ 44 483 66. One of Antsirabe's longest-established hotels. Rooms often in use by army.

🛏 **Tantely** [175 B6] (6 rooms) Rue Ernest Renan; \ 44 491 37; m 032 55 156 44. One of the oldest houses in Antsirabe (1920); retains its Malagasy features. Comfy dbl & family rooms.

🛏 **Chez Billy (Maharitrafo)** [175 B6] (8 rooms) \ 44 484 88/952 00; m 032 45 740 71; e chezbilly@moov.mg; www.chez-billy.fr.gd. B&B with rooms for 2–5 people; shared facilities with hot water.

🛏 **Avenir** [175 A3] (4 rooms & 1 bungalow) m 032 02 482 70/033 02 495 39. Dbl rooms, some en suite (hot water).

Penny-pincher €

🛏 **Domoina** [175 B6] (3 rooms) Rue Kleber Antsenakely; m 034 10 852 81/034 13 255 41. Cheap rooms with shared cold-water facilities. Also an annexe at Mahazoarivo with 7 rooms.

🛏 **Njato** [175 B3] (10 rooms) Nr Galana. Simple hotel with en-suite cold-water facilities. No food.

✘ **WHERE TO EAT** Some of the hotel restaurants serve very good food. Particularly recommended is the **Trianon** [175 C4], which specialises in French food but also serves Malagasy and Italian. The **Nouveau Synchro Pub** [175 A4] serves good European, Malagasy and Chinese food.

✘ **Arche** [175 A3] Rue Stavanger; m 032 02 479 25; ⊕ Mon–Sat 11.30–00.00, Sun closed. Small, French-owned place with good food & sometimes live music.

✘ **Razafimamonjy** [175 C6] Antsenankely; \ 44 483 53. Opposite the market. Good-value excellent food & cabaret Tue–Sat from 20.00.

✕ **Manambina** [175 B2] Rte d'Antananarivo; ☎ 44 493 02; ⏱ Tue–Sun 11.00–14.30 & 17.30–21.00, Mon closed. Malagasy, French, Chinese & vegetarian dishes.

✕ **Truffe** [175 B3] Rue Jean Ralaimongo; ▥ 033 11 335 55. Below Nouveau Baobab. Restaurant, snack bar & patisserie.

✕ **Chez Jenny** [175 C6] ▥ 033 12 127 78/032 07 751 16; ⏱ Tue–Sun, Mon closed. Very homely bar, creperie & pizzeria. Much recommended.

✕ **Insolite** [175 D6] RN7; ▥ 032 02 158 14; ⏱ Tue–Sun 11.00–15.00 & 17.00–late, Mon closed. Bar & restaurant with recreation park (mini-golf, bowling, badminton etc). Malagasy & European food.

✕ **Venise** [175 C4] Nr railway station; ▥ 034 04 792 27/033 11 411 61; ⏱ 08.00–00.00. Bar & restaurant; good atmosphere; pool table.

✕ **Gaëlle** [175 A3] ⏱ Sun–Fri 06.00–00.00, Sat closed. Snack bar & Chinese food. Also bike hire (till 18.00).

✕ **Tarantella** [175 C6] ▥ 033 11 520 89. Restaurant & piano bar with pool table.

✕ **Mihaja** [175 C5] ☎ 44 914 90; ⏱ Wed–Mon 07.00–21.00, Tue closed. Reasonable restaurant.

✕ **Sarabanda** [175 A3] ▥ 032 51 822 95/032 44 173 07; ⏱ 10.00–late. Small Italian restaurant with pizza & Malagasy food. Cocktail bar.

✕ **Oasis** [175 B7] ▥ 032 07 591 56; ⏱ 11.00–21.00. Small restaurant with extensive Chinese menu.

✕ **Pousse-Pousse** [175 B6] ▥ 032 40 275 26/032 07 191 97; ⏱ Thu–Tue 11.00–22.30, Wed closed. Restaurant alongside the market. Cocktails & live music.

✕ **Danielle** [175 B7] ⏱ Mon & Wed–Sat 10.00–14.00 & 17.00–21.00, Sun 16.00–21.00, Tue closed. Simple restaurant; good prices.

✕ **Terrasse** [175 B4] 5 Rue Foch ☎/f 44 480 66; ▥ 034 02 003 02/034 08 724 55; ⏱ 11.00–14.30 & 18.30–22.00. Restaurant, pizzeria & cybercafé.

✕ **Jovenna** [175 B1] A surprisingly good & very inexpensive eatery at the fuel station.

▭ **Mirana** [175 A3] Av Jean Ralaimongo; ☎ 44 491 81; ▥ 033 11 044 28. Good for b/fast & take-away meals including pizza, ice cream & pastries.

▭ **Au Bon Coin** [175 A3] Rue Stavanger; ☎ 44 492 48. Inexpensive & simple but tasty Malagasy & Chinese food.

▭ **Ritz** [175 A3] ☎ 44 490 27. Snack bar with sandwiches, ice cream, pizza & fries.

▭ **Gastro Pizza** [175 C5] ⏱ 10.00–22.00. Ice cream & pizza, including takeaway.

▭ **Gastro Glace** [175 A4] Roadside kiosk with juice & more than a dozen flavours of ice cream.

NIGHTLIFE The main nightclub is **Tahiti** at Hôtel Diamant [175 B3], which has been running for decades. It's open every night from 21.00. Another discotheque is **Atlas**, at the defunct Ritz cinema [175 A3] opposite BNI bank. **Mozika Kafe** [175 C4] (▥ 032 53 443 53/034 10 423 17), near the railway station, has live music in the evenings and karaoke each afternoon.

INTERNET

🖳 **Cyber Kool** [175 C6] ⏱ 08.00–00.00. Has 11 computers & costs 30Ar/min. Quite fast & if you stay long enough (3hrs) you get a free drink.

🖳 **Cyber SEN** [175 B6] ☎ 44 101 14/965 73; ⏱ Mon–Sat 08.00–18.00, Sun closed. 10 computers; 30Ar/min.

🖳 **Multi-Service** [175 B4] At Terrasse restaurant; ⏱ 08.00–12.00 & 14.00–20.00. 30Ar/min.

SHOPPING For groceries and general supplies, the **Shoprite** supermarket [175 C6] near the market is the best stocked (⏱ *Mon–Sat 08.00–19.00, Sun 08.30–13.00*).

Several nice **handicraft boutiques** are centrally located on the same street as the Arche, a restaurant which has **paintings** by local artists for sale.

WHAT TO SEE AND DO Saturday is market day in Antsirabe, an echo of Tana before they abolished the *zoma* but with an even greater cross section of activities. It's enclosed in a walled area of the city on the hill before the road to Lake Tritriva.

Workshops Antsirabe has a thriving handicrafts sector and it's well worth visiting the workshops to see the skill and ingenuity of the craftsmen. Local handicrafts and products include jewellery made from zebu horn, toys crafted from old tin cans, wooden carvings, billiard tables, polished minerals, embroidered tablecloths and clothing. You can take a *pousse-pousse* tour round several workshops. The demonstrations are generally free but you are expected to buy something after.

Kololandy, situated 800m west of the town centre, does traditional weaving of silk, cotton, sisal and raffia (m *032 07 927 76/033 11 921 77*; e *odilerao@yahoo.fr*; *www.kololandy.com*; ⊕ *08.00–17.00*).

It is also possible to visit local producers to see wine, beer (see below), honey, cheese (*www.lactimad.com*), and sweets (*Chez Marcel*; \ *44 499 71*; ⊕ *05.00–13.00*) being made.

Star Brewery [175 D4] Don't miss a visit to this factory to see the famous Three Horses Beer in production. Tours are only possible on Tuesday/Wednesday/Thursday at 09.00 and 14.00 and it is necessary to book in advance (\ *44 481 71*; e *a.razafindrabe@star.mg*).

TOURIST OFFICE, TOUR OPERATORS AND VEHICLE HIRE

Z ORTVA (regional tourist office) m 032 07 186 42; e etravel@moov.mg

Rando Raid Madagascar [175 A3] m 032 04 900 21; e randoraidmadagascar@yahoo.fr. Opposite Arche. Bike & motorbike hire, horseriding, microlights, trekking (guided & unguided), tent hire & multi-day tours.

DiscoverMad [175 B3] m 033 12 232 08/034 10 145 77; e discovermad@yahoo.com. Based at Nouveau Baobab. Small group exploratory tours. Boat trips on the Tsiribihina & visits to Tsingy de Bemaraha.

Red Island Tours [175 A3] Next to Ville d'Eau; m 033 14 417 03/032 52 872 99; e lucky.adventures@mail.org; ⊕ 08.00–18.00.

Trips to *tsingy*, Tsiribihina & Baobabs Amoureux; horseriding; bike hire; camping trips.

RaVaKa [175 A3] Tombotsoa Bldg (next to Arche); \ 44 498 87; m 032 42 638 22/034 01 683 47/033 12 462 75; e ravekarando1@yahoo.fr; ⊕ Mon–Sat 08.30–18.00. Trips of 1–4 days around local village communities to see Malagasy way of life.

Travel Flying Service [175 D6] m 033 11 177 70/032 40 199 90; f 44 498 03; e tfsmadagascar@yahoo.fr. Travel agency, car hire, Tsiribihina cruises & fishing trips.

Aina Princy Andriambololona m 032 50 806 53/034 08 704 95; e jeuneguide@yahoo.fr. Local English-speaking guide.

BICYCLE HIRE [175 C6] Rabemananjara Mamisoa is your man. Find him at the hotel Green Park (*or* m *032 02 176 05*; e *rabemananjaram@yahoo.fr*). 'He has a stack of good bikes which he hires out for a reasonable price. He provided a good map and even gave me a puncture repair kit and tools for no extra cost. A lovely bloke!' (Stuart Riddle). Mamisoa can also organise excursions on foot, by bike or by car, or even trekking trips further afield.

EXCURSIONS FROM ANTSIRABE

Lakes Andraikiba and Tritriva Just 7km west of Antsirabe, **Lake Andraikiba** is a large volcanic lake often overlooked in favour of the more spectacular **Lake Tritriva**. The scenery here is picturesque and the area very peaceful. *Taxi-brousses* heading for Betafo pass close to the lake, or you can go by hired bicycle as a day trip – or longer if you bring a tent. Alternative accommodation is available at **Dera**, a mid-range hotel with rooms and bungalows on the lake shore (\ *44 052 42/938 01*).

Lake Tritriva's name comes from *tritry* – the Malagasy word for the ridge on the back of a chameleon(!) – and *iva*, 'deep'. And this emerald-green crater lake is indeed deep – 80m, some say. It is reached by continuing past Lake Andraikiba for 12km on a rough, steep road (4x4 only) past small villages of waving kids. You will notice that these villages are relatively prosperous-looking for Madagascar; they grow the barley for the Star Brewery.

Apart from the sheer beauty of Lake Tritriva (the best light for photography is in the morning), there are all sorts of interesting features and legends. The water level rises in the dry season and debris thrown into the lake has reappeared down in the valley, supporting the theory of underground water channels.

Look across the lake and you'll see two thorn trees with intertwined branches growing on a ledge above the water. It is said that these are two lovers, forbidden to marry by their parents, who drowned themselves in Lake Tritriva. When the branches are cut, blood oozes out, so they say. You can walk right round the lake for impressive views. There is an entrance fee of 2,500Ar.

Betafo About 22km west of Antsirabe, off the tarred road to Morondava, lies Betafo, a town with typical highlands red-brick churches and houses. Dotted among the houses are *vatolahy*, standing stones erected to commemorate warrior chieftains. It is off the normal tourist circuit, and gives you an excellent insight into the Merina way of life. Monday is market day. There is no hotel in Betafo but you should be able to find a room by asking around.

At one end of the town is the crater lake **Tatamarina**. From there it is a walk of about 3km to the **Antafofo** waterfalls among beautiful views of rice fields and volcanic hills. You will need to find someone to show you the way. 'It's very inviting for a swim,' observed reader Luc Selleslagh, 'but they told me there are ghosts in the pool under the falls which will grab your legs and pull you to the bottom'.

On the outskirts of Betafo there are hot springs, where for a few ariary you can have a lingering hot bath.

CONTINUING SOUTH ON RN7

Leaving Antsirabe you continue to pass through typical highland scenery of rice paddies and low hills. Some 20km south of Antsirabe you enter the Amoron'ny

ASSOCIATION MADALIEF/FITIAVANA

This inspiring Dutch/Malagasy organisation demonstrates how visitors can work with local people to make a real difference in Madagascar. Fitiavana was founded in 2000 by Malagasy women in Ambositra who used their own money to help needy children in their town. They were joined by three Dutch women who, after their visits to Madagascar, wanted to do something for the Malagasy children. They founded their organisation, Madalief, in the Netherlands to raise funds for the projects in Ambositra.

In 2003 they had raised enough funds to build an orphanage for 17 children (not all of these children are strictly orphans; some have mothers who are unable to care for them properly). By 2006 the group had built another three houses for homeless women, which include a crèche and a sewing room. Gradually these women are rebuilding their lives, and their children (now more than 40) are provided with clothes, schooling and medical care. Fitiavana has also helped families repair their houses, built two new classrooms for the local school, and runs their kindergarten. They prepare a daily snack and once a week a good meal for the children.

They have also recently opened a guesthouse to the south of Antsirabe, providing the children with employment after they complete their education and generating funds for the organisation's social project. See **Résidence Madalief** on page 174.

For further information or to arrange a visit contact Mme Honorine Razafindranoro (m 033 14 155 91), Vice President of the Association in Ambositra, or Remi Doomernik (e remi.madagaskar@gmail.com; www.madalief.nl).

Mania region, Betsileo country, and the province of Fianarantsoa. It's another 76km along winding roads to Ambositra.

AMBOSITRA (PK 259)

Ambositra (pronounced 'am*boostr*') is a friendly little Betsileo town. Many of the 30,000 inhabitants are students so in July and August the population is much reduced. Most visitors stop only briefly, but the countryside around the town is very scenic, so it merits a few days' stay if you have time. Market day is Saturday (best mid-morning); raffia products are particularly plentiful.

Ambositra is the centre of Madagascar's woodcarving industry. Even the houses have ornately carved wooden balconies and shutters. There is an abundant choice of carved figures and marquetry (see *Shopping* on page 182).

Several readers have complained that this town has particularly persistent beggars. The problem area is in front of Grand Hotel with its profusion of tour buses. You are unlikely to be bothered in other parts of the town, which is notably safe and friendly.

🏠 WHERE TO STAY

🏠 **Artisan (Chez Victor)** (18 rooms) m 032 51 996 09/034 04 642 53; e artisan_hotel@yahoo.fr. Opened in 2007, this is a very nice hotel with wonderful woodwork. All rooms en suite with fan. €€€

🏠 **Mania** (17 rooms) \ 47 710 21; m 033 12 453 96/032 04 620 91; f 47 711 21; e toursmania@moov.mg. Malagasy-owned, central; clean en-suite dbl, twin & family rooms. Tours organised; bikes & cars for rent. €€€

🏠 **Jonathan** (13 rooms) \ 47 713 89; m 032 07 019 72; e madtrade@moov.mg. Rooms with TV, some en suite. €€€

🏠 **Angelino Tsaralaza** (7 rooms) \ 47 711 92; m 032 54 420 38; e angelino-hotel@moov.mg. Traditional Malagasy house with clean, spacious rooms, high ceilings, wooden floors & nice view. Rooms have TV. Also 5-bed dorm. €€–€€€

🏠 **Violette** (6 rooms & 6 bungalows) Madiolahatra; \ 47 710 84; f 47 715 89; e violette@moov.mg.

North end of town. Elegantly furnished bungalows with TV. Great views, but cheaper rooms face the road. €€–€€€

🏠 **Relais des Tropiques** (12 rooms) \ 47 711 26; m 033 02 711 26/032 07 742 80. Simple rooms, some with shared facilities. Good restaurant. €€–€€€

🏠 **Grand Hotel** (13 rooms) \ 47 712 62. The oldest hotel in Ambositra; a beautiful old building. Some rooms en suite. Also dormitory. €–€€€

🏠 **Mahatsinjo** \ 47 710 36; e jeannoeltours@yahoo.fr. A short walk up the hill. Very attractive, quiet & rural surroundings, but near town. €€

🏠 **Prestige** (7 rooms) \ 47 711 35. A charming, small guesthouse with garden & beautiful views. Helpful owner. Sgl, dbl, twin & family rooms. €–€€

🏠 **Miora** (12 rooms) m 032 40 735 73. Cheap rooms with shared facilities. €€

✕ WHERE TO EAT

✕ **Tanamasoandro** Rue de Commerce. A budget restaurant which also has rooms.

✕ **Oasis** Restaurant with reasonable prices, nice seating upstairs & tasty food with vegetarian options. Sometimes live music.

✕ **Oasis Annexe** Reliable good-value snacks & meals.

✕ **Grand Hotel** A hangout for travellers, so even if

you're not staying here it's useful to have a drink & swap stories. The food is (usually) good.

✕ **Voajanahary** m 032 02 996 32/033 12 247 52; ⏰ 08.00–22.00. Simple food with a lovely view.

🍽 **Boulangerie du Betsileo/Le Bon Grain** Bakery.

🍽 **Hotely Basile** Typical Malagsy *hotely*.

MONEY AND COMMUNICATIONS Ambositra has branches of BFV, BNI and BOA banks, all with 24-hour ATMs. The BFV has a Western Union service and also opens Saturday mornings. There is a post office and branch of Colis Express (\ 47 713 38). At the time of writing, there are no longer any operational internet cafés

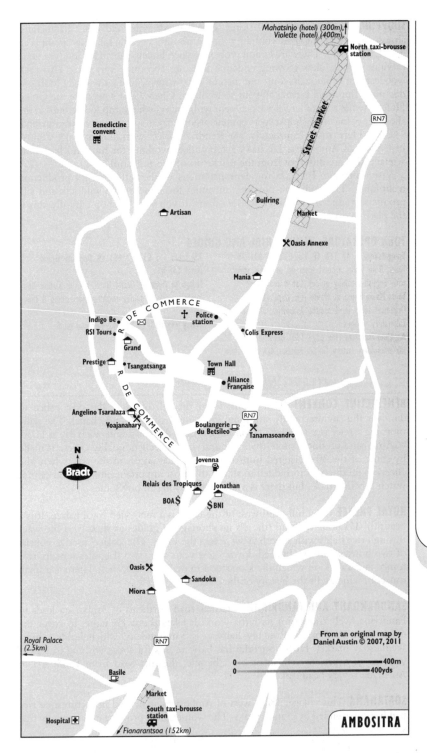

Mahatsinjo (hotel) (300m),↑
Violette (hotel) (400m),

North taxi-brousse
station

RN7

Benedictine
convent

Street market

Bullring

Artisan

Market

Oasis Annexe

Mania

R DE COMMERCE

Indigo Be

Police
station

RSI Tours

Colis Express

Grand

Prestige

Town Hall

Tsangatsanga

Alliance
Française

R DE COMMERCE

Angelino Tsaralaza

Voajanahary

Boulangerie
du Betsileo

RN7

Tanamasoandro

N

Jovenna

Bradt

Relais des Tropiques

Jonathan

BOA $

$ BNI

Oasis

Sandoka

Miora

Royal Palace
(2.5km)

RN7

From an original map by
Daniel Austin © 2007, 2011

0 ———— 400m
0 ———— 400yds

Basile

Market

South taxi-brousse
station

Hospital

Fianarantsoa (152km)

AMBOSITRA

SHOPPING There are some 30 stores selling woodcarving and other handicrafts, almost all on the 'ring road' running round Ambositra's central hill (this circuit is an easy 1.5km walk). There are ethical problems when buying palisander and rosewood carvings – these slow-growing endemic trees are becoming very rare. That said, woodcarving is the main source of income for the town, so it's a typically Malagasy dilemma. But avoid buying all your souvenirs at Chez Victor's opposite the Grand Hotel. He has a commercial arrangement with drivers who dump tour groups at the shop, depriving other shopkeepers of their custom. Try to spread your custom around.

Clare Hermans recommends 'Mr Randrianasolo's workshop at Ilaka Centre, just north of Ambositra. He has 25 apprentices working for him and has some artefacts that are different from the usual run-of-the-mill stuff.'

Visit Angelino Tsaralaza for demonstrations of the different silk production techniques. This initiative provides an outlet for some of the wild silk and silk products produced by women's associations. If you want to shop ethically, this is the place to do it.

TOUR OPERATORS, VEHICLE HIRE AND GUIDES

Tsangatsanga \ 47 714 48; m 032 04 621 28. Tours, from walks around town up to 7-day treks with English-speaking guides. Car & tent hire.
Tours Mania Based at Mania (see page 180). Organises tours in & around Ambositra; also to Zafimaniry villages.
Angelino Tsaralaza (see page 180) Excursions to silk/embroidery factory. Guides; minibus, 4x4 & car hire.

RSI Tours m 032 12 693 49. Opposite Grand Hotel. Car hire.
Indigo Be Opposite Grand Hotel, a little further up. English-speaking guides; trekking, horseriding & bike hire.
Mamy m 033 13 415 43. Regional guide.

PLACES OF INTEREST NEAR AMBOSITRA

BENEDICTINE CONVENT Walk 500m down the hill opposite the post office to discover this architecturally stunning 75-year-old convent and chapel. The daily morning service is at 06.30 (07.00 on Sunday) and there is singing each day at 11.30.

Ambositra produces more than woodcarvings: excellent quality cheese is made by some of the 30 cloistered nuns here. Note that access to the area where the cheese is produced is forbidden to all but the most important nuns, so you cannot watch it being made, but there is a shop where you can buy some.

ROYAL PALACE On a hill southwest of the town is a renovated royal palace. It is a beautiful 1½ hour walk up (there's no shortage of guides to show you the way) through rice fields with superb views across the valley. The 'palace' used to consist of two houses, but one burned down a few years ago. Two flagpoles remain, two tombs and a rock on which the king stood to make his speeches. There is a small museum which tells the history of the place.

SANDRANDAHY AND FANDRIANA A tarmac road northeast of Ambositra leads to Fandriana, well known for its raffia work. It takes about 1½ hours to cover the 45km from Ambositra. Roughly halfway is Sandrandahy, which holds a huge Wednesday market. **Hôtel Sariaka** has basic rooms for those wishing to stay. If you are in a private vehicle or on a bicycle, the dirt road from Fandriana to Antsirabe is very beautiful.

SOATANANA This village, 38km west of Ambositra, is nestled in picturesque rice paddies surrounded by granite peaks. The women here produce exceptionally fine silk cloth.

The region has the largest remaining area of *tapia* forest in Madagascar – *tapia* is the staple diet of the endemic silkworm (*Borocera madagascariensis*). Feedback Madagascar, Ny Tanintsika, oversees a project in this area to reintroduce the wild silkworm to the *tapia* forest and supports a weavers' union, Tambatra. A tour of this area provides the opportunity to see all the stages in silk production, from the cocoon to weaving, including dyeing of the threads using natural dyes.

The trip to Soatanana can be made in an hour by private vehicle. You can organise a tour from Ambositra, hire a taxi, or cycle. Take the paved RN35 (the turn-off from RN7 is 12km south of Ambositra) for 15km west to Anjoman' Akona, then ask for directions to Soatanana – you will need to take the dirt road that goes to Ambohimahazo. Alternatively you can get as far as Anjoman' Akona or Ambohimahazo by *taxi-brousse* from Ambositra.

AMBATOFINANDRAHANA If you want to explore more of the area, Mark and Kyley provide the following information: 'If you continue on RN35 west past Anjoman' Akona, 50km down the paved road is Ambatofinandrahana. Much of Madagascar's marble and granite is cut and processed here in a factory 3km south of town. Some of the stone is quarried 5km from the factory, but most comes on flatbed trucks from the hinterlands west of 'Ambato' (as the locals call it). MAGRAMA is the name of the factory and they are happy to give free tours. The finished stone is sold to wealthy Tana residents and some is exported to Europe.

'Just north of Ambato (5km on a dirt road) are some wonderful hot springs. Buildings put up by the French have fallen into disrepair and now look like Roman ruins, lending the place a charming sense of disorientation. Go in the early morning, when the air is cool and the water is clean. Ask anybody in town how to get to the *ranomafana*.'

There is one tourist hotel in Ambato: **Hôtel du Marbre**. The rooms are nice and the hotel has a garden full of native plants.

ZAFIMANIRY VILLAGES For the past few years I have downplayed the attractions of the Zafimaniry region following reports in the 1990s of severe deforestation, but this woodcarving region is now benefiting from controlled ecotourism. However, persistent begging has become a problem. Be firm and resist, as giving in only exacerbates the issue. The community charge (a compulsory fee of 3,000Ar payable to the mayor of each village you visit) is a much fairer way of giving to the villagers.

Taxi-brousses only run on Wednesdays (market day), otherwise you will need to find private transport to get here.

Antoetra This is no longer a typical Zafimaniry village, but nevertheless is worth a visit for the chance to see woodcarvers at work and to buy their crafts. French is spoken, but not English.

Basic dorm accommodation may be found here at **Papavelo**, where camping is permitted and tents can be hired. A better hotel, **Sous le Soleil de Mada** (m *033 07 344 14;* e *resa.souslesoleildemada@yahoo.fr; http://souslesoleildemada.monsite-orange.fr;* €€), has ten Zafimaniry-style bungalows on the road to Ivato.

Trekking circuits Guides may be found in Antoetra or via one of the hotels. They charge about 20,000Ar per day for tours of villages in the area. Apart from their craft, the Zafimaniry are known for their unique houses. The area's woodcarving culture was proclaimed a Masterpiece of the Oral and Intangible Heritage of Humanity by UNESCO in 2003.

Sakaivo Nord, approximately 3½ hours from Antoetra at the foot of a mountain, is one of the best villages to visit. Closest to Antoetra is **Ifasina** ('place of dirt'), about 1½ hours away on foot. Also recommended are **Faliarivo** (on a hilltop with splendid views), **Fempina** and **Tetezandrotra**.

AMBOSITRA TO FIANARANTSOA

About 6km south of Ambositra, near PK 266, is a turning for a cave, signposted Toerana Masina ('sacred place'). It is 500m west of RN7.

Continuing south, the scenery becomes increasingly spectacular. You pass remnants of the western limit of the rainforest (being systematically destroyed). The road runs up and down steep hills, past neat Betsileo rice paddies interspersed with eucalyptus and pine groves. The steepest climb comes about two hours after Ambositra, when the vehicle labours up an endlessly curving road, through thick forests of introduced pine, and reaches the top where stalls selling fruit or baskets provide an excuse for a break. Just after **Ambatofitorahana**, for a few kilometres after PK 302, you will see stalls along the road selling carved kitchenware. Half an hour further on, for a couple of kilometres either side of PK 340, the road is lined with sellers of delicious eucalyptus honey for much of the year.

Then it's down to **Ambohimahasoa**, where good snacks are served at **Nirina** and basic rooms may be found at **Mimosa** (m *033 04 236 43*). Beyond this, you pass more remnants of forests, then open country, rice paddies and houses as you begin the approach to Fianarantsoa.

RICE   *Hilary Bradt*

The Malagasy have always had an almost mystical attachment to rice. King Andrianampoinimerina declared: 'Rice and I are one,' and loyalty to the Merina king was symbolised by industry in the rice paddies.

Today the Betsileo are masters of rice cultivation (they manage three harvests a year, rather than the normal two) and their neat terraces are a distinctive part of the scenery of the central highlands. However, rice is grown throughout the island, either in irrigated paddies or as 'hill rice' watered by the rain. Rice production is labour-intensive. First the ground must be prepared for the seeds. Often this is done by chasing zebu cattle round and round to break and soften the clods – a muddy, sticky job, but evidently great fun for the boys who do it. Seeds are germinated in a small plot and replanted in the irrigated paddies when half grown. In October and November you will see groups of women bent over in knee-deep water, performing this back-breaking work.

The Malagasy eat rice three times a day, the average annual consumption being 135kg per capita – the highest of any nation in the world – although this is declining because of the availability of other foods and reduced productivity. Rice marketing was nationalised in 1976, but this resulted in such a dramatic drop in the amount of rice reaching the open market that restrictions were lifted in 1984. By that time it was too late to reverse the decline, which was mainly due to the decay of irrigation works. Despite a steady increase in acreage at the expense of the precious forest, production continues to fall.

Small farmers grow rice only for their own consumption but are forced to sell part of their crop for instant cash. Richer families in the community store this grain and sell it back at a profit later. To solve this small-scale exploitation, village co-operatives have been set up to buy rice and sell it back to the farmer at an agreed price, or at a profit to outsiders if any is left over.

IALATSARA LEMUR FOREST CAMP (PK 344) (e *reservation@madagascar-lemuriens.com; www.madagascar-lemuriens.com; entry 15,000Ar pp; half-day guided walks 20,000Ar per group, max 4; night walks 5,000Ar pp; sgl/dbl chalets 27,000/50,000Ar; meals 22,000Ar*) Created in 2002, this private reserve is on RN7, just north of Ambohimahasoa. It is 65km from Fianar and 84km south of Ambositra. It has 2,500ha of forest to the south of the road, comprising 1,000ha natural forest and 1,500ha of managed pine and eucalyptus, and a separate 600ha on the north side. Several species of lemur can be seen here, including Milne-Edwards' sifaka. Chameleons, snakes, tenrecs, frogs, geckos and birds may also be found.

Seven wood-frame canvas chalets have been built on stilts in the forest. They are very basic for the high price, with shared facilities, but the beds are soft and comfy.

FIANARANTSOA (PK 408)

The name means 'place of good learning'. Fianarantsoa ('Fianar' for short) was founded in 1830 as the administrative capital of Betsileo. The lower and upper towns are separated by a fairly steep climb, and still further up the hill is the attractive old town, reachable only on foot and definitely worth a visit. The majority of the hotels, however, are in the drearier lower town.

Fianar is an ideal base from which to do a variety of excursions: Andringitra, Ranomafana and Andrambovato are within easy(ish) reach.

GETTING THERE AND AWAY The journey by *taxi-brousse* takes between six and ten hours from Tana (23,000Ar). The onward trip to Toliara takes nine to 14 hours (30,000Ar) or, going east, seven hours to Manakara (13,000Ar). **Mazabus** (see page 189) operates comfy buses to Toliara (depart Friday, return Saturday; 75,000Ar) and Manakara (depart Sunday/Wednesday, return Monday/Thursday; 55,000Ar).

Fianar is also connected to Manakara by the FCE railway (see page 190).

WHERE TO STAY
Upper range €€€€

🏠 **Tsara Guest House** (14 rooms) Ambatolahikosoa; \ 75 502 06; f 75 512 09; m 032 05 516 12; e tsaraguest@moov.mg; www.tsaraguest.com. Popular & universally praised by readers. An old house & garden that began life as a church; terrace has wonderful view of town. Most rooms are en suite with TV & safe; also some cheaper rooms with shared facilities. Many tours offered. Visa & MasterCard accepted.

Mid-range €€€

🏠 **Tombontsoa** (8 rooms) Bd Hubert Garbit; \ 75 514 05; e contact@hotel-tombontsoa.com; www.hotel-tombontsoa.com. Highly recommended hotel, well situated for upper & lower towns. Sgl, dbl, twin & trpl rooms, en suite with TV, some with bath; 1 studio with kitchenette. Pool, sauna, tennis court, bar, restaurant & secure parking.

🏠 **Zomatel** (34 rooms) Pl du Zoma; \ 75 507 97; f 75 513 76; m 032 40 509 67/033 12 801 97; e zomatel@zomatel-madagascar.com; www.zomatel-madagascar.com. Plain en-suite rooms with TV, minibar & AC. Also apartment with kitchenette. Visa accepted.

🏠 **Cotsoyannis** (21 rooms) 4 Rue Ramaharo; \ 75 514 72; m 032 40 209 86; e cotso@

malagasy.com. A long-established hotel; en-suite dbl rooms with good views.

🏠 **Soafia** (83 rooms) Zorozoroana Ambalakisoa; \ 75 503 53/513 13; e soafia.hot@moov.mg. Curious rabbit warren of a hotel with cartoonesque décor. En-suite sgl to family rooms with TV & minibar. Swimming pool; good restaurant; pool table in bar.

🏠 **Plazza Inn** (38 rooms) \ 75 515 72. Sgl, dbl, twin & family rooms, some en suite with TV. Conference centre but no restaurant.

🏠 **Peniela** Rue du Rova; m 032 40 486 56/032 02 739 63/033 07 602 90; e peniela.house@yahoo.fr. Beautiful renovated traditional house in old town. Great tranquil location; no vehicle access.

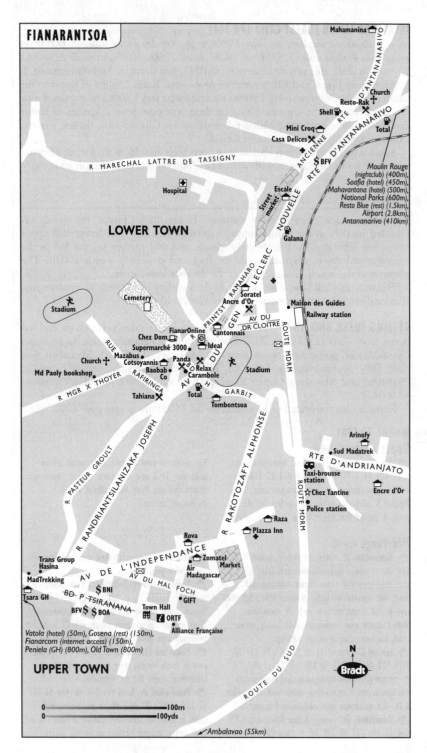

FIANARANTSOA

Mahamanina

RTE D'ANTANANARIVO

Church

Resto-Rak

Shell

RTE ANCIENNE

Mini Croq

Casa Delices

Total

RTE D'ANTANANARIVO

$ BFV

NOUVELLE

R MARECHAL LATTRE DE TASSIGNY

Hospital

Escale

Street market

Moulin Rouge
(nightclub) (400m),
Soafia (hotel) (450m),
Mahavantana (hotel) (500m),
National Parks (600m),
Resto Blue (rest) (1.5km),
Airport (2.8km),
Antananarivo (410km)

LOWER TOWN

Galana

Stadium

Cemetery

RAMAHARO

PRINTSY GEN LECLERC

Soratel
Ancre d'Or

Maison des Guides

Railway station

FianarOnline

Chez Dom

Supermarché 3000

Mazabus

Church

Cotsoyannis

Md Paoly bookshop

Baobab Co

AV DU DR CLOITRE

Cantonnais

Ideal

Panda

Relax

Carambole

RUE RAFIRINGA

AV DU B

Stadium

ROUTE MDRM

R MGR X THOYER

Tahiana

Total

GARBIT

Tombontsoa

Arinofy

Sud Madatrek

RTE D'ANDRIANJATO

R PASTEUR GROULT

R RANDRIANTSILANIZAKA JOSEPH

R RAKOTOZAFY ALPHONSE

Taxi-brousse
station

Chez Tantine

Encre d'Or

ROUTE MDRM

Police station

Raza

Plazza Inn

Rova

AV DE L'INDEPENDANCE

Zomatel

Air Madagascar

Market

Trans Group
Hasina

MadTrekking

Tsara GH

AV DU MAL FOCH

$ BNI

BD P TSIRANANA

BFV $ $ BOA

GIFT

Town Hall

ORTF

Alliance Française

Vatola (hotel) (50m), Gosena (rest) (150m),
Fianarcom (internet access) (150m),
Peniela (GH) (800m), Old Town (800m)

UPPER TOWN

ROUTE DU SUD

N

Bradt

0 ———————— 100m
0 ———————— 100yds

Ambalavao (55km)

186

The children of Fianar have learned (from whom?) an irresistible method of getting money – and more – from tourists. When my group met for dinner, each had a similar story and each (including myself) was charmed by it. A little boy came up to me in the street and said, in impeccable English: 'Excuse me, I wonder if you would be willing to buy these cards I have made. I shall use the money to buy a copybook for school. I also collect foreign coins. Perhaps you have one for me?' I asked his age (12) and a few questions about his family. Each question was answered courteously and in the same fluent English. I gladly bought some of his nicely drawn cards and found a shiny English penny for him. Every town in Madagascar has its child beggars, but only Fianar seems to have these courteous, well-educated ones. I would love to know who taught them that courtesy succeeds better than aggression. A recent visitor to Fianar reports being followed by one such child for some distance: 'This cute kid was just staring at my feet, then eventually – in timid but flawless English – said, "Excuse me, can I have your shoes?" What do you say to that?'

🏠 **Soratel** (32 rooms) Ampazambazaha; ✆ 75 516 66; f 75 516 78; m 033 08 988 88; e info@ soratel.com; www.soratel.com. Central rooms with TV, minibar, hairdryer & en-suite bath. B/fast inc.

🏠 **Mahamanina** (22 rooms) Rte d'Andriamboasary; ✆ 75 521 11/502 50; m 032 04 931 48; e hotel-mahamanina@moov.mg. Very pleasant dbl, twin & family rooms; some en suite with balcony. Excellent restaurant. B/fast inc.

Budget €€

🏠 **Arinofy** (10 rooms) ✆ 75 506 38; m 032 43 091 99; e arinofy_hotel@yahoo.fr. Perennially popular. Various rooms, mostly with communal facilities. Tent hire & camping (12,000Ar/tent). Organises treks & homestays.

🏠 **Raza** (4 rooms) ✆ 75 519 15; m 032 12 342 42/034 03 593 29; e kotoarivonyfils@yahoo.fr. Large, quiet, well-furnished & spacious rooms with shared bathroom. Camping permitted (8,000Ar/person).

🏠 **Mini Croq** (29 rooms) Ancienne Rte d'Antananarivo; ✆ 75 505 87/907 68; m 033 12 202 02; e mini.croq@yahoo.fr. Parking. Clean,

Penny-pincher €

🏠 **Mahavantana** (8 rooms) m 032 02 395 33/033 09 873 59. Cheap dbl & group rooms with shared hot-water facilities; dorm beds for 3,000/Ar. Pool table.

✗ WHERE TO EAT

✗ **Gosena** ✆ 75 516 16; ⊕ Mon–Fri 06.30–14.00 & 16.30–20.30, Sat 06.30–09.30, Sun closed. Charming old town family restaurant with soups, sandwiches & pastries.

🏠 **Cantonnais** (14 rooms) ✆ 75 521 30. En-suite dbl, twin & trpl rooms with TV. No food.

🏠 **Ruche d'Or** (10 rooms & 3 bungalows) ✆ 75 506 14; e laruchedor@moov.mg. Out of town 5.5km towards Tana. An excellent alternative to the city for those who prefer leafier surroundings. Various rooms for 2–5 people, including some budget rooms with shared toilet.

bright rooms, mostly en suite. Good value. Popular with groups so booking advised.

🏠 **Ideal** (14 rooms) m 032 43 592 63. Basic hotel. Rooms mostly with shared facilities, some with TV.

🏠 **Encre d'Or** (6 rooms) ✆ 75 906 10; m 032 02 944 95. Guesthouse in quiet area not far from *taxi-brousse* station. Rooms with shared bathrooms.

🏠 **Vatola** (6 rooms) ✆ 75 515 98. Marvellously friendly upper-town guesthouse. Dbl, trpl & family rooms with communal hot showers. Excellent value including food.

🏠 **Escale** (7 rooms) ✆ 75 504 41. Simple but cheap dbl & family rooms.

🏠 **Rova** (14 rooms) m 033 08 501 68. Typical basic trpl & family rooms for low prices.

✗ **Panda** Bd Garbit; ✆ 75 505 69. Very good Chinese meals but questionable décor of crocodile skins & turtle shells.

✕ **Relax** Av Leclerc; ☎ 75 518 59; ⏰ 10.00–22.00 (closed Mon in high season & Sun in low season). Small but smart restaurant with excellent pizzas (including takeaway) & snacks.

✕ **Tahiana** 📱 032 02 786 75; ⏰ Mon–Fri 12.00–23.00, w/end 07.00–late. A pleasant pizza & grill restaurant.

✕ **Ancre d'Or** Spacious bar. Sometimes live music at w/ends. Great food & friendly staff.

✕ **Dragon d'Or** 📱 033 01 557 32; ⏰ 06.30–14.00 & 17.00–22.00. Downstairs at Soratel. Chinese/Malagasy restaurant.

✕ **Resto Blue** Very good, inexpensive food. Friendly.

✕ **Casa Delices** ⏰ Mon–Fri 08.30–21.00, Sat 08.00–21.00, Sun closed. Good value snacks & meals.

✕ **Resto-Rak** ⏰ 08.00–21.00. Malagasy food & salads.

🍽 **Chez Dom** A fast-food café & bar; popular with *vazaha*. Internet access (1 computer). Some local guides base themselves here.

🍽 **Snack Imanoela** 📱 033 11 891 23; e snackimanoela@yahoo.fr; ⏰ Mon–Sat 09.00–18.30, Sun closed. Splendid little café in the old town.

NIGHTLIFE

☆ **Moulin Rouge** Once the best nightclub in town, but still worth a visit. On the outskirts of town. Busiest on Sun.

☆ **Soafia Dance** ⏰ Tue–Sat. For a hot sweaty experience, slightly more upmarket than the Moulin Rouge. Entry 4,000Ar for men, free for women.

☆ **Chez Tantine** By the *taxi-brousse* station, a very Malagasy style disco.

MONEY AND COMMUNICATIONS Most of the banks/ATMs are clustered in the upper town on the main boulevard, but there is now also a branch of BFV in the lower town; this is the only one open on Saturdays. There are post offices in both the upper and lower towns, with internet access at the latter.

📧 **Cyberpaositra** ⏰ Mon–Fri 07.00–19.00, Sat 08.00–18.00. There's 11 computers for 30Ar/min at the lower town post office; also printing & scanning services.

📧 **FianarOnline** ⏰ daily 08.00–19.00. Cybercafé (40Ar/min) & T-shirts.

📧 **Fianarcom** ☎ 75 504 39; 📱 032 40 187 57. Cybercafé.

SHOPPING

Supermarché 3000 ☎ 75 509 31. A fairly well stocked supermarket. Recently changed name from Supermarché 2000; perhaps it will have upgraded again by the time you read this?!

Md Paoly ⏰ Mon–Fri 07.45–11.30 & 14.00–17.30, Sat 07.45–11.30. Bookshop. Sells beautiful handmade greeting cards, wooden carvings, a massive range of postcards, books, maps, religious items & other handicrafts.

Labo Men ☎ 75 500 23; 📱 032 07 729 85; e pieromen@moov.mg; www.pierrotmen.com. Near Hôtel Soafia. Home to renowned photographer Pierrot Men, this shop has posters, postcards & books.

Carambole T-shirts & handicrafts.

WHAT TO SEE AND DO Take time to explore the old town and then visit the upper town market (best on Tuesday/Friday). On the road up to the old town is a small museum: **Musée Diocèse Fianarantsoa**.

There is little to do in Fianar itself, but one recommended visit is to a family-run **Antaimoro paper workshop**. Head down Route d'Andrianjato from the *taxi-brousse* station, over the bridge, then turn right and follow the power lines up the hill past the *gendarmerie*. At the top, turn right and just past the water tap on the left you will see the paper drying on frames outside the workshop.

TOURIST INFORMATION, TOUR OPERATORS, VEHICLE HIRE AND GUIDES

🎫 **ORTF** (regional tourist office) Tranom-Pokonolona Bldg; ☎ 75 904 67; e ortfianar@moov.mg; ⏰ Mon–Fri 08.30–12.00 & 14.30–17.30

National Parks office ☎ 75 512 74; ⏰ Mon–Fri 08.00–12.00 & 14.00–18.00. The office is 250m up the dirt track opposite Jovenna fuel station on the road near the Soafia.

Air Madagascar Nr Zomatel; ✆ 75 508 77/507 97; ⏰ Mon–Fri 08.00–12.00 & 14.00–17.00, Sat 08.30–11.00

Maison des Guides ▣ 034 03 255 26/032 40 481 99; ℮ coeurmalgache@hotmail.com; ⏰ Mon–Fri 08.00–11.30 & 14.00–17.30, Sat 08.00–11.30. In wagon in front of railway station. Organises all types of tours in the area & can arrange cheap accommodation.

Sud Madatrek ✆ 75 932 68; ℮ sudmadatrek@hotmail.com. Pirogue trips, car hire, trekking & excursions to Ranomafana, Isalo & Andringitra.

MadTrekking ✆ 75 503 73/901 73; ▣ 032 02 221 73; ℮ mad.trekking@moov.mg. Recommended; walks, pirogue trips, car hire & excursions including Ranomafana, Isalo & Andringitra.

Trans Groupe Hasina ✆/f 75 520 79; ℮ rhasina@moov.mg; ⏰ Mon–Fri 09.00–12.00 & 14.30–17.30. Local tours & car hire.

Fianar Touring ✆ 75 502 98; ▣ 032 07 722 26; ℮ fianartouring@yahoo.fr; http://fianar.touring.ifrance.com. Based at Carambole shop. Tours, trekking & car hire.

GIFT (Groupement Interprofessionnel Fianarois de Tourisme) ✆ 75 514 72; ▣ 034 08 652 17; ℮ cotso@malagasy.com; ⏰ 08.00–12.00 & 14.00–17.00. Town & regional tours.

Mazabus Rue Thoyer; ✆ 75 903 77; ▣ 033 07 825 67/032 02 566 67; ⏰ Mon–Sat 08.30–12.00 & 14.00–18.00, Sun 14.00–18.00. Comfy bus connections to Toliara & Manakara.

Marao ▣ 032 04 064 95; ℮ aurelienmada@yahoo.fr. Professional local guide.

EXCURSIONS FROM FIANARANTSOA

Sahambavy This pretty valley with its lake and tea estate has its own resort-style hotel, making it well worth a stay of a day or two if you want to relax.

If you don't have your own vehicle, the easiest way to get here is by train to the Sahambavy station on the way to Manakara (see page 190). It's also possible to get here by *taxi-brousse*. With your own transport, take the turning at the Shell fuel station 10km north of Fianar; Sahambavy is 13km from here by road, of which the last 4km is quite rough.

The **Sahambavy Tea Estate** (✆ 75 916 08/919 62; ℮ sidexam@yahoo.fr; ⏰ 07.30–15.30), which employs 120 workers, has been manufacturing black tea for over forty years and green tea since 2004. The 335ha plantation produces some 550 tonnes of tea each year, of which more than half is exported to Kenya. Guided tours of the factory take about an hour, cost 7,000Ar, and end with a tasting.

The nearby mid- to upper-range **Lac Hotel** (✆ 75 518 73; f 75 519 06; ℮ lachotel@moov.mg; www.lachotel.com; €€€€) has 35 bungalows, including a honeymoon suite and fantastic tree house! All rooms are en suite and some are built out over the water. The lakeside location is a peaceful and romantic spot, safe for swimming. Other activities include horseriding, pedalos, boat trips, cycling and hiking.

Vineyards The famous **Lazan'i Betsileo** (✆ 75 901 27; ▣ 032 05 292 29/032 02 313 75; ℮ lazan_i_betsileo@yahoo.fr; ⏰ Mon–Fri) produces red, white, rosé, and 'grey' wines, as well as some liqueurs and aperitifs. It is located some 12km south of Fianar. It's best to book ahead for a visit.

Alternatively, you can also witness the wine-making process at the **Cistercian-Trappist Monastery of Maromby**. You can get most of the way there by *taxi-brousse* (1,000Ar) or taxi (40,000Ar return).

Andrambovato Peace Corps volunteers Ben and Kendall Badgett sent me this information about a ecotourism project 45km from Fianar and accessible by rail.

'Andrambovato is a small village in the rainforest. A Malagasy NGO is working with the locals to establish ecotourism. The villagers are very excited about the project and are welcoming to all visitors. The emphasis is on hiking, with short and long walks to suit all levels of fitness and ability.

'The easiest hike, which can be done as a day trip from Fianar, is an hour's walk to a gorgeous waterfall. Bring a picnic and soak your feet in the cool streams. More strenuous is the hike to the top of the granite rock face. You'll get to see wildlife as well as a breathtaking view of the valley below. The trail is the same as that used in colonial times to extract timber from the forest for the construction of the FCE railway. Another hike takes you to the Tanala village of Ambalavero, where you can see traditional village life and meet the local *mpanjaka* (king). Finally there's a two- to three-day trek through the forest corridor from Andrambovato to Ranomafana. Along this route you will see typical Tanala villages, wonderful flora and fauna, and traditional agriculture.'

A local guide is obligatory and an entrance fee is payable to the local community association. Provisions in the village are quite limited so bring what you need with you. If you have your own tent there are plenty of places to camp, or you can find lodging with a local family. Alternatively, there are basic bungalows nearby owned by Lac Hotel (Sahambavy) and Tsara Guesthouse (Fianar), which can be booked via those hotels.

The train is the only way to get to Andrambovato (unless you hike in from Ranomafana or Sahambavy); it takes about two hours.

Fianarantsoa–Côte Est Railway The 163km trip between Fianar and Manakara (see page 272) is justifiably popular. The train leaves for Manakara Tuesday/Thursday/Saturday at 07.00 and the journey takes eight to ten hours, returning on Wednesday/Friday/Sunday. Tickets can be bought in advance (25,000Ar for first class, including seat reservation, or 13,000Ar for second class) from the ticket office in Fianar railway station (\ 75 513 55; e *fce@blueline.mg*; ⏲ *Mon 14.00–17.00, Tue–Fri 07.00–11.00 & 14.00–17.00*).

If travelling second class, board just before departure to get a spot by the door. This is nice and breezy, ensures you get a good view, and avoids the smell of the toilet. The train stops frequently (there are 18 stations *en route*) allowing time for photography and for buying fruit and snacks from vendors.

The line, which was constructed between 1926 and 1936, passes over 67 bridges, through 48 tunnels (one is more than 1km long) and crosses the runway at Manakara airport! Many of the rails once formed part of a track in Alsace, but were seized from the Germans after WWI, and were eventually shipped to Madagascar by the French.

The lives of more than 100,000 people along the line depend exclusively on the FCE to bring supplies in and to send their produce to market. So it was a tragedy when, in 2000, cyclones caused almost 300 landslides that buried the track – and took months to clear. Locals came to understand that it was due to deforestation and poor farming methods that the mudslides had been so severe, and so new agricultural practices were quickly adopted. Now vetiver grass is planted between crops on slopes along the track to protect against washouts. A nice booklet describing the history of the FCE is available from the ticket office.

RANOMAFANA

The name Ranomafana means 'hot water' and it was the waters, not the lemurs, that drew visitors in the colonial days and financed the building of the once-elegant Hôtel Station Thermale de Ranomafana.

These days the baths are often ignored by visitors anxious to visit Ranomafana National Park, which was created in 1991. This hitherto unprotected fragment of mid-altitude rainforest first came to the world's attention with the discovery of the golden bamboo lemur in 1986 and is particularly rich in wildlife.

Ranomafana has experienced a welcome explosion of accommodation in recent years (for nearly a decade after it opened there was just one, dire hotel) so now pleases almost everyone. I have always loved it! First you have the marvellously scenic drive down, with the dry highland vegetation giving way to greenery and flowers. Then there are the views of the tumbling waters of the Namorona River, and the relief when the hillsides turn to that lovely unbroken, knobbly green of virgin forest that indicates you are nearing the park. Hidden in these trees are 12 species of lemur: Milne-Edwards' sifaka, red-fronted brown lemur, red-bellied lemur, black-and-white ruffed lemur and three species of bamboo lemur. At night you can add mouse lemur, woolly lemur, sportive lemur, greater dwarf lemur and aye-aye. Then there are the birds: more than 100 species with 36 endemic. And the reptiles. And the butterflies and other insects. Even if you saw no wildlife, there is enough variety in the vegetation and scenery, and enough pleasure in walking the well-constructed trails, to make a visit worthwhile. And – I nearly forgot – in the warm summer months you can swim in the cold, clear water of the Namorona while a Madagascar malachite kingfisher darts overhead. On the downside, the trails are steep and arduous, it often rains and there are leeches.

GETTING THERE AND AWAY Ranomafana is about 1½ hours from Fianar and 3½ hours from Ambositra. Plenty of *taxi-brousses* leave Fianar throughout the morning, and there is no shortage of drivers or tour operators able to supply a private vehicle.

WHERE TO STAY AND EAT

Setam Lodge (14 bungalows) ⊃ 22 234 31; e setamlodge@setam-madagascar.com; www.setam-madagascar.com. The best hotel in Ranomafana, about 1km from the park entrance. Spacious semi-detached bungalows on 3 levels with stunning views of the forest & Namorona valley. Good food, though limited choice. €€€€

Domaine Nature (20 bungalows) m 032 02 611 18/033 12 001 88/033 05 558 61; e domnat7@yahoo.fr. Excellent setting on a steep hillside halfway between village & park, with gorgeous river views. The quality of the service & food is only mediocre, however. €€€€

Centre-Est (8 bungalows & 13 rooms) ⊃ 75 523 02. Beyond the museum, on the left as you enter Ranomafana. Sgl, dbl, twin & trpl en-suite rooms; very pleasant & reasonably priced thatched bungalows with shared bathrooms. €€€

Ihary (14 bungalows) ⊃ 75 523 02. Located just beyond the village of Ranomafana. Bungalows in a nice riverside setting; en-suite facilities. But rooms can be noisy. €€€

Forêt Australe (10 bungalows) m 033 09 873 61; e austral@netclub.mg. About 2km from the park. €€€

Chez Gaspard (8 bungalows) A variety of rooms at different prices; most have shared bathrooms. €€€

Cristo m 033 08 376 69. Simple rooms with en-suite bathrooms. €€ €€€

Palmerie (6 rooms) A good budget option with hot water & shared toilets. Restaurant on opposite side of road. €€

Manja (10 bungalows & 4 rooms) On RN26 to Mananjary, 5min walk east along river. Excellent food. €€

Ravenala (9 rooms) Located opposite the museum. Basic, funky, very friendly, beautiful views & good food. €

Rian'ala (24 dorm beds) Dormitory accommodation (8 beds/room) near park entrance. €

✗ **Varibolo** Near park entrance, with nice views overlooking forest. An ideal place to have lunch after hiking in the forest. B/fast available.

✗ **Chez Tantely & Claire** A nice welcoming little restaurant in the village.

Out of town For those with their own transport these hotels on the way to Mananjary are recommended.

Tropic Village (14 rooms) ⊃ 22 695 76; f 22 695 76; e tropic.r@moov.mg. An upmarket hotel in Mahatsinjorano, about 9km from Ranomafana. Spacious rooms with nice view. Good restaurant. €€€

Relax Situated 5km from Ranomafana. Recommended with its restaurant **Le Terrace**. Lovely setting, away from the bustle of Ranomafana. €€

Camping There is a campsite at the park entrance. There are six tent pitches, with open-sided A-frame thatched shelters giving shade as well as protection from the rain, and one centrally located covered picnic table. There are basic toilets and showers, a tap for drinking water and a bungalow with kitchen facilities. No food is available here but the **Varibolo** restaurant is nearby.

RANOMAFANA AND CONSERVATION
The Ranomafana National Park Project, set up by Dr Patricia Wright, is engaged in numerous activities, from education and health care for the villagers on the periphery of the park to an ecological monitoring team that works at several sites within the park. The national park is now one of the country's flagship conservation projects, with the involvement of local communities playing an important role.

Much scientific research takes place here and there have been some clashes between researchers and tourists. Tourists have been known to push researchers aside in order to get a better photo, and to encourage guides to shake or bang on trees to persuade a lemur to move. It goes without saying that this is irresponsible behaviour and is counter-productive since some researchers withhold information on the whereabouts of the rarer lemurs for fear of being disturbed in their work.

A world-class research station near the park entrance (Centre Valbio) was completed in 2003 under the initiative of an international consortium, bringing great possibilities for scientific research in the area.

VISITING THE NATIONAL PARK
Permits and guides Permits (see page 72 for prices) are obtainable from the park office. You are not allowed into the park without a guide. There is an official four-person limit per group; guides may allow five but for larger numbers you need an additional guide. The quality of the guides at Ranomafana is now every bit as good as those from Andasibe. Official guide fees are posted in the office.

In the forest There is a large network of maintained trails. Most of the standard routes take a few hours, but if you are fit you could opt for the longer tours taking six to eight hours. You will see primary forest, where the vines are thicker, the trees bigger and it will be quieter. Even for the shorter walks you need to be reasonably fit – the paths are moderate to steep, and frequently slippery.

Your guide will assume that it is mainly lemurs you have come to see; so, unless you stress that you are interested in other aspects such as botany or insects, he will tend to concentrate on mammals and birds. You are most likely to see red-fronted brown lemurs, grey bamboo lemurs and the rarer red-bellied lemur. Star attractions such as greater bamboo lemur and golden bamboo lemur are now fairly frequently seen. There is also the spectacular Milne-Edwards' sifaka – dark brown with cream-coloured sides.

A delightful walk is to the waterfall on the River Namorona. If the circular route is taken it is quite strenuous, with a long steep descent to the cascade. This is a dramatic and beautiful place and it's worth lingering to watch for kingfishers. A hydroelectric scheme diverts some of the water plunging over the cliffs, but is not intrusive. The walk back, along the river, is outside the park boundary so gives you a chance to see small farming communities. Another waterfall, Le Petite Cascade, is hidden in the forest. A long ribbon of water falls into a deep pool which provides a chilly but invigorating swim (so bring your swimsuit). Allow three hours for this round trip.

Another trail system has been established on flatter ground at Vohiparara, near the boundary of the park, 12km west of Ranomafana on the main road. It only takes about three hours to do all the trails here with a guide. Birders should be able

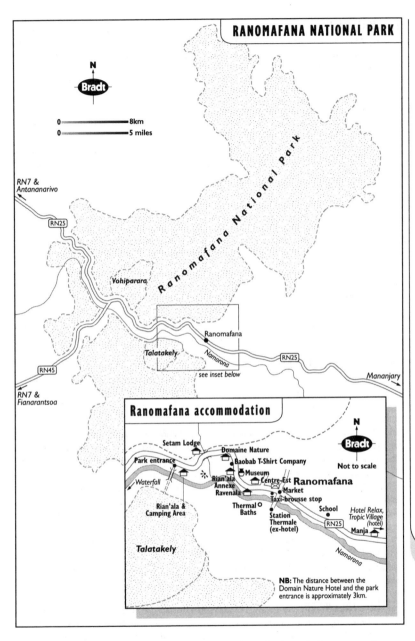

RANOMAFANA NATIONAL PARK

N
Bradt

0 ━━━━━ 8km
0 ━━━━━ 5 miles

RN7 &
Antananarivo

RN25

Ranomafana National Park

Vohiparara

Ranomafana

Talatakely

Namorona

RN25

see inset below

RN45

Mananjary

RN7 &
Fianarantsoa

Ranomafana accommodation

N
Bradt

Not to scale

Setam Lodge

Domaine Nature

Park entrance

Baobab T-Shirt Company

Museum

Waterfall

Rian'ala
Annexe
Ravenala

Centre-Est **Ranomafana**

Market

Taxi-brousse stop

Rian'ala &
Camping Area

Thermal
Baths

Station
Thermale
(ex-hotel)

School

Hotel Relax,
Tropic Village
(hotel)

RN25

Manja

Talatakely

Namorona

NB: The distance between the
Domain Nature Hotel and the park
entrance is approximately 3km.

to see brown emutail, Madagascar snipe, Meller's duck and the extremely rare slender-billed flufftail. According to Nick Garbutt this is also the best place for the rufous-headed ground-roller, Pollen's vanga and yellow-bellied sunbird-asity.

Museum and gift shop This is part of the Ranomafana National Park Project to improve visitor understanding of the area. It is an interesting museum and the handicrafts are of a high standard, including beautifully embroidered T-shirts.

THERMAL BATHS (⏰ *Wed–Mon 08.00–16.30; Tue closed*) These are close to the former Station Thermale hotel. For a minimal payment you can have a wonderful warm swim in the pool. I love it, but note that the pool water is not chlorinated so there's algae on the bottom.

CONTINUING SOUTH: FIANARANTSOA TO IHOSY

The next leg of the journey on RN7 is 206km. Coming from Fianar the landscape is a fine blend of vineyards and terraced rice paddies (the Betsileo are acknowledged masters of rice cultivation), then after 20km a giant rock formation seems almost to hold the road in its grasp. Its name is, appropriately, Tanan' Andriamanitra, or 'hand of God'. From here to Ihosy you will see some of the finest mountain scenery in Madagascar.

AMBALAVAO (PK 461)

Some 56km southwest of Fianarantsoa is my favourite highlands town: Ambalavao. The road drops steeply down to the town providing excellent views across the landscape. But RN7 does not pass through the attractive part of Ambalavao; I strongly urge people to stop here for a few hours or at least to amble through the car-free streets which are thronged with people, and take in the once-grand houses with their pillars, carved balconies, and steep, red-tiled roofs. If travelling south, this is the last time you'll see typical highland architecture. The town is famous as the centre for Antaimoro paper-making, so a lot of tour buses stop here. Market day is Wednesday.

🏠 WHERE TO STAY AND EAT

🏠 **Bougainvillées** (24 bungalows) 📞 75 340 01/08; m 034 08 206 01/032 46 351 35; e auxbougainvilleesambalavao@gmail.com. Adjacent to the Antaimoro paper shop. Bungalows with en-suite bathrooms & solar-heated water. Pleasant restaurant but popular with tour groups. €€€–€€€€

🏠 **Tsienim-parihy** (16 rooms) 📞 75 341 28; m 033 02 607 22/032 44 284 62; e tsienimpari@moov.mg. Obvious tall orange building. Nice en-suite dbl, twin & trpl rooms. Very good restaurant & patisserie. Car hire & tours organised. €€€

🏠 **Résidence du Betsileo** (11 rooms) m 033 02 863 89/032 44 285 60; e sorafahotel@moov.mg. Centrally located & highly recommended. En-suite rooms with nice décor. Good restaurant too. €€€

🏠 **Tropik** (30 rooms) 📞 75 340 55; m 033 14 183 83/034 06 883 53; e letropikhotel@yahoo.fr. Clean & spacious en-suite sgl to family rooms with TV. €€€

🏠 **Samoina** (4 bungalows & 8 rooms) RN7; 📞 75 341 48; m 033 05 029 61. Northeast outskirts of town. Bungalows have en-suite bathrooms; rooms share facilities. Restaurant recommended. Good value. €€

🏠 **Notre** (6 rooms) Cheap but rather scruffy rooms with shared facilities. €

✗ **Fraîche Heure** ⏰ Mon–Sat 06.00–19.00, Sun closed. Good value Malagasy food & pizza.

🍺 **Ah-Tsin-Tsen** 📞 75 341 97; ⏰ Tue–Sun 09.00–20.00, Mon closed. Snack bar owned by the Chan Foui family who have a local winery. You can buy the wine here.

GETTING ORGANISED There are no taxis in Ambalavao, but most hotels can help with organising transport or tours to places nearby. Alternatively, **JB Trekking** (m *033 11 774 30/032 46 596 36;* e *jbtrekking@gmail.com;* ⏰ *Mon–Sat 08.00–18.00, Sun 15.00–18.00*) near the north *taxi-brousse* station rents out bicycles and motorbikes, as well as camping equipment and arranging tours and treks. **Tsara Aventure** is another operator organising treks and mountain biking tours, based next to Résidence du Betsileo.

The **National Parks office** (⏰ *Mon–Fri 08.00–12.00 & 14.00–18.00*) is about 1km northeast of town on the main road. The Total fuel station has a small **shop** selling groceries and supplies including toiletries, batteries and gas canisters.

There are no banks in Ambalavao, but if you get stuck the Tropik hotel can usually change euros.

WHAT TO SEE

Antaimoro paper (⊕ *Mon–Sat 07.30–11.30 & 13.00–17.00, Sun 07.30–15.00*) Ambalavao is the home of the famous Malagasy Antaimoro paper. This papyrus-type paper impregnated with dried flowers is sold throughout the island made into such items as wall-hangings and lampshades. The people in this area are Betsileo, but paper-making in the area copies the coastal Antaimoro tradition which goes back to the Muslim immigrants who wrote verses from the Koran on this paper.

Antaimoro paper is traditionally made from the bark of the *avoha* tree from the eastern forests, but sisal paste is now sometimes used. After the bark is pounded and softened in water it is smoothed onto linen trays to dry in the sun. While still tacky, dried flowers are pressed into it and brushed over with a thin solution of the liquid bark to hold them in place.

The open-air factory where all this happens is to the east of the town in the same compound as the hotel Bougainvillées. It is fascinating to see the step-by-step process, and you get a good tour. A shop sells the finished product in dozens of forms: from bookmarks and greeting cards to photo albums and picture frames. Oh, and bring along your business card or a passport photo to add to the collection that covers one wall of the shop!

Silk production (m *033 14 987 45/032 43 799 63;* ⊕ *07.30–17.00*) Witness the process of silk production, from silkworm to silk scarf, at **Soalandy**. The workshop is opposite the Tropik hotel, 100m beyond the National Parks office at the northeast end of town, and you can buy silk products here too.

If you have time to spare, combine this with a visit to **Nathocéane** (⊕ *Mon–Sat 08.00–12.00 & 14.00–17.00*), 250m back towards town, where you can buy T-shirts, bags and scarves and watch these items being embroidered.

Cattle market Held on Wednesday and Thursday on the outskirts of town. It gets going at about 03.00, so you need to be an early riser! To get there take RN7 south and after about 1km you'll see the zebu on a hill to the left.

After the market, the herdsmen take a month to walk the zebu to Tana, and you'll see these large herds on the road. Look out for the yellow ear tags: these are 'zebu passports' giving the owner the right to take his cattle across regional boundaries.

EXCURSIONS FROM AMBALAVAO

Soavita Winery (⊕ *Mon–Sat 07.00–11.00 & 13.00–17.00, Sun closed*) This place offers tours on weekdays where you will be shown the various stages of winemaking by one of the workers, followed by a tasting. The turning for the winery is 3.5km from Ambalavao towards Fianar, from which point it is 1km down a track. You are advised to go to the Ah-Tsin-Tsen snack bar in town first to make an appointment to visit. Tours cost 3,000Ar per person.

Anja (Anjaha) Park About 13km south from Ambalavao on RN7 is a community-run park which offers superb scenery, intriguing plants adapted to the dry southern climate, some interesting Betsileo history and several troops of cheeky ring-tailed lemurs.

The local people have long recognised the tourist potential here and so a few years ago they organised themselves to gain some income from it. The region is

The humpbacked cattle, zebu, which number more than half the country's human population, produce a relatively low yield in milk and meat. These animals are near-sacred and are generally not eaten by the Malagasy outside of important social or religious ceremonies. Zebu are said to have originated from northeast India, eventually spreading as far as Egypt and then down to Ethiopia and other parts of East Africa. It is not known how they were introduced to Madagascar but they are a symbol of wealth and status as well as being used for burden.

Zebu come in a variety of colours, the most sought-after being the *omby volavita*, which is chestnut with a white spot on the head. There are some 80 words in the Malagasy language to describe the physical attributes of zebu, in particular the colour, horns and hump.

In the south, zebu meat is always served at funerals, and among certain southern tribes the cattle are used as marriage settlements, as in mainland Africa. Whenever there is a traditional ritual or ceremony zebu are sacrificed, the heads being given to the highest-ranking members of the community. Blood is smeared on participants as it is believed to have purification properties, and the fat from the hump of the cattle is used as an ingredient for incense. I have seen a Vezo village elder wearing a domed hat apparently made from a zebu hump. Zebu milk is an important part of the diet among the Antandroy; it is *fady* for women to milk the cows but it is they who sell the curdled milk in the market.

Tourists in the south will see large herds of zebu being driven to market, a journey that may take several days. All cattle crossing regional borders must wear a 'zebu passport' in the form of yellow ear tags. Cattle-rustling is now a major problem. Whereas before it was mainly confined to the Bara, as an initiation into manhood, it is now organised by large, Mafia-like gangs. In former times the punishment matched the crime: a fine of ten zebu would have to be paid by the thief, five for the family from whom the cattle were stolen and five for the king.

To the rural Malagasy a herd of zebu is as symbolic of prosperity as a new car or a large house in Western culture. Government aid programmes must take this into account; for instance improved rice yields will indirectly lead to more environmental degradation by providing more money to buy more zebu. The French colonial government thought they had an answer: they introduced a tax on each animal. However, local politicians were quick to point out that since Malagasy women had always been exempt from taxation, the same rule should apply to cows!

---

sacred to the Betsileo; their ancestors are buried here and it has always been *fady* to hunt the lemurs. The caves have provided a useful sanctuary in times of trouble and were inhabited up to a century or so ago.

The reserve covers 8ha and is home to about 300 ring-tails. Given the health problems affecting the lemurs of Berenty (see page 244) this park provides a worthwhile alternative for tourists wanting a lemur fix and to benefit the local people. It costs 7,000Ar to visit the park, where you are provided with a guide (8,000Ar for two people). The well-maintained short trail winds past some impressive rocks, topped by waiting lemurs, to a sacred cliff where there is an apparently inaccessible tomb high in the rock face. The tour takes one to two hours. A longer circuit incorporating several stunning viewpoints can take up to six hours. There is a simple campsite at the trailhead.

Most hotels and tour operators in Ambalavao and Fianar can help organise a visit to Anja Park.

AMBOHIMAHAMASINA

Some 40km southeast of Ambalavao, Ambohimahamasina is home to Madagascar's most sacred mountain: Ambondrombe. A community ecotourism project, FIZAM, has set up a network of trails and homestays in the area, giving travellers an opportunity to experience how rural Malagasy people really live. Bordering the rainforest corridor that runs from Ranomafana to Andringitra, the beautiful Betsileo villages around Ambohimahamasina are surrounded by spectacular scenery.

The **Angavoa** trail (3 hours) is the shortest, passing wonderful scenery and interesting tombs. Of the three one-day trails, **Ambohitrampanefy** and **Ambohitravo** show you the traditional livelihoods of the region and allow you to try your hand at blacksmithing and basket weaving, while **Itaolana** incorporates more flora and fauna and shows you the cultural value of the sacred mountain. The two-day **Ambondrombe** trail climbs to the 1,936m summit of Ambondrombe. And the three-day **Andriapiaka and Tsipoapoaka** trail passes through the rainforest to Vohipeno on the east coast. The trails are all interconnected so can be combined to make longer treks, with several homestays and campsites providing accommodation *en route*.

Trained guides can be found at the FIZAM office in Ambohimahamasina. There are fixed rates for guides, accommodation and meals, and the profits are used to benefit local communities.

GETTING THERE There are daily *taxi-brousses* from Ambalavao (departing very early on Monday and Thursday – market days). Or you can go by private vehicle. It takes about an hour. Try to arrive in Ambohimahamasina in the morning, in good time to make arrangements for your first night's homestay. Alternatively, there are guides in Ambalavao and Fianarantsoa who can organise your trip.

ANDRINGITRA MOUNTAINS

These spectacular granite peaks and domes have entranced me since I first travelled the length of RN7, so I am thrilled that they can now form the focus for a trekking holiday. The wonderful Andringitra National Park does not cover the entire area – there are other lodges and camps on the outskirts of the park which offer equally good scenery.

WHERE TO STAY AND EAT

⌂ **Tsara Camp** (15 tents) e tsaracamp@ boogiepilgrim-madagascar.com; www.tsaracamp-madagascar.com. Owned by Boogie Pilgrim (see page 86), this tented camp is located outside the park's northwest boundary, about 2hrs from RN7. The camp is open Apr–Nov. The large en-suite tents are pitched on wooden floors under thatched shelters, set in a spectacular plain bounded by the Andringitra Massif. Although the main trekking routes of the national park are not easily accessible from here, half-day to 5-day trips can be arranged. €€€€

⌂ **Camp Catta** e campcatta@campcatta.com; www.campcatta.com. Up the road from Tsara Camp, this place is a centre for paragliding & climbing (note that technical climbing is not allowed in the park). There are basic brick huts & lots of ring-tailed lemurs,

as the name implies. Arrangements to stay here can be made through Hôtel Cotsoyannis in Fianar. Camping permitted (8,500Ar). €€€€

⌂ **Tranogasy** m 033 11 264 27/033 14 306 78; e contact@tranogasy.com; www.tranogasy.com. The ideal blend of comfort & scenery. Well-sited chalets (some en suite), but reportedly starting to become run down. Can arrange complete package for trekkers, including transfer from Ambalavao, guides & porters. €€€

⌂ **Gîte** This basic hut near Ambolamandary, 7km from park entrance, is comfy, but it's a 1hr drive from the trail system. Shared cold-water facilities. You need to bring your own food, but there is a cook to prepare it for you. Book through the WWF in Ambalavao (🕿 75 340 81). €€

Camping There are five campsites within the national park, each with a capacity of around a dozen tents, a cooking hut, running water, and either a long-drop or flush toilet. A couple of them also have a shower. Pitches cost 5,000Ar per night, and a further 5,000Ar to hire a tent. Sleeping bags and mats are also available to rent.

ANDRINGITRA NATIONAL PARK Created in 1999, this park protects the flora and fauna around Madagascar's second highest peak: Pic d'Imarivolanitra (2,658m), meaning 'close to the sky' (formerly known as Pic Boby). Andringitra has some wildlife, but landscape, vegetation and trekking are the chief attractions. And what attractions! I would put Diavolana (see *Trekking* below) in the top ten of all mountain walks that I have ever done: the combination of granite peaks and gneiss formations, endemic succulent plants and ring-tailed lemurs (though at a distance) makes this an utterly different – and utterly marvellous – walking experience. Each circuit covers different terrain, from forest and waterfalls to the frosty peak of Imarivolanitra. In the warmer, wet season the meadows are carpeted with flowers, including 30 species of orchid.

Great care has been taken in creating the trails which are beautifully engineered through difficult terrain to make them as safe and easy as possible. Although the trail system covers a variety of ecosystems, the park also protects an area of montane rainforest in the east, which is closed to visitors. This provides a sanctuary for such rare species as golden and greater bamboo lemurs.

Local guides The guides are well-trained and knowledgeable, particularly on the medicinal use of plants, though few speak English. Fees are roughly 15,000Ar per day for guides and 8,000Ar for porters.

Getting there and away Travelling here by public transport is problematic, but for true backpackers carrying a tent and food, it would be worth the effort. You may find a *taxi-brousse* to take you at least part of the way, but be prepared for a lot of walking. Alternatively hire a car and driver in Fianar. The vast majority of visitors arrange an all-inclusive trip from a Fianar tour operator (see pages 188–9).

There are two entry points: east (Namoly) and west (Morarano). Access is usually via Namoly. All visitors need to go to the *gîte* where the park office is located to pick up their permit, which takes around two hours. A map of the trail system and visitor guidelines are available here. It's another hour or more (depending on the condition of the road, and whether the four toll booths are manned) to the parking area and a further 20-minute walk to the campsite, so aim to leave Ambalavao by 14.00 at the latest to avoid setting up your tent in the dark.

Equipment There is no point in going to Andringitra unless you are equipped for walking. This means boots or tough trainers, hiking poles, daysack, good raingear and a water bottle. Remember also that at this altitude the nights can be very cold (close to freezing between June and September) so you need warm sleeping bags, thermal underwear, gloves and thick socks for overnight. Days are pleasantly warm, but it can rain – hard – at any time. It's worth bringing a swimsuit for the freezing (but refreshing) dip in the pool on the Diavolana circuit.

Trekking There are four main circuits:

Asaramanitra This circuit (6km/3–4 hours) begins at the Belambo campsite and climbs up to two sacred waterfalls, Riambavy and Riandahy (the queen and king), which plunge 250m off the edge of the escarpment. These falls are said to be the embodiment of an ancient king and queen who, unable to conceive a child,

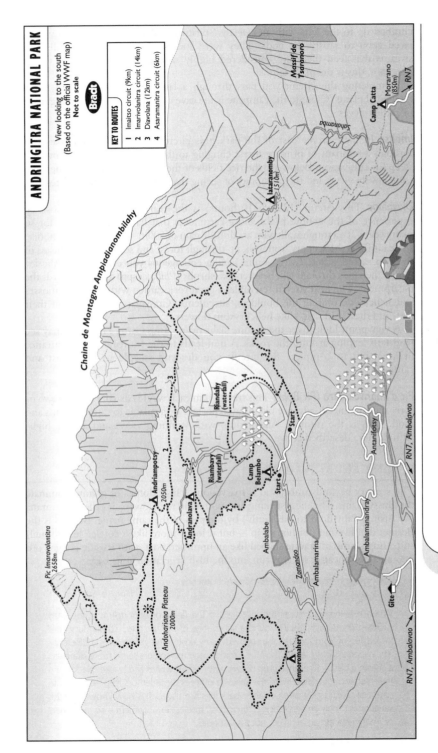

ANDRINGITRA NATIONAL PARK

View looking to the south
(Based on the official WWF map)
Not to scale

Bradt

KEY TO ROUTES

1 Imaitso circuit (9km)
2 Imarivolanitra circuit (14km)
3 Diavolana (12km)
4 Asaramanitra circuit (6km)

Chaine de Montagne Ampiadianombilahy

Pic Imarovolanitra
2658m

Andriampotsy
2050m

Andranolava

Andohariana Plateau
2000m

Amporomahery

Riambavy
(waterfall)

Riambahy
(waterfall)

Camp
Belambo

Start

Start

Iataranomby
1510m

Sahambo

Massif de
Tsaranoro

Camp Catta

Morarano
(850m)

RN7

Ambalabe

Zomandoo

Ambalamarina

Antanifotsy

Ambalamanandray

RN7, Ambalavao

Gite

RN7, Ambalavao

RN7, Ambalavao

climbed up to the falls with an *ombiasy* (spiritual healer) and sacrificed a white-faced zebu to satisfy the gods. They were successful: now the waterfalls and streams that feed them are considered highly sacred. And if you want to get pregnant, this is the place to go!

Completing the circuit you pass through a large area of forest with many medicinal plants. Close to the campsite is the cave of Ijajofo, a former hiding place of cattle thieves.

Imaitso In the extreme east of the park, this circuit (9km/3–4 hours) takes you through a remnant of primary forest clinging to the side of a mountain and too steep for cultivation. Below are the rice fields of the local communities. There are some lovely views and the possibility of seeing five lemur species in the forest.

Diavolana This circuit (12km/6–10 hours) is the real Andringitra – a close-up experience of the granite peaks and escarpments that have intrigued me for so many years. It's a tough walk with an altitude gain of 500m – but you hardly notice, so beautiful is the scenery. You walk up through forest and soon cross the heads of the two sacred waterfalls (if you're feeling courageous you can swim in the icy pools) then pass through tall, heather-like shrubs (*Phillipia* spp) and up towards the escarpment. The next stretch resembles a giant rock garden with colourful mosses and lichens decorating the boulders, succulents (Crassulaceae) nestling at their feet, and masses of daisy-like helichrysum flowers.

A viewpoint looks over the granite slabs near Camp Catta. Here you may see ring-tails leaping around the rocks. A trail leads to the Mororano park entrance (17km), but to complete the circuit you descend steeply to the forest and campsite.

Pic d'Imarivolanitra (Pic Boby) This trek (14km each way) is usually done in two or three days and needs advance planning so porters are available to carry the tents and food. This is the ultimate Andringitra, with stunning views and all the high-altitude flora described above.

BEYOND AMBALAVAO ON RN7

The scenery beyond Ambalavao is marvellous. Huge domes of granite dominate the grassy plains. The most striking one, with twin rock towers, is called Varavarana Ny Atsimo ('the door to the south') by the pass of the same name. Beyond is the Bonnet de l'Evêque ('bishop's cap' – but it looks more like a cottage loaf to me!) and a huge lump of granite shaped like an upturned boat, with its side gouged out into an amphitheatre; streams run into the lush vegetation at its base.

THE RING-TAILED LEMURS OF ANDRINGITRA   *Hilary Bradt*

When researchers first started investigating the fauna of Andringitra, in the early 1990s, they thought they'd found a subspecies of *Lemur catta*. The lemurs here look different from those in the southern spiny desert and gallery forest of Berenty. They appear slightly larger, their fur is thicker, and the colours seem more dramatic: a chestnut back, rather than grey-brown, with whiter whites and blacker blacks. And their behaviour is different. In the absence of trees these lemurs leap from rock to rock with great agility, often on their back legs like sifakas. It is now known that this variation is simply an adaptation to their cold, treeless environment – so the lemurs of Andringitra are an ecotype, not a subspecies.

You will notice that not only the scenery but the villages are different. Bara houses are solidly constructed from red earth (no elegant Merina pillars here) with small windows. Bunches of maize are often suspended from the roof to dry in the sun.

Shortly after Ambalavao you start to see tombs – some painted with scenes from the life of the deceased.

Cyclists can find accommodation at **Ankaramena** (PK 519), where a cattle market takes place on Fridays, or at Hôtel Tongasoa in **Zazafotsy** (PK 576) – the name means 'white child'. The next town of importance is Ihosy (see page 204).

HOPE IN A PLASTIC BOTTLE
Theresa Haine

In Toamasina, on a monitoring trip for the charity Money for Madagascar, I found myself enthralled by a story of rubbish! Whilst visiting SAF – a Malagasy development organisation – I talked with my friend Charnette about her project to tackle the mountains of rubbish polluting the town.

She had decided to start at grassroots level by setting up training courses in recycling and vegetable growing. For pots, they use are an assortment of plastic bags and soft drinks bottles from the rubbish heaps. These are cleaned and the people are taught how to make compost from the vegetable peelings and other scraps that are normally thrown away. The first seeds are given free of charge.

I visited several households in the backstreets of Toamasina and was impressed to see a wonderfully healthy assortment of salad vegetables, and even strawberries, growing on every available ledge, step and windowsill. Many even have a surplus to sell at the market. The enthusiasm of all involved was infectious.

One memorable visit was to a disabled man of 29 who lives in a tiny two-room shack with his 11-year-old son. He lost his wife nine months ago and sent his younger son to live with his grandmother in the forest. The older boy chose to remain with his father, but the loss of his mother affected him very badly. His father has great difficulty walking but can ride a bicycle. He earns his living mending computers and other electronic equipment. After the death of his mother the boy became very withdrawn. His school grades plummeted and he spent every spare moment riding obsessively up and down their lane on his father's bicycle.

The father has some ancestral land a short distance away that he wants to cultivate with the help of four of his handicapped friends, so he signed up for one of Charnette's training courses. His son noticed his father collecting plastic bags from the rubbish heap and was intrigued to see him planting seeds in them. A little while later the boy came home with some empty plastic drinks bottles which he cut in half and cleaned and then asked his father for help to plant some seeds.

They planted some aubergines, but had to take them to Grandma's once they were growing well as they have so little space in their tiny house. From the moment he started growing his aubergines the boy's school grades started to improve, and he finished that academic year third in his class – to the great delight of his father.

I visited them towards the end of the school holidays, but the boy was not at home. 'He's gone to his grandmother's because he was so desperate to see how his aubergines are doing,' his father commented with a smile.

I left Toamasina feeling quite uplifted by the ingenuity I had seen. It was heart-warming to see how just a few seeds and a lot of resourcefulness were starting to clean up the face of a town and improve the lives of its inhabitants – sometimes in quite unexpected ways.

Theresa Haine is the co-ordinator of Money for Madagascar, a charity that has been funding development work in Madagascar for 25 years. See page 134 for details.

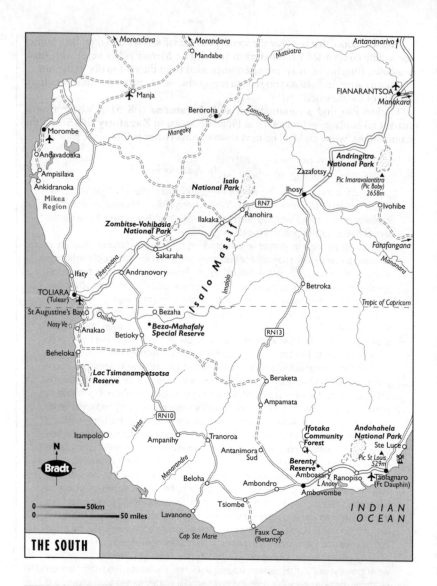

THE SOUTH

Morondava · Morondava · Antananarivo · Matsiatra · Mandabe · FIANARANTSOA · Manakara · Manja · Beroroha · Zomandao · Mangoky · Moromba · Andavadoaka · Ampisilava · Ankidranoka · Zazafotsy · **Andringitra National Park** · Pic Imaravolantitra (Pic Boby) 2658m · **Isalo National Park** · Ihosy · Ivohibe · Mikea Region · **Zombitse-Vohibasia National Park** · Ilakaka · Ranohira · RN7 · Farafangana · Sakaraha · Mananara · Ifaty · Fiherenana · Andranovory · Betroka · TOLIARA (Tulear) · Tropic of Capricorn · St Augustine's Bay · Onilahy · Bezaha · Nosy Ve · Anakao · Betioky · **Beza-Mahafaly Special Reserve** · RN13 · Beheloka · Imaloto · Isalo Massif · **Lac Tsimanampetsotsa Reserve** · Beraketa · Linta · Ampamata · Itampolo · Ampanihy · Tranoroa · **Ifotaka Community Forest** · **Andohahela National Park** · Ste Luce · Antanimora Sud · Pic St Louis 529m · **Berenty Reserve** · Amboasary · Ranopiso · Taolagnaro (Ft Dauphin) · Menarandra · Beloha · Ambondro · L Anony · Ambovombe · Tsiombe · Lavanono · Cap Ste Marie · Faux Cap (Betanty) · INDIAN OCEAN · N · Bradt · 0 50km · 0 50 miles

DISTANCES IN KILOMETRES

Ihosy–Taolagnaro	506km	Toliara–Morombe	290km
Ihosy–Betroka	132km	Bezaha–Ampanihy	199km
Ihosy–Ranohira	91km	Ampanihy–Taolagnaro	334km
Ranohira–Sakaraha	110km	Taolagnaro–Betroka	374km
Sakaraha–Toliara	133km	Taolagnaro–Amboasary	75km
Toliara–Anakao	56km	Taolagnaro–Berenty	89km
Toliara–Ifaty	27km	Tsiombe–Faux Cap	30km
Toliara–Andavadoaka	338km	Tsiombe–Lavanono	94km
Toliara–Bezaha	129km	Itampolo–Anakao	134km

9

The South

This is the most exotic and the most famous part of Madagascar, the region of 'spiny desert' where weird cactus-like trees wave their thorny fingers in the sky, where fragments of 'elephant bird' eggshells may still be found, and where the Mahafaly tribe erect their intriguing and often entertaining *aloalo* stelae above the graves. Here also are some of the country's most popular national parks and reserves, as well as its best beaches and coral reefs. No wonder the south features on almost all tour itineraries.

BACKGROUND INFORMATION

HISTORY Europeans have been coming to this area for a long time. Perhaps the earliest were a group of 600 shipwrecked Portuguese sailors in 1527. Later, when sailors were deliberately landing in Madagascar during the days of the spice trade in the 16th and 17th centuries, St Augustine's Bay, south of modern-day Toliara (Tulear), became a favoured destination. They came for reprovisioning – Dutch and British – trading silver and beads for meat and fruit. One Englishman, Walter Hamond, was so overcome with the delights of Madagascar and the Malagasy, 'the happiest people in the world', that fired by his enthusiasm the British attempted to establish a colony at St Augustine's Bay. It was not a success. The original 140 settlers were soon whittled down to 60 through disease and murder by the local tribesmen who became less happy when they found their favourite beads were not available for trade and that these *vazaha* showed no sign of going away. The colonists left in 1646. Fifty years later St Augustine was a haven for pirates.

THE PEOPLE TODAY Several ethnic groups live in the south: the Vezo (fishermen), Mikea and Masikoro (pastoralists) are subclans of the Sakalava. The Mahafaly, Antanosy, Antandroy and Bara all have their homes in the interior. These southern Malagasy are tough, dark-skinned people with African features, accustomed to the hardship of living in a region where rain seldom falls and finding water and grazing for their large herds of zebu is a constant challenge. The Bara are particularly known for their association with cattle – this warlike tribe resisted Merina rule and were never really subdued until French colonial times. Cattle rustling is a time-honoured custom – a Bara does not achieve manhood until he has stolen a few of his neighbours' cows.

In contrast to the highland people, who go in for second burial and whose tombs are the collective homes of ancestors, those in the south (with the exception of the Bara) commemorate the recently dead. There is more opportunity to be remembered as an individual here, and a Mahafaly or Masikoro man who has lived eventfully, and died rich, will have the highlights of his life perpetuated in the form of wooden carvings (*aloalo*) and colourful paintings adorning his tomb.

Antandroy tombs may be equally colourful. They are large and rectangular (the more important the person the bigger his tomb) and, like those of the Mahafaly, topped with zebu skulls left over from the funeral feast; a very rich man may have over a hundred. They usually have 'male and female' standing stones (or more recently cement towers) at each side. Modern tombs may be brightly painted, though unlike those of the Mahafaly the paintings do not necessarily represent scenes from the life of the deceased.

In Antandroy country, burial sometimes takes place several months after the day of death, which will be commemorated by the sacrifice of cattle and ritual mourning or wailing. A few days later the body is placed in the coffin – and more zebu are sacrificed. Meanwhile finishing touches will be made to the tomb, before the internment ceremony, which takes place over two days or more. The tomb is finally filled in with stones and topped with the horns of the sacrificed zebu. Then the house of the deceased is burnt to the ground. The burial ceremonies over, the family will not go near the tomb again.

The Antanosy have upright stones, cement obelisks or beautifully carved wooden memorials. These, however, are not over the graves themselves but in a sacred and secret place elsewhere.

GETTING AROUND Road travel in the south can be a challenging affair, but all of RN7 to Toliara is now paved. Cyclists and motorists alike will find the deep sand a problem on many of the unmade roads, so many visitors prefer to fly.

IHOSY (PK 611)

Pronounced 'ee*oosh*', this small town is the capital of the Bara tribe. It is about five hours from Fianar by *taxi-brousse* and lies 15km north of the junction for Toliara and Taolagnaro. The road to the former is good; to the latter, bad. An almost impassable road also runs to Farafangana on the east coast (see page 274).

Ihosy is a medium-sized town whose role is to feed and accommodate those travelling south on RN7. There is a post office, a small hospital and a branch of BOA bank (but no ATM). Try opposite Evah for internet. In town there is a nice little square of open-sided *hotelys* serving good Malagasy food.

 WHERE TO STAY AND EAT

🏠 **Zaha** \ 75 740 83. Pleasant, comfortable bungalows with en-suite bathrooms 1km from centre (towards Toliara). €€€€

🏠 **Relais Bara** (16 rooms) \ 75 800 17. Opposite post office. Dbl rooms, mostly en suite, some with hot water. €€€

🏠 **Nirina** (3 rooms) m 032 07 521 95. Opposite Total fuel station, not far from *taxi-brousse* station. Shared facilities but hot water. €€

🏠 **Ravaka** (18 rooms) m 033 12 444 06. Basic dbl & family rooms, a few en suite (cold water). €€

🏠 **Evah** (5 rooms) A reasonable budget hotel, 450m from centre towards Toliara. Shared bathrooms. €

FROM IHOSY TO TAOLAGNARO (FORT DAUPHIN)

This difficult route sees few tourists (most go via Andranovory). Pablo and Itziar, who recently made the journey, report that it takes 7 hours to get as far as Betroka – an unappealing town but with a reasonable hotel (**Trois Fleurs**), lots of supplies, and the last bank before Taolagnaro. The next section of road is in much better condition: 2½ hours to Isoanala and a further 2½ hours to Bereketa – both villages worth a stop. The road deteriorates again beyond that. It takes 4½ hours to Antanimora, with only basic accommodation, then 3 hours to Ambovombe. The final 4½ hours to Taolagnaro are on a tarred but potholed road.

After leaving Ihosy, RN7 crosses the Horombe Plateau. These monotonous grasslands look rather dull from a distance, but up close you can find all kinds of wonderful plants and fungi.

As you approach Ranohira, *Medemia* palms enliven the scenery. Henk Beentje of Kew Gardens explains: 'The palms are properly called *Bismarckia*, but the French didn't like the most common palm in one of their colonies being called after a German so changed the name, quite illegally according to the Code of Botanical Nomenclature!'

RANOHIRA (PK 702)

The small town of Ranohira lies 91km south of Ihosy and is the base for visiting the popular Isalo National Park.

GETTING THERE AND AWAY Getting to Ranohira is no problem. If coming from Toliara (23,000Ar) note that the *taxi-brousses* and buses depart early, so try to book the day before. Continuing south can be difficult since there is no *taxi-brousse* station, and services are usually full by the time they reach Ranohira. *Taxi-brousse* operator **Sonatra** has an agent in town (m *032 57 268 85*) who should be able to reserve a seat, otherwise the best option may be to take a taxi to Ilakaka (5,000Ar) and get a *taxi-brousse* from there.

 WHERE TO STAY AND EAT
Top end €€€€€
🏠 **Jardin du Roy** (27 bungalows) \ 22 351 65/336 23; m 032 07 843 44/033 07 123 07; f 22 351 67; e mda@mda.mg; www.hotels-isalo.com. Luxurious hotel built in grey stone, echoing the landscape of rocky outcrops amongst which it is nestled. The beautifully designed bungalows are attractively furnished, with AC, spacious bathrooms & broad verandas. Excellent restaurant, bar & big pool.
🏠 **Relais de la Reine** (30 rooms) Contact details as Jardin du Roy, which is next door & under same ownership. Blocks of 6 rooms grouped around a courtyard blend into the 40ha gardens. Water is drawn from a stream & is solar-heated for en-suite

showers. 2 deluxe rooms have AC & bath. Pool, tennis court, basketball & horseriding tours in Isalo.
🏠 **Satrana Lodge** (40 bungalows) \ 22 219 74; m 034 14 260 87/032 07 760 59; f 22 213 40; e satranalodge@cortezexpeditions.mg; www.satranalodge.com. Lovely wood-frame bungalows with canvas walls, swish en-suite facilities & wooden deck overlooking Isalo. Newly opened, set in 60ha of bushland. Credit cards accepted. See ad on page 249.
🏠 **Isalo Rock Lodge** (60 rooms) \ 22 328 60; e eres@lifehospitality.com; www.signaturehotels.co.za. Blending in with its rocky surroundings, the impressive new lodge sits high amid the sandstone with breathtaking views. Luxurious rooms & spa.

Upper range €€€€
🏠 **Isalo Ranch** (20 bungalows) \ 24 319 02; f 23 309 28; e info@isalo-ranch.com; www.isalo-ranch.com. Branding itself as an eco-lodge, this hotel has comfy bungalows, mostly en suite with solar-heated water. Public swimming pool & restaurant. Recommended by several readers. Car hire. Camping permitted (8,000Ar/person).

🏠 **Palme de l'Isalo** (19 bungalows) m 032 05 017 64/033 02 534 56; e austral@netclub.mg. Beautifully located, opposite turn for La Fenêtre. Dbl, twin & trpl rooms, en-suite bathrooms. Electricity evenings only.

Mid-range €€€
🏠 **Orchidée d'Isalo** (30 rooms) m 032 44 676 89; www.orchidee-isalo.com. At the centre of the village, attractive en-suite dbl & twin rooms, mostly

with hot water. Reception is at **Zebu Grillé**, their spacious & smart restaurant.

🏠 **Joyau de l'Isalo** (20 bungalows) ☎ 22 536 64; m 033 12 680 92/032 43 832 27; e joyaudisalo@yahoo.fr. Sgl, dbl, twin, trpl & family rooms with en-suite hot water.

🏠 **Motel d'Isalo** (62 bungalows) ☎ 22 330 82; m 032 02 621 23/032 40 892 59; e motelisalo@moov.mg; www.motelisalo.com. The 1st hotel, coming from the north. Nice bungalows with en-suite rooms, solar heating & swimming pool. Much-praised, but away from the centre of town. HB only.

🏠 **Toiles de l'Isalo** (10 bungalows) ☎ 22 245 34/24 223 01; m 032 51 534 30/033 12 327 95.

Dbl, twin & trpl rooms with hot water facilities. Pool & recommended restaurant.

🏠 **Berny** (18 rooms) ☎ 75 801 76; m 032 05 257 69/75; f 94 419 20. Central dbl & trpl rooms, mostly en suite.

🏠 **Momo Trek** (4 rooms & 7 bungalows) m 032 44 187 90/033 90 050 07; e momo_trek@yahoo.fr. Near park office. Bara-style huts with shared cold-water facilities & trpl rooms with en-suite hot water. Camping: 3,000Ar/person with own tent or 10,000Ar/tent inc 2-man tent hire.

Budget €€

🏠 **Chez Alice** m 032 04 042 22/032 02 055 68. Bungalows & Bara-style huts (*paillottes*) on a meadow 500m from town, overlooking Isalo & its spectacular sunsets. The gregarious proprietor speaks some English. Excellent food. Camping: 3,000Ar/person; tent hire 6,000Ar.

🏠 **Maison Jumelle (Chez Thomas)** (17 rooms) m 032 43 708 69. Basic dbl & family rooms with shared cold-water facilities.

MONEY AND COMMUNICATIONS Ranohira has no bank, but if you get stuck hotels Berny and Orchidée will change cash. Internet is available at the **Orange Boutique** and at **Telecentre Communal** (at the town hall) for 200Ar/minute.

SHOPPING Located opposite Orchidée, **Joyeux Lemuriens** (⊕ *06.30–21.00*) is an *épicerie* well stocked with drinks, biscuits and a few tinned goods. Much bigger is **Supermarché de l'Isalo** (⊕ *Mon–Sat 08.00–12.00 & 14.30–18.00, Sun 14.30–18.00*), 850m from Ranohira centre towards Tana. It sells food and a surprisingly good range of camping equipment as well as clothing.

ISALO NATIONAL PARK

The combination of sandstone rocks (cut by deep canyons and eroded into weird shapes), rare endemic plants and dry weather (between June and August rain is almost unknown) makes this park particularly rewarding. For botanists there are pachypodiums and a locally endemic aloe; and for lemur-lovers there are sifakas, brown lemurs and ring-tails. Isalo is also sacred to the Bara tribe. For hundreds of years they have used caves in the canyon walls as burial sites.

☞ **WARNING!** Hiking should not be undertaken lightly at Isalo. It can get very hot and many trails offer little shade. Avoid taking valuables to La Fenêtre as there have been muggings there.

PERMITS, GUIDES AND VEHICLES You will need to buy a permit (prices on page 72) from the park office in Ranohira (m *033 13 172 58; e parc.isalo@yahoo.fr; ⊕ 07.00–17.00*). It doesn't open until 07.00, meaning that by the time you have bought permits and got organised it's the hottest time of the day. So, if possible, make your arrangements at the office the day before. They also sell simple maps of the park.

Almost half of the 60 guides speak English; check the noticeboard for information on the specialities of each one. Guide fees are also posted on the wall. They range from 16,000Ar for the Piscine Naturelle or Cascade des Nymphes, or

20,000Ar for the Canyon des Makis, to 52,000Ar for a combination of all three. For trekking with camping, guides are 25,000Ar per day and porters cost 10,000Ar.

For most excursions you will need a vehicle to get to the appropriate start point to avoid the rather dull one- to two-hour walk from Ranohira to the park boundary. Guides can organise a car and driver for you but note that they will take a commission; so if you're on a tight budget it may be cheaper to find a driver yourself.

ISALO INTERPRETATION CENTRE (MAISON DE L'ISALO) (m *033 04 496 05/032 55 487 69;* ⏰ *06.30–18.00*) This is a tremendous museum in a beautiful building, well worth a visit to learn more about the wildlife of the park and the people who live locally. The well-designed exhibits have English, French and Malagasy explanations (Italian is also in the pipeline at the time of writing). Sited almost 10km south of Ranohira, a visit may most conveniently be combined with La Fenêtre.

HIKING AND TREKKING There are several established circuits with campsites, providing all the Isalo specials of lemurs, cool leafy canyons, and hot, dry plains with extraordinary rock formations and accompanying succulent plants. If possible, arrange to camp overnight in the park. That way you can hike in the cooler parts of the day.

Momo Trek (see page 206) organises trekking packages with guide, porters, meals and camping equipment included for 90,000–165,000Ar per person (price depends on group size) for two days, and longer treks up to 305,000–490,000Ar for six days.

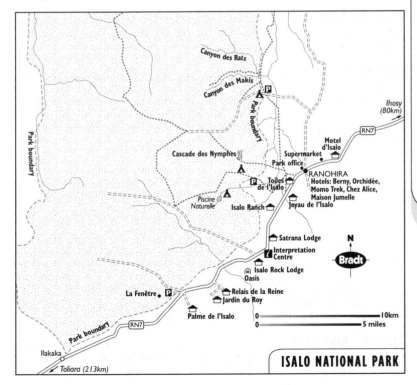

ISALO NATIONAL PARK

Circuit Namaza This has you following a stream (some scrambling) up a leafy canyon to the Cascade des Nymphes. The walk takes 30–45 minutes and you are rewarded at the end with a refreshing swim in surprisingly cold water. The pool is very deep, and you need to swim to see the waterfall and the imposing, fern-fringed black cliffs which almost hide the sky. The campsite here is regularly visited by ring-tails, brown lemurs and hoopoes.

Canyon des Makis This is 18km by track from Ranohira (4x4 only) or 9km on foot. At the canyon a path goes over rocks and along the edge of the tumbling river; there are pools into which you can fling yourself at intervals and, at the top, a small waterfall under which to have a shower. The sheer rocks hung with luxuriant ferns broaden out to provide views of the bare mountain behind, and trees and palms provide shade for a picnic. A visit may be combined with the neighbouring **Canyon des Rats** for a full-day trip.

Piscine Naturelle (natural swimming pool) This is justifiably the most popular destination for hikers in Isalo, so can be crowded. The palm-fringed pool, constantly filled by a waterfall, is both stunningly beautiful and wonderful for swimming. There is also an open-sided shelter where Benson's rock thrushes flirt with bathers. The nearby campsite has a flush toilet, shower and barbecue stoves.

La Fenêtre This is another popular site – perhaps too popular at times. A natural rock formation provides a window to the setting sun. It is just off RN7 so no hiking is necessary, nor do you need a permit or guide. A taxi from Ranohira should cost about 30,000Ar for the round trip.

Grotte des Portugais Some 45km from Ranohira at the northern extremity of the national park, this 32-metre-long cave is reachable by 4x4 or four to six days' trekking. This picturesque area is the place to head for to get away from other tourists.

BEYOND THE PARK Those with a 4x4 can explore some of the dirt roads bordering the park. Wendy Applequist 'got a guide from Ranohira and went up a dirt road west of the park towards the valley of the Malio River. In a small forest patch we rediscovered a liana previously known from only two 50-year-old collections. This is an interesting piece of forest. When you hit sand you have to park and walk through dense, liana-filled jungle with gigantic butterflies flitting through the gloom. Our guide told us that when he was a boy, they used to roast and eat the huge spiders that spin webs across the trail to catch *vazaha*. "But that was when I was a boy," he said while I was gagging. "I wouldn't do that now, of course – because they're endemic!" I thought this was a young man who had a real future in science!'

ILAKAKA (PK 729)

This extraordinary settlement has sprung up over the past decade or so as the centre of the sapphire trade. Tour buses drive straight through with the windows up for fear of bandits, but providing you are sensible over security it is worth a visit for the Wild West atmosphere. Every other shop has the word *saphir* above its doorway, and the quantity of high-priced consumer goods for sale is remarkable. If you decide to stay, **Les Jokers** has rooms with air conditioning and TV.

SAPPHIRE MINE TOUR (m *033 14 737 57/033 14 780 42/032 02 624 85;* e *colorlineilakaka@gmail.com*) Sapphire company **Color Line** runs visits to the open mines allowing you to see first-hand the massive effort (and danger) involved in

The crystalline rocks and gravels available to today's miners, sifters and washers-of-gravel were once 10–30km deep within the earth – not necessarily underground but perhaps at the heart of ancient mountains now eroded away. Millions of years ago, the land flexed upwards so the rocks now on the surface were in fact formed under tens of kilometres of other rock in conditions of great pressure and great heat – ideal for the formation of crystalline gems. Gemstones are, by their nature, dense and durable, so they survive the ravages of time. Mountains and rocks were gradually ground down and washed away towards the sea and in some areas of the west coast gem-hunters have to trace and chase the old river channels in search of deposits of the hard, bright and valuable survivors of barely imaginable eruptions and upheavals.

Elsewhere, traditional mining is necessary. To retrieve gemstones at Ilakaka, for example, an exploratory shaft is sunk until miners recognise a likely combination of rock types. Then a few bags of local gravel are washed; if the results are good, a pit is sunk and more work begins. One miner said that half a dozen bags of gravel from an exploratory hole might yield four million ariary's worth of sapphires. The catch is that the payload layer is often around 15m deep in the earth, yet only about one metre thick – a big, deep hole for what might prove to be a small yield.

When a find is made, the Malagasy miners will often arrive in great numbers from far away, willing to break their backs shifting dirt with shovels for the duration of the rush – two years? ten years? a hundred years? Curiously, the government has precluded the use of heavy machinery by the Malagasy people while outsiders are free to mine in whatever fashion they wish. Thai and Sri Lankan miners use earth-moving equipment to dig the efficient way. Strange enough; but add to this the shady nature of the gem industry: riches and smuggling. Instead of Madagascar getting rich now that its treasures are reaching the marketplace, money floods out of the country at a rate beyond anyone's wildest dreams. The richest Malagasies in the business seem not to be digging but instead are the ones providing security for the foreign buyers.

The jewellery industry worldwide is trying to rebalance the distribution of money so that countries with a natural abundance of gemstones, and the indigenous miners of those riches, will get a better deal. The Kimberly Process is working well for the diamond industry and something might emerge from that for the coloured stone trade. In the meantime, if you are thinking of buying loose gemstones, remember that specialists and big business will have creamed the top off the supply. Buy something you fall in love with – there's plenty to choose from – but don't expect to get rich quick by selling it when you get home.

finding these tiny gems. A visit costs 24,000Ar per person and takes about an hour. The company also does cutting and polishing demonstrations in their showroom. Enquire at the bar called **Al$_2$O$_3$**.

CONTINUING SOUTH TO TOLIARA

The drive from Isalo to Toliara (243km) takes a minimum of four hours. The sapphire rush is moving south and you will pass the temporary grass huts and piles of earth dug by fortune seekers for many kilometres.

After Ilakaka the rugged mountains give way to grasslands, and following the rains there are many flowers – the large white *Crinum firmifolium* and the Madagascar periwinkle – but in the dry season it's quite monotonous.

ZOMBITSE-VOHIBASIA NATIONAL PARK (PK 795) (e *angaptle@gmail.com;* ⊕ *07.00–16.00*) Zombitse is a stark example of the effects of deforestation. Years of continuous felling have turned the surrounding areas into an arid moonscape and what remains is an isolated pocket of forest, thankfully now protected. The park covers 36,300ha, straddling RN7. It is an important example of a boundary zone between the western and southern domains of vegetation and so has a high level of biodiversity.

Zombitse is of major significance to birdwatchers as it offers the chance to glimpse one of Madagascar's rarest endemics, Appert's greenbul, which is confined to this forest. In addition to birds you have a good chance of seeing sifaka, red-fronted brown lemurs, and the nocturnal sportive lemur peering out of its nest hole. The locally endemic Standing's day gecko is also easily found.

The park office is on the southern side of RN7. There are four easy circuits (each 1.5–5km/1–2½ hours) costing 3,000Ar for the guide per circuit.

It takes just over an hour to reach the park from Isalo, or two to three hours from Toliara, so serious birdwatchers should leave as early as possible in the morning to avoid the heat. Better still, stay in Sakaraha, 17km to the west. It is also possible to camp at the park entrance, but there are no facilities and no water source.

SAKARAHA (PK 812) Ilakaka's sapphire rush is spreading southwards, with several gemstone stores now open along RN7 in Sakaraha. This small town offers some of the closest accommodation to Zombitse National Park and the reserve's welcome centre is also here.

Where to stay and eat

🏠 **Zombitse Ecolodge** (10 bungalows) m 033 12 325 64; e ecolodge@zombitse.de; www.zombitse.de. Situated 7km from the park entrance, this lodge is on RN7, 10km east of Sakaraha. Fairly simple bungalows, 3 of which are en suite. B/fast inc. €€€

🏠 **Relais de Sakaraha** (8 chalets) Hotel, bar, restaurant & disco. Each chalet has a dbl room upstairs, another downstairs, an en-suite squat toilet & bucket shower. The semicircular upper level with curved balcony is reminiscent of a lighthouse! Close to south *taxi-brousse* station but noisy on disco nights. €€

🏠 **Palace Club** (3 rooms) French-run hotel on the southwest side of town with a bar & nightclub. Rooms with bucket showers; shared toilets. Excellent food & helpful staff. €€

🏠 **Venus** (9 bungalows) A short walk out of town. Mostly en suite with shower, but 3 cheaper ones have shared facilities. €

SAKARAHA TO TOLIARA Beyond Sakaraha you will start to see painted tombs, some with *aloalo*, near the road. As you get closer to Toliara you'll see your first baobabs and pass through a cotton-growing region. Look out for the enormous nests of hamerkop birds in roadside trees.

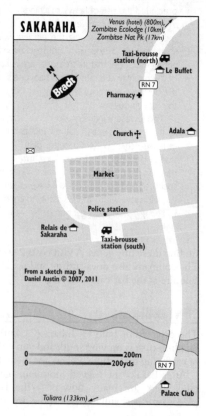

SAKARAHA

Venus (hotel) (800m),
Zombitse Ecolodge (10km),
Zombitse Nat Pk (17km)

Taxi-brousse station (north)

Le Buffet

RN 7

Pharmacy ✚

Church ✚

Adala

Market

Police station

Relais de Sakaraha

Taxi-brousse station (south)

From a sketch map by
Daniel Austin © 2007, 2011

0 ———— 200m
0 ———— 200yds

RN 7

Palace Club

Toliara (133km)

About two hours from Sakaraha is the small village of **Andranovory**, which has a colourful Sunday market. Another hour and Toliara's table mountain comes into view on the right; half an hour later you pass the airport and head for the town.

TOLIARA (TULEAR) (PK 945)

The pronunciation of the French (Tulear) and the Malagasy names is the same: 'tool*ea*r'. Toliara's history is centred on St Augustine's Bay, described at the beginning of this chapter, although the name of the town is said to derive from an encounter with one of those early sailors who asked a local inhabitant where he might moor his boat. The Malagasy replied: '*toly eroa*' ('mooring down there'). The town itself is relatively modern – 1895 – and was designed by an uninspired French architect. His tree planting was more successfully aesthetic, and the shady tamarind trees (*kily*) give welcome respite from the blazing sun.

There are three good reasons to visit Toliara: the rich marine life with good snorkelling and diving, the Mahafaly and Masikoro tombs with a museum that puts it all in context, and the remarkable spiny forest and its accompanying fauna. Don't miss a visit to the Arboretum d'Antsokay and/or the Reniala Forest. These two privately run places can give you an experience as good as many national parks, at a fraction of the cost.

The beaches south of the town have fine white sand, but those in the north are often rocky. Beyond the beaches is an extensive coral reef, sadly now suffering from coral bleaching so no longer particularly rewarding for snorkellers. Toliara itself, regrettably, has no beach, just mangroves and mud flats.

☞ **WARNINGS!** In the cool season (June to September) the nights in Toliara are quite cold but cheaper hotels rarely supply enough blankets. Businesses close 12.00–15.00; banks are usually closed 11.30–14.00. There have been a few muggings after dark so take a taxi if going out late.

GETTING THERE AND AWAY

By road *Taxi-brousses* run regularly on RN7, and cost 45,000Ar to Tana (about 18 hours), 30,000Ar to Fianar (10 hours), 20,000Ar to Ranohira/Isalo (4½ hours) and 7,000Ar to Sakaraha/Zombitse (2 hours). **KoFiFiVo** operates daily services on the more adventurous route to Taolagnaro in a *camion-brousse*: 36,000Ar to Taolagnaro (2 days), 30,000Ar to Tsihombe, 20,000Ar to Ampanihy and 13,000Ar to Betioky. To take the same route at a more leisurely pace, **Boogie Pilgrim** (see page 86) do 4x4 connections to Taolagnaro taking seven days, so plenty of time to see the sights *en route*. For the even more difficult overland route to Morondava, see page 221.

By air There are flights most days from Tana, Morondava and Taolagnaro, but in the high season these tend to be fully booked. However, it's always worth going to the airport, whatever they say in the office.

GETTING AROUND Distances can be far, but *pousse-pousses* are plentiful. A typical trip at the *vazaha* price should cost around 1,500Ar; more at night or in the rain. For taxis, the going rate is 3,000Ar for any trip in town (4,000Ar after 20.00) or 15,000Ar to the airport. See also *Tour operators and vehicle hire* on page 216.

⌂ **WHERE TO STAY** Most visitors spending any time in the Toliara area stay at the beach resorts (see pages 218–27) but there are some good-value hotels in or near the town.

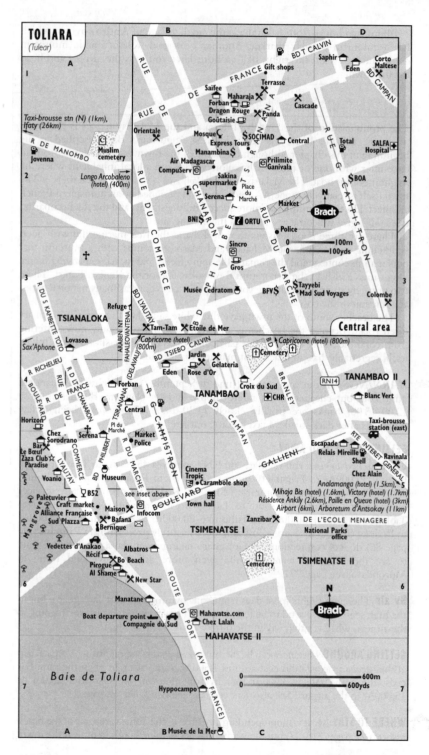

TOLIARA
(Tulear)

Taxi-brousse stn (N) (1km),
Ifaty (26km)

R DE MANOMBO

Jovenna

Muslim cemetery

Longo Arcobaleno
(hotel) (400m)

RUE DE FRANCE

RUE DE LT SIRANANA

RUE DU COMMERCE

BD LYAUTAY

ARABEN NY FAHALEOVANTENA (DELAVAU)

BD TSIEBO CALVIN

BD T CALVIN

Saphir

Eden

Corto
Maltese

BD CAMPAN

Gift shops

Terrasse

Saïfee

Maharaja

Forban
Dragon Rouge
Goûtaisie

Panda

Cascade

Orientale

Mosque

Express Tours
Manambina

Air Madagascar
CompuServ

Sakina
supermarket

SOCIMAD

Central

Prilimite
Ganivala

Total

SALFA
Hospital

RUE DU MARCHE

RUE G CAMPISTRON

BOA

Serena

Place
du
Marché

Market

Bradt

N

BNI

ORTU

Police

0   100m
0   100yds

Sincro

Gros

Musée Cedratom

BFV

Tayyebi
Mad Sud Voyages

Colombe

Central area

TSIANALOKA

Refuge

Lovasoa

Sax'Aphone

Tam-Tam

Etoile de Mer

Capricorne (hotel)
(800m)

Cemetery

Capricorne (hotel) (800m)

BD BRANLEY

Jardin

Gelateria

Eden

Rose d'Or

TANAMBAO I

Croix du Sud

CHR

RNI4

TANAMBAO II

Blanc Vert

R RICHELIEU

R DU S KAHBETTE TOTO

R LT CHANARON

RUE DE FRANCE

BOULEVARD

Forban

Central

Horizon

Chez
Sorodrano

Bar

Le Bœuf
Zaza Club
Paradise

Serena

Pl du
Marché

Market
Police

Museum

Voanio

BD PHILIBERT

BD CAMPAN

GALLIENI

RTE INTERET GENERAL

Taxi-brousse
station (east)

Escapade

Relais Mireille
Shell

Ravinala

Chez Alain

Analamanga (hotel) (1.5km),
Mihaja Bis (hotel) (1.6km), Victory (hotel) (1.7km),
Résidence Ankily (2.6km), Paille en Queue (hotel) (3km),
Airport (6km), Arboretum d'Antsokay (11km)

Paletuvier

Craft market

Alliance Française

Sud Plzaza

BD LYAUTAY

B52

Maison

Bafana
Bernique

see inset above

Cinema
Tropic

Carambole shop

Town hall

Infocom

Mangrove

Vedettes d'Anakao
Récif

Bo Beach

Pirogue
Al Shame

New Star

Albatros

Manatane

TSIMENATSE I

Zanzibar

R DE L'ECOLE MENAGERE

National Parks
office

TSIMENATSE II

Cemetery

N

Bradt

Boat departure point
Compagnie du Sud

Mahavatse.com
Chez Lalah

MAHAVATSE II

ROUTE DU PORT (AV DE FRANCE)

Baie de Toliara

Hyppocampo

0   600m
0   600yds

B Musée de la Mer

Top end €€€€€

⌂ **Hyppocampo** [212 B7] (8 rooms & 2 suites) \ 94 410 21; e info@hyppocampo.com; www.hyppocampo.com. Beautifully designed, this recently opened luxurious hotel at the south of town offers spacious rooms with AC, internet, TV & DVD player. Suites also have hydro massage shower & bath. Massage, pool & sea-view bar.

Upper range €€€€

⌂ **Victory** [212 D5] (43 rooms) Rte de l'Aeroport; \ 94 440 64; m 032 42 820 87; f 94 443 35; e hotelvictory.tulear@gmail.com; www.hoteltulear-victory.com. Away from town, a very good hotel with clean, airy rooms that have AC, hot shower, hairdryer, TV, minibar, fridge, safe & free Wi-Fi. Good restaurant & large swimming pool (8,000Ar for non-guests).

⌂ **Capricorne** [212 B3] (34 rooms) \ 94 426 20/24 743 49; f 94 431 66; m 032 05 465 30; e capricorne@madagascar-resorts.com; www.madagascar-resorts.com. Well-run with a good restaurant. Most rooms with AC. B/fast inc.

⌂ **Paille en Queue** [212 D5] (18 bungalows) Andranomena; \ 94 447 00; e socoeto@simicro.mg; www.pailleenqueue.com. Only 5mins from airport. En-suite bungalows, with AC & TV, arranged round a central pool. The once-excellent service reportedly becoming less reliable.

⌂ **Eden & Saphir** [212 D1] (34 rooms) Tanambao; \ 94 415 66/442 59; f 94 442 60; e eden.hotel@yahoo.fr. Great central location & nice atmosphere; en-suite AC rooms with TV & most with minibar. Car hire.

⌂ **Serena** [212 C2] (10 rooms) \ 94 411 73; f 94 434 05; e serenatulear@gmail.com; www.serenatulear.com. Attractive new AC rooms with minibar, TV & free Wi-Fi. Nice b/fast terrace overlooking market. Airport transfers inc.

⌂ **Saïfee** [212 B1] (21 rooms) Rue de l'Eglise; \ 94 410 82; m 032 05 410 82; e saifee_hotel@tulear.org; www.tulear.org. Dbl, twin & trpl en-suite rooms with AC, TV & balcony; Wi-Fi. B/fast inc.

⌂ **Paletuvier** [212 A5] (55 rooms) Bd Lyautey; \ 94 440 39; f 94 444 10; e hotelpaletuvier@yahoo.fr; www.hoteltulear-lepaletuvier.com. En-suite sgl, dbl & trpl rooms (but sgl has cold water only). Internet café.

Mid-range €€€

⌂ **Longo Hotel Arcobaleno** [212 B2] (12 rooms) m 032 40 454 23/032 02 506 12; e longo.hotel@yahoo.it. En-suite rooms with TV, a few also with AC & balcony.

⌂ **Sud Plazza** [212 A5] (32 rooms) \ 94 903 02; m 032 46 761 89; e sud_plaz@yahoo.fr. En-suite rooms in spacious gardens facing the sea, some with AC. Casino **Le Joker** on site. Cards accepted. Airport transfer inc.

⌂ **Escapade** [212 D5] (10 bungalows) Bd Gallieni; \ 94 411 82; m 032 02 202 05; e escapade@moov.mg. En-suite dbl & twin bungalows in peaceful garden. Visa accepted.

⌂ **Récif** [212 A6] (16 rooms) Bd Lyautey; \ 94 446 88; m 032 40 755 39. En-suite bathrooms (hot water), some with AC & ocean view. Nice swimming pool (5,000Ar for non-guests) & restaurant.

⌂ **Manatane** [212 B6] (23 rooms & dorm) Bd Lyautey; m 032 05 267 24/032 05 309 09; e hotel.manatane@yahoo.fr. Brand new seafront hotel. Rooms have balcony, TV & en-suite hot-water facilities. 10-bed dorm for groups. Nice restaurant.

⌂ **Albatros** [212 B6] (14 rooms) Av de France; \ 94 432 10; m 032 40 414 08; e hotelalbatros@moov.mg. Dbl, twin & trpl rooms with en-suite hot water & some with TV.

⌂ **Chez Alain** [212 D5] (15 bungalows & 5 rooms) \ 94 415 27; f 94 423 79; e c.alain@moov.mg. Deservedly popular with rooms to suit a range of budgets: from simple bungalow to suite with AC & hot water. Bike & 4x4 hire. ReefDoctor has an information point here.

⌂ **Résidence Ankily** [212 D5] (10 rooms) \ 94 445 50; m 032 40 328 77; f 94 445 51; e laresidenceankily@yahoo.fr. En-suite rooms with AC & TV, some with minibar & bath.

Budget €€

⌂ **Refuge** [212 B3] (11 rooms) \ 94 423 28; f 94 425 94. Very pleasant central hotel. En-suite dbl & trpl rooms, some with AC & TV. Small pool (4,000Ar for non-guests). 4x4 hire.

⌂ **Al Shame** [212 A6] (31 rooms & 1 bungalow) Bd Lyautey; \ 94 447 28; m 032 05 267 24. Simple hotel in seafront location with en-suite rooms (cold water).

⌂ **Arboretum d'Antsokay** (4 bungalows) The arboretum (see page 216) has en-suite bungalows (cold water); perfect for early-rising birdwatchers & other wildlife fans.

⌂ **Forban** [212 C1] (3 rooms) m 032 04 781 15. Dbl rooms with en-suite cold shower. They also have bungalows in Ifaty.

⌂ **Pirogue** [212 A6] (12 bungalows) \ 94 415 37; m 032 02 892 35. Dbl bungalows with en-suite cold-water facilities. Can be noisy.

⌂ **Chez Lalah** [212 B6] (11 rooms) Av de France; \ 94 434 17. Quiet, inexpensive & comfy. Some rooms en suite, a couple with AC. Quad hire.

Penny-pincher €

⌂ **Voanio** [212 A5] (4 bungalows) Bd Lyautey; m 033 14 088 73. Tin-roofed bungalows are surrounded by palm trees in a breezy setting. Cold showers & some rooms with en-suite toilet.

⌂ **Central** [212 C2] (8 rooms) m 032 02 553 25/034 01 410 80. Aptly named, bang in the centre of town. Large dbl & twin rooms with en-suite hot shower, balcony, TV & optional AC.

⌂ **Relais Mireille** [212 D5] (6 rooms) m 032 54 043 44. Dbl & family rooms, en suite (cold water).

⌂ **Blanc Vert** [212 D4] (20 rooms) m 032 07 701 34. Good value dbl rooms with en-suite hot shower.

⌂ **Analamanga** [212 D5] (13 rooms) RN7; m 032 44 442 42. Bungalows on stilts in quiet setting. Basic dbl rooms & a few more expensive en-suite ones.

⌂ **Mihaja Bis** [212 D5] (11 rooms) m 032 04 361 66. En-suite dbl rooms, some with TV. Car hire.

⌂ **Croix du Sud** [212 C4] (3 rooms) \ 94 916 05/905 93; m 032 05 250 05. Basic *chambres d'hôtes* above restaurant **Relax**.

⌂ **Chez Sorodrano** [212 A5] (4 rooms) m 032 07 905 20. Sgl & dbl rooms with en-suite shower.

✗ WHERE TO EAT

✗ **Etoile de Mer** [212 B3] Bd Lyautey; m 032 02 605 60; ⏲ 06.00–15.00 & 18.00–23.00. This place has maintained high standards since I first visited in 1982. Excellent pizza (including vegetarian options), great seafood; also good Afghan & Indian dishes.

✗ **Jardin** [212 B4] ⏲ Tue–Sun 09.30–12.30 & 16.00–22.30, Mon closed. Exceptional, Italian-run restaurant decorated in a pub style. Jovial owner; English & Italian spoken. Lasagne & seafood platter especially recommended; also takeaway ice cream, pastries, cakes & pizza.

✗ **Gelateria** [212 C4] ⏲ Tue–Sun 09.30–12.30 & 16.00–22.30, Mon closed. Much recommended ice creams; also cakes & snacks. Pizza each eve.

✗ **Zanzibar** [212 C5] Rte de l'Ecole Ménagère; m 032 46 185 30; ⏲ Fri–Wed 10.00–14.00 & 16.00–22.00, Thu closed. Malagasy snacks, huge pizzas, friendly atmosphere.

✗ **Corto Maltese** [212 D1] m 032 02 643 23/032 04 657 42; ⏲ Mon–Fri, closed w/end. An upmarket restaurant serving really delicious Italian food. Menu varies day to day.

✗ **Bernique** [212 A5] Bd Gallieni; m 032 02 606 55; ⏲ Mon–Sat, Sun closed. French-owned bar with snacks & comprehensive collection of malt whiskies.

✗ **Panda** [212 C1] ⏲ Mon–Sat, Sun closed. Excellent Chinese cuisine at good prices.

✗ **Terrasse** [212 C1] m 032 02 650 60. Typical menu with some Malagasy dishes. They serve English breakfasts! Also ice cream & takeaway pizza. Nice shady outdoor eating area.

✗ **Bar Le Bœuf** [212 A5] m 032 53 397 61; ⏲ 07.00–00.00. A pleasant grill bar/restaurant. Great steak; also pizza.

✗ **Orientale** [212 B2] French family-owned restaurant.

✗ **Maison** [212 B5] Bd Gallieni; \ 94 919 62; ⏲ Tue–Sat 08.30–late, Sun 18.00–late. An airy restaurant with thatched roof & attractive dining area. Pizza, seafood, good steaks & bar with pool table.

✗ **New Star** [212 B6] m 032 04 563 56; ⏲ Tue–Sun 07.30–late, Mon closed. Restaurant & bar.

✗ **Tam-Tam** [212 B3] m 032 04 035 12; e tamtamcafe@moov.mg; ⏲ Mon–Sat 16.00–late, Sun closed. Newly opened tapas bar. Pool table.

✗ **Maharaja** [212 C1] Mid-price restaurant; menu has a section of 'Indian specialities' (one of which, curiously, is spaghetti bolognaise!).

✗ **Cascade** [212 C1] \ 94 938 25; m 032 50 106 90; ⏲ daily except Sun lunch. Upstairs restaurant above Blackwear shop. Fairly upmarket.

✗ **Bo Beach** [212 A6] m 032 04 009 13; ⏲ 07.30–late. Breezy seafront restaurant & bar with pool table, darts, Wi-Fi & small cybercafé.

✗ **Ravinala** [212 D5] ⏲ Sun–Fri 06.00–21.00, Sat closed. Traditional Malagasy food.

🍷 **Dragon Rouge** [212 C1] \ 94 917 69; ⏲ Tue–Sun, Mon closed. Snack bar.

🍷 **Rose d'Or** [212 B4] ⏲ Wed–Mon except Sun afternoon, Tue closed. Boulangerie & patisserie.

☕ **Gros** [212 C3] ⏰ 07.00–12.00 &
15.30–19.30. *Salon de thé.*
☕ **Goûtaisie** [212 C1] ⏰ Mon–Sat 06.30–19.00,
Sun closed. Snack bar with small terrace. A wonderful
place to have b/fast; also chocolate, pastries &
Indian dishes.
☕ **Horizon** [212 A4] Snack bar.

NIGHTLIFE

☆ **Zaza Club Paradise** [212 A5] This nightclub has
long been popular but hassling from prostitutes &
local girls looking for a *vazaha* boyfriend has
worsened in recent years.

♀ **B52** [212 A5] m 032 56 278 48;
⏰ 11.00–15.00 & 18.00–02.00 (w/end till 03.00).
Lounge bar with cocktails & snacks. Pool table &
casino with roulette & poker. Free Wi-Fi.
♀ **Casino Capricorne** [212 B3] Pleasant hangout with
entertainment including darts & pool table.

INTERNET

🅴 **Prilimite Ganivala** [212 C2] ⏰ Mon–Sat
08.00–12.00 & 14.45–18.30, Sun closed. Internet for
35Ar/min.
🅴 **CompuServ** [212 B2] ⏰ Mon–Sat 07.00–12.00
& 14.00–17.30, Sun 08.30–11.00. Has 9 computers
for 30 Ar/min.
🅴 **Sincro** [212 C3] ⏰ Mon–Sat 08.00–12.00 &
15.00–18.30, Sun closed. Has 8 computers for
30Ar/min.

🅴 **Mahavatse.com** [212 B6] ⏰ 08.00–18.00. In
front of Chez Lalah. AC & facilities for printing. Can
be slow; price 35Ar/min.
🅴 **Infocom** [212 B5] ✆ 94 444 89. Small cybercafé
with 7 computers; 40Ar/min, cheaper if prepaid.
🅴 **Cyberpaositra** [212 B5] At the post office on Bd
Gallieni; ⏰ Mon–Sat 08.00–20.00, Sun closed.
30Ar/min.

MONEY

$ **Tayyebi** [212 C3] Rue du Marché; ✆ 94 442 51;
f 94 423 20. Recommended bureau de change. Visa
cash advances.
$ **SOCIMAD** [212 C2] Corner of Rue Père Joseph
Castan & Rue de l'Eglise; ✆ 94 216 91. Fast &
efficient bureau de change.

$ **Manambina** [212 C2] ✆ 94 416 98; m 032 02
550 81. Money changer, including travellers' cheques
& Visa.
$ **BNI** [212 B2] Pl du Marché. ATM & Western
Union.
$ **BFV** [212 C3] Bd Lyautey. ATM & Western Union.
$ **BOA** [212 D2] Rue Campistron. 2 ATMs.

SHOPPING For general supplies, **Sakina** [212 C2] is a well stocked small
supermarket (✆ 94 417 35).

The main **craft market** [212 A5] in Toliara is towards the end of Boulevard
Gallieni near the monument. There is also a seashell market but tourists should
resist buying these (the creatures are harvested alive to ensure an intact shell
despite many species being threatened with extinction).

Bafana [212 A5] This boutique near the craft
market sells a range of good-quality local crafts; run
on a co-operative basis.
Carambole Shop [212 B5] Bd Gallieni. Part of the
bright orange bldg of NGO Bel Avenir. A nice little
boutique with a variety of souvenirs.
Univers de la Pierre [212 C2] m 032 02 532 02;
⏰ Mon–Sat. Precious stones from Madagascar
including sapphires, rubies & emeralds. Visa accepted.

The Mohair Man [212 A5] m 032 07 767 16;
e letapismalgache@moov.mg;
www.letapismalgache.com. Handmade carpets from
Ampanihy. Thick & hardwearing, these mats & rugs
are produced from goat hair with both Malagasy &
contemporary designs using natural vegetable/plant
dyes. Showroom near the craft market.

MEDICAL The **Centre Hôpital Régional** [212 C4] (✆ 94 418 55; e *chrpu@
moov.mg*) is the main hospital for the southwest and can handle serious
emergencies. **Clinique St Luc** at Andabizy (✆ 94 422 47; m *032 02 294 51;*

e cliniquesaint-luc@dts.mg) is a private clinic, on the road to the airport, that can handle most medical problems.

WHAT TO SEE AND DO The very helpful regional **tourist office** [212 C2] is located near the market in an office raised on stilts (\ 94 446 05; m 032 51 296 56; e ortu@ tulear-tourisme.com; www.tulear-tourisme.com; ⏰ Mon–Fri 08.30–12.00 & 15.00–18.00).

The **National Parks office** [212 D5] is on Rue de l'Ecole Ménagère (\ 94 435 70; m 032 07 606 77; e angaptle@gmail.com; ⏰ Mon–Fri 07.30–12.00 & 14.30–18.00).

Tour operators and vehicle hire

Air Madagascar [212 B2] \ 94 415 85; ⏰ Mon–Fri 08.00–11.30 & 15.00–17.00, Sat 08.00–10.00, Sun closed

Mad Sud Voyages [212 C3] \ 94 423 20; ⏰ Mon–Fri 08.00–12.00 & 15.00–18.00, w/end 08.00–12.00

Express Tours & Voyages [212 C2] Bd Philibert Tsiranana; \ 94 419 04; m 032 07 235 25; f 94 419 05; e etvtul@moov.mg; ⏰ Mon–Fri 08.00–12.00 & 15.00–18.00. Travel agency including flights.

🚗 **Budget** \ 94 434 94; m 032 05 403 01; www.budget.mg. Car & 4x4 hire (with driver) by the day, week or month.

🚗 **Vedettes d'Anakao** [212 A6] \ 94 930 44/45; m 032 04 624 09/032 43 555 74; e vedettes@ tulear-tourisme.com. 4x4 rentals. Runs day trips to

Anakao, Nosy Ve, Sarondrano & further afield to Tsimanampetsotsa etc. They can also organise transport to Morondava (3 days; €180).

🚗 **Compagnie du Sud** [212 B6] \ 94 437 21; m 032 04 624 09; e info@compagniedusud.com; www.compagniedusud.com. Car rental & boat transfers to Anakao & Ifaty.

🚗 **Trajectoire** On road to airport; \/f 94 433 00; m 032 07 433 00; e trajectoire@moov.mg; www.trajectoire.it. Motorbike & quad hire. Runs small-group adventure tours in remote areas, including Makay Massif (motorbike) & Mangoky River (canoe).

🚗 **Quad du Capricorne** [212 A5] \ 94 437 17; m 032 02 680 89/032 40 463 40; e quad@ moov.mg; www.quad-du-capricorne.com. Near the craft market. Quad hire & guided quad tours.

Museums
The small museum **Musée Cedratom** [212 C3] (⏰ Mon–Sat 07.30–11.30 & 14.30–17.30 except Sat afternoon; entry 4,000Ar) on Boulevard Philibert Tsiranana is run by the University of Toliara. There are some remarkable exhibits, including a Mikea mask (genuine masks are rare in Madagascar) with real human teeth. These are well-displayed and labelled, and include some Sakalava erotic tomb sculptures.

Marine enthusiasts should visit the **Musée de la Mer** [212 C7] (m 032 40 956 64; ⏰ Mon–Fri 08.00–11.30 & 14.30–17.30, Sat 08.00–11.30, Sun closed; entry 10,000Ar), also run by the university, on Route de la Porte. The main attraction is the preserved coelacanths: seven have been caught around Toliara of which three are on display here. The fascinating collection also includes shells, coral, whale teeth and bones, crustaceans and lots of other marine curiosities – as well as a somewhat out-of-place ostrich skeleton!

Arboretum d'Antsokay
(12km from Toliara, just north of the turn to St Augustine on RN7; m 032 02 600 15; e info@antsokayarboretum.org; www.antsokayarboretum.org; entry inc tour 10,000Ar) This botanical garden should not be missed by anyone with an interest in the flora – and accompanying fauna – of the southwest. Around a thousand plant species are showcased, mostly endemic to the region, and many with medicinal qualities.

English-speaking guides take you on a two-hour tour of the 7ha planted area of the 50ha arboretum where you will see around 100 species of *Euphorbia* and 60 species of *Kalanchoe*, as well as an abundance of birds and reptiles. Indeed,

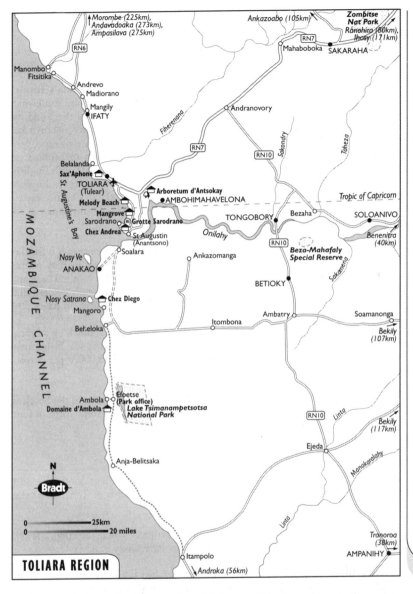

with the spiny forest fast disappearing, this is one of the best places in the region for birders. Try to arrive as early as possible to avoid the heat of the day. Better still, stay overnight in one of the smart bungalows of **Auberge de la Table**, or camp (10,000Ar/tent). Excellent meals are served at their restaurant **The Dry Forest**.

Tombs The most spectacular tombs within easy reach of the town are those of the Masikoro, a subgroup of the Sakalava. This small tribe is probably of African origin, and there is speculation that the name comes from *mashokora* which, in parts of Tanzania, means 'scrub forest'. There are also Mahafaly and Bara tombs here.

The tombs are off RN7, a little over an hour from Toliara, and are clearly visible on the right. There are several large, rectangular tombs, flamboyantly painted with scenes from the distinguished military life of the deceased, with a few mermaids and Rambos thrown in for good measure. Oh, and a scene from the film *Titanic*. These are known as the **Tombs of Andranovory**.

Another, on the outskirts of town beyond the university, is **King Baba's Tomb**. This is set in a grove of *Didierea* trees and is interesting more for the somewhat bizarre funerary objects (an urn and a huge, cracked bell) displayed there and its spiritual significance to the local people (you may only approach barefoot) than for aesthetic value. This King Baba, who seems to have died a century or so ago, was presumably a descendant of one of the Masikoro kings of Baba mentioned in British naval accounts of the 18th century. These kings used to trade with English ships calling at St Augustine's Bay and gave their family and courtiers English names such as the Prince of Wales and the Duke of Cumberland. On the way to King Baba's Tomb you may visit a little fenced-off park of banyan trees, all descending from one 'parent', known as 'the sacred grove'.

Watersports For many people the main reason to visit the Toliara region is for the coral reefs. Most of the dive centres are attached to beach hotels in Ifaty to the north of Toliara, and there are a couple more in Anakao to the south. These are listed in their respective sections. Dead or dying coral is disturbingly evident but some diving and snorkelling sites can still be rewarding. See boxes on pages 399 and 400 for information on marine conservation.

Sailing and pirogue trips, typically lasting all day with a picnic lunch on a beach or small island, offer an alternative and relaxing way to enjoy the sea. Fishermen with sailboats who are willing to take tourists out for around 15,000Ar per person are easily found in Anakao and Ifaty.

☞ *WARNING!* Sea urchins are a problem in the shallows off many of the beaches (see box on page 222). Be careful not to touch them and wear some form of foot protection when swimming or snorkelling.

IFATY

Ifaty (and Mangily with which it has now merged) offers sand, sea and snorkelling, plus beach bungalows. It lies only 27km north of Toliara, but the road is fairly poor.

☞ *WARNINGS!* There are no money-changing facilities. When selecting a hotel, bear in mind that only those in the north of Ifaty have sandy beaches.

GETTING THERE AND AWAY It takes a little under two hours by *taxi-brousse* from Toliara and costs 4,000Ar. Private vehicles can be rented at a much higher cost and take 30 minutes to one hour.

🏠 **WHERE TO STAY AND EAT** Note that the hotels and beach bungalows are strung out over several kilometres of coastline.

Luxury ♨

🏠 **Dunes** (22 rooms & 19 villas) \ 22 258 12/94 914 80; f 032 07 109 16; f 22 339 33; e dunesifaty@apma.mg; www.lesdunesdifaty.com. Swish en-suite accommodation with TV & 24hr electricity; sea-view villas for up to 4 people. Splendid pool, beachfront bar, excellent food & internet. Credit cards accepted.

Top end €€€€€

🏠 **Paradisier** (21 bungalows) ✆ 94 429 14;
m 032 07 660 09; e paradisier@paradisier.net;
www.paradisier.net. Comfy en-suite bungalows with
fan; also a luxury suite. Infinity edge pool & good
food. B/fast inc. Nature walks great for birds &
reptiles.

🏠 **Hôtel de la Plage** (8 bungalows) ✆ 94 906 92;
m 032 04 362 76; e hotelplagetulear@
blueline.mg; www.hotelplage-tulear.com. Well-run hotel
with attractive en-suite bungalows, some with AC.
Diving, fishing, kayaking & other activities.

🏠 **Nautilus** (22 rooms & 1 villa) ✆ 94 418 74;
m 032 07 418 74; f 94 413 80; e nautilus@
moov.mg. Upmarket hotel on a nice beach. AC
bungalows for up to 6 people & an 8-bed villa.
Excellent restaurant, especially for seafood. New
swimming pool. Diving, whale-watching & glass-
bottom boat. Visa accepted.

Upper range €€€€

🏠 **Lakana Vezo** (20 bungalows) ✆ 24 743 49/94
920 38; m 032 05 416 84/032 05 465 30; f 22
466 89; e lakanavezo@madagascar-resorts.com;
www.madagascar-resorts.com. Sgl, dbl, trpl & family
rooms, many with sea view onto Ranobe lagoon.
Diving & boat trips. B/fast inc.

🏠 **Bamboo Club** (25 bungalows) ✆ 94 902 13;
m 032 04 004 27; e bambooclubifaty@
gmail.com; www.bamboo-club.com. Good-value
Belgian-owned bungalows, en suite with solar power,
in pleasant beachfront spot. Nicely planted 14ha
garden with small pool. Also apts for rent by
day/week/month. Diving & other watersports.

🏠 **Tonga Soa** (21 bungalows) m 032 02 788 98.
Nicely decorated dbl, trpl & family bungalows, mostly
with balcony & sea view. Bike & 4x4 hire; boat for
fishing, whale-watching & sea trips. Pool & internet.

🏠 **Vovotelo** (16 bungalows) ✆ 94 937 18;
m 032 02 621 48; e hotelvovotelo@simicro.mg.
Much recommended bungalows with en-suite hot-
water facilities & fan. Excellent (but fairly expensive)
food & local dancing weekly. Diving & fishing.

Mid-range €€€

🏠 **Mangily** (7 bungalows) ✆ 94 915 30; m 032
02 554 28; f 94 414 19; e Mangily-hotel@
moov.mg. Bungalows for up to 5 people right on
the beach with shower, toilet & big terrace.

🏠 **Ifaty Beach Club** (15 bungalows) m 032 02 600
47; e ifatyclub@ifaty.mg; www.ifaty.com. En-suite
bungalows for up to 4 people. Beachfront restaurant
with good but expensive meals. Small pool & dive club.

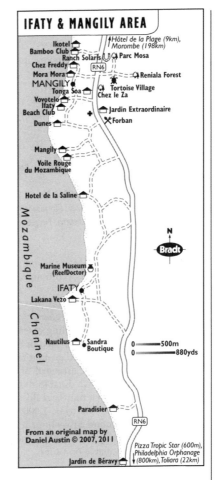

IFATY & MANGILY AREA

Ikotel
Bamboo Club
Ranch Solaris
Chez Freddy
Mora Mora
MANGILY
Tonga Soa
Vovotelo
Ifaty
Beach Club
Dunes
Mangily
Voile Rouge
du Mozambique
Hotel de la Saline
Marine Museum
(ReefDoctor)
IFATY
Lakana Vezo
Nautilus
Sandra
Boutique
Paradisier

Hôtel de la Plage (9km),
Morombe (198km)
Parc Mosa
RN6
Reniala Forest
Tortoise Village
Chez le Za
Jardin Extraordinaire
Forban

Mozambique Channel

N
Bradt

0 ——— 500m
0 ——— 880yds

RN6

**From an original map by
Daniel Austin © 2007, 2011**

Pizza Tropic Star (600m),
Philadelphia Orphanage
(800km), Toliara (22km)
Jardin de Béravy

🏠 **Mora Mora** (10 bungalows) ✆ 94 915 39;
m 032 51 615 26. One of the oldest hotels in
Ifaty. Sgl, dbl & trpl bungalows, some with sea view.
Swimming pool & diving.

🏠 **Ikotel** (13 rooms) ✆ 94 901 14; m 032 42
856 84/032 41 887 32; e mahayanahotels@
yahoo.fr. Waterfront rooms for 2–6 people, all en
suite with solar electricity.

🏠 **Voile Rouge du Mozambique** (10 bungalows)
m 032 04 311 42/032 04 841 55;
e voilerougedumozambique@yahoo.fr. Basic
traditional dbl & trpl bungalows, some en suite with
sea view. Solar electricity.

🏠 **Jardin Extraordinaire (Chez Pauline)** (9 rooms)
✆ 94 936 13; m 032 51 721 82; e jecp@
moov.mg. On main road 250m from beach. Simple

clean rooms, some en suite (cold water). Bar with pool table.

⌂ **Jardin de Béravy** m 032 40 397 19; e jardin.beravy@yahoo.fr. Rooms in a peaceful spot on the edge of the lagoon.

⌂ **Chez Daniel** (4 bungalows) \ 94 930 39; m 032 04 678 53; e bigorno@malagasy.com. Comfy seafront bungalows owned by a French-Malagasy couple.

Budget €€

⌂ **Auberg'in'** (12 rooms) m 032 41 821 33. Dbl rooms, a few of which are en suite.

⌂ **Chez Freddy** (8 bungalows) \ 94 907 00; m 032 40 375 48; e chezfreddy2003@yahoo.fr. En-suite bungalows, some with kitchenette. Pirogue trips & whale-watching.

⌂ **Coq du Village (Chez Alex)** (18 bungalows) \ 94 903 12; m 032 04 658 73. Basic mostly en-suite beachfront bungalows with shared toilet/shower block. Can be noisy Fri & Sat nights.

⌂ **Maroloko** (5 rooms) m 032 04 861 39/033 19 029 16. En-suite dbl, trpl & family rooms.

⌂ **Princesse du Lagon** (6 rooms) m 032 02 268 87. Seafront dbl & trpl rooms, en suite with cold water. 4x4 hire.

WHAT TO SEE AND DO Diving is one of the main attractions but there are some super inland reserves that even non-naturalists will enjoy.

Reniala Forest (\ 94 417 56/906 76; m 032 02 513 49; e reniala-mada@blueline.mg; www.reniala-madagascar.com; ☉ summer 08.00–18.00, winter 07.30–17.30; entry 9,000Ar inc guided tour) This outstanding reserve protects 45ha of spiny forest, especially recommended for those interested in birds and flora. An early-morning visit more or less guarantees long-tailed ground roller and subdesert mesite. Guides, who live at the reserve and can be arranged on arrival, are excellent at locating these two species and are also knowledgeable about the area's unique plant life. In addition to birds there are around a thousand *Adansonia rubrostipa* baobabs (including one 13m in circumference and said to be 1,000 years old) as well as *Didierea* and *Euphorbia*. There is a one-hour and a two-hour trail. Night walks are also possible.

There are bungalows (15,000Ar) and a campsite (10,000Ar/tent) with toilet and shower. Food is available on order.

Parc Mosa (m 032 43 259 90/032 61 129 09; entry 10,000Ar) This is another private reserve with excellent birding prospects. Sadly, several readers have complained of unethical practices and overcharging here, and Mosa's staff are known to ambush tourists *en route* to Reniala Forest to persuade them to visit here instead.

Chez le Za (m 032 02 514 36; entry 7,000Ar for 1hr guided walk or 9,000Ar for 1½hrs) Near to Reniala Forest and Parc Mosa, this small reserve also offers guided tours of ornithological and botanical interest. You will learn about traditional medicinal plants in the botanical garden area.

Tortoise Village (\ 94 425 67; m 032 02 072 75/032 40 307 50; e creadedaniel@yahoo.fr; www.villagetortues.com; entry adults 5,000Ar, children 1,000Ar; ☉ daily 09.00–17.00) Tortoise Village was set up by a group of conservation organisations for the protection of the two southwestern species: spider and radiated tortoises. Both are seriously threatened by illegal trade (for pets abroad) and hunting (by locals for food). Around 1,200 are resident including some confiscated by customs.

Set in 7ha of spiny forest with small baobabs, with a further 7ha of fenced areas, the guided tour will show you the tortoises and explain the efforts to conserve them. Allow an hour for a visit; you may see other reptiles, birds and brown lemurs.

Horseriding Contact **Ranch Solaris** (✆ *94 903 14;* m *032 02 477 75;* e *ranch@ atimoo.com; www.ranch-solaris.com*) for a variety of activities, including horseriding on the beach (1 hour; 41,000Ar), in the baobab forest (2½ hours; 82,000Ar), half-day treks (135,000Ar) and lessons for beginners.

Marine Museum This small information centre was created by ReefDoctor (see page 213) for tourists, locals and schoolchildren alike. Information posters accompanied by exhibits such as shells educate visitors about the local and marine environments.

Mangrove Information Centre (e *honkomad@yahoo.com; www.honko.org*) At Ambondrolava, midway between Toliara and Ifaty (look for the signpost with a waving crab), is this new wetland centre created by Honko, a Belgian NGO. The organisation works to restore nearby mangroves and teach locals to use them sustainably. Trained guides lead visitors along a 400m elevated boardwalk to experience the mangrove habitat and a hide enables close viewing of birdlife.

Diving (and other watersports) Most dive centres are based at beach hotels (indicated in brackets in the following list). Where contact details differ from the hotel they are given here; otherwise refer to the *Where to stay* section above.

꙳ **Atimoo Plongée** (Mora Mora) ✆ 94 937 01; m 032 04 529 17; e club@atimoo.com; www.atimoo.com. PADI.
꙳ **Club de Plongée** (Hôtel de la Plage) PADI.
꙳ **Club Nautique** (Dunes) ✆ 94 428 85; e gino@moov.mg
꙳ **Deep Sea Club** (Nautilus) CMAS.

꙳ **Grand Bleu** (Vovotelo) m 032 07 822 12; f 94 414 19
꙳ **Centre Nautique d'Ifaty** (Lakana Vezo) Also pirogue, catamaran & glass-bottom boat trips; whale-watching & fishing.
꙳ **Ifaty Plongée** (Ifaty Beach Club)
꙳ **Fifi Diving** (Bamboo Club) m 032 04 659 47; e fifidiving@moov.mg

MADIORANO

This village a few kilometres north of Ifaty (38km from Toliara) offers a more peaceful setting.

 WHERE TO STAY

🏠 **Mira** (12 rooms) m 032 02 621 44; e lamira.hotel@moov.mg; www.hotel-lamira.com. Spacious & very comfortable. French/Malagasy ownership. Great fresh food. Fishing, boat trips & quad hire. €€€€

🏠 **Chez Bernard** (5 bungalows) Comfy bungalows near a quiet beach, but not far from the road. Excellent food. €€€

NORTH TO MOROMBE AND MORONDAVA

A *camion-brousse* runs regularly along the coastal road to Manombo and then to Salary, which is about halfway between Ifaty and Andavadoaka. It's four hours to Manombo and another four to Salary with breathtaking views of the coastline and spiny forest. The onward journey to Andavadoaka and Morombe is possible by pirogue or speedboat.

Despite the relative proximity of Toliara to Morondava (340km as the crow flies) the direct overland journey can take several days – certainly much slower than taking the circuitous 1,320km route on good roads via the *hauts plateaux*. Thus, those whose main goal is to reach the other end rather than seeking adventure tend to fly. **Vedettes d'Anakao** (see page 216) operate sea transfers from Toliara to Morondava.

SALARY A rather nondescript Vezo fishing town along a beautiful coastline with difficult access. It can be reached by boat or 4x4 from Ifaty. The town is in two parts: Salary Avaratra (north) and Salary Atsimo (south).

Where to stay and eat

🏠 **Salary Bay** (10 bungalows) ☎ 75 514 86; 📱 032 49 120 16; 📧 salarybay@malagasy.com; www.salarybay.com. An upmarket set of comfortable, thatched bungalows in a good beach location. Diving, snorkelling, pirogue/boat trips & walks to Mikea forest. €€€€

🏠 **Chez Francesco** Salary Avaratra; 📧 salaryfrancesco@yahoo.it. Francesco is an ebullient Italian who has lived in the area for many years. Bungalows with bucket shower & squat toilets. Tremendous Italian food. €€€

🏠 **Chez Jean-Louis** Salary Atsimo. Basic bungalows. €

🏠 **Takaliko** Reasonably priced simple bungalows. €

MARINE BEASTIES
Rob Conway & Jane Wilson-Howarth

One of the main reasons that people enjoy snorkelling and diving is the contact with marine species in their natural habitats, and Madagascar has one of the most beautiful and diverse marine environments in the western Indian Ocean. But not all these creatures are harmless. Most injuries from marine creatures are due to inexperience, unfamiliarity with the local environment, or self defence on the part of the animal. Below are some of the marine nasties that you may encounter in Madagascar and the first aid measures should you get hurt.

SEA URCHINS The most common injury to swimmers and snorkellers is from sea urchins, often from stepping on one. Such injuries are painful but not dangerous. Treat by washing the wound and then remove as many of the spines as possible with tweezers or, if little bits remain in your sole and you have nothing else, use a toothpick or similar; the wound will not heal until all the bits are out.

BITES Most marine animals are not interested in human beings. The majority of bites are in self defence. The primary concern for the first aider is to control bleeding and minimise the risk of infection. Sharks and moray eels are the two animals that could attack swimmers or divers on the reef, as well as titan triggerfish during the nesting season; the titan is up to 75cm long and will defend her nest ferociously.

- Control bleeding by applying firm bandages or strips of cloth.
- Clean wound and flood with lots of water to minimise infection.
- Seek medical advice.

RAY, SCORPIONFISH, LIONFISH AND STONEFISH STINGS Symptoms include immediate pain, laceration, nausea, vomiting, shock, swelling and occasionally collapse. This situation is one where good first aid will help more than anything doctors can offer.

- Immerse wound in hot water (43–45°C) for 30–90 minutes. The stung body part will be so painful that you won't be able to tell whether the water is too hot, so use a non-stung hand to check that the water isn't likely to scald.
- Repeat the immersion if pain recurs; it may be necessary to top up the water, but remove affected limb from the water before doing so.
- Remove any visible pieces of the stinger and irrigate vigorously with fresh water.
- Once the worst of the pain has subsided get someone to clean and dress the wound.
- Over the next few days look out for spreading redness, throbbing and/or fever; these symptoms imply infection which will need antibiotic treatment.

Two correspondents have raved about this unspoiled area northeast of Toliara. Valerie Middleton writes: 'By turning right some 17km from Toliara on RN7 it is possible to reach the Onilahy River at a point where virtually every salad and vegetable crop known is grown on the rich sediments. If the rough road is followed eastwards the attractively situated village of Tolikisy is reached (not 'Tokilisy' as shown on maps). A meeting with the village *président* may elicit an invitation to camp up the delightful Atsodroka Valley at the entrance to the village. Small cliffs and exotic trees like Moringa and banyans dominate the hillsides. The many ring-tailed lemurs may also keep you awake at night with their continuous screaming! From the head of the valley a local guide, again with the good grace of the *président*, can take you on a 7km

STINGS FROM FIRE CORAL, ANEMONE, HYDROID OR JELLYFISH Anemones are beautiful creatures that live amongst the coral and have stinging tentacles. Often small clown fish will live amongst these tentacles, protected by a mucous layer on their skin. Brushing against any coral will give a nasty abrasion which is inflamed and slow to heal. Fire coral looks like coral, but on closer examination there are fine stinging cells. Hydroids are small marine creatures, that look like plants, also with stinging cells. Jellyfish are commonly encountered whilst diving or swimming in tropical waters and often do not sting; they may cause minor skin irritation. If stung by any of these:

- Rinse with seawater (not fresh water).
- If the stinger was a box jellyfish there will be characteristic cross-hatched tentacle-prints on the skin surface and irrigation with vinegar will inactivate the stingers. Vinegar actually makes things worse if the jellyfish is a Portuguese man-of-war but most stings are mild and the following treatments suffice.
- Shave off area with credit card to remove stinging cells, being very careful not to sting yourself.
- Apply hydrocortisone cream to reduce inflammation.
- If collapse occurs, offer cardio-pulmonary resuscitation since the severe effects of the venom fade quite quickly. Next get medical help as soon as you can.

CONE SHELLS Cone shells are beautiful shells that contain a dart-like projection at the front. Do not touch as they can deliver a painful and potentially deadly sting. If stung:

- Apply pressure bandage and immobilise limb.
- Seek medical attention.

SEA SNAKES The beautiful *Pelamis platurus* spends most of its life out at sea but they are occasionally encountered around the coasts of Madagascar. Sea snake venom is some of the most potent known to man. Fortunately for us they are usually timid, sluggish creatures that avoid humans. You are unlikely to be bitten unless you tease or handle one, or if you go close to a mating bundle of sea snakes – they resent disturbance of their orgy. If you are unfortunate enough to be bitten, symptoms may include: stiffness and aching, respiratory distress, difficulty swallowing or speaking, or weakness.

- Apply pressure bandage and immobilise limb.
- Seek medical attention.
- Do not use suction technique.

trip onto the plateau to visit the chasm of Ankikiky Velo. This is well worth the effort and measures around 80m diameter and 60m deep. A further 15 minutes away is the new village of Ankikimaty where another cave of impressive dimensions can be descended to nearly 90m in an enormous passage. The forest now remains good only at the edge of the plateau and on the steep riverside slopes.

'Continuing upriver from Tolikisy the scenery becomes quite dramatic until, about 2km before Ifanato, a crystal-clear stream gushes beneath the road. There is a place to park here and by following the footpath on the left for 50m a superb flat campsite can be found above the first of the "Seven Lakes". These beautiful blue lakes are connected by yellow to orange tufa (a form of calcite) cascades and waterfalls extending for over 700m. Apart from the first lake upon which there is a *fady*, swimming can be done in most of them. The surrounding gallery forest is superb. It is possible to follow a zebu trail into the mountains where there is yet another vertical shaft known as Ankikiky Lava. Ifanato, 2km further on, has a couple of reasonable restaurants including one run by a Frenchman, but to follow the road further into Tongobory is extremely difficult.'

ST AUGUSTINE'S BAY This large bay some 15km southeast of Toliara is an area of history and natural wonders, including dramatic sand dunes and a cave swimming pool. The bay, which was mentioned by Daniel Defoe in *The King of Pirates*, was the site of an ill-fated British colony, abandoned in 1646, and later frequented by pirates.

Getting there The hotels in the region will arrange transfers from Toliara, but there is a daily *taxi-brousse* to Sarodrano (3,000Ar) on a sandy spit at the southern end of the bay. The village of St Augustin lies about 5km beyond, at the Onilahy river mouth.

Where to stay

🏠 **Mangrove** (11 rooms) \ 94 936 26; e arthur.jeannin@gmail.com; www.hotelsud-tulear.com. Located 8km from RN7 (the turn-off is signposted). Same ownership as Chez Alain in Toliara. Rocky shore; no beach. Diving, fishing & boat excursions to Nosy Ve & Anakao. €€€

🏠 **Chez Andréa** (10 rooms) m 032 02 258 43. Italian-owned beach bungalows near Sarodrano.

Thoughtfully designed, very friendly, excellent food & service. €€€

🏠 **Melody Beach** (15 bungalows) m 032 02 167 57; e moukar@moov.mg. Overlooking a sandy beach in the middle of the bay with good swimming. Just 5km from RN7 so easily accessible. €€–€€€

🏠 **Longo Mamy** m 032 04 344 64. Nice but basic bungalows in St Augustin village. €€

GROTTE SARODRANO Under a rocky overhang is a deep pool of clear blue water. Swimmers will find the top layer of warm water only mildly salty, while the cooler lower layer is saline. Fresh water flows from the mountain into the pool, on top of the heavier layer of saltwater from the sea. Grotte Sarodrano is a 4km walk south from the Mangrove hotel (along an easy road). Kids with pirogues hang around there to take you back. Well worth it!

ANAKAO

Anakao is a pretty little Vezo fishing village with colourful boats drawn up on the sands. Hotels catering for all budgets have opened in recent years so it now competes with Ifaty for beaches and opportunities for snorkelling, diving and birdwatching.

GETTING THERE AND AWAY Anakao is accessible from Toliara via a 56km dirt road, or much more easily by boat. All the hotels provide a transfer service. The typical cost is 50,000Ar (or 80,000Ar return). Because of the varying tides and wind, this journey may involve a vehicle trip as well as the boat ride.

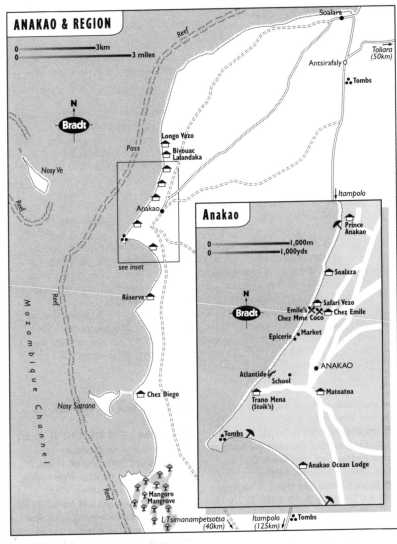

ANAKAO & REGION

Soalara

Toliara (50km)

Antsirafaly

Tombs

Reef

0 ___ 3km
0 ___ 3 miles

Bradt

N

Pass

Longo Vezo

Bivouac Lalandaka

Nosy Ve

Anakao

Reef

see inset

Réserve

M o z a m b i q u e   C h a n n e l

Reef

Nosy Satrana

Chez Diego

Reef

Mangoro Mangrove

L Tsimanampetsotsa (40km)

Anakao

Itampolo

Prince Anakao

0 ___ 1,000m
0 ___ 1,000yds

Soalaza

N

Bradt

Safari Vezo

Emile's
Chez Mme Coco

Chez Emile

Epicerie   Market

ANAKAO

Atlantide

School

Matoatoa

Trano Mena (Stoik's)

Tombs

Anakao Ocean Lodge

Itampolo (125km)

Tombs

The South ANAKAO

9

☞ **WARNINGS!** Fresh water is a problem in Anakao: there is not enough of it, and only a couple of hotels have running water. The beach around the village itself is very busy (local life being centred around fishing) and not particularly clean, so for swimming/sunbathing head further along the shore. If seafood is not your thing, your dining options in Anakao will be very limited; consider bringing some supplementary tinned food from Toliara.

WHERE TO STAY

Anakao Ocean Lodge (18 bungalows) ✆ 94 919 57; m 032 07 602 57; e eres@ lifehospitality.com; www.signaturehotels.co.za. Wonderful Italian-owned boutique hotel with beautiful bungalows, perfect beach, impeccable service, delicious food & relaxed atmosphere. Diving, kayaking, sailing, surfing, fishing & excursions. €€€€€

Prince Anakao (27 bungalows) ✆ 94 439 57/902 00; e prince.anakao@gmail.com;

THE DILEMMA OF PET LEMURS

Hilary Bradt

Several hotels in the Toliara region keep pet lemurs. The pathetic sight of these animals in cramped cages or tied by a cord around their loins upsets all visitors. Here's a report from a South African tour leader, written a few years ago, who decided that action speaks louder than words.

The hotel has a cage with three ring-tails. I was shocked to see this and so were the clients so we designed this bold plan to liberate the lemurs. It was working like clockwork. Our transport was waiting and I had the clients in position. The manager, cooks, and receptionist all duly entertained by their barrage of questions as I slinked through the back and opened the cage door just enough to let them out. Then we all casually made our way to the truck. I peeped over my shoulder and saw the lemurs come out, stand up and sniff – that sweet scent of freedom – and then the Stockholm Syndrome kicked in and they made a bee-line for the kitchen window. We drove off to screams and pots and pans clanging. I laughed but wanted to cry. Bloody idiots.

As this story demonstrates, you cannot 'liberate' an animal accustomed to captivity. It will not know what to do with itself and will return to its cage. The solution, as always in Madagascar, is more complicated than it seems. The reason these adorable animals are kept caged or tied is that as they grew from charming babies into assertive adults they started biting the hand that fed them.

'So what can we do?' a hotelier in Toliara asked me, her hands thrown wide in Gallic gesture. 'A kid brings us a little baby lemur and says that the mother is dead and do we want to buy it? I say yes because I think I will treat it more kindly than the kid. Maybe I shouldn't, because then he started biting my guests so now I have to keep him tied up.'

www.princeanakao.com. Comfy bungalows & good food (fixed menu). €€€€

🏠 **Chez Diego** \ 94 903 70; m 032 04 047 99; e laltraluna @ hotmail.it. Characterful new hotel with wooden bungalows sited about 8km south of the village, opposite Nosy Satrana. €€€€

🏠 **Bivouac Lalandaka (Chez Olivier)** (6 bungalows) \ 94 914 35; m 032 04 341 42/032 02 275 20; e lalandaka @ moov.mg; www.lalandaka.com. Bungalows with bucket showers (hot water on request) & shared toilets. €€€€

🏠 **Safari Vezo** (23 bungalows) \/f 94 413 81/410 81; m 032 02 638 87; e safarivezo @ netclub.mg. Bungalows with balconies & bucket showers. Diving, whale-watching, snorkelling & excursions. €€€

🏠 **Réserve** (6 bungalows) m 032 02 141 55; e quad @ dts.mg. Peaceful spot on the bay south of the village. French-run place with simple en-suite

bungalows & excellent food. Whale-watching & fishing. €€€

🏠 **Longo Vezo** \/f 94 901 27/437 64; m 032 02 631 23; e longo.vezo @ yahoo.fr; www.longovezo.org. Comfy bungalows in quiet location well north of the village. Whale-watching, surfing, diving (CMAS) & excursions. €€€

🏠 **Soalaza** (3 bungalows) \ 94 445 07; m 032 04 180 93; e lacombe-christian @ voila.fr. Small cosy hotel. No restaurant. €€€

🏠 **Trano Mena** (6 bungalows) Run by Stoick, a mechanic from Taolagnaro. Bungalows with bucket showers; communal squat toilet. Bar & terraced eating area. €–€€

🏠 **Chez Emile** (6 bungalows) In the village. Bucket showers & shared squat toilet. Very friendly. Bar popular with the locals. Shop sells snacks & a few postcards. €–€€

✗ **WHERE TO EAT** Good food is served at **Le Prince** and **Safari Vezo** (fixed menus). **Chez Emile** is centrally located with some non-seafood options, but pricey with slow service. **Trano Mena** serves food if you book in advance; likewise **Chez Mme Coco** (near Chez Emile), whose prawns with garlic and curry are particularly recommended.

WHAT TO SEE AND DO

Tombs, wildlife and *Aepyornis* eggshells A day spent exploring on foot is rewarding. Take the track behind the village heading south. On the outskirts of Anakao you will find some interesting tombs (one has a satellite dish on the roof to provide eternal entertainment for the ancestors) and will then come to a small peninsula with a couple more tombs. It is still possible to find fragments of subfossil eggshell from the long-extinct elephant bird here, but please keep your collecting instincts under control so that others can enjoy this extraordinary glimpse of the past. It is illegal to take these eggshells out of the country.

Birders would be well advised to take an early-morning walk on one of the tracks through the spiny forest, setting off shortly before sunrise.

Diving With dead coral reducing the attraction of shallow reef for snorkellers, the emphasis has switched to diving. The best months for diving are between April and December when the water is clear of sediment from the Onilahy river. Most of the hotels offer diving, or can help with arrangements. Particularly recommended is **Atlantide** (\ *94 940 08;* m *032 40 720 00;* e *lalbatross_8@yahoo.fr*), near Trano Mena, which is PADI and CMAS accredited.

Nearby islands Lying 4km west of Anakao is **Nosy Ve** (the name means 'is there an island?'!), which is a sacred site. It has a long history of European domination since a Dutchman landed there in 1595; it was officially taken over by the French in 1888 before their conquest of the mainland, although it is hard to see why: it is a flat, scrub-covered little island.

What makes Nosy Ve special to modern-day invaders is the tranquillity of its white beaches, the snorkelling on its fringing reef, and the world's southernmost breeding colony of red-tailed tropic-birds. They breed year-round so you can be sure of seeing them at their nest sites under bushes at the southern end of the island, as well as flying overhead.

A 2,000Ar fee must be paid to visit the island. Camping is not allowed and there are no buildings. Visits are dependent for their success on wind and tide (strong wind makes snorkelling difficult; high tide is equally unrewarding for snorkellers and beachcombers). For this reason visits with fishermen using pirogues, which can land at low tide, are more successful than by large motorboats. With little natural shade on the island, make sure your boatman erects a sail on the beach to provide respite from the burning sun. There are *fady* prohibiting harming the tropic-birds and defecating on the beach, and tourists should also respect the ancestors by keeping away from the tombs.

Further south, **Nosy Satrana** is a small peaceful island closer to the shore (in fact you can walk out to it on a sandbar at low tide). It offers excellent diving and good snorkelling, but no tropic-birds.

Mangoro mangrove This mangrove is about an hour's walk down the beach from Chez Diego, but it is more rewarding to explore this place by boat. The birdlife is good with bee-eaters, vasa parrots, flamingoes, harrier-hawks and plovers amongst species seen here.

BEHELOKA AND AMBOLA

These two fishing villages offer the nearest accommodation to Tsimanampetsotsa National Park. Beheloka is 20km north of the lake and Ambola is 6km to its west. The park office is at Efoetse, just 2km from Ambola. Once-weekly *taxi-brousses* run between Toliara and Beheloka. Compagnie du

Sud make the transfer by boat, and Vedettes d'Anakao do boat connections from Toliara to Ambola (see page 216).

The villages also act as stop-offs for rugged travellers heading south along the almost impassable road to Itampolo. The beaches are good, with clear water. Note that, besides bottled water, only brackish water is available in Beheloka, so coffee and tea taste salty.

🏠 WHERE TO STAY

🏠 **Domaine d'Ambola** (11 rooms) Ambola; ✆ 94 930 44; m 032 45 326 21; e contact@ ambola-madagascar.com; www.ambola-madagascar.com. Seafront location on 1km private beach; the closest hotel to the lake. Spacious, bright rooms of surprisingly good quality given the hotel's remoteness. The rooms are en suite, mostly with sea views. €€€

🏠 **Vahombe** (3 bungalows) Ambola. Simple dbl rooms on beautiful beach. €€€

🏠 **Canne à Sucre** (4 rooms & 4 bungalows) Beheloka; ✆ 94 437 21; m 032 04 624 09. Cheap rooms & more expensive bungalows. Good food. €€€

🏠 **Finaritra** (6 rooms) Beheloka. Very basic but cheap accommodation on the beachfront. €

LAKE TSIMANAMPETSOTSA NATIONAL PARK

The large, shallow soda lake – 15km long by 2km at its widest point – is the focus for this terrific national park of 43,200ha. The large limestone plateau here has some of the most striking spiny forest vegetation in Madagascar, with countless locally endemic species. There are two quite extraordinary baobabs, pachypodiums, and also a magnificent banyan tree with its aerial roots hugging the side of a cliff face to find purchase in the soil some 20m below.

The park sits on a large underground aquifer that runs north, evidenced by the numerous sinkholes and caves. The lake is renowned for its waterfowl, notably flamingoes, and other rare endemic birds including the Madagascar plover, but the emblem of the park is the very rare Grandidier's mongoose.

Lying about 50km south of Anakao, down a very bad road, a visit is only just manageable as a day trip. To see the park properly you need to be pretty fit to cope with the heat, and carry enough water (bring water-purifying tablets so you can top up from the well). The lake, with its greater and lesser flamingoes, is starkly beautiful, but the dry forest is interesting at every step. You can visit Mitoho Cave (a sacred site) where a rare endemic species of blind fish, *Typhleotris madagascariensis*, is easily seen.

The usual park fee must be paid (see page 72) at the office at Efoetse, a couple of kilometres from the park entrance. You pick up your guide here as well. The park has four circuits of one to three hours in length. Guide fees are 10,000–15,000Ar per circuit.

If you are here between August and October, you stand a good chance of witnessing a passing funeral ceremony, for in this region burials may officially take place only during this period.

GETTING THERE AND AWAY Tsimanampetsotsa is not accessible by public transport. You need your own vehicle or to sign up for a tour with a hotel/operator in Anakao, Ambola or Toliara.

🏠 WHERE TO STAY
There are two campsites in the reserve (with water but no other facilities) which are ideal for birders and other naturalists who want to see this extraordinary place in the early morning. Camping costs 10,000Ar per person. If you don't want to camp, stay in nearby Ambola, Beheloka (an hour's drive away), or – at a stretch – Itampolo.

The far south is gradually being developed and you can drive on a barely motorable, sandy road until you join RN10, which links Toliara with Taolagnaro. The beaches in this region are littered with fragments of *Aepyornis* eggshell. Intrepid drivers with a 4x4 can continue to the very tip of Madagascar, Cap Sainte Marie (see page 231).

ITAMPOLO This village about 180km south of Toliara is said by some to have the most beautiful beach in Madagascar, with pinkish-coloured sand. Valerie Middleton writes: 'An interesting excursion can be made to a cenote (a vertical-sided collapsed doline – or sinkhole – floored by a lake whose surface is level with the local water table). This is situated barely 3km south of Itampolo and is just 50m east of the road. It is locally known as Vintana and measures around 35m in diameter and is 5m to the water surface at its lowest point.'

 Where to stay

🏠 **Gite d'Etape Sud Sud** (4 bungalows & 3 rooms) ↘ 94 415 27; f 94 423 79; e c.alain@moov.mg. Under same ownership as Chez Alain in Toliara. Simple, comfortable bungalows & rooms above restaurant (good food). Camping permitted (8,000Ar). €€€

🏠 **Chez Nany** (I bungalow) Located 1.5km northwest of the village behind the dunes, 75m from the sea. No electricity; outdoor latrine & bucket shower; a well provides fresh water. Camping permitted. €

BEZA-MAHAFALY SPECIAL RESERVE

This reserve was established at the request of local people who volunteered to give up using part of the forest, in return for help with a variety of social and agricultural projects such as schools and irrigation channels.

The reserve protects two distinct types of forest: spiny forest and gallery (riverine) forest, with habituated ring-tailed lemurs and sifakas much in evidence. In Beza-Mahafaly, researchers and the local Malagasy come first but visitors with a serious interest in natural history will find this a hugely rewarding place. In addition to lemurs, the forest has four species of tenrec including the rare large-eared one, *Geogale aurita*, three species of carnivores including the fossa, and lots of reptiles. Over 100 species of birds have been recorded.

Dana Whitelaw, who spent a year there studying ring-tailed lemurs, can hardly contain her enthusiasm: 'Come here to enjoy the lemurs trooping into camp in the morning, and the well-cut trails in the reserve just across the road from your tent. Walk to the canyon, the sacred forest and visit a village. Hire the local cook and have someone (very inexpensively) clean your travel-worn clothes. Request a chicken, local tomatoes and some fruit to be brought from the local villages. These simple acts help ensure the economic viability of the reserve and keep money in the local people's pockets proving the value of this special reserve.'

GETTING THERE Well, there had to be a downside! Beza-Mahafaly is 35km north of Betioky along a terrible – but very scenic – road. To get there you need a 4x4, motorbike, bicycle (maybe) or zebu cart. Dana reports that she met two groups of tourists who hired zebu carts from Betioky 'and absolutely loved their trip down. I used zebu carts to go back and forth to market day in Betioky and it was one of my most memorable experiences. We were asked to leave in the middle of the night to make sure the zebu didn't overheat. A moonlit/starlit ride through the bush is enchanting! It takes about six hours. Take a cushion.'

CAMPING The campsites are situated under groves of tamarinds which are the sleeping trees for the friendly groups of ring-tailed lemurs and Verreaux's sifakas. If you don't have your own tent, you can hire one or stay in a local house. There is water from a well for showers and to drink (bring purifying tablets or a filter). Toilet facilities are simple but clean. Camping costs 10,000Ar per night.

WHAT TO SEE There are well-marked trails in the gallery forest directly across the road from the research camp, with habituated ring-tail and sifaka groups. The spiny forest is worth the hike and heat (but go early). Guides cost 5,000Ar per circuit, which vary in length up to 12km. Night hikes (7,000Ar) are not to be missed: lepilemurs and mouse lemurs abound and their vocalisations are the last sound you'll hear as you drift to sleep under the tamarinds.

To fully appreciate Beza you need to stay a few days. That way there is time to visit Ehazoara Canyon, a 3km (1½ hour) hike from the campsite which takes you through a local Mahafaly village. There is also a lovely sacred banyan forest 30 minutes' walk along the river to the northeast of the reserve, protected by a local *fady*. Several sifaka and ring-tailed lemur groups live here, although it is in the midst of agricultural fields.

THE ROAD TO TAOLAGNARO (FORT DAUPHIN)

A *taxi-brousse* from Toliara to Taolagnaro takes two to three days. It's a shame to pass straight through such an exciting area, however. Much more interesting is to rent a vehicle and driver, or to do the trip by *taxi-brousse* in stages, staying at Betioky, Ampanihy and Beloha or Ambovombe, or – most interesting of all – by a combination of walking and whatever transport comes along, taking pot luck on where you'll spend the night.

TOLIARA TO BETIOKY The turning for RN10 is at **Andranovory**, 70km from Toliara. It takes about four hours to get to **Betioky** by 4x4, or eight hours by *taxi-brousse* (10,000Ar) on a very poor road. Market day is Tuesday and **Mahasoa** is a simple hotel here – each room is named after a different car manufacturer!

A side trip to **Bezaha** is worthwhile if you have time: wonderful scenery, fascinating flora and interesting Mahafaly tombs. The village lies 17km east of the road and the turning is 46km before Betioky.

BETIOKY TO AMPANIHY Beyond Betioky the bad road gets considerably worse. Some 20km to the south is the small village of **Ambatry**. Next comes **Ejeda**, about 2½ hours from Betioky on a reasonable dirt road. Ejeda to **Ampanihy** takes about five hours by truck on a very bad, rocky road. All along this route you will see Mahafaly tombs.

Ampanihy means 'the place of bats' but it is now the place of the goats. Mohair carpet weaving has long been a local industry; carpets can even be purchased from **The Mohair Man** showroom in Toliara (see page 215). **Hôtel Angora** provides comfortable accommodation, and camping is allowed in the garden.

AMPANIHY TO AMBOVOMBE After Ampanihy you enter Antandroy country and will understand why their name means 'people of the thorns'. The road deteriorates (if you thought that possible) as you make your way to **Tranoroa** (which means 'two houses') in about five hours. This is one of the main weaving towns in the south. Another five hours and you approach **Beloha** on an improving road (much favoured by tortoises, which thrive in the area since it is *fady* to eat them) and with tombs all around.

If you stop in Beloha, visit the Catholic church with its beautiful stained glass made by a local craftsman. This is also the departure point for the coastal village of Lavanono (see below).

Between Beloha and **Tsiombe** is the most interesting stretch of the entire journey. There are baobabs, tortoises and tombs about 33km before Tsiombe. Two roads lead from this village to **Faux Cap** and **Cap Sainte Marie**. You might want to stop overnight in Tsiombe where there are reasonable hotels: **Paradis du Sud** (\ *92 727 28*) and **La Sirène**.

Just beyond Tsiombe are yet more interesting tombs. The next place you come to is **Ambondro**, the main centre for weaving in the region. Though much of the cloth is now being made in surrounding villages and brought into the town to sell, you can still purchase woven cloth direct from the makers. There is an impressive zebu market held on Saturdays. From there it is 30km to **Ambovombe**.

AMBOVOMBE TO AMBOASARY AND TAOLAGNARO
Meaning 'place of many wells', Ambovombe is a bustling town (now with a BOA bank) in the heart of Androy country. It holds a colourful Monday market and hosts the annual Androy music festival, which showcases a wonderful mix of local and regional musicians. It is a free, three-day event held around the end of October.

Most travellers prefer to press on to Taolagnaro but there are a few hotel options on the main street if you decide to stay the night.

Some 35km from Ambovombe is **Amboasary**, the town that marks the turn-off to Berenty. Unfortunately you cannot visit Berenty under your own steam as the expensive transfer from Taolagnaro is part of the package and you may be refused entry on your own. The thriving town of Amboasary with its busy marketplace makes a worthwhile stop if you are visiting Lake Anony or Amboasary Sud. From here you are three to four hours (75km) away from Taolagnaro on a paved but very potholed road. Amboasary's best accommodation is **Discovery**, with its bungalows quietly tucked away from the town centre to the south.

About 12km south of Amboasary is a brackish lagoon, **Lake Anony**. There are flamingoes here and a large number of other wading birds in a lunar landscape – a paradise both for birdwatchers and botanists.

THE FAR SOUTH
Adventurous travellers are increasingly seeking out the extreme southwest. The coastal village of Lavanono has been recommended by several tough travellers, and the whole area is worth investigating.

This is a good area to see humpback whales; between September and November they can be observed quite close to shore with their calves.

LAVANONO The 'road' to this lovely place runs from Beloha via Tranovaho, a total of 39km. Access is difficult without your own 4x4, but worth the effort. For accommodation, Rupert Parker recommends eco-lodge **Chez Gigi** (m *033 07 971 64; www.lavanono.com;* €€): 'Gigi is from Réunion but all profits are ploughed back into the village. It's a very beautiful spot: nicely constructed, right by the sea with good surfing close by. The bungalows are simple but cosy, food is good and prices reasonable'.

CAP SAINTE MARIE Cap Sainte Marie is the southernmost tip of Madagascar and is as spectacular as its neighbours, with high sandstone cliffs and dwarf plants resembling a rock garden. Note that since the area is a protected reserve, a permit must be purchased (see page 72), and this is best arranged in Tana.

Bill Love notes that the heaviest occurrence of radiated tortoises is between Lavanono and Cap Sainte Marie: 'We counted 110 just on the coastal road in about two hours of driving. On the drive out to the lighthouse at Cap Sainte Marie, we literally had to move them off the track many times. The "road" was so narrow in places where the prickly pear cactus had grown up that we frequently had to back up hundreds of feet to find places wide enough to open the 4x4's doors, get out, and shove torts into "holes" in the wall of cactus. The cactus was scraping the car mirrors as we drove; a man on an open zebu cart would get flayed alive unless he sat in the exact centre of his cart!'

FAUX CAP I made my first visit to this dramatic, lonely place in 1997, and then predicted that it would soon be developed for tourism. This hasn't happened yet, but with the recent improvement of the road it has become more accessible so it is only a question of time.

Faux Cap is a small community (the village here is called **Betanty**; market day Monday) isolated from the outside world not only by the poor roads, but by wild seas and a treacherous coral reef. The huge, shifting sand dunes are littered with fragments of *Aepyornis* shell. It is an extraordinary place which is worth making a considerable effort to visit.

The best accommodation is the mid-range **Libertalia** (\ *92 211 13/904 55;* m *032 07 560 41;* e *madalibertalia@yahoo.fr; www.madalibertalia.com;* €€) with five beautiful solar-powered stone bungalows. Nearby is the cheaper and rather more basic **Cactus** with bungalows, some en suite with bucket showers.

Getting there and away The starting point for a trip to Faux Cap is Tsiombe. Ask around for ongoing transport. With your own 4x4 the 30km journey should take about 3½ hours. If you decide to hike, be prepared to carry all that you need in case you don't catch a lift.

TAOLAGNARO (FORT DAUPHIN)

HISTORY The remains of two forts can still be seen in or near this town on the extreme southeast tip of Madagascar: Fort Flacourt built in 1643; and another that dates from 1504 – thus making it the oldest building in the country – which was erected by shipwrecked Portuguese sailors. This ill-fated group of 80 reluctant colonists stayed about 15 years before falling foul of the local tribes. The survivors of the massacre fled to the surrounding countryside where disease and hostile natives finished them off.

A French expedition, organised in 1642 by the Société Française de l'Orient and led by Sieur Pronis, had instructions to 'found colonies and commerce in Madagascar and to take possession of it in the name of His Most Christian Majesty'. An early settlement at the Bay of Sainte Luce was soon abandoned in favour of a healthier peninsula to the south, and a fort was built and named after the Dauphin (later Louis XIV) in 1643. At first the Antanosy were quite keen on the commerce part of the deal but were less enthusiastic about losing their land. The heavily defended fort survived only by use of force and with many casualties on both sides. The French finally abandoned the place in 1674, but their 30-year occupation formed one of the foundations of the later claim to the island as a French colony. During this period the first published work on Madagascar was written by Pronis's successor, Etienne de Flacourt. His *Histoire de la Grande Île de Madagascar* brought the island's amazing flora and fauna to the attention of European naturalists, and is still used as a valuable historical source book.

TAOLAGNARO TODAY This laid back coastal town is one of the most beautifully located of all popular destinations in Madagascar. Built on a small peninsula, it is bordered on three sides by beaches and breakers and backed by high green mountains which dwindle into spiny forest to the west. One eye-catching feature of the bay is the shipwrecks. A romantic imagination associates these with pirates or wreckers of a bygone era. In fact they are all unfortunate insurance scams. Pity!

People generally still use the French name, Fort Dauphin, but to be consistent with the rest of the book I shall stick to Taolagnaro in the text. The Malagasy name is also used on maps and Air Mad schedules.

Taolagnaro has recently experienced an unprecedented influx of new residents, most especially as a result of the controversial ilmenite (titanium ore) mine. As a consequence, the face of the town is changing and prices here have risen faster than in any other part of the country.

The southeast region gives the best opportunity in all of Madagascar for wildlife-viewing to suit all budgets and levels of energy. Whilst **Berenty** is rightly world-famous, adventurous visitors should give equal consideration to **Andohahela National Park**, whilst those on a tight budget can consider the **Mandena Conservation Zone** or the community project of **Ifotaka.**

☞ *WARNING!* There have been muggings and assaults on some Taolagnaro beaches. Shipwreck Bay may be risky around dawn or dusk, but Libanona Beach and Baie des Galions are safer. Attacks have also occurred on beaches to the north towards Evatraha.

GETTING THERE AND AWAY
By road The overland route from Tana (90,900Ar) is reportedly best done with the operator Sonatra (m *032 62 811 63*). These buses go via Ihosy, Betroka and Ambovombe. Book your seat well in advance. For the journey overland from Toliara, see page 211; and from Vangaindrano, see page 277. A *camion-brousse* leaves for Vangaindrano each Wednesday.

By air There are flights (often heavily booked) to Taolagnaro from Tana and Toliara every day and twice weekly to Morondava. Check with Air Mad for the latest schedules; their office in town is near the BOA bank (✆ *92 211 22;* m *032 05 222 80;* ⊕ *Mon–Fri 08.00–11.30 & 14.30–17.00, Sat 08.30–11.00*).

GETTING AROUND
Taxis cost 2,000Ar per person for short trips in town, or 6,000Ar to the airport. The official rate for longer private hire is 20,000Ar per hour.

WHERE TO STAY
Top end €€€€€
🏠 **Kaleta** (41 rooms) ✆ 92 212 87; f 92 210 97; e kaletaresa@moov.mg; www.kaletahotel-fortdauphin.com. Classy new hotel under same ownership as Colbert in Tana. En-suite rooms with safe, minibar, AC, fan & TV; some with bath. Free Wi-Fi in lobby; public pool & spa. Visa accepted.

Upper range €€€€
🏠 **Azura** (19 rooms) ✆ 92 211 17/23/36; f 92 211 38; e azura.hotel@moov.mg; www.hotel-azura.com. Smart contemporary rooms with TV, AC, minibar, Wi-Fi (not free) & en-suite bathroom. Spa, pool & tour operator.

🏠 **Libanona Beach View** m 033 12 510 46; e libanonabeachview@fortnet.net. Suites & self-catering units. Very nice with stunning views of the beach & to Pic St Louis; spacious rooms with TV & fridge. All guests have access to kitchen facilities; some rooms with private kitchenette. B/fast inc.

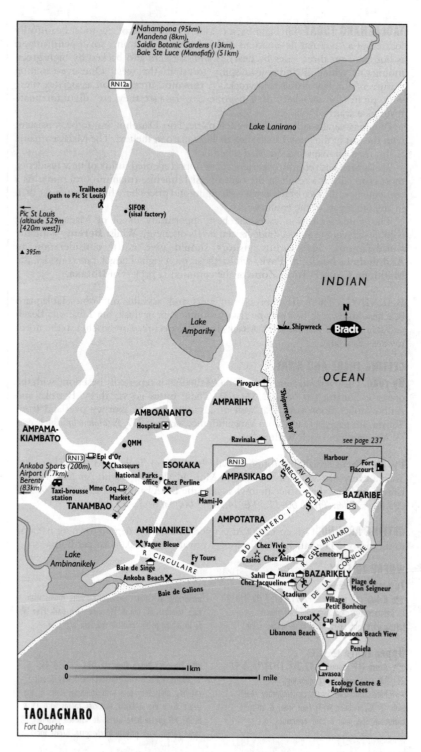

Nahampona (95km),
Mandena (8km),
Saidia Botanic Gardens (13km),
Baie Ste Luce (Manafiafy) (51km)

RN12a

Lake Lanirano

Trailhead
(path to Pic St Louis)

SIFOR
(sisal factory)

← Pic St Louis
(altitude 529m
[420m west])

▲ 395m

INDIAN

N

Lake
Amparihy

🕊 Shipwreck   **Bradt**

OCEAN

Pirogue 🏛

AMPARIHY

AMBOANANTO

'Shipwreck Bay'

Hospital ✚

Ravinala 🏛

see page 237

AMPAMA-
KIAMBATO

● QMM

Harbour

Fort
Flácourt 🏰

Epi d'Or 🏛
RN13

Chasseurs ✕

ESOKAKA

RN13

Ankoba Sports (200m),
Airport (1.7km),
Berenty
(83km)

National Parks
office

✕ Chez Perline

AMPASIKABO

BAZARIBE ✉

Taxi-brousse
station

Mme Coq 🏛

Mami-Jo ✕

🛈

Market

✚

AV DU MARECHAL FOCH $

$

TANAMBAO

✚

AMPOTATRA

$

AMBINANIKELY

BD NUMERO I

R GEN BRULARD

✕ Vague Bleue

Chez Vivie 🏛

R. CIRCULAIRE

Casino ☆ Chez Anita

Cemetery

CORNICHE

Lake
Ambinanikely

Fy Tours ✕

BAZARIKELY

Baie de Singe
Ankoba Beach ✕

Sahil 🏛 Azura 🏛
Chez Jacqueline 🏛

✕

Plage de
Mon Seigneur

Baie de Galions

Stadium 🏛

R DE LA

Village
Petit Bonheur

Local ✕ ● Cap Sud

Libanona Beach ✕   🏛 Libanona Beach View

0   I km   Peniela 🏛
0   I mile

TAOLAGNARO
Fort Dauphin

Lavasoa 🏛
● Ecology Centre &
Andrew Lees

🏠 **Hotel du Phare** (14 rooms) \ 92 905 10; m 033 11 254 29/034 03 659 27; e hotelduphareftu@hotmail.fr. Dbl rooms with TV, AC, minibar & hot water. Free Wi-Fi. B/fast inc.

🏠 **Dauphin, Croix du Sud & Galion** (75 rooms) \ 92 217 58; m 032 05 416 83; e contact@ madagascar-resorts.com; www.madagascar-resorts.com. This cluster of hotels is under the same ownership as Berenty Reserve. You are expected to stay here if you want to visit Berenty. Meals are taken in the Dauphin which has a lovely garden. Expensive airport transfers.

Mid-range €€€

🏠 **Peniela** (10 bungalows & 10 rooms) \ 92 906 34; m 032 07 905 77/034 15 230 23; e hotel.peniela@yahoo.fr. Newly opened with AC, TV & internet in rooms.

🏠 **Ravinala** (5 rooms) \ 92 910 94; m 033 12 197 65/032 02 380 07; e favilaclaris@yahoo.fr. Cosy rooms for 2–6 people, all en suite with fan & TV, including a family room with kitchenette. No food.

🏠 **Pirogue** (5 rooms) m 032 04 075 70/033 08 246 09. Small dbl & trpl beachfront bungalows with TV; en suite.

🏠 **Soavy** (10 rooms & 6 bungalows) Ampasikabo; \ 92 213 59; m 032 40 657 46; e deriazi@ yahoo.fr. Rooms & bungalows of various price/standard, some with hot water, AC & electricity. Restaurant **Vanille** is recommended.

🏠 **Village Petit Bonheur** (13 rooms & 5 bungalows) \ 92 212 60; e villagepetitbonheur@ fortnet.net. Comfy dbl rooms & family apartments including 1 with kitchenette. Good restaurant with great views. Organises trips. Visa accepted.

🏠 **Motel Gina** (14 bungalows & 2 rooms) \/f 92 217 24; e motelgina2005@yahoo.fr. Attractive bungalows & rooms around tranquil garden. Various standards. Excursions & vehicle/bike hire. Credit cards accepted.

Budget €€

🏠 **Sahil** (7 rooms) Bazarikely; \ 92 912 39. A modest, clean hotel; 2nd floor panoramic view of Baie de Galions. Dbl en-suite rooms.

🏠 **Mahavoky** (12 rooms) Bazaribe; \ 92 902 32/914 15. Inexpensive, large dbl & twin rooms with communal (outside) hot showers & toilet. Games room & good-value restaurant.

🏠 **Lavasoa** (2 rooms & 4 bungalows) \/f 92 211 75; m 033 12 517 03/033 12 911 75; e info@lavasoa.mg; www.lavasoa.com. Bungalows have en-suite bathroom & balcony overlooking Libanona beach. B/fast but no restaurant. Offers excursions to hard-to-reach places such as Lokaro; 4x4 rental.

🏠 **Marina** (18 rooms) m 033 08 287 95/032 49 834 42; e hotelpanorama_lamarina@yahoo.fr. Same ownership as Panorama. Dbl rooms & 6-person suites, all with en-suite hot water, AC & TV.

🏠 **Népènthes** (13 bungalows) Ampasikabo; m 032 04 455 54. Dbl bungalows & restaurant in quiet, spacious grounds. Can supply guides & transport for day trips to Lokaro/Evatraha by boat.

🏠 **Panorama** (5 bungalows) m 033 12 516 04; e hotelpanorama_lamarina@yahoo.fr. En-suite bungalows with balcony overlooking Shipwreck Bay. Wi-Fi. Restaurant **La Terrasse**.

🏠 **Tournesol** (8 bungalows, 1 room & 3 studios) \ 92 216 71; m 033 12 513 16/032 42 613 77. On outskirts of town. Rooms with TV in nice communal garden; stunning views of Pic St Louis. Resident guide Narcisse can organise just about any local excursion.

🏠 **Gina Village** (10 bungalows) \ 92 915 14; m 032 43 904 49/033 07 987 66; e ginavillage@yahoo.fr. Dbl & twin bungalows with en-suite bathrooms.

🏠 **Chez Anita** (8 rooms & 6 bungalows) \ 92 904 22; m 032 40 323 36; e anitahotel@fortnet.net. Bungalows nestled in a quiet garden tucked away from the main road. Dbl & trpl with hot water & TV.

🏠 **Baie de Singe** (16 rooms) m 033 12 616 49. Good-value en-suite rooms for up to 4 people.

🏠 **Chez Flora** (5 rooms) \ 92 905 87. Guesthouse with dbl rooms; communal facilities. 4x4 hire.

🏠 **Mahavoky Annexe** (9 rooms) m 032 07 990 70. Centrally located. Most rooms have a balcony with dramatic views of the shipwrecks in the bay. Cheaper rooms facing road. Nice restaurant.

🏠 **Chez Jacqueline** (6 rooms) Ampasimasay; \ 92 900 73; m 032 41 109 07. Popular with budget travellers. Basic en-suite rooms, some with hot water.

✖ **WHERE TO EAT** Restaurants in Taolagnaro offer a wonderful mix of Malagasy dishes and international cuisine, with an emphasis on freshly caught seafood. Lobster, ocean fish, oysters, crab and shrimp are a must if you are staying in town.

✗ **Dauphin** ⊕ 12.00–late. Lovely restaurant with a wide selection of consistently good fare; impeccable service. Great seafood & fresh fruit sorbets.

✗ **Las Vegas** m 032 11 530 55; ⊕ 06.00–late. Pizza, seafood & many Malagasy dishes. Good terrace for relaxing.

✗ **Mirana** ✆ 92 903 73; ⊕ Mon–Sat, Sun closed. Much recommended restaurant.

✗ **Local** m 032 44 540 60; ⊕ 07.30–20.30. A lovely pub-restaurant with stunning sunset views over Libanona Bay. Fantastic seafood. Service can be slow, so it is recommended that you order, go for a swim, then come back after 1hr.

✗ **Recréat** ⊕ Tue–Sun 07.00–late, Mon closed. A lovely outdoor café/restaurant. A great place to come if you want to sit back & people-watch. Generous portions of seafood & zebu brochettes.

✗ **Chez Perline** Specialises in seafood dishes such as lobster & crab. The curried shrimp with sauce comes highly recommended.

✗ **Chasseurs** m 033 14 368 61; ⊕ 07.30–late. Quick service, late opening & reliable food.

✗ **Oasis** m 033 12 205 09. Popular among locals, offering Malagasy *plats du jour*. There is also a selection of *vazaha* dishes including cheeseburgers.

✗ **Chez Vivie** Bazarikely; ✆ 92 214 40. Family-run restaurant serving Malagasy dishes at bargain prices.

Portions are not large, but the food is tasty & service amenable.

✗ **Vague Bleue** m 032 12 784 40; ⊕ 07.00–22.00. Typical Malagasy cuisine.

✗ **Ankoba Beach (Chez Marceline)** m 032 40 287 15; ⊕ Tue–Sun, Mon closed. Nice restaurant but doesn't open late.

✗ **Filao** m 032 44 672 14; ⊕ Mon–Sat 11.30–22.00, Sun closed. Lunch sandwiches & European cuisine.

✗ **Maxi Pizza** m 032 55 671 49; ⊕ Tue–Sun 10.00–23.00, Mon 16.00–23.00. Big range of pizza, including takeaway.

⊡ **Kaleta** ⊕ Tue–Sun, Mon closed. This hotel has a wonderful patisserie with divine almond croissants, ice cream & Belgian-style chocolates.

⊡ **Mahavoky Escale** This family-run hotely is a lively local place for drinks & brochettes.

⊡ **Epi d'Or** Bazaribe. A bakery-cum-café with a wide selection of cakes, pastries, desserts & ice cream.

⊡ **Mami-Jo** Esokaka. This small but popular Malagasy & Chinese cuisine *hotely* is great for a quick, cheap meal. Patisserie too.

⊡ **Madame du Coq's** In the heart of the market area, this place is great for a quick snack.

NIGHTLIFE

♀ **Tranobongo (Chez Martine's)** A great bar for a few cheap drinks before heading to the disco. Also great for *tsaky-tsaky* (Malagasy for 'snack food').

♀ **Las Vegas** At the restaurant of the same name. They have a wide selection of flavoured rums. Good music & often cabaret at the w/end.

☆ **Nana Club (Motel Gina)** ⊕ Wed–Sun 21.00–04.00. This dance club is very popular with

the locals & can be a great night out if you are with a group. Every Fri/Sat night DJs play Malagasy music to a lively packed crowd. Outdoor bar serves beer & spirits. Be warned: sex workers are notoriously aggressive here.

☆ **Casino** ⊕ Thu–Sat 20.00–02.00, Sun 17.00–00.00. Arcade-style machines open late.

MONEY AND COMMUNICATIONS The post office has Western Union services (⊕ *Mon–Fri 08.30–12.00 & 13.30–17.00, Sat 08.30–11.00*), as do the BFV, BOA and BNI banks, which close at weekends but have 24-hour ATMs. There is a DHL office at Air Fort Services (see page 238).

Internet is available at **Mendrika** for 60Ar/minute (⊕ *Mon–Fri 08.00–11.30 & 14.00–17.30*). **Cybersnack Arisoa** is an alternative cybercafé which also serves snacks.

SHOPPING On Avenue Gallieni, **SMAR** (✆ *92 213 26*) is a supermarket well stocked with groceries. The main **market** is on the west side of town.

Taolagnaro has some distinctive local crafts. Most typical are the heavy (and expensive) silver bracelets worn traditionally by men. Also on offer are handmade shoes and raffia handbags. The souvenir shops, such as **Au Bout du Monde** and **Baz'Arts** are mostly along the main road. Handicrafts and souvenirs are also on sale at the small shops in Kaleta hotel.

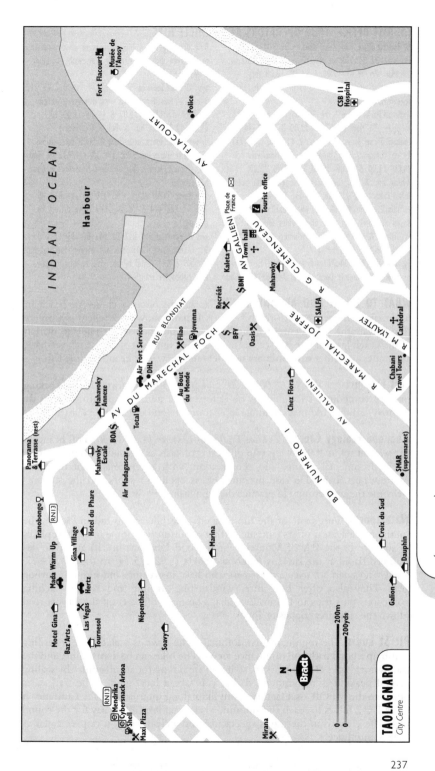

TAOLAGNARO
City Centre

INDIAN OCEAN

Harbour

Fort Flacourt
Musée de l'Anosy
Police
AV FLACOURT
CSB II Hospital

Tourist office
Place de France
Kaleta
GALLIENI
BNI AV Town hall
Mahavoky
SALFA
BFV
Oasis
R LYAUTEY
Cathédral
Chabani Travel Tours
Recréat
RUE BLONDIAT
Filao
Jovenna
MARECHAL FOCH
AV DU
Air Fort Services
DHL
Total
Au Bout du Monde
Chez Flora
R MARECHAL JOFFRE
AV GALLIENI
BD NUMERO I
SMAR (supermarket)
Mahavoky Annexe
Panorama & Terrasse (rest)
BOA
Mahavoky Escale
Air Madagascar
Tranobongo
RNJ3
Gina Village
Hotel du Phare
Marina
Croix du Sud
Dauphin
Galion
Motel Gina
Mada Warm Up
Baz'Arts
Las Vegas
Hertz
Tournesol
Népenthès
Soavy
Mendrika
Cybersnack Arisoa
Shell
Maxi Pizza
RNJ3
Mirana

200m
200yds
N
Bradt

0
0

237

TOURIST OFFICE, TOUR OPERATORS AND VEHICLE HIRE

⛿ Tourist office Rue Realy Abel; \ 92 904 12;
m 032 02 846 34; e officetourismeftu@moov.mg;
⊙ Mon–Fri 08.30–12.00 & 14.30–18.00. Very
helpful staff who can arrange excursions with tour
operators.

National Parks Office \ 92 904 85; e angapfd@
yahoo.fr; ⊙ Mon–Fri 07.30–12.00 & 14.30–18.00

Chabani Travel Tours m 033 12 415 00; f 92 217
43; e chabanitravel@gmail.com; ⊙ Mon–Fri
08.00–12.00 & 14.00–18.00, Sat 08.00–12.00.
Vehicle hire & tours/excursions throughout the south.

Safari Laka \ 92 212 66; m 032 02 329 96;
e safarilakatours@yahoo.fr; www.safarilaka.com.
Based at Motel Gina, they offer guides for local
excursions & adventure trips, including mountain
biking, trekking & canoeing.

Fy Tours m 032 04 212 04; f 92 211 71;
e fytourl@yahoo.fr. Located near Ankoba Beach on
Baie des Singes. 4x4 hire & tours to all destinations
in the area including camping trips with car, guide
& food.

🚗 Air Fort Services \ 92 212 24; m 032 05 212
34; e air.fort@moov.mg; www.airfortservices.com;
⊙ Mon–Fri 08.00–12.00 & 14.00–17.00, Sat
08.00–12.00. Car, bus & 4x4 hire including
driver/guide. Tours, excursions & flight reservations.

🚗 Mada Warm Up \ 92 211 39; m 032 61 440
06; e madawarmup@gmail.com. Motorbike & quad
bike rental.

🚗 Hertz SICAM Bldg; \ 92 210 76; m 032 05
221 53. Car, 4x4 & minibus hire (with driver) by
the day.

🚗 Madarental m 032 02 943 88/033 12 178
91; e madarental@yahoo.com; www.madarental.com.
Minibus & 4x4 rental by the day, month or year.
Also helicopter transfers.

WHAT TO DO IN AND AROUND TOWN Taolagnaro offers a choice of beach or
mountain. The best easy-to-reach beach is **Libanona**, with excellent swimming
(but beware the strong current), snorkelling and tide-pools. The pools to the left
of the beach (as you face the sea) seem best. Look out for a bizarre, frilly sea-hare,
anemones and other extraordinary invertebrates, as well as beautiful little fish.

Fort Flacourt (⊙ *Tue–Sat 08.00–11.00 & 14.30–17.30*) This fort is now a working
military compound so a guide is obligatory for a tour. A museum, **Musée de
l'Anosy**, exhibits old maps, photographs, uniforms and other cultural artefacts.

Libanona Ecology Centre (⊙ *Mon–Fri 08.00–12.00 & 14.30–17.30*) This beautiful
site was set up in 1996 by a group of local ecologists as a regional training centre
for environmental science and conservation, with a generous grant from the
Andrew Lees Trust. Do stop by: the LEC is open to visitors and the students
welcome the opportunity to practice their English.

Watersports With some of the most superb coastline of the Indian Ocean, the
south of Madagascar offers fantastic surfing opportunities. Some of the best places
to surf are in the Bay of Monseigneur (beyond Libanona beach) and Baie des
Galions. Based at the latter is **Ankoba Sports** (\ *92 215 15; m 033 12 514 17;
e ankoba@fortnet.net; www.ankoba.com*) who have instructors and hire our surfing
gear. They also offer boat hire, windsurfing, fishing and whale-watching
excursions plus trips to Lokaro/Evatraha. The main office is on the airport road
(down the side street opposite Total).

Pic St Louis The mountain that dominates the town is scaled by a rewarding
climb up a good path and offers nice views. The hike can be demanding, and the
trail is not always clearly marked, so if you are not up for an adventure by scaling
several peaks it is recommended that you take a local guide. The trail starts
opposite the SIFOR sisal factory about 3km along the road to Lake Lanirano. It
takes 1½–2 hours to reach the summit, so allow at least a half day for the round
trip. The view from the top is spectacular: on a clear day you can see as far as
Baie Sainte Luce.

LA DOMAINE DE LA CASCADE, MANANTANTELY (m *032 07 678 23; entry 10,000Ar*)
Meaning 'place of honey', this tranquil park contains tree nurseries, fruit plantations, an apiary and a natural waterfall. There are rooms if you want to stay and campsites too. Located about 8km west of Taolagnaro, on the way to Amboasary, this is a great place to take a picnic, hike, or swim in the waterfall pools.

NAHAMPOANA RESERVE (*Entry 16,000Ar pp inc guided tour, min 2 people*) This is an easily accessible zoo-cum-reserve and botanical garden owned by Air Fort Services (see opposite) who can provide transport to get there. The 67ha park is just 7km (15 minutes) from Taolagnaro on the way to Sainte Luce. Although some species are from other parts of Madagascar, it provides the usual tame lemurs, reptiles and regional vegetation. Allow a full day for a visit or stay in one of the en-suite rooms (70,000Ar including breakfast).

RANOPISO ARBORETUM (\ *92 213 25;* e *sear_ftu@yahoo.fr*) About an hour out of Taolagnaro lies this 2ha botanical garden, founded in 1980 by the Société d'Exploration Agricole de Ranopiso (SEAR). The arboretum harbours 160 species, including more than 60 endemic to the south of Madagascar. Nearby is a factory where SEAR produces leukaemia drugs from the endemic Madagascar periwinkle.

PORTUGUESE FORT/ILE AUX PORTUGUAIS The tour to the old fort involves a pirogue ride up the River Vinanibe, about 6km from Taolagnaro, and then a short walk to the sturdy-looking stone fortress (the walls are 1m thick) set in zebu-grazed parkland. This is the oldest building in Madagascar, and worth a visit for the beautiful surroundings. Despite its name it pre-dates Portuguese visitors and is probably of 14th-century Swahili origin. The fort is built on an islet in Lake Vinanibe (if you want to stay in the area, see below for nearby accommodation).

MULTI-DAY TRIPS

LAKE VINANIBE Less than 10km west of Taolagnaro is this large lake, famous for its prawns. The lake is perfect for sailing and the whole area of hills and dunes is great for strolling. The upper-range **Vinanibe Lodge** (\ *92 910 56;* m *032 05 416 83;* e *vinanibe@madagascar-resorts.com; www.madagascar-resorts.com;* €€€) has charming en-suite rooms and bungalows in a tranquil spot on the lakeshore.

BAIE SAINTE LUCE (MANAFIAFY) About 65km (3 hours) northeast of Taolagnaro is the beautiful and historically interesting bay where the French colonists of 1638 first landed. There is a superb beach and a protected area of humid coastal forest here under the same ownership as Berenty. It is possible to reach Manafiafy by *taxi-brousse* or with a tour operator such as Air Fort Services.

Where to stay
Manafiafy Beach & Rainforest Lodge (6 bungalows) \/f 22 022 26; m 032 05 619 99/00; e erika@madaclassic.com; www.manafiafy.com. A brand new community-based eco-lodge owned by Madagascar Classic Camping. Entirely solar-powered, the en-suite luxury dbl & family bungalows with huge beds are discreetly tucked into the forest a stone's throw from the water's edge. Private terraces with hammock. B/fast, meals & soft drinks inc. Forest walks, whale-watching, fishing & boat trips to nearby islands & canoeing in the mangrove. See ad after page 408.

EVATRAHA AND LOKARO Evatraha is a very attractive coastal village to the north of Taolagnaro, situated on the mouth of a small river just south of Lokaro. Day trips here, by boat, can be organised through many tour operators, or a longer stay through Fy Tours. There are two cheaply priced en-suite double bungalows if you decide to stay.

There is no public transport, but Evatraha can be reached from Taolagnaro either by pirogue (a peaceful sail downriver), 4x4 (2 hours), mountain bike (but the last 15km is tough due to deep sand), or on foot – a three-hour (10km) walk along the beach running north from Taolagnaro. From Evatraha, it is an hour's walk through hills and forest to the beach at Lokaro.

The isolated Bay of Lokaro is perhaps the most beautiful spot on the southeast coast. Given the beauty of the area there is a strong case for staying longer than a day trip. There are some beautiful spots to camp and three bungalows and an open-air restaurant can be found at **Camp Pirate**, run by Hôtel Lavasoa (see page 235).

BERENTY

This is the key destination of most package tours and most visitors love it. The combination of tame lemurs, comfortable accommodation and the tranquillity of the forest trails makes this *the* Madagascar memory for many people. The danger is that Berenty is already becoming overcrowded, and too many groups bring problems. Fortunately, there is only a limited amount of accommodation, so if you can arrange to spend a night or two you will at least have the reserve to yourself in the magical hours of dawn and dusk when the daytrippers are gone.

Visits must be organised with Madagascar Resorts – through one of their hotels: Dauphin in Taolagnaro (see page 235) or Capricorne in Toliara (see page 213) – or online (e *berenty@madagascar-resorts.com; www.madagascar-resorts.com*). Note that you cannot turn up without a booking or with your own transport.

THE ROAD TO BERENTY The reserve lies some 87km to the west of Taolagnaro, amid a vast sisal plantation, and the drive there is part of the experience. For the first half of the journey the skyline is rugged green mountains. Traveller's trees (*Ravenala*) dot the landscape, and near **Ranopiso** is a grove of the very rare triangle palm, *Neodypsis decaryi*.

Your first stop will be a visit to some **pitcher plants**, *Nepenthes madagascariensis*, whose nearest relatives are in Asia, and you may stop at an **Anosy tomb**. While driving, look out for what look like clusters of missiles lurking in the forest. These Antanosy cenotaphs commemorate those buried in a communal tomb or instances where the body could not be recovered.

Ranopiso marks the end of the hills and the landscape soon flattens out. The bizarre fingers of *Didierea* and *Alluaudia* appear on the skyline, interspersed with the bulky trunks of baobabs – the unique flora of the spiny forest (see page 67).

The exhilaration of driving through the spiny forest is dampened by the sight of all the **charcoal sellers** waiting by their sacks of ex-*Alluaudia*. These marvellous trees are being cut down at an alarming rate by people who have no other means of support. While condemning the practice, give uneasy thought to the fact that your sumptuous meals in Berenty will be cooked on stoves fuelled with locally produced charcoal. And that it is city-dwellers who consume the most charcoal in Madagascar: on average two sacks a month.

En route, one enterprising community sells **woodcarvings** of lemurs, tortoises, chameleons and other local fauna. If you pass through the village of **Ankaramena** (28km from Taolagnaro) on a Thursday, do stop to experience the fascinating **zebu**

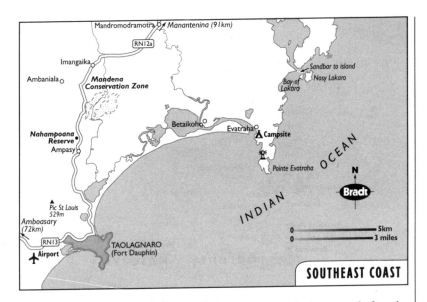

SOUTHEAST COAST

market. There is also a terrific market at **Amboasary**, the last town before the bridge across the River Mandrare and the turn-off to Berenty. The rutted red road takes you past acres of sisal and some lonely looking baobabs, to the reserve.

THE RESERVE Berenty is most famous for its population of ring-tailed lemurs and sifakas. If you have ever seen these in a TV documentary, chances are they were filmed here. The de Heaulme family have made this one of the best-studied 260ha of forest in Madagascar. Although in the arid south, its location on the River Mandrare ensures a good water supply for the habitat of gallery or riverine forest, which is divided into two sections: **Malaza** (near the tourist bungalows) and **Ankoba** to its northwest.

The joy of Berenty is its broad forest trails that allow safe wandering on your own, including nocturnal jaunts. Remember, many creatures are active only at night and are easy to spot in the light of a torch. A dusk visit (with a guide) to the reserve's area of spiny forest is a must – not only for the mouse lemurs but also the surreal, magical experience of those weird giant trees in silhouette.

Get up at dawn for the best birdwatching, and to see the lemurs opening their arms to the sun. Enjoy the coolness of the forest before going in to breakfast.

WILDLIFE Lemurs are what most people come here for: brown lemurs, ring-tails and sifakas are all guaranteed sightings. They have not been hunted here for nearly a century, so they trust people. They were fed bananas by tourists in the 1980s and 1990s, but this is no longer allowed. Disappointed that an outstretched hand no longer offers food, they will try to sneak into your cabin to find it for themselves. **Ring-tailed lemurs** (*Lemur catta*) have an air of swaggering arrogance, are as at home on the ground as in trees, and are normally highly photogenic with their grey, black and white markings and waving striped tails. These fluffy tails play an important part in communication and act as benign weapons against neighbouring troops which might have designs on their territory. However, Berenty's ringtails don't always look so photogenic (see box on page 244).

There are approximately 500 ring-tailed lemurs in Berenty, and the population has stayed remarkably stable considering only a quarter of babies survive to

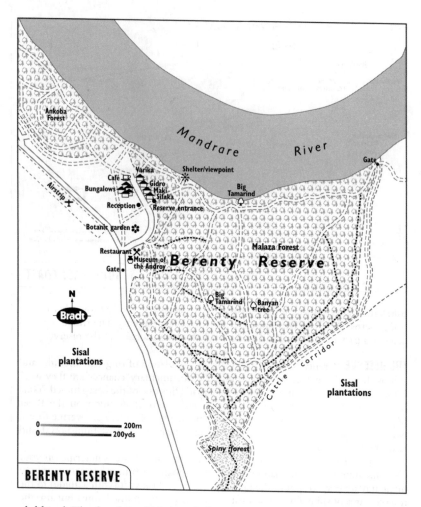

BERENTY RESERVE

adulthood. The females, which are wholly dominant over the males, are receptive to mating for only a week or so in April or May, so there is plenty of competition amongst the males for this once-a-year treat. The young are born in September and at first cling to their mother's belly, later climbing onto her back and riding jockey-style.

Attractive though the ring-tails are, no lemur can compete with the **Verreaux's sifaka** for soft-toy cuddliness, with its creamy white fur, brown cap, and black face. The species here is *Propithecus verreauxi* and there are about 300 of them in the reserve. Unlike the ring-tails, they rarely come down to the ground, but when they do the length of their legs in comparison with their short arms necessitates a comical form of locomotion: they stand upright and jump with their feet together like competitors in a sack race. The best places to see them do this are on the trail to the left at the river and across the road by the aeroplane hangar near the restaurant and museum. The young are born in July.

The **red-fronted brown lemurs** (*Eulemur rufus*) were introduced from the west and are now well established and almost as tame as the ring-tails. These are the only sexually dimorphic lemurs in Berenty – in other words you can tell the

Hilary Bradt

When I first started leading trips to Madagascar in the 1980s we always visited Berenty. It was one reliable success in an island of mishaps. So once a year I would make the drive from Taolagnaro and stop at a tiny settlement beside the road to see the Tomb of Ranonda. The village was a scattering of huts, like every other village along that road except for one thing: the collection of wooden carvings commemorating the dead. Unlike their more famous neighbours, the Mahafaly, the Antanosy people rarely use figurative carvings or paintings in their memorials. They prefer to mark the burial place with a cluster of concrete cenotaphs. So this was a rarity, but what set it apart from any other tomb I've seen was the exquisite craftsmanship. We even know the sculptor's name: Fiasia. Ranonda herself was evidently a religious young woman – she holds a bible and a cross – but much livelier is the man losing a leg to a crocodile and an expertly carved boatload of people, their expressions tranquil except for the helmsman who poles his overloaded canoe to its end: the vessel sank and all on board were drowned. His face shows some anxiety as he looks round, perhaps at the oncoming waves.

The boat-people were the most famous but my favourite was a group of three zebu. These animals, destined to be sacrificed to the ancestors, are usually portrayed in a stylised form with an exaggeratedly large hump. So it was with the two bulls but among them was a cow and her calf. Here the sculptor has moved away from symbolism and used his chisels with real affection for his subject. Like all southerners, he would have lived with cattle all his life, and his knowledge is revealed in the way the cow's head is turned as she licks her suckling calf. The youngster responds by flicking its tail across her muzzle. Towering above them was their protector – a wooden herdsman.

For seven years I stopped my bus-load of tourists and showed them the carvings. The first year the children were too shy to approach us but peeped, bright-eyed, from the dark doorways of their huts. As years passed they became bolder. Tourists didn't linger, and no-one thought of giving anything back to the village whose beautiful memorial provided so much pleasure. And these children were starving. Literally. I'm haunted by a photo I took of a sombre little girl with matted reddish hair, about six years old, carrying her little brother whose distended stomach and stick-like limbs show the classic signs of malnutrition. I used to fantasise about somehow persuading an NGO to set up a health clinic here, funded from income generated by tourists visiting the tomb. But I did nothing.

In 1989 I stopped as usual and led my group to the tomb. Where the carved cattle used to stand under the watchful eye of their guard, only the herdsman remained. The cow and her calf, and the two bulls, had been ripped away leaving only the jagged remains of their wooded plinth. In their place was a row of fresh zebu skulls, their horns sprouting fungi as they decomposed in the humid air. 'A tourist stole it' explained our driver. The skulls were from the cattle slaughtered by this impoverished village to calm the ancestors' rage at this desecration.

Buses no longer stop at the village. There's no point. The tomb is surrounded by a high fence of sharpened stakes. To take a photograph, tourists must pay €5. 'Not worth it', they mutter after peering though the fence with binoculars. Not worth it, I agree. The carvings have deteriorated, the wood has darkened and split, and lichen blotches the formerly smooth features of the boat-people. Somewhere, in a private collection of 'primitive art', the cow still licks her calf. Their wood retains its original grey smoothness, denied its destiny to grow old and return to the earth. And I ache for that village and its loss. Which is worse: its loss of trust or the loss of something that was not art but the tangible soul of an ancestor?

males from the females by their colour: males have a fluffy orange cap while females have greyish heads and bodies that are a more chestnut brown than males'. Both sexes have long, black noses and white 'eyebrows'.

Berenty is the perfect place to observe one of the unique aspects of lemur behaviour: female dominance. Ring-tail and sifaka males are always submissive to females, while brown lemurs are much less so. Alison Jolly, who has written so absorbingly about Berenty in her book *Lords and Lemurs* (see page 416) says 'I have seen a male brown lemur at Berenty throw a female out of a tree, which scandalised me as a ring-tail watcher. Female dominance is very odd among primates and other mammals. Of around 400 primate species, only the lemurs tend toward female dominance as a group. No monkeys or apes show the full-time chivalry of many lemur males. I call it chivalry rather than wimpishness, because males fight and wound each other, and could certainly fight females if they chose – but it is built-in that they don't confront females.'

There are other lemurs which, being nocturnal, are harder to spot, although the **white-footed sportive lemur** (*Lepilemur leucopus*) can be seen peering out of its hollow tree nest during the day. **Grey mouse lemurs** (*Microcebus murinus*) may be glimpsed in the beam of a flashlight, especially on spiny forest night walks.

Apart from lemurs there are other striking mammals. **Fruit bats** or flying foxes live in noisy groups on 'bat trees' in one part of the forest.

Birdwatching is rewarding in Berenty, and even better in Bealoka, beyond the sisal factory. Nearly 100 species have been recorded. You are likely to see several families unique to Madagascar, including the hook-billed vanga, crested coua, giant coua, coucal, grey-headed lovebirds and the beautiful Madagascar paradise flycatcher. Male flycatchers come in two colour morphs: chestnut brown, and black and white. Two-thirds of Berenty's paradise flycatchers are black and white. If you visit from mid-October to May you will see a variety of migrant birds from southeast Africa: broad-billed roller, Malagasy lesser cuckoo and lots of waders (sanderlings, greenshank, sandpiper, white-throated plover).

Then there are the **reptiles**. Although Berenty's two chameleon species are somewhat drab, they are plentiful. There is also a good chance of seeing Dumeril's boa (a huge but placid snake). In captivity there is a sulky crocodile (its companion escaped after its enclosure was damaged in a cyclone) and some tortoises.

Finally, don't forget the **insects**. One of my favourite activities in Berenty is visiting the 'cockroach tree,' a large tamarind on the left of the main trail to the river. This is pockmarked with small holes, and if you visit at night and shine your torch into them, you will see pairs of antennae waving at you. These belong to Madagascar giant hissing cockroaches. If you are able to catch one of these 5–8cm insects it will give a loud, indignant hiss. (I have kept them as pets in England; they brought me endless enjoyment!) Another equally entertaining insect is the ant lion (see boxes on pages 48 and 395). Look for their conical holes on the sandy paths, then find an ant as a drop-in gift.

THE BALD LEMURS OF BERENTY
Alison Jolly

Some ring-tailed lemurs in troops near Berenty cafeteria go nearly bald during the dry season, but grow their fur back in the wet season. This is not a contagious disease or anything to do with tourism. It is the result of feeding on *Leucaena*, a toxic introduced tree. If you see a team of veterinarians among the tourists, ask them for the latest information. Workmen have worked hard to eradicate much of the *Leucaena* in an effort to prevent this problem. Meanwhile lemurs in the rest of the forest away from the *Leucaena* areas are as furry as ever.

WHERE TO STAY AND EAT There are 13 bungalows and 17 rooms. Generators are switched off at 22.00, after which there is no electricity (without the electric fans it can get very hot).

There is a snack bar near the bungalows where breakfast is served, and the bar/restaurant (near the museum) offers fixed-menu meals, and cool outdoor seats for your pre-dinner drink.

EXCURSIONS Tourists staying more than a day should take the two excursions offered. The area of **spiny forest** here is superb (though hot) and may be your only chance to see mature *Alluaudia* trees. Some tower over 15m – an extraordinary sight. A visit to the **sisal factory** may sound boring but certainly is not.

MUSEUM OF THE ANTANDROY This is undoubtedly the best ethnological museum in Madagascar, and if your interest in the region extends beyond the wildlife, you should allow at least an hour here. Several of the rooms are given over to an explanation (in English and French) of the traditional practices of the Antandroy people, illustrated by excellent photos. There are some beautiful examples of handicrafts and a small but interesting natural history section including a complete elephant bird egg. This museum should be seen in conjunction with the replica Antandroy 'village' near the botanical garden, where you can step inside a traditional house.

MANDENA CONSERVATION ZONE

This protected reserve was established by QMM to protect 230ha of rare littoral forest in the region that is the centre of their controversial ilmenite mining project and is now mainly community-managed. The conservation area includes 160ha of the least degraded fragments of forest and 60ha of wetlands. Twenty-two species of flora are endemic to this region, with about 200 species of large trees. In 2001 a troop of collared brown lemurs (*Eulemur collaris*) were relocated to Mandena from a small, threatened area of forest outside the conservation zone.

I have visited Mandena twice and absolutely love it! It is completely different from the Berenty experience, has been thoughtfully conceived to give tourists as much variety as possible, and the local Antanosy people are involved. At present this is primarily a botanical experience. The six species of lemur in the Mandena area are still shy; no doubt they will become habituated in time, but you'll see plenty of birds and reptiles meanwhile. There is an easy circuit which takes three to four hours and a boat trip which takes you down a *Pandanus*-fringed waterway. Then it's a walk back along another forest trail to the visitor centre and tree nursery.

VISITING MANDENA (*Entry 10,000Ar inc guided walk & boat trip*) The main hotels and tour operators in Taolagnaro run day trips, but independent travellers can contact QMM (m *033 12 815 04*). The reserve is about 10km from Taolagnaro (a beautiful drive) so is within cycling distance. A taxi costs around 50,000Ar for the round-trip. There is a campsite just outside the boundary of the reserve (tent hire 2,000Ar) and in this area you can walk unguided. There is also a restaurant where you can eat lunch.

ANDOHAHELA NATIONAL PARK

This national park (pronounced 'andoowa*hela*') opened to tourists in 1998, and is a model of its kind. Much thought has gone into the blend of low-key tourist facilities and the involvement of local people.

This crop was introduced to Madagascar in the inter-war years, with the first exports taking place in 1922 when 42 tons were sent to France. By 1938, 2,537 tons were exported and 3,500ha of sisal were planted in the Toliara and Taolagnaro region. By 1950 production reached 3,080 tons. In 1952 a synthetic substitute was developed in the US and the market dropped. The French government stepped in with subsidies and bought 10,000 tons.

The Toliara plantations were closed in 1958 leaving only the de Heaulme plantations in Taolagnaro. In 1960 these covered 16,000ha and, by the mid-1990s, 30,000ha of endemic spiny forest (over 100 square miles!) had been cleared to make way for the crop, with plantations under the ownership of six different companies. Workers earn 32,000Ar per month (1999 figure). There is no sick pay or pension provision. The de Heaulme plantation alone employs 15,000 people who cut 300,000 leaves per day.

And here's something to think about: in the late 1990s there was a resurgence of demand for sisal, with exports reaching 5,000 tons in the year 2005, putting more spiny forest at risk. Why? Because we 'green' consumers in the EU are demanding biodegradable packaging. And what is the best biodegradable substance? Sisal!

The reserve spans rainforest, spiny forest and transition forest, and thus is of major importance and interest. These three distinct zones make Andohahela unique in its biodiversity.

ANDOHAHELA INTERPRETATION CENTRE Even if you are not able to visit Andohahela itself, do spend some time in this beautifully organised centre set up both for tourists and locals. It is a green building on the left-hand side of the road just after Ranopiso. Through clear exhibits (in English, French and Malagasy) it emphasises the importance of the forest and water to future generations, and explains the use of various medicinal plants. Local initiatives include the introduction of fuel-efficient cooking stoves that burn sisal leaves. Wind power is also being investigated. Schools are being built in the area, with education on the importance of preserving the environment a priority. For those in need of accommodation, there are two rooms at the centre and camping is permitted.

VISITING ANDOHAHELA A visit to most areas of the national park requires a 4x4 and camping gear (all can be provided by tour operators) but fit and properly equipped hikers or cyclists can make it independently. There are campsites with toilets and showers at Tsimelahy and Mangatsiaka (5,000Ar/night) and simple campsites without facilities at Malio, Manangotry and Ihazofotsy (3,000Ar).

From the Interpretation Centre to Tsimelahy is 5km on the main road then a further 8km from the turn-off. Cyclists would be better to go via Mangatsiaka.

Local tour operators offer packages to Andohahela. They can arrange guides and permits; these can also be obtained from the National Parks office in Taolagnaro (for prices see page 72). Guide fees are 7,000Ar per group.

THE NATIONAL PARK
Malio (rainforest) The rainforest area has a trail system and campsites, plus all the rainforest requisites: waterfalls, orchids and lemurs (*Eulemur fulvus*), but without the crowds of Andasibe or Ranomafana. It is also popular with birders who come here looking for the rare red-tailed newtonia. To get there (dry season only) take the paved road out of Taolagnaro for approximately 15km,

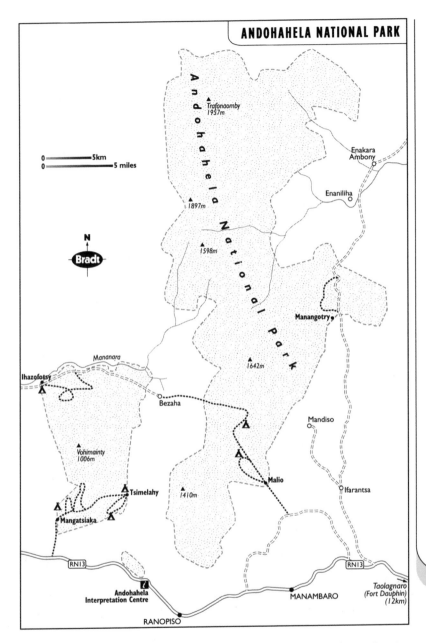

turn north on a dirt road before the town of Manambaro and go 6km to the nice little village of Malio.

Ihazofotsy and Mangatsiaka (spiny forest) Visitors should remember that spiny forest is very hot and often shadeless, so camping/walking here can be quite arduous. That said, for the committed adventurer this is a wonderful area for wildlife, birding and botany. Even if you were to see no animals, the chance to walk through untouched spiny forest – the real Madagascar – gives you a glimpse of how extraordinary this land must have seemed to the first Europeans.

Apart from the fascinating trees and plants unique to this region, if you're lucky you should see sifakas, small mammals such as tenrecs, reptiles, and plenty of birds endemic to the south, such as running coua and sickle-billed vanga.

Of the two areas, **Mangatsiaka** is the easier to visit, being only 6km off the main road to Amboasary, so ideal for self-sufficient independent travellers. There is a well-laid-out trail system and a simple campsite. **Ihazofotsy** is more popular with groups because you need a 4x4 to tackle the two-hour access track. Camping is permitted near the village and there is a good trail system through the superb *Alluaudia* trees. An added bonus is the view from a huge domed rock, which is crawling with iguanas.

Tsimelahy (transition forest) I loved this place! Apart from reptiles (lizards and snakes), we saw little wildlife, but the scenery and plants are utterly wonderful. This region is the only area in which the triangle palm is found; it says something for the rest of the botany that seeing this was *not* the highlight of our stay. The campsite for Tsimelahy is within a stone's throw of a large deep pool (perfect for swimming), fed by a waterfall, and fringed with elephant-ear plants.

Tsimelahy is clearly marked on the main road, from where the trailhead is 8km. The rocky dirt road is pretty tough on cars, so it is recommended that you hire a knowledgeable driver. You can take a 4x4 to within a few kilometres of the campsite, then you have a marvellous walk. Two trails run along both shores of River Taratantsa, affording super views of white-flowered *Pachypodium lamerei*, and green forest. My favourite plant was the 'celebrity tree' (*lazar* in Malagasy, genus *Cyphostemma*). It seems to start as a tree, then change its mind and become a liana, draping its top over neighbouring plants. Young Malagasy seeking popularity or success will ask a *mpanandro* (soothsayer) to request help from this tree.

IFOTAKA COMMUNITY FOREST (ICF)

This admirable project began in 2001, following a government initiative encouraging communities to manage their own natural resources. The local Tandroy people allow woodcutting for fuel, building and cattle grazing in some parts of the protected area, while preserving sacred and environmentally important areas for ecotourism. All the characteristic animals of the south (including Verreaux's sifakas and ring-tailed lemurs) can be seen here at a fraction of the cost of Berenty, while visitors have the happy knowledge that their fees go directly to the local community.

Owen Beaton, who has worked here since it opened, explains that 'Ifotaka is not for the fainthearted; it is usually very hot and dry, and the living conditions are quite basic. But for the adventurous visitor who prefers to see lemurs in the wild and wants a real taste of Tandroy village life, Ifotaka is an unforgettable experience.'

A variety of treks can be organised in the area, costing from 5,000Ar for a visit to the forest to 12,000Ar for an overnight camping trip. Porters are also available for 4,000Ar.

GETTING THERE ICF is to the northwest of Amboasary, 110km from Taolagnaro. *Taxi-brousses* leave Amboasary between 12.00 and 17.00. If you start from Taolagnaro you should leave before 08.00, in order to make the connection in Amboasary. *Taxi-brousses* return to Amboasary between 17.30 and 19.00.

WHERE TO STAY AND EAT For those on a budget, there are eight wooden bungalows (no electricity or running water) built by the Tandroy Conservation Trust with the community of Ifotaka. There is also a campsite. For food you should either be self-sufficient, or organise meals with a local family, who can either cook with ingredients that you bring or prepare local food for you.

Alternatively, much more upmarket accommodation may be found 3km from Ifotaka village at **Mandrare River Camp** (\f *22 022 26;* m *032 05 619 99/00;* e *erika@madaclassic.com; www.madaclassic.com;* 🍴), owned by Madagascar Classic Camping. There are six luxury furnished tents here, with solar electricity and en-suite facilities. See ad after page 408.

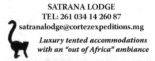

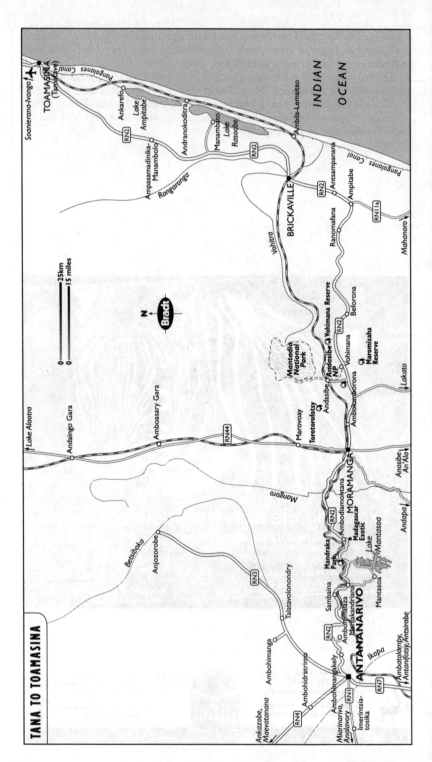

TANA TO TOAMASINA

10

Tana to Toamasina

Since the early days of the Merina kingdom, there has been a link from the country's main port to its capital. The route between the two cities will have been established during the expansionist days of King Radama I, when dignitaries were carried by palanquin and goods were transported on the heads of porters. It gained greater importance after the arrival of teachers from the London Missionary Society, the first Europeans to have a significant influence on Madagascar. They arrived in Tamatave bearing not only the word of God, but technology in the form of printing presses. The track up the escarpment was narrow, difficult and slippery in the rainy season (most of the year) but the royal government refused to build a proper road, fearing this would facilitate an invasion from outside (in the event, the French later invaded via Mahajanga). The first road was built by the French, but maintenance was never a high priority, especially after independence, partly to reduce competition with the state-owned railway. The collapse of the economy in the Second Republic meant that there was no money at all for maintenance and the road became at times almost impassable. However in the 1990s the road was rehabilitated to a high standard with aid from Switzerland and China.

These days many visitors take RN2 from the capital. Most are heading for Andasibe but some continue to the coast. The route description here is aimed at those travelling in a private vehicle or by bicycle, but of course *taxi-brousse* travellers may choose to break their trip at any of the stops along the way.

☞ **WARNING!** RN2 is notorious for its reckless drivers and high death toll. Keep alert, especially if on a bicycle. Even if you don't usually suffer from motion sickness, take precautions on this trip; the macho drivers and winding road are a challenge to any stomach.

ANTANANARIVO–COTE EST RAILWAY

Passenger trains have recently been reinstated on the Tana to Toamasina line (although scheduled services currently only run beyond Moramanga) so this offers an alternative to RN2.

The passenger service, called **Dia Soa**, comprises trains with three 72-seat carriages. They depart Moramanga Mondays at 14.00 and Thursdays at 07.00 and make the return journey from Toamasina or Brickaville Wednesdays and Saturdays at the same departure times. The route is divided into five zones. You pay 1,800Ar for each zone you pass through – 9,000Ar for the full trip.

A tourist class service, the **Trans Lémurie Express**, has two 52-seat 'Palisander Class' carriages equipped with a bar and electrical sockets and takes 15 hours between Tana and Toamasina. It does not currently run to a regular timetable but check with Madarail for the latest.

Donald Wilson

In the 1930s, the Michelin tyre company collaborated with several builders to design a self-propelled rubber-tyred railcar which could give a smoother ride on tracks and avoid the 'clickety-clack' produced by the wheels of conventional trains as they pass over track joints.

Most countries were reluctant to place orders for this innovative technology, but some of the French colonial railways used them successfully, including Madagascar which received three new trains to the original design in 1952.

Disused for 25 years, no 517 (named 'Viko-Viko' after an endemic bird, the Madagascar pratincole) was restored to its former glory at the Antananarivo workshops of Madarail, and finally returned to service in 2010.

Weighing in at almost seven tonnes and measuring over 13m in length, Viko-Viko has a theoretical top speed of 80kph. With its 19 comfortable wicker armchairs, bar and toilet, this 12-wheeled vehicle is powered by a Perkins 100hp 4-cylinder diesel engine and glides effortlessly along, stopping at scenic locations for passengers to alight and admire the stunning views.

Punctures are an occasional hazard, and when this happens the train is jacked up where it stops so that one of the six spare wheels can be fitted. The process takes just 15 minutes.

At the time of writing, services run every Saturday from Antananarivo's impressive railway station – either east to Andasibe (perfect for an overnight visit to the national park) or south to the elegant town of Antsirabe – returning the following day.

Madagascar's Micheline is a working museum piece that lives up to its marketing slogan – the 'train unlike any other'. Where else in the world could your train suffer a puncture?

Donald Wilson is a former stationmaster of London Marylebone and Commercial Director of Kent & East Sussex Railway. He travels the world in search of unusual rail experiences and gives lectures on his travels (e stationmasterdon@aol.com).

Even more exciting for rail enthusiasts is the refurbished **Micheline 'Viko-Viko'** (see box above). Michelines were rubber-tyred trains pioneered in France in the 1930s and this is the only one still in regular operation anywhere in the world. More reminiscent of a bus, the vehicle averages just 30mph, giving you plenty of time to enjoy the view. At present it operates mainly on a private hire basis so you have full flexibility in choice of destination and departure time, although scheduled services have started to run from Tana at weekends to Andasibe or Antsirabe (130,000Ar return). These usually depart Tana at 08.00 Saturday, heading back at 14.00 Sunday, but check with Madarial for dates and times.

Madarail is based at the Soarano railway station in Tana (✆ 22 345 99; f 22 218 83; e tourisme@madarail.mg; www.madarail.mg).

TANA TO MORAMANGA

After the hectic atmosphere of Tana, the journey to Moramanga offers first-time visitors to Madagascar a gentle introduction to rural life. Rice fields, *hotelys* and roadside stalls selling seasonal fruits line the route, and it is a fine opportunity to observe activities that make up the daily routine of the vast majority of Malagasy people living outside the major cities.

The 20km of road to **Ambohimangakely** is surrounded by rice fields which, in the early morning, will be filled with local people pursuing the all-important business of supplying their families with rice: digging paddies, sowing rice, transplanting the mature plants, weeding and eventually harvesting.

The following 20km takes you through the town of **Ambohimalaza**, steeped in history and tradition.

Manjakandriana is the last major town before you descend from the *hauts plateaux*. Here the flat, straight stretches of road give way to a long series of steep, winding sections and hairpin bends as you head towards the plain below and the small town of **Ambodiamontana**. This descent offers fine views of the forest clinging to the precipitous slopes of the mountains to your left, and a good vantage point from which to survey the next phase of your journey across the flat plains towards Moramanga. If you can take your eyes off the scenery, look out for enterprising locals transporting goods in oil drums balanced on tiny carts down the hair-raisingly steep stretches of road. To your left, water plunges down the flank of a nearby mountain, powering the neighbouring hydroelectric station.

As the mountains of the *hauts plateaux* recede into the distance behind you, the road to Moramanga takes you through numerous small villages and stretches of thinly populated countryside, with occasional charcoal sellers along the way.

SAMBAINA (PK 42) This small village 40km from Tana gives an opportunity to stop for a good breakfast. **Pizza Nino** (⏱ *06.30–18.30*) serves various dishes as well as pizza. The early morning weather is likely to be misty and cold.

MANJAKANDRIANA (PK 48) This town has a good choice of *hotelys* so is an alternative breakfast stop if you have made a pre-dawn start from Tana. The small **Manja Motel** on the left has basic rooms. The town also has a BOA bank, hospital, pharmacy and fuel station.

This is also where you should turn if you are heading south to Lake Mantasoa (see page 166).

MANDRAKA PARK (PK 61) (✆ *22 431 27;* f *22 431 27;* e *mandrakapark@moov.mg*) This Malagasy-run collection of wooden bungalows offers accommodation, outdoor tables, prepared meals (grilled dishes a speciality) and hikes in the neighbouring forest. It is a popular picnic spot for Malagasy families from Tana.

MADAGASCAR EXOTIC (PK 72) (✆ *22 321 01;* m *032 04 108 87;* ⏱ *07.00–17.00; entry 10,000Ar; guide 2,000Ar farm only or 6,000Ar inc lemurs*) Also known as Réserve Peyrieras and Mandraka Reptile Farm, this is a small farm-cum-zoo at Marozevo owned by naturalist André Peyrieras. The centre provides the opportunity for close viewing of some of the island's most extraordinary reptiles and invertebrates: chameleons, leaf-tailed geckos, butterflies, crocodiles and a few mammals.

Sadly, all this comes at a price: most of the animals are kept in crowded and stressful conditions, and although one purpose of the centre is the breeding (for export) of butterflies and moths, the demand for reptiles for the pet trade is also satisfied, reportedly through illegal collecting from the wild.

There is an adjacent patch of forest with (relocated) Verreaux's sifakas and common brown lemurs that are habituated. There is also a small handicraft shop, a restaurant (fixed menu) and some mid-range en-suite rooms.

AMBODIAMONTANA (PK 73) Just beyond the farm is this village where you can have a meal in one of the traditional Malagasy *hotelys* along the roadside. Rabbit is a speciality here.

Moramanga means, prosaically, 'cheap mangoes'. The area is being transformed by the new Ambatovy nickel and cobalt mine. As the stopping point for public transport travelling between Tana and Toamasina, there is heavy traffic day and night so hotels with rooms facing the street can be noisy. On the plus side you can always find an open restaurant.

GETTING THERE AND AWAY A *taxi-brousse* from Tana costs 5,000Ar and takes less than three hours.

The passenger train is back after several years' inactivity, with regular services now connecting Moramanga with Toamasina. There are departures from Moramanga on Monday and Thursday mornings, with return services from Toamasina on Wednesdays and Saturdays. More details are on page 251.

 WHERE TO STAY

⌂ **Bezanozano** (13 rooms & 18 bungalows) m 033 28 761 66/032 69 769 03; e bezanozanohotel@yahoo.fr; www.bezanozano-hotel.com. New Chinese-owned hotel. €€€€

⌂ **Diamant** (12 rooms) \ 56 823 76; m 032 52 865 02. Opposite the church. Comfortable clean rooms with small veranda, some en suite. €€–€€€

⌂ **Nadia** (19 rooms) \ 56 822 43. Sgl, dbl & twin rooms with facilities; some with TV. €€–€€€

⌂ **Emeraude** (47 rooms) \ 56 821 57; f 56 822 35. Centrally located dbl & family rooms, some en suite with TV. €€

⌂ **Fihavanana** (11 rooms & 6 bungalows) \ 56 820 63; m 033 12 591 23/032 46 097 39. On the right-hand side as you enter town from Tana, near Jovenna. Basic rooms with shared facilities & en-suite bungalows. €–€€

⌂ **Maitso an'Ala** (5 rooms) Very simple dbl & twin rooms. €

✕ **WHERE TO EAT**

✕ **Coq d'Or** \f 56 820 45; ⊕ Mon–Sat 08.00–20.00, Sun 08.30–15.00. Down a side road in front of Emeraude. Chinese, Malagasy & European menu & good pastries. A favourite stop-off for tour groups.

✕ **Sirène Dorée** On RN2 at the west of town. Good standard restaurant with Chinese & European menu.

✕ **Flore Orientale** A deservedly popular Chinese restaurant near the market.

✕ **Jovenna** On RN2 at the east of town, the Jovenna fuel station has a surprisingly good restaurant with reasonable prices.

MONEY AND COMMUNICATIONS There are several cybercafés here, mostly on RN2 near the Emeraude. Moramanga also has a branch of BOA bank and a post office.

WHAT TO SEE AND DO Turn left on entering the town and drive 800m to have a quick look at the **mausoleum** for the people who died during the uprising in 1947, and then the **Police Museum**. Ask at the *gendarmerie* gatehouse for permission to visit. The curator speaks English and will show you around this comprehensive collection, mainly of police history, but also local cultural exhibits. There are displays of transport, guns, cannons (one a gift from George IV to Radama I in 1817), police uniforms and even an intriguing array of genuine murder weapons.

HEADING NORTH OR SOUTH

Moramanga lies at a crossroads. To the north is RN44 which leads to Lake Alaotra, described opposite. To the south is a rough but interesting road to Anosibe an'Ala and the Chutes de Mort, a large waterfall 53km from Moramanga.

Continuing east along RN2 you reach Andasibe (Périnet) in about half an hour (see page 257).

Rupert Parker

We were travelling back from a *famadihana* in Ambatondrozaka to Moramanga early one morning and decided to stop halfway at a small *hotely* for breakfast. My Malagasy friends decided to order chicken and rice, but I was feeling a bit queasy and asked if they could do me *'œuf sur le plat'* – fried egg. This sounded like the safest bet. But, this being Madagascar, they asked for money in advance to buy the egg. We sat and waited for our food and eventually coffee was served; we also saw a girl going out and returning with an egg. Soon the chicken and rice arrived but there was nothing for me. We asked what the problem was and they said they had no oil and needed to buy some before they could start the cooking. I produced a little more money and my friends tucked into their food.

After 20 minutes, by now very hungry, there was still no fried egg. I enquired what was going on. A very worried man emerged from the kitchen and beckoned for us to enter the dark, smoke-filled space at the back. He explained that the problem was that they had bought an egg without a yolk and he wanted us to see it in case we didn't believe him. This was news indeed, so we all crammed inside to behold this Malagasy marvel – a world first perhaps. Of course the truth was somewhat more mundane: as we peered into the pan there was a sticky yellow mess. They'd broken the yolk, or maybe stirred the egg, and created a perfect omelette. It was delicious, but obvious that they'd never fried an egg before.

The moral is don't take anything for granted in Madagascar.

LAKE ALAOTRA

This is the largest lake in Madagascar and looks wonderful on the map; one imagines it surrounded by overhanging forest. Sadly, forest has made way for rice, and this is one of the country's most abused and degraded areas. Half a million people now live around the lake, and deforestation has silted it up so that its maximum dry-season depth is only 60cm. Introduction of exotic fish has done further damage. However, all is not lost. Since 1997 an environmental campaign led by Durrell Wildlife Conservation Trust has led to strong local support to ban marsh-burning and lemur-hunting and introduce larger net mesh sizes and a closed season for fishing. Local people recognise the role the marshes play in maintaining local hydrology, providing a spawning ground for fish and weaving materials for basketry, an important source of income for women here.

In 2006 the entire area, including watershed, rice fields, marshes and lake, was given protected status as part of The Durban Vision, and an ecotourism project developed to give tourists a chance to see one of Madagascar's most endangered species: the Lac Alaotra gentle lemur. Annual monitoring has shown that lemur populations have stabilised and that fish catches are on the increase. Alaotra provides a great example of conservation providing benefits for biodiversity and for local livelihoods and deserves some foreign visitors to support these local efforts.

GETTING THERE AND AWAY A *taxi-brousse* from Tana to Ambatondrazaka takes around six hours, or four hours to travel the 157km from Moramanga (9,000Ar).

AMBATONDRAZAKA AND NEARBY VILLAGES This is the main town of the area, and a good centre for excursions. A tour of the lake by road needs a full day and takes you through village after village where rice, cattle, fishing and geese – along with tomatoes and onions – are the mainstays of rural life. The village **Imerimandroso** gives good views over the lake and nearby **Vohitsoa** is famed for its delicate baskets

10

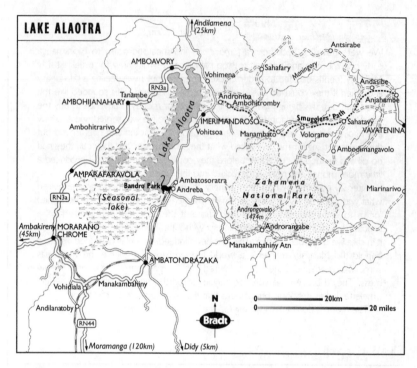

and mats woven with papyrus from the marshes. You should certainly visit **Bandro Park** near Andreba and enjoy an early-morning pirogue ride on the lake.

Where to stay and eat

🏠 **Max-Irene** ✆ 54 813 86. Near the train station, with some en-suite rooms. Friendly & clean. €€

🏠 **Voahirana** Simple rooms with shared facilities & hot water. Local tours organised. €

✕ **Bonne Ruche, Manantena & Zamaeva** are recommended places to eat.

BANDRO PARK The main reason to come to Lake Alaotra these days is to visit Bandro Park at **Andreba** and to support this new ecotourism project. *Bandro* is the Malagasy name for the rare and locally endemic Alaotra gentle lemur. In order to see the *bandro* you will need to book an early-morning pirogue trip, which is also a good way to see the area's aquatic birds. A two-hour guided boat tour on the lake and into the park costs 10,000Ar per two-person pirogue. There is also a park entry fee of 10,000Ar per person. The best time to visit is from March to June when the water level is highest.

Andreba is 45 minutes from Ambatondrazaka by *taxi-brousse* (2,000Ar). **Camp Bandro** (✆ 26 347 87; m 034 10 147 60; e *reservation@mwc-info.net*; €), a Madagascar Wildlife Conservation project, has two double rooms (10,000Ar), camping facilities (5,000Ar/tent) and a kitchen area but no restaurant.

THE SMUGGLERS' PATH A steady trickle of adventurers come to Lake Alaotra in order to hike the Smugglers' Path to the east coast. Much of the feedback I've received has been quite negative. It's very tough, very steep, and not particularly rewarding (lots of deforestation). The route takes four to five days, beginning in Andromba. The trail passes through Ambohitromby, Manambato, then various small villages before ending in Anjahambe. From there *taxi-brousses* go to Vavatenina, and thence to the east coast. Hotel Voahirana can arrange guides.

ZAHAMENA NATIONAL PARK

Zahamena (\ 57 300 33; e *cimateza@dts.mg*) is a wonderful but somewhat difficult to reach and thus little-visited national park, which has only recently become accessible to tourists. Its 64,370ha protects 13 lemur species (including indri), over 100 varieties of reptile and amphibian, and a diverse range of flora – including two locally endemic ferns.

Access is usually from the east: from Ambatondrazaka it is a 70km road to the park office at Antanandava (2 hours) then 8km to the park entry at Ankosy on a track that is passable in a 4x4 from July to November (otherwise it's two hours on foot). It is also possible to reach the park from the east coast around Fenoarivo, where there is also an office.

Guides (8,000Ar) and porters (5,000Ar) are available, but best arranged in advance. There are two circuits of roughly 6km (3 hours) each, with camping possible for 2,000Ar/night. You will need to bring with you all food and other supplies for your visit. See page 72 for permit prices.

CONTINUING EAST ON RN2: MORAMANGA TO ANDASIBE

The turning for Andasibe is just 23km beyond Moramanga. Along this stretch of RN2 it is interesting to stop at **Ambolomborona** (PK 124) to visit Hôtel Juema, a simple traditional *hotely*. You can take a tour of the family business to watch the fascinating process of bamboo furniture being made. There is no fee but they expect a small donation if you don't make a purchase.

ANDASIBE-MANTADIA NATIONAL PARK/ASSOCIATION MITSINJO

In the late 1990s the long-established reserve of Analamazaotra Forest, sometimes known by its colonial name of Périnet, was combined with Mantadia, 20km to the north, to form **Andasibe-Mantadia National Park**. Because of its proximity to Tana and its exceptional fauna, this is now one of Madagascar's most popular reserves. These two areas of moist montane forest (altitude: 930–1,049m) are home to a variety of lemurs, birds, reptiles and invertebrates. The experience is enhanced by the quality of the local guides.

Association Mitsinjo is an NGO which protects a portion of Analamazaotra forest separate from the national park. It offers all the same wildlife but at a lower price, making it perfect for independent travellers. Mitsinjo also offers night walks (not permitted in the main park). The entrance to Mitsinjo is on the left, coming from RN2, and the national park is just beyond on the right.

Although the vast majority of visitors spend one or two nights here it is possible to visit Andasibe as a day trip from Tana. You will need to leave at 06.00 to arrive in time to see and hear the indri.

☞ *WARNING!* In the winter months (May–August) it can feel very cold in Andasibe, especially when it rains (as it does at that time of year). Hotels without heaters can be quite an ordeal. At any time of year bring warm clothing and waterproofs.

ANDASIBE VILLAGE This is really just a simple Malagasy village – no bank, no internet, no taxis. It is 2km from RN2 and 1km from the park office. Taking a

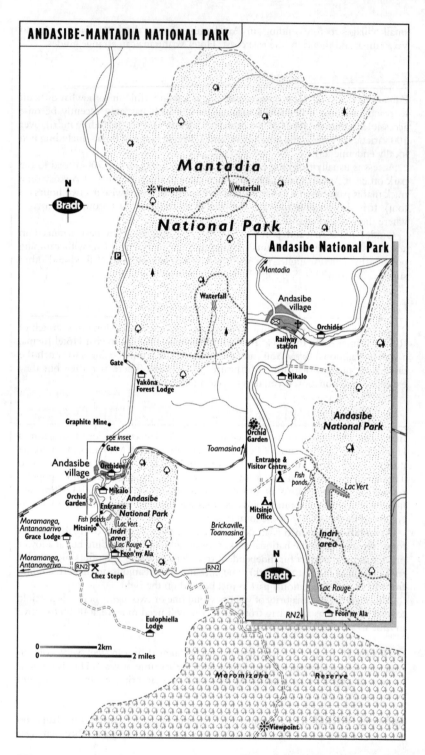

ANDASIBE-MANTADIA NATIONAL PARK

Mantadia

National Park

☀ Viewpoint   ≋ Waterfall

N
Bradt

P

Waterfall

Gate
⌂ Vakôna
Forest Lodge

Graphite Mine

see inset
Gate
Orchidée
Andasibe
village
⌂ Mikalo
Orchid
Garden
Entrance
Andasibe
National Park
Moramanga,
Antananarivo
Grace Lodge
Fish ponds
Mitsinjo
Lac Vert
Indri
area
Lac Rouge
⌂ Feon'ny Ala
Moramanga,
Antananarivo
RN2
✗ Chez Steph

Toamasina

Brickaville,
Toamasina

RN2

Eulophiella
Lodge
⌂

0 ——— 2km
0 ——— 2 miles

Maromizaha *Reserve*

☀ Viewpoint

Andasibe National Park

↑ *Mantadia*

Andasibe
village
⊠ ✝ Orchidée
Railway
station

⌂ Mikalo

☀ Orchid
Garden

Andasibe
National Park

Entrance &
Visitor Centre
⛺ *Fish*
ponds
Lac Vert

⛺ Mitsinjo
Office

Indri
area

N
Bradt

Lac Rouge

RN2

⌂ Feon'ny Ala

room at Orchidée offers the opportunity to sit on the balcony observing the comings and goings of local daily life. At the post office, you can watch bats emerging at dusk (see box on page 62).

GETTING THERE AND AWAY

By road Plenty of *taxi-brousses* ply RN2 from Tana, but taking one direct to the junction for Andasibe is expensive (20,000Ar). Far cheaper and not much slower is to get one to Moramanga (5,000Ar), then find local transport for the last few kilometres. You can then be dropped at your chosen accommodation, which is quite a bonus since all the hotels except Feon ny'Ala are some way from RN2.

By rail The train journey from Moramanga takes 45 minutes and costs 1,800Ar; and from Toamasina it's 11 hours for 9,000Ar. The Micheline makes the trip from Tana some weekends. For more information see page 252.

WHERE TO STAY AND EAT

🏠 **Vakôna Forest Lodge** (24 bungalows) ✆ 22 624 80; m 033 02 010 01; f 22 625 67; e vakona@ moov.mg; www.hotelvakona.com. The name is Malagasy for the *Pandanus* plant. Andasibe's best hotel, located just over 1km from the park, is thoughtfully designed with an octagonal reception area, bar & lounge-dining room with central log fire. The bungalows are quiet & comfortable; staff efficient & courteous; & the food delicious. Vakôna deserves longer than the normal couple of days so you can relax, swim & go horseriding as well as visit the rainforest. The hotel owns a little island which is a sanctuary for ex-pet lemurs & a small zoo, providing a great opportunity for close-up lemur photos. €€€€€

🏠 **Eulophiella Lodge** ✆ 22 242 30; m 032 07 567 82; e eulophiellandasib@eulophiella.com. About 600m towards Tana along RN2 from the Andasibe junction is the start of the 5km track to this hotel named after an endemic white orchid that only grows in the bases of *Pandanus*. Well-spaced en-suite bungalows in 2 sizes. Recommended restaurant. There's a small private reserve where night walks are possible. €€€€

🏠 **Grace Lodge** (9 bungalows) ✆ 24 308 66; m 032 05 308 66/033 03 308 66; e gracelodge@blueline.mg; www.grace-lodge.com. Down a 1km track opposite the turning to Eulophiella, a new hotel run by a very friendly English-speaking Malagasy woman. Lovely bungalows,

small swimming pool & on-site chapel! Car & bike hire. €€€ €€€€

🏠 **Feon'ny Ala** (36 bungalows) ✆ 56 832 02; m 033 05 832 02. Near RN2 & 1km from park entrance. It is a popular place in a prime location facing the national park – close enough to hear the indri call, hence the name which means 'voice of the forest'. Most bungalows en suite but 7 cheaper ones with shared facilities, all with hot water. No heaters for colder months. Excellent restaurant. Kids' play area. €€€

🏠 **Mikalo (Buffet de la Gare)** (15 bungalows) ✆ 56 832 08; m 033 11 817 85. Until 1993 this was the only place to stay in Andasibe & its list of distinguished guests includes Prince Philip, Gerald Durrell & David Attenborough. Now with newly built dbl/twin bungalows (very comfy with fireplace) & chalets. Splendid but slightly pricey restaurant. €€€

🏠 **Orchidée** (8 rooms) ✆ 56 832 05; e hotelorchideeandasibe@yahoo.fr. In Andasibe village, good value sgl, dbl & trpl rooms with hot water. €€ €€€

✕ **Chez Steph** On the south side of RN2 between the turnings for Eulophiella & Andasibe, this is a recommended small restaurant. Glorious *poulet au coco*!

✕ **Park Snack** Conveniently located eatery at the entrance to the national park.

Camping There are tent shelters (5,000Ar/tent) at Mitsinjo (where you can also hire two-man tents) and at the entrance to the national park. Camping is permitted on the lawn at Feon'ny Ala as well.

PERMITS AND GUIDES The Andasibe guides are among the best in Madagascar and an example to the rest of the country for knowledge, enthusiasm and an awareness of what tourists want. All the guides know where to find indri and other lemurs, but particularly recommended for birds are Maurice, Luc, Florent, Julien and Patrice; Patrice is also knowledgeable about plants, as is Simon; reptile and frog specialists are Jacques and Donna. Circuits range from two hours (15,000Ar for the guide) to five hours (35,000Ar). In addition, for the national park you must also buy a permit at the park office (prices on page 72), and guides expect a tip. Andasibe and Mantadia are open from 06.00 to 16.00.

At Mitsinjo your guide and permit are included in the same ticket price. There is a short trail that takes about two hours (30,000Ar) and a longer one of four hours or so (40,000Ar). Night walks (highly recommended) cost 15,000Ar for up to 90 minutes, or 20,000Ar for longer.

VISITOR CENTRE The visitor centre at the national park office is terrific. It offers excellent explanations of animal behaviour and the whole ecology of this montane rainforest, as well as some nice souvenirs (and a surprisingly splendid toilet!)

ANDASIBE NATIONAL PARK (PÉRINET) This 810ha reserve protects the largest of the lemurs (*Indri indri*). Standing about a metre high, with a barely visible tail, black-and-white markings and a surprised teddy-bear face, the indri looks more like a gone-wrong panda than a lemur. The long back legs are immensely powerful, and an indri can propel itself 10m, executing a turn in mid-air, to hug a new tree and gaze down benevolently at its observers. And you *will* be an observer: everyone now sees indris here, and most also hear them. For it is the voice that makes this lemur extra special: whilst other lemurs grunt or swear, the indri sings. It is an eerie, wailing sound – a cross between whale song and a siren – and it carries for up to 3km as troops call to each other across the forest. They generally call at dawn, mid-morning, and sometimes shortly before dusk. During the middle of the day they take a long siesta in the canopy so you are unlikely to see them.

Indri are monogamous, live in small family groups of up to five animals, and give birth around June in alternate years. In Malagasy the indri is called *babakoto* which means 'father of Koto'. It is *fady* to kill them, the legend being that a boy called Koto climbed a tree in the forest to collect wild honey, and was severely stung by the bees. Losing his hold, he fell, but was caught by an indri which carried him on its back to safety.

There are 11 species of lemur altogether in Andasibe, although you will not see them all. You may find grey bamboo lemurs, common brown lemurs and perhaps a sleeping avahi (woolly lemur) curled up in the fork of a tree. Diademed sifakas and black-and-white ruffed lemurs have been translocated here from Mantadia and from forest cleared to make way for the Ambatovy mining project.

In addition to lemurs there are tenrecs, beautiful and varied insects, spiders and reptiles – especially chameleons and boas. Birdwatchers will want to look out for the velvet asity, blue coua and nuthatch vanga.

Leeches can be an unpleasant aspect of the reserve if you've pushed through vegetation and it's been raining recently. Tuck your trousers into your socks and apply insect repellent.

The trails in Andasibe have been carefully constructed, but nevertheless, there is quite a steep ascent (up steps) to the plateau where the indri are found, and to follow these animals you may have to scramble a bit.

Night walks are not allowed in the national park itself (but are in Mitsinjo's reserve), though it's worth going on a guided nocturnal stroll along the road for the frogs and chameleons which are easier to see at night. On one memorable occasion our group disturbed a streaked tenrec that fell/jumped into the lake. When the little animal reached the far shore in safety our cheers could have woken every sleeping indri for miles!

MANTADIA NATIONAL PARK While Andasibe is for almost everyone, Mantadia, 20km to the north, is for the enthusiast. The trails are rugged but the rewards are exceptional. Mantadia varies more in altitude (800–1,260m) than the more popular section and consequently harbours different species. What makes it so special is that, in contrast to Andasibe, it comprises virtually untouched primary forest. There are 10,000ha with just a few constructed trails – visitors must be prepared to work for their wildlife – but this is a naturalist's goldmine with many seldom-seen species of mammals, reptiles and birds.

The forest is bisected by the road, with the three trails on the eastern side. Here you may see the beautiful golden-coloured diademed sifaka (*simpona*) and some indri (curiously much darker in colour than in Andasibe). Both these lemur species are getting easier to see as they become habituated to humans. This section of Mantadia has some good, but steep, trails with gorgeous views across the forest and super birdwatching possibilities, including specials such as the scaly ground-roller, pitta-like ground-roller and red-breasted coua.

There are two main trail areas: the northern Tsokoko circuit at 14km is the toughest and best for wildlife, and a couple of trails to the south. One is an easy two-hour trail which leads up through the forest to a waterfall and lake (Cascade and Lac Sacré). Bring your swimsuit for a cooling dip in the pool beneath the waterfall. The alternative is the longer Rianasoa circuit.

To do justice to Mantadia you should spend the whole day there, bringing a picnic, and leave the hotel at dawn. You will need your own transport and, of course, a guide. Most guides can help you find a vehicle (60,000–80,000Ar) or you can enquire at Mitsinjo's office.

ASSOCIATION MITSINJO (\ 56 832 33; m 033 14 474 89; e *mitsinjo@hotmail.com*; ⊕ 07.00–17.00 & 18.30–21.00) While offering the same attractions as the national park, this local NGO is promoting reforestation and other conservation measures. They also operate the reserve of Torotorofotsy and run a handicrafts shop in Andasibe village. They have six tree nurseries, some of which you can visit. Thousands of seedlings of 151 endemic species are being raised to help re-establish corridors between blocks of isolated forest (see the box on page 263). In other community work, Mitsinjo has ongoing projects in family planning and

---

NATURALIST'S PROMISED LAND

Joseph-Philibert Commerson has provided the best-known quote on Madagascar:

C'est à Madagascar que je puis annoncer aux naturalistes qu'est la véritable terre promise pour eux. C'est là que la nature semble s'être retirée dans un sanctuaire particulier pour y travailler sur d'autres modèles que ceux auxquels elle s'est asservie ailleurs. Les formes les plus insolites et les plus merveilleuses s'y rencontrent à chaque pas.

Here in Madagascar I have truly found the naturalist's promised land. Nature seems to have retreated into a private sanctuary, to work on models unlike any she has created elsewhere. At every step one encounters the most strange and marvellous forms.

Commerson was a doctor who travelled with Bougainville on a world expedition in 1766, arriving at Mauritius in 1768. He studied the natural history of that island, then in 1770 journeyed on to Madagascar where he stayed for three or four months in the Fort Dauphin region. His famous description of 'nature's sanctuary' was in a 1771 letter, written from Madagascar, to his old tutor in Paris.

providing clean water. The latter has seen the construction of more than 20 wells for local communities.

Close to the national park entrance you'll find Mitsinjo's office and visitor centre. This is the entrance to their 700ha of Analamazaotra Forest. There are seven groups of indri here, but only two groups are habituated. I was thrilled by my visit here, not only for what I saw (my first ever mossy leaf-tailed gecko, *Uroplatus sikorae*) but the enthusiasm of the guide and the work the association is doing. Chris Howles agrees: 'We look back at the 4½-hour trek we did as one of the highlights of the holiday. Our guide spoke good English and had a very good knowledge of all the local flora and fauna. He worked hard to find everything for us, including of course a family of indri. They came really close to us and we stayed with them for about 45 minutes, stopping when our necks started to ache from all that looking up in the trees!'

This is a rewarding place for night walks, especially since these are not permitted in the national park. Derek Schuurman reports: 'The recently described (2005) Goodman's mouse lemur is readily seen. Your chances of seeing reptiles such as Parson's chameleons and *Uroplatus* geckos are better here and you are bound to see a lot of frogs and other nocturnal creatures.'

Mitsinjo has a vehicle which may be hired (with driver) for transfers to Mantadia (65,000Ar), Vakôna (15,000Ar) or Moramanga (25,000Ar).

ORCHID GARDEN (⏱ *07.30–12.00 & 13.30–17.00*) Near to the road, between the park offices and Andasibe village, this small lake is a particularly attractive spot in October and November. Being a joint project between the national park and Mitsinjo, visitors who have purchased a permit from either may visit it.

MAD'ARBRES (☎ *22 417 54;* m *033 12 343 17;* e *madarbres@yahoo.fr; prices 50,000Ar/half-day, 80,000Ar/day*) This association of Malagasy and French climbers offering canopy tours is specialised in teaching novices the ropes – literally – and, just as importantly, ensuring you experience the canopy up close without causing it any damage. Open from April to November, they operate from the same office as Mitsinjo. Only small groups are taken at a time so book in advance if possible.

OTHER PROTECTED AREAS NEARBY

TOROTOROFOTSY RESERVE This marsh 11km west of Andasibe – an important part of any birding trip – was declared a Ramsar Site in 2005.

Including forest as well as wetlands, the 12,000ha reserve is also famous for its golden mantella frogs (easily seen) and a recently discovered population of rare greater bamboo lemurs. It's an excellent area for trekking and has five bungalows. Enquire at Mitsinjo to organise a visit.

MAROMIZAHA RESERVE (m *033 02 568 18;* e *gerp@moov.mg*) In the 1990s this forested but unprotected area provided some excellent hiking, distant lemur viewing, and an impressive variety of weevils, some wearing little yellow tutus. Then the loggers arrived, and in a few years there was nothing to see except cleared hillsides. Now Maromizaha is being rehabilitated as a protected area under the management of GERP (Groupe d'Etude et de Recherche sur les Primates de Madagascar). It is still a beautiful walk and the sound of the chainsaws has been silenced.

The wildlife is similar to that found at Mantadia. There is a cave full of fruit bats and botanists will be interested to see the locally endemic *marola* palm. Enquire at the Andasibe park office.

MITSINJO AND THE ANDASIBE FOREST CORRIDOR PROJECT

Rainer Dolch, Coordinator, Association Mitsinjo

Over the last hundred years or so, population growth and poverty have taken their toll on Madagascar's eastern rainforest belt. The increasing need for timber, charcoal and new agricultural land has led to extensive deforestation. This loss of trees contributes to greenhouse gas emissions and climate change (both local and global), which further exacerbates poverty and environmental degradation in a downward spiral.

One of the larger remaining forests is Ankeniheny-Zahamena, which is soon to gain protected status. But even this has become severely fragmented, especially around the village of Andasibe. Forest fragmentation spells disaster because numerous isolated patches of forest cannot support the same diversity of species as a single larger one. When an area of forest gets cut off, the wildlife it contains risks becoming inbred and these small populations are less able to recover from problems such as outbreaks of disease and cyclones. Extinctions are inevitable.

The Andasibe Forest Restoration Project (better known by its Malagasy acronym TAMS) aims to halt deforestation in the region by restoring 3,000ha of rainforest, reconnecting fragments with forest 'corridors' and improving livelihoods for local people. Association Mitsinjo, a Malagasy NGO that itself evolved out of a community project, has been a driving force in this innovative programme, in partnership with international and national NGOs, as well as government agencies. In total, more than 25 nurseries grow some 500,000 seedlings of 150 mostly endemic trees each year. By the end of the project more than 3 million trees will have been planted.

Local farmers who voluntarily make part of their fallow land available for reforestation benefit both in terms of security of land tenure and other forms of sustainable and more productive agriculture provided by the project. Carbon credits generated will be traded via the BioCarbon Fund of the World Bank, and it is hoped that farmers will also benefit in terms of direct payments.

The restoration project fits into Mitsinjo's philosophy of conservation work going hand-in-hand with rural development. Working closely with local communities on agricultural and health issues is the key to success. Several conservation and research projects are carried out together with local communities, the most important being the study and protection of the greater bamboo lemur, one of the world's rarest primates, which was rediscovered in the area by Mitsinjo in 2007.

Mitsinjo also generates local income by promoting ecotourism at two sites – Analamazaotra and Torotorofotsy – which can be visited in the company of the association's guides. In addition to enjoying the wildlife of these areas, tourists may actively contribute to conservation efforts by participating in tree-planting and lemur-tracking. Donations are also most welcome. Contact details are on page 261.

VOHIMANA RESERVE (PK 148) (📞 *22 674 90;* e *vohimana@mate.mg; www.madagascar-environnement.com*) This forest reserve, a few kilometres east of Andasibe, is protected through a partnership with local villagers and the NGO Man And The Environment (MATE). They are working towards reducing the local community's dependence on slash-and-burn farming. Clearly this is a project worth supporting, but Vohimana is much more than that – it provides arguably the best 'herping' experience in the area. Anyone with a serious interest in Madagascar's reptiles and frogs should plan a visit here. The reserve is roughly the same size as Andasibe but it includes rainforest of a great range of elevations (700–1,080m) and is known for its frog diversity (over 80 species) and various chameleons not found in Andasibe, including the spectacular *Calumma gallus* with an ultra-long nasal extension.

The reserve has some simple accommodation with shared facilities and a nice communal dining area. Accommodation and meals should be prebooked.

Getting there Vohimana is on the north side of RN2 about 10km after the turn-off to Andasibe, near the village of Ambavaniasy. The walk to the reserve takes about 45 minutes, although it is now possible to get halfway by vehicle on a road built by the Ambatovy mining project.

What to see and do You can divide your time between seeing what MATE is doing to help Madagascar's environmental crisis, such as visiting the tree nursery (like at Mitsinjo, these saplings are used to establish forest corridors linking isolated areas of forest), the essential oil distillery which demonstrates that revenue can be earned from the leaves of trees without having to cut them down (*www.huiles-essentielles-madagascar.com*), the model farm running trials with new agricultural methods – and searching for wildlife.

There are several circuits varying from two to 12 kilometres, passing through beautiful rainforest, cultivated fields and spectacular viewpoints. Some of the trails follow the railway line, including a century-old disused tunnel now home to four bat species.

ANDASIBE TO TOAMASINA

The start of the journey from Andasibe down to Toamasina is lovely, taking you through lush, mist-enshrouded rainforest.

This eventually gives way to eucalyptus woods, and those in turn to *savoka* (secondary vegetation) dotted with travellers' palms, and then finally *bozaka* – the stubbly grassland that results from continual slash-and-burn. This journey provides a stark illustration of the severity of Madagascar's environmental crisis, and a reminder of the huge importance of the work of conservation groups, such as the rainforest corridor project described in the box on page 263.

A ROLLING STONE GATHERS NO MOSS
Rupert Parker

Many *taxi-brousses* ply the route from Tamatave to Tana, all in various states of disrepair. The trick is to ensure you get a good one, so we opted for a VW camper van on the basis that it was built like a tank and was relatively modern compared with everything else on offer. So we squeezed in and off we went. After about an hour there was a huge bang from the back and we immediately came to a stop. Everyone piled out to look, but it was only the back tyre that had blown, so a spare was produced and we were on our way again. I fully expected the driver to stop in Brickaville and get the tyre repaired but he carried on and didn't even pause in the last village before the steep ascent up to the *hauts plateaux*. And as we began to climb, there was another familiar bang: it was another tyre and we were in the middle of nowhere. I thought that maybe he carried two spares, but this was Madagascar and there was another solution – of sorts.

They removed the damaged wheel and the passengers were deputed to gather as much grass as they could. This was packed hard inside the damaged tyre. With the wheel back in place we set off again, but had hardly gone a hundred metres before we had to stop and re-stuff the tyre. Only another 200km to Tana! We stayed with the process for a few more times, then decided to cut our losses and try hitchhiking. Fortunately a rather full Peugeot 406 stopped, and we left the other passengers by the side of the road still stuffing the tyre.

BEFORONA (PK 169) Christina Dodwell recommends a visit to the agro-ecology project here: 'Their guided tour shows how they tackle erosion on the mountain slopes using vetiver grass, and their terraces of fish ponds and rice fields have an ingenious bamboo pipe water supply, each pond flowing to another lower down the slope. The centre is run by a local farmers' cooperative and a representative is happy to explain to you about their conservation and development work. The tour takes an hour. It is free but donations are greatly appreciated (all proceeds go to the cooperative). They have a cheerful little canteen and dormitories for study groups and overnight visitors. Reserve in advance by contacting Mparany (e *HBP@ chemonics.mg and nyrapa@yahoo.fr*).'

AMBODIAVIAVY (PK 173) Ony Rakotoarivelo reports: 'While driving down the road I was attracted by the nice garden with flowers and green grass on the left-hand side, where you can see a waterfall called Andriampotsimbato. So I stopped and talked to a young man called Lezoma who has built a chalet with a garden for people passing by. He charges a small fee to picnic here.'

RANOMAFANA (PK 214) This is a name encountered often in Madagascar since it simply means 'hot water'. Here the name refers to a natural hot spring that is considered sacred by locals, who use it to ask for blessings from the ancestors. A local couple whom Ony spoke to had been childless for seven years; after asking for blessing in this place they had a baby. The path is just beyond the village before the bridge; ask locals to direct you to '*la source sacrée*'.

ANTSAMPANANA (PK 227) Some 1½ hours' drive beyond Andasibe is this small town at the junction of RN2 with the road to Vatomandry (see page 270). This is where to look for a *taxi-brousse* going south.

The town is brimming with stalls offering a huge variety of fruit and vegetables: good for reprovisioning and photography. If you want to dally longer, **Espérance** offers basic accommodation and **Fantasia** is a recommended restaurant.

BRICKAVILLE (AMPASIMANOLOTRA) (PK 257) Everyone knows this town as Brickaville, but its official Malagasy name is often used on maps. After the relatively smooth RN2 passing through wide open spaces, the pot-holes, noise and industry of Brickaville can come as a bit of a shock. It is the centre of sugarcane and citrus production and has a few hotels, but few people would stay intentionally. The bungalows of **Bricka Cool** are perhaps the best of a poor lot.

However fruit, vegetables and friendly *hotelys* can be found in abundance, allowing ample opportunity for refreshment before embarking on the final 104km to Toamasina across an enormous, ageing (but sturdy) iron bridge over the Rianala River.

AMBILA-LEMAITSO This quiet town, where you can happily get stuck for a day or so, is stretched along a narrow strip of land between the sea and the Pangalanes Canal. Situated some 17km (by road) from Brickaville, it is most easily reached by train. From Ambila is a two- to three-hour walk north to Lake Ampitabe.

Where to stay and eat

Relais Malaky \ 56 720 22/260 13. Probably the best hotel; in a good situation close to the station & overlooking the ocean. A range of bungalows & rooms, some en suite; good food. Canoe rental. €€–€€€

Ambila Beach About 3km from the station, overlooking the Pangalanes. Nice bungalows, some with cooking facilities. Camping permitted. €€

Nirvana m 033 14 763 55. Efficient, French-run hotel near the ferry point. €€

Tropicana Basic wooden dbl & family bungalows near the station. €

MANAMBATO Manambato is a picturesque lakeside resort further north. The turn-off is 11km beyond Brickaville on a 7km road which gets muddy after rain. Although easily reached by private car, there is no public transport; you need to take a taxi or go on foot from Ambila.

Lake Rasoabe is part of the Pangalanes Canal system, and, perched on its southwestern shore, Manambato is popular with Tana families for weekend getaways (the bathing is much safer than in the ocean). It is also an access point for boat trips up the canal to Lake Ampitabe and Toamasina. A few hotels face the lake and there are wide beaches of white sand.

Where to stay and eat

Chez Luigi ✆ 56 720 20; m 033 02 720 20. Spacious & comfy bungalows, rooms & excellent restaurant; en suite. Boat transfers & canoe hire. €€€

Acacias ✆ 22 404 29; m 033 12 338 35/034 04 244 97; e info@acaciasbungalows.com; www.acaciasbungalows.com. Dbl, twin & family bungalows. Boat hire. €€€

Rasoa Beach (10 bungalows) ✆ 56 720 18; m 032 02 361 87; e rasoab@dts.mg. Rooms for 2–6 people, some with lake views & a 'Tarzan' hut on stilts! Good food; HB only. €€€

Au Bon Coin Zanatany At the entrance to the village. Malagasy-run chalets for budget travellers. Shared facilities. Great food. €€

Hibiscus (4 bungalows) Simple bungalows with shared facilities & bucket showers. €

Beyond Brickaville, a few glimpses of the ocean and Pangalanes lakes convinces you that you've reached the coast, beyond which it's a relatively uneventful 94km to Toamasina through degraded forest and palm plantations.

South of Toamasina

This chapter covers the increasingly visited Pangalanes lake resorts to the south of Toamasina. It touches on the little-visited (but that's part of the attraction) towns that may be accessed via the Pangalanes Canal, before rejoining the good road which connects the two seaside towns of Mananjary and Manakara, and continues to the town of Farafangana. After Vangaindrano the road becomes unpredictable, although a trickle of adventurous travellers manage to reach Taolagnaro (Fort Dauphin).

PANGALANES

This series of lakes was linked by artificial canals in French colonial times for commercial use, a quiet inland waterway being preferable to an often stormy sea. Over the years the canals became choked with vegetation and no longer passable, but they are gradually being cleared so that in future there may once again be an unbroken waterway stretching 665km from Toamasina to Vangaindrano (see box on page 270). Currently 430km are, in theory, navigable, and some tour operators offer one- to four-day trips down the canal.

The quiet waters of the canal and lakes are much used by local fishermen for transporting their goods in pirogues and for fishing. In recent years Pangalanes has been developed for tourism, with lakeside bungalows and private nature reserves competing with the traditional ocean resorts.

The tourist centre is **Lake Ampitabe**, 55km south of Toamasina. It has broad white beaches, clean water for swimming, a private nature reserve with several introduced species of lemur and the Lac aux Nepenthes where there are literally thousands of insect-eating pitcher plants. Only really accessible by boat, it is beautifully quiet and peaceful. In 2000, Hotel Ony (see page 269) opened on **Lake Rasoamasay**, 10km further south.

GETTING THERE AND AWAY Each hotel provides boat transfers for guests as part of the package. Reaching the lodges from RN2 involves a drive to Manambato on Lake Rasoabe (see page 266) followed by a boat journey north (25 minutes to Lake Rasoamasay; 45 minutes to Lake Ampitabe) or you can take a motor launch from the Port Fluvial in Toamasina (1½–2 hours).

DISTANCES IN KILOMETRES			
Toamasina–Vatomandry	189km	Mananjary–Manakara	152km
Vatomandry–Mahanoro	70km	Manakara–Farafangana	109km
Mahanoro–Nosy Varika	91km	Farafangana–Vangaindrano	75km
Nosy Varika–Mananjary	109km		

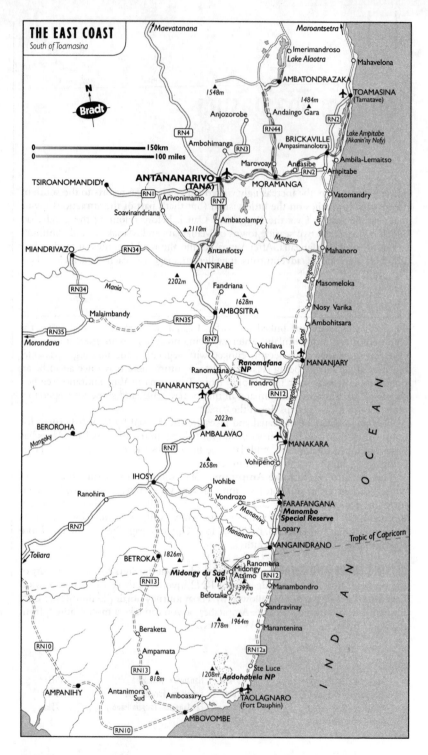

Bradt

N

0 ————— 150km
0 ————— 100 miles

Maevatanana

Maroantsetra

Imerimandroso
Lake Alaotra

Mahavelona

AMBATONDRAZAKA

1548m

TOAMASINA
(Tamatave)

Anjozorobe

Andaingo Gara
1484m

RN44

RN4

Ambohimanga

RN3

BRICKAVILLE
(Ampasimanolotra)

Lake Ampitabe
(Akanin'ny Nofy)

RN2

Marovoay

Andasibe

Ambila-Lemaitso

TSIROANOMANDIDY

ANTANANARIVO
(TANA)

MORAMANGA

RN2

Ampitabe

RN1

Arivonimamo

Vatomandry

RN7

Soavinandriana

Ambatolampy

2110m

Mangoro

Canal

MIANDRIVAZO

RN34

Antanifotsy

Mahanoro

RN34

Mania

ANTSIRABE

2202m

Fandriana

Masomeloka

Pangalanes

1628m

Nosy Varika

Malaimbandy

RN35

AMBOSITRA

Ambohitsara

RN35

RN7

Morondava

Vohilava

Canal

Ranomafana
NP

MANANJARY

Ranomafana

Irondro

FIANARANTSOA

RN12

Pangalanes

2023m

BEROROHA

AMBALAVAO

MANAKARA

Mangoky

RN7

2658m

Vohipeno

IHOSY

Ivohibe

Ranohira

Vondrozo

FARAFANGANA

RN7

Mananivo

Manombo
Special Reserve

Lopary

Mananara

Tropic of Capricorn

VANGAINDRANO

BETROKA

1826m

Ranomena
Midongy
Atsimo

RN12

RN13

Midongy du Sud
NP

Manambondro

1399m

Befotaka

Sandravinay

Beraketa

1778m 1964m

Manantenina

RN10

Ampamata

RN12a

RN13

818m

1208m

Ste Luce

AMPANIHY

Andohahela NP

Antanimora
Sud

Amboasary

TAOLAGNARO
(Fort Dauphin)

AMBOVOMBE

RN10

I N D I A N   O C E A N

WHERE TO STAY The first three sets of beach bungalows below are at Ankanin'ny Nofy ('house of dreams') on Lake Ampitabe; Ony is on Lake Rasoamasay.

Bush House (11 bungalows) m 033 05 530 71; e bushhouse@boogiepilgrim-madagascar.com; www.bushhouse-madagascar.com. Operated by Boogie Pilgrim (see page 86). Highly praised by many readers. €€€€

Palmarium (10 bungalows) ☏ 57 908 83; m 033 14 847 34/032 41 330 39; e hotelpalmarium@yahoo.fr; www.palmarium.biz. Also highly praised. Spacious en-suite bungalows with hot water & electric sockets. Nice restaurant. Private reserve (see below). €€€€

Pangalanes (12 bungalows) ☏ 53 334 03/321 77. Dbl, twin & family bungalows. The cheapest option on Lake Ampitabe. €€€

Ony (20 bungalows) ☏ 53 011 26/918 40; m 033 14 732 21/033 11 587 25; e onyhotellaoka@moov.mg; http://onyhotel.free.fr. Malagasy-owned hotel in marvellous setting between 2 lakes, affording guests the double pleasure of watching the sun both rise & set across the water. Beachfront en-suite dbl & family bungalows. Camping permitted. Within walking distance of pitcher plants. The hotel helped build & supports a school in the local village, Ampanotoamaizina, which you can visit. €€€

PALMARIUM RESERVE Alongside the Palmarium hotel this 50ha reserve of littoral forest protects a wide variety of palms, hence its name. It has broad, well-maintained trails on flat terrain and some ten different species of very tame (and mostly transplanted) lemurs. There are also lots of 'orchids, chameleons, frogs, birds, colourful green lynx spiders and interesting plants including the only endemic Malagasy cactus, which grows as a bizarre epiphyte, and both the island's species of pitcher plants' (Derek Schuurman).

Entry (including a guided walk) costs 13,000Ar, but is free for guests of the Palmarium hotel.

VOHIBOLA FOREST This is a project run by MATE (Man And The Environment) which is being developed for tourism. The forest, which stretches 9km northwards from Lake Ampitabe, is one of the two largest remaining fragments of littoral forest in Madagascar. 'Among the flora are a number of critically endangered trees, notably *Humbertiodendron saboureaui*, which had not been seen for 50 years and was thought extinct. Several dozen mature trees were found, so the species was effectively rediscovered. It exists nowhere else' (Derek Schuurman). Vohibola has an extensive tree nursery and tourists have the hands-on opportunity to give something back by planting an indigenous tree as part of the reforestation programme.

There are two interesting and contrasting circuits, the Discovery Trail and the Wetlands Trail, and with other activities planned this is a super place for independent travellers.

11

The Canal des Pangalanes was created in colonial times to provide a safe means of transport along the east coast. The shore is surf-beaten and the few harbours are shallow and dangerous. The inland water passage provided a safe alternative and around the turn of the century regular ferry services were in operation. The canal interconnected the natural rivers and lagoons, where necessary cutting through the low-lying coastal plain. At intervals it crosses rivers which flow to the sea, providing access for fishermen and ensuring that the level is stable.

The waterways fell into disuse, but in the 1980s a grand project to rehabilitate them was carried out. Silted canals were dredged, new warehouses built and a fleet of modern tug barge units purchased to operate a cargo service. That may once have worked, but now the warehouses and quaysides are empty and the tug barge units lie in a jumble in the harbour at Toamasina.

Meanwhile, local people make good use of the waterways. Mechanised ferries run from Toamasina and every house along the way seems to have a wooden pirogue. The communities face the water and for many people it is the only reliable means of transport, especially in the wet season. It is also a vital source of livelihood and the stakes of fish traps almost fill the channels, while fields of cassava line the banks. Piles of dried fish, wood and charcoal stand in heaps awaiting collection by the returning ferries. Coming from the town, they are overflowing with people competing for space with beer crates, bicycles, sacks of food and all the other paraphernalia of life.

To travel on the Pangalanes is a joy – well, mostly. Start at Toamasina and you get the worst bit over and done with quickly. Boats leave from the bleak Port Fluvial, with its empty warehouses and discarded tugs. The first, manmade, cut of the canal runs south from the town, past the oil refinery. The air is thick with the smell of hydrocarbons and greasy black outfalls show all too clearly the source of the grey slime that coats the water hyacinth – seemingly the only thing capable of growing. But persevere and soon you start to pass family canoes tied to the bank and the slender, deeply loaded ferry boats pushed by struggling outboard motors. As the water starts to clear, the vegetation recolonises the riverbank and the pervasive odour of industrialisation slips away.

The artificial straightness of the first sections gives way to twisting channels and the wider expanses of lagoons and lakes – a world where communities of thatched wooden houses cluster around small landing places, grey rectangles in a canvas of green and blue, delineated here and there by the stark white of sandy beaches.

Those planning an exploration of the Pangalanes in their own canoe should buy maps number 6 and number 8 of the 1:500,000 series published by FTM (see page 158). French sea charts also show the canal.

THE SOUTHEAST COAST

Formerly a visit to this region usually began in Mananjary or Manakara. But the once nearly impassable road from RN2 to Vatomandry has been improved so it is now practical for adventurous travellers to take this rewarding route. The journey, which in the old days took up to three days, now takes less than an hour by car.

VATOMANDRY The name means 'sleeping rocks', from two flat, black rocks close to the shore. This was an important town in its time, growing from a small settlement on the east bank of the River Sandramanongy to the administrative centre of the Hova government in the pre-colonial 19th century. At this time, Vatomandry was a prosperous port and merchandise was carried by porters to the capital along the paths of the eastern forest. This is also the birthplace of former President Ratsiraka.

Espace Zazah Robert (\ *53 821 03;* m *032 02 257 52;* €€–€€€) on the northern outskirts offers budget to mid-range accommodation. Some rooms have air conditioning.

MAHANORO The name means 'happy-making' but whether Mahanoro will have this effect on all visitors is debatable. The town is to the north of the Mangoro River, so most of the places of interest are watery (although there is said to be a Merina fortress here). The impressive Chutes de la Sahatsio are 18km to the north. The best place to stay is **Tropicana's** bungalows (\ *53 901 33*).

NOSY VARIKA Nosy Varika means 'lemur island' although you'd be lucky to see any *varika* (brown lemurs) here now. The most interesting excursion in the area is to the Chutes de la Sakaleona, a waterfall which plunges 200m, but this requires an expedition of several days.

AMBOHITSARA This isolated village 60km north of Mananjary is only accessible by boat, yet there is an upmarket hotel here. **Auberge d'Ambohitsara** (\ *22 267 21;* m *032 07 267 21*) is a set of pleasant bungalows overlooking the canal, owned and run by German-born Mme Manambelona who also organises local tours. Apart from the opportunity to relax on and around the Pangalanes, one of Madagascar's most enigmatic sights is here: a stone elephant. Depending on whose version of the story you believe, the carving is said to have been brought here from Mecca or Yemen by the ancestors, perhaps 800 years ago.

MANANJARY AND MANAKARA

These two pleasant seaside towns have good communications with the rest of Madagascar and are gaining popularity among discerning travellers, especially now the railway from the highlands to the coast has been rehabilitated.

MANANJARY This is a rather sleepy little town with a good choice of places to stay and a couple of banks (BFV and BOA). The weekend fish market held at the river mouth is well worth a visit. 'The fishermen sell their daily catches from their canoes parked up on the shore. Like all markets in Madagascar, there's a lot of action. In addition to the fish-selling, the ladies wash their clothes there and lay them out to dry on the beach while their children play in the water.' (Sheena Jones)

Every seven years, mass circumcision ceremonies known as *sambatra* are performed in the area. The next is due around October 2014.

GETTING THERE AND AWAY Mananjary is usually reached by road from Ranomafana. There are also weekly Air Mad flights connecting it with Tana and Farafangana.

 Where to stay and eat

🏠 **Plantation (Vahily Lodge)** (11 bungalows) \ 72 090 01; m 033 04 630 87/032 53 520 67; e laplantation@moov.mg. A resort hotel on the edge of town near the airport. Classy restaurant, swimming pool & attractive bungalows. The hotel also runs a spice business; tours of the fruit plantation can be arranged. 👑

🏠 **Jardin de la Mer** (7 bungalows) \ 72 092 70. Comfy en-suite sgl & twin beach bungalows, swimming pool & restaurant. €€€
🏠 **Sorafahotel** (9 rooms & 5 bungalows) Bd Maritime; \ 72 092 01. Pleasant beach bungalows, some with verandas. Sgl & dbl rooms, pool & top restaurant with great pizza. €€€

🏠 **Yvonna** m 032 02 049 93. Good-value simple bungalows. €€

🏠 **Chez Stenny** (2 rooms & 3 bungalows) \ 72 942 66. Small, friendly guesthouse. Cold water only. €

🏠 **Ideal** Next to the cathedral. Cold water only. €

🏠 **Bons Amis** Nr JIRAMA. Cold water only. €

✖ **Route des Epices** Best restaurant in town. On R25, just before the cathedral. Also runs birding tours.

✖ **Grillion** Nr cathedral. Good-value food.

MANAKARA This town at the end of the line is experiencing a surge of popularity. Shaded by filao trees, the path running between the ex-colonial buildings and the ocean makes the waterfront a very attractive part of town. Plentiful *pousse-pousses* provide the best means of getting around, especially to the *taxi-brousse* station which is 2km north of the centre.

You should not swim in Manakara because of dangerous currents and sharks. But the sea is rewarding anyway: from the broad beach you can watch the captivating waves breaking on the reef 450m offshore.

Getting there and away Manakara is the end of the railway journey from Fianarantsoa. At the time of writing trains depart for Fianar every morning except Tuesday and Saturday at 06.45. The ticket office at the station is open for reservations Tuesday/Thursday/Saturday 13.30–17.30. Full details of this rail route are on page 190.

By *taxi-brousse* Fianar and Mananjary are both about seven hours away and cost 13,000Ar. It takes three hours to Farafangana (7,000Ar) or 4½ hours to Vangaindrano (11,000Ar). A direct *taxi-brousse* to Tana should cost 30,000Ar.

🏠 **Where to stay**

🏠 **Ampilao Beach** (7 bungalows) \ 72 216 68; m 034 03 746 33; e ampilaobeach.hotel@ yahoo.fr. Seafront location. Restaurant recommended. €€€

🏠 **Sidi** (56 rooms) \ 72 212 85; m 033 02 803 90/034 12 301 32; e mariejocelyneveroniquerasoanirina@galana.com. En-suite rooms with TV. Nightclub from 21.00 Fri–Sun. €€€

🏠 **Antemoro** (4 bungalows) m 032 43 705 33. Quiet en-suite bungalows near beach. €€€

🏠 **Vanille** (9 rooms & 8 bungalows) \ 72 210 23; m 033 14 710 40; e hotellavanillemanakara@ yahoo.fr. En-suite rooms with TV. The bungalows are 8km north of town. €€€

🏠 **Flamboyants** (11 rooms) m 032 52 459 51. Owned by the French consul. €€–€€€

🏠 **Parthenay Club** (13 rooms) \ 72 216 63; m 033 14 712 19; f 72 215 36. En-suite rooms & a 4-bed dorm. Prime seafront spot with sandy beach. Bike hire. €€–€€€

🏠 **Vent de la Mer** (6 rooms) m 034 12 221 59. Dbl en suite with hot water. €€

🏠 **Bungalows du Sud** (5 rooms & 5 bungalows) \ 72 211 00. Some en suite. €€

🏠 **Leong** (25 rooms) \ 72 216 88; m 032 09 270 06; f 72 213 86. Budget rooms with TV; 2 with AC; 3 cheap sgl rooms. €€

🏠 **Padoula** (9 rooms) \ 72 216 23; m 033 14 085 28/033 11 441 73. Basic with cold water. €€

🏠 **Eden Sidi** (8 rooms & 10 bungalows) Nice bungalows 13km south of town. €€

🏠 **Recif** (8 rooms) \ 72 211 89; m 032 41 366 17. En-suite dbl rooms. €€

🏠 **Orchidées** (7 rooms) m 033 14 715 24. En suite (cold water). €€

🏠 **Celeste** (4 bungalows) m 032 47 393 36/033 08 433 28. Cold water only. €€

🏠 **Delices d'Orient** (15 rooms & 9 bungalows) \ 72 217 34. Good centrally located en-suite rooms with splendid restaurant & an annexe of bungalows at the river mouth. €–€€

🏠 **Mangrove** (11 rooms & 11 bungalows) m 032 46 452 02. Simple rooms in 3 locations. €–€€

🏠 **Morabe** (15 rooms) \ 72 210 70; m 032 45 859 92. Dbl with shared facilities. €–€€

🏠 **Fenosoa, Miadana, Mamy, Rizière (Lilie), Tsy Manavaka & Gare Routière** are very basic cheap options. €

✖ **Where to eat**

✖ **Gourmandise** ⊕ 09.00–late. Highly recommended.

✖ **Chez Clo** ⊕ 08.00–21.00, Thu closed. Restaurant & *salon de thé*.

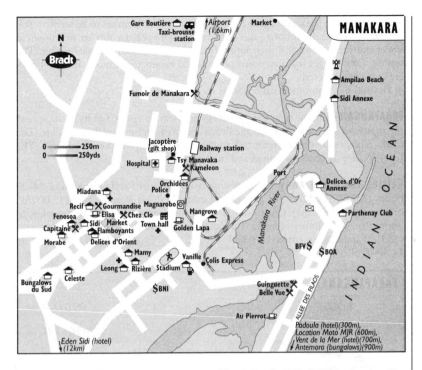

MANAKARA

✕ Capitaine ⊕ 12.00–late. Popular with *vazaha*.
✕ Fumoir de Manakara ⊕ Daily except Wed lunch. Nice French-owned restaurant.
✕ Kameleon Restaurant, pizzeria & bar.
✕ Guinguette ⊕ 08.00–23.00 except Tue morn. Riverfront restaurant with canoe hire.

✕ Belle Vue ⊕ 07.00–00.00. Waterfront bar with meals & snacks.
⊑ Golden Lapa Pleasant little café.
⊑ Au Pierrot Waterfront snack bar.
⊑ Chez Elisa ⊕ 09.00–late. Snack bar. Also runs boat trips.

Money and communications Manakara has branches of all the major banks: BFV, BNI and BOA. There is a post office (⊕ *Mon–Fri 09.00–17.00, Sat 08.00–12.00*) and Colis Express (✆ *72 210 30*). Cybercafé **Magnarobo** (⊕ *Mon–Fri 08.00–12.00 & 14.00–18.00, Sat 08.00–12.00*) has four computers and costs 200Ar/minute.

What to see and do There is an interesting **entomological museum** in Manakara Be owned by an eccentric Frenchman, Yves Escarnot, who also runs a small shop called **Jacaoptère** opposite the train station selling curiosities and handicrafts.

A couple of restaurants by the river run **boat trips** and hire out **kayaks** for exploring the Pangalanes. If you need a local guide try Gilbert (m *032 51 254 66*) or Frostin (m *032 46 875 91/032 55 376 68*). **Location Moto MJR** (m *032 43 561 37*) rents motorbikes.

CONTINUING SOUTH

VOHIPENO Situated some 45km south of Manakara, this village is the centre of the Antaimoro tribe who reportedly came from Arabia six centuries ago, bringing the first script to Madagascar. Their Islamic history is shown by their clothing (turban and fez, as well as Arab-style robes). They are the inheritors of the 'great writings',

11

sorabe, written in Malagasy using Arabic script. *Sorabe* continues to be written, still in Arabic, still on Antaimoro paper. The scribes who practise this art are known as *katibo* and the writing and their knowledge of it gives them a special power. The writing itself ranges from accounts of historical events to astrology and the books are considered sacred.

Beyond this point the road becomes more potholed.

FARAFANGANA On the map this appears to be a seaside resort, but its position near the mouth of a river means that the beach and ocean are not easily accessible. The town is a prosperous commercial centre with a busy market (Tuesday). The Jovenna shop is good for tinned and packet foods.

Getting there and away A *taxi-brousse* from Tana to Farafangana takes 14–20 hours (33,000Ar), but most people will come here via Ranomafana (15,000Ar) or Manakara (7,000Ar). Continuing to Vangaindrano costs 4,000Ar and takes an hour. Air Mad flights connect Farafangana with Tana and Mananjary once a week (Farafangana office: m *033 03 222 19*; ⊕ *Mon–Fri 07.30–12.00 & 14.30–17.30*).

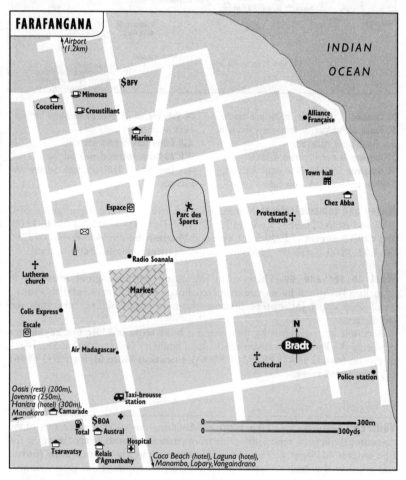

My alarm clock went off at a quarter to four in the morning. I quickly got up and cycled the half mile or so to the Antaimoro fishermen's village at the northern end of Farafangana, with a half moon lighting the way. The village was fast asleep but soon one of the fishermen, with whom I had arranged to go sea-fishing, appeared. He quietly took my bicycle, pulled it into his little wooden house and fastened it to the wall behind the bed. The other members of the family were still sleeping but a cock was already beginning to crow.

With an oar each in hand, we set off to the nearby river where the pirogues lie on the sandy beach. We waded through the warm water to reach the long sandy bank that separates river from ocean. There we were joined by another two fishermen and we all clambered into a larger, wider pirogue shaped more like a banana in order to better tackle the waves. I thought we would have more difficulty getting over the violent breakers, but our departure was timed perfectly and we were past them in no time. Away from the coast the waves move more slowly and do not break, so there is little danger of being turned over. We paddled away from the coast, where lone fishermen in small boats were casting their nets. Every so often we saw a fish coming to the surface and the fishermen, instead of exclaiming '*trondro!*' ('fish'), said '*laoka!*' which means 'food to accompany rice'!

About half a mile out to sea we came across our first float. It was pulled aboard followed by the net. The net had been left for two days, as the fishermen normally go out on alternate days – weather-permitting, of course. The net was 50m long, with a heavy stone to anchor it to the seabed. We checked five or six nets that morning. One contained a kind of flat fish, whose wings were cut off and tied to the net as bait before it was put back in the water. Another contained three small, toothless sharks, brown and white in colour.

At first I didn't feel seasick, but by the end the smell of the sea, the fish and the constant rise and fall of our small vessel on the large waves combined to make me ill. The fishermen said they were not sick – even on their first ever outing – saying they were 'already used to it'. They meant they already had the sea in their blood, since their forefathers were all fishermen. They had no idea where Europe, America, Japan and so on lie, and they were fascinated when I pointed out the general direction of these places.

Our arrival on the beach was as perfect as the departure: beautifully executed despite the large waves. We all happily jumped out of the narrow boat in which we had been sitting or crouching for almost fours hours. Others on the beach expressed surprise at the sight of a white fisherman!

On the way back across the river it began to rain heavily, but it was actually an incredibly pleasant feeling; you don't mind getting wet when it's warm and you feel at one with nature and the locals.

Where to stay and eat

🏠 **Austral** (30 rooms) ✆ 73 000 97; m 032 05 017 65; e austral@netclub.mg. Good rooms, some with AC. Well sited for *taxi-brousse* station. €€€

🏠 **Coco Beach** (10 bungalows) ✆ 73 911 87/88; e ranarson@dts.mg. Beachside bungalows 3km south of the centre. En suite with hot water. €€€

🏠 **Cocotiers** (15 rooms) ✆ 73 911 87/88; e ranarson@dts.mg. Dbl, twin & trpl en-suite rooms, some with AC. €€€

🏠 **Chez Abba** (15 bungalows) m 032 41 033 89/033 12 639 01/032 44 369 84. Seafront bungalows with simple bucket showers. €€

🏠 **Miarina** (7 rooms) m 032 07 586 70/032 05 586 70. Newly renovated dbl rooms, some en suite. €€

🏠 **Tsaravatsy, Camarade, Hanitra & Relais d'Agnambahy** are very basic cheap options. Hanitra is recommended for food. €

🛏 **Laguna** Bungalows 4km south of town. Being rebuilt at time of writing.
✗ **Oasis** ⏲ 07.00–22.00. Recommended simple restaurant.

🍴 **Croustillant** ⏲ 07.00–12.00 & 15.00–19.00. Bakery; also confectionery.
🍴 **Mimosas** ⏲ 09.00–13.30 & 16.00–late. *Salon de thé* with good selection.

Money and communications There are BOA and BFV banks here; the latter now has an ATM. Near the market are the post office (⏲ *Mon–Fri 08.30–12.00 & 14.00–17.30*) and Colis Express (\ *73 007 32*). Internet places keep opening and closing but try Escale, Espace and Radio Soanala.

WEST TO IHOSY For the seriously adventurous, the road to Ihosy is now just about passable in the dry season by 4x4 or motorbike. *Taxi-brousses* run as far as **Vondrozo**. You can continue by car to the **Vevembe** region, at which point the passable road ends and jungle takes over. You will probably need a guide to help you reach the next stretch of passable road at **Ivohibe** because of the numerous trails that have been created by the locals. If you make it to Ivohibe you're home and dry; there are *taxi-brousses* to Ihosy. But beware: the area is said to be infested with *dahalo* (bandits).

MANOMBO SPECIAL RESERVE This reserve 25km south of Farafangana protects around 5,000ha of littoral forest. It is home to eight species of lemur including the southernmost population of black-and-white ruffed lemurs and the extremely rare grey-headed lemur (*Eulemur cinereiceps*) which is among the world's 25 most endangered primates. Manombo also has the highest diversity of land snails of any rainforest in the world. There is no accommodation but visitors can camp at the park office on the main road, 4km from the forest.

LOPARY This village is near the Mananivo river mouth, 23km before Vangaindrano. Lopary market (actually held 1km north of the village at Mahabo) is an important Saturday market where you will find a wide variety of produce. It draws people from as far as Farafangana and Vangaindrano.

VANGAINDRANO This has the atmosphere of a frontier town, and indeed it marks the end of the good road heading south. Few tourists come here which gives it a certain appeal. Market day is Monday.

🏠 **Where to stay and eat**
🛏 **Tropic** (12 rooms) m 032 44 343 49. Reasonable rooms just past the stadium 1km southwest of the market; some en suite. Restaurant **Mandarine** has grill & seafood specialities. €€–€€€

🛏 **Shell Motel** (11 bungalows) m 032 45 500 12. So named for its proximity to the fuel station at the north of town. €€
🛏 **Guerit, Jupiter, Hunotel & Antsika** are basic hotels with cheap rooms & bucket showers. €
✗ **Mini-Resto Ezaka** ⏲ 05.30–late. Malagasy hangout with loud music.

Money and communications Vangaindrano has a BOA bank which can change major foreign currencies but not travellers' cheques and there's no ATM (⏲ *Mon–Fri 08.00–11.30 & 14.30–17.00*). The town also has a post office and a branch of Colis Express (m *032 44 564 52*). At the time of writing there is no internet access.

What to see and do The town itself has little of interest but it is a nice excursion to follow the enormous River Mananara the 12km to the sea. If spices are your thing, head 20km south from Vangaindrano then turn east for 9km to Matanga –

the capital of cloves ('*jirofo*' in Malagasy). Some 30km south of Vangaindrano is an out-of-the-way regional museum, Papan'ny Do Mahasianaka.

The owner of Tropic Hotel, M Ronaldo, is president of the region's tourist board so this is the best place to come for the latest information, including the above trips and finding transport to Taolagnaro.

MIDONGY DU SUD NATIONAL PARK Well off the beaten track, this park is challenging to reach (impossible in the rainy season) and has little tourist infrastructure. It comprises 192,000ha of mountainous and often rainy terrain.

From Vangaindrano head east. You can cover the 94km to Ranomena in two hours but the remaining 42km to Midongy Atsimo, where there is basic accommodation, is much slower going. One reader took six hours but it's highly weather-dependent. Visit the park office (the yellow building on the hill as you enter town) to arrange permits and a guide (see page 72 for permit prices).

FROM VANGAINDRANO TO TAOLAGNARO (FORT DAUPHIN) The road to Taolagnaro is terrible and much of the 230km requires a 4x4. The journey involves no fewer than ten river crossings. If you're lucky and none of the ferries stationed at the crossing points is broken down, then in a good vehicle and good weather the trip can be achieved in one long day. However, most vehicles make the journey over two days, overnighting at **Manantenina** just after the fifth river crossing. The best hotel there is **Chez Mme Pety**, with eight simple bungalows.

The first of the river crossings is 32km south of Vangaindrano. It is *fady* to wear red or gold (including jewellery) on this crossing. All the ferries are free and operate from dawn till 18.00. A tip of 2,000Ar or so per vehicle is usual, but you'll have to pay more if you want to be taken across after 18.00.

A two-day *camion-brousse* departs Vangaindrano each Sunday morning (m *032 62 811 63*). Delays are common and it's not unknown for travellers to take four or five days to reach Taolagnaro.

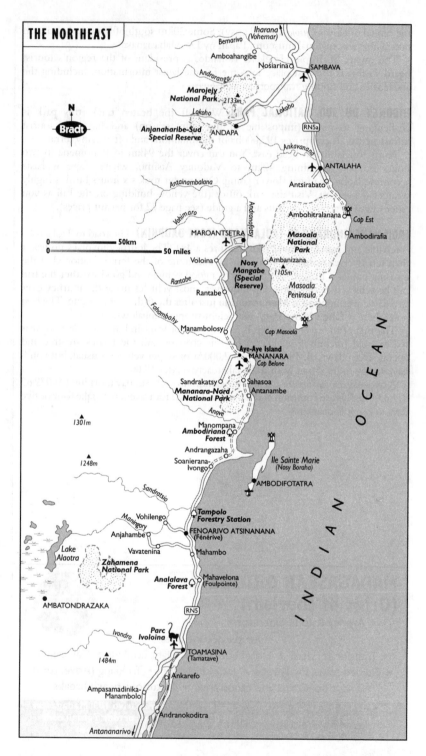

THE NORTHEAST

Iharana
(Vohemar)
Bemarivo
Amboahangibe
Nosiarina
SAMBAVA
Androranga
Marojejy National Park
2133m
Lokoho
Lokoho
Anjanaharibe-Sud Special Reserve
ANDAPA
RN5a
Ankavanana
ANTALAHA
Antainambalana
Antsirabato
Ambohitralanana
Cap Est
Vohimaro
Ambodirafia
MAROANTSETRA
Masoala National Park
Voloina
Nosy Mangabe (Special Reserve)
Ambanizana
1105m
Rantabe
Rantabe
Masoala Peninsula
Fahambahy
Manambolosy
Cap Masoala
Aye-Aye Island
MANANARA
Cap Belone
Sandrakatsy
Sahasoa
Antanambe
Mananara-Nord National Park
Anove
1301m
Manompana
Ambodiriana Forest
Andrangazaha
1248m
Soanierana-Ivongo
Ile Sainte Marie
(Nosy Boraha)
AMBODIFOTATRA
Sandratsio
Vohilengo
Tampolo Forestry Station
Maningory
Anjahambe
FENOARIVO ATSINANANA (Fénérive)
Vavatenina
Mahambo
Lake Alaotra
Zahamena National Park
Analalava Forest
Mahavelona
(Foulpointe)
AMBATONDRAZAKA
RN5
Ivondro
Parc Ivoloina
1484m
TOAMASINA
(Tamatave)
Ankarefo
Ampasamadinika-Manambolo
Andranokoditra
Antananarivo

I N D I A N   O C E A N

0 ――――――― 50km
0 ――――――― 50 miles

N
Bradt

12

Toamasina and the Northeast

Punished by its weather (rain, cyclones), eastern Madagascar is notoriously challenging to travellers. In July 1817 James Hastie wrote in his diary: 'If this is the good season for travelling this country, I assert it is impossible to proceed in the bad.' With this in mind you'd be better avoiding the wettest months of February and March, and remembering that June to August can be very damp as well. The driest months are September to November, with December and January worth the risk. April and May are fairly safe apart from the possibility of cyclones. The east coast has other problems: sharks and dangerous currents. So although there are beautiful beaches, swimming is safe only in protected areas.

Despite – or perhaps because of – these drawbacks, the northeast may be Madagascar's most rewarding region for independent travellers. It is not yet on the itinerary for many groups, yet has a few beautifully situated upmarket hotels for that once-in-a-lifetime holiday, and wonderful exploratory possibilities for the intrepid backpacker. Much of Madagascar's unique flora and fauna is concentrated in the eastern rainforests and any serious naturalist will want to pay a visit. Other attractions are the rugged mountain scenery with rivers tumbling down to the Indian Ocean, the friendly people, abundant fruit and seafood, and access to the lovely island of Ile Sainte Marie. The chief products of the east are coffee, vanilla, bananas, coconuts, cloves and lychees.

HISTORY

This region has an interesting history dominated by European pirates and slave traders. While powerful kingdoms were being forged in other parts of the country, the east coast remained divided among numerous small clans. It was not until the 18th century that one ruler, Ratsimilaho, unified the region. The half-caste son of Thomas White, an English pirate, and briefly educated in Britain, Ratsimilaho did so in response to the attempt by Chief Ramanano to take over all the east coast ports. His successful revolt was furthered by his judiciously marrying an important princess; by his death in 1754 he ruled an area stretching from the Masoala Peninsula to Mananjary.

The result of this liaison of various tribes was the Betsimisaraka, now the second-largest ethnic group in Madagascar. Some (in the area of Maroantsetra) practise second burial, although with less ritual than the Merina and Betsileo.

DISTANCES IN KILOMETRES			
Toamasina–Mahambo	90km	Iharana–Sambava	153km
Toamasina–Soanierana-Ivongo	163km	Sambava–Antalaha	89km
Toamasina–Mahavelona	61km	Sambava–Andapa	119km

Although maps show roads of some sort running almost the full length of the east coast, this is deceptive. Rain and cyclones regularly destroy bridges so it is impossible to know in advance whether a selected route will be passable even in the 'dry' season. The rain-saturated forests drain into the Indian Ocean via numerous rivers, many of which can be crossed only by ferry. And there is not enough traffic to ensure a regular service. For those with limited time, therefore, the only practical way to get to the less accessible towns is by air. There are regular planes to Ile Sainte Marie and flights between Toamasina (Tamatave) and Antsiranana (Diego Suarez). Planes go several days a week from Toamasina to Maroantsetra, Antalaha and Sambava.

For the truly adventurous it is possible to work your way down (or up) the coast providing you have plenty of time and are prepared to walk.

TOAMASINA (TAMATAVE)

HISTORY As in all the east coast ports, Toamasina began as a pirate community. In the late 18th century its harbour attracted the French, who already had a foothold in Ile Sainte Marie, and Napoleon I sent his agent Sylvain Roux to establish a trading post there. In 1811, Sir Robert Farquhar, governor of the newly British island of Mauritius, sent a small naval squadron to take the port of Toamasina. This was not simply an extension of the usual British-French antagonism, but an effort to stamp out slavery at its source, Madagascar being the main supplier to the Indian Ocean. The slave trade had been abolished by the British parliament in 1807. The attack was successful, and Sylvain Roux was exiled. During subsequent years, trade between Mauritius and Madagascar built Toamasina into a major port. In 1845, after a royal edict subjecting European traders to the harsh Malagasy laws, French and British warships bombarded Toamasina, but a landing was repelled leaving 20 dead. During the 1883–85 war the French occupied Toamasina but Malagasy troops successfully defended the fort of Farafaty just outside the town.

Legend has it that the name Toamasina comes from King Radama I who is said to have tasted the seawater here and remarked '*Toa masina*' – 'It's salty'.

TOAMASINA TODAY Toamasina (still popularly known as Tamatave) has always had an air of shabby elegance with some fine palm-lined boulevards and once-impressive colonial houses. Every few years it's hit by a cyclone, and spends some time in a new state of shabbiness before rebuilding. As you'd expect, it's a spirited, bustling city with a good variety of bars, snack bars and restaurants. Not many tourists stay here for any length of time, which is a shame; there is plenty to see and do. For instance the wonderful Parc Ivoloina (see page 287) provides one of the most accessible and delightful natural history experiences in Madagascar.

GETTING THERE AND AWAY

By road and rail RN2 is one of the country's best roads and is the fastest and cheapest way of reaching Toamasina from Tana. *Taxi-brousses* run twice a day, morning or night, and take from six to 12 hours. Information on train connections is on page 251.

By air There are daily flights between Tana and Toamasina. A taxi from the airport into town costs 7,000Ar. There is an Air Mad office in Toamasina (⊕ *Mon–Fri 07.30–11.00 & 14.00–16.30, Sat 08.00–11.00*).

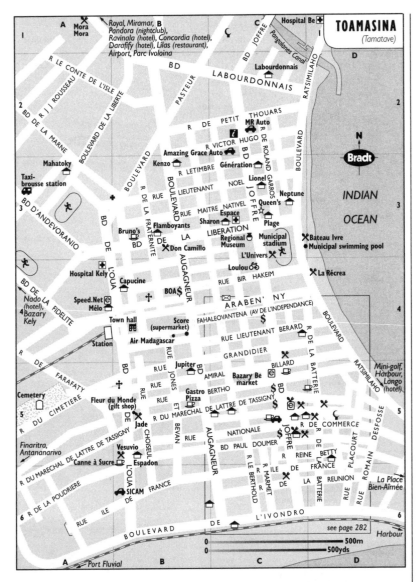

By the map:

By boat Toamasina is one of the starting – or finishing – points for a trip down the Pangalanes Canal. Boats leave from the Port Fluvial at the southwest edge of the town (separate from the harbour).

GETTING AROUND A taxi ride in the town should cost 2,000Ar. There is an abundance of *pousse-pousses*, which should cost around 1,000Ar for a short trip in town. Recent years have also seen the appearance of numerous *cyclo-pousses*, or bicycle rickshaws.

☞ **WARNING!** Walking around certain parts of town after dark is inadvisable; there have been some late-night muggings. In any case this is best avoided as several

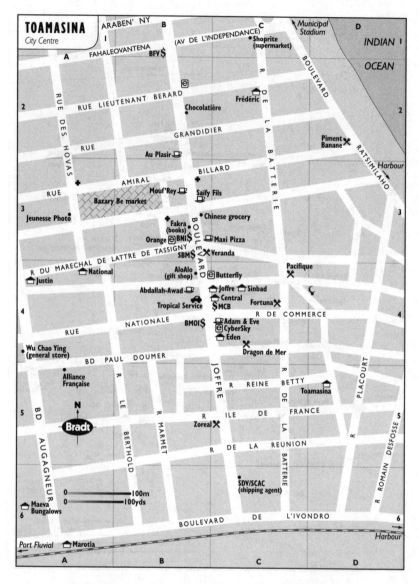

TOAMASINA
City Centre

ARABEN' NY
FAHALEOVANTENA
(AV DE L'INDEPENDANCE)
• Shoprite
(supermarket)
• Municipal
Stadium

BFV$

INDIAN

OCEAN

RUE LIEUTENANT BERARD

Chocolatière

Frédéric

GRANDIDIER

Piment
Banane

Harbour

Au Plasir

BILLARD

AMIRAL

RUE

Mouf'Rey

Saify Fils

Bazary Be market

Jeunesse Photo

Fakra
(books)

• Chinese grocery

Orange BNI$

Maxi Pizza

SBM$

Veranda

R DU MARECHAL DE LATTRE DE TASSIGNY

Justin

National

AloAlo
(gift shop)

Butterfly

Pacifique

Abdallah-Awad

Tropical Service

Joffre

Central

MCB

Sinbad

Fortuna

R DE COMMERCE

NATIONALE

BMOI$

Adam & Eve
CyberSky

Eden

RUE

Dragon de Mer

Wu Chao Ying
(general store)

BD PAUL DOUMER

Alliance
Française

REINE BETTY

Toamasina

Bradt

Zoreal

ILE DE FRANCE

DE LA REUNION

SDV/SCAC
(shipping agent)

0   100m
0   100yds

Maeva
Bungalows

BOULEVARD   DE   L'IVONDRO

Harbour

Port Fluvial   Marotia

holes in the town's pavements are impossible to see in the dark and large enough to swallow an unsuspecting pedestrian.

WHERE TO STAY
Upper range €€€€

Sharon [281 C3] (44 rooms) Bd de la Libération; ☎ 53 304 20 to 26; f 53 331 29; e sharonhotel@moov.mg; www.sharon-hotel.com. The nicest hotel in town; popular with businesspeople. Rooms have AC, minibar, safe, TV & internet (but it's 30,000Ar/day). There is a new

gym & nice pool (free for guests); also beauty salon with massage & sauna. Good Italian/European restaurant **Rose des Vents** & an excellent pizzeria. Visa accepted.

Neptune [281 C3] (47 rooms) 35 Bd Ratsimilaho; ☎ 53 322 26; f 53 324 26;

e neptune@moov.mg; www.hotel-neptune-tamatave.com. Once the poshest hotel in town & still not bad but rooms lack character. Good seafront setting. Dbl, twin & family rooms with AC. Pool, good food & nice bar. Free Wi-Fi in restaurant/reception area. Disco most nights. Credit cards accepted.

Mid-range €€€

🏠 **Longo** [281 D5] (22 rooms) Rue Amiral Pierre; \ 53 339 54; f 53 344 13; e longohotel@yahoo.fr. Near port entrance. Comfortable, en-suite rooms with AC & TV. Chinese/European restaurant.

🏠 **Joffre** [282 C4] (20 rooms) 18 Bd Joffre; \ 53 323 90; f 53 332 94; e hotel.joffre@moov.mg. Atmospheric old hotel with good restaurant (closed Sun, except b/fast). Rooms & studios have AC & en-suite bath/shower. Credit cards accepted.

🏠 **Labourdonnais** [281 C2] (6 rooms) Bd Labourdonnais; \/f 53 350 67; m 032 49 970 34; e labourdonnais@yahoo.fr; http://labourdonnais.free.fr. Near French consulate, 200m from ocean. Reasonable rooms with AC, TV, fridge, safe & balcony. Excellent restaurant with charming décor & Creole specialities (closed Sun).

🏠 **Royal** [281 B1] (15 rooms) Rte d'Ivoloina; \ 53 311 15; f 53 312 81. Clean but rather characterless concrete high-rise on road to airport. Large rooms with AC & TV; mostly en suite; some with fridge.

🏠 **Génération** [281 C3] (30 rooms) 129 Bd Joffre; \ 57 220 22/53 328 34; e generationhotel@moov.mg; www.hotel-generation.com. Large, pleasant rooms. Restaurant serves good food including vegetarian options.

Budget €€

🏠 **Lionel** [281 C3] (19 rooms) \ 53 348 04. Good-value en-suite rooms in somewhat seedy part of town.

🏠 **National** [282 A4] (15 rooms) 13 Rue Lattre de Tassigny; \ 53 322 90. Near the market, en-suite rooms, some with AC. Rooms available for long-term rent.

🏠 **Nado** [281 A4] (15 rooms) opposite Eglise Sacré Cœur; \ 53 333 11; f 53 333 14; e sedo@moov.mg. Not far from bus station. Pleasant rooms, some with AC, TV, phone & bath. Cheapest rooms are very small with shared facilities.

🏠 **Sinbad (Salama)** [282 C4] (20 rooms) Rue Lt Hubert; \ 53 971 54; f 53 932 98;

Penny-pincher €

🏠 **Eden** [282 C4] (8 rooms) Bd Joffre; m 032 40 247 78/032 04 628 82. Appropriately situated near Adam & Eve Snack Bar. Good budget option; basic

🏠 **Toamasina** [282 D5] (24 rooms) 13 Rue de la Colonne; \ 53 335 49; f 53 336 12; e letoamasinahotel@moov.mg. Comfortable rooms with TV, safe, phone, minibar & some have AC. Reasonable food in restaurant **Pousse-Pousse**.

🏠 **Central** [282 C4] (12 rooms) 16 Bd Joffre; \ 53 340 86; f 53 341 19; e central_hotel_mada@yahoo.fr; www.central-hotel-tamatave.com. Charmless 2nd-floor rooms with AC, TV, phone & safe but reportedly becoming run-down. Visa accepted.

🏠 **Flamboyants** [281 B3] (36 rooms) Bd de la Libération; \/f 53 323 50. Recommended hotel with decent-sized rooms that are en suite with TV; some with AC. Good value. Bar & restaurant (closed Sun, except b/fast).

🏠 **Espadon** [281 B5] (36 rooms) Bd de l'OUA; \ 53 303 86; f 53 303 87; e espadon-hotel@moov.mg. Fairly basic rooms but some with AC, TV & minibar.

🏠 **Fréderic (Capricorne)** [281 C2] (21 rooms) 33 Rue de la Batterie; \ 53 347 40; f 53 347 39. Newly renovated; excellent value. Large, clean, en-suite rooms on a central backstreet. Most have AC & TV; some with fridge & balcony.

🏠 **Kenzo/Auberge des Iles** [281 B3] (4 rooms) 35 Bd Augagneur; \ 53 349 10. Modest, but large en-suite rooms with AC, TV & hot water. Convenient for taxi-brousse station.

e sinbad_hotel@yahoo.fr. Basic dbls & trpls. The 5-times-daily call to prayer broadcast over speakers from nearby mosque can be heard loudly in rooms.

🏠 **Plage** [281 C3] (45 rooms) Bd de la Libération; \ 53 320 90; f 53 307 24; e hotel_plage@simicro.mg. In the heart of the red-light district & quite run-down, but within easy walking distance of the beach. Nightly disco.

🏠 **Jupiter** [281 B5] (8 rooms) 21 Bd Augagneur; \ 53 321 01. Concrete building close to market. Simple rooms with hot water & fan. Nightclub next door Fri–Sun.

rooms with fan & hot water; some en suite with balcony. Check room before accepting as some are quite run-down.

☖ **Capucine** [281 B4] (12 rooms) Rue Guynemer; m 032 04 517 27/032 07 787 14. Basic dbl & family rooms; some en suite.
☖ **Mahatoky** [281 A3] (14 rooms) Bd de la Liberté; ☎ 53 300 21. Basic, but ideally located for *taxi-brousse* station. Some rooms en suite (cold water only).

Beach hotels and bungalows
☖ **Miramar** [281 B1] (20 bungalows) Bd Ratsimilaho, Salazamay; ☎ 53 332 15; m 032 65 993 74; f 53 330 13; e miramar-hotel-tmv@netcourrier.com; www.miramar-hotel-tamatave.com. Comfortable chalets & bungalows in a good location to the north, near the beach & convenient for airport. Chalets (fan) & bungalows (AC). Deep pool. €€€€
☖ **Ravinala** [281 B1] (9 rooms) Bd Ratsimilaho; ☎ 53 942 63; e vdbdtruong@belgacom.net. Highly recommended. On the beach 200m north of Miramar. Rooms with fans, mostly en suite with hot water; nice décor. Quiet & peaceful. €€€
☖ **Darafify** [281 B1] (20 bungalows) Ampanalana (north end of town); ☎ 53 960 80; e daraftamatave@moov.mg. Seafront location between airport & Miramar. En-suite bungalows of various types. Kids' playground. Very popular restaurant (closed Tue eve). €€–€€€

☖ **Justin** [282 A4] (16 rooms) Rue Lattre de Tassigny; m 033 14 458 54. Humble establishment popular with Malagasy. Good budget rooms; en suite (cold water).
☖ **Mélo** [281 A4] (11 rooms) Bd de l'OUA. No fan/AC but clean & extremely cheap dbl rooms with en-suite cold shower.

☖ **Concordia** [281 B1] (14 rooms) Rte de l'Aéroport; ☎ 53 317 42; e chanpowoo@moov.mg. Within walking distance of airport. Pleasant bungalows in an attractive setting; en-suite facilities with hot water, fan & TV. Restaurant closed Sun. €€
☖ **Maeva Bungalows** [282 A6] (3 bungalows) m 032 02 278 69. Simple Malagasy-run bungalows, each for up to 5 people. €€
☖ **Marotia** [282 A6] (20 bungalows) Bd de l'Ivondro; ☎ 53 949 22; m 032 04 325 44/033 14 896 14. Quiet palm grove near the ocean but not a very nice area (take a taxi after dark) & said to be popular with prostitutes. En-suite bungalows; some with hot water. €€
☖ **Finaritra** [281 A5] (9 bungalows) Mangarano II; ☎ 53 339 79; m 033 11 907 07/032 40 122 74. Pleasant en-suite bungalows with hot water. Close to university. €–€€

✗ **WHERE TO EAT** Toamasina is known for its many restaurants. One speciality is *soupe Chinoise*, which can be a meal in itself. Several hotels also have excellent restaurants worth trying. Particular thanks are due to researcher Lauren Leigh Hinthorne for feedback on Toamasina's restaurants and hotels.

✗ **Piment Banane** [282 D2] 23 Bd Ratsimilaho; ☎ 53 312 64; m 034 08 043 09; ⏰ 10.00–15.00 & 18.00–22.30 or later. Swish new restaurant on the seafront. Wonderful décor; free Wi-Fi; extensive wine list.
✗ **Bateau Ivre** [281 C1] Bd Ratsimilaho; ☎ 53 302 94; ⏰ 09.00–23.30. Adjoins the old municipal

swimming pool. Characterful beachfront bar & restaurant. Moderately priced European food; seafood a speciality. Live music.
✗ **Veranda** [282 B3] Bd Joffre; ☎ 53 334 35; ⏰ Mon–Sat 07.30–14.00 & 19.00–22.00, Sun closed. An old Creole house with nice décor; popular & full of character. Duck in honey particularly recommended.

THE LEGEND OF DARAFIFY   *Hilary Bradt*

Many, many years ago, when Madagascar was still young, the land was surrounded by fresh water. One day a giant named Darafify came striding down the eastern shoreline, carrying a bag of salt over one shoulder. He paused for a rest. A fisherman paddling his pirogue saw what he thought were two enormous trees standing on the edge of the water. These were splendid trees, with fine, straight, brown trunks, just the thing for a new pirogue. So he started to cut the nearest one down with his axe.

Darafify let out a roar of pain and dropped his bag of salt in the water. Since then the sea has been salty.

✗ **Pacifique** [282 C4] 22 Rue G Clemenceau; ☏ 53 322 23; ⏲ 11.00–14.00 & 18.00–22.00 (restaurant); 09.00–13.30 & 18.00–21.30 (*soupe Chinoise*); both closed Mon. Chinese restaurant serving very good meals at reasonable prices.

✗ **La Récrea** [281 D4] Bd Ratsimilaho; ▥ 032 04 610 71; ⏲ 10.00–23.00. Pleasant setting on the beach. Good food & nice place for a drink. Live music some w/ends. Bar, billiards & boutique.

✗ **Zoreal** [282 C5] 11 Bd Joffre; ☏ 53 332 36; ⏲ Tue/Thu/Fri/Sat 11.00–14.30 & daily 17.30–00.00. Local hangout with pool tables, darts & bar. French & Creole food, plus excellent pizzas.

✗ **Lilas** [281 B1] Rte d'Ivoloina; ☏ 53 324 12; ⏲ Tue–Sun 07.30–13.00 & 15.30–19.30, Mon closed. Small but clean & pleasant family-run Chinese restaurant. Tasty meals & soups at good prices.

✗ **Mora Mora** [281 A1] Bd Labourdonnais; ▥ 032 02 775 99; ⏲ Mon–Sat 12.00–14.30 & 18.00–24.00, Sun closed. Good food with a diverse menu featuring French & Malagasy dishes, as well as crêpe specialities. Nice décor with TV & bar.

✗ **L'Univers** [281 C3] Bd Joffre; ⏲ 24hrs. Rather gritty outfit in the west side of the stadium. Serves grills & simple dishes.

✗ **Don Camillo** [281 B3] Bd de la Libération; ▥ 032 07 668 10; ⏲ Tue–Sat 10.00–21.00, Sun/Mon 17.00–21.00. Italian food & bar. Eat in, take away or delivery. The thin crispy pizzas gets great reviews from local expats.

✗ **Fortuna** [282 C4] Rue de la Batterie; ☏ 53 338 28; ⏲ 11.00–13.30 & 18.00–21.30 (restaurant); 07.15–11.00 & 17.00–20.30 (*soupe Chinoise*); both closed Mon. Very good Chinese restaurant (but slow service) & adjacent *soupe Chinoise* serving the eponymous soup & noodle specialities.

✗ **Jade** [281 B5] 44 Rue Lattre de Tassigny; ☏ 53 335 65; ⏲ Mon–Sat 11.00–13.30 & 18.00–21.30, Sun closed. Chinese restaurant with excellent food, including vegetarian options. Reasonably priced lunch specials.

✗ **Vesuvio** [281 B5] Bd de l'OUA; ☏ 53 935 19; ⏲ 11.30–14.00 & 17.30–21.30, closed Wed lunch. Pizza competes favourably with Don Camillo. Also Creole food. Eat in, takeaway & delivery.

✗ **Dragon de Mer** [282 C4] 8 Rue Paul Doumer; ▥ 033 11 635 60; ⏲ Wed–Mon 08.00–13.30 & 17.30–21.00, Tue closed. Chinese restaurant with good food at reasonable prices.

Snack bars and cafés

▭ **Bruno's** [218 B3] Bd de la Libération; ⏲ 08.00–12.00 & 15.00–19.00 or later. Best pastries & cakes in town, but get there early. Great coffee & ice cream; good for b/fast.

▭ **Saïfy Fils** [282 B3] 30 Bd Joffre; ☏ 53 928 80; ⏲ 06.30–12.00 & 15.30–18.30, closed Sun afternoon. Average pastries, but decent coffee & fruit juices in season. B/fast & other savouries available.

▭ **Adam & Eve** [282 C4] 13 Rue Nationale; ☏ 53 334 56; ⏲ Mon–Sat 08.00–20.30, Sun closed. A long-time *vazaha* favourite with good prices. Particularly good value for b/fast. Delectable milkshakes. Always busy.

▭ **Maxi Pizza** [282 B3] Bd Joffre. Hole-in-the-wall pizza kiosk with a few pavement tables.

▭ **Gastro Pizza** [281 B5] Good pizzas & ice cream from this popular chain.

▭ **Abdallah-Awad** [282 B4] Off Bd Joffre; ⏲ Mon–Sat 08.00–12.00 & 14.30–18.30, Sun closed. Coconut & coffee ice creams highly recommended by local expats.

▭ **Mouf'Rey** [282 B3] Reliable bakery with good bread & a range of pastries.

▭ **Au Plasir** [282 B2] 10 Bd Joffre. Centrally located *salon de thé*.

▭ **Canne à Sucre** [281 B5] Bd de l'OUA; ⏲ Mon–Sat 07.00–00.00, Sun closed. Karaoke bar with Malagasy & Creole specialities.

NIGHTLIFE

☆ **Neptune** [281 C3] ⏲ Mon–Sat. At the hotel of the same name, this is the most popular disco venue in town.

☆ **Pandora Station** [281 B1] ⏲ Tue–Sun. Near the Miramar. An interesting & imaginatively decorated nightclub. Simple snacks served including pizza.

☆ **Queen's Club** [281 C3] Bd Joffre. Discotheque near Plage.

☆ **Stone Club** [281 B5] At Jupiter, this is a simple nightclub frequented mainly by Malagasy.

INTERNET There are many internet facilities in Toamasina, especially around Boulevard Joffre and the Bazary Be.

◎ Orange Cyber [282 B3] Bazary Be;
⏱ 07.30–19.30. Fastest internet in town; 40Ar/min.
◎ CyberSky [282 C4] Bd Joffre; ✆ 53 940 29;
e cyberskytmm@yahoo.fr; ⏱ 09.00–19.30. Price
25Ar/min. Upstairs near Adam & Eve.
◎ Speed.Net [281 A4] Bd de l'OUA; ✆ 53 916 03;
m 033 11 908 80/032 40 750 86;

e speedcomputertamatave@yahoo.fr; ⏱ Mon–Sat
07.30–19.30, Sun closed. Price 15Ar/min.
◎ Butterfly [282 C4] Bd Joffre; ✆ 53 317 04;
e bnc@moov.mg; www.chez.com/bnc/; ⏱ Mon–Sat
08.30–12.00 & 14.30–18.00, Sun closed. Smart
cybercafé with 5 computers & AC; 30Ar/min.

MONEY Toamasina has branches of all the major banks – BFV, BNI, BOA and
BMOI – all now with ATMs and Western Union services. There are many money
changers around town and Neptune also changes travellers' cheques.

SHOPPING

Score [281 B4] Av de l'Indépendance; ⏱ Mon–Fri
08.30–13.00 & 14.30–19.00, Sat 08.30–19.00, Sun
08.30–12.30. The largest supermarket in town. It
stocks mostly European & local brands, including
some T-shirts. Decent deli & bakery.
Shoprite [282 C1] Av de l'Indépendance;
⏱ Mon–Thu 08.30–13.00 & 14.30–19.00, Fri/Sat
08.30–19.00, Sun 09.00–13.00. Supermarket near the
beach. It carries mainly South African & local products.
Chocolatière [282 B2] Bd Joffre. For a chocolate fix, or
to buy locally made candy gifts, look for the Robert's
chocolate shop along from the defunct Ritz cinema.
Fakra [282 B3] 29 Bd Joffre; ✆ 53 321 30;
⏱ Mon–Fri 08.00–12.00 & 14.30–18.00, Sat
08.00–12.00. This mainly French bookshop has a
decent selection of postcards & some coffee-table
photo books & CDs of Malagasy music.
AloAlo [282 B4] 25 Bd Joffre; ⏱ Mon–Sat
08.30–12.00 & 14.30–18.00, Sun closed. Interesting
selection of handicrafts, different from that found
elsewhere.

Fleur du Monde [281 B5] 16 Bd de l'OUA;
⏱ Mon–Sat 08.30–12.00 & 14.30–17.00, Sun
closed. Unique souvenirs & some imported items.
Worth a visit if you're at this end of town.
Nulle Part Ailleurs [282 B4] 69 Bd Joffre; ✆ 53 325
06; ⏱ Mon–Fri 08.30–12.00 & 14.30–17.45, Sat
08.30–12.00. A diverse collection of quality gifts:
from T-shirts & baskets to handbags & items made
from semi-precious stone. Visa accepted.
Bazary Be ('big market') [282 A3–B3] In typical
Malagasy logic, the big market in Toamasina is
actually much smaller than the small market, bazary
kely. Toamasina is known for its baskets & other
woven items; the bazary be is a great place to find
such souvenirs. Pause for a fresh coconut on the
north side. After drinking the juice, have the coconut
cracked open so that you can enjoy the flesh. The
vendor will make you a nifty scoop from the shell.
T-shirts & CDs are available at shops surrounding
the market. **Jeunesse Photo** on the west side has an
excellent selection of postcards.

CAR AND BICYCLE HIRE Renting a car in Toamasina is more expensive than in Tana.
Most agencies require advance booking. Alternatively ask at your hotel reception
(staff usually know someone willing to hire out a private vehicle) or stop a decent-
looking taxi and negotiate. You'll be obliged to accept the driver's services, but that
isn't necessarily a bad thing since they know the area. The bulletin board at Score
supermarket frequently displays vehicles for hire.

🚗 **Amazing Grace** [281 C2] Villa Rabary, Rue Victor
Hugo; ✆ 53 301 52; f 53 339 58
🚗 **MR Auto** [281 C2] Bd Joffre; ✆ 53 308 70;
m 033 11 049 91. Recommended by an expat
who frequently uses this business; reasonable rates.
🚗 **SICAM** [281 B6] Bd de l'OUA; ✆ 53 321 04;
f 53 334 55; e sicam@sicam.mg or
sicam.tamatave@simicro.mg. Hertz representative.

🚗 **Tropical Service** [282 B4] 23 Bd Joffre; ✆ 53
336 79; f 53 334 80; e tropicalservice@moov.mg;
www.croisiere-madagascar.com. General travel agent;
full details on website under 'locations voitures'. They
also take booking for the ferry to Ile Sainte Marie.
🚲 **Loulou Location Velos** [281 C4] Bd Joffre;
m 032 04 414 83/033 14 701 78. Bike hire:
12,000Ar/day, 6,000Ar/half-day, 2,000Ar/hr.

WHAT TO SEE AND DO The regional **tourist information office** [281 C2]
(ORTT) is based at 83 Boulevard Joffre (✆ 53 912 14; m 032 41 581 16;

e *officetouristmv@yahoo.fr; www.tamatave-tourisme.com;* ⏲ *Mon–Fri 08.00–11.30 & 14.30–17.00, Sat 08.00–12.00).*

Regional Museum [281 C3] (*Bd de la Libération, at intersection with Bd Joffre;* ⏲ *Tue–Sun 09.00–16.00*) Don't plan on making a day of it, but if you have some time to kill this small regional museum is a decent filler. The entrance is opposite the fuel station near the Sharon hotel. Calling itself a museum of ethnology, history and archaeology, there are exhibits from around the island relating to traditional village life, religious beliefs, musical instruments etc. Signboards include text in English.

La Place Bien-Aimée [281 D6] Kim Loohuis recommends this botanical garden near the port, with its magnificent banyan trees: 'People play *pétanque* here. Very tranquil and a good place to meet the real Malagasy.'

Mini-golf [281 D5] (⏲ *Mon–Sat 08.00–21.00; games 1,000Ar*) 18-hole course at the end of Rue de Commerce, down from the port entrance opposite Bonnet et Fils. 'Sounds corny but is nicely laid out and kept up with bar and grillade restaurant' (Charlie Welch). Great if you're looking for something completely different to do.

Horseriding (\ *53 342 93;* f *53 324 25*) For those who have ever harboured romantic notions of riding a horse down a tropical beach, here's your chance. The equestrian centre is located off the main airport road, just before the street to the Miramar (coming from town). The sandy road is marked by two signs ('Domaine des Haras: Masteva'). Contact in advance.

PARC IVOLOINA

(\ *53 931 68;* e *tim@savethelemur.org; www.seemadagascar.com;* ⏲ *09.00–17.00; entry 10,000Ar, guide 10,000Ar, nocturnal visit 5,000Ar, camping 4,000Ar*) This began life more than two decades ago as a rather grand botanical garden but is now a conservation centre and zoo. It is funded by the Madagascar Fauna Group, a consortium of some 30 zoos from around the world with a special interest in Madagascar. It supports Ivoloina and the reserve of Betampona. See their excellent website for more information (*www.savethelemur.org*).

A visit here is rewarding both for what you see and what the MFG is doing in terms of educating the local population about conservation. First the lemurs: in total there are 13 species here, including a female aye-aye (phone in advance to arrange an after-hours visit to see the nocturnal aye-aye active). Free-ranging lemurs include black-and-white ruffed lemurs, white-fronted brown lemurs, red-bellied lemurs and crowned lemurs. These offer great photo opportunities, as well as the pleasure of seeing 'zoo animals' living in freedom. There are also reptiles (tortoises, chameleons and boas), tenrecs, vasa parrots and tomato frogs which are unique to the Maroantsetra area.

You can explore the forest around the zoo on a network of seven forest and lakeside trails of varying levels of difficulty, which include wildlife interpretation boards, two waterfalls, a small pool and a viewpoint overlooking the park and the surrounding countryside to the Indian Ocean. An abundance of birds, reptiles and lemurs can be seen from the trails. Guides are not obligatory except for big groups.

There is a botanical tour, with labelled native trees and also a new invertebrate trail. A snack bar also sells souvenirs near the entrance and you can even take a leisurely pirogue trip on the lake.

Do visit the education centre to learn about the importance of conservation in the area. The centre runs a teacher-training project and a teachers' manual for environmental education. Children from the local primary school come here on Saturdays to learn about conservation, and two more Saturday Schools have recently been built, one at Ambodirafia (near Betampona) and one at Ambodiriana.

A Conservation Training Centre runs courses in forest management, nursery management, reforestation, composting, intensive rice culture and more. The agro-forestry model station, which you see near the entrance, helps teach sustainable agriculture techniques to Malagasy cultivators.

GETTING THERE Ivoloina is 12km north of Toamasina. It is possible to get there by *taxi-brousse*, although to the village only. From here there is a 4km track to the park, but those on foot can take the 2km shortcut (turn left off the track 60m past the small bridge and welcome arch). The easiest way is to take a taxi or transport arranged through a hotel in town. Alternatively hire a bicycle in Toamasina.

The ideal way to see the park and its animals is by camping overnight; you'll need to provide your own tent and food.

THE ROUTE NORTH

The road is tarred and in good condition as far as Soanierana-Ivongo. Beyond that it is usually passable (just) as far as Maroantsetra. Then you have to take to the air or journey on foot across the neck of the road-free Masoala Peninsula. An increasing number of good-quality seaside hotels are being built along the coast.

MAHAVELONA (FOULPOINTE) The town of Mahavelona is unremarkable, but nearby is an interesting old circular fortress with mighty walls faced with an iron-hard mixture of sand, shells and eggs. There are some old British cannons marked 'GR'. This fortress was built in the early 19th century by the Merina governor of the town, Rafaralahy, shortly after the Merina conquest of the east coast. The entry fee is 3,000Ar and guided tours are available (in French).

This beach resort with calm waters is becoming popular with the Malagasy as well as *vazaha*, and there's a growing number of places to stay.

 Where to stay and eat

⌂ **Manda Beach** (42 rooms) ⟍ 57 220 00; m 033 15 220 00/034 11 220 00; f 57 220 02; e mandabeach@moov.mg; www.mandabeach-hotel.com. Good accommodation located on the Toamasina side of town. Bungalows & safe swimming. €€€

⌂ **Grand Bleu** (8 bungalows & 3 rooms) ⟍ 57 220 06; m 032 02 311 61; e hotel.joffre@

moov.mg; www.grandbleu-tamatave.com. En-suite beachfront accommodation. €€€

⌂ **Au Gentil Pêcheur** Beachfront, next to Manda Beach. Less expensive bungalows & excellent food. €€

✕ **Foulpointe** This restaurant is receiving rave reviews.

Analalava Forest This is a 200ha fragment of low-elevation humid forest 7km southwest of Mahavelona. Although small and degraded, it is of high conservation importance, being the only forest remaining in the area and supporting a rich biodiversity. It has started to open up to ecotourism so is worth checking out.

MAHAMBO A lovely beach resort with safe swimming (but nasty sandflies, called *moka fohy*), offering a more tranquil alternative to Mahavelona.

Where to stay and eat

🏠 **Pirogue** (10 bungalows & 6 rooms) \ 57 301 71; m 033 08 768 10/18; e la.pirogue@ gmail.com; www.pirogue-hotel.com. Wonderful bungalows to suit a broad range of budgets, very tastefully decorated with all sorts of artisanal products & minerals. Fishing & boat trips. €€€–♨

🏠 **Dola** (20 bungalows) \ 57 331 01/302 35; m 032 02 396 14; e hoteldola_madagascar@

voila.fr; http://hoteledola.site.voila.fr. Small windowless bungalows. €€€

🏠 **Orchidées** (6 bungalows) Good-value dbl & family rooms in lovely location. €€

🏠 **Ylang-Ylang** \ 57 331 00/300 08; e mamitina@moov.mg. A very nice bungalow complex set in a quiet garden. Bungalows for up to 6 people; all with hot water. Restaurant has good cheap food. €€

HEADING WEST Between Mahambo and Fenoarivo Atsinanana is a road leading inland to Vavatenina, where there is basic accommodation in bungalows, and on to Anjahambe. This town marks the beginning (or end) of the Smugglers' Path to Lake Alaotra (see page 255).

FENOARIVO ATSINANANA (FÉNÉRIVE EST) Beyond Mahambo is the former capital of the Betsimisaraka Empire. There is a clove factory in town which distils the essence of cloves, cinnamon and green peppers for the perfume industry. They are not geared up for tourist visits but will show you round if you ask.

There are several basic hotels, including **Belle Rose Bungalows** (\ 57 300 38; €€) on the road leading to the hospital, an excellent Chinese bakery, and a BOA bank – the last on the route north until Mananara.

VOHILENGO From Fenoarivo a road leads west to Vohilengo. This makes a pleasant diversion for those with their own transport, especially during the lychee season. Clare Hermans 'arrived at the start of a six-week lychee bonanza. Along the road to Vohilengo were pre-arranged pick-up points where the pickers would bring their two 10kg panniers. Vohilengo is a small village, perfumed with the scent of cloves laid out to dry'.

TAMPOLO FORESTRY STATION About 10km north of Fenoarivo is this small forestry station. It is managed by the agricultural branch of Tana university (*www.essa-forets.org*) and partly supported by the Lemur Conservation Foundation (*www.lemurreserve.org*). There is an interpretive museum and paths into the coastal forest that can be taken with guides, offering a good opportunity to see some of Madagascar's most endangered flora: the littoral forest.

A project has just been completed to build an environmental classroom, Centre EnviroKidz, which will double as a community centre.

SOANIERANA-IVONGO Familiarly known as 'S-Ivongo', this little town is the main starting point for the boat to Ile Sainte Marie. It is also the end of the tarred road.

S-Ivongo has only the most basic accommodation. **Les Escales** (m 032 43 174 63; €) is well located for the boat departure point and **Relais Sainte Marie** has pleasant bungalows.

CONTINUING NORTH (IF YOU DARE!)

From S-Ivongo the road is unreliable to say the least. As fast as bridges are repaired they wash away again. You may have a fairly smooth *taxi-brousse* ride with ferries taking you across the rivers, or you may end up walking for hours and wading rivers or finding a pirogue to take you across. You should get local advice before setting out, especially if you have a lot of luggage to carry or are on a tight schedule.

MANOMPANA This charming and characterful village, once the departure point for boats to Ile Sainte Marie, is a peaceful destination in itself. There is good surfing and swimming in the area and an attractive lagoon at Pointe Titingue. A French volunteer-run cultural centre for local children, called **La Marmaille à La Case** (*http://marmaillealacase.free.fr*), makes for an inspiring visit.

Ambodiriana Forest is a small reserve protecting 65ha of lowland rainforest, home to eight resident lemur species and administered by ADEFA (*www.adefa-madagascar.org*). A visit to the forest costs 5,000Ar per person plus 5,000Ar for the obligatory guide. There are three dramatic waterfalls connected by well-marked paths including a botanical trail. A day visit is quite possible but there are basic camping facilities for those wishing to stay a night.

They also run fascinating tours of the village during which you will learn about shipbuilding, clove distillation and local customs. You will see the baker's oven, coffee being dried on mats, vanilla pods drying in glass Coca-Cola bottles, sea cucumbers drying on mats before being shipped to Japan for sushi, and witness production of *betsabetsa*, a bitter local alcoholic drink made in a week using sugarcane juice. Visit ADEFA's office in Manompana for more information.

 Where to stay and eat

⌂ **Chez Wen-Ki's** (5 bungalows) Secluded spacious beachfront bungalows with bucket showers. Bikes for hire. 'Meals were superb, bungalows delightful & M Wen-Ki the most enchanting & courteous gentleman imaginable' (FRB). €

⌂ **Chez Lou Lou** (6 bungalows) Central beachfront bungalows; clean with good toilets. Great seafood. €
⌂ **Mahle** On Mahle Point, a beautiful oceanfront place 1km from the village. Run by affable brother & sister. Excellent food. Good diving & lovely forest nearby. €

MANOMPANA TO MAROANTSETRA

The road north can be an adventure in itself: 'Intending to set out on foot one morning I found myself in the back of a vehicle bound for a nearby village and was

---

BEWARE OF SANDFLIES   *Duncan Murrell*

The thing about sandflies, as I discovered, is that you don't know the extent of the damage until it's too late. They seem to home in on your back as if they realise that they're evading your detection. I was busy trying to swat a relatively small number on my arms, unaware that my back was being ravaged. Their insidious approach is also abetted by the apparent lack of any noticeable pain from the bites. On two separate occasions my back and the backs of my arms were covered in the horrendously itchy spots. They didn't last for weeks but they certainly itched for days and days and days – and nights especially! Every night I was compelled to emerge from my hammock for a two-handed scratching frenzy. My advice is to put on a long-sleeved shirt when the first sandfly is spotted – even if it appears to be only one – because it's just a decoy. Otherwise they could ruin the whole trip.

subsequently transferred to a lorry. The experience of watching happy and unconcerned Malagasy cutting down saplings to reinforce bridges, diving into the river to retrieve bits of erstwhile bridge and unloading/reloading the lorry to get it safely across – then repeating the process just a few kilometres on – together with negotiation of the near impossible "road" in between, will stay with me forever! I suspect too that images of the astounded *vazaha* may stay with those with whom I shared this journey!' (FRB).

Bill French notes that this stretch is tough-going for cyclists, especially the part north of Antanambe, the worst part being around Ivontaka.

ANTANAMBE Some 37km north of Manompana, on the edge of the Mananara-Nord National Park, is this pretty town with one of the east coast's nicest hotels.

Where to stay

Chez Grandin This lodge is deservedly popular. Considering its remote location it is rather luxurious, with gas cooking, filtered running water, pressure showers, flush toilets & comfortable beds, not to mention a great restaurant with Creole & French cooking & fresh fish. Diving/fishing excursions & tours to Mananara-Nord. €€€

Vahibe Budget accommodation next to the ferry some 2km north of town. €

SAHASOA The 15km or so from Antanambe to Sahasoa is in a dreadful state and it may take several hours in a 4x4. But the views from this coast-hugging road are spectacular. Many travellers choose to tackle some or all of the 47km section between Antanambe and Mananara on foot.

Sahasoa is the gateway to Mananara-Nord National Park. The park office is at the southern end of the village. They have built three spacious seafront bungalows, which are run by the village women's association and cost 20,000Ar for a double. A cheaper option is a basic bungalow for 3,000Ar at the **Hôtel du Centre** (€).

MANANARA-NORD NATIONAL PARK (✆ *22 415 38;* e *angaptmv@gmail.com*) This UNESCO Biosphere Reserve covers an area of 140,000ha, with a variety of ecosystems including tropical humid forest, sandy coastal plains with littoral vegetation, river vegetation, mangrove formations, marshlands and coral reefs. Despite its name and apparent proximity to Mananara, the state of the road means that the entry (at Sahasoa) is half a day's journey away by 4x4.

A handful of adventurous tourists visit the park's marine reserve that protects, among other things, dugongs. At its centre is the small island of **Nosy Atafana**, where Madagascar flying foxes can be seen in great numbers. You can arrange a boat via the park office; the trip takes two hours each way and costs around 300,000Ar (per boat). There is a campsite on the island.

Very few people visit the forest, which from Sahasoa is a two-hour hike inland across degraded habitat. Camping is now possible at the edge of the park. The terrain is moderately tough going, with three trails of 16–20km and many impressive views.

Guides for both the terrestrial and marine areas cost 12,000Ar/day, porters 8,000Ar/day and camping 5,000Ar/tent. The park has welcome centres in both Antanambe and Mananara, which you would be well advised to visit since the park cannot always cater for unexpected visitors.

SAHASOA TO MANANARA Ongoing transport becomes increasingly scarce and the condition of the road doesn't get any better. If you are on foot (or break down/get stuck) **Seranambe** is conveniently located halfway along this 32km leg. The **Capital** hotel has a basic bungalow (4,000Ar).

MANANARA This friendly small village 127km north of Soanierana-Ivongo sees few visitors despite the fact that it is the only place in Madagascar where one is very likely to see an aye-aye in the wild. There is a lively market and the ocean for relaxation. About 3km south of the village is a secluded bay, protected by a reef, with safe swimming.

Getting there and away Mananara is sometimes served by Air Mad flights from Toamasina, but domestic routes change often so check www.airmadagascar.com.

To reach Mananara by road is certain to be an adventure. From Toamasina it takes at the very least 24 hours; from Maroantsetra it's even slower and more perilous. Taking the route in from the north or south on foot is always an option, but it is neither a quick nor an easy undertaking. If you don't want to subject your body to this sort of torture, the only way to reach Mananara without flying is by speedboat from Maroantsetra.

Where to stay

⌂ **Aye-Aye** On the beachfront opposite the airport. Pleasant en-suite bungalows, enlivened by free-ranging bamboo & brown lemurs. €€

⌂ **Chez Roger** (6 bungalows) If visiting Aye-Aye Island is your main reason for coming to Mananara you should stay here, since M Roger owns the island

& will deal with all the arrangements. Good en-suite bungalows with hot water & reliable restaurant. €–€€

⌂ **Ton-Ton Galet** A friendly, modest set of bungalows near the hospital. Good meals & convivial atmosphere. €

Money and communications The town has a post office and a bank (BOA), the only one on the 297km stretch between Fenoarivo and Maroantsetra. There is mobile phone coverage but no landlines or internet access.

AYE-AYE ISLAND This is *the* reason most people come to Mananara. The privately-owned river island of about 10ha has a few resident aye-ayes as well as white-fronted brown lemurs. Normally aye-ayes live high in the rainforest canopy and have large territories. On Aye-Aye Island, however, their range is restricted by the island's small size and the trees are much lower and less dense, so they are comparatively easy to see. They are partial to coconuts and coconut palms are found in abundance here.

A sighting is by no means guaranteed, but at least half of the tourists who make an evening visit to the island are lucky. Chances are increased for those staying overnight (you can camp or there's a small hut) but not everyone is successful. Wybe Rood wonders if the elusive animal even exists: 'Didn't see any! After having spent almost two years in Madagascar, and having been to Nosy Mangabe and Aye-Aye Island, I am now convinced this creature is a fabrication!'

Botanically the island is interesting; not only are there coconuts, but bananas, pineapples, jackfruits, papayas, vanilla, coffee, cloves and maize are all cultivated.

Visits can be arranged at the hotel Chez Roger. The cost is 16,000Ar per person, including the pirogue crossing.

MANANARA TO MAROANTSETRA To continue the journey north is a serious adventure. It is possible (just) by road and also by sea. Since the mid 1990s, readers have recounted their experiences using both forms of transport, most resulting in extreme hardship with some near-deaths. As the road continues to deteriorate, the trek on foot is at least safe, if hard work.

Getting there and away

By road Reader Jeremy Sabel reports: 'This 114km journey took 14 hours in a 4x4 *taxi-brousse*. The road was terrible and the passengers were packed in like sardines, and two suffered from motion sickness. *Taxi-brousses* leave when there are sufficient passengers (roughly once every two days).'

By boat It is worth enquiring at the port of Mananara if there are any cargo boats heading north as they regularly ply the route.

On foot/by bicycle Dylan Lossie did it (from Maroantsetra): 'The first 20km from Maroantsetra we went by *taxi-brousse* but the vehicle completely collapsed after 18km and we had to leave the poor driver and his destroyed vehicle behind. We walked 2km to **Voloina**. Then another 12km to **Rantabe**, where we camped on a beach.' After that, Dylan's journey was a combination of walking, bicycle and *taxi-brousse* for the final leg from **Manambolosy** to Mananara. 'Not an easy ride! All along the way bridges were collapsed, or just about to. The roads are in a terrible state. Nevertheless, the area is beautiful and I would not have missed it!'

MAROANTSETRA AND THE MASOALA PENINSULA

Despite difficulty of access and dodgy weather, this is perhaps the leading destination for ecotourists who want to see Madagascar's most important natural habitat in terms of biodiversity – the eastern rainforest, exemplified by Nosy Mangabe and the Masoala Peninsula.

These places require fitness and fortitude but the rewards for nature-lovers are great. Fitness is needed for the hills and mud which are an aspect of all the reserves, and fortitude because this is the wettest place in Madagascar, with annual rainfall exceeding 500cm. The driest months tend to be November and December.

MAROANTSETRA Nestled at the far end of the Antongil Bay, Maroantsetra is Madagascar at its most authentic. Well away from the usual tourist circuits, it is a prosperous, friendly little town, with enough comfortable hotels to make a visit a pleasure for both packaged and independent travellers.

☞ *WARNING!* There is no ATM here and Visa cards are not accepted anywhere.

Getting there and away
By air Most people fly. Consequently flights are often booked up well in advance. Currently four flights a week connect Maroantsetra with Tana, Toamasina, Antalaha and Sambava, but check the latest schedules with Air Mad (*www.airmadagascar.com*). The airport is 8km from town (10,000Ar by taxi).

By land You can come on foot (and occasional vehicle) from Mananara (see page 292) or hike from Antalaha (see page 301).

There are two *taxi-brousse* operators in Maroantsetra: **KoFiMan** next to Pagode and **KoFiFen** (m *032 41 404 67/033 11 640 95*) at Hôtel du Centre. A *taxi-brousse* to Mananara costs 30,000Ar and takes 12–15 hours on a treacherous road.

By sea There are regular cargo boats (*boutres*) between Toamasina and Maroantsetra. They will stop *en route* at Ile Sainte Marie if requested. The cost is approximately 20,000Ar to Ile Sainte Marie (10 hours) and 30,000Ar to Toamasina (18 hours). Beware of stopovers and choppy seas.

⌂ Where to stay
⌂ **Relais du Masoala** (15 bungalows) ☎ 22 219 74; m 034 14 577 24; e relaisdumasoala@ cortezexpeditions.mg; www.relaismasoala.com. Spacious bungalows with swimming pool set in 7ha of gardens

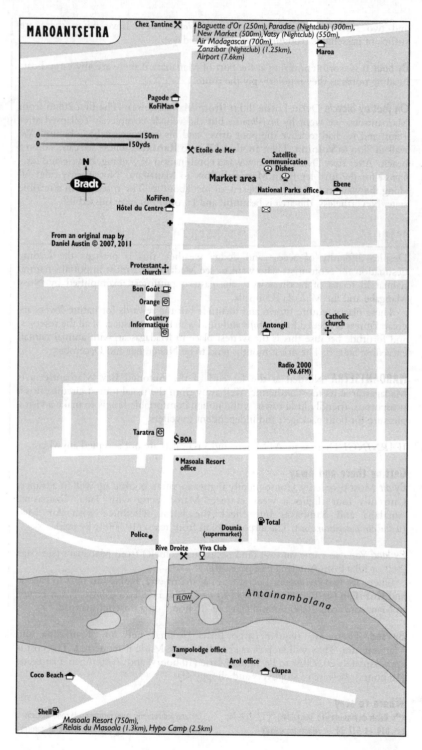

MAROANTSETRA

Chez Tantine ✕

↑Baguette d'Or (250m), Paradise (Nightclub) (300m),
New Market (500m), Vatsy (Nightclub) (550m),
Air Madagascar (700m),
Zanzibar (Nightclub) (1.25km),
Airport (7.6km)

Maroa

Pagode 🏠
KoFiMan ●

0 ————————— 150m
0 ————————— 150yds

N

Bradt

✕ Etoile de Mer

Satellite
Communication
☼ Dishes ☼

Market area

National Parks office ●

Ebene
🏠

KoFiFen ●
Hôtel du Centre 🏠

✉

✝

From an original map by
Daniel Austin © 2007, 2011

Protestant ✝
church

Bon Goût 🖳
Orange ℮

Country
Informatique
℮

Antongil
🏠

Catholic
church ✝

Radio 2000
(96.6FM) ●

Taratra ℮
$ BOA

● Masoala Resort
office

Police ●

Dounia
(supermarket) ●

🅿 Total

Rive Droite
✕

Viva Club
🍷

FLOW ▷

Antainambalana

Tampolodge office ●

Arol office ●
🏠 Clupea

Coco Beach 🏠

Shell 🅿
Masoala Resort (750m),
Relais du Masoala (1.3km), Hypo Camp (2.5km)

& coconut groves overlooking Antongil Bay. A super place & very comfortable. Very good food Can arrange all activities in the area. See ad on page 313. €€€€

🏠 **Masoala Resort** (13 bungalows) m 032 40 213 81; e masoala.resort@yahoo.fr. Indian-owned beachfront hotel, new in 2007. Beautifully built dbl en-suite bungalows with TV, minibar & balcony with hammock & great view; most with AC. Swimming pool. Camping pitch (10,000Ar). Visa accepted. €€€€

🏠 **Coco Beach** (10 bungalows) \ 57 720 06; e maroatours@gmail.com. Various en-suite dbl bungalows, some with hot water. Meals in the spacious dining-room are of variable quality & service is slow. Striped tenrecs may be seen in the garden at night. For excursions contact Rakotovazaha (see

Maroa Tour under *Tour operators*). €€–€€€

🏠 **Hypo Camp** Brand new accommodation about 1km past Relais du Masoala. €€–€€€

🏠 **Ebene** (4 bungalows) m 033 14 908 73; e mahafenokathy@yahoo.fr. Basic en-suite rooms with cold water next to parks office. €€

🏠 **Pagode** (16 bungalows) m 032 54 681 67/032 75 373 03/033 05 198 99. Dbl bungalows with hot or (much cheaper) cold water. Good restaurant. €€

🏠 **Antongil** (8 rooms) Rooms have fans, wide (shared) balconies, showers & shared toilets. €

🏠 **Hôtel du Centre** \ 57 721 31; e tsimanova@yahoo.fr. Across from the market; inexpensive rooms & bungalows. €

🏠 **Maroa** Quiet bungalows with en-suite bathrooms at the north of town. €

✕ Where to eat

✕ **Rive Droite** Open-air restaurant & bar built out over the river. To the right as you come into town from the Coco Beach. Good food but flies sometimes a nuisance.

✕ **Chez Tantine** Recommended Malagasy eatery near the north market.

✕ **Baguette d'Or** Chinese restaurant 300m north of Pagode. Excellent seafood in big portions & good *soupe Chinoise*. Sometimes karaoke.

✕ **Etoile de Mer** A simple Chinese restaurant behind the central market.

☕ **Bon Goût** A *salon de thé*; good for b/fast. Nice bread, croissants, *pains au chocolat* & cakes.

Nightlife The best discotheque is said to be **Paradise** (m *032 42 039 73/032 57 172 46*) near Chez Tantine. Two others are **Vatsy**, in the same area, and **Zanzibar**, about 1km past Baguette d'Or. They generally open on Friday and Sunday nights. Next to Rive Droite is **Viva Club**, a bar/disco right on the river.

Money and communications Maroantsetra has just one bank, a branch of BOA, which only handles MasterCard – no Visa. There is no ATM; cash withdrawals can take a long time. This has led many unprepared travellers into financial difficulties so try to come to Maroantsetra with sufficient local currency. If you're in a rush or the bank is closed, there's a nearby shopkeeper who changes dollars and euros, but his rate is usually a little worse than the bank's. The post office has a Western Union service.

Internet has finally arrived here and there are at least four places to get online, mostly clustered just north of the bank. The price is usually 100Ar/minute.

Shopping There are two markets: the central one is smaller than the new market on the main road 600m north of Pagode.

Dounia is a well-stocked supermarket with items suitable for taking as provisions on camping trips such as tinned food and cartons of drinks.

Tour operators Here, more than anywhere else in Madagascar, you need the services of a local tour operator to secure a boat to Nosy Mangabe or Masoala, as well as other excursions which are difficult to do on your own. The **National Parks office** is near the post office.

Maroa Tour m 033 12 057 19/032 43 482 09; e maroatours@gmail.com; www.maroatours.com.

Run by the indefatigable **Rakotovazaha**, a guide who seems to be able to organise just about anything in the region including treks & forest visits. With boundless energy he exists in a perpetual whirlwind of arranging & planning. Rakoto speaks English & will organise a complete package (boats, guides, permits, accommodation etc) according to your budget & needs. He has also started hiring out camping equipment & bikes. You'll often find him at the airport when flights arrive or at Coco Beach. **Explorer Madagascar** (at Tampolodge office) \ 57 721 49; m 033 14 471 20. Trips to Masoala & Nosy Mangabe, boat hire, trekking, whale-watching & bird-watching.

Adrien Bemirhary \ 57 721 42; m 032 02 039 10. Speedboat owner. He is a tough negotiator. Best to form a group before meeting him.
Relais de Masoala (see *Where to stay*) The hotel has been organising trips to Masoala & other hard-to-reach places longer than anyone. Not cheap, but you can be assured of the quality of the equipment.
Paul Harimala Clememt \ 53 339 12; m 033 02 259 43; f 53 313 50; e laly_son@yahoo.fr. An experienced guide who organises tours that allow tourists to experience & contribute to social aspects of the region.

LOCAL EXCURSIONS Sil Westra did a full-day tour organised by Rakotovazaha. 'This was excellent and I really recommend it! You can see lots of things in a short time. You can see kingfishers and Parson's chameleons on the banks of the river while you try to balance yourself inside the ever-unstable pirogue. You can taste local sugar cane wine *betsabetsa* in a traditional small village where you will constantly be surrounded by curious children. You can hike through the rural countryside and be pulled across the river on a raft. You can experience the petrol-saving driving techniques of the taxi drivers rolling to a standstill with the engine shut off before the massive acceleration starts again. A farmer will show you around his vanilla plantation and explain how cinnamon is grown and harvested. And you can have a look at the huge endemic tomato frog in people's backyards.' It's good to hear of a tour that involves local people in this way.

Andranofotsy and Navana It is worth taking a pirogue trip up the Andranofotsy River to the village of the same name. The vegetation and river-life viewed on the way are fascinating, and the relatively unspoilt village is delightful.

Equally worthwhile is a visit to Navana. Follow the coast east along a beach backed by thickets, through waterways clogged with flowering water hyacinths and past plenty of forest. You need to cross a lot of water on a pirogue, a regular local service. It takes an hour through little canals and costs very little.

NOSY MANGABE In fine weather the island of Nosy Mangabe is superb. This special reserve has beautiful sandy coves, marvellous trees with huge buttress roots and also strangler figs. And it's bursting with wildlife including, of course, its famous aye-ayes which were released here in the 1960s to prevent what was then thought to be their imminent extinction. If aye-ayes are what you're after, there's little point in coming here just for the day (they are nocturnal) but there is plenty to see on a day visit, including the weird and wonderful leaf-tailed gecko (*Uroplatus fimbriatus*), green-backed mantella frogs, white-fronted brown lemurs and black-and-white ruffed lemurs.

Leo Barasi spent six days on the island: 'I don't regret on any of it. OK we didn't manage to see any aye-aye, but the rest of the wildlife and the scenery more than made up for it. I loved the leaf-tailed geckos, particularly at night when they took on a completely new appearance. Lots of chameleons, including *Brookesia*, some very nice boas and several other attractive snakes. The black-and-white ruffed lemurs could be heard from all points of the island and sounded like dying pigs. Best of all, though, were the dolphins and sea turtles that we saw swimming around the bay on our last day – fantastic!'

Another reader who stayed five days (also no aye-ayes) 'took the circuit to the summit. Our guide assured us that the round-trip would take no more than four hours, but we encountered so much wildlife along the route that we had not even reached the summit in this time! It seemed that every few paces we were pausing to examine another frog or gecko.'

You can see from the above that though it's famous for its aye-ayes very few see them here these days. However, Simon Jackson got lucky: 'We were fortunate enough to have the island to ourselves for two days in perfect weather at the beginning of December. Our guide, Armand, feared that he had lost face on the first evening, having presented himself as Mr Aye-Aye, then had us sit on a log in the middle of the forest for an hour in the pitch black waiting in vain for the animals to betray their presence by dropping partially consumed fruit on our heads. The next morning, just after dawn, he woke us in our tent in a state of high excitement. Determined to make amends, he had risen in the dark

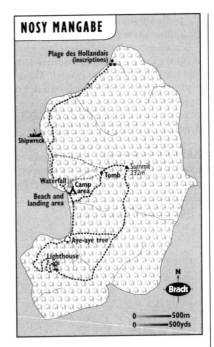

to follow some cries. He dragged us off the path up a steep slope, our hearts racing from the rapid transition from deep sleep to violent exercise, and there at eye-level, not five metres away, were two aye-ayes making more aye-ayes while a rejected suitor slunk off. The female was grasping a vertical bamboo stem while the smaller male hung on doggedly below/behind her. They seemed bemused but unfazed by our presence, and were still blissfully conjoined when we left them 20 minutes later.'

If you don't get time to take the trail to Plage des Hollandais to see the fascinating 17th-century Dutch inscriptions carved on the rocks, then ask your boatman to stop by there when you leave. There is also a recent shipwreck.

Practicalities There is no accommodation on the island – you must camp in the thatched shelters which cost 5,000Ar per night with your own tent. The trails are well-made and vary from easy to moderately difficult. In rain – and it rains often –

THE BREAST-LEAPER

The breast-leaper is a small animal which attaches itself to the bark of trees and being of a greenish hue is not easily perceived; there it remains with its throat open to receive the flies, spiders and other insects that approach it, which it devours. This animal is described as having attached to the back, tail, legs, neck and the extremity of the chin, little paws or hooks like those at the end of a bat's wing with which it adheres to whatever it attaches itself in such a manner as if it were really glued. If a native happens to approach the tree where it hangs, it instantly leaps upon his naked breast, and sticks so firmly that in order to remove it, they are obliged, with a razor, to cut away the skin also.

Samuel Copland, History of the Island of Madagascar, 1822

the paths are slippery and it can be pretty unpleasant. Permits are purchased at the park office on the island; for prices see page 72.

Experienced English-speaking guides cost 35,000Ar/day plus 10,000Ar for a night walk. Particularly recommended are Ursula, Seraphine, Armand, Felix (bird specialist) and Paul (for plants). There are less qualified guides for about half this price but they don't normally speak English.

Boats can be arranged through hotels and tour operators in Maroantsetra. The crossing takes about 30 minutes and costs 35,000–100,000Ar return per person depending on the size of the group.

MASOALA PENINSULA Masoala (pronounced 'mash*wahl*') is one of the largest and most diverse areas of virgin rainforest in Madagascar, and probably harbours the greatest number of unclassified species. The peninsula's importance was

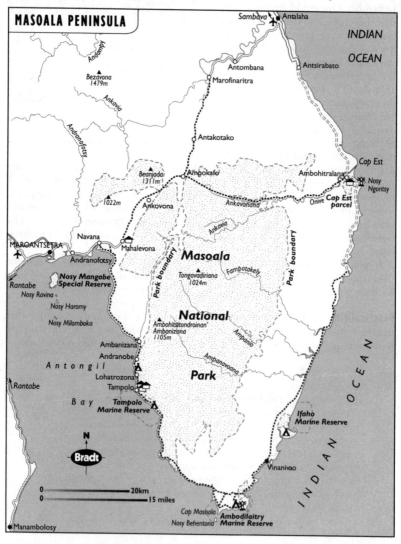

Matthew Hatchwell

One of the most fascinating episodes in the history of European presence in the Masoala region is the extraordinary story of Count Auguste de Benyowski, who established a French colony named Louisbourg on the site of modern-day Maroantsetra in 1774.

An aristocrat of mixed Hungarian, Slovak and Polish descent, Benyowski first arrived in Madagascar in 1772 at the culmination of a series of adventures that had taken him all the way across Russia to the Kamchatka Peninsula, down the Pacific coast of mainland Asia in a commandeered battleship, and finally across the Indian Ocean. Following a brief reconnoitre, Benyowski travelled on to France where he persuaded Louis XV to fund the creation of a new French colony at Maroantsetra which, he argued, could serve later as the basis for claiming Madagascar for France. Like every other early attempt to establish a permanent European settlement in Madagascar, the enterprise was a failure. Benyowski returned to France in 1776, where he met the famous American scientist and diplomat Benjamin Franklin, who inspired him to sail to the New World where he played a minor role in the American War of Independence against the British. Ten years later, he returned to Madagascar with American backing and was killed by French troops after establishing a trading station near Cap Est across the Masoala Peninsula from Maroantsetra.

All traces of Benyowski's original colony have been lost, but at least one 19th-century traveller observed finding a stone engraved with the names of some of Benyowski's fellow colonists at a second settlement which they established inland to escape the ravages of malaria. On Nosy Mangabe, many traces remain of European occupation in the 17th and 18th centuries, when first the Dutch and later the French established slave-trading stations there to supply labourers for their colonies elsewhere in the region. It is unknown which of these date from Benyowski's day, although one of the main tourist trails on the island retraces an earlier path complete with stone steps which he must have used when he established a quarantine station on the island. Many European sailors did not survive the rigours of their long sea journeys and are buried on Nosy Mangabe. One, a Dutchman named Willem Cornelisz Schouten, is famous as the navigator of the first European fleet to round the southern tip of South America, which he named after his native village in the Netherlands: Hoorn.

We know too that Nosy Mangabe was one of the first sites in Madagascar settled by humans when they first arrived more than 1,500 years ago. Another historical site worth visiting on the island is an enormous boulder at the Plage des Hollandais where Dutch sailors left carved messages during the 1600s. A few decades later, Antongil Bay and nearby Ile Sainte Marie became infamous to sailors as the strongholds of pirates such as Henry Avery and James Plantain. Traces of many of these eras can still be seen in the Masoala region. Others remain to be rediscovered!

Summarised from Masoala: The Eye of the Forest *(see page 418).*

12

recognised by the French back in 1927 when they created a small reserve there, but independent Madagascar was swift to remove the protection in 1964. However, 230,000ha has now been set aside as a national park.

Visitors should be warned that logging and clearance for agriculture still persists (see box on page 302) and maps of the peninsula tend to be deceptively green. That said, there are still large expanses of virgin forest along with stunning beaches of golden sand dotted with eroded rocks. Some parts of the peninsula, seen on a sunny day, can arguably be described as the most beautiful in Madagascar.

The wildlife is equally stunning. You will need to work for it, but nevertheless the opportunity to see red ruffed lemur in its only habitat, helmet and Bernier's vangas, scaly ground-roller and other rare endemic birds plus a host of reptiles and invertebrates is not to be missed.

Switzerland's Zoo Zürich has established a link with Masoala and finances development projects to encourage conservation. Their Masoala Kely exhibit – an 11,000m² indoor replica rainforest at their Zürich zoo – is well worth visiting (*www.zoo.ch/masoala*) – see box below.

How to visit Masoala National Park (e *infos@masoala.org; www.masoala.org*)

Unless you're up for some serious trekking, Masoala can be reached from Maroantsetra only by boat (1½–2 hours). For independent travellers, finding a safe but affordable vessel is the main difficulty. The trip should be made as early in the morning as possible to avoid rough seas. It may be possible to get a local cargo boat to Ambanizana, Andranobe or Lohatrozona, but they don't run every day. If you are staying in one of the Masoala lodges the boat transfer will be part of the package, otherwise you will need to make arrangements through one of Maroantsetra's tour operators.

For recommended guides see page 298. Park permits should be purchased in Maroantsetra; prices are on page 72.

MASOALA COMES TO ZURICH   *Janet Mears*

A unique ecosystem project has recently come to fruition at Zoo Zürich in Switzerland and is well worth a visit. With input from the Wildlife Conservation Society and Masoala National Park, Zoo Zürich is now home to the Masoala Biome, some 11,000m² of Madagascar rainforest. The brainchild of zoo director Dr Alex Rübel, the idea was first conceived in 1992. The biome, known as Masoala Kely, gives an impressive snapshot of the Malagasy rainforest and has really captured the natural relationships between the tropical plant and animal worlds.

There are approximately a hundred different plant and tree species, with 55% of the trees being endemic to Madagascar. About 20% of the 17,000 trees, shrubs and plants in the exhibit were brought in directly from a specially established nursery in Madagascar while others were located in various botanical gardens around the world. With a temperature of 26°C and 80% humidity, there are plants in flower year-round.

About 30 species of Malagasy animals, reptiles and birds live in the biome, including a superb group of Aldabra giant tortoises – a species now extinct in Madagascar. As in the real rainforest, you need to use your ears and eyes as you wander between lush green-fringed pathways with the occasional glint of water from the streams running through to lakes. A rustling overhead gives notice that flying foxes are on the move. Then the tiniest of movements on a traveller's palm shows up a large day gecko, slowly making his way along a frond, which takes your eye to a chameleon sitting silent and stationary a few feet away. And, suddenly, a cacophony of noise from deep in the forest disturbs the whispering conversation of the viewing public as four red ruffed lemurs chase each other out onto the branches above the path. Round bright eyes staring out of dark faces, they look at us, realise we are not a threat, and then run up and down the trees, onto a fallen branch before disappearing back into the forest. Magical.

In Madagascar an area of rainforest as large as the entire Masoala Kely biome is destroyed every five minutes. This is a project that is helping to stop the destruction.

See *www.zoo.ch* and *www.masoala.ch*.

Where to stay Tent shelters cost 7,000Ar per night. While camping is popular and gives instant access to the rainforest, there are three lodges that allow a more comfortable stay, all near Tampolo, arguably the most picturesque beach in Madagascar. The orange-gold sand is backed by the dark green of the rainforest; fresh water runs down from the hillsides into the sea, and comet orchids shine like stars against the dark eroded rocks. You can book through Rakotovazaha (Maroa Tours), Relais de Masoala or at the lodges' Maroantsetra offices.

Masoala Forest Lodge (5 canvas bungalows) \ 22 261 14; e mea@moov.mg; www.masoalaforestlodge.com. An upmarket South African/Swiss-owned camp with swish African safari-style tents. The furnished tents under thatched shelters are on hard-wood decks. Toilets & bathrooms with hot water are in separate huts. Excursions include kayak trips, snorkelling, rainforest walks & village visits. €€€€–💶

Tampolodge m 033 11 338 70/032 40 217 98; e tampolodge@yahoo.fr; www.masoalamadagascar.com &

http://tampolodge.marojejy.com. Maroantsetra office near Coco Beach. This Italian-owned collection of rustic huts boasts a superb location at Tampolo. Fairly basic accommodation; excellent food. €€€€

Chez Arol Ecolodge (9 bungalows) m 032 40 889 02/033 12 902 77; e masoala@free.fr; http://arollodge.free.fr. Maroantsetra office near Coco Beach. Comfortable palm-thatched huts, mostly en suite, set back from the beach. Fairly simple: cold water, 3hrs electricity each eve & solar oven. Camping permitted (3,000Ar/person). Treks & excursions organised. Canopy viewing tower in the forest. €€€

CAP EST The most easterly point of Madagascar, Cap Est is gradually opening up to adventurous travellers. It can be accessed via boat and on foot from Maroantsetra or Antalaha. It takes about three hours to reach the town nearest to the cape, **Ambodirafia**, from Antalaha by *taxi-brousse*, including two river crossings by ferry.

The littoral forest inland from Cap Est is part of Masoala National Park and an excellent place to see the insectivorous Masoala pitcher plant. Cap Est is also the closest access point on the coast to the impressive Bevontsira Waterfall, two to three days' walk inland towards Maroantsetra. Avoid hiking during periods of high rainfall because river crossings may be a problem.

Where to stay

Résidence du Cap (5 bungalows) m 032 04 539 05. Once an upmarket hotel, it was virtually destroyed by the cyclones of 2004, then rebuilt only to be wiped out by another cyclone 3 years later. Impressively they are again open for business & no

doubt praying there's truth in the saying 'third time lucky'. €€

Voyageur (16 bungalows) A straightforward setup of huts with beds, mosquito nets & buckets for washing. No electricity. €

MAROANTSETRA TO ANTALAHA THE ADVENTUROUS WAY Guided treks offered from tour operators in Maroantsetra include to Antalaha (four days), to Cap Est (six days), and to Andapa (eight days). It is also possible to hike right round the coast of the peninsula. You will need the relevant FTM map (number 4), best bought in Tana. As most of these routes pass through parts of the national park, you are obliged to take a guide and buy a park permit.

Maroantsetra to Antalaha: across the neck of the peninsula I have heard mixed reports of this five-day hike. The distance is 152km, and in the heat it is very strenuous. Considering that you are mainly passing through secondary forest and cultivated areas, it doesn't attract me much, but most readers report it to be an enjoyable trek with plenty of friendly people to meet along the way.

This is the route – Day 1: Maroantsetra to Mahalevona, the village beyond Navana, which is described under *Local excursions* on page 296. A pleasant 5km walk. Day 2: Mahalevona to Ankovona. The track climbs into the mountains and there

Toamasina and the Northeast   MAROANTSETRA AND THE MASOALA PENINSULA

12

are rivers to cross. Day 3: Ankovona to Ampokafo. A long trek to Ampokafo which marks the halfway point. Very hilly and very beautiful, with lots of streams and orchids. The village has a small shop. Day 4: Ampokafo to Analampontsy. Less wild, but still orchids along the way. Most villages *en route* have shops. Day 5: Analampontsy to Antalaha. You emerge onto the road at the village of Marofinaritra, about 30km from Antalaha. From here you can get a *taxi-brousse* to Antalaha.

Via Cap Est A more scenic (but equally tough) route to Antalaha from Maroantsetra is via Cap Est. The route is the same as Maroantsetra–Antalaha as far as Ampokafo, then you turn east and climb 600m up a muddy slope into Masoala National Park.

Jeremy Sabel 'went in the dry season but it was raining constantly. If you don't mind leeches, slipping, falling, getting muddy and crossing rivers up to your chest,

---

ILLEGAL LOGGING
Derek Schuurman

The 2009 coup left a political vacuum which was swiftly exploited by loggers who began plundering protected areas for precious wood. The majority of this illegal activity took place in Masoala and Marojejy. In just a few months, at least 100,000 rosewood and ebony trees worth hundreds of millions of dollars were felled.

The logs, mostly destined to be shipped to China, begin their journey to the ports by being floated down rivers, but the density of the wood is such that every tree needs to be strapped to half a dozen lighter-weight species to prevent it from sinking. Further trees are cut just so the loggers can get access to the precious timber. Consequently total losses to the forests over the year must be in excess of a million trees.

Driven by demand in China, where the burgeoning middle class has developed a penchant for Ming-style rosewood furniture, a number of locals, including some hoteliers, snatched the opportunity to make a quick buck. Soon the Chinese mafia became involved, considerably increasing criminal activity and silencing those daring to speak out. Conservative estimates put the number of rosewood-laden shipping containers to flood out of Madagascar's east coast ports over the first year at around 1,500, but the reality may be many more.

Corrupt officials at all levels were implicated in the trade: export was legalised, several timber harvesters were given official licences and most who had been brought to justice mysteriously walked free. This political involvement is nothing new; in recent decades, illegal logging activity has peaked prior to elections, indicating this form of revenue is used to fund political campaigns.

International pressure, orchestrated by a global underground network of conservationists and others, focussed on the three shipping companies transporting the cargo. Faced with publicity of the controversial nature of their activities, two soon gave in, but French-owned Delmas continued. Under immense pressure, they too eventually agreed to stop, but were forced to resume exports by the transitional government who reportedly threatened to cancel all their other contracts in Madagascar.

Shipments carried on into 2010, but halted in April when a decree was finally signed by the deputy prime minister declaring that those cutting and exporting rosewood and ebony would be prosecuted. But alas the decree was not worth the paper it was written on, for barely a month after the morotorium came into force the prime minister authorised a new export of 79 containers of rosewood. This shipment left Madagascar with a Singapore-registered shipping company after the French embassy advised Delmas against accepting the contract.

then this is the hike for you. It's definitely not the option for those who just want a stroll and I recommend taking porters. You must have camping equipment, bring food and be prepared to hike for up to eight hours per day. I really enjoyed the experience, and even got to see the elusive fossa. The final day of the trip is a four-hour pirogue ride down the Ankavanana River to the village of Ambohitralalana. From here it is a 5km walk to the village of Ambodirafia which is on Cap Est. Here I visited a small portion of the national park which is separated from the rest and just 1km from Ambodirafia. I also saw freshwater turtles and many birds. The 40km north to Antalaha should only take three hours.'

Wybe Rood reports on his walk in the reverse direction: 'I did the trek in five days. Day 1 was in a pirogue and nice; Day 2 we hiked to Bizono, crossed the river about 20 times: waist-high water, slippery rocks. Bizono is a relatively new village, created for relocated forest dwellers. Then the hardest day involved another 20 times of river crossing. I'd recommend to bring shoes to protect your feet from the rocks, as well as hiking boots. The forest was a bit disappointing though. Most of the time you walk through parts that have been lived in. We saw no wildlife apart from geckos. The bit from Ampokafo to Maroantsetra was very pretty and relatively easy.'

Via Masoala Sebastian Bulmer and Jamie Gibbs did a variation of the Cap Est walk from Antalaha to Maroantsetra following the coast down to the tip of the peninsula. Here is their report: 'Walk from Ambodirafia to the southern tip of the peninsula; seven days, including one day off. Walking at a gentle pace, staying in villages along the way, empty beaches, mangrove swamps, cleared woodland and a little rainforest towards the end as well as the scars of previous cyclones. Plenty of rivers to ford, either with log bridges, pirogues or on foot. On entering villages the children tended to run away screaming. It seems their mothers tell them that if they misbehave they will be taken to market and sold to the *vazaha* who will cook and eat them! From Masoala village there is an irregular boat service to Maroantsetra, 10,000Ar per person, slow going and very heavily loaded. Visitors should budget for an additional few days whilst awaiting the boat.'

ANTALAHA AND BEYOND

ANTALAHA This prosperous, vanilla-financed town suffered devastating damage from cyclones Gafilo in 2004 and Indlala in 2007. In true Malagasy fashion it was swiftly rebuilt after each one.

Getting there and away The only easy way to get to Antalaha is by plane (the Air Mad office is on the seafront) or by road from the north. The alternatives are to trek across the peninsula from Maroantsetra, or come by sea (there are regular cargo boats from Maroantsetra and Toamasina).

Where to stay and eat

🏠 **Océan Momo** m 032 02 340 69; e momo@ moov.mg; www.ocean-momo.com. AC bungalows. Boycotted by some tour operators as a result of the owner's alleged involvement with illegal rosewood logging. €€€€

🏠 **Hazo Vola (Palissandre)** m 032 05 000 65. Upmarket with fridge, minibar, safe & TV. The owner of this hotel has also been implicated in logging. €€€€

🏠 **Vitasoa** m 032 40 765 74. A good-value hotel with hot water & good restaurant. €€

🏠 **Chez Nanie** m 032 40 051 89/032 02 232 51. Basic bungalows, right next to the sea opposite the pier. The more expensive ones have AC. €€

🏠 **Cocotier & Florida** are other inexpensive options. €–€€

✗ **Fleur de Lotus** A recommended Chinese restaurant.

✗ **Corail** French/Malagasy-owned. Good for b/fast & pizza.

Money and communications Antalaha has at least one good cybercafé (at the Kodak shop, 100Ar/minute), a post office and branches of the main banks (BFV, BNI and BOA) with ATMs.

Trekking and nature

Masoala trekking A Swiss-run organisation, Projet d'Analalava (*www.projet-analalava.com*), organises various treks in Masoala as well as Marojejy. They are in partnership with the tour operator PRIORI in Tana. Once in Antalaha you can contact the manager Mme Olga (m *032 04 340 27*) or the guide Ilderic (m *032 07 713 64*).

La Colline de Vinany This private reserve just off the main road after the bridge on the way into town is a botanical wonderland with gorgeous views of the river and Indian Ocean. The owner has established several villages in the area for recovered lepers and employs them in tree nurseries where they propagate seedlings for reforestation projects in Masoala.

CONTINUING NORTH The road from Antalaha to Sambava is in excellent condition. The journey takes 1½ hours.

SAMBAVA

The centre of the vanilla- and coconut-growing region, and an important area for cloves and coffee production, Sambava merits a stay of a couple of days. The town essentially comprises two very long, parallel streets. There is a good beach and a dramatic sea with, at times, huge – and dangerous – waves.

GETTING THERE AND AWAY Sambava has air connections with Tana, Toamasina and Maroantsetra (for current schedule see *www.airmadagascar.com*). The airport is not far from town: you can even walk it. The Air Mad office (⏰ *Mon–Fri 08.00–11.00 & 14.00–19.00*) is at the tourist end of town.

The town is accessible by good road from Iharana (Vohemar), taking approximately two hours. The *taxi-brousse* station is on the northwest outskirts, 30 minutes' walk from the market.

🏠 WHERE TO STAY AND EAT

🏠 **Mimi Hotel** (11 rooms) m 032 07 610 28/032 40 288 55; e mimi.hotel.resto@gmail.com; http://mimi-hotel.marojejy.com. Smart new en-suite rooms with balconies. Great restaurant. Experts in organising tours to Marojejy & Anjanaharibe-Sud. €€€

🏠 **Las Palmas** (6 bungalows & 2 rooms) \ 88 920 87; m 032 40 073 72; e las.palmas@laposte.net. A nicely-situated beachfront hotel. The rooms & some bungalows have AC. They organise excursions including to a nearby vanilla plantation. €€€

🏠 **Orchidea Beach II** (2 bungalows & 8 rooms) \ 88 923 24; m 032 04 383 77; e orchideabeach2@moov.mg. This replaced the original Orchidea Beach which was flattened by Cyclone Gafilo. Lovely beachfront hotel set in a beautifully planted garden, with an excellent

restaurant (big portions) & bar. Rooms have AC, balcony & en-suite bathrooms. €€–€€€

🏠 **Paradis** Only the top-price rooms have hot water, but all have a shower/bath & fan. It is above a disco, so ask for a 2nd-floor room if staying on Fri or Sat. Restaurant not recommended. €€–€€€

🏠 **Carrefour** (36 rooms) \ 88 920 60; f 88 923 22. Near the beach, with en-suite bathrooms, some with hot water & some with AC, TV & minibar. €€–€€€

🏠 **Cantonais** (8 rooms) A hotel in a quiet part of town. A range of rooms from cold shower only to en-suite toilet & hot shower; most with balcony. Good value. €–€€

🏠 **Chez l'Ambassadeur** m 032 02 113 47. A good backpacker place. €–€€

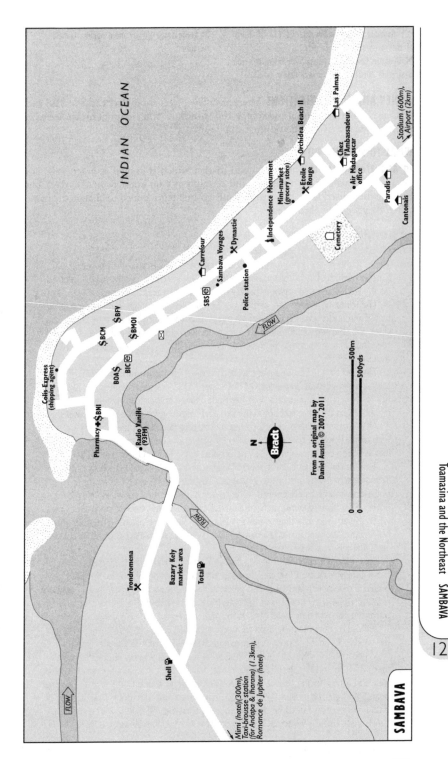

SAMBAVA

INDIAN OCEAN

Trondromena

Bazary Kely
market area

Shell

Total

*Mimi (hotel)(300m),
Taxi-brousse station
(for Andapa & Iharana) (1.3km),
Romance de Jupiter (hotel)*

FLOW

FLOW

FLOW

Colis Express
(shipping agent)

Pharmacy BNI

Radio Vanille
(93FM)

BCM

BFV

BMOI

BOA

BIC

BS

Carrefour

Sambava Voyages

Dynastie

Police station

Independence Monument

Mini-market
(grocery store)

Etoile
Rouge

Orchidea Beach II

Las Palmas

Chez
l'Ambassadeur

Air Madagascar
office

Paradis

Cantonais

Cemetery

*Stadium (600m),
Airport (2km)*

N

Bradt

From an original map by
Daniel Austin © 2007, 2011

0   500m
0   500yds

Romance de Jupiter m 032 04 633 89. North of the *taxi-brousse* station. €

✗ **Dynastie** Chinese restaurant with extensive menu & sizeable portions; open breezy dining area.

✗ **Etoile Rouge** Slightly more opulent Chinese restaurant.

MONEY AND COMMUNICATIONS There are a few places for internet access: **SBS** and **BIC** are both quite central and charge 100Ar/minute. You are spoilt for choice with banks: there are five in the centre.

WHAT TO SEE AND DO

In and around town There is a good market which is known as *bazary kely*, not because it's small or *kely* (it isn't – and certainly not on Tuesday, market day), but because there used to be two markets and no-one felt inclined to change the name when they were amalgamated.

VANILLA IN MADAGASCAR
Clare & Johan Hermans

Vanilla is the major foreign currency earner for Madagascar, which together with Réunion and the Comoros grows 80% of the world's crop. Its cultivation is centred on the eastern coastal region around Andapa, Antalaha and Sambava.

The climbing plants are grown supported on 1.5m-high moisture-retaining trunks and under ideal conditions take three years to mature. When they bloom the vines are checked on alternate days for open flowers to hand-pollinate. The pod then takes nine months to develop. Each 15–20cm pod will contain tens of thousands of tiny seeds.

They go to a processing plant to be prepared for the commercial market. First they are plunged into a cauldron of hot water (70°C) for two minutes and are kept hot for two days. During this time the pods change colour from green to chestnut brown. Next they are laid out in the sun each morning for three to four weeks.

After maturing, the pods are sorted by size and bundles of sorted pods are tied with raffia. They are checked for quality by sniffing and bending before being packed into wooden crates, with most of the product going to the US for use in ice cream.

The vanilla used in cultivation in Madagascar is *Vanilla planifolia* which originates from Mexico. It was brought to Madagascar by the French once the secret of hand-pollination had been discovered – the flower has no natural pollinator in its foreign home. The culinary and pharmaceutical use of vanilla dates back to pre-Aztec times when it was used as a drink or as an ingredient of a lotion against fatigue for those holding public office. Similarly a native Malagasy vanilla stem can be found for sale on Tana markets as a male invigorator.

Four different species of vanilla orchid occur naturally in Madagascar, most of them totally leafless. One can be seen on the roadside between Sambava and Antalaha resembling lengths of red-green tubing festooned over the scrub. Another is found in the spiny forest near Berenty. Most of the native species contain sap that burns the skin and their fruits contain too little vanillin to make cultivation economic.

Although conventionally used for cooking, vanilla is also an insect repellent, and the wonderful-smelling pods can be put in drawers to scent clothing or linen.

When cooking you can reuse the pods for as long as you remember to retrieve them – wash and dry them after each use. Vanilla does wonders for tea or coffee (just add a pod to the teapot or coffee filter, or grind a dried pod with the coffee beans) and can be boiled with milk to make a yummy hot drink (add a dash of brandy) or custard. Put some beans in your sugar tin and the flavour will be absorbed. Vanilla adds a subtle flavour to chicken or duck, rice or... whatever you fancy.

This is one of the main vanilla-producing areas of Madagascar and a tour of the Lopat vanilla factory will open your eyes to the laborious process of preparing one of the country's main exports.

North of Sambava is a beautiful beach with safe swimming.

Excursions further afield Many of the hotels can organise excursions, as can the tour operator **Sambava Voyages** (\ *88 921 10*).

River Bemarivo A pleasant do-it-yourself excursion is up the Bemarivo (not possible at the end of the dry season). Take a *taxi-brousse* to Nosiarina on the road north and look for a pirogue to take you on the five-hour journey upriver to Amboahangibe. It's a relaxing and picturesque trip.

It is also possible to find a cargo boat to Amboahangibe. This is quite a large village with several grocery stores and places to stay (look for the sign '*misy chambres*' – 'rooms available') which fill up with vanilla-pickers during the harvest. As an alternative to taking a boat back, it is a pleasant hike along the river, with some interesting tombs.

CONTINUING NORTH Two hours further up the good road is the next town of importance, Iharana (Vohemar) – see *Chapter 14*, page 344.

ANDAPA AND AREA

Andapa lies in a fertile and beautiful region, a 105km drive southwest of Sambava, where much of north Madagascar's rice is grown. This is also a major coffee-producing area. To help facilitate export, the EEC provided funding to build an all-weather road in the 1960s. It has been resurfaced subsequently and remains in good condition. The journey to Andapa is really beautiful, with the jagged peaks of the Marojejy Massif to the right, and bamboo and palm-thatch villages by the roadside. The journey takes three to four hours by *taxi-brousse*.

The town itself is one of my favourites in Madagascar. The relative wealth of the area shows in the goods available in the many shops, but because it sees relatively few tourists – and only the very best sort (those willing to hike up steep slopes in pouring rain) – the people are exceptionally friendly and easygoing. It is also wonderfully compact, which comes as a relief after straggly Sambava, and cool. Even if you are not doing the major trek in Marojejy there are numerous wonderful walks in the area.

 WHERE TO STAY AND EAT

🏠 **Riziky** \ 88 072 31; m 032 40 214 22; e riziky@yahoo.fr; http://riziky.marojejy.com. Quiet bungalows in Ambendrana, on the Sambava side of town. Rooms to suit all budgets, all with hot water & comfy en-suite bungalows with TV. €–€€€€

🏠 **Soaland Chalet** Rue Ramandraibe; m 032 40 118 82; e flavienne@marojejy.com. New guesthouse with nice rooms. €€€

🏠 **Beanana** (10 rooms) \ 88 070 47/072 20; m 032 40 226 10; e hsbeanana@yahoo.fr; http://beanana.marojejy.com. Rooms are grouped round a courtyard & overlook a beautiful garden. Excellent service & value for money. €€

🏠 **Vatosoa** \ 88 070 78; m 032 02 603 89. This once-popular hotel is starting to become run down, but is still comfortable with en-suite rooms & hot water. Superb food. €€

✕ **Maroantsetra** A mediocre eatery opposite the Vatosoa.

WHAT TO SEE AND DO Visit **Pièces Auto** in Andapa for help and advice on visiting the region (see *http://travel.marojejy.com*).

This is a wonderful area for wandering. At every step you see something interesting from the people or wildlife perspective (in the latter category butterflies, snakes and chameleons) and the scenery is consistently beautiful.

Refer to the wall map in Vatosoa hotel to plan a variety of day hikes. Almost any dirt road through the villages would make for an enjoyable walk watching the locals go about their daily lives.

PROTECTED AREAS

Marojejy National Park and Anjanaharibe-Sud Special Reserve are two of Madagascar's most exciting wilderness areas, in what are perhaps the most remote pristine rainforests remaining.

ANJANAHARIBE-SUD SPECIAL RESERVE (\ 88 070 27; e info@marojejy.com; http://anjanaharibe.marojejy.com) This comprises 28,624ha of mountainous rainforest. The name means 'Place of the Great God' and although only 20km southwest of Andapa, it is appropriately difficult to reach. The wildlife is not easy to see since it was hunted until recently, but repays the effort. This is the most northerly range of the indri, which here occurs in a very dark form – almost black. The silky sifaka is also found here, but you are more likely to see the troops of white-fronted brown lemurs. Birders will be on the lookout for four species of ground-roller.

Even without seeing any mammals it is a most rewarding visit, with an easy-to-follow (though rugged) trail through primary forest to some hot springs. The reserve is also a vital element in the prosperity of the area. The Lokoho River,

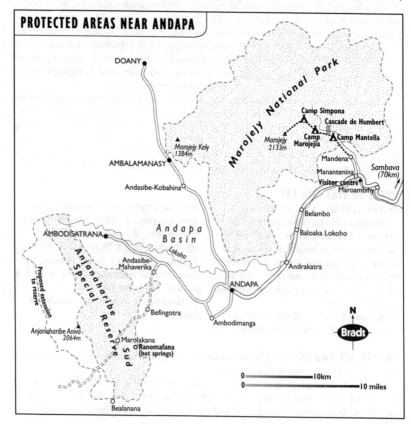

PROTECTED AREAS NEAR ANDAPA

We set off from the village of Ambodihasina and, having crossed a deep river, we climbed fairly steeply, crossing a 1,200m ridge that is largely clothed in primary forest. The path was absolutely incredible – only ever wide enough for one person, but in some places eroded up to 5m into the soil, so that the tree roots were above our heads. It was also a great place to see Malagasy life – people passed us carrying rice, chickens, bicycles, suitcases, and even driving zebu along the narrow paths. Eventually, we crossed a large river by a pirogue ferry, then followed it downstream for a while. It was fast and furious, with many rapids. On the other side was the northern end of the Anjanaharibe mountain chain, which must be entirely inaccessible.

The path eventually left the river and ascended a ridge of more open, upland heath vegetation. This gave us superb views towards the forested mountains of Anjanaharibe. We reached a summit of 1,500m, before descending to the open, agricultural valley of Ambalaromba. This is quite a large town, with most of the houses being built of clay bricks rather than wood. I don't think they had ever seen a foreigner before, and so the whole town clustered around me as one of my colleagues talked to the mayor!

Next day we set off to walk south to another town on the western side of the mountain range. This path was much less well frequented, and we often had to clamber over logs or find a way round an obstacle. For much of the day, we were walking on hills with fairly open vegetation, affording us wonderful views of the emerald forests and sparkling waterfalls. Towards the end of the day, high on a ridge, we entered an area of primary forest, and just as we did so we saw a family of brown lemurs in the trees. We descended, sliding on tree roots and treacherous muddy chutes, and constantly stopping to flick off leeches! Eventually we emerged into a more populous, agricultural area with many small villages, and finally arrived at the town, on what was once the main road from Bealanana to Andapa. At Marolakana, where the road is broken because a bridge has failed, we were picked up by one of our drivers – the road is only just passable in a 4x4. To complete the trek, one could walk out to Ambodipont, towards Andapa.

which rises in Anjanaharibe-Sud, is the only source of water for the largest irrigated rice producer in the country.

Visiting the reserve The normal route is from the east, via Andasibe-Mahaverika and Befingotra, along the now very poor road.

The trailhead is indicated with a rusty, barely legible WWF board marking 'Piste Touristique'. It takes about an hour to reach the campsite and a further hour to the hot springs. Once there, your efforts are worthwhile. There are three springs: one is too hot to keep your feet in but the others – one shallow and one deep – merge with cool stream water and make the temperature much more pleasant.

If you are looking for a serious challenge you can follow the route of Kathryn Goodenough, an impressively fit geologist whom I met whizzing up Marojejy in 2006. Her account is in the box above.

MAROJEJY NATIONAL PARK (\88 070 27; *www.marojejy.com*) This stunningly beautiful national park was established in 1998 and designated a UNESCO World Heritage Site in 2007. You need to be reasonably fit – and able to tolerate the heat – to enjoy it fully, but there are few other areas in Madagascar to compare to Marojejy for awesome splendour and the feeling of ultimate wilderness. Imposing mountains and craggy cliffs are surrounded by lush rainforests full of wildlife. Having made a return

Toamasina and the Northeast   PROTECTED AREAS   12

visit in 2006 after being disastrously lost there in 1976, I can echo Dylan Lossie who says: 'Marojejy is how I once imagined Madagascar as a child, long before I first went there: exotic, rugged, isolated and prehistorical!' And then there is the wildlife. This is the best place in Madagascar to see the silky sifaka, one of the five rarest primates in the world, and the helmet vanga. The panther chameleons are as I remember from 30 years ago – huge, and outrageously coloured – and there are leaf-tailed geckos, frogs galore, huge millipedes, wonderful spiders... and lots of leeches.

☞ **WARNING!** Marojejy is a vulnerable area and cannot support large numbers of visitors. There is just one path to the top of the mountain which is suffering from the booted feet of tourists. The maximum number of beds is 17 (including guides and porters) so the park cannot accept large groups. Because you will be expected to share a hut, a group of three or four friends is ideal.

Organising your visit
My two companions and I put our arrangements into the hands of Eric Mathieu (m *032 40 118 81;* e *info@marojejy.com*), a charming Frenchman living in Andapa with his wife Flavienne. He did a great job organising the guides, cook, porters, food and transport from Sambava. You can also just turn up at the visitor centre mid-way between Sambava and Andapa. One reader wrote in especially to sing the praises of 'Primo the cook and his fantastic banana flambées'.

There are three 'camps' at different altitudes, each with its own distinctive flora and fauna. Individually they comprise four comfortable bunk beds in wooden chalets with a shared shower and flush toilet, and separate cooking/eating area. Marojejy requires advance planning. You will need proper hiking boots, and I found a hiking pole very useful. Pack warm clothing for the nights and a bandana to mop your streaming face during the very hot days. Don't forget a good headlight torch and binoculars. If you are travelling on your own you would be safer to bring a tent or team up with other travellers.

The best times to visit are April to May and September to December when there's less rain.

Visitor centre
The staff here are helpful and the place is well set up for visitors. It sells a series of excellent leaflets on the flora and fauna of the massif. Coming from Sambava it's 200m before Manantenina on the left side of the road.

In the national park
The first part of the trip can be done by vehicle. It's a lovely walk, however, taking you through rice paddies and cultivated areas. It can also be very hot. After 2.7km you arrive at the village of Mandena, a delightful place with a private school (!) full of friendly, well-behaved children. Then it's a further 2.9km to the park entrance. This is the best stretch for finding panther chameleons so keep an eye on the track-side bushes. At the park entrance there's a good map showing the trails, and a chance for a rest under a shelter. It's 4.3km through rainforest to the first camp. From road to camp will take four to five hours.

Camp Mantella (425m) is situated in the heart of superb lowland rainforest. There are 17 beds and a nice eating area. A night walk is particularly rewarding, revealing *Brookesia* chameleons, *Uroplatus* and many frogs.

Camp Marojejia (750m) is an hour from the first camp, and lies at the transition between lowland and mid-altitude rainforest opposite an amazing outcrop of rock cloaked in rainforest. This peak, called Ambatotsondrona, or 'Leaning Rock', is one of the most spectacular views in Madagascar. To eat your breakfast watching the changing light on its flank is perfection, which is a good thing because the path beyond this camp is very, very tough. The compensation is that the areas above Camp Marojejia offer the best chance of seeing a silky sifaka.

Few classes of invertebrates elicit more disgust than leeches. Perhaps some facts about these extraordinarily well-adapted animals will give them more appeal.

Terrestrial leeches such as those found in Madagascar are small (1–2cm long) and find their warm-blooded prey by vibrations and odour. Suckers at each end enable the leech to move around in a series of loops and to attach itself to a leaf by its posterior while seeking its meal with the front end. It has sharp jaws and can quickly – and painlessly – bite through the skin and start feeding. When it has filled its digestive tract with blood the leech drops off and digests its meal. This process can take several months since leeches have pouches all along their gut to hold as much blood as possible – up to ten times their own weight. The salivary glands manufacture an anticoagulant which prevents the blood clotting during feeding and digestion. This is why leech wounds bleed so spectacularly. Leeches also inject an anaesthetic so you don't feel them biting.

Leeches are hermaphrodites but still have pretty exciting sex lives. To consummate their union they need to exchange packets of sperm. This is done either the conventional way via a leechy penis or by injection, allowing the sperm to make its way through the body tissues to find and fertilise the eggs.

Readers who are disappointed with the small size of Malagasy leeches will be interested to hear that an expedition to French Guiana in the 1970s discovered the world's largest leech: at full stretch 45cm long!

Wherever there are blood vessels there are leeches, and travellers compete for the worst leech story. Here's one from Frankie Kerridge, a researcher in the southeast rainforest: 'A highlight was my guide getting a leech on his eyeball. Mega shouting and screaming. Got it off by killing it (slowly) with a tobacco leaf.'

Reader T T Terpening had an equally gruesome experience: a leech in his nose. This he dealt with thus: 'I pushed on my left nostril with my finger and blew hard. Some blood, a little snot, and a big glossy leech flew out into the rainforest litter.' But then: 'My guide says a dab of tobacco will keep my respiratory system leech-free for the remainder of the hike. I take a scoop and plug both nostrils. Immediately I feel dizzy and sick and my nose burns. I brace myself against a tree and my head clears. My nose definitely still feels weird. Over the next minute I come to the realisation that another leech is travelling the length of my sinus. "Probably running away from the tobacco," says my guide helpfully. Within 12 hours the leech has run its course, journeying the length of my nose, then sinus to my throat where I eventually swallow it. Most of Madagascar's wildlife is found nowhere else on earth. Thank God!'

See page 115 for advice on dealing with leeches.

Camp Simpona (1,250m) is a welcome sight. There are just eight beds here, and room for only one tent. The forest is more stunted because of the altitude, but there are still silky sifakas and birds such as rufous-headed ground-roller and yellow-bellied sunbird-asity. A viewing platform shortly before the camp offers a breathtaking vista.

The camp is used to facilitate treks to Marojejy peak at 2,132m, a four- to five-hour climb. Not much harder than the previous day, but you need good weather and that's pretty rare. If you're in luck then the view from the top is awesome and the feeling of space and wilderness unmatched.

Visitors to Madagascar are often pleasantly surprised to discover its cuisine is as unique and varied as its ecology. The culinarily adventuresome can experience new dishes, sweets, snacks and food traditions in each region. In the highlands, *laoka* (a catch-all word for whatever accompanies the obligatory mound of rice) are often vegetables, pulses or animal proteins in tomato-based sauces flavoured with pork, while coastal dishes reflect even more variety, adding coconut sauces and a wider range of seafood. The historic influence of Islam in coastal areas means zebu meat may be substituted for pork (often *fady*).

In the north, steak or poultry *au poivre vert* (creamy green peppercorn sauce) and poultry or seafood *à la vanille* (vanilla sauce) blend French and local influences. In Mahajanga the specialty is *khimo* (curried ground beef), while near Morondava *kabaro* (lima beans with curry or coconut) are a filling alternative to meat. On the coast you can try treats like *godro-godro* (cardamom-coconut pudding), *boatamo* (coconut cookies) or *mokary* (a coconut-flavoured *mofo gasy*; see below), or spice up your dishes with tart *lasary* – a chutney-like condiment of lemon, mango or papaya sold in a colourful array of recycled bottles at roadside stands. While in the highlands, you can try other *lasary* made of tomato (*voatabia*), peanuts (*voanjo*), mango (*manga*) or vegetables (*legioma*) in a curried vinaigrette, or tuck into a bowl of scrumptious, peanut-flavoured *voanjobory* (bambara groundnuts with pork).

Under the 19th-century Merina monarchy, New Year was celebrated with rich and distinctive dishes. Among these were *tatao* (boiled rice, honey and milk) and *jaka* (beef conserved in clay pots for a year). The main seven dishes have become iconic of highland cuisine: *romazava* (beef stew), *varanga* (fried slivered beef) and *sesika* (a sort of poultry blood sausage), as well as pork with *ravitoto* (shredded cassava leaves), *vorivorin-kena* (beef tripe), *amalona* (stuffed eel) and *vorontsiloza* (turkey) – a staple of highland celebrations, especially weddings and Christmas.

Certain foods are also traditionally associated with specific life events. At a *famadihana* it is customary to eat *vary be menaka* – rice prepared with beef and lots of fatty pork. After the birth of a baby, thinly-sliced strips of pan-fried smoked beef called *kitoza* are traditionally prepared to help the new mother regain her strength. She may also be offered *ro-patsa*, a bouillon made of potato and tiny dried shrimps believed to aid in nursing – although its reputation for restoring health and vitality makes it a popular home remedy for any ill.

Madagascar's array of doughnut-like treats is surprisingly diverse in flavour and texture. In the highlands, rice is used to make sweet *mofo gasy*, savoury *ramanonaka* and half-sweet *mofo grefy*, as well as rice flour doughnut rings (*menakely*) or balls (*mofo baolina*). Savory ones are made from chopped greens (*mofo anana*), chilli sauce (*mofo sakay*), various veggies or prawns. The more common sweet ones are made from baguette (*makasaoka*), banana (*mofo akondro*), pumpkin (*mofo voatavo*), sweetcorn (*mofo katsaka*), sweet potato (*mofo bageda*), cassava (*mofo mangahazo*) or yam (*bokoboko*).

Most *laoka* involve some sort of sauce or juice to flavour the rice. You can find almost anything curried (*au curry*) or in coconut milk (*au coco* or *voanio*), and if no sauce is specified then expect something mild and tomato-based. *Ritra* means 'simmered in its own juices'. Green and red *sakay* (chilli sauce) are usually available on the side to spice things up to your taste. You will find more basic food vocabulary for decoding Malagasy menus on pages 101 and 413. *Mazotoa homana!*

Carrie Antal has worked throughout Madagascar and brings the delights of Malagasy cuisine to the world through online cookery videos: www.youtube.com/lemurbaby.

above left   The weirdest of all lemurs, the aye-aye was once believed to be a type of squirrel (DA) page 57

above right   Eastern grey bamboo lemur. Bamboo lemurs are the smallest lemurs active by day (DA) page 59

left   Diademed sifaka, Vakôna, Andasibe (DA) page 259

below   Golden-crowned sifaka mother and baby. Fewer than 4,000 individuals are thought to remain in a tiny area in the northeast (NG/NHPA) page 343

above left Ring-tailed lemurs live in large social groups with female leaders. They spend more time on the ground than other lemurs so are easy to see (NG/NHPA) page 58

above The brown mouse lemur belongs to a group of 18 mouse lemurs, including the world's smallest primate which weighs a mere 30g (DA) page 60

left The largest living lemur is the indri. This species cannot survive in captivity so conservation of wild populations is particularly critical (NG) page 59

opposite

top A Striped civet or *fanaloka* (DA) page 64

middle upper left Highland streaked tenrec (DA) page 64

middle lower left Commerson's leaf-nosed bat (DA) page 62

middle right The fossa is Madagascar's largest predator. This one is captive at Tsimbazaza Zoo (DA) page 64

bottom Humpback whale fluke. Whale-watching is a popular activity in Malagasy waters from July to September (NG/NPL) page 320

top left   The aptly named tomato frog burrows underground to survive dry periods (DA)

top right   White-spotted reed frog (DA)

above   Twig-mimic snakes have extraordinary 'noses'. This is a female; the male's nose is sharply pointed (HB)

left   *Stenophis arctifasciatus* snake (DA)

above	Giant Madagascar day gecko (DA)
above right	Leaf-tailed geckos (*Uroplatus*) are masters of camouflage, almost impossible to see by day (DA)
right	*Brookesia vadoni* chameleon (PN/FLPA)
below right	Panther chameleon (DA)
bottom left	The ploughshare is the world's rarest tortoise with fewer than 200 left in the wild. A captive-breeding programme aims to reverse the population decline (DA) page 380
bottom right	The blade chameleon showcases one of many varied and spectacular 'noses' in the chameleon world (DA) page 263

left   **Madagascar paradise flycatcher in nest** (DA) page 244

below   **Grey-headed lovebirds** (NG/NHPA)

bottom left   **Madagascar malachite kingfisher** (DA)

bottom right   **Common sunbird asity** (NG/NHPA)

top   **Helmet vanga** (NG/NPL)

above   **Long-tailed ground-roller** (NG/NHPA)

right   The Madagascar fish eagle is critically endangered with a population of fewer than 100 breeding pairs (NG/NHPA)

below   **Giant coua** (NG/NHPA)

above left	**Pair of giant millipedes** (DA)
above right	**Comet moth** (NG/NPL) page 47
left	**Day-flying *Euchromia* moth** (DA)
below left	**Flatid leaf bugs: adult and nymphs** (NG/NPL)
below	**Rainbow milkweed locusts mating** (DA)
bottom right	**Giraffe-necked weevil male** (NG/NHPA) page 46

Toamasina and the Northeast

12

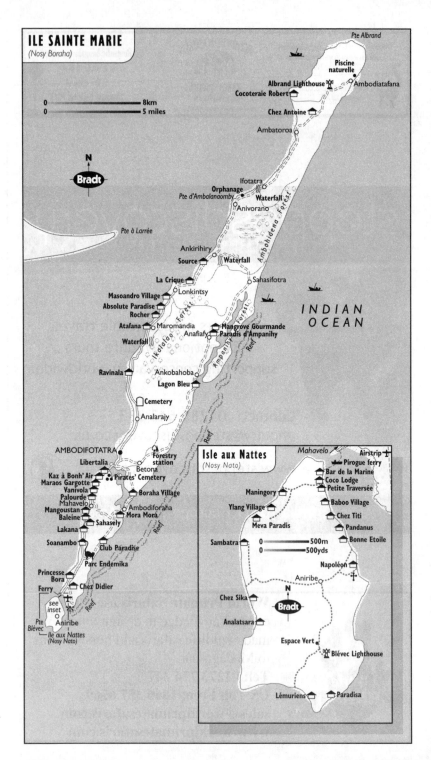

ILE SAINTE MARIE
(Nosy Boraha)

Pte Albrand

Piscine
naturelle

Albrand Lighthouse ⚓ Ambodiatafana
Cocoteraie Robert

Chez Antoine

Ambatoroa

0 ─────── 8km
0 ─────── 5 miles

N

Bradt

Ifotatra
Orphanage
Pte d'Ambalanaomby   Waterfall
Anivorano

Ambohdena forest

Pte à Larrée

Ankirihiry
Source   Waterfall

Sahasifotra

La Crique

Masoandro Village   Lonkintsy
Absolute Paradise
Rocher
Atafana   Maromandia
Anafiafy   Mangrove Gourmande
Waterfall   Paradis d'Ampanihy

INDIAN
OCEAN

Reef

Ikalalao forest

Ampanihy forest

Ravinala   Ankobahoba
Lagon Bleu

Cemetery

Analarajy

AMBODIFOTATRA
Libertalia   Forestry
Betona   station
Kaz à Bonh' Air   Pirates' Cemetery
Maraos Gargotte
Vanivola   Boraha Village
Palourde
Mahavelo   Ambodiforaha
Mangoustan   Mora Mora
Baleine
Lakana   Sahasely
Soanambo
Club Paradise
Parc Endemika

Princesse
Bora
Ferry   Chez Didier
see
inset
Pte
Blévec   Aniribe
Ile aux Nattes
(Nosy Nato)

Isle aux Nattes
(Nosy Nato)

Mahavelo   Airstrip
Pirogue ferry
Bar de la Marine
Maningory   Coco Lodge
Petite Traversée
Ylang Village   Baboo Village
Chez Titi
Meva Paradis
Pandanus
Sambatra   0 ─────── 500m   Bonne Etoile
0 ─────── 500yds
Napoléon
Aniribe
Chez Sika

N

Bradt

Analatsara

Espace Vert
Blévec Lighthouse

Lémuriens   Paradisa

Ile Sainte Marie (Nosy Boraha)

Here is a cliché of a tropical island with endless deserted beaches overhung by coconut palms, bays protected from sharks by coral reefs, hills covered with luxuriant vegetation, and a relative absence of unsightly tourist development. Most travellers love it: 'As soon as we saw the island from the air, we were ready to ditch our travel plans and spend the rest of our trip nestled in paradise. Everything about the island is intoxicating: the smell of cloves drying in the sun, the taste of coco rum and the warmth of the sea.' In addition to this heady, holiday atmosphere, Ile Sainte Marie is the best place in Madagascar for whale-watching.

The island, due east of Soanierana-Ivongo, is 50km long and 7km at its widest point. The only significant town is **Ambodifotatra**; other small villages comprise bamboo and palm huts. The island is almost universally known as Sainte Marie – few use its Malagasy name: Nosy Boraha. Sainte Marie unfortunately – or perhaps fortunately, given the dangers of overdevelopment – has a far less settled weather pattern than its island rival, Nosy Be. Cyclones strike regularly, although not usually with the ferocity of Cyclone Ivan which destroyed three-quarters of the island's buildings in 2008. At any time of year expect several days of rain and wind, but interspersed with calm sunny weather. The best months for a visit tend to be June and mid-August to December, but good weather is possible anytime.

Note that on Sainte Marie, in addition to the daily *vignette touristique*, there is a one-off tax of 10,000Ar per person (payable at your first hotel).

HISTORY

The origin of the Malagasy name is obscure. It means either 'island of Abraham' or 'island of Ibrahim', with probable reference to an early Semitic culture. It was named Ile Sainte Marie by European sailors when the island became the major hideout of pirates in the Indian Ocean. From the 1680s to around 1720 these pirates dominated the seas around Africa. There was a Welshman (David Williams), Englishmen (Thomas White, John Every and William Kidd) and an American (Thomas Tew) among a Madagascar pirate population which, in its heyday, numbered nearly one thousand.

Later a Frenchman, Jean-Onésime Filet ('La Bigorne'), was shipwrecked on Sainte Marie while escaping the wrath of a jealous husband in Réunion. La Bigorne turned his amorous attentions with remarkable success to Princess Bety, daughter of King Ratsimilaho. Upon their marriage the happy couple received Nosy Boraha as a gift from the king, and the island was in turn presented to the mother country by La Bigorne (or rather, put under the protection of France by Princess Bety). Thus France gained its first piece of Madagascar in 1750.

GETTING THERE AND AWAY

BY AIR Air Mad flies every day from Tana and Toamasina to Sainte Marie. Flights are heavily booked, especially in July and August, so try to make your reservations well in advance. Air Mad's local office is in the north of Ambodifotatra (↘ 57 400 46/403 23; m 032 07 222 08; ⊕ Mon–Fri 07.30–11.30 & 14.30–17.00, Sat 08.00–10.30), down the side street opposite Hortensia hotel.

BY LAND/SEA Four companies (Dolphin, Cap Sainte Marie, Gasikara and Tropicana) run daily ferry services from Soanierana-Ivongo to Sainte Marie. The cheapest option is to take a *taxi-brousse* north from Toamasina to S-Ivongo and buy your ferry ticket there (about 60,000Ar). However, it is safer to buy a combination bus and ferry ticket in Toamasina. This way you don't risk missing the crossing if you get delayed, or turning up to find the ferry fully booked. The combined ticket costs around 100,000Ar one way or 180,000Ar return.

GETTING AROUND THE ISLAND

A limited *taxi-brousse* service runs up part of the west coast, but it's worth flagging down any vehicle; most will stop and charge the standard rate.

Taxis are easily found in the centre of Ambodifotatra and at the airport, or can be summoned by any hotel reception. A short trip in town costs 3,000Ar. From Ambodifotatra to the airport should cost 20,000Ar, or 30,000Ar to go north to Lonkintsy. Beyond Lonkintsy the road is bad and you need a 4x4 or motorbike.

Most hotels have bikes for rent (about 10,000Ar/day). Many also rent scooters (40,000Ar), motorbikes (55,000Ar) and quads (220,000Ar), though sometimes for guests only.

AMBODIFOTATRA

This town is growing; it has several boutiques and a patisserie which runs out of bread in the late morning. Market days are Tuesday and Thursday, and there's a small but well-stocked supermarket, **Super-Mahafapou** (⊕ Mon–Sat 07.30–12.00 & 14.30–19.00, Sun 07.30–12.00), on the north side of the harbour.

The tourist information office is situated nearby (↘ 57 901 47; m 034 57 901 47; e info@tourisme-sainte-marie.com; www.tourisme-sainte-marie.com; ⊕ Mon–Sat 08.00–12.00 & 14.00–18.00).

⌂ WHERE TO STAY

⌂ **La Bigorne** (5 bungalows) ↘ 57 401 23. About 400m north of the harbour. A good bar & restaurant with en-suite bungalows crowded in the back garden. €€€

⌂ **Hortensia** (12 rooms) ↘ 57 403 69. Just 250m north of the harbour. Clean, spacious rooms with hot water. Family rooms have sea views; dbl rooms have balconies facing the road. Good, reasonably priced restaurant. €€–€€€

⌂ **Drakkar** (8 bungalows) ↘ 57 400 22. About 650m north of harbour. Simple bamboo bungalows

with cold shower. Rather grim, but cheap. €€–€€€

⌂ **Palmiers** (6 bungalows) ↘/f 57 402 34; m 032 04 960 94. Some 200m up a track from Drakkar. Simple bungalows, some with kitchenette. €€–€€€

⌂ **Zinnia** (6 bungalows & 5 rooms) ↘ 57 400 09. Right by the harbour wall. Dbl bungalows with cold showers, fans & outside flush toilet. Rooms with shared facilities. Pleasant restaurant, excellent food & great coffee. €€

✕ WHERE TO EAT

✕ **Barachois** Across from the harbour. Outside tables good for people-watching. Very comprehensive menu.

✕ **Banane** m 032 02 280 26/032 02 663 85. 200m north of the harbour. A *vazaha* hangout with sea-view terrace, bar, pool table & good food. Also has rooms & dorm.

✗ **Gargotte à Bord 'Eaux** Small cosy restaurant-bar on the path to the pirate cemetery.

✗ **P'tit Chez Vous (Chez Jeremy)** m 032 04 270 30. Pleasant little restaurant 1km north of the harbour. Not always open as the owner reportedly has a habit of shutting up shop & heading off travelling whenever he has enough money.

✗ **Vazimba** Snack bar near Air Mad (take the turning opposite Hortensia).

MONEY There are two banks: a BFV with an ATM (Visa) and a BOA where you can change travellers' cheques. Be warned that MasterCard is not very useful on Ste Marie; most hotels don't accept cards and the BOA can take up to two days to clear a cash withdrawal.

INTERNET The best place seems to be **Cyber Corsair**, 650m north of the harbour. There are four computers and connection costs 50Ar/minute. A second cybercafé, **Nir.Info**, is near the harbour but more expensive.

WHAT TO SEE AND DO There are some interesting sights around Ambodifotatra which are an easy cycle ride from most of the hotels. In the town itself there is a **Catholic church** built in 1837, which serves as a reminder that Sainte Marie was owned by France from 1750. As a further reminder of French domination there is a **war monument** to a French-British skirmish in 1845.

The **pirates' cemetery** is just after the bay bridge south of town. A signposted track leads to the cemetery. It's impassable at high tide but you can cross by pirogue (agree a price in advance). This is quite an impressive place, with gravestones dating from the 1830s, including one carved with a classic skull and crossbones. There is a 2,000Ar charge to visit the cemetery or 10,000Ar with a guide.

The **town cemetery** is worth a visit too, though it lacks the story-book drama of the pirates' final resting place. It's about 5km north of Ambodifotatra at Bety Plage on the right-hand side of the road.

⌂ BEACH HOTELS

Most of the beach hotels are ranged along the west coast, with only a few in the east. Several more are on Ile aux Nattes to the south (see page 322).

Bear in mind that airport transfers to the more isolated hotels north of Ambodifotatra are most expensive and there are fewer alternatives to eating (perhaps expensive) meals at your hotel. Those on a tight budget would do best to stay in Ambodifotatra where there is a choice of eateries and other facilities.

Prices for high season (September to mid-November, Christmas and school holidays) tend to be substantially higher than for low season and be aware that – unusually for Madagascar – prices here tend to be quoted per person, not per room.

HOTELS BETWEEN THE AIRPORT AND AMBODIFOTATRA
Luxury ⌂

⌂ **Princesse Bora Lodge & Spa** (20 villas) ☎ 57 040 03; m 032 07 090 48; e resa@ princessebora.com; www.princessebora.com. Within walking distance of the airport, but transfers are usually by zebu cart. Owned by François-Xavier Mayer, whose family has been on Ste Marie for over 200 years, & his partner (architect of the hotel) Sophie de Michelis. Beautifully designed, this hotel is the best on the island – excellent in every respect. In whale-watching season (Jul–Sep) the hotel becomes a centre of scientific study, with guests going out with research teams to participate in data collection. The new **Jungle Spa** offers relaxation & pampering. Visa accepted. See ad after page 408.

🏠 **Soanambo** (40 rooms) 📞 57 902 98/22 640 54; e resa@hsm.mg; www.hsm.mg. A large hotel with lovely orchid garden & terrace bar/restaurant

Top end €€€€€
🏠 **Vanivola** (9 bungalows & 10 rooms) 📞 57 900 90; m 032 42 357 67; e info@vanivola.com; www.vanivola.com. French-run hotel with pool, TV lounge, atmospheric bar & funky

Upper range €€€€
🏠 **Lakana** (15 bungalows) 📞 57 902 96; m 032 07 090 22; e lakana@moov.mg; www.sainte-marie-hotel.com. Simple but very comfortable wooden bungalows, including 6 perched on the sea along the jetty. Friendly staff & personal service.
🏠 **Libertalia** (13 bungalows) 📞 57 403 03/903 33; m 032 02 763 23; e libertalia@moov.mg; www.lelibertalia.com. French-owned. Popular, friendly hotel in a very nice setting; often fully booked. There's a jetty out to a small private islet. Excellent food in stunning restaurant, with an ambience that belies its reasonable prices.

Mid-range €€€
🏠 **Baleine** (10 bungalows) 📞 57 903 36; m 032 40 257 18/032 02 378 26; e lantoualbert@moov.mg; www.hotel-la-baleine.com. Rustic bungalows, mostly en suite with hot water, owned by Albert Lantou, who sponsors a youth football club & other local projects. Great food but beach not so good here.
🏠 **Kaz à Bonh'Air** (3 bungalows) 350m south of Libertalia; m 032 45 362 57; e lesponsasaintemarie@yahoo.fr; www.lakazabonhair.com. En-suite bungalows in peaceful garden near beach. Free bike use.
🏠 **Sahasely** (5 rooms) Between Palourde & Baleine; 📞 57 901 57; m 032 04 962 20;

Budget €€
🏠 **Mangoustan** (7 bungalows) Nr Baleine; m 032 04 760 28; e mangoustanhotel@yahoo.fr. En-suite bungalows of various sizes.
🏠 **Chez Didier** (4 bungalows) Barely 200m from airport; m 032 40 843 87. Noisy & basic with shared facilities & cold water.

HOTELS NORTH OF AMBODIFOTATRA
🏠 **Masoandro** (18 bungalows) 📞 57 040 05/22 640 54; e resa@hsm.mg; www.hsm.mg. One of the best hotels on Ste Marie. Bungalows in 2 categories: 'luxe' (with TV, minibar, safe, lounge & huge terrace)

from which you can watch whales. Good long private beach; swimming pool. Credit cards accepted.

restaurant. The vivacious wife, Fabienne, speaks perfect English. Seafront bungalows with AC & good-value rooms, some with TV. Attentive personal service.

🏠 **Le Pirate** (4 bungalows) Opposite Libertalia; 📞 57 902 42; m 032 02 672 44/032 02 030 18; e lepiratehotelsm@yahoo.fr. Bungalows with hot shower & sea-view balcony; 2 with kitchenette. True to the pirate cliché, 2 vasa parrots live in the bar.
🏠 **Vanilla Café** (5 bungalows) Just north of Palourde; 📞 57 900 56; m 032 43 821 67/032 40 698 38; e ylangvillage@yahoo.fr; www.vanillacafe.com. En suite; b/fast inc.

e reservation@sahasely.com; www.sahasely.com. Set among rice paddies 150m from beach, a (pretty accurate) sign announces 'broken English spoken perfectly'. German-Malagasy owners Holger & Félicité run an admirably ethical establishment, aiming for self-sufficiency where possible (the restaurant uses almost entirely home-grown produce). Come for lunch or a drink & enjoy the pleasant forest trail to a waterfall & viewpoint. Camping permitted (5,000Ar/tent).
🏠 **Palourde** (7 bungalows) 📞 57 910 05; m 032 02 157 80. Clean en-suite bungalows on a mediocre beach. The friendly Malagasy/Mauritian owner is a great cook. There is a cybercafé opposite.

🏠 **Manaos Gargotte** (4 bungalows) Nr Vanivola; m 032 40 019 94. Traditional Malagasy bamboo bungalows; shared toilets. Good food. Camping permitted (5,000Ar/tent).

are significantly better than 'superior'. All en suite with AC. Infinity edge pool, lovely location & beautiful views. Top notch dinner & buffet b/fast inc. Credit cards accepted. €€€€–👑

🏠 **Ravinala** (2 bungalows) m 032 04 996 95. Plush en-suite bungalows, small private beach & communal lounge. Excellent buffet lunch. B/fast inc. €€€€€

🏠 **La Crique** (12 bungalows) ☎ 57 902 45; m 034 03 117 24/25; e lacrique@moov.mg; www.lacrique.net. One of Ste Marie's longest-established hotels; deservedly popular so book ahead. Extremely pretty location, right on the beach. Mostly en suite with hot water but also a couple of cheaper basic bungalows. Good beach for snorkelling (equipment available). Wonderful ambience & delicious, good-value meals. €€€–€€€€

🏠 **Atafana** (9 bungalows) ☎ 57 040 54; m 032 04 637 81; e hotel_atafana@yahoo.fr; http://atafana.chez-alice.fr. In a beautiful bay of its own, this resort offers good value for a great location. En-suite bungalows, good snorkelling & tasty food. Highly recommended for relaxation. Bike, motorbike & 4x4 hire. €€€

HOTELS ON THE EAST COAST

🏠 **Boraha Village** (9 bungalows) ☎ 57 400 71/912 18; e boraha@moov.mg; www.boraha.com. French-owned sgl, dbl & family bungalows facing the water; no beach, but a lovely jetty-style veranda. Specialises in deep-sea fishing; also water-skiing & canoeing. Minimum stay 2 nights. €€€€€

🏠 **Club Paradise** (6 bungalows) ☎ 57 901 16; e clubparadise@moov.mg; www.stmarie-clubparadise.com. Take the turning at Parc Endemika. Bungalows right on the beach in a tranquil bay. €€€€€

🏠 **Mora Mora** (10 bungalows) ☎ 57 040 80/913 78; m 032 07 090 98; e moramora@malagasy.com; www.moramora.info. En-suite dbl &

🏠 **Rocher (Chez Emilienne)** (7 bungalows) ☎ 57 040 16/912 98. Emilienne's charming & cheerful character (& splendid cooking) make this an unforgettable place to stay. Bungalows en suite with hot water. €€€

🏠 **Cocoteraie Robert** (13 bungalows) ☎ 57 901 76; m 034 04 168 63. En-suite (cold water) sgl & dbl bungalows in the far north. €€€

🏠 **Absolute Paradise** (4 rooms) ☎ 57 900 20; m 032 02 369 36; e absolute-paradise@wanadoo.fr; www.absolute-paradise.com. A simple *chambre d'hôte*. €€€

🏠 **Source** (4 rooms) ☎ 57 912 02. Good value basic rooms with shared facilities. €€

🏠 **Chez Antoine** (3 bungalows) ☎ 57 906 22. Malagasy-owned trpl bungalows with shared facilities (cold water) in inland location. Ideal for those planning to explore the north as more than a day trip. €€

family bungalows. Italian-owned place specialising in boat trips to watch whales & watersports including diving. No beach & quite isolated. €€€€

🏠 **Paradis d'Ampanihy** ☎ 57 042 06. On the river close to Anafiafy. Run by Helène, a Malagasy woman & her family. Basic bungalows; some with en-suite shower. Great meals in a beautiful dining-room with outside tables & several tame lemurs. €€–€€€

🏠 **Lagon Bleu** On the east coast, near Marofilao, 7km from Anafiafy. A small & cosy site, but clean & peaceful. €€

🏠 **Mangrove Gourmande** Just north of Anafiafy. Low price bungalows & excellent value food. €

WHAT TO SEE AND DO

WHALE-WATCHING July to September is the best time to see humpback whales but you could be lucky in June or October. You can watch them from any of the beachfront hotels or take a boat excursion (offered by most hotels and dive centres). For a really hands-on experience, stay at Princesse Bora where you'll get the chance to assist whale researchers.

If you go out whale-watching on a boat, be sure the operator subscribes to the Megaptera code of conduct – guidelines on the viewing distance, boat speed, maximum observation period, approach angle etc – to ensure your presence does not stress the whales. Take plenty of water, suncream and a waterproof jacket.

SNORKELLING AND DIVING The shallows around Sainte Marie are ideal for snorkelling and diving, despite the inshore waters being overfished. Most of the coral reefs are in good condition and the water is usually clear, although some of

Duncan Murrell

Every year humpback whales migrating from their summer feeding-grounds in Antarctica arrive in the waters off Madagascar between July and September to mate, give birth and nurture their young. Humpback whales, like several other species of whale, migrate between their colder, high latitude feeding-grounds to the warmer shallow waters around tropical islands or on continental shelves. There is more food available in the nutrient-rich waters of polar regions than in tropical waters but the calves have insufficient insulating blubber to protect them from colder water. It takes 1½ months for the whales to travel the 5,000km journey from Antarctica, during which they lose up to a third of their bodyweight. As with all of the baleen whales, the gestation period of 10–12 months is closely linked to the timing of their annual migration.

The majority of the whales end up in the relatively protected, shallow waters of Antongil Bay but many can be observed either in transit or lingering between Sainte Marie and the mainland, often in very close viewing distance of the shore; this is especially true between Atafana and Antsara where the channel narrows considerably. They can also be seen passing Taolagnaro (Fort Dauphin) early and late in the season, and a few travel up the west coast and can be viewed near Anakao and Morondava.

Humpback whales are undoubtedly one of the most entertaining of whales because of their exuberant displays of breaching (jumping), lobtailing (tail-slapping) and pec-slapping (flipper-slapping). Males competing for females often indulge in forceful displays of head-lunging and slapping to create surges and explosions of water to intimidate their rivals. In their feeding-grounds they often deploy a unique feeding strategy where they herd their prey with bubbles.

But probably the behaviour that the humpback whale is most renowned for is its singing. The male produces one of the most complex songs in the animal kingdom using sounds spanning the highest and lowest frequencies audible to the human ear. These songs constantly evolve; as the season progresses new themes may be added or old ones changed. Each whale changes its song to keep in tune with other singers. As a result the song heard at the end of the season is quite different from that at the beginning. When the whales return the following year, they resume singing the version in vogue at the end of the previous season. Many whale-watching boats are now equipped with hydrophones to enable visitors to listen to this singing. The haunting songs elicit both the mystery and the majesty of these incredible animals.

Until recently the humpbacks of Madagascar were one of the least-studied and least-understood populations in the world. In the last few years researchers have been using DNA testing, satellite-tagging, photographic identification and other methods to increase our knowledge of this significant population. In 2000 Madagascar's Ministry of the Environment wholeheartedly endorsed new laws governing whale-watching to protect the whales along their migration route. Training has been provided to instruct local students and faculties from Malagasy universities in research techniques, and for local ecotourism representatives to encourage safe, enjoyable, conservation-oriented whale-watching procedures. The humpback whales are a fantastic offshore bonus for the visitor, and as with the rest of Madagascar's dwindling natural treasures there is no room for complacency.

Humpback whales have been protected since 1966 and their numbers are recovering very slowly. Before they were hunted intensively in the 19th century, humpbacks probably numbered about 150,000 worldwide; today's estimates range from 25,000 to 35,000. Increased demands on their habitat, including unregulated whale-watching, continue to threaten the likelihood that they will ever recover fully.

the huge table corals have been broken off by fish traps. The best snorkelling sites are near Atafana and La Crique, and also the west side of Ile aux Nattes.

Divers should read the safety box on page 116; and everyone should watch out for the vicious spines of sea urchins (see page 222).

⤙ **Le Lémurien Palmé** Ambodifotatra (120m north of harbour); ☎ 57 040 15; m 032 04 816 56; e lemurienpalme@moov.mg; www.lemurien-palme.com. Dive centre with over 15yrs' experience. Offers try-dives, PADI/CMAS/FFESSM training, exploration diving, 2-day wreck diving to La Cocoteraie, open-sea outings & whale-watching.

⤙ **Mahery Be** 400m south of Lakana hotel; ☎ 57 911 08; m 032 04 757 77/033 01 308 14;

e maherybe@live.fr. Offers try-dives, CMAS/FFESSM/ANMP/CEDIP training, boat hire, sea fishing & whale-watching. They also have 4 basic rooms (30,000Ar) & will pick up from hotels south of Ambodifotatra.

⤙ **Il Balenottero** Ambodifotatra (at the harbour); ☎ 57 400 36; e ilbalenottero@simicro.mg. Dive centre under new Belgian ownership. Wreck & reef diving; whale-watching.

EXPLORING THE ISLAND The best way to explore Sainte Marie is by bike (hard work), motorbike or on foot. In the low season, if you are fit and energetic, you could walk or cycle around most of the island and take your chance on places to stay, but during peak seasons most of the hotels may be full. The bad road north of Lonkintsy requires a motorbike or 4x4.

CROSSING FROM WEST TO EAST From Ambodifotatra or Ankirihiry the walk across the island takes about 2½ hours. Although possible to do on your own, it's easy to get lost, so several young men make a lucrative business of guiding visitors; many overcharge and have no information except for the route, so be sure to agree the price first.

It is well worth taking a pirogue trip to explore the coast around the northeastern peninsula with its Forêt d'Ampanihy. Most of the northern hotels run excursions there.

WATERFALL AND NATURAL POOL At the far northeast, beyond the end of the road, is a beautiful and impressive *piscine naturelle* with a waterfall, a big pool and enormous basalt rocks. The beach here is spectacularly beautiful. Also in the area is Albrand Lighthouse, dating from colonial times.

PARC ENDEMIKA (*Entry 15,000Ar, under-10s 5,000Ar, under-5s free*) A small park-cum-zoo at the village of Vohilava in the south of the island. The owner, Arnaud, rescues animals (mainly lemurs) that are captured for sale or are kept as pets by hotels. His aim is to establish an educational centre for the island, but in the short term he has opened the zoo to visitors. There's a good guide, Prosper, who is knowledgeable about the plants and animals.

HORSERIDING (☎ 57 905 45; m 032 43 739 45) Mandrakata Ranch, 750m north of Lakana hotel, is an Italian-owned horseriding centre. It costs 25,000Ar for an hour or 100,000Ar for a full day.

PANORAMA At the southern tip of Sainte Marie there is a viewpoint from which you can see Ile aux Nattes and watch the sunset. Head 1km or so past the airport and follow the signs for 'Panorama'.

ILE AUX NATTES (NOSY NATO)

To many people this little island off the south coast of Sainte Marie is even better than the main island. Being car-free it is much more peaceful. Debbie Fellner reflects: 'If I were to do the trip again, I'd split my time equally between both islands. Nosy Nato is about as fantasy-islandesque as it gets. Pristine beaches, quiet village, hidden bungalows, excellent restaurants'.

A pirogue transfer here from near the airport on Sainte Marie costs 2,000Ar, or more to be taken directly to your chosen hotel.

WHERE TO STAY AND EAT
Upper range €€€€

Maningory (10 bungalows) ☎ 57 040 69/902 58; m 032 07 090 05; e maningoryhotel@ moov.mg; www.maningoryhotel.com. Well-equipped bungalows built in the local style in an idyllic location. Internet available. Dive centre & boats for whale-watching & fishing.

Petite Traversée (7 bungalows) ☎ 57 900 22; m 032 42 360 52; e jolene@madxperience.com; www.madxperience.com. South African owner Ockie goes out of his way to make guests feel at home. Described by one reader as 'heaven on earth'. Snorkelling, & glass-bottom boat trips for those who prefer to stay dry.

Baboo Village (14 bungalows) ☎ 57 042 07; m 032 04 791 26; e infos@baboo-village.com; www.baboo-village.com. En-suite bungalows, large & airy with hot water on request; 4 are right on the water. Wonderful dining area on a jetty. Boutique, massage, netball, bikes & boats for excursions.

Meva Paradis (8 bungalows) m 032 46 802 81; e hotel@mevaparadis.com;

www.mevaparadis.com. Owned by a Malagasy-American couple, these palm-thatched bungalows fronting the white-sand beach are close to perfection. Restaurant-bar with homely atmosphere.

Napoléon (10 bungalows) ☎ 57 042 04/26; m 032 05 635 75; e napoleonhotel@freenet.mg; www.hsm.mg. Virtually destroyed in 2008's cyclone, rebuilding should be finished by the time you read this. Nice spot not far from the village. Special honeymoon discounts.

Coco Lodge (3 villas) ☎ 22 755 01; www.cocolodge.com. Self-catering accommodation for up to 8 people.

Ylang Village (8 bungalows) ☎ 57 900 56; m 032 43 821 67/032 40 698 38; e ylang2@ wanadoo.fr; www.vanillacafe.com. Simple local-style bungalows.

Analatsara (3 bungalows) ☎ 57 906 11; m 032 02 127 70; e jean-pierre.briois@ wanadoo.fr. Sgl & dbl with TV, fridge, fan & toilet on HB basis.

Mid-range €€€

Sambatra (Chez Régine) (5 bungalows) ☎ 57 042 14; m 032 04 726 16/032 02 317 58; e lsambatra@freenet.mg. Quiet, basic accommodation (some en suite); beautiful beach; excellent swimming.

Chez Sika (5 bungalows) m 032 42 478 86/032 41 656 98. Dbl & family bungalows; communal kitchen for guests' use.

Pandanus In a prime seafront spot, these Malagasy-owned bungalows were totally wiped out in Cyclone Ivan. At the time of writing they are still trying to raise funds for rebuilding from their now-reopened restaurant.

Paradisa (8 bungalows) m 032 07 920 78; e paradisa@franef.net. New en-suite bungalows; the ones set back are cheaper than those nearer the beach. Tennis court, bar & snack bar; a good stop-off when walking the coastal circuit.

Lémuriens (10 bungalows) ☎ 57 401 25; e leslemuriens@vanivola.com. The bungalows were destroyed in the 2008 cyclone but are being rebuilt. In any case it's worth the walk down here for the excellent restaurant & fantastic view across the lagoon. Nice bar with pool table.

Budget €€

Chez Titi (5 bungalows) m 034 04 362 03. Simple but nice huts, some en suite (cold water). Visa accepted.

Bar de la Marine (4 bungalows) ☎ 57 910 80; m 032 41 041 02/032 46 233 18; e contact@ bardelamarine.com; www.bardelamarine.com. Basic accommodation with shared cold showers. New

restaurant & boutique right at the pirogue crossing point.

Bonne Etoile (2 bungalows & 4 rooms) m 032 02 886 84/034 13 198 88; e enockpaul@ yahoo.fr. Very cheap sgl & dbl rooms; also dbl & family bungalows. The hotel supports a local orphanage.

WHAT TO SEE AND DO The circumference of the island is 8km, and it takes at least three hours to walk round it, but some parts are impassable at high tide.

There is much to see during a short walking tour, including the island's unique and amazing orchid, *Eulophiella roempleriana*, known popularly as *l'orchidée rose*. It is 2m high with deep pink flowers.

The best beaches are in the north of the island: calm, shallow, crystal clear water, with soft white sand overhung by picture-postcard palms.

A small trip to the interior of the island is also recommended. Aniribe village at the centre is pure unspoiled Madagascar. Head south from there up to the old lighthouse. At the junction in the path 200m before the lighthouse, stop to visit **Espace Vert**, a small shop selling cloves, lemongrass, honey, vanilla, cinnamon and other local spices. Ralai, the owner, loves to practice his English and if you ask he will proudly show you the English grammar book he has written in Malagasy.

Ile Sainte Marie   ILE AUX NATTES (NOSY NATO)

13

323

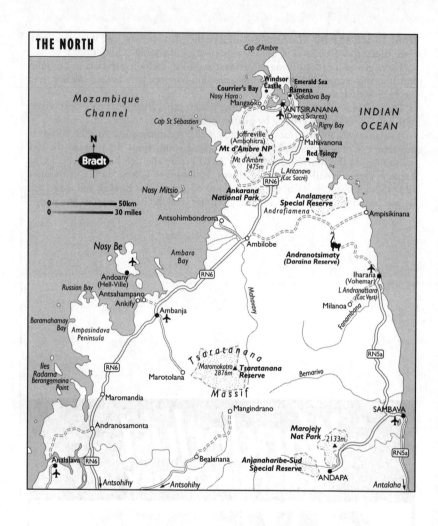

Cap d'Ambre

Windsor Castle
Emerald Sea
Courrier's Bay
Nosy Hara
Ramena
Sakalava Bay
Mangaoko
ANTSIRANANA
(Diego Suarez)

Mozambique Channel

INDIAN OCEAN

Cap St Sébastien

Rigny Bay

Joffreville (Ambohitra)
Mt d'Ambre NP
Mahavanona
Red Tsingy

N
Bradt

Mt d'Ambre
1475m

L. Antanavo
(Lac Sacré)

RN6

Nosy Mitsio

Ankarana National Park

Analamera Special Reserve
Andrafiamena

Ampisikinana

0 ────── 50km
0 ────── 30 miles

Antsohimbondrona

Ambilobe

Andranotsimaty (Daraina Reserve)

Nosy Be

Ambaro Bay

RN6

Iharana (Vohemar)
L. Andranotsara (Lac Vert)

Andoany (Hell-Ville)
Russian Bay
Antsahampano
Ankify

Milanoa

Mahavavy

Fanambana

Baramahamay Bay
Ambanja

Ampasindava Peninsula

Iles Radama
Berangomaina Point

RN6

Tsaratanana

Marotolana

Maromokotro
2876m ▲ **Tsaratanana Reserve**

Bemarivo

RN5a

Maromandia

Massif

Mangindrano

SAMBAVA

Andranosamonta

Marojejy Nat Park
2133m ▲

Analalava   RN6

Bealanana

Anjanaharibe-Sud Special Reserve

RN5a

↙Antsohihy

←Antsohihy

ANDAPA

Antalaha↓

DISTANCES IN KILOMETRES			
Ambondromamy—Antsiranana	756km	Antsiranana—Ambanja	240km
Antsohihy—Ambanja	217km	Antsiranana—Anivorano	75km
Antsiranana—Ambilobe	138km	Antsiranana—Daraina	245km
Antsiranana—Ankarana	108km	Antsiranana—Vohemar	301km

14

The North

The north of Madagascar is characterised by its variety. With the Tsaratanana Massif (including Maromokotro, Madagascar's highest peak) bringing more rain to the Nosy Be area than is normal for the west coast, and the pocket of dry climate around Antsiranana (Diego Suarez), the weather can alter dramatically within short distances. The Antsiranana area has seven months of dry weather, with almost all of its 90cm annual rainfall concentrated between December and April. With changes of weather come changes of vegetation and its accompanying fauna, making this region particularly interesting to botanists and other naturalists.

This is the domain of the Antankarana people. Cut off by rugged mountains, the Antankarana were left to their own devices until the mid 1700s when they were conquered by the Sakalava; they in turn submitted to the Merina King Radama I, aided by his military adviser James Hastie, in 1823.

The road connection between Antsiranana and Tana is now reasonably good, but it is a journey of around 1,200km so those with limited time may prefer to fly.

ANTSIRANANA (DIEGO SUAREZ)

HISTORY Forgivingly named after a 16th-century Portuguese explorer who arrived and proceeded to murder and rape the inhabitants or sell them into slavery, this large town has had an eventful history with truth blending into fiction. An often-told story, probably started by Daniel Defoe, is that pirates in the 17th century founded the Republic of Libertalia here. Not true, say modern historians.

Most people still call the town Diego. The Malagasy name simply means 'port' and its strategic importance as a deep-water harbour has long been recognised. The French installed a military base here in 1885, and the town played an important role in World War II when Madagascar was under the control of the Vichy French (see box on page 332). To prevent Japanese warships and submarines making use of the magnificent harbour, and thus threatening vital sea routes, Britain and the Allies captured and occupied Diego Suarez in 1942. There is a British cemetery honouring those killed.

ANTSIRANANA TODAY This is Madagascar's fifth-largest town and is of increasing interest to visitors for its diverse attractions and superb location. The harbour is encircled by hills and to the east is a large bay with a 'sugarloaf', Nosy Lonja ('conical island'), in the middle. The port's isolation behind its mountain barrier and its long association with non-Malagasy races have given it an unusually cosmopolitan population and lots of colour: there are Arabs, Creoles (descendants of Europeans), Indians, Chinese and Comorans.

Almost everyone enjoys Antsiranana. Lee Miller writes: 'The area north of Place Foch is the old colonial sector, with an atmosphere of faded French occupation. Big brick colonial buildings, with street arcades topped by upper-story verandas, crumbling in disuse, abandon and neglect. Here is where you find most of the tourist activity: hotels, restaurants and handicraft shops. It has a languid, empty feel. But walk south down Rue Lafayette, then Rue du Suffren, and the activity increases exponentially as you find yourself in the bustle of the Malagasy centre.'

A set of pamphlets giving historical background to a series of self-guided walking tours of the town is available from the tourist office.

If you want to relax on a beach for a few days, stay at **Ramena** (see page 331).

GETTING THERE AND AWAY

By air There are flights to and from Tana most days, and also weekly services to Nosy Be, Sambava and Mahajanga. The local Air Mad office [327 C5] is on Avenue Surcouf (✆ *82 233 89;* m *032 07 666 15;* e *airmaddi@moov.mg;* ⏰ *Mon–Fri 07.30–11.00 & 14.30–17.00, Sat 08.00–10.00*).

Taxis are easily found at the airport for the 8km trip into town (10,000Ar), but a considerably cheaper alternative is to walk 250m to the main road and wait for a *taxi-brousse*.

By road The overland route between Ambaja (nearest town to Nosy Be) and Antsiranana is scenically beautiful and on a good road. Much tougher, but possible, is the road to Iharana (Vohemar). Both routes are described later in this chapter.

GETTING AROUND Within the town, taxis should cost a flat rate per person of 800Ar (1,200Ar at night) – or more on a private hire basis. You can also rent bicycles.

WHERE TO STAY
Upper range to luxury

⌂ **Grand Hotel** [327 B4] (66 rooms) 46 Rue Colbert; ✆ 82 230 63/64; f 82 225 94; m 032 40 881 43/033 14 168 59; e grandhotel_diego@ yahoo.fr; www.grand-hotel-diego.com. Centrally located high-standard rooms with TV, AC & minibar; Wi-Fi in lobby & a few rooms. Large public pool, patisserie, 2 restaurants, bar & boutique. ♨

⌂ **Allamanda** [327 B1] (24 rooms) Rue Richelieu; ✆ 82 210 33/231 47; f 82 221 80; m 032 07 666 15; e hotelallamanda@gmail.com; www.allamanda-hotel.com. Upmarket hotel at the north end of town. En-suite rooms with AC, minibar & TV. Cards accepted. €€€€€

⌂ **Colbert** [327 B3] (34 rooms) 51 Rue Colbert; ✆ 82 232 89; f 82 232 90; e hlcdiego@moov.mg; www.hlcdiego.com. Popular en-suite rooms with AC, safe & TV in 4 standards. Good restaurant, but expensive. €€€€

⌂ **Emeraude** [327 C5] (20 rooms) Rue Rigault; ✆ 82 225 44; m 032 02 783 81/032 07 546 59; e contact@hotelemeraude.com; www.hotelemeraude-diego.com. Centrally located, comfortable, classy; some suites with large bathrooms. €€€€

⌂ **De la Poste** [327 B1] (100 rooms) ✆ 82 239 24; f 82 239 23; e contact@diego-hoteldelaposte.com; www.diego-hoteldelaposte.com. A great location & totally renovated. Dbl en-suite rooms with AC & TV. Price depends on view: road, garden or sea/docks. Free Wi-Fi. €€€€

⌂ **Imperial** [327 B3] (39 rooms) 65 Rue Colbert; ✆ 82 233 29/39; f 82 233 11; e accueil@ hotelimperial-diego.com; www.hotelimperial-diego.com. Dbl rooms with AC, TV, minibar & balcony. €€€€

⌂ **Firdoss** [327 B4] (34 rooms) 11 Rue Lavigerie; m 032 57 746 01/033 13 983 53; f 82 223 84; e reservation@hotelfirdoss.com; www.hotelfirdoss.com. Smart new hotel; TV, AC & minibar in rooms; some with small balcony; 2 suites with kitchenette. €€€€

Mid-range €€€

⌂ **Baie de Diego Suarez** [327 B1] (6 rooms) 5 Rue Richelieu; m 032 40 250 59; e baiedediegosuarez@moov.mg. B&B at the far north of town with stunning bay view. Comfortable, attractive rooms; some en suite.

⌂ **Rascasse** [327 B5] (22 rooms) Rue Surcouf; ✆/f 82 223 64; e sglveni@moov.mg. A range of good-value rooms in a convenient location. All rooms en suite; some with fans, others with AC & TV.

A   **B**   **C**   **D**

Dordogne Cove

Pointe de Corail

Baie de Diego Suarez

Allamanda
Melville
Monument
Guetali de Veronique
R JOFFRE
R GOURAUD

RUE RICHELIEU

BFV
Ocean
Hospital

De la Poste
Port de la Nièvre
R DE L REPUBLIQUE

R FLACOURT
BOA

VILLE BASSE

Marina
Mada Quad
Metisses
Baobab
Bodega
Pl Kabary
Kikoo
Grillade
Leong-Hoi
(grocery store)

R DE L'OUREG
Iris

R DE CORAIL

Market
Voky Be

New Sea Roc
AV DE FRANCE
BNI
Vahinée
Valiha
Gis

V MAREUIL

Melville Cove

Tsara Be Yaovao
Boit Noir

RUE CARNOT
Rosticceria
Fian-Tsilaka
Colbert
BMOI
Imperial
Concorde
Nouvel Hôtel
Etincelle
Diego Raid
Taverne
Grand

RUE DES QUAIS

BOULEVARD MILITAIRE

BD SAKARAMY

R DE LE VAUCHERET

N
Bradt

R FREPPEL

Diego
Ambassador
Côte
Place
Foch
King de la Piste
Libertalia
Town hall
Arcades
Loft
San Diego Rock Café
Espace
Medical
Firdoss
Amicale
Balafomanga
Blue Note
Housseni
Belle Vue

RUE MONSEIGNEUR COURBET

RUE DE LE ABATTOIR

BD DE G BAYER
LAVIGERIE

RUE DUGAY
RUE

AMIRAL

LAFAYETTE

Nature et Océan
Venilla
Ecotours
Rascasse
Maymoune
Emeraude
Casa Nostra
Air Madagascar
Orchidée
Place du 14 Octobre
Petit Paradis

PIERRE
AV SURCOUF
RIGAULT
R CABOTO
DE VILLERS
MAHEY
BENJOWSKY
DU GL CHARLES DE GAULLE

Taxi-brousse
station

TANAMBAO II

Market
Suffren
Moramora
Cybercafé

Municipal
stadium

RUE DUGAY
AV PASTEUR
R DES COMORES
BD DU SUFFREN
BEZARA
AV P TSIRANANA

TROUIN
MONTCALM
BD SYLVAIN ROUX
BD TOLLENDAL
BOULEVARD CAYLA

TANAMBAO I
Police

BD DE L'AMIRAL MIOT

TANAMBAO V
Royale
Market
Paradis du Nord
Espa.com

Bambou
Halmah
(rest)(200m)

Mada (hotel)(100m),
Taxi-brousse stn (South)
(200m), Airport (6.8km)

French
war cemetery
British
war cemetery

Ramena (17.4km),
Andovobazaha Bay

Taxi-brousse stn (West)
(200m)

0 ——— 200m
0 ——— 200yds

🛏 **Arcades** [327 B4] (8 rooms) 3 Av Tollendal; ☎ 82 231 04; e arcades@blueline.mg. Typical colonial building with courtyard, restaurant & bar, but becoming rundown. Most rooms en suite; some with AC. Popular restaurant. Free Wi-Fi.

🛏 **Paradis du Nord** [327 B7] (12 rooms) Av Villaret Joyeuse; ☎/f 82 214 05; m 032 04 859 64; e paradisdunord@moov.mg; www.leparadisdunord-diego.com. Sgl & dbl en-suite rooms, mostly with AC & TV. Rooms are cell-like, but comfy & good value. Excellent organiser of excursions & 4x4 hire.

🛏 **Valiha** [327 C3] (18 rooms) 41 Rue Colbert; ☎ 82 221 97/236 44; f 82 293 55; e valiha@ddt.mg. Clean rooms with AC & TV.

🛏 **Fian-Tsilaka** [327 B3] (20 rooms) 13 Bd Etienne; ☎ 82 223 48; m 032 04 067 95;

Budget €€

🛏 **Orchidée** [327 B5] (6 rooms) Rue Surcouf; ☎ 82 210 65. En-suite dbl rooms with fan or AC; cold water.

🛏 **Mada** [327 C7] (11 rooms) m 034 07 717 22/034 07 717 23. Excellent value rooms with TV & fan; hot water, some en suite.

e dom.bigot@wanadoo.fr. En-suite dbl rooms, some with hot water & AC.

🛏 **Belle Vue** [327 C4] (11 rooms) 35 Rue François de Mahy; ☎ 82 210 21; m 032 02 000 94; e bellevue@blueline.mg. Dbl rooms, some en suite. Good value; b/fast inc.

Also in this category: **Balafomanga** [327 C4] (m 032 41 738 70), **Concorde** [327 B3] (☎ 82 902 13), **Diego Ambassador** [327 B4] (☎ 82 228 51), **Gis** [327 C2] (☎ 82 238 36), **Iris** [327 C2] (☎ 82 900 79), **Kikoo** [327 C2] (www.kikoohotel.com), **Maymoune** [327 B5] (☎ 82 218 27), **Moramora** [327 C6] (☎ 82 226 55), **Ocean** [327 C1] (www.hotelocean-diego.com), **Petit Paradis** [327 C5] (m 032 47 891 13).

🛏 **Suffren** [327 B6] (12 rooms) 6 Rue Suffren; ☎ 82 212 82; m 032 59 209 67. Range of en-suite rooms, some with AC & hot water.

🛏 **Royale** [327 B7] (16 rooms) 10 Rue Justin Bezara; ☎ 82 228 15; m 032 04 590 39. Cell-like rooms but clean, with fan & safe; cold water.

🛏 **Baobab** [327 C2] (6 rooms) ☎/f 82 236 35. Basic accommodation; cheap & central.

Hotels on Andovobazaha Bay
At the bay just to the east of town you will find some of the nicest hotels in the area, along the road to Ramena, offering a quieter and more scenic location than hotels in Antsiranana itself.

🛏 **Note Bleue Park** (26 rooms) m 032 07 125 48/032 07 666 26; e bleudiego@gmail.com; www.diego-hotel.com. Boutique hotel with spectacular view overlooking sugarloaf island. Huge swimming pool, watersports, gym & even crèche — everything that goes with conventional luxury. Colourful sgl to 4-person en-suite rooms & suites with AC, TV, minibar & balcony. Reliable restaurant with Thai chef. B/fast inc. Cards accepted. New botanic garden & 6-hole pitch-n-putt golf. See ad on page 347. 🛏

🛏 **Meva Plage** (8 bungalows) m 032 07 935 94; e mevaplage@yahoo.fr; www.mevaplagehotel.com. A pleasant beach hotel 3km before Ramena (although the beach is more mangrove mud than sand); en-suite waterfront bungalows with AC. Small pool. Jet ski hire. €€€€

🛏 **Panorama** (12 bungalows) ☎ 82 225 99; m 032 04 908 10; e info@kingdelapiste.com; www.kingdelapiste.de. Comfy & efficient with good food. Bungalows have private shower & terrace set in spacious gardens with large pool. €€€€

🛏 **King's Lodge** (8 rooms) Contact details as for Panorama. An excellent base for climbing Montagne des Français & seeing the rare plants there (see pages 330–1). Well designed, set on a gentle slope with a shaded terrace & sea view. Good restaurant. There is also a 26ha botanical garden here. €€€

🛏 **Capitaine Boregar** (10 bungalows) m 032 51 402 73; e baylodgediego@gmail.com. Just 2km before Ramena. Comfy wooden bungalows arranged around a pool. €€€

🛏 **Cocotiers** (12 rooms) ☎ 82 907 43; m 032 02 386 73/032 71 893 14; e claudecocotiers@moov.mg; www.lescocotiers-diego.com. En-suite rooms in waterfront location 13km from town. €€€

🛏 **Pain de Sucre** (12 rooms & 7 apts) ☎ 82 901 10; e residencepaindesucre@yahoo.fr. Dbl rooms with AC & bath; trpl apartments with AC, shower, kitchenette & terrace. Boat, 4x4, car & bike hire. €€€

🛏 **Jungle Park** A unique hotel constructed in the tree canopy. See page 331. €€€

✖ WHERE TO EAT

✖ **Bodega** [327 C2] 5 Rue Colbert; m 032 04 734 43; e bodegadiegosuarez@gmail.com. Lively Spanish-owned tapas bar with fantastic atmosphere & very personal service. Restaurant menu changes daily. Also has 3 rooms.

✖ **Rosticceria** [327 C3] Rue Colbert. A wonderful little Italian restaurant with veranda. Highly recommended for its excellent food, great atmosphere & jovial owner.

✖ **San Diego Rock Café** [327 B4] Av Tollendal; m 032 56 982 46. Open-fronted bar & restaurant with tremendous pizzas & burgers. Ice cream sundaes recommended.

✖ **Venilla** [327 B5] \ 82 229 25. Among the best restaurants in town, yet keeps its prices reasonable.

✖ **Libertalia** [327 B4] Offers good meals at good prices on 1st floor & in a nice garden.

✖ **Tsara Be Vaovao** [327 B3] Rue Colbert. Nice restaurant with excellent food, but pricey.

✖ **Melville** [327 B1] m 032 05 606 99. Swish restaurant under same ownership as Allamanda. Local & French menu served on a fantastic terrace.

✖ **Loft** [327 B4] 5 Av Tollandal; m 032 50 975 64. Upstairs restaurant & pizzeria with pool table.

✖ **Halmah** [327 B7] Rue Roi Tsimiaro. Good-value local eatery at south end of town.

Other recommended good-value restaurants: **Casa Nostra** [327 C5], **Etincelle** [327 B3], **Grillade** [327 C2], **Guetali de Veronique** [327 B1], **Marina** [327 B2], **Saveurs Metisses** [327 C2].

Snack bars

🍴 **Boulangerie Amicale** [327 B5] Excellent hot rolls & *pains au chocolat*.

🍴 **Pâtisseries du Grand Hotel** [327 B4] Good range of quality pastries & cakes.

🍴 **Voky Be** [327 C2] Snack bar with burgers & salads. Considering the name means 'very full' the portions are pretty small.

🍴 **Côte** [327 B4] Fast food from hamburgers to brochettes; also salads.

🍴 **Bambou** [327 B7] Small but popular snack bar.

NIGHTLIFE

♀ **Vahinée Bar** [327 B2] Rue Colbert. Recommended for its wonderful atmosphere & staff.

♀ **Taverne** [327 B4] Conveniently located bar opposite Grand Hotel.

☆ **Boit Noir** [327 C3] Rue Colbert. The most stylish of the nightclubs.

☆ **Nouvel Hôtel** [327 B3] Rue Colbert. A popular disco with the locals.

INTERNET Antsiranana has several internet cafés which typically cost around 25Ar/minute. The largest is **Housseni** [327 C4] in the Ny Havana building opposite the fuel station on Avenue Tollendal, where you can connect your laptop by Wi-Fi.

SHOPPING Antsiranana has some high-quality souvenir shops, mostly along Rue Colbert and Rue Lafayette.

Leong-Hoi [327 C2] is a well-stocked Chinese-run grocery store, and by the fuel station on Avenue Tollendal there is a 24-hour shop [327 B5] that stocks tinned foods, yoghurt, ice cream, fruit juice and other basic necessities.

MONEY There are branches of all the major banks: BFV, BNI, BOA and BMOI, mostly now with ATMs and Western Union. The BNI is reportedly the most efficient for changing travellers' cheques. Good English is spoken at the small BFV office inside Grand Hotel.

MEDICAL Antsiranana has plenty of pharmacies dotted around town. There is a hospital [327 D1] (\ 82 218 61) and the services of Espace Medical [327 B4] are recommended for emergencies (m 034 05 096 96; e espamed.diego@yahoo.fr; ⊕ Mon–Fri 08.00–12.00 & 14.30–18.00, Sat 08.00–10.00).

TOURIST OFFICE, GUIDES AND TOUR OPERATORS The well-organised regional tourist office [327 C1] is located at the intersection of Rue Colbert and Rue

Flacourt (☎ 82 917 99; e info@office-tourisme-diego-suarez.com; www.office-tourisme-diego-suarez.com; ⊕ Mon–Fri 08.00–12.00 & 15.00–18.00, Sat 08.00–12.00) and also runs an information kiosk in Place Foch [327 B4] .

If you are in need of a local guide, contact the local guides association (m 032 04 790 76/032 52 931 61; e chrismarvao@yahoo.fr).

King de la Piste [327 B4] Pl Foch; m 032 04 908 10; e info@kingdelapiste.com; www.kingdelapiste.de. This highly recommended agency, run by York & Lydia Pareik can organise trips to most of the region, including hard-to-reach places such as Windsor Castle, Cap d'Ambre, Analamera & Sakalava Bay. Excursions by 4x4, motorbike & bike. Personal & efficient service. See ad after page 408.

Paradis du Nord [327 B7] Av Villaret Joyeuse; ☎/f 82 214 05; m 032 04 859 64; e paradisdunord@moov.mg; www.leparadisdunord-diego.com. A reliable operator with a fleet of 4x4s & mini-buses with good drivers. Arranges visits to most attractions in the north.

Blue Note Voyages [327 B4] m 032 07 125 48/032 07 666 26; e bleudiego@gmail.com; www.diego-hotel.com. This regional tour agency has been leading the way in opening up some new destinations to tourists. They serve all usual destinations as well as offering boat trips, including camping trips to Nosy Hara, fishing & snorkelling. Quad, 4x4 & scooter hire.

Cap Nord Voyages [327 B3] ☎ 82 235 06; m 032 07 188 74; e cap.nord.voyages@moov.mg; www.cap-nord-voyages.com. Based at Hotel Colbert they specialise in multi-day tours of the north but also do day trips. Mini-bus & 4x4 hire.

Evasion Sans Frontière [327 B4] ☎ 82 230 61; f 82 217 23; e esf.diego@moov.mg. A knowledgeable operator based at Grand Hotel; they work throughout the north & especially around Nosy Be.

New Sea Roc [327 B2] 26 Rue Colbert; ☎ 82 218 54; m 032 04 724 46; e newsearoc@moov.mg; www.newsearoc.com. Adventure sporting excursions including climbing, caving & mountain biking. Closed mid-Dec to end of Jan.

Nature et Océan [327 C5] 5 Rue Cabot; ☎ 82 226 32. They run 4x4 excursions to a variety of local places of interest.

Ecotours [327 B5] 14 Av Surcouf; m 032 40 118 14; e madagascarecotours@yahoo.fr. Good prices & English-speaking guides.

VEHICLE HIRE Most of the tour operators listed above hire out 4x4s, and some also cars, motorbikes, quads and mountain bikes. Other rental options are:

🚗 **Location 4L** (PK 2); ☎ 82 901 71; m 032 52 200 25; e loc4ldiego@gmail.com. Renault 4s (some convertible) with & without driver.

🚗 **San Diego Rock Café** [327 B4] (see page 329) Rents motorbikes.

🚗 **Diego Raid** [327 B4] m 032 58 890 77/032 40 001 75. Quad hire & guided excursions by quad up to 8 days.

🚗 **Mada Quad** [327 C2] m 032 40 888 14. Quad rental & excursions.

🚲 **Bicycles** [327 B3] Rue Colbert. Just north of the Colbert you may find bikes for rent.

WHAT TO SEE AND DO

British war cemetery [327 D7] On the outskirts of town on the road that leads to the airport, the British Commonwealth Cemetery is well signposted on a side road opposite the main Malagasy cemetery. Here is a sad insight into Anglo-Malagasy history: rows of graves of the British troops killed in the battle for Diego in 1942 (see box on page 332) and the larger numbers, mainly East African and Indian soldiers serving in the British army, who died from disease during the occupation of the port. Impeccably maintained by the Commonwealth War Graves Commission, this is a peaceful and moving place.

The **French war cemetery** [327 C7] is nearby, alongside the local cemetery.

Botanical gardens The **Parc Botanique des Mille Baobabs** at King's Lodge is worth a visit. Covering 26ha, it is planted with interesting, unusual, rare and endangered plants from across northern Madagascar, arranged into zones according to their place of origin. A 2.5km trail passes through all the biotope regions. Entry costs 10,000Ar per person.

Note Bleue Park Hotel has also recently opened a 3ha botanical garden with rare plants from the region.

Montagne des Français (French Mountain) Now officially a protected area, the mountain gets its name from the memorial to the French and Malagasy killed during the Allied invasion in 1942 – another reminder of a war about which the locals can have little understanding.

The start of the trail is just before King's Lodge, 8km from Antsiranana. At the foot of the mountain, close to the road, are some specimens of the critically endangered locally endemic baobab species, *Adansonia suarezensis* (they are the ones with smooth reddish bark; the grey-barked ones are *A. madagascariensis*).

It is a hot but rewarding climb, with splendid views and some nearby caves. Go early in the morning for the best birdwatching (and to avoid the heat of the day). The footpath is marked with red paint about 300m along the track on the left. If you are lucky you may spot Sandford's brown lemurs, snakes and chameleons.

Since early 2000 these cliffs and the interior of the cave have become a Mecca for rock climbers where French groups have put up many bolted routes. Enquire at King's Lodge for details.

For those seeking accommodation with a difference, why not try living like lemurs in the forest canopy? Local climbing specialists New Sea Roc have recently constructed **Jungle Park** (\ *82 218 54*; m *032 04 724 46*; e *newsearoc@moov.mg*; *www.jungle-park-nature.com*; €€€), a series of tree houses interconnected by steps, rope bridges and aerial runways, built around a central kitchen at ground level. The park at Vallée des Perroquets is also an environmental interpretation centre keen to forge close community ties, with reforestation, irrigation and school-building among their current projects. Activities include caving, rock climbing, tree climbing and birdwatching. Advance booking is essential.

RAMENA AND THE EAST COAST

The beach resort of Ramena provides a pleasant alternative to staying in Antsiranana. It is about 18km from the town centre, 45 minutes from the airport. Get there by *taxi-brousse* or by private taxi (about 40,000Ar round-trip). It's a beautiful drive around the curve of the bay, with some fine baobabs *en route*. Alternatively you can arrange a boat to take you there across the bay.

 WHERE TO STAY AND EAT

Le 5 Trop Près (10 bungalows) \ 82 908 82; m 032 07 740 60; e le5troppres@gmail.com; www.normada.com/5TROPI/. The name is pronounced 'Saint-Tropez'. New bungalows right on the beach. Good restaurant. €€€

Palm Beach (6 bungalows) m 032 02 409 04; e palmbeach@netcourrier.com. En-suite bungalows with fans. €€€

Casa en Falafy (20 bungalows) m 032 02 674 33; e contact@case-en-falafy.com; www.case-en-falafy.com. En-suite thatched bungalows for 3–7 people; quiet location 70m from beach. €€–€€€

Nautica (1 room) m 032 49 593 21. Trpl beachfront room with TV. €€€

Badamera (4 rooms & 3 bungalows) m 032 07 733 50; e badamera@hotmail.com. Attractive garden in breezy location. Buffet lunch with live music every Sun; theatrical performance on garden terrace every Sun eve. €€€

Ramena Nofy (15 bungalows) \ 82 920 30; m 032 49 822 71. En-suite bungalows with very comfy beds & en-suite cold showers, 2mins from beach. Delicious food, especially fish. €€€

Oasis (4 rooms & 1 bungalow) \ 82 925 08; m 034 08 261 70; e tony_oasis@moov.mg. Basic

In the days before mass air transportation, Madagascar's geographical location gave the island immense strategical importance. In World War II, British convoys to the Middle East and India sailed round the north of Madagascar, passing the great French naval base of Antsirane (now Antsiranana) at Diego Suarez. Antsirane, its harbour facilities completed in 1935, was France's most modern colonial port with a dry dock that could accommodate 28,000-ton battleships and an arsenal capable of repairing the largest of guns.

It was evident to both the Allied and Axis Powers that whoever held Diego Suarez controlled the western Indian Ocean. As the French authorities in Madagascar were firm supporters of the German-influenced Vichy Government, Britain believed that it had to occupy the island before it was handed over to her enemies. So, in the spring of 1942, Britain mounted Operation Ironclad, its first ever large-scale combined land, sea and air operation, to capture Diego Suarez as the initial step in occupying the whole island.

A force of some 13,000 troops with tanks and artillery, supported by 46 warships and transport vessels and 101 aircraft of the Fleet Air Arm, assembled to the north of Cap d'Ambre before dawn on 5 May 1942. The narrow entrance to Diego Suarez Bay was known to be powerfully defended by large-calibre artillery so the British decided to land in Courrier's Bay and march across country to take Antsirane from the landward side.

The first troops to land were Commandos, who captured the small battery that overlooked Courrier's Bay. The French and Senegalese defenders were still asleep and the position was taken with little loss of life. However, a small French force ensconced in an observation post on the summit of Windsor Castle could not be dislodged. For two days the French clung to their eyrie, despite repeated bombardments from the Royal Navy and attacks by the Fleet Air Arm and the Commandos.

With the beaches secured, the main British force landed and began its march upon Antsirane. Meanwhile, the Fleet Air Arm depth-charged and torpedoed the French warships and submarines at anchor in Diego Suarez Bay and bombed Arrachart airfield. But the defenders were now at their posts and an intense battle for possession of Diego Suarez began.

Some three miles to the south of Antsirane the French had built a strong defensive line across the isthmus of the Antsirane Peninsula. Devised by General Joffre in 1909, it comprised a trench network and an anti-tank ditch strengthened by forts and pillboxes

---

dbl rooms with AC & en-suite facilities (cold water). Internet (200Ar/min). €€

🛏 **Chez Grand-mère Jeanette** Very simple cheap accommodation. Food on request. €€

✗ **Emeraude** Restaurant & bar right on the beach.

✗ **Gargotte Chez Marie** Small place with cheap but excellent food.

DIVING Based in Ramena, **MadaScaph** (m *032 48 012 52;* e *info@madascaph.com; www.madascaph.com*) offers PADI-accredited scuba diving in the bays of the region.

MINI-GOLF (m *032 02 010 66*) About 1km from the centre of the village, on the road to Antsiranana, is a new French-owned 14-hole mini-golf course, which costs 10,000Ar per person. There is also a grill restaurant and swimming pool at the site.

BAIE DES DUNES A walk here makes a nice excursion from Ramena with good birdwatching prospects. Since part of the route passes through a military zone you will need to buy a permit from one of the sentries (take your passport).

From the village of Ramena, walk along the metalled road towards the headland

housing artillery and machine-guns. For two days the British forces assaulted the French line without success and with mounting losses.

The breakthrough came on the evening of 6 May when a British destroyer charged through the entrance of Diego Suarez Bay under the guns of the French batteries. The destroyer successfully landed a body of 50 Marines onto the quay. This tiny force stormed through the town, capturing the main barracks and the artillery headquarters. This disruption in their rear finally broke the defenders' resolve and when the main frontal attack was renewed the French line was overrun.

The fighting resulted in more than 1,000 casualties. The British commander submitted recommendations for more than 250 decorations, including three posthumous Victoria Crosses.

Britain's vital route to the east had been secured – but only in the nick of time. Barely three weeks after the capture of Antsirane, a Japanese submarine flotilla arrived off the coast of Madagascar. In a daring night raid the Japanese attacked the ships in Diego Suarez Bay, sinking one supply ship and severely damaging the flag ship of the British expedition, the battleship *Ramillies*.

With the island's main naval base in British hands, it was expected that the French Governor General, Armand Annet, would bow to the inevitable and relinquish control of the whole island. However, despite months of negotiations, Annet refused to surrender and Britain was forced to mount further military operations.

In September 1942, British and Commonwealth troops landed at Majunga and Tamatave. Brushing aside all attempts to stop and delay them, the Allies captured Tananarive only to find that Annet had retreated to the south of the island. But when a South African force landed at Tulear, Annet realised that he was trapped.

The French strung out surrender negotiations until one minute after midnight on 6 November – exactly six months and one day after the start of the British attack upon Diego Suarez. The significance of this was that French troops involved in a campaign lasting longer than six months were entitled to a medal and an increased state pension!

After a brief period of British Military Administration, the island was handed over to General de Gaulle's Free French movement. The key naval base of Antsirane, however, remained under British control until 1944.

John Grehan is the author of The Forgotten Invasion; *see page 415.*

John Grehan is the author of The Forgotten Invasion; *see page 415.*

– straight on from the bungalows rather than down to the beach – which will take you to the military installation where you show your pass at the gatehouse. Follow signs to the lighthouse/dunes past the barracks then along an open stretch to the hillside. The track continues past some ruined buildings and there is a signpost to the lighthouse. Carry on along the track, and the view opens up seaward as you approach Baie des Dunes.

The bay itself is overlooked by an old gun emplacement. On the beach to the right of this there is a stretch of white sand gently sloping to the sea; to the left there is a remnant reef with pools, then a steep drop off into the water; excellent for snorkelling. In front of the emplacement there is a small island which is accessible from the beach.

The whole area is excellent for wildlife, especially the pools, and there is the potential to spend the whole day here exploring if you bring a packed lunch.

SAKALAVA BAY On the far side of the Ramena peninsula is the beautiful and isolated Sakalava Bay. The turn-off is 8km beyond Ramena, after which it is a further 6km. A taxi here from Antsiranana should cost around 75,000Ar return.

On the 5km-long beach are the bungalows of **Sakalava Lodge** (\ *82 907 95;* m *032 04 512 39;* e *informations@sakalava.com; www.sakalava.com;* €€€€) where you will find a windsurfing and kitesurfing school. There is now also smarter mid-range accommodation at **Royal Sakalava** (\ *82 926 36/22 207 88;* m *032 05 777 05;* e *royal@relais-normand.mg; www.royalsakalava.com;* €€€€).

EMERALD SEA A little way to the north, opposite the headland, are the gorgeous turquoise waters of La Mer d'Emeraude, reachable only by boat from Ramena or Antsiranana. The shallow water is perfect for swimming and snorkelling, and windsurfing and kitesurfing are also available. Come for a day trip or stay at the newly opened **Babaomby Island Lodge** (m *032 55 009 39;* e *babaomby@hotmail.com; www.babaomby.com;* ◥) which has ten 'African safari'-style furnished tents.

EXCURSIONS WEST FROM ANTSIRANANA

WINDSOR CASTLE A few hours' drive due west from Antsiranana, this 390m-high monolith is steep-sided and flat-topped, so made a perfect lookout point during times of war. The views from there are superb. It was fortified by the French, occupied by the Vichy forces, and liberated by the British. A ruined staircase still runs to the top (if you can find it) but it is a hot, shadeless climb so take plenty of water and sun protection. There are many endemic succulents including a local species of pachypodium, *P. windsorii*.

To get there, a 4x4 is advised, but ordinary taxis can just about make it in good weather. Take the road that runs west across the salt pans to Antsahampano, then turn north for 12km before making a left turn and heading a further 5km.

COURRIER'S BAY Courrier's Bay, half an hour beyond Windsor Castle, is an exceptionally fine beach. This west-coast area of rugged beauty is the starting point for a number of hiking, fishing, climbing and diving activities, as well as visits to Nosy Hara.

NOSY HARA Nosy Hara, together with its surrounding islets, is a new marine reserve in Courrier's Bay where dolphins and turtles are often sighted. The area is reached by a two-hour drive through salt pans and mango plantations, then a tour of the islands can be made by pirogue. A camping trip of at least three days is recommended. To arrange a visit enquire at Note Bleue or, if you are interested in climbing, contact New Sea Roc who have a base there (contact details for both are on page 330).

CAP D'AMBRE Remote and rarely visited, Cap d'Ambre – the northernmost part of Madagascar – is reached via the route to Windsor Castle. Driving from Antsiranana to the disused lighthouse at the point of the cape takes about seven hours in a 4x4, the best route being via Bedarabe and Ambatonjanohavy.

The area has fantastic views, with both the Indian Ocean and the Mozambique Channel visible at once. There are good opportunities for hiking or mountain biking and areas of *tsingy* to explore.

MONTAGNE D'AMBRE (AMBER MOUNTAIN) NATIONAL PARK

This 18,500ha national park was created in 1958, the French colonial government recognising the unique nature of the volcanic massif and its forest. The park is part of the Montagne d'Ambre Reserves Complex which also includes Ankarana, Analamera and Forêt d'Ambre. The project was the first to involve local people in

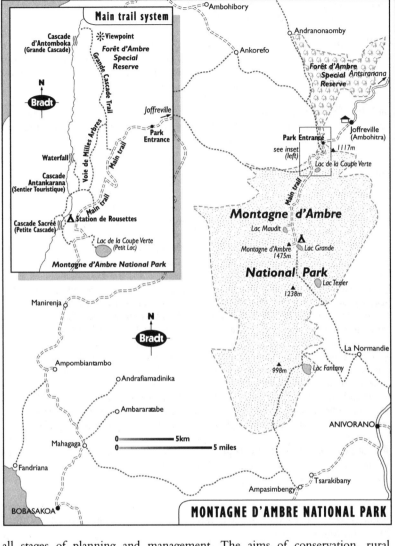

Main trail system

☀ Viewpoint

Cascade d'Antomboka (Grande Cascade)

Forêt d'Ambre Special Reserve

Grande Cascade Trail

N Bradt

Joffreville

Park Entrance

Voie de Milles Arbres

Main trail

Waterfall

Cascade Antankarana (Sentier Touristique)

Main trail

Cascade Sacrée (Petite Cascade)

▲ Station de Rousettes

Lac de la Coupe Verte (Petit Lac)

Montagne d'Ambre National Park

Ambohibory

Andranonaomby

Ankorefo

Forêt d'Ambre Special Reserve

Antsiranana

Park Entrance

see inset (left)

Joffreville (Ambohitra)

1117m

Lac de la Coupe Verte

Montagne d'Ambre

Lac Maudit

▲ Montagne d'Ambre 1475m

▲ Lac Grande

National Park

▲ Lac Texier

1238m

Manirenja

N Bradt

Ampombiantambo

Andrafiamadinika

Ambararatabe

La Normandie

▲ 998m

Lac Fantany

Mahagaga

ANIVORANO

0 — 5km
0 — 5 miles

Fandriana

BOBASAKOA

Ampasimbengy

Tsarakibany

MONTAGNE D'AMBRE NATIONAL PARK

all stages of planning and management. The aims of conservation, rural development and education have largely been achieved. Ecotourism has been encouraged successfully with good information and facilities now available.

Montagne d'Ambre National Park is a splendid example of montane rainforest. The massif ranges in altitude from 850m to 1,475m and has its own micro-climate with rainfall similar to the eastern region. It is one of the most visitor-friendly of Madagascar's protected areas, with broad trails, fascinating flora and fauna, a comfortable climate and readily available information. In the dry season vehicles can drive right up to the main picnic area, giving a unique opportunity (in Madagascar) for elderly or disabled visitors to see the rainforest and its inhabitants.

☞ **WARNING!** Antsiranana is now firmly on the itinerary of cruise ships, with Montagne d'Ambre the focus of the day's excursion. This means that a hundred or more passengers will pour into the park. Independent travellers may wish to visit the port to check if a ship is due before planning their visit.

PERMITS AND GUIDES Permits are available from the park office at the entrance or the National Parks office on the outskirts of Antsiranana towards the airport. Guides can also usually be found at the park office. All tour operators and most hotels can assist in planning a visit here.

GETTING THERE The entrance to the park is 27km south of Antsiranana, 4km from the town of Joffreville (Ambohitra). *Taxi-brousses* take about an hour and cost 4,000Ar. A taxi to Joffreville costs around 45,000Ar, or 55,000Ar to the park entrance 4km further up the hill.

 ## WHERE TO STAY AND EAT
Joffreville

Domaine de Fontenay (8 rooms & 1 suite) \ 82 908 71; m 033 11 345 81; e contact@ lefontenay-madagascar.com; www.lefontenay-madagascar.com. A delightfully quirky hotel. In a beautifully furnished & renovated manor house owned & run by couple Karl-Heinz Horner & Marie-José de Spéville, with brother Raymond. Warm hospitality, spacious chic rooms & delightful cooking. The house has a library & CD collection (for use in the car stereos installed in the sides of wardrobes in rooms!) & the gardens are home to Galileo the giant tortoise. Their 300ha private **nature park** is particularly good for reptiles & is running an active reforestation programme. 🐾

Nature Lodge (12 bungalows) m 032 07 123 06; e naturelodge@blueline.mg; www.naturelodge-ambre.com. Very comfortable dbl & trpl bungalows

with en-suite hot showers; tastefully designed bar & restaurant with excellent food. See ad on page 347. €€€€€

Litchi Tree m 033 12 784 54; e thelitchitree@hotmail.com; www.thelitchitree.com. Opened in 2008, this charming guesthouse is a meticulously restored villa originally built in 1902. Spacious rooms with solar-heated water. €€€€€

Hôtellerie du Monastère (8 rooms & dorms) m 032 04 795 24/032 04 795 34; e contact@gitesaintbenoit.com; www.gitesaintbenoit.com. Benedictine convent with good-value en-suite rooms & dorms with 5–7 beds. Communal meals; b/fast inc. €€€

Auberge Sakay-Tanay m 032 04 281 22; e contact@sakay-tany.com; www.sakay-tany.com. Good-value simple guesthouse. €€ €€€

Accommodation in the national park There are tent shelters and a hut with bunks in the park for visitors equipped with sleeping bags. From the wildlife point of view, staying in or near the park is far preferable to making a day trip from Antsiranana.

A campsite at the picnic area, known as Station des Rousettes, has running water, shower, toilet and barbeque facilities. Firewood is available from the warden, but bring your own food.

WEATHER The rainy season is from December to April. It is usually dry from May to August, but there is a strong wind, *varatraza*, almost every day and it can feel quite cold. The temperature in the park is, on average, 5°C cooler than in Antsiranana. It is often wet and muddy and there may be leeches – so be wary of wearing shorts and sandals however hot and dry you are at sea level. Bring waterproofs, insect repellent and even a light sweater.

The most rewarding time to visit is during the warm season: September to November. There will be some rain, but most animals are active and visible, and the lemurs will have babies.

FLORA AND FAUNA Montagne d'Ambre is as exciting for its plants as for its animals. All visitors are impressed by the tree ferns and the huge, epiphytic bird's nest ferns which grow on trees. The distinctive *Pandanus* is also common and you can see Madagascar's endemic cycad. Huge strangler figs add to the spectacle.

Most visitors want to see lemurs and two diurnal species have become habituated: Sanford's brown lemur and crowned lemur. Male Sanford's lemurs have white/beige ear-tufts and side-whiskers surrounding black faces, whilst the females are more uniform in colour with no whiskers and a grey face. Crowned lemurs get their names from the triangular head markings, most distinctive in the male. Young are born from September to November. There are also five species of nocturnal lemur.

Another mammal often seen is the ring-tailed mongoose, and if you are really lucky you could see a fossa or its relative the falanouc.

At eye level you may spot some large chameleons, also often seen crossing the road during the drive up from Antsiranana. A good guide should be able to find some of the tiny *Brookesia* chameleons that David Attenborough came here to film in 2007 for his *Life in Cold Blood* series, and also the most amazingly camouflaged of all lizards, the mossy leaf-tailed gecko. You won't find it yourself, believe me! Plus there are many frogs, pill millipedes rolling into perfect balls, butterflies and other invertebrates.

Even non-birders will be fascinated by the numerous species here: the Madagascar crested ibis is striking enough to impress anybody, as is the Madagascar paradise flycatcher with its long, trailing tail feathers. The locally endemic Amber Mountain rock thrush is tame and ubiquitous, and the black-and-white magpie robin is often seen. The jackpot, however, is one of Madagascar's most beautiful birds: the pitta-like ground-roller.

TRAILS, WATERFALLS AND LAKES The park has over 30km of paths, many of which are quite flat and easy. Three waterfalls provide the focal points for day visitors. If time is short and you want to watch wildlife rather than walk far, go to the **Cascade Sacrée**, an idyllic fern-fringed grotto with waterfalls splashing into a pool. This is only about 100m along the track beyond the picnic area (Station des Rousettes) and on the way you should see lemurs, chameleons, orchids and birds galore. Take a small path on your left to the river for a possible glimpse of the white-throated rail and the Madagascar malachite kingfisher.

The **Sentier Touristique** is also easy and starts near the Station des Rousettes. The path terminates at a viewpoint above **Cascade Antankarana**: a highly photogenic spot.

The walk to the **Cascade d'Antomboka** is tougher, with some up-and-down stretches, and a steep descent to the waterfall. There is excellent birdwatching here, some lovely tree ferns and a good chance of seeing lemurs.

On your way back you'll pass a path marked '**Voie des Mille Arbres**'. It's a roller-coaster of a walk, but very rewarding, and eventually joins the main track. Ring-tailed mongooses are often seen along this stretch.

Sadly wildlife is reportedly becoming harder to see near the busier main trail system, so if you're visiting for more than a day trip then one of the longer hikes is recommended.

Beyond the Cascade d'Amtomboka, the trail eventually reaches a river and the rarest of all baobab species: *Adansonia perrieri*. There are two or three in the area, and the largest stands at a truly impressive 25m or so tall with a massive girth. This is a tough walk; allow three to four hours for the round-trip.

Other walks from Station des Rousettes include the easy climb to the viewpoint above the crater lake, **Lac de la Coupe Verte**. A full day's walk takes you to a crater lake known as **Lac Maudit**, or Matsabory Fantany, then on for another hour to **Lac Grand**. Beyond that is the highest point in the park, the peak of **Montagne d'Ambre** itself (1,475m). Unless you are a fit, fast walker it would be best to take two days on this trek and camp by Lac Grand. That way you can wait for weather conditions to allow the spectacular view.

EXCURSIONS SOUTH FROM ANTSIRANANA

RIGNY BAY On the east coast, an hour from Antsiranana, this natural harbour is home to an attractive new hotel. **Ile aux Baobabs** (\ *82 919 47*; m *032 40 487 87*; e *ileauxbaobabs@gmail.com;* €€€€) offers upper-range accommodation in the form of bungalows along a private beach. Activities include hiking, quad biking and fishing.

The hotel is reached from Andrafiabe, 26km south of Antsiranana, via a 17km road to the coast.

RED TSINGY About an hour south of Antsiranana are these spectacular geological features. Like the true *tsingy* of Ankarana and Bemaraha, the Red Tsingy are erosion phenomena, but are formed from laterite rather than limestone, giving them a striking orange-red hue and a rather more rounded Daliesque appearance then their duller spiky cousins.

Three main patches of red *tsingy* are accessible on a 17km track that begins 46km south of Antsiranana. An entry fee of 2,000Ar is charged per vehicle. You will need a 4x4 to get there and it's not accessible at all during the wet season (roughly December–March).

ANALAMERA (ANALAMERANA) SPECIAL RESERVE (e *angapdie@gmail.com*) This 34,700ha reserve is in remote and virtually unexplored deciduous forest southeast of Montagne d'Ambre, and is the last refuge of the very rare Perrier's sifaka (*Propithecus perrieri*). You may also see crowned lemurs, Sanford's brown lemurs and endangered birds such as the white-breasted mesite and Van Dam's vanga. The park merits a couple of nights' camping, but there are no facilities of any kind, so visitors must be totally self-sufficient.

To reach the reserve from Antsiranana drive 60km south on the main road, and then a further 25km on a dreadful stretch which is impassable in the rainy season. An alternative route in starts 45km south of Antsiranana. Guides and porters can be organised in the nearby village of Menagisy, but it is more sensible to arrange the visit through a tour operator in Antsiranana (essential if you need an English-speaking guide). Visit the park office in Anivorano (PK 75) first to get permits.

LAKE ANTANAVO (LAC SACRÉ) The turning is 75km south of Antsiranana at Anivorano, where you must buy a permit (4,000Ar/person) before proceeding to the sacred lake along a 4km track that is impassable in the rainy season. It attracts visitors more for its legends than for the reality of a not particularly scenic lake, and the possibility of seeing a crocodile. Locals feed them occasionally, so ask a tour operator in Antsiranana when the next croc-feeding day is.

The story is that once upon a time Anivorano was situated amid semi-desert and a thirsty traveller arrived at the village asking for a drink. When his request was refused he warned the villagers that they would soon have more water than they could cope with. No sooner had he left than the earth opened, water gushed out, and the mean locals and their houses were inundated. The crocodiles which now inhabit the lake are considered to be ancestors and to wear jewellery belonging to their previous selves. The most important crocodile was said to wear a bracelet. In 1990, so I've heard, a big croc came up into the rice fields and was killed by a mob of young locals. But when they saw that it was the famous bracelet-wearing one, the worried villagers gave him a proper burial in the cemetery. Then one by one all those involved in the killing mysteriously died.

Two to three hours south of Antsiranana is the limestone massif of Ankarana. An 'island' of *tsingy* (limestone karst pinnacles) and forest, the massif is penetrated by numerous caves and canyons. Some of the largest caves have collapsed, forming isolated pockets of river-fed forest with their own perfectly protected flora and fauna. Dry deciduous forest grows around the periphery and into the wider

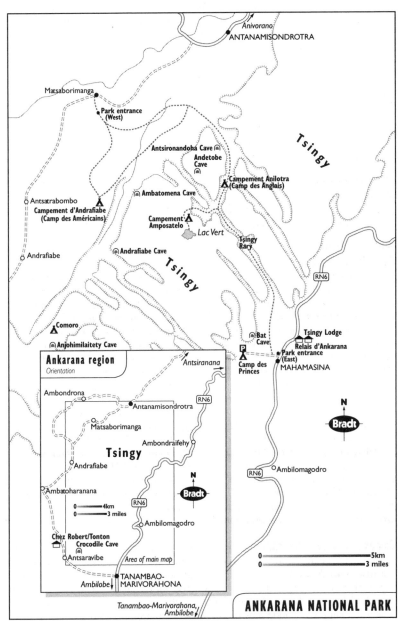

canyons. The caves and their rivers are also home to crocodiles, some reportedly 6m long. The reserve is known for its many lemur species, including crowned and Sanford's brown lemurs, and also the inquisitive ring-tailed mongoose, but it is marvellous for birds, reptiles and insects as well. Indeed, the wow-factor is as high here as anywhere I have visited.

GETTING THERE AND AWAY The main entrance to this reserve is on the east side at Mahamasina on RN6, 108km south of Antsiranana. By *taxi-brousse* it is about three hours from Ambanja or 2½ hours from Antsiranana. There is a park office near the trailhead, from where it is a couple of hours' walk into the reserve.

There are two other gateways, but a 4x4 is required to access them: the southwest entry point is near Amboandriky, and the northwest one (not reachable in the rainy season) is at Matsaborimanga.

ORGANISED TOURS It is not difficult to do Ankarana independently, provided you have your own tent or settle for a day visit only, but most visitors prefer to let a local tour operator take care of the logistics. Levels of organisation and comfort vary considerably, so your choice will depend on your budget. Any Antsiranana-based tour operator can arrange an all-inclusive camping visit.

PERMITS AND GUIDES A permit for Ankarana may be purchased at the entrance or alternatively from the National Parks office in Antsiranana or Tana. See page 72 for permit prices. Guides are compulsory and can be found at the park office in Mahamasina. Guide fees range from 12,000Ar to 30,000Ar per circuit.

 WHERE TO STAY
Outside the park

⌂ **Ankarana Lodge** (3 bungalows & 7 rooms) ☏ 82 225 99; m 032 04 908 10; e info@ankaranalodge.com; www.ankarana-lodge.com. Located 1km from Mahamasina, this brand new hotel has dbl rooms & large shelters with luxury tents with shared facilities as well as en-suite bungalows. See ad after page 408. €€€€

⌂ **Relais de l'Ankarana** (6 bungalows) m 032 02 222 94; e ankarana_lerelais@yahoo.fr; www.relaisdelankarana.unblog.fr. Situated 1km north of Mahamasina, this hotel is popular with tour operators so advance booking is essential. Quite simple but comfortable & reliable. €€€

⌂ **Ankarana Village** (6 bungalows) Mahamasina. Pretty dbl & trpl bungalows with electricity & en-suite cold shower; communal toilet. €€

⌂ **Chez Robert/Tonton** (17 rooms) Ambatomitsangana (10 km off RN6). Palm-thatch pavilion with dining & lounge space, simple rooms & shared toilets but no running water. Independent travellers can catch a *taxi-brousse* from Ambilobe to Antsaravibe (only dependable May–Nov); get out at Maromena & walk the last 2km. €€

⌂ **Chez Laurent** (14 bungalows) Mahamasina; m 032 07 992 89. Basic bungalows with shared facilities (cold water). No electricity. €–€€

⌂ **Goulam Lodge** (12 bungalows) Mahamasina; m 032 52 682 82/032 02 691 06; e goulamguide_ds@yahoo.fr. Dbl & family bungalows with electricity; shared facilities. Goulam speaks excellent English & is an experienced guide specialised in reptiles. €–€€

⌂ **Chez Aurelien** (18 bungalows) Mahamasina; m 032 02 786 00/032 40 630 14; e aurelien_ank@yahoo.fr. Basic bungalows, some en suite. No electricity. Very good food. Camping for 3,000Ar/tent. €

Campsites inside the park The main campsite, formerly known as Camp des Anglais (following a British expedition in the 1980s), has been renamed **Campement Anilotra**. It is equipped with long-drop toilets and picnic tables. Note that the camp offers considerably more shade than Campement d'Andrafiabe, as well as a chance to bathe in the river running through the cave. The water supply is a good ten-minute walk down a slippery slope.

Daniel Austin & Kelly Green

This was one of our most testing reserve visits, and the suffering began as soon as we left Antsiranana. Hiring a car and driver for this four-day trip 108km to the south was not a viable option on our budget, so instead we caught a *taxi-brousse*. Sardines don't even know what 'crammed in' means – there were fully thirty of us in this small 15-seater minibus for the majority of the three-hour trip.

On arrival at Ankarana, the relief of having the use of our limbs again soon turned to irritation: this time by the local cicadas. These pesky insects are about 7cm long and look like a cross between a cockroach and a gigantic bluebottle. All day long a cicada's job is to sit on a tree and screech. Their shrill tones fill the forest with chainsaw-like screams. We've often seen and heard solitary cicadas elsewhere, but at Ankarana there were literally thousands of them vibrating their tymbals (noise-making membranes) in unison.

But even when the calls of the cicadas subsided, there was no respite. Large, orange-brown flies – like horseflies – followed us everywhere, circling, buzzing constantly and occasionally diving in for a bite. Killing them was fruitless; reinforcements were always ready to take their place. And then there were the swarms of mosquitoes, which found Kelly's anklebones particularly tasty, biting them (through her socks) until they were red raw and infuriatingly itchy.

On top of all this we had to be particularly wary of scorpions, carefully checking inside our shoes and rucksack pockets. And there were tarantulas. And crocodiles…

But we would be lying if we said Ankarana wasn't one of our most fantastic experiences during the whole six-month trip. All of its downsides combined don't even come close to equalling the positives; it is a magical place of stunning landscapes and fascinating creatures.

Visitors must not be put off by our experiences. We later discovered that December can be one of the most difficult times to visit this reserve.

The usual alternative campsite is **Campement d'Andrafiabe** (Camp des Américains), which is handy for the Andrafiabe Cave. It has a water supply and toilets, but can get crowded.

An increasingly popular camp is **Camp des Princes**, which has long-drop toilets and picnic tables. Water is a problem: it's hard to get in the dry season so you need to bring your own. There is a bat cave nearby and some small *tsingy* about half an hour's walk away, but to reach the main *tsingy* you must walk a 32km round-trip.

Camp Amposatelo is about two hours from Campement Anilotra and is a good base for visiting Lac Vert and some of the best *tsingy*.

☞ *WARNING!* If you are going to happen upon a scorpion anywhere in Madagascar, it is likely to be at Ankarana. Be cautious and check carefully inside pockets, bags and shoes to avoid a very nasty sting.

WHAT TO SEE AND DO

***Tsingy* and lake** Although found in other countries, *tsingy* is very much a Madagascar phenomenon and you won't want to leave Ankarana without seeing it. If staying at Anilotra Camp, the best *tsingy* is about two hours away, over very rugged terrain, just beyond the beautiful crater lake, **Lac Vert**. This is a very hot, all-day trip (start early and take plenty of water) and is absolutely magnificent. Board walks have been constructed to allow safe passage over the *tsingy*, protecting

14

the fragile rock while you admire the strange succulents such as pachypodiums which seem to grow right out of the limestone.

Lac Vert is as green as its name, and if you are crazy enough you can hike down a steep, slippery slope to the water's edge. An easier alternative is the **Petit Tsingy** which is found just 15 minutes from the campsite. Although smaller, there are similar plants and also lemurs.

Caves From Andrafiabe Camp you can explore the gigantic passageways of **Andrafiabe Cave**. This is well worth a visit with an exit halfway through into one of the spectacular canyons from where an interesting return can be made.

At the south, the **Crocodile Cave**, so named because it is home to the world's only known cave-dwelling crocs, is little-visited but is well worth the effort – the situation is spectacular and the passageways are huge. It is easily walkable in about 30 minutes from the entrance to the eastern end, from where it is a steep, rocky climb out into the sunken forest.

Don't miss the wonderful bat caves, many of which also feature incredible sparkling stalagmites and stalactites.

Shrimp and sugar factories There is an aquaculture centre, **Gambas of Akarana**, 12km from Campement d'Andrafiabe. You can visit to learn the ins and outs of shrimp-breeding, and witness the manufacture and packaging of shrimp products.

Not far away, it is also possible to visit the **Sirama** sugar factory and stroll through the fields of sugar cane.

FROM ANTSIRANANA TO IHARANA (VOHEMAR) BY ROAD

From Antsiranana to Ambilobe RN6 is a good road; by *taxi-brousse* it takes about three hours to cover the 138km. The next 163km to Iharana on RN5a, however, is in rather worse condition and may take ten hours or more.

If you can possibly afford it, hire a private car. This is not just because it cuts the trip down to a manageable seven hours or so but it gives you the chance to visit the highly rewarding reserve of Daraina.

AMBILOBE This is a very gritty transit town, busy at all hours with traffic. It lies at an important junction linking Antsiranana in the north with Iharana on the east coast, so you may need to stop here. There are some basic hotels and a superb pizzeria which almost makes the stop worthwhile in itself.

If you're passing through in late July or early August, you may catch the annual regional cultural festival which combines traditional oratory, music and dance.

Getting there and away There are frequent *taxi-brousses* to Ambanja (6,000Ar; 2 hours) and Antsiranana (9,000Ar; 3 hours). They cruise around town from early in the morning collecting customers, so pick an almost-full one if you want a reasonably quick getaway. There are also *bachés* for the very rough journey to Vohemar via Daraina.

Where to stay and eat

Noor (14 rooms) m 032 42 509 00. Behind the Jovenna fuel station at the north of town. It's a pleasant old-fashioned place built around a courtyard with en-suite bathrooms & some AC rooms; a few have hot water & TV. €€€

National (10 rooms) \ 82 065 41; m 032 42 577 84. Good en-suite dbl rooms, some with AC & TV. €€–€€€

Diana (14 bungalows) m 032 43 055 33/032 45 921 10. Dbl rooms with en-suite cold showers;

some with AC & TV. Situated 2.5km from centre (towards Ambanja) so more peaceful. Restaurant (🕑 06.00–late). €€–€€€

🛏 **Amicale** (16 rooms) m 032 02 902 61. Very noisy with cold water only & poor security – but cheap. €

✕ **Coco Pizza** By far the best eatery; opposite Jovenna. Range of delicious thin-crust pizzas cooked in a wood-fired oven.

✕ **Escargot** An acceptable restaurant down a side street in the centre.

DARAINA Daraina is a small town 56km northwest of Iharana (3 hours), or 114km (5 hours) from Ambilobe. If you are taking that road anyway, it makes the whole journey worthwhile; if you're in Iharana it's worth making it a day's excursion.

The reason to go here is to see the beautiful golden-crowned sifaka (*Propithecus tattersalli*), one of the rarest of all lemurs and listed as one of the 25 most threatened primates in the world. Yet you *will* see the sifaka, and close-up (see box below) and this is probably the only place in Madagascar where you can have this sort of experience without crowds sharing it with you. The sifaka tend to sleep in the heat of midday (and it's murderously hot then for humans too) so if coming for a day trip make a really early start.

A Malagasy NGO called FANAMBY is working with the local communities to preserve the forests and the sifakas. The region has deposits of gold and is rich in semi-precious stones – one of the factors causing conflict with the establishment of a protected reserve.

Guides charge 25,000Ar. Allow about three hours for a visit to the sifakas. It takes an hour to reach them: drive 20 minutes west from Daraina then turn right onto a very bad track for a further 20 minutes. It's then a 20-minute walk through forest to Andranotsimaty, where you'll start seeing sifakas and as soon as they see you watching them they'll come down to investigate.

SEEING SOME OF THE RAREST PRIMATES IN THE WORLD

Lee Miller

On arriving in Daraina, we find a guide and head to the forest. The forest floor is pock-marked with holes in the ground, five feet across and equally deep. We realise that these are dug by gold miners; and indeed we come upon a group of people panning for gold.

After hiking in the heat for another half hour, our guide points to the top of a tree where we see a sifaka! Soon enough, he motions us along further, and there is a group of eight more, all far up in the trees. As we watch them, they begin to come down to us, scrambling down the trunks, and leaping from tree to tree. Their leaping is one of the most amazing things I've ever seen. They are spring-loaded. With barely a sign that it is about to leap, a sifaka will suddenly thrust with its back legs and shoot 20–30 feet horizontally to another tree, grabbing effortlessly to cling to that trunk. Beautiful and thrilling.

They keep coming down, peering around the trees at us, until some are just five feet away, watching us with their curious brown eyes. A little baby clings to his mother's back as she approaches. As she settles in to watch us, he asserts his independence and climbs onto a nearby branch, only to leap again onto her back at the slightest sound. Later we watch as she walks on her hind legs across the forest floor, walking in a kind of dance with her baby riding along. It is *fady* to kill them in this area and so they have no fear of humans. These are among the rarest primates in the world; yet here, in their home, they are so easily viewed. It is a remarkable and delightful opportunity, well worth the discomforts of the journey.

In Daraina, cheap food and simple accommodation can be found at **Hôtel Camarade**. For more information contact FANAMBY (\/f *22 288 78;* e *fanamby@fanamby.org.mg; www.fanamby.org.mg*).

IHARANA (VOHEMAR) This seafront town, known almost universally as Vohemar, marks the end of the good road north from Sambava and Andapa, and the start of the rather bad road connecting the east coast with RN6.

Part of its charm is a near absence of tourists, but there are a couple of beachfront hotels. And in contrast to the roaring ocean further down the coast, Iharana's bay is sheltered and protected by a reef. If you potter along the low tide pools you can find a wealth of sea creatures. Keep walking and you'll pass a sacred tree, hung with white cloth and zebu skulls. It's a reminder that the local culture is still very much intact in this isolated place.

The town itself is nothing special. There is a BOA bank, an internet café, a pharmacy, a lively nightclub (Zanzibar), a few restaurants and some surprisingly good gift shops.

Getting there and away The easiest way to get here is to fly to Sambava then take a *taxi-brousse* for the two-hour road journey. The route from Antsiranana is described earlier in this chapter.

Where to stay and eat

Baie d'Iharana (16 rooms) m 032 07 131 46/032 05 131 49; e mcmahvo@moov.mg. Italian-owned upmarket hotel set in a beautiful garden with super views of the bay from comfortable AC rooms with balconies. The spacious dining room has ocean views. Easy beach access. Excursions organised, including to Daraina. €€€€

Sol y Mar (20 rooms) \ 88 063 56; m 032 62 493 98/032 41 969 90; e solymar-hotel.vohemar@blueline.mg; http://hotelsolymar-vohemar.ifrance.com. Very pleasant en-suite bungalows, some with ocean views. Frogs in the toilet at no extra charge. Superb meals. €€€

Floride (5 rooms) m 032 04 590 68. Simple rooms with shared facilities. €€

AMBILOBE TO AMBANJA (AND ON TO NOSY BE)

RN6 is now a pretty good road so this route is popular with travellers heading for Nosy Be – but there is plenty to see in the area so it is a shame to rush. The Ambilobe to Ambanja section is 102km.

AMBANJA This is a pleasant little town set amid lush scenery. There's a BOA bank, a post office, several pharmacies and a cybercafé called Fiesta near the covered market.

Getting there and away Most people stopping at Ambanja are on their way to or from Nosy Be. Ankify (the ferry departure point for Nosy Be) is 22km away but takes about an hour because the last 16km is on a very bad road; transport costs 4,000Ar.

Taxi-brousses run north and south: Antsiranana (5 hours/20,000Ar), Antsohihy (4 hours/20,000Ar), Mahajanga (14 hours/50,000Ar) and Antananarivo (16 hours/60,000Ar).

Where to stay and eat

Auberge Eco-Ethnique Alamita (15 bungalows) m 032 02 043 57; e robian@moov.mg; www.mangrove-madagascar.com. Situated some distance north of town in the mangroves of Ambaro Bay this lodge is surrounded by nature. €€€€

🏠 **Diamant IO** (6 rooms & I suite) ✆ 86 502 59. En-suite rooms with AC & fridge. €€€

🏠 **Palma Nova** (10 rooms) ✆ 86 900 41; m 032 48 140 49; e palma_nova@yahoo.fr. Peaceful setting 1km from centre. Dbl, twin & trpl en-suite rooms, some with AC. Bike hire. €€€

🏠 **Meridien** (10 rooms) ✆ 86 500 11; m 032 47 782 29; e houshm@yahoo.fr. Nice place; en-suite (cold water) rooms with TV, some with AC. €€€

🏠 **Ylang-Ylang** (12 rooms) ✆ 86 502 40; m 032 05 502 40. Range of rooms with TV, some en suite with hot water & fridge. Internet. €€–€€€

🏠 **Cocotiers** (13 rooms & I villa) m 032 04 847 93. Dbl rooms with en-suite cold showers, a few with AC. Also 8-person villa with hot water. Good restaurant. €€–€€€

🏠 **Bougainvilleas** (m 032 40 659 53), **Chez Sachine** (m 032 40 876 74), **Patricia** (✆ 86 500 22) & **Salama Rose** (m 032 45 243 27) offer the cheapest accommodation. €€

ANKIFY AREA This beautiful area of coast is being developed as a resort, and has some very good hotels. But don't expect a proper village here – there are no shops or other ways of whiling away the time as you are waiting for the ferry.

Hotel transfers to the ferry port typically cost 15,000Ar, but you should be able to find a local vehicle for 5,000Ar – or walk.

🏠 Where to stay and eat

🏠 **Baobab** (20 bungalows) m 032 40 478 68/032 07 208 87; e baobabankify@yahoo.fr. Nestled between rocky cliffs & a beach that overlooks Nosy Komba, 1.5km from ferry. Pleasant dbl bungalows with separate bathrooms (cold water) in beautifully planted grounds. Electricity in evenings. Good food. €€€€

🏠 **Chez Nono** (2 bungalows & 4 rooms) m 032 04 664 22/032 07 927 97. En-suite rooms (cold water), I with kitchenette; 4.5km from ferry. €€€€

🏠 **Dauphin Bleu** (8 bungalows) ✆ 86 926 11; m 032 45 334 61; e info@ledauphinbleu.eu; www.ledauphinbleu.com. Stone bungalows, en-suite cold water for 2–4 people, 4km from ferry. Private beach; snorkelling possible. €€€€

🏠 **Ankify-Marina** (2 bungalows & 4 rooms) ✆ 86 920 80; m 033 17 846 03. Dbl Rooms, 3km from ferry. Electricity in evenings. €€€

🏠 **Mangroves & Porte Rouge** both offer very basic cheap rooms right at the port. €

BAOBAB BEACH On the opposite side of Ampasindava Bay from Ankify is a new ecolodge only really accessible by boat. **Eden Lodge** (m *032 02 203 61/034 86 931*

PRISON DETAIL   *Rupert Parker*

With many years' experience of travelling by *taxi-brousse* I know that they carry anything and everything – bicycles, chickens, baskets of fish all crammed in with people filled to bursting point. On New Year's Eve we were on the way to Iharana from Sambava on the newly surfaced road. Strapped to the roof were a gaggle of geese ready for the festive pot, baskets of mangos and other fruit, as well as everybody's luggage – oh, and a large sofa. About halfway we were flagged down by the police. Just the obligatory security check, I thought, and we'd soon be on our way. The driver was called into the police hut and a few minutes later emerged with two gun-toting officers, a couple of geese, and a rather desperate-looking prisoner handcuffed to one of the policemen. He cleared the seat in front of us and the prison detail took their places.

Now, what happens in a crowded *taxi-brousse* when a prisoner tries to make a break for it? Do the police start shooting, and what happens if he leans over and grabs me as a hostage? I spent a very tense couple of hours mulling all this over, but of course we reached Vohemar safely and the prisoner was taken off to spend an unhappy Christmas in a Malagasy cell.

Wandering into the Tsaratanana Massif to ascend Maromokotro – Madagascar's highest peak at 2,876m – is a task rarely undertaken by any climber. Its remoteness requires a 14-day round trip on foot, crossing waist-deep rivers, bashing through dense jungle and summiting on a peak reminiscent of the Pennines. The peak is held sacred by the locals so we took a plentiful supply of white chickens with us to appease the ancestors! The climate varies incredibly from burning grassland to freezing moorland in only a few days, and requires stamina for the 30-plus kilometres you have to cover each day. A local guide with porters led the way for me through the maze of hills and valleys, walking barefoot as I followed on in walking boots. Theirs was the last laugh however as my boots fell apart from the combination of dry, wet, dust and mud. I finished in sports sandals.

Initially we followed the river out of Ambanja before breaking off into the hills and leaving the last villages behind. Suddenly we were in a world of tall grass, then thick forest, before the moorland opened up. Being a Derbyshire lad it almost felt like home as we approached the summit and soon I overlooked most of northern Madagascar. It was here we left a white chicken along with money, tobacco and alcohol as a blessing. Quite what a chicken does at almost 3,000m I'm not sure! Heading home was an epic in itself as the jungle paths were almost nonexistent and dawn-till-dark days were spent cutting through the dense undergrowth hoping we were going in the right direction. Soon the first villages appeared and once again the savanna opened up before us on the long walk home.

Scaling Maromokotro marked the completion of a four-year challenge in which Nigel climbed the seven highest mountains of the world's seven largest islands; see www.into-thin-air.co.uk.

19; **f** *86 932 75;* **e** *resa@edenlodge.net; www.edenlodge.net;* 🍽) has good food and facilities in a tremendous location with a marvellous beach and lush forest. Its eight bungalows are entirely solar powered

CONTINUING SOUTH FROM AMBANJA TO MAHAJANGA For a description of this journey see *Chapter 16*, page 372.

BAYS AND INLETS ACCESSIBLE TO YACHTS

The bays below could be reached by adventurous hikers or cyclists (many are near villages) but are visited mainly by yachties (lucky devils!).

RUSSIAN BAY (HELONDRANON' AMBAVATOBY) This is a beautiful and remote place opposite the Nosy Be archipelago. It provides excellent anchorages, all-round shelter and is a traditional 'hurricane hole'. The marine life in the bay itself is terrific, offering wonderful snorkelling and diving, especially on the reefs outside the entrance. There is excellent fishing too and in the right season (October to December) whales are commonly sighted. This is also one of the best spots in which to seek the very rare whale shark. The beaches are known turtle-nesting sites. The moist tropical deciduous woods harbour abundant birdlife, reptiles and lemurs, and there is a choice of trails for day hikes.

The bay's name dates back to the 1905 Russo-Japanese War when a Russian fleet spent nine weeks harboured there. On their departure, they left behind a leaky transport ship to sink at anchor in the bay.

BARAMAHAMAY BAY (MAROAKA) The Baramahamay River is navigable for about 3km inland and provides a beautiful, well-sheltered anchorage with verdant hills behind sunny, white beaches. The wide bay is conspicuous as a large gap in the coastline. Yachties should approach on the north side of the bay and anchor near the villages in 8m over sand and mud. These villages are known also for their blacksmiths, who make large knives and pangas, and another is famous for its wild honey. Your chances of seeing rare Madagascar fish eagles here are good.

BERANGOMAINA POINT The bay inside this headland is an attractive, well-sheltered anchorage. Good visibility is needed to access the bay, however, as there are many scattered reef patches. The channel is at its deepest on the north side, where the depth exceeds 15m right up to the reef. Anchor off the beach before the village, in 10m over a mud bottom. This place is for self-sufficient travellers only; no provisions are available.

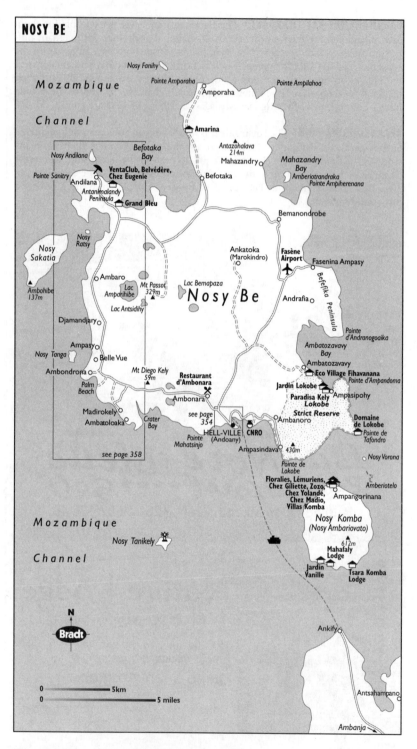

NOSY BE

Mozambique

Channel

Nosy Fanihy

Pointe Amporaha

Amporaha

Pointe Ampilahoa

Befotaka
Bay

Amarina

Antazohalava
214m

Mahazandry

Mahazandry
Bay

Amberiotrandraka
Pointe Ampiherenana

Nosy Andilana

Pointe Sanitry

Andilana

VentaClub, Belvédère,
Chez Eugenie

Antanimalandy
Peninsula

Grand Bleu

Befotaka

Bemanondrobe

Nosy
Sakatia

Nosy
Ratsy

Ankatoka
(Marokindro)

Fasène
Airport

Fasenina Ampasy

Ambohibe
137m

Ambaro

Lac
Amparihibe

Mt Passot
329m

Lac Bemapaza

Nosy Be

Andrafia

Befefika Peninsula

Lac Antsidihy

Pointe
d'Andranogoaika

Djamandjary

Ampasy

Nosy Tanga

Belle Vue

Ambatozavavy
Bay

Ambondrona

Mt Diego Kely
59m

Restaurant
d'Ambonara

Ambatozavavy

Eco Village Fihavanana

Pointe d'Ampandoma

Jardin Lokobe

Palm
Beach

Ambonara

see page
354

Paradisa Kely
Lokobe

Ampasipohy

Madirokely

Ambatoloaka

Crater
Bay

Strict Reserve

Domaine
de Lokobe

Pointe de
Tafondro

HELL-VILLE
(Andoany)

CNRO

Ambanoro

Pointe
Mahatsinjo

Ampasindava

430m

Nosy Vorona

see page 358

Pointe de
Lokobe

Floralies, Lémuriens,
Chez Giliette, Zozo,
Chez Yolandé,
Chez Madio,
Villas Komba

Amberiotelo

Ampangorinana

Mozambique

Channel

Nosy Tanikely

Nosy Komba
(Nosy Ambariovato)

612m

Mahafaly
Lodge

Jardin
Vanille

Tsara Komba
Lodge

N

Bradt

Ankify

Antsahampano

0   5km

0   5 miles

Ambanja

15

Nosy Be

The name means 'big island' and is pronounced '*nossy bay*' by the local Sakalava people, although '*nooss bay*' is nearer the highland pronunciation. It is blessed with an almost perfect climate for much of the year. Fertile and prosperous, with the heady scent of ylang-ylang blossoms giving it the tourist-brochure name of 'Perfumed Isle', this is the place to come for a rest – providing you can afford it. Compared with the rest of Madagascar, Nosy Be is expensive.

Tourism developed here long before the mainland, so inevitably the island seems touristy to adventurous travellers. Since the recent demise of the sugar industry, all available land is being bought up for hotel development. This, in turn, has pushed prices ever higher. That said, Nosy Be provides a taste of everything that is special to Madagascar – from good seafood and beaches to chameleons and lemurs – so it is ideal for those with limited time looking for a hassle-free holiday. It also has several options for real luxury – rare in the rest of Madagascar.

The only significant town is **Hell-Ville**, where you'll need to go if you require such services as banks or airline offices. It has some basic accommodation but no beach; most tourists will want to stay at the better hotels stretching along the west coast. The beachfront village of **Ambatoloaka** in the southwest comprises a couple of dozen hotels and restaurants, so this is the place to stay if you want to be within walking distance of a good choice of places to eat. Heading north, the hotels become progressively more isolated and the beaches better. For an even more remote experience, consider staying on one of the islets surrounding Nosy Be.

Thanks are especially due to Nosy Be resident Harriet Joao of MadagasCaT Charters & Travel for updates to this chapter.

HISTORY

Nosy Be's charms were recognised as long ago as 1649 when the English colonel Robert Hunt wrote: 'I do believe, by God's blessing, that not any part of the world is more advantageous for a plantation, being every way as well for pleasure as well as profit, in my estimation.' Hunt was attempting to set up an English colony on the island, known then as Assada, but failed because of hostile natives and disease.

Future immigrants, both accidental and intentional, contributed to Nosy Be's racial variety. Shipwrecked Indians built a magnificent settlement several centuries ago in the southeast of the island, where the ruins can still be seen. The crew of a Russian ship that arrived during the Russo-Japanese War of 1904–05 are buried in the Hell-Ville cemetery. Other arrivals were Arabs, Comorans and – more recently – Europeans flocking to Madagascar's foremost holiday resort.

When King Radama I was completing his wars of conquest, the Boina kings took refuge in Nosy Be. First they sought protection from the Sultan of Zanzibar, who sent a warship in 1838 then, two years later, they requested help from Commander Passot who had docked his ship at Nosy Be. The Frenchman was only too happy to oblige and asked Admiral de Hell, the governor of Bourbon Island (now Réunion), to place Nosy Be under the protection of France. The island was formally annexed in 1841.

GETTING THERE AND AWAY

BY AIR There are now several direct international flights to Nosy Be. Air Mad runs services from Paris, Milan and Réunion; Air Austral flies from Paris, Mayotte and Réunion; Corsairfly runs a service from Paris; and Air Italy connects with Rome and Milan.

There are daily Air Mad flights to/from Tana and less regular services from Antsiranana and Mahajanga (domestic routes change often so check *www.airmadagascar.com* for schedules).

BY BOAT Nosy Be's nearest mainland town is Ambanja; *taxi-brousses* leave from outside the town hall for Ankify (the departure point for Nosy Be) and take about an hour. Speedboats to Hell-Ville leave as and when they fill up (roughly hourly) and take 30 minutes. It should cost 20,000Ar but operators have a habit of overcharging *vazaha* or trying to impose a fee for luggage.

GETTING AROUND THE ISLAND

There is one good road running in a loop around the island from the airport past Hell-Ville, Ambatoloaka, most of the west-coast hotels, and back to the airport. All the others are tracks, often completely impassable in a normal vehicle. Occasional *taxi-brousse* services run on the main road. There are also plenty of taxis, operating on either a private hire or a (much cheaper) shared basis. A private taxi from Hell-Ville to the airport or Ambatoloaka takes 25 minutes and costs 15,000Ar.

Bikes, scooters, motorbikes, quads and cars are hired out by several rental agencies (see under *Hell-Ville* and *Ambatoloaka*) and also many hotels.

ACTIVITIES

The tourist office in Hell-Ville is very helpful (\ *86 920 62*; e *ortnb@moov.mg*; *www.nosybe-tourisme.mg*; ⊕ *Mon–Fri 08.00–12.00 & 15.00–18.00, w/end 08.00–12.00*). In their office you will also find a desk for the Nosy Be guides association, often manned by the association's president, Jean-Pierre (m *032 40 507 61*).

TREKKING, MOUNTAIN-BIKING AND ISLAND TOURS The following companies offer treks or cycling tours of Nosy Be and boat trips to the nearby islands. For visits to islands further afield, see *Sailing* opposite.

Green Adventures Galerie Ankoay, Hell-Ville; m 032 07 573 12/033 12 260 50; e greenadventures@ hotmail.it. Mont Passot trekking; biking; visits to Lokobe, Nosy Komba & Nosy Sakatia.
Evasion Sans Frontière Hell-Ville (nr BFV); \ 86 062 44 ; m 032 11 002 96; f 86 610 60; e esf.nosybe@moov.mg. General travel agency.
Nosy Be Expedition Ambatoloaka; m 032 44 155 93; e nosy_bexpedition@yahoo.fr; ⊕ 07.30–11.00 & 15.00–20.00. Trips to Nosy Komba, Nosy Tanikely, Nosy Iranja, Nosy Sakatia & Lokobe.

Libertalia Aventure Delastelle bldg, Hell-Ville; \ 86 925 41; m 032 04 611 21; e libertaliaventure@ yahoo.fr; www.libertalia-aventure.com. Island trips of 1–10 days; trekking; biking; 4x4 circuits.
Escapades Nord Madagascar Hell-Ville; \ 86 927 66; m 033 12 126 24; e escapades@moov.mg; www.nosybe-madagascar.com. Excursions, fishing & diving.
Kekeh m 032 02 211 76/034 29 010 65. Recommended English-speaking guide & boatman for trips to nearby islands.

SAILING

⚠ **MadagasCaT** Cratère; ☎ +27 21 858 1574 (South Africa); ℯ info@madagascat.co.za; www.madagascat.co.za; Skype: madagascat. Highly recommended catamaran cruises, especially to the Radamas or Mitsios (6 days) or both (10 days) with possibility of incredible snorkelling, diving & fishing. Excellent personal service. MadagasCaT also supports a local village school near Nosy Iranja. See ad on page 367.

⚠ **Ulysse Explorer** ⓜ 032 04 802 80; ℯ ulyssexplorer@gmail.com; www.ulyssexplorer.com. 8-berth catamaran for trips to the Radamas, Mitsios etc; diving & fishing. See ad on page 367.

⚠ **Alefa** Madirokely (nr Aviavy); ☎ 86 060 70; ⓜ 032 07 127 07; ℯ alefa@simicro.mg; www.pirogue-madagascar.com. Round-island luxury sailing pirogue trips lasting 2–21 days, camping with cooks, tents etc provided.

⚠ **Madavoile** Ambatoloaka; ☎ 86 065 55; ⓜ 032 04 223 55; ℯ mad.planet@simicro.mg; www.madavoile.com. Well-run sailing trips; also deep-sea fishing & diving.

⚠ **Tropical Adventure** Madirokely; ☎ 86 620 37; ℯ starcat@moov.mg. The *Star Cat* catamaran.

⚠ **Bossi** ☎ +27 16 341 6134 (South Africa); ℯ info@bossiadventures.com; www.bossiadventures.com. Live-aboard yachts for trips of 2–5 days.

⚠ **Dream** ☎ +248 23 26 81 (Seychelles); ℯ dream.customer@dreamyachtcharter.com; www.dreamyachtcharter.com. Crewed yacht charters in the Nosy Be archipelago.

DIVING The once-lovely coral around Nosy Be itself has sadly been destroyed, but the pristine little islands of the region offer some of the best diving in Madagascar. The recommended time is May to October. For the best chance of sighting a whale shark or manta ray, come in late October or November.

➷ **Océane's Dream** Ambatoloaka; ☎ 86 614 26/610 17; ⓜ 032 07 127 82/032 07 127 85; ℯ oceaned@moov.mg; www.oceanesdream.com. PADI, CMAS. Reputable operator with over 20yrs' experience.

➷ **Madagascar Dive Club** Madirokely (nr Marlin Club); ☎ 86 060 46; ⓜ 032 04 386 77/032 04 750 48; ℯ madiro@simicro.mg. PADI.

➷ **Akio** Ambatoloaka; ⓜ 032 02 814 55; ℯ nicolasricher@free.fr or akiodiving@yahoo.fr

➷ **Madaplouf** Bemoko (nr Vanila); ☎ 86 921 37/938 65; ⓜ 033 14 248 33; ℯ madaplouf@moov.mg; www.madaplouf.com. PADI, CMAS, FFESSM.

➷ **Blue Océane** Madirokely; ☎ 86 928 10; ⓜ 032 07 058 80; ℯ bluedive@blueline.mg; www.diving-madagascar.com. PADI.

➷ **MantaDiveClub** Madirokely (at Madiro); ⓜ 032 07 207 10; ℯ manta@moov.mg; www.mantadiveclub.it. CMAS, CEDIP, SSI.

➷ **Coral Diving Club (Aventura Diving)** Ambondrona (at Domaine Manga Be); ⓜ 032 58 168 96/032 52 160 67; www.coralgardendiving.com. PADI.

➷ **Tropical Diving** Ambataloaka (at Coco Plage); ⓜ 032 49 462 51/032 02 493 16; ℯ tropical.diving@moov.mg; www.tropical-diving.com. PADI, CMAS.

➷ **Aqua Diving** Ambaro; ☎ 86 921 95; ⓜ 033 02 020 40; ℯ info@aquamadagascar.com; www.aquamadagascar.com. PADI, CMAS.

➷ **Nomade** Ambatoloaka; ⓜ 032 04 838 89; ℯ nomade.diving@yahoo.com; http://nomadeplongee.free.fr

➷ **Forever Dive** Madirokely; ⓜ 032 07 125 65; ℯ info@foreverdive.com; www.foreverdive.com. NAUI.

➷ **Mitsiky Plongée** Nr Vanila; ⓜ 032 02 203 55; www.123plongee-madagascar.com. PADI, CMAS, SSI, FFESSM.

➷ **Sakatia Lodge** ⓜ 032 02 770 99; ℯ sakatialodge@sakatia.co.za; www.sakatia.co.za. NAUI. Diving on Nosy Sakatia (see page 363).

➷ **Nosy Komba Plongée** ☎ 86 931 46; ⓜ 032 44 410 30/032 44 901 30; www.nosykombaplongee.com. PADI, CMAS, FFESSM.

SNORKELLING The prospects for snorkelling around the coastline of Nosy Be itself are not great, although the **Andilana** area is reasonable. Significantly better are the surrounding islets: the protected **Nosy Tanikely** has wonderful snorkelling, as does the tiny **Nosy Fanihy**, 3km offshore from Amarina hotel. **Nosy Sakatia** and **Nosy Komba** are also recommended.

But serious enthusiasts should consider heading to islands further afield. **Nosy Tsarabanjina** is excellent and the **Radama** and **Mitsio** archipelagos are truly world-class spots both for snorkelling and diving.

DEEP-SEA FISHING

Manou Madirokely; \ 86 062 12; m 032 04 444 84; e manoufishing@simicro.mg or amatmc@moov.mg; www.manou-fishing.com. Fishing trips of 1–12 days.

Fishing World m 032 07 125 13; e fishingworld@moov.mg; www.fishingworld-nosybe.com. Fishing trips of 1–8 days.

Barracuda Ambatoloaka; \ 86 620 66; m 032 02 629 92; e contact@barracuda-mada.com; www.barracuda-mada.com. Hotel specialising in fishing.

Bouana Pêche Ambatoloaka; \ 86 920 19/063 04; m 032 04 944 48; e bouanapeche@moov.mg; www.nosybefishing.com; Skype: nosybe81. Experienced fishing operator.

Nosy Be Fishing Club Madirokely; \ 86 925 03; m 032 04 306 03/032 04 416 14; e nosybefishingclub@moov.mg; www.nosybe-fishingclub.com. Hotel specialised in sport fishing, including trips to Radama islands.

WATERSPORTS

Nosy Be Kite Surf Ambondrona (nr Domaine Manga Be); m 032 02 316 87; e mg-tourisme@moov.mg; www.nosybekitesurf.com. Kitesurfing for beginners to experienced. Season: Jul–Nov.

Kokòa Andilana; \/f 86 921 22; m 032 04 414 26/033 11 241 22; e kokoa@simicro.mg; www.kokoa-nosybe.com. Comprehensive range of watersports including windsurfing, kitesurfing, waterskiing, wakeboarding & parasailing.

KayakinMadagascar e info@kayakinmadagascar.co.za; www.kayakinmadagascar.co.za. Runs sea kayaking tours around Nosy Tanikely, Nosy Komba, Lokobe & Russian Bay.

GLASS-BOTTOM BOAT

Experience the coral reef wonders around Nosy Komba and Nosy Tanikely from the dry comfort of a boat. Based in Ambatoloaka, and at the Saloon in Hell-Ville, **Aqua-bulle** (m *032 42 104 80;* e *erobinault@yahoo.fr*) operates half-day and full-day trips.

QUAD BIKING

Quad Run Andilana; \ 86 921 51; m 032 40 169 99/033 14 146 31. Hire of dbl quads for 120,000Ar/day.

Nosy Be Quad Ankibanivato (at Explora Village); m 032 07 210 79/032 04 968 82/032 55 898 94; e nosybequad@moov.mg; www.exploravillage.com. Sgl & dbl quad hire from 170,000Ar/half-day.

HORSERIDING

Located near hotel Chanty Beach, opposite the departure point for ferries to Nosy Sakatia, **Ambaro Ranch** (m *032 43 691 78*) offers horseriding from 45 minutes (45,000Ar) to half-day (130,000Ar) as well as riding lessons for children.

PLEASURE FLIGHTS

Madagascar Helicopter Ankibanivato (nr Explora Village); m 032 07 212 32/032 07 212 54; e contact@madagascarhelicopter.com or madaheli@simicro.mg; www.madagascarhelicopter.com. Choppers for pleasure flights or transfers.

Nosy Be ULM Ankibanivato (at Explora Village); \ 86 920 00; m 032 07 210 79; e nosybequad@moov.mg. Floatplane for overflights of Nosy Be.

MUSIC FESTIVAL

The four-day Donia music festival is held each Pentecost (May/June) in the Hell-Ville football ground with groups coming from across the Indian Ocean. Sebastian Bulmer highly recommends this 'great party with a friendly crowd and good music' but warns about the lack of toilet facilities! Hotels get very booked up at this time.

MUSEUMS

Marine research centre **CNRO** has an interesting oceanographic museum on the hill east of Hell-Ville, towards Lokobe. And there's a small museum of cultural history, **Espace Zeny** (m *033 14 669 31;* e *espace_zeny@moov.mg*), on the site of a sacred tree at Mahatsinjo west of Hell-Ville.

The name comes from Admiral de Hell rather than an evocation of the state of the town. Hell-Ville is actually quite a smart little place (at least by Malagasy standards), its main street lined with boutiques and tourist shops. There is a market selling fresh produce and an interesting cemetery, especially if you are around on All Souls' Day (1 November).

WHERE TO STAY There are plenty of basic hotels in Hell-Ville. For budget travellers a night or two here while you investigate the cheaper beach hotels is almost essential.

Mid-range €€€

🏠 **Diamant IO** (14 rooms) Bd Dr Manceau; ☏ 86 614 48; m 032 07 739 14; e madexof@metclub.mg. Comfortable en-suite rooms with AC.

🏠 **Villa Fany** (7 rooms) ☏ 86 611 70; m 032 02 343 79; e fany@dts.mg. Pleasant rooms a short distance out of town; most en suite with hot water. Great view over Hell-Ville towards Nosy Komba.

🏠 **Plantation** (6 rooms) m 032 07 934 45/032 40 045 08; e mdbr-plantation@hotmail.com. Small & intimate; better known as a restaurant.

🏠 **Belle Vue** (19 rooms) Rue R Tsiomeko; ☏ 86 613 84; e bellevuehotel_nosybe@yahoo.fr. Dbl & trpl rooms, some with AC & some en suite.

🏠 **Hôtel de la Mer** (16 rooms) Bd Dr Manceau; ☏ 86 617 53; e hdlm@moov.mg. Basic rooms, some en suite with sea view.

🏠 **Abud** (30 rooms) Rte Principal; ☏ 86 610 55/612 57; m 032 45 885 23. A central 5-storey hotel with comfortable small rooms, some en suite (cold water).

🏠 **George V** (6 rooms) La Poudrière; m 032 04 005 88. Inexpensive dingy en-suite rooms with fans. No food.

🏠 **Tatamo** (7 rooms) Senganinga; m 032 40 449 52. About 50m down a side road. Dbl rooms, some en suite.

Budget €€

🏠 **Royal Pacifique** (9 rooms) ☏ 86 926 40; m 032 04 028 30. Dbl & trpl rooms with hot water. Also a self-catering apartment.

🏠 **Clérac** (11 rooms) Senganinga; ☏ 86 632 62; m 032 40 778 83. About 20m from main road. En-suite (cold water) dbl & trpl rooms.

🏠 **Rahim's** (23 rooms) Rue Poncaré; ☏ 86 927 54; m 032 48 971 29/032 02 652 87. Simple cheap dbl & family rooms.

✖ WHERE TO EAT

✖ **Manava** ☏ 86 610 36; m 032 04 394 54. Above Moulin Rouge disco. Considered by local resident Irene Boswell to be the best on Nosy Be. Tasty food, huge quantities, reasonable prices & pool table. Live music Tue & Fri–Sun.

✖ **Plantation** (see *Where to stay*) French cuisine served on pleasant veranda, rather overpriced but often delicious.

✖ **Restaurant de la Mer** ☏ 86 610 32. Bar & restaurant with nice sea-view terrace — peaceful evening view of pirogues returning from a day's fishing.

✖ **Saloon** ☏ 86 921 77. Bar & restaurant with pool table. They also have rooms.

🖳 **Oasis** ☏ 86 611 79. Snack bar & café with fresh croissants & *pains au chocolat* daily. Also cakes & ice cream. Terrace good for people-watching.

NIGHTLIFE

♀ **Vieux Port** A popular place at the old port. Wild nights. Usually gets going around 22.00, with live music. Great *salegy* & reggae music.

♀ **Nandipo** Rue Albert I; m 032 04 482 32/032 44 394 12; ⊕ 07.00–00.00. Central French-run pub, popular with expats. Serves pizzas, snacks & ice cream. Pool table & darts. Wi-Fi.

☆ **Moulin Rouge** ☏ 86 610 36; ⊕ Fri–Mon & Wed 22.00–dawn. Discotheque near the market. Serves pizzas during the day.

☆ **Disco Number One** ⊕ Thu & Sat. In a basement beneath Hôtel de la Mer.

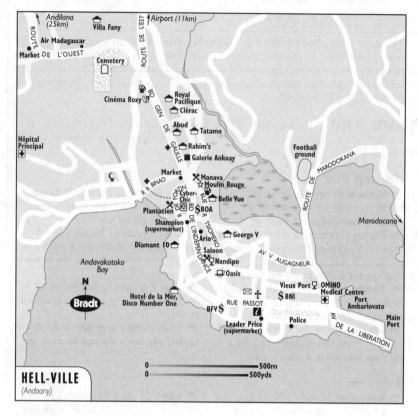

Map labels:
Andilana (25km), Air Madagascar, Villa Fany, Airport (11km), ROUTE DE L'EST, ROUTE DE L'OUEST, Market, Cemetery, Cinéma Roxy, BD GEN DE GAULLE, Royal Pacifique, Clérac, Abud, Tatamo, Hôpital Principal, Rahim's, Galerie Ankoay, Football ground, ROUTE DE MARODOKANA, Market, R R. BINAO, Manava, Moulin Rouge, Cyber-Chic, Belle Vue, Plantation, BOA, BD DE L'INDÉPENDANCE, Shampion (supermarket), Ario, George V, Marodocana, Diamant 10, Saloon, Nandipo, Oasis, AV V AUGAGNEUR, Andavakotoko Bay, N, Bradt, Hotel de la Mer, Disco Number One, BFV, RUE PASSOT, Vieux Port, OMINO Medical Centre, BNI, Port Ambariovato, Leader Price (supermarket), Police, DE LA LIBERATION, Main Port, 0—500m, 0—500yds

HELL-VILLE
(Andoany)

SHOPPING The large number of tourists visiting Nosy Be has made it a centre for souvenir production, giving you the opportunity to buy direct from the makers and benefit local people. Mind you, much of the stuff comes from Tana. Unique to Nosy Be are the carved pirogues, clay animals and Richelieu-embroidered curtains and tablecloths. Handicraft sellers frequent the road to the port and there are some high-quality goods in Hell-Ville's many boutiques.

The recently refurbished **indoor market** is well worth a visit and is the best place for vanilla and spices, both for quality and price. A short distance to the north is a small mall, **Galerie Ankoay**, with its restaurant and two floors of shops built around a central bar shaped like a ship. There are two supermarkets: **Shampion** (⊕ *Mon–Sat 07.00–13.00 & 15.00–19.00, Sun 07.30–12.30*) and a small **Leader Price** (⊕ *Mon–Fri 08.00–12.00 & 15.00–18.00, Sat 08.00–12.00*).

INTERNET Of Hell-Ville's half-dozen cybercafés, **Cyberchic** (⊕ *08.00–22.00*) opposite the BOA bank is the fastest but also most expensive. **Ylang.Net** in Galerie Ankoay (see *Shopping* above) is cheaper and also open every day. And near the tourist office is **Perle d'Ocean** (⊕ *Mon–Sat 08.00–12.00 & 14.00–19.00*).

VEHICLE HIRE
🚗 **Nosy Easy Rent** \ 86 063 08; m 033 11 611 00; e nosyeasy.rent @ moov.mg; www.nosyeasyrent.com. Motorbikes, cars & 4x4s.

🚗 **ZigZag** \ 86 921 81; m 032 04 159 84; e zig.zag @ waika9.com. Self-drive 2CVs; also bikes, mopeds & bus trips.

🚐 **Nosy Velo** ⟍ 86 614 15/500 41; m 032 04 611 21; e nosyvelo@yahoo.fr; www.vtt-trekking.com. Mountain bikes, including guided excursions.

MEDICAL Based midway between Hell-Ville and Ambatoloaka, **Espace Médical** (⟍ *86 925 99;* m *032 04 431 15*) provides excellent 24-hour medical services. In Hell-Ville itself are **OMINO** medical centre (⟍ *86 611 91/93*) and the **Hôpital Principal** (⟍ *86 613 95*).

Pharmacies **Tsarajoro** (*Bd Gen de Gaulle;* ⟍ *86 613 82*) and **Nouroudine** (*Rue Binao;* ⟍ *86 610 38*) are well stocked.

MONEY AND BANKS

$ **BNI** Rue Passot; ⊕ Mon–Fri 08.00–15.30. Visa; MasterCard; Western Union; 24hr ATM.

$ **BFV** Rue Gouhot; ⊕ Mon–Fri 07.30–11.30 & 14.00–16.00. Visa; Western Union; 24hr ATM.

$ **BOA** Rue Gallieni; ⊕ Mon–Fri 07.30–11.30 & 14.30–16.30. MasterCard; Western Union.

$ **Western Union** service at Abud hotel; ⊕ Mon–Fri 08.00–11.30 & 14.30–17.00, Sat 09.00–13.00

AIRLINE OFFICES

✈ **Air Madagascar** North Hell-Ville; ⟍ 86 613 13/57/60; m 032 05 222 51; e noskk@airmadagascar.com; ⊕ Mon–Fri 08.00–11.00 & 14.30–17.00, Sat 08.00–09.30

✈ **Agence Ario** Rue Passot; ⟍ 86 612 40; e arionos@dts.mg; ⊕ Mon–Fri 08.00–12.00 & 14.00–17.30, Sat 08.00–11.00. Represents Air Mauritius & Air Austral.

AMBATOLOAKA

Once a charming fishing village, Ambatoloaka is now full of bars and good-time girls. In an effort to clamp down on sex tourism, some of the hotels are wary about taking single men.

However, this lively centre offers the best options for inexpensive places to stay in Nosy Be and is the place to be if you're looking for nightlife rather than somewhere to relax. Most of the hotels are positioned along the beach, which is the most popular in Nosy Be despite being inferior to those further north.

🏠 WHERE TO STAY
Upper range €€€€

🏠 **Coco Plage** (13 rooms) m 032 40 178 54; e coco.plage@moov.mg. Dbl & twin rooms with AC & safe; some with sea view.

🏠 **Ylang Ylang** (12 rooms) ⟍ 86 928 13; m 032 07 126 93; e hotel.lylang@moov.mg; www.hotel-lylangylang.com. HB sgl & dbl en-suite rooms with safe & minibar; some with AC. British-owned & very good value. Great beachfront location, excellent cuisine & friendly service. B/fast inc.

🏠 **Clair de Lune** (6 bungalows) m 032 04 197 18; e lescheres@netclub.mg. Charming, quiet B&B on a breezy hillside 500m west of the village. Bungalows with lovely bathrooms set in a lovely garden with swimming pool. No single men. Airport transfers included for stays of 3+ nights. Closed Jan–Mar.

🏠 **Chez Gérard et Francine** (10 rooms) ⟍ 86 061 05; m 032 07 127 93; e geretfra@simicro.mg.

Set in a beautiful peaceful garden at the south of the village, a delightful place ideal for those wanting to steer clear of the local nightlife. Rooms with fridge; some en suite with balcony. Deservedly popular. B/fast inc.

🏠 **Barracuda** (8 rooms) ⟍ 86 620 66; m 032 02 629 92; e contact@barracuda-mada.com; www.barracuda-mada.com. Sgl to family-size rooms with AC & shared facilities (cold water).

🏠 **Boucaniers** (17 bungalows) m 032 02 675 20; e boucaniers@moov.mg; www.hotellesboucaniers.com. Tastefully furnished bungalows, some with ocean views. AC option.

🏠 **Benjamin** (6 rooms & 1 villa) ⟍ 86 927 64; m 032 02 408 13; e hotelbenjamin@simicro.mg; www.hotelbenjamin-nosybe.com. Very comfortable bungalows with terraces set in a nice garden. Also 4-bedroom **Villa Razambe** for up to 8 people, with pool.

15

⌂ **Résidence Ambatoloaka** (12 rooms) ✆ 86 920 66; m 032 02 062 16; e alexranaivo@mel.moov.mg. Good beachfront restaurant

Mid-range €€€

⌂ **Chez Pat** (6 rooms) m 032 40 247 86/032 04 793 15; e patricia.chaponnay@wanadoo.fr. Beachfront dbl & family en-suite rooms (cold water). Bar & restaurant on terrace; French dishes & pizza.

⌂ **Caravelle** (5 bungalows) m 032 40 284 54; e pascal@hotel-nosybe.com; www.hotel-nosybe.com. Good value bungalows, en suite with (hot water) with small lounge & balcony, at far north of village.

⌂ **Coucher du Soleil** (7 bungalows) ✆ 86 928 42; m 032 02 087 21; e coucherdusoleil@moov.mg. Hotel & restaurant; clean, comfy en-suite bungalows (cold water). Not on the beach, but sea view.

⌂ **Villa Francesca** (5 rooms) m 032 51 282 47/032 02 293 61. Guesthouse with en-suite rooms (hot water), 250m from beach.

⌂ **Dauphin** (14 rooms) m 032 46 686 21/032 02 994 58; e hotelledauphin@moov.mg. Dbl en-suite rooms (cold water), some with balcony, at north of village.

⌂ **Espadon** (20 rooms & 4 bungalows) ✆ 86 921 47; m 032 07 125 03; e contact@hotelespadon-nosybe.com; www.hotelespadon-nosybe.com. Beachfront hotel & restaurant with pleasant garden. Comfy rooms with TV, AC & minibar. Specialises in deep-sea fishing. Visa & MasterCard.

⌂ **Villa Catherine** (5 rooms) m 034 13 204 89; e cjjnosybe@moov.mg. Dbl rooms, including 1 en suite. At the time of writing they're finishing 14 new self-catering units with sea-view balconies called **Les Hauts d'Ambatoloaka**.

⌂ **Chambre Authentique** (10 bungalows) ✆ 86 937 85; m 032 07 798 23. Centrally located en-suite (cold water) rooms 250m from beach. Simple (no garden or view) but cheap.

✕ **WHERE TO EAT** Most of the main hotels have good restaurants, with Ylang Ylang particularly recommended. There is also a handful of restaurants and snack bars clustered in the centre of the village.

✕ **Karibou** ✆ 86 616 47; m 032 04 664 75. Italian food, including pizzas; bar.

✕ **Chez Angeline** ✆ 86 616 21; m 032 07 798 55; ⊕ Tue–Sun, Mon closed. Popular long-established restaurant, famous for seafood & *poulet au coco*.

✕ **Bel Rose** m 032 40 452 04. A small pink & white restaurant that wouldn't look out of place in *Hansel & Gretl*.

✕ **Gargotte Chez Papa Bebetto** Inexpensive good food.

🍹 **Baobab Kafé** ✆ 86 620 35. Serves mainly snacks: sandwiches, crepes etc. Cocktail bar.

🍹 **Amicale** Snack bar & pizzeria.

NIGHTLIFE The nightclubs are all situated along the road between hotels Espadon and Dauphin at the northern end of town.

☆ **Djembe** Well-equipped nightclub with AC, high-tech lighting, special effects, mirrored walls & a waterfall behind the bar. Also pool tables & pizza.

☆ **Casino** Fruit machines, roulette, blackjack etc. Live music Sat nights.

☆ **Jackpot** Nightclub & gambling place next to Djembe. More downmarket than Casino.

☆ **Sirène** Discotheque sited opposite Djembe (at least one of the two is open every night).

☆ **Lion d'Or** Near Djembe, with mainly Malagasy clientele, but said to have gone downhill in recent years.

SHOPPING Ambatoloaka has limited options for shopping so you may wish to stock up in Hell-Ville first. There is a small supermarket, **Big Bazar**, in nearby Daresalama.

INTERNET Cybercafé **Nosy-Ylang.Com** (m *032 04 038 11/033 12 747 78;* e *nosy.ylang@moov.mg;* ⊕ *Mon–Sat 09.00–12.00 & 16.00–21.00*) next to hotel Barracuda offers connections for 100Ar/minute.

VEHICLE HIRE

🚗 **Nosy Red Cars** 📞 86 620 35; 📱 032 41 547 82; 📧 nosyredcars@simicro.mg. Self-drive 2-seat cars & Renault 4s.

🚗 **Moto Mada** 📱 032 02 680 25; 📧 solcud@simicro.mg. Motorbikes.

🚗 **Locamad** 📱 032 42 062 42. Motorbikes.

🚗 **Location Jeunesse** 📱 032 04 663 87; ⏱ 07.00–19.00. Bikes, scooters & motorbikes. Also hires tents & snorkelling gear.

EMERGENCIES There is a **police** post near Casino nightclub at the north end of the village. Pharmacy **Toko** (📞 86 927 82) in the centre is reliable, and for medical care **Espace Médical** (see page 355) is 4.5km away on the road to Hell-Ville.

🏠 BEACH HOTELS AND OTHER ACCOMMODATION

Hotels are now dotted all along the sandy western coast, mostly in beachfront locations, and a few in the north and southeast too. Nosy Be now competes with other tropical islands in the quality of its hotels, most of which have ocean views, swimming pools and extras such as massage and jacuzzi. Prices tend to vary between the high season (usually mid-July to mid-September, and Christmas) and low season, and are often quoted per person (not per room) on Nosy Be.

LUXURY 👑

🏠 **Amarina** (58 rooms) 📞 86 921 28/30; 📱 032 07 307 47; 📠 86 921 26; 📧 reservation@amarinahotel.com; www.amarinahotel.com. This hotel has all the facilities you'd expect (AC, private balconies, Wi-Fi, massage, swimming pool) & plenty you might not (trampoline, DVD library, Malagasy language lessons, babysitting service). Set on 900m of beautiful isolated beach. The spacious en-suite rooms have a sea view facing the sunset. Snorkelling is excellent (although tide-dependent) in the lagoon & at the beautiful coral island of Nosy Fanihy opposite the hotel. Boats for excursions/transfers & activities from biking, kayaking & fishing to archery, gym & volleyball, although watersports are limited to those that do not consume fuel. In fact, the hotel takes its environmental & community responsibilities seriously: they've built a medical clinic for villagers & support various local arts, education & other projects. See ad after page 408.

🏠 **Domaine de Lokobe** (10 bungalows) 📞 86 921 33; 📱 032 05 650 40/70; 📧 domaine@nosybe-lokobe.com; www.nosybe-lokobe.com. Pleasant upmarket hotel in attractive surroundings accessible only by boat. But somewhat overpriced & some readers have been disappointed by the rather poor beach.

🏠 **Corail Noir** (9 bungalows & 31 rooms) 📞 86 920 52/53; 📠 86 920 54; 📧 corailnoir@moov.mg; www.corailnoirhotel.com. An attractive, comfy & relaxing place to unwind. There are ground-floor rooms with little front garden, 1st floor with balcony & bungalows with decks out front. Set within beautiful & well-maintained grounds, with a fabulous open-air bar/restaurant & swimming pool, the whole complex sits next to the beach looking out across the sea & to Nosy Sakatia. Buildings are mostly made from stone, bamboo & palm leaves & decorated very simply in natural colours & accessories. Boat trips, diving school, ping-pong etc.

🏠 **Loharano** (24 rooms) 📞 86 921 90; 📱 033 14 334 20; 📧 info@loharanohotel.com; www.loharanohotel.com. New hotel with AC rooms in 10 bungalows. Closed Jan–Feb.

🏠 **Belle Plage** (16 bungalows) 📞 86 927 34; 📧 hotel@belleplage.com; www.belleplage.com. Swiss-owned en-suite bungalows with AC in a wonderful garden right on a private beach.

🏠 **Vanila** (35 rooms & 6 suites) 📞 86 921 01/02/03; 📱 032 02 203 60; 📠 86 921 05; 📧 info@vanila-hotel.com; www.vanila-hotel.com. Very comfortable rooms with AC, TV & private terrace. Prestige suites also have hi-fi, DVD player & jacuzzi. One of the better hotels in Nosy Be; very well managed; lovely garden with 2 rim-flow swimming pools; 2 restaurants. Quite large; no feeling of intimacy.

🏠 **Royal Beach** (42 rooms & 6 suites) 📱 032 05 322 44/032 05 323 44/033 11 122 44; 📧 reservation@royalbeach.mg; www.royalbeach.mg. New 3-storey 4-star hotel. Rooms are en suite with TV, AC & balcony (many with sea view); suites also have baths. B/fast inc. Sauna, *hamam*, massage, pool & gym; Italian-managed pizzeria & swish restaurant.

🏠 **Andilana Beach (Bravo Club)** (208 rooms) 📞 86 932 81; 📱 033 15 250 00/01; 📠 86 932 80;

e booking@andilana.info; www.nosybe.com.
Madagascar's only all-inclusive hotel using the Club
Med format: meals, snacks, drinks, numerous sports &
all other activities are included in the price. Only
possible to book via a tour operator (although walk-
in trade is accepted if they have spare rooms). Don't
expect to experience the 'real' Madagascar here; with
every facility imaginable within the security perimeter
few venture out of the resort. Disabled facilities.

TOP END €€€€€

⌂ **Nosy Be Hotel** (50 rooms) ✆ 86 061 49/51;
m 032 40 011 46; **e** nosy.be.hotel@simicro.mg;
www.nosybehotel.com. Various rooms, suites &
attractive bungalows in a pleasant garden with pool.
Outdoor restaurant with sea view. Many activities
including diving & fishing.

⌂ **Chanty Beach** (2 bungalows & 3 rooms) ✆ 86
928 16; **e** cherz@moov.mg; www.chantybeach-
hotel.com. Charming self-catering bungalows & en-
suite rooms with AC on a private beach.

⌂ **Orangea Village** (11 rooms & 9 bungalows)
✆ 86 927 90; m 032 04 200 85; **e** orangea@
moov.mg; www.orangea-nosybe.com. Owned & run by
an enthusiastic French-Belgian couple, this is an
exceptionally attractive & relaxing place. Rooms (some
with AC) set in beautiful garden with pool. Top food.

⌂ **Madiro** (22 rooms) ✆ 86 060 46; m 032 04
386 77; **e** madirohotel@moov.mg;
www.madirohotel.com. Tastefully decorated en-suite
rooms, some with AC, arranged around central
swimming pool in a lovely garden alongside a good
beach. Free gym. Restaurant with Italian specialities.

⌂ **Marlin Club** (16 rooms & 6 suites) ✆ 86 610
70; m 032 07 127 62; **e** marlin.club@simicro.mg;
www.marlin-club.com. Newly rebuilt. Mainly a deep-
sea fishing centre.

⌂ **Aviavy** (13 rooms) ✆ 86 922 23; m 032 07
207 87; **e** contact@letempsduneile.com;
www.aviavy-hotel.com. Swiss owner Jean-Claude first
came to Madagascar in 1953. This beachfront hotel
specialises in fishing & catamaran trips to their
lodges in the Ampasidava & the Radamas.

⌂ **Explora Village** (10 bungalows) ✆ 86 920 00;
m 032 07 210 79; **e** nosybequad@moov.mg;
www.exploravillage.com. Stylish Italian-owned en-suite
bungalows with solar-heated water. B/fast inc.

⌂ **Heure Bleue** (11 bungalows) ✆ 86 060 20;
m 032 02 203 61; **e** resa@heurebleue.com;
www.heurebleue.com. Traditional en-suite bungalows
with fridge & balcony. Stunning views over
Ambatoloaka Bay although the beach is a little
rocky here. B/fast inc.

NOSY BE WEST

UPPER RANGE €€€€

🏠 **Domaine Manga Be** (50 rooms) \ 86 060 88; m 032 42 092 82; e domainemangabe@ moov.mg; www.domainemangabe.com. Various rooms, suites & villas for 2–6 people, some with sea view.

🏠 **Maison des Parfums** (2 villas & 11 rooms) \ 86 924 09; m 032 40 483 07; e mirellanosybe2@ yahoo.fr. From dbl rooms to waterfront villas with kitchenette.

🏠 **Jardin Lokobe (Jungle Village)** (2 bungalows & 1 villa) \ 86 938 11; e tropic.construction@ gmail.com. Beautifully located in a hidden paradise accessible only by boat, but seems to have gone downhill recently.

🏠 **Belvédère** (6 rooms) \ 86 928 08; m 032 04 619 96; e belvedereandilana@yahoo.fr;

www.hotel-nord-madagascar.com. Set on a hill close to the beach; lovely view over Andilana Bay. B/fast inc. Restaurant *Chez Loulou* does excellent meals & Sunday buffet lunch.

🏠 **Grand Bleu** (15 bungalows) \ 86 920 23; m 033 14 248 16; e legrandbleu@moov.mg; www.legrandbleunosybe.com. On a hill overlooking the sea this place specialises in all kinds of fishing. Great infinity edge pool; 3mins from the beach.

🏠 **Chez Eugénie** (5 rooms) \ 86 923 53; m 032 40 634 48; e chezeugenie@yahoo.fr; www.chez-eugenie.com. Intimate & friendly out-of-the-way place with en-suite rooms & fantastic food. Praised by countless readers. B/fast inc.

MID-RANGE €€€

🏠 **Aladabo** (8 bungalows) \ 86 937 71; m 032 02 323 93; e aladabo@moov.mg; www.aladabo.com. Traditional en-suite bungalows owned by a doppelganger of TV chef Gordon Ramsey.

🏠 **Paradisa Kely** (6 bungalows) \ 86 938 68; m 032 04 944 21; e paradisakely@aliceadsl.fr; www.madagascar-paradisakely.com. Beachfront hotel on the edge of Lokobe, accessible only by boat; en-suite bungalows for 2–6 people.

🏠 **Tsara Loky** (4 bungalows & 8 rooms) \ 86 610 22; m 032 04 853 97/032 04 343 85;

e tsar_lok@yahoo.fr. Malagasy-run. Simple en-suite bungalows (2 with kitchenette) & rooms with shared facilities (cold water).

🏠 **Chez Senga** (6 bungalows) m 032 40 378 01; e hotelsenga@moov.mg. Simple en-suite bungalows with fan. Highly regarded restaurant, well known for its local specialities. Very good value.

🏠 **Villa Vero** (9 bungalows) \ 86 939 70; m 032 02 171 34/034 02 070 00; e villavero2@yahoo.fr. Bungalows with fan & en-suite cold showers.

CAMPING Camping is possible and accepted around Nosy Be. Just be sure to ask permission from the locals before pitching your tent, even if you plan to do so in an apparently public space such as a beach.

✘ **WHERE TO EAT** Most of the main hotels have good restaurants but there are also a few independent eateries.

✘ **Restaurant d'Ambonara** \ 86 613 67; m 032 02 611 12; e ambonara@moov.mg. A distinctive restaurant situated in an old coffee plantation.

✘ **Tsy Manin' Kafé** Madirokely; m 032 40 021 40; ⏰ Wed–Mon eves, Tue closed. Next to Aviavy hotel.
✘ **Alexander** Orangea; \ 86 635 19; m 033 14 247 22. Friendly restaurant with excellent cuisine.

EXCURSIONS

MONT PASSOT A popular excursion is the trip to the island's highest point, Mont Passot. The road there is rather bad but most hotels can help you find a suitable vehicle and driver. *En route* there are good views of a series of deep-blue crater lakes, which are said to contain crocodiles, as well as being the home of the spirits of the Sakalava and Antakarana princes. Supposedly it is *fady* to fish there, or to smoke, wear trousers or any garment put on over the feet, or a hat, while on the lakes' shores. That said, it may be that the tourists have frightened the spirits away, since my local informant has never heard of these prohibitions. It is, in any case, difficult to get down to the water since the crater sides are very steep.

LOKOBE STRICT RESERVE Nosy Be's only protected area, Lokobe, has been on the brink of opening up to ecotourism for years but at the time of writing those plans have still not come to fruition. However, it is possible to visit the buffer zone on the northeastern side of the peninsula where permits are not required. The two little villages here, Ambatozavavy and Ampasipohy, have embraced tourism with enthusiasm and the whole area now bears little similarity to the unspoilt place I so delighted in three decades ago. Nevertheless, a visit here still offers a glimpse of village life in Nosy Be and is an informative and enjoyable excursion.

Guided day trips are now commonplace: it takes around an hour by pirogue from Ambatozavavy to Ampasipohy. During the course of the day you are served a traditional lunch and taken on a tour of the forest (now sadly very degraded) where you are bound to see a grey-backed sportive lemur that often spends its day dozing in the fork of a favourite tree or tangle of vines, and you should also see black lemurs, ground boas and chameleons. The villagers grow vanilla and peppers, and a wide range of handicrafts can be bought direct from the makers.

If you want to come to the area for more than a day trip, there are a few options to suit a range of budgets: see **Paradisa Kely**, **Jardin Lokobe** and **Domaine de Lokobe** in the previous section.

ISLANDS AROUND NOSY BE

No visit to Nosy Be is complete without an excursion to Nosy Tanikely and Nosy Komba. Most Nosy Be hotels do excursions to these islands and will let you do the sensible thing of taking an overnight break on Nosy Komba.

Both Nosy Komba and Nosy Sakatia now have decent accommodation and offer tranquil alternatives to the increasingly crowded Nosy Be. Or for the ultimate isolation stay on the tiny Nosy Vorona.

LEMUR BEHAVIOUR   *Alison Jolly*

Female lemurs tend to be dominant over males. This is drastically different from our nearer relatives, the monkeys and apes, where males dominate females in the vast majority of species. In some lemur species, like the ring-tails and the white sifakas of Berenty, males virtually never challenge females. In others, like brown lemurs, it is nearer fifty-fifty, depending on the individual's character. The black lemurs of Nosy Komba are intermediate. Their females are likely to dominate males but are not certain to. If you are feeding them, the blond females are apt to be in the forefront of the scrimmage with only a few of the black males. Watch to see who grabs food from whom and – even more telling – who does not dare grab.

Female dominance also applies to sex. An unwilling female chases off a male, or even bites him. Or she may just sit down with her tail over her genitals – a perfect chastity belt. A lemur's hands can't hold another's tail, so if she puts it down, or just sits down, he is flummoxed. And in most lemur species, he would never dream of challenging her desires.

Also note the way the males rub their wet, smelly testicles and anal region on the females. Some females do not appreciate this and tell them off with a snarl. Males may also rub their bottoms on branches to scent-mark them. Then they may rub their heads on the branch in order to transfer the scent to their forehead.

You can tell a lot about a lemur's mood by where it is looking – a long hard stare is a threat, quick glances while head-flagging away is submissive. The tail, though, won't tell you much except how the animal is balanced on a branch or your shoulder. They use tails to keep track of each other, but not to signal mood.

NOSY KOMBA (NOSY AMBARIOVATO) When I first visited Nosy Komba in 1976 it was an isolated island with an occasional boat service, a tiny, self-sufficient village (Ampangorinana), and a troop of semi-tame black lemurs that were held to be sacred. Now all that has changed. Tourists arrive by the boatload from Nosy Be and passing cruise ships, which can land over a hundred people on this small island.

Komba means 'lemur' and it is the lemurs that bring in the visitors. During the 1980s the villagers made nothing out of these visits apart from the sale of clay animals which they glazed with the acid of spent batteries. Then they instigated a modest fee for seeing the animals and increased the variety of handicrafts. Now that Nosy Komba is on cruise-ship itineraries they have taken on the works: 'tribal dancing', face-decoration, escorted walks… anything that will earn a dollar or two.

With all the demands on your purse, it may take a bit of mental effort to see the underlying charm of Ampangorinana, but it is nevertheless a typical Malagasy community living largely on fishing and *tavy* farming (witness the horrendous deforestation of their little island; at the time of my 1976 visit it was almost completely forested) but it is the black lemurs that provide the financial support (and help prevent further degradation of their environment). If you want the lemur-on-your-shoulder experience and the chance to see these engaging animals at close quarters you should definitely come here. Only the male *Eulemur macaco* is black; the females are chestnut brown with white ear-tufts. There is a 2,000Ar entry fee for Lemur Park.

En route, everyone in the village will try to sell you something. Since you are buying direct from the grower/maker, this is the best place to get vanilla and handicrafts. The handicrafts here are unlike any found on the mainland, so it is worth bringing plenty of small change.

The once-plentiful coral of Nosy Komba has sadly almost completely disappeared so snorkelling is no longer rewarding. The sea and beach near the village are polluted with human waste, but there is a good swimming beach to the east. Beaches on the south of the island are clean and peaceful.

The best way to visit Nosy Komba is alone, or in a small group, avoiding the mid-morning rush.

Take a hike up the hill for spectacular views of the whole area (the peak, at 630m, is higher than any point on Nosy Be), but start early before it gets too hot. A guide costs 15,000Ar and the round trip should take four to five hours.

The cheapest way to get here is by pirogue from Port Ambariovato (east of the main port in Hell-Ville). Most pirogues leave at around 11.00 each day. Motor boat crossings from either Hell-Ville or Ankify cost about 5,000Ar one way. Yachties approaching from Nosy Be should wait until Nosy Vorona then bear 020°; there's good anchorage in 3–7m over sand and mud. Note that drinks etc are much more expensive on Nosy Komba than Nosy Be because of the carriage costs.

⌂ Where to stay

⌂ **Tsara Komba Lodge** (8 bungalows) m 032 07 440 40; e eden@moov.mg; www.tsarakomba.com. Exclusive, beautiful lodges with solar-heated water overlooking a tiny beach. Diving, trekking & canoeing offered. The high price is justified by the owners by the profits they put back into the village, renovating the houses & school, building a dispensary & working to provide safe water & solar power. ☙

⌂ **Jardin Vanille** (8 bungalows & 1 suite) m 032 07 127 97; e jardinvanille@moov.mg. Delightful mangrove-wood bungalows on stilts set into the hillside above the beach (62 steps up!) on the south side of the island away from the hordes of day-trippers. En-suite bungalows with minibar & balcony; the suite is right on the sea. Wild black lemurs often pass through in the evenings but are not habituated. ☙

⌂ **Floralies** (8 bungalows) m 032 02 200 38; e floralieskomba@yahoo.fr; www.bungalows-floralies.com. Dbl bungalows,

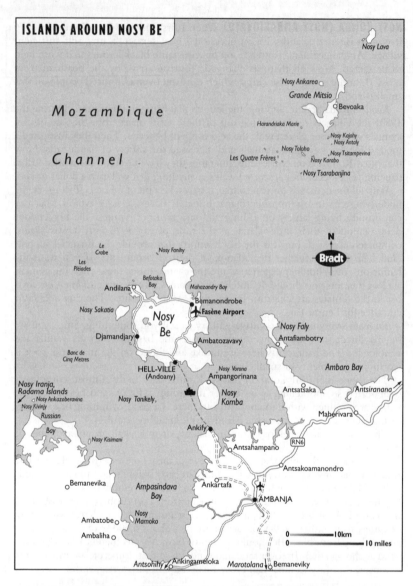

ISLANDS AROUND NOSY BE

Nosy Lava

Nosy Ankarea
Grande Mitsio
Bevoaka

Harandriaka Marie

Nosy Kajohy
Nosy Antaly
Nosy Toloho
Nosy Tsitampevina
Les Quatre Frères
Nosy Karabo

Nosy Tsarabanjina

Mozambique

Channel

N
Bradt

Le
Crabe
Nosy Fanihy
Les
Pléiades
Befotaka
Bay
Andilana
Mahazandry Bay
Bemanondrobe
Nosy Sakatia
Fasène Airport
Nosy
Be
Djamandjary
Ambatozavavy
Nosy Faly
Antafiambotry
Banc de
Cinq Metres
Ambaro Bay
HELL-VILLE
(Andoany)
Nosy Vorona
Ampangorinana
Nosy Iranja,
Radama Islands
Nosy Ankazoberavina
Nosy Tanikely
Nosy
Komba
Antsatsaka
Antsiranana
Nosy Kivinjy
Russian
Bay
Maherivara
Nosy Kisimani
Ankify
Antsahampano
RN6
Antsakoamanondro
Bemanevika
Ampasindava
Bay
Ankartafa
AMBANJA
Ambatobe
Nosy
Mamoko
Ambaliha
0 ———— 10km
0 ———— 10 miles
Antsohihy
Ankingameloka
Marotolana
Bemaneviky

beautifully situated at the end of a quiet beach opposite Lokobe, with en-suite cold-water shower & toilet. Bar & restaurant. B/fast inc. Hiking, diving & fishing can be arranged. €€€€€ —🛥️

🏠 **Mahafaly Lodge** (4 suites & 1 bungalow) m 032 07 126 57; e guyramanantsoa@moov.mg. Owned by an English-speaking Malagasy prince of the region who delights in enlightening guests about local culture, tradition & history. Wonderful garden with beautiful rooms & splendid views. €€€€ €€€€€

🏠 **Villas Komba** (6 rooms) m 032 04 740 53; e villakomba@gmail.com; www.locations-villas-nosy-komba.com. Villa for 4–10 people. €€€€

🏠 **Chez Yolande** (8 bungalows) \ 86 921 40; e casinca@hotmail.com; www.casinca.com. Seafront bungalows, some en-suite but cold water. Solar electricity. €€ €€€

🏠 **Lémuriens** (10 bungalows) \ 86 923 28; m 032 44 986 88; e hotel.lemuriens@yahoo.fr. Basic bungalows with en-suite toilet & cold shower or (cheaper) shower only. €€

🏠 **Zozo** (10 rooms) m 032 02 215 74. Dbl bungalows with shared facilities & some with balcony. €€
🏠 **Chez Giliette** (5 bungalows) m 033 14 470 34. Simple bungalows with shared facilities (cold water). €€

🏠 **Chez Madio** (6 bungalows) ☎ 86 926 72; e c3chicco@hotmail.com; www.chezmadamemadionosykomba.com. Mme Madio is as welcoming as her web domain is long! Basic good value bungalows for 2–4 people; squat toilets & bucket showers. €€

NOSY SAKATIA This 4km-long island, just 750m off the west coast of Nosy Be, has some well-run hotels. Ferry crossings cost 10,000Ar return (but are free for those staying on the island). Once seriously denuded, Nosy Sakatia is now on the road to recovery under a programme encouraging locals to plant pineapples instead of rice. It is *fady* to take a dog to Nosy Sakatia. It is also *fady* to wash laundry in the river there on a Tuesday or to go to the toilet in the sacred forest of Ambohibe.

 Where to stay

🏠 **Sakatia Towers** (7 rooms) ☎ 86 922 30; m 032 02 019 86; e sakatiatowers@mel.moov.mg; www.sakatiatowers.com. Excellent beachfront hotel with 7 en-suite trpl rooms in 4 bungalows; 24hr solar power. B/fast inc. €€€€€
🏠 **Sakatia Passions** (12 bungalows) ☎ 86 060 22; m 032 41 325 49/032 07 126 75; e sakatia1@moov.mg; www.sakatia-passions.com. Lovely bungalows with private terraces, set amid coconut palms on a private beach. En-suite bathrooms with hot water. B/fast inc. €€€€€

🏠 **Sakatia Lodge** (8 bungalows) ☎ 86 615 14; m 032 07 126 75; e sakatialodge@sakatia.co.za; www.sakatia.co.za. Smart bungalows & a larger villa; family-style dining. Excellent dive centre. €€€€
🏠 **Delphino Villa** (4 bungalows) ☎ 86 060 68; m 032 04 844 05/032 02 323 84; e delphino.villa@simicro.mg. Right at the water's edge with good snorkelling (mask & fins provided). €€€

NOSY TANIKELY This marine reserve (visit fee 5,000Ar) lures snorkellers and bird enthusiasts. Although now much visited, indeed sometimes overcrowded, it is still a lovely little island. In clear water you can see an amazing variety of marine life: coral, starfish, anemones, every colour and shape of fish, turtles, lobsters… (With this captivating world beneath your gaze there is a real danger of forgetting the passing of time and becoming seriously sunburnt, so wear a T-shirt and shorts.)

Don't think you have finished with Nosy Tanikely when you come out of the water; at low tide it is possible to walk right round the island. During the 1.5km circumambulation you will see, going anticlockwise, a broad beach of white sand covered in shells and bleached pieces of coral, a couple of trees full of flying foxes and – in the spring – graceful white-tailed tropic-birds flying in and out of their nests in the high cliffs. The walk involves some scrambling round rock pools, but nothing too challenging. Then there is the short climb up to the lighthouse at the top of the island for the view.

LEMURS ARE WILD ANIMALS *Alison Jolly*

Be careful when feeding lemurs. They may scratch you with their fingernails in their eagerness, or give you an accidental nip while trying to get the food. Much more important: never try to catch a lemur with your hands, just let it jump on you as it wants. If you constrain it, it will react as though a hawk has grabbed it and give you a slash with its razor-sharp canines. Especially do not let children feed lemurs unless they are warned never to hold on. These are wild animals, not pets.

15

NOSY VORONA (BIRD ISLAND) This speck of an island northeast of Nosy Komba offers you the chance to live out your desert island fantasy. Barely covering 1ha, and complete with a hammock slung between palm trees on a sandy beach, it comes as close to the remote desert island cliché as you'll get. The single four-room bungalow (accommodating up to eight people) shares the island only with an old lighthouse and costs around €100 per person per night on a full-board basis (m *032 02 367 03/032 46 590 97;* e *nosyvorona@gmail.com; www.nosy-vorona.com;* €€€€€).

NOSY MAMOKO This little island is at the southwest end of Ampasindava Bay. Known among the yachting fraternity for its exceptional shelter in all weather, it is a lovely, tranquil spot for a few days' relaxation. There is good fishing here and whale-watching from October to December. Good anchorage is found in the channel between the island and the mainland, in 15m over a sandy bottom.

OTHER NEARBY UNINHABITED ISLANDS The apple-core-shaped **Nosy Tanga**, measuring 400m across, lies opposite Nosy Be Hotel on the west coast. Less than 1km offshore it is easily reached by canoe. In the bay to the east of Nosy Sakatia is the sacred rocky island of **Nosy Ratsy** ('Bad Island'), just 100m across. At the northwest of Nosy Be, 700m offshore, is **Nosy Andilana** with striking white beaches of dead coral. Opposite Amarina Hotel the picturesque coral island of **Nosy Fanihy** ('Bat Island') is great for snorkelling but harder to reach without a motor boat, being 3.5km offshore. In Mahazandry Bay lies the crescent-shaped **Amberiotrandraka** ('Tenrec Island'). It's a tidal island (ie: connected to the shore at low tide) and, being on the east side of Nosy Be, is rarely visited by tourists. Just south of Nosy Vorona is **Amberiotelo**, a chain of three islets (which is what the name means) connected by an S-shaped sandbar. It's a nice vantage point from which to watch the sun set behind Nosy Komba.

MITSIO ISLANDS (NORTHEAST OF NOSY BE)

The Mitsio archipelago lies some 50km from Nosy Be, so is beyond the range of a day trip, but a number of yacht/catamaran charters offer multi-day excursions here from Nosy Be. This is the Maldives of Madagascar, with world-class diving, perfect beaches and an exclusive fly-in resort.

GRANDE MITSIO The largest island is populated by local Malagasy – Antakarana and Sakalava – who survive on their denuded island through farming, cattle and goats. Overgrazing has devastated the island but some forest remains in the southern part. Huge basalt columns are a prominent feature on the northwest tip, used as an adventure playground by enterprising goats. There is a basic campsite on the southwest coast.

The island attracts yachties to its coral reefs and good anchorages. Maribe Bay provides good anchorage, protected between two hills. Manta rays can often be seen in this area.

NOSY TSARABANJINA The name means 'good-looking' and this is indeed a small but incredibly beautiful island. The red, grey and black volcanic rocks, rising quite high at its centre, have a mass of lush, green vegetation clinging to them, including baobabs and pachypodiums. But its real glory is the pure white beaches of coarse sand, along which laps crystal-clear ocean. Turtles and rays rest near the beaches. Divers can be kept busy for a couple of days, and there are walking trails. Yachties can anchor off the southwest, at 6m over a sandy bottom.

This highlight of **Tsarabanjina** is the luxury hotel of the same name (m *032 05 152 29;* e *resa@tsarabanjina.com; www.tsarabanjina.com;* 🛥). This is a beautifully designed collection of 25 en-suite chalets constructed predominantly of natural materials. Despite the exclusivity there is a total lack of pretension as guests are encouraged to cast aside their footwear and go barefoot. Besides relaxing on the island's three beaches, other free activities at your disposal include snorkelling, water-skiing, tennis, volleyball, sailing and morning aquagym. Massage, fishing and boat excursions are on offer, and Tsarabanjina is also a world-class scuba-diving centre (PADI); most diving takes place round Les Quatre Frères (see below) where you may see batfish, scorpionfish, hawksbill turtles and rays, as well as colourful coral. For those who can't quite let go from the rest of the world, Wi-Fi internet is available in the reception area.

NOSY ANKAREA This island is now privately owned so get permission before visiting. There are some gorgeous, sun-drenched beaches and the low hills make for pleasant walking excursions in relatively undisturbed forest.

LES QUATRE FRÈRES (THE FOUR BROTHERS) These are four imposing lumps of silver basalt (Nosy Beangovo, Nosy Betalinjona, Nosy Antsoha and Nosy Betanihazo) rising 51–88m from the sea. Two of them are home to hundreds of nesting seabirds, including brown boobies, frigate birds and white-tailed tropic-birds; and a pair of Madagascar fish eagles nests on one. The sides drop vertically to about 20–30m, and divers come here because three of the boulders can be circumnavigated during one vigorous dive. Yachties can anchor to the southeast of Nosy Beangovo, roughly 100m from the mouth of a cave, at a depth of about 10m. Currents reach up to one knot. The best marine life is in the lee. There are huge caves, spectacular overhangs and rockfalls in the area.

NOSY LAVA This elongated reef, 3.5km by 1.5km, rises to 160m at its peak and is covered in vegetation. It is the northernmost island in the archipelago and home to another pair of fish eagles. A good beach runs along the northern side. Not to be confused with the former prison island of the same name 230km further down the coast (see page 386).

ISLANDS SOUTHWEST OF NOSY BE

The islands are listed below in the order they are encountered heading away from Nosy Be. It is possible to get as far as Nosy Iranja for a day trip (1½ hours each way) but visiting the Radamas requires a multi-day cruise.

NOSY ANKAZOBERAVINA True to its name (meaning 'island with big-leaved trees') this 14ha paradise, 26km from Nosy Be, has plenty of large trees. The forest is home to flying foxes, chameleons and a few lemurs, and there are mangroves and a beautiful palm-lined beach on the northern side. The area is a marine reserve and turtles come to the island to lay their eggs.

Eco-Lodge Ankazoberavina (m *032 04 802 80/032 04 496 94;* e *ulyssexplorer@ gmail.com; www.ankazoberavina.it;* €€€€€), which owns the whole island, has eight simple but comfortable en-suite bungalows, each designed to accommodate a family of four. Accommodation is on a full-board basis. Closed January–March.

NOSY KIVINJY (SUGARLOAF ROCK) This is a great dome-shaped basalt boulder with 'organ-pipe' formations on one side. Not recommended for diving or anchorage. There are strong northeast-flowing currents around the islet.

15

NOSY IRANJA Nosy Iranja, 50km southwest of Nosy Be, is actually a pair of small islands connected by a 1.25km sandbar (walkable at low tide). When I visited in the mid 1990s it was a beautiful peaceful place inhabited by fisherfolk, and an important breeding reserve for both hawksbill and green turtles. Then the luxury hotel was built amid considerable controversy. It has been owned since 2006 by Legacy Hotels of South Africa who seem to be taking their conservation responsibilities seriously. Nevertheless, whether the hotel – whose 29 bungalows encircle the whole southern island – can co-exist harmoniously with the turtles in the long term remains to be seen. The northern island is home to a charming old lighthouse designed by Gustave Eiffel.

The luxury resort of **Nosy Iranja Lodge** (\ *86 616 90 or +27 11 806 6888;* m *032 07 341 31/032 41 628 12;* f *22 480 81;* e *hotels@legacyhotels.co.za; www.iranjalodge.co.za;* ☎) has double and family bungalows with en-suite facilities and private terraces. Activities on offer include water-skiing, parasailing, windsurfing, diving (PADI), snorkelling, pedalos and kayaks, as well as the possibility of manta ray-, dolphin- and whale-watching.

RADAMA ISLANDS The Radama Islands, which lie 90km to the southwest of Nosy Be (and thus are only really accessible by yacht) compete with the Mitsios for the best diving sites in Madagascar. They are set in a breathtaking coastline of bays backed by high mountains. Most of these high sandstone islands are steep-sided above and below the water and covered with scrub, grass and trees. Sharp eroded rock formations, however, render the remaining forest rather difficult to explore.

Nosy Kalakajoro The northernmost island of the group features dense, impenetrable forest on the south side. There are good beaches on the southern side and snorkelling is worthwhile off the southeast. Yachts should anchor 100m off the southeast side in 10–12m over good holding sand and mud, to get protection from the north-to-west winds.

Nosy Berafia (or Nosy Ovy – 'Potato Island') This is the largest of the Radamas, but the environmental degradation is terrible. Nearly all the trees have been cut and goats have completed the destruction of its flora. Red soil weeps from gaping scars into the surrounding water. But if you want to visit, boats can anchor off the east side, near a protected rocky outcrop.

Nosy Antanimora With its broad sandy beaches and turquoise water Nosy Antanimora lives up to its name, which translates loosely as 'land of relaxation'.

Nosy Valiha A small island which is privately owned, so you should not visit without permission.

NOSY SABA, NOSY IFAHO AND (THE OTHER) NOSY LAVA These islands some 40km further southwest are covered on page 386.

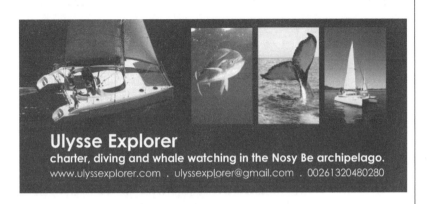

Nosy Be

15

Accurate statistics for rates of HIV are particularly hard to come by in Madagascar as a result of low levels of testing and a historical lack of data collection. According to recent government and WHO estimates, prevalence amongst vulnerable groups is thought to be between 1.0% and 1.8%. That this figure is notably lower than other African countries may be partially attributed to the island's geographical isolation.

However, social indicators suggest that Madagascar could well be following in the footsteps of mainland Africa, with low condom use (around 2% amongst women in rural communities), the relative prevalence of polygamous relationships and partners, and high birth rates (see box on page 135).

In the southeast region of Anosy, indicators suggesting the likelihood of an HIV epidemic are all too apparent. Almost 90% of the population lives below the poverty line, illiteracy is as high as 80% and malaria, bilharzia, typhoid and respiratory diseases are widespread. HIV prevention efforts in the regional capital of Taolagnaro (Fort Dauphin) were initiated during the development of the Rio Tinto ilmenite mine which briefly caused a boom in migration and working tourism.

HIV testing in the town is low, but indications are that infection levels have risen by around 64% in the last four years. In 2010 the first child was diagnosed with the virus. Other factors which increase the likelihood of the spread of HIV are underage sex and marriage (from as young as 12) and low levels of sexual health knowledge. Sex work is common and considered culturally acceptable amongst both men and women; acceptance is as high as 90% amongst impoverished groups. There are strong *fady* around the discussion of sex and access to information is typically low. Another indicator used to predict potential or actual levels of HIV is the prevalence of sexually transmitted diseases, which are estimated by doctors to be around 40% in the town.

The Malagasy government has responded to the threat of HIV with the implementation of a national strategy as part of the country's development plan. This has involved the establishment of regional HIV/AIDS Task Forces to coordinate community-based activities in prevention, counselling, treatment and aftercare. However, as a result of the 2009 political crisis, withdrawal of international funding and restructuring of governmental ministries, coordination has completely collapsed.

The youth representative for the Anosy HIV/AIDS Task Force, Azafady began HIV prevention efforts in 2006. A pilot study was conducted, from which a major three-year behaviour change programme in the town was developed, followed by a specialised maternal HIV prevention project in 2010. During this time, Azafady has managed to increase HIV knowledge amongst young people by an average of 25% and has distributed over 65,000 condoms as well as information, education and communication materials. This has been achieved through local peer group educators and the implementation of a range of community-based activities including focus groups, home visits, the first antenatal group, school workshops, film screenings, sport and culture events, and mass mobilisations.

The biggest community mass mobilisation is the well-established World AIDS Day street carnival, held annually on 1 December and supported by diverse community groups. Participants wear traditional clothing and brightly coloured *lamba hoany*, and decorate themselves with red ribbons and body paint, to perform energetic and synchronised routines. It is an extremely uplifting and enjoyable celebration well worth visiting Taolagnaro for.

Ailie Tam is a qualified social worker and HIV specialist working for Azafady (see pages 77 and 133), having won a year's funding from the Vodafone World of Difference competition. She is preparing a PhD based on her maternal HIV prevention programme.

16

The West

The west of Madagascar offers a mostly dry climate, deciduous forest (with some excellent reserves to protect it), and endless sandy beaches with little danger from sharks. It is effectively divided into two sections: the north, with its gateway town of Mahajanga, and the south with Morondava providing access. No roads directly link these two regions – the traveller is obliged to return to Tana or face the uncomfortable but adventurous journey by *boutre* (cargo boat). Otherwise you can fly: Air Mad Twin Otter services connect a dozen towns throughout the region (see map on page 97). There are also daily flights from Tana to Mahajanga and Morondava.

The lack of roads and agreeable climate makes this the ideal area for mountain bikers and walkers. Adventurous travellers will have no trouble finding a warm welcome in untouristed villages, their own deserted beach and some spectacular landscapes. This is the region in which to see one of Madagascar's extraordinary natural wonders: the *tsingy*. Pronounced *zing*, this is exactly the sound made when one of the limestone pinnacles is struck (they can be played like a xylophone!). It is also a word for 'sharp' in Malagasy. Limestone karst is not unique to Madagascar, but it is rare to see such dramatic forms, such an impenetrable forest of spikes and spires. The endemic succulents that struggle for a foothold in this waterless environment add to the otherworldly feeling. Three national parks showcase *tsingy*.

Opposite major rivers the sea water along the west coast is a brick-red colour: 'like swimming in soup' as one traveller put it. This is the laterite washed into the rivers from the eroded hillsides of the highlands and discharged into the sea: Madagascar's bleeding wounds.

HISTORY

The west is the home of the Sakalava people. For a while in Malagasy history this was the largest and most powerful tribe, ruled by their own kings and queens. The Sakalava kingdom was founded by the Volamena branch of the Maroserana dynasty which emerged in the southwest during the 16th century. Early in the 17th century a Volamena prince, Andriamisara, reached the Sakalava River and gave its name to his new kingdom. His son, Andriandahifotsy (which means 'white man'), succeeded him around 1650 and, with the aid of firearms acquired from European traders, conquered the southwestern area between the Onilahy and Manambolo rivers. This region became known as the Menabe. Later kings conquered first the

DISTANCES IN KILOMETRES			
Antananarivo–Ankarafantsika	453km	Antananarivo–Morondava	701km
Ankarafantsika–Mahajanga	108km	Miandrivazo–Morondava	286km
Antananarivo–Mahajanga	561km	Morondava–Belo-sur-Tsiribihina	106km

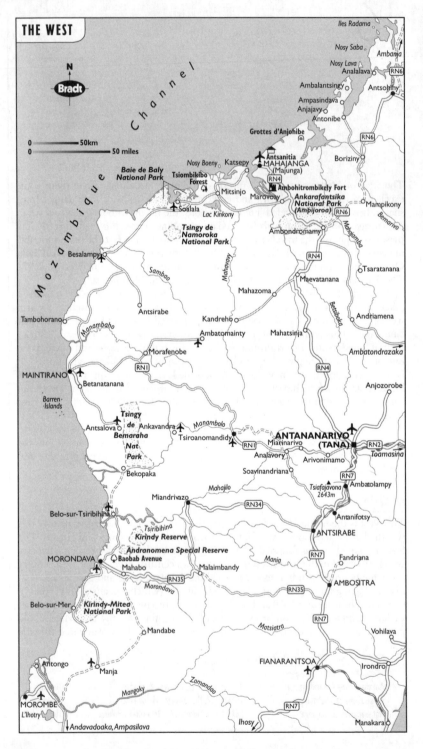

THE WEST

N

Bradt

0   50km
0   50 miles

Mozambique   Channel

Iles Radama

Nosy Saba   Ambanja

Nosy Lava   *Analalala*   RN6

Ambalantsingy   Antsohihy

Ampasindava
Anjajavy
Antonibe   RN6

Grottes d'Anjohibe

Nosy Boeny Katsepy **Antsanitia**   Boriziny
Baie de Baly   MAHAJANGA
National Park   (Majunga)
Tsiombikibo   RN4
Forest   Mitsinjo   **Ambohitrombikely Fort**
     Soalala   Marovoay   **Ankarafantsika**   Mampikony
                          National Park
     Lac Kinkony   **(Ampijoroa)**   RN6
Tsingy de   *Bemarivo*
Namoroka   Ambondromamy
National Park

Besalampy   RN4
                      Maevatanana   Tsaratanana
     Sambao
                  Mahazoma
Tambohorano   Andriamena
          Manambaho   Kandreho   Mahatsinja
     Antsirabe
                  Ambatomainty   *Ambatondrazaka*
          Morafenobe   RN4
MAINTIRANO   RN1
     Betanatanana   Anjozorobe

Barren
Islands   **Tsingy**
     Antsalova **de** Ankavandra   *Manambolo*
          Bemaraha   Tsiroanomandidy   **ANTANANARIVO**
          Nat   Miarinarivo   **(TANA)**   RN2
          Park   Analavory   *Toamasina*
     Bekopaka   Soavinandriana   Arivonimamo   RN7
Belo-sur-Tsiribihina   *Tsiafajavona* Ambatolampy
          Tsiribihina Miandrivazo   *2643m*
          Kirindy Reserve   Antanifotsy
          Andranomena Special Reserve   RN34
MORONDAVA   **Baobab Avenue**   *Mania*   **ANTSIRABE**
          Mahabo   RN7   Fandriana
          Morondava Malaimbandy
Belo-sur-Mer **Kirindy-Mitea**   RN35   RN35   **AMBOSITRA**
          National Park
               Mandabe   *Matsiatra*   RN7   Vohilava

Antongo   **FIANARANTSOA**   Irondro
     Manja   RN7
Mangoky
MOROMBE   *Zomandao*
L'lhotry
  Andavadoaka, Ampasilava   *Ihosy*   Manakara

Boina, the area from the Manambolo to north of present-day Mahajanga, and then the northwest coast as far as Antsiranana.

By the 18th century the Sakalava Empire occupied a huge area in the west, but was divided into the Menabe in the south and the Boina in the north. The two rulers fell out, unity was abandoned, and in the 19th century the area came under the control of the Merina. The Sakalava did not take kindly to domination and sporadic guerrilla warfare continued in the Menabe area until French colonial times.

The Sakalava kingdom bore the brunt of the first serious efforts by the French to colonise the island. For some years France had laid claims (based on treaties made with local princes) to parts of the north and northwest, and in 1883 two fortresses in this region were bombarded. An attack on Mahajanga followed. This was the beginning of the end of Madagascar as an independent kingdom.

THE SAKALAVA PEOPLE TODAY The modern Sakalava have relatively dark skins. The west of Madagascar received a number of African immigrants from across the Mozambique Channel and their influence shows not only in the racial characteristics of the people, but also in their language and customs. There are a number of Bantu words in their dialect, and their belief in *tromba* (spirit possession) and *dady* (royal relics cult) is of African origin.

The Sakalava do not practise second burial. The quality of their funerary art (in one small area) rivals that of the Mahafaly; birds and naked figures are a feature of Sakalava tombs, the latter frequently in erotic positions. Concepts of sexuality and rebirth are implied here. The female figures are often disproportionately large, perhaps recognising the importance of women in the Sakalava culture.

Sakalava royalty do not require elaborate tombs since kings are considered to continue their spiritual existence through a medium with healing powers, and in royal relics. The box on page 390 describes an encounter with the present-day royal family.

KING RADAMA II   *Hilary Bradt*

The son of the 'Wicked Queen' Ranavalona, King Radama II was a gentle ruler who abhorred bloodshed. He was pro-European, interested in Christianity (although never formally a Christian) and a friend of William Ellis, missionary and chronicler of 19th-century Madagascar. After Radama's death, Ellis wrote: 'I have never said that Radama was an able ruler, or a man of large views, for these he was not; but a more humane ruler never wore a crown.' With missionaries of all denominations invited back into Madagascar, intense rivalry sprang up between the Protestants sent by Britain, and the Jesuits who arrived from France. Resentment at the influence of these foreigners over the young king, and disgust at the often rash changes he instigated, boiled over in 1863, and only eight months after his coronation he was assassinated – strangled with a silken sash so that the *fady* against shedding royal blood was not infringed.

The French–British rivalry was fuelled by the violent death of the king, even to the extent that Ellis was accused of being party to the assassination. But was Radama really dead? Both Ellis and Jean Laborde believed that he had survived the strangling and had been allowed to escape by the courtiers bearing him to the countryside for burial. Uprisings, supposedly organised by the 'dead' king, supported this rumour. In a biography of King Radama II, the French historian Raymond Delval makes a strong case that the ex-monarch eventually retreated to the area of Lake Kinkony and lived out the rest of his life in this Sakalava region.

MAHAJANGA (MAJUNGA)

HISTORY Ideally located for trade with East Africa, Arabia and western Asia, Mahajanga has been a major commercial port since 1745, when the Boina capital was moved here from Marovoay. One ruler of the Boina was Queen Ravahiny, a very able monarch who maintained the unity of the Boina which was threatened by rebellions in both the north and the south. It was Mahajanga which provided her with her imported riches and caught the admiration of visiting foreigners. Madagascar was at that time a major supplier of slaves to Arab traders and in return received jewels and rich fabrics. Indian merchants were active then, as today, with a variety of exotic goods. Some of these traders from the east stayed on, the Indians remaining a separate community and running small businesses. More Indians arrived during colonial times.

During the 1883–85 war, Mahajanga served as the base for the military expedition to Antananarivo which consolidated the French Protectorate. Shortly thereafter the French set about enlarging Mahajanga and reclaiming swampland from the Bombetoka River delta. Much of today's extensive town is on reclaimed land.

In World War II Mahajanga was seized from the Vichy French by British forces (see boxes on page 332 and below).

MAHAJANGA TODAY Mahajanga is a hot but breezy town with a large Indian population. The province is slowly opening up to ecotourism, with easily accessible hotspots such as Ankarafantsika National Park and the fly-in resorts contrasting with the barely accessible region to the southwest.

A wide boulevard follows the sea along the west part of town, terminating near a lighthouse. At its elbow is the Mahajanga baobab, said to be at least 700 years old with a circumference of 14m. This area comes alive after dark: indulge in the local life by sampling the delicious zebu brochettes being barbecued along the street.

GETTING THERE AND AWAY Mahajanga is 560km from Tana on a good road (RN4). By *taxi-brousse* it takes around ten hours and the price is 32,000Ar. Heading further north costs 44,000Ar to Antsohihy, 66,000Ar to Ambanja and 77,000Ar all the way to Antsiranana.

There are daily Air Mad flights between Mahajanga and Tana, and weekly flights direct to Antsiranana and Nosy Be. Twin Otter services connect with Analalava, Soalala, Besalampy and Maintirano once or twice a week. Check

---

BEWARE OF THE LOCAL WILDLIFE!   *John Gehan*

The port of Majunga was seized by British forces from the Vichy French in September 1942. To prevent any French troops from retreating to Antananarivo, a party of British Commandos was taken up the Ikopa River to the south of Majunga in small boats.

Unfortunately, as the boats travelled up the river, they ran aground on a sandbank. The simple solution to this was for the men to climb out of the boats and drag them into the main channel – but the river was full of crocodiles!

The Commandos found that the only way they could keep the crocs at bay was by throwing hand grenades at them. The soldiers fought their way through the crocodiles and finally reached their objective, only to find that their perilous journey had been in vain. Instead of trying to retreat, all the French had simply surrendered!

MAHAJANGA
(Majunga)

Hotels & restaurants in central area

Hotels
1 Coco Lodge
2 Badamier
3 Vieux Baobab
4 Nouvel
5 Akbar
6 Fayyaaz
7 Kismat
8 Tropic
9 Anjary
10 Ravinala
11 New Continental

✕ Restaurants
12 Saify
13 Le Sud
14 Pakiza
15 Quai Ouest
16 Red Bulle
17 Filibuste
18 ParadIce
19 De la Mer
20 Abad
21 Kohinoor

TSARANO AMEANY
AMBALAVOLA
MANJARISOA
MORAFENO
ABBATOIR
AMBOVOALANANA
MANGA
MANGARIVOTRA

RTE D'ANTANANARIVO
CHARLES-DE-GAULLE
AV DES COMORES
AV DE L'EGLISE
BD MARCOZ
AV D'AMBOROVY
AV PHILIBERT TSIRANANA
AV DU GL AV DU BIA
14 AV
RANAIVOSON
RUE GEORGES
BRICE
OCTOBRE
RUE DE VICTOR HUGO
RUE LARROUY
AV DU ROVA
BD POINCARE
RUE M JOFFRE
QUAI MAROFOTOTRA
QUAI BARRIQUAND
RUE BOSTANY
GUINAMBERT
AV GALLIENI
RUE RICHELIEU
RUE RIGAULT
BARRE
RUE MORICEAU
QUAI VUILLEMIN
AV DE FRANCE
R EMMANUEL
R EDOUARD
Q ORSINY
AV VII
BOULEVARD MARCOZ
R BARRIOUAND
BOULEVARD CORNICHE
R M BARRIOUAND
AV DE LA REPUBLIC

Terasse (rest) (400m),
Marco Pizza (600m),
Mozea Akiba (museum) (2.5km),
Airport (5.8km)

Escale de la Plage (800m),
Karon (hotel) (1km)

Police
National Parks office
Rabemananjara
Alexis Stadium
Yahiny House
Chez Chabaud
BFV $
Town hall
Taxi-brousse station
Market
Aventure et Découverte
Cathedral
Shakira
Bookshop
Score
BMOI
Locasoa
Tabany
BENENI
GEO
BOA
Madeci Tour
Tropicana
Hospital
Tranquillile
Baobab
Air Madagascar
BFV $
BNI $
Thi-Lan
Bel Air
Petite Cour
Piscine
Kanto
San Antonio
Hotel du Phare
Lighthouse
Fishing Residence
Boina Beach
Ruche des Aventuriers
Key Largo
Cap Ouest
Lighthouse
Katsepy

Bay
Bombetoka
Mozambique Channel
Pointe du Sable
Pointe du Caiman

Bradt

N

500m
500yds

www.airmadagascar.com for the latest schedules. Air Austral (*www.air-austral.com*) also flies here weekly from Mayotte and Réunion.

Taxi-brousses pass close to the airport if you want to avoid getting a taxi the 6km into town.

For the truly adventurous the cargo boats – *boutres* – plying the west coast will take passengers (see box on page 384).

WHERE TO STAY

Upper range and top end

🏠 **Piscine** (31 rooms) La Corniche, Bd Marcoz; ☏ 62 241 72/73/74; f 62 239 65; e piscinehotel@moov.mg; www.piscinehotel.com. En-suite dbl rooms & 2 suites with TV, AC, minibar, free Wi-Fi & balcony, some with sea view. Large pool, massage & nightclub/casino. Credit cards accepted. €€€€–€€€€€

🏠 **Coco Lodge** (17 rooms) 49 Av de France; ☏ 62 230 23/238 18; f 62 226 92; e cocolodge@moov.mg; www.coco-lodge.com. Recently renovated smart, spacious en-suite rooms with AC & minibar built around central courtyard with lovely pool. No food except b/fast. €€€€

🏠 **Tropicana** (16 bungalows) Oasis Gatinière, Rue Lacaze, Mangarivotra; ☏ 62 220 69; e hotel-tropicana@tiscali.fr; www.hotel-majunga.com. Up the hill from Don Bosco school behind the cathedral. Pleasant bungalows away from the centre. €€€€

🏠 **Badamier** (32 rooms) Av de la République; ☏ 62 240 65/67; m 032 57 435 75/033 13 122 17; f 62 242 49; e hotelebadamier@moov.mg; www.hotelmajunga-lebadamier.com. New smart 4-floor hotel; centrally located. En-suite dbl rooms with AC, TV, free Wi-Fi, safe & balcony; more expensive suites also have minibar, lounge & sea view. €€€€

Mid-range €€€

🏠 **New Continental** (25 rooms) Av de la République; ☏ 62 225 70. Dbl, trpl & family rooms with en suite facilities, AC, TV & safe.

🏠 **Ravinala** (11 rooms) Quai Orsini; ☏ 62 902 18; m 032 40 400 37/034 03 937 69; e ravinalahotel@moov.mg; www.majunga-hotel-ravinala.com. Clean dbl, trpl & family rooms with TV, AC, Wi-Fi (not free) & en-suite bathroom. Also 6-person room with kitchenette. Good value.

🏠 **Hotel du Phare** (23 rooms) Bd Marcoz, La Corniche; ☏ 62 235 00; f 62 222 00; e hotelduphare@moov.mg. En-suite dbl & twin rooms, some with AC & minibar.

🏠 **Fishing Residence** (10 rooms & 7 bungalows) 58 Bd Marcoz; m 032 04 682 20/032 05 682 20/032 02 003 35; e fevedaniel@yahoo.fr. Family bungalows & dbl AC rooms, all with en-suite (cold water) facilities & TV. Restaurant with seafood specialities & swimming pool.

🏠 **Escale de la Plage** (10 bungalows) ☏ 62 221 41; m 032 40 442 34/034 08 252 89/033 01 214 26; f 62 248 25; e escaledelaplage@moov.mg; www.escaledelaplage.com. En-suite dbl & trpl rooms, some with hot water & TV.

🏠 **Tranquilllle** (6 rooms) La Corniche; m 032 07 524 59/032 43 962 89; e gladys-coll@yahoo.fr. Yes, the name really is spelled with a quadruple 'L'! Tiny pool. Small, cosy, quiet place; rooms with en-suite toilet but shared showers.

Also in this category: **Akbar** (www.hotel-akbar.com), **Anjary** (www.anjary-hotel.com), **Corniche** (m 032 40 154 95), **Fayyaaz** (☏ 62 227 40), **Karon** (☏ 62 226 94), **Kismat** (☏ 62 235 62), **Nouvel** (☏ 62 221 10), **Vahiny House** (☏ 62 243 41), **Vieux Baobab** (☏ 62 223 20).

Penny-pincher and budget

🏠 **Chez Chabaud** (28 rooms) ☏ 62 233 27; m 032 40 530 05/032 40 028 57. Near town hall. Some very cheap rooms with shared facilities; also very good-value rooms with AC &/or TV. €€

🏠 **Boina Beach** (20 rooms) Bd Marcoz, La Corniche; m 032 02 032 16. En-suite (cold water) dbl & family rooms. Very friendly & helpful Malagasy owner. Pool table. €€

🏠 **Tropic** (7 rooms) ☏ 62 236 10. Simple rooms, one of which is en suite (cold water). No food. €€

🏠 **Kanto** (11 rooms) La Corniche; ☏ 62 229 78. Overlooking the sea to the north of town. Dbl rooms with fans, some en suite. €

✗ WHERE TO EAT

✗ **Marco Pizza** Pavillion 53, Rte Amborovy, Tsaramandroso; m 032 11 110 32/033 11 110 33. Top quality pizza: eat-in, take-away & delivery. Also ice cream & cocktails.

✗ **Bel Air** ⊕ 09.00–late. French & Malagasy dishes in ocean-view setting.

✗ **Kohinoor** Rue Henri Garnier; ⊕ 07.30–23.00. Indian restaurant with good food, including snacks, & kitsch décor. Vegetarian options.

✗ **Pakiza** Av de la République; ⊕ Wed–Mon, Tue closed. Pizzas & Indian food; also ice creams, milkshakes & juices.

✗ **Flibuste** ✆ 62 941 93. Particularly recommended for its seafood.

✗ **Red Bulle** m 032 45 178 39; ⊕ Mon–Sat 11.00–14.30 & 18.00–04.00, Sun closed. Pub-grill with big screen & dance floor.

✗ **Petite Cour** La Corniche, Bd Marcoz; ✆ 62 021 94; m 032 07 750 57; ⊕ Mon–Sat, Sun closed. Reliable upmarket restaurant.

✗ **De la Mer (Boulé)** ✆ 62 242 68; m 032 04 621 60/033 01 623 74; ⊕ Wed–Mon 09.00–late, Tue closed. On seafront boulevard. Karaoke Wed–Fri at 20.00; cabaret w/end.

✗ **Key Largo** Restaurant & snack bar.

✗ **Terrasse** m 033 05 644 09. Bar & restaurant with wood-oven pizza, including take-away.

✗ **Thi-Lan** ✆ 62 229 61; ⊕ Mon–Sat 10.00–14.00 & 18.00–22.00, Sun closed. Vietnamese specialities.

⊑ **Quai Ouest** 5 Rue Georges V; ✆ 62 233 00. Posh café serving a variety of coffees, teas, juices & pastries; also good handicraft boutique.

⊑ **Saify** Av de Mahabibo; ✆ 62 222 33; ⊕ Mon–Sat 07.00–12.00 & 15.00–20.00, Sun 07.00–12.00. Perennial favourite for breakfast, ice cream & snacks.

⊑ **Parad'Ice** Off Bd Poincaré; ⊕ Mon–Sat 08.00–22.00, Sun closed. Splendid ice cream & good b/fast.

⊑ **Cap Ouest** m 033 12 151 33; ⊕ 08.00–22.00. Snack bar.

⊑ **Le Sud** m 032 02 540 66/032 45 923 69; ⊕ Wed–Mon 09.00–01.00, Tue closed. New bar & snack bar with pool table.

⊑ **Abad** ✆ 62 238 46. Bakery with cakes; also b/fast.

NIGHTLIFE The Italian-owned **Shakira** lounge bar and club is a chic venue, usually busy on Thursday to Saturday nights, and there's a respectable discotheque (**Jacaranda**) at the Piscine hotel. **Ravinala** (near the hotel of the same name) has pool tables open from 18.00, then the nightclub gets going around 22.00. **San Antonio** is another nightclub near Boina Beach.

SHOPPING There is a **Score supermarket** (⊕ *Mon–Fri 08.30–13.00 & 15.00–19.30, Sat 08.30–19.30, Sun 08.30–12.30*) at the intersection of Rue du Colonel Barre and Rue Henri Paul, two blocks south from the Galana fuel station.

The bookshop **Librairie de Madagascar** sells a few postcards and sometimes has local maps.

TOURIST INFORMATION, TOUR OPERATORS AND VEHICLE HIRE

▨ **Regional tourist office (ORTM)** m 032 07 668 87; e ortmajunga@moov.mg; www.mahajanga.org. They publish a weekly flyer (available at most hotel receptions) with local news & events.

National Parks office 14 Av Philibert Tsiranana; ✆ 62 226 56; e angapmjg@gmail.com

Air Madagascar ✆ 62 222 59; m 033 11 222 07; f 62 293 75; e mjnkk@airmadagascar.com; ⊕ Mon–Fri 07.30–11.30 & 14.30–17.00, Sat 08.00–10.00

Maderi Tour Rue Jules Ferry; ✆ 62 023 34; m 032 07 600 50; e maderitour@yahoo.fr; www.maderi-tour.com; ⊕ Mon–Fri 08.00–12.00 & 14.30–18.00, Sat 08.00–12.00. Various local excursions & tours;

also transfers to Tana incorporating a visit & overnight stay at Ankarafantsika.

Axius Tourisma 6 Rue de l'Artillerie; m 034 14 100 27; e tourisma@axiusmada.com; www.axiusmada.com. Tour operator, vehicle rental & flights.

Aventure et Découverte ✆ 62 934 75; m 034 08 521 96/033 02 069 79; www.aventure-decouverte.com; ⊕ Mon–Sat 08.00–12.00 & 14.30–18.00. Fishing, pirogue trips & tours. Also hires quads, motorbikes & 4x4s (with/without driver).

Ruche des Aventuriers Rue Richlieu; ✆ 62 247 79; m 032 47 488 98/033 07 631 27; e laruchedesaventuriers@moov.mg;

www.laruchedesaventuriers.net. Tours & packages including guide, tent, camping gear etc. Also 4x4 hire.

Locasoa \ 62 931 27; m 032 40 053 70; e locasoa@yahoo.fr; ⏱ 08.00–12.00 & 15.00–18.30. Car & 4x4 rental.

WHAT TO SEE AND DO IN AND AROUND MAHAJANGA

Mozea Akiba (Museum) (⏱ *Tue–Fri 09.00–11.00 & 15.00–17.00, w/end 15.00–17.00*) This museum is situated near the entrance of the University at Ambondrona in Mahajanga. It has displays showing the history of the region, as well as an exhibition of palaeontology and ethnology. There are also photos and descriptions of some of Mahajanga's tourist sights such as the Cirque Rouge and Grottes d'Anjohibe. Signs are in French but some are also in English.

Katsepy Katsepy is a fishing village across the bay from Mahajanga, which is reached by a ferry (one or two crossings each day) that takes 45 minutes. Katsepy is the starting point for exploring the wildlife areas to the southwest of Mahajanga.

For at least three decades there has been only one reason to go to Katsepy as a day trip: to dine at **Chez Chabaud** (m *032 07 067 34*). I still go weak at the knees remembering my meal there in 1984, while researching the first edition of this book. There is accommodation here too in the form of comfy en-suite bungalows.

Amborovy Beach This sandy beach also known as **Petite Plage**, 5–7km north of town, is popular with locals for weekend outings. A couple of kilometres further north is another good beach, **Grand Pavois**, near to the Cirque Rouge.

There is upper-range accommodation at Amborovy Beach: **Zaha Motel** (\ *62 225 55/237 20*; e *zahamotel.mjn@moov.mg*; €€€€) has 12 double rooms and 22 family bungalows with TV, air conditioning, Wi-Fi (not free) and en-suite hot water. The mid-range **Dohatel** (\ *62 224 91*; m *034 13 090 06/034 01 153 71*; e *dohatel@gmail.com*; *www.dohatel-madagascar.com*; €€€) in the same area has some rooms with air conditioning. And reader Sunniva Gylver recommends the **Convent Sacré Cœur** (€), which has rooms from 6,000Ar.

Cirque Rouge About 10km from Mahajanga and 4km past the airport (as the crow flies), this is a canyon ending in an amphitheatre of red-, beige- and lilac-coloured rock eroded into strange peaks and spires. It is a beautiful and dramatic spot and – with its stream of fresh water running to the nearby beach – makes an idyllic camping place. For a day visit, give yourself at least an hour to look around. Late afternoon is best, when the low sun sets the reds and mauves alight.

Fort Ambohitrombikely This impressive fort, 20km southeast of Mahajanga, was built on the highest point in the region in 1824 by King Radama I. It is worth a visit for the views and sense of history.

Antsanitia (\ *62 023 34/911 00/913 63*; m *032 07 600 50/032 05 196 90*; e *antsanitia@antsanitia.com*; *www.antsanitia.com*; €€€€€) This upper-range place, about an hour's drive north of Mahajanga, is much praised by readers. The hotel, restaurant, location, and beach are all excellent. And as a bonus the hotel works with the local community and tries to be ecologically responsible. The hotel arranges transfers from Mahajanga, but otherwise you will need a 4x4 as the road is bad.

La Dune offers budget accommodation nearby (contact details as for Tranquilllle on page 374).

Mangatsa (m *032 40 032 48/034 06 775 29/032 43 035 45*; e *kalotody@moov.mg*) There is a small sacred lake here, on a site once owned by Madagascar's first

ANKAFOBE FOREST
Chris Birkinshaw, Missouri Botanical Gardens

Ankafobe Forest is a complex of several small and degraded forest fragments located in valleys on the Tampoketsa (high plateau savanna) of Ankafobe in central Madagascar. We selected this site because it contains much of the remaining population of one of Madagascar's most threatened trees: *Schizolaena tampoketsana*. One of the forest fragments is immediately adjacent to RN4, linking Tana and Mahajanga (some 30km northwest of Ankafobe, near PK 131).

It is here that we have built a simple chalet with educational signs and seats, and also constructed a 1km trail, passing through savanna, valley-bottom marsh and forest, with labelled trees. Although the forest here is small it is of general interest as a living remnant of the type of forest that presumably covered much of the *hauts plateaux*. The site supports much else of interest (including three lemur species) for the road-weary tourist needing a short break from the journey between Tana and Mahajanga. I think many tourists will also appreciate that here we do not hassle them with guides or even entry fees – rather they can just park next to the road enjoy the scenery and wander around the trail themselves. We ask that anyone who appreciates the project stops at the shop in the nearby village of Firarazana (5km southeast of the site on the left) to buy a project T-shirt. Profits are used to support the various activities necessary to conserve this site.

president: Philibert Tsiranana. Aside from the lake, which is home to crocodiles, there are mangroves, baobabs, mango and coconut plantations, and you may see sifakas. There is a restaurant and bungalows at **Espace Kalatody**, and it is also possible to camp. The site is 16km to the north of Mahajanga, 30 minutes by car beyond the airport.

Belobaka Caves Although classed as a tourist site since the 1940s, these six caves are little known. The first is a sacred place where people come to make wishes, but the other five are more spectacular for stalactites and stalagmites. It is said a fence and gate were once erected to manage the tourism, but the resident spirits objected to this arrangement and sent lightning which struck and destroyed the barrier.

Local tour operators can arrange a visit, or you can get here in 20 minutes or so by car: take RN4 12km out of town then turn left for 2km. Caretaker Tahiana should be on hand to show you the path. There is also an ostrich farm nearby.

Anjohibe Caves and beyond Anjohibe means 'big cave' so this name is common in the region. The famous Grottes d'Anjohibe are 82km northeast of Mahajanga and accessible only by 4x4, and only in the dry season. There are two places to visit: the caves themselves and a natural swimming pool above the Mahafanina waterfalls. The caves are full of stalactites and stalagmites (and bats), and have several kilometres of passages. Dan Carlsson excavated them in 1996: 'It seems as though the caves have been used for normal living but also as a place of sacrifice. We found pottery with ash, charcoal and animal bones; also several hippopotamus bones believed to be some million years old.'

To reach the caves turn left at Antanamarina and continue for 5km. It takes about four hours from Mahajanga. Don't forget to take a torch.

John and Valerie Middleton add: 'Two thirds of the way to the caves the river Mariarano is crossed next to the small village of Posima. The area is very beautiful with many cone-shaped hills often with caves, most with large passageways and beautiful formations.'

(✆ *62 780 00;* e *ankarafantsika@gmail.com*) This is a super national park; it's easy to get to, thrilling to visit with abundant wildlife, and with clear, level or stepped paths which make hiking a pleasure. With accommodation now available next to the park, this is a must for naturalists.

Ankarafantsika straddles RN4 about 120km from Mahajanga. The most-visited part of the reserve is on the southern side of the road, with Lac Ravelobe to the north – but the park covers over 130,000ha stretching all the way north to the Mahajamba river. The name Ankarafantsika comes from the word *garafantsy*, which means either 'hill of thorns' or 'nail in the skull'.

GETTING THERE AND AWAY It takes two hours by road from Mahajanga, and if you are in a private vehicle it is worth stopping at Lac Amboromalandy, a reservoir which is a great place to see waterfowl. Note the excellent examples of Sakalava tombs near PK 16, on your left as you're driving to Ankarafantsika. The park is at PK 114. Coming from Tana, it takes about eight hours by *taxi-brousse*.

The park has a minibus available for airport transfers (45,000Ar/person; four people minimum).

⌂ **WHERE TO STAY AND EAT** The **Gîte d'Ampijoroa** (€€€) has mid-range accommodation right at the entrance. Book directly with the park (contact details above). The six double rooms share facilities, while the seven newer bungalows each sleep up to four and have en-suite bathrooms (cold water only).

More basic Malagasy-run accommodation may be found at Andranofasika, 4km towards Tana. You can arrange a transfer with the park minibus.

There are good facilities for **camping** at the park entrance: 11 sheltered tent pitches with nice communal showers, toilets, kitchen and dining area. The pitches themselves have power sockets and lights and cost 6,000Ar per night. Double/triple tents may be rented for 15,000/25,000Ar (price includes the pitch).

A simple restaurant provides breakfast from 3,000Ar and meals from 10,000Ar.

PERMITS AND GUIDES Permits are available at the park office (see page 72 for prices). There are 15 guides, 11 of whom speak English. They cost from 15,000Ar per circuit; maximum six people per guide.

VISITORS' CENTRE The visitors' information centre and souvenir shop are worth seeing, with good information on the local customs, including the *tromba* (trance) ceremony. One such ceremony takes place on New Year's Day at Lake Ravelobe.

There are several *fady* in the area, mostly pertaining to the lake (women must not wash in the lake during menstruation and nothing can be washed – or sacrificed – at the lake on a Saturday). There is also a *fady* against eating pork.

FLORA AND FAUNA This is typical dry, deciduous forest with sparse understorey and lots of lianas. In the dry winter season many of the trees have shed their leaves, but in the wet months the forest is a sea of bright greens. Conspicuous is the tree with menacing spines, *Hura crepitans*, which is actually not a native species – it was introduced from Central America. There are 130 bird species (with highlights like the Van Dam's vanga, Madagascar fish eagle and white breasted mesite), eight easily seen lemur species and reptiles galore.

Wildlife-viewing in Ankarafantsika starts as soon as you arrive. Right beside the parking area is a tree that Coquerel's sifakas use as a dormitory. They are extremely handsome animals with the usual silky white fur but with chestnut-brown arms

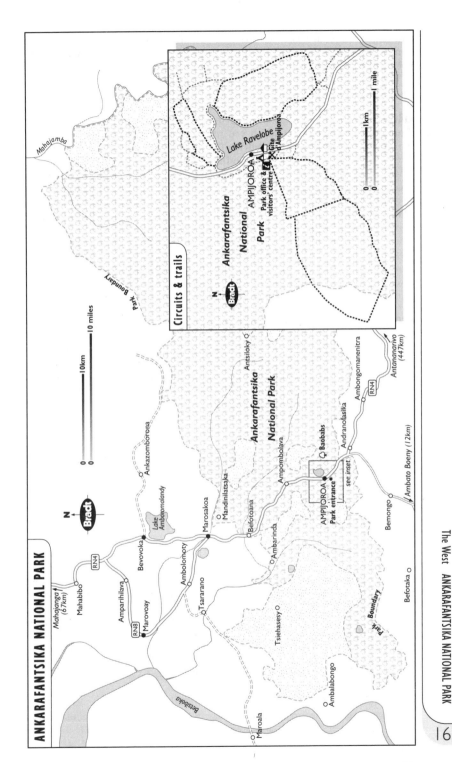

ANKARAFANTSIKA NATIONAL PARK

Circuits & trails

Lake Ravelobe

Ankarafantsika National Park

AMPIJOROA

Park office & visitors' centre

Gîte d'Ampijoroa

Mahajamba

Park Boundary

0   1km
0   1 mile

Mahajanga (67km)

Mahabibo

RN4

Amparihilava

Marovoay

RNB

Tsararano

Lake Ambondromalandy

Bevovoka

Ambolomoty

Marosakoa

Ankazomborona

Ankazomborona

Mandinilatsaka

Befotoana

Ambarinda

Tsiehasey

Ambalabongo

Ambalongo

Maroala

Betsiboka

Park Boundary

Antsiloky

Ampombolava

Baobabs

AMPIJOROA

Park entrance

see inset

Andranofasika

Ambongomanenitra

RN4

Antananarivo (447km)

Ambato Boeny (12km)

Bemongo

Befotaka

0   10km
0   10 miles

and thighs. On your walks you may also see mongoose lemurs, western woolly lemurs and sportive lemurs; and this is the only place where you might see the golden-brown mouse lemur, *Microcebus ravelobensis*.

If you're keen to see crocodiles they may be sighted year round, but the best months are July to October.

CIRCUITS There is a very good trail system. The shortest and easiest is **Circuit Coquereli** (1½ hours), on which you may see sifakas and brown lemurs. More botany-focussed is **Circuit Retendrika** (2–3 hours), which is also good for birding. A visit to the park's famous **pachypodiums** will take about two hours. A similar length of time is required to go and see the tall *Adansonia madagascariensis* **baobabs**, but if you're pressed for time you can drive part of the way. On **Circuit Source de Vie** (3–4 hours) you will gain an insight into local culture and everyday rural life. **Circuit Ankarokaroka** (3 hours) offers a hike through forest and savanna to the **canyon**, an amazing multicoloured erosion feature. There's plenty of wildlife to see *en route*, or you can go to the canyon by vehicle (25,000Ar per person in the park 4x4). **Night walks** (1½ hours) will give you the chance to see mouse lemurs and chameleons. **Boat trips** (1–2 hours) are the best way to see **Lake Ravelobe** – particularly rewarding for birders and a good chance of sighting crocs. The cost including guide is 50,000Ar for two people, then 15,000Ar for each additional person.

PROJET ANGONOKA Ankarafantsika is also home to the Angonoka Tortoise Programme operated by the Durrell Wildlife Conservation Trust (see box on page 68). This is one of Madagascar's most successful captive breeding projects. After many years of research, ploughshares – the world's rarest tortoises – are now breeding readily and are being reintroduced to their original habitat. Almost as rare, the attractive little flat-tailed tortoise (*kapidolo*) is also being bred here, as is the Madagascar big-headed/side-necked turtle.

The site is fortified as a result of thefts, so it is possible for tourists to glimpse them only through a chain-link fence.

FLY-IN BEACH RESORTS NORTHEAST OF MAHAJANGA

If you look on a map of Madagascar, you'll see a glorious expanse of nothingness along the indented coastline between Mahajanga and Nosy Be. This is where three entrepreneurs have established fly-in resorts which come (in my opinion) as close to perfection as you could hope for.

LODGE DES TERRES BLANCHES (m *032 05 151 55;* e *lodgeterresblanches@gmail.com; www.lodgeterresblanches.com;* 🏊) About 100km from Mahajanga and 25km south of Anjajavy. This lodge really does qualify for the cliché 'best kept secret' (at least from English-speaking tourists) since it sees far fewer visitors than Anjajavy or Marovasa-Be (see below) and no tour groups. Access is by light aircraft or boat.

There is quite simple, but comfortable, accommodation in six double bungalows next to a gorgeous white beach fringed with forest. Compared with the luxury lodges this is a simple, do-it-yourself resort. Guests eat together in the lodge, and there is a bar with fridge for guests to help themselves. Electricity is by generator. If you want to go on a longer hike, or to be dropped off in a cove somewhere for the day, picnics can be arranged.

This is a popular resort for sport-fishermen, and the two boats are largely used for fishing trips. However, you can arrange to be taken to some beautiful coves along the coast, or to baobab-arrayed islands, or to an area of *tsingy*. See the ad on page 406.

LA MAISON DE MAROVASA-BE (\ +33141496010 in France; e lodge@marovasabe.com; www.marovasabe.com; ☕) Located some 15–20km north of Anjajavy in Moramba Bay this lodge is accessible by light aircraft from Mahajanga (45 minutes) or Tana (2 hours). There are three suites and six luxury rooms, all with en-suite bathrooms and balconies.

The location is, perhaps, not as attractive as that of the other two lodges, and its forest has suffered from slash-and-burn agriculture (*tavy*). However, the hotel itself is beautifully thought-out and offers true luxury with a beautiful swimming pool and other amenities. The owners are also involved with Ecole du Monde, a local NGO working to benefit local communities. Their work includes reforestation projects, and guests can contribute by planting a tree. As with all these lodges, the rates are full board and include a motorboat for exploring the area.

ANJAJAVY (\ +33144691503 in France; e contact@anjajavy.com; www.anjajavy.com; ☕) Anjajavy is about as good as you can get in Madagascar. This is not just a luxury seaside hotel: in addition to its 24 villas it protects 450ha of Madagascar's dwindling dry deciduous forest. In some places this grows right on the *tsingy* limestone.

Wildlife viewing here is effortless, including Coquerel's sifakas, brown lemurs, mouse lemurs and sportive lemurs. Birds include flocks of bright green grey-headed love-birds, sickle-billed vangas, crested ibises, crested couas and vasa parrots, to name just a few. You may also see ground boas, hognose snakes and plenty of chameleons and beautiful butterflies. There's a couple of caves too, spectacular enough with stalactites and stalagmites (and bats), and one with the skulls of an extinct lemur species embedded in the rocks. Perhaps most startlingly for botanists, Anjajavy and Moramba Bay hold an undescribed species of cycad trees. Then there are the coral reefs, *tsingy*, pristine beaches and extensive mangroves... not to mention total comfort, brilliant service and superb food!

Three nights is the minimum stay, five allows you to appreciate all that this amazing place has to offer. Note that arrivals/departures must be scheduled to coincide with flights (Tuesday/Thursday/Saturday at the time of writing) unless your group is large enough to warrant an additional flight of the 8-seater Cessna. Anjajavy offers a range of land- and water-based activities. Some, such as guided forest walks, are included in the rates. Other free activities include sailing, windsurfing, snorkelling, mountain biking and visits to the surrounding villages. For an additional fee you can indulge in deep-sea fishing, waterskiing and massages. For a longer excursion there's the magnificent **Moramba Bay** (15km/45minutes by boat) – a must for any nature enthusiast. To fit as much into a day as possible, Anjajavy operates in its own time zone bubble – an hour ahead of the rest of Madagascar!

It is an equally wonderful spot for relaxation, with a good beach, lovely swimming pool and 'oasis' garden. There is free Wi-Fi in the restaurant/pool area and some villas. Anjajavy works with a local school and NGO to benefit the local communities.

CONSERVATION AREAS TO THE SOUTHWEST OF MAHAJANGA

From Katsepy (see page 376) a road, of sorts, provides access to the *tsingy* and wetlands which are of great interest to anyone who loves Madagascar's diversity of landscape, plants and wildlife. Access is exceptionally difficult, however, so even adventurous travellers may prefer an organised tour.

Dr Jonathan Ekstrom

Anyone who has spent time in Madagascar will realise that the Malagasy are not the most monogamous of peoples. The same is true for the island's parrots. The greater vasa parrots of Madagascar are those big black squawking things you see flying around the forest canopy. They are not the prettiest of parrots, having drab brownish-black plumage, long necks and even bald heads for some of each year. But vasa parrots have one of the most exhilarating sex lives of any animal on Earth. It's the females that are dominant over the males (they're 25% bigger) and they pursue the little chaps ardently all through September and October. It's the girls that do the chasing. And they seem to know what they're doing as most females end up with four to eight mates.

You can imagine what a headache this is for the males, having to compete to fertilise the eggs of the female with all your best buddies. The male parrots have risen to the challenge, however, with some utterly unbelievable evolutionary adaptations. For a start they have a penis. Birds in general don't have penises; both sexes just have cloacal openings which are pressed together to transfer the sperm. Not so for vasa parrots: the males have evolved a penis somewhat bigger than a golf ball which they erect out of their cloaca as and when they need it. Courtship before sex takes an appropriately long time – several weeks in fact – and on the big day the female might consort with a half dozen males before settling down with one at midday. And of course this is not ordinary love-making.

Sex in most bird species doesn't look that fun to be honest – it's all over pretty quickly with a kiss of the cloacas lasting a couple of seconds, and both partners then wander off in different directions pretending they don't know each other. Not so in vasa parrots: sex lasts a full two hours with the male and female locked together in passionate coitus. Tied together for two hours you can see them crooning over each other, preening their partner's plumage, squawking when things get a bit rough. So much so that it frequently attracts onlookers: a whole crowd of parrots can turn up to watch. Sometimes things get a bit out of hand and some of her other boyfriends get a bit frisky and try jumping on top of the copulating pair, sometimes managing to disturb them and have a go themselves. However, it's all down to the female's choice as she has the beak and claws to control her diminutive boyfriends.

After such persistent promiscuity, when it comes to feed the chicks you can imagine the confusion. The males have normally found several girlfriends for themselves as well, and these avian harems often mean it's not clear which chicks belong to which dad. It's the males that do all the work bringing in the food and you can see the lads vexing over which of their girlfriends to feed next. Once again the females don't just sit back and see what happens; they sing long, complex songs to get attention. Each female has her own unique song, so November in the forests of Madagascar is rather like a huge singing contest where females with chicks compete to be the best singer. And it works; females singing longer or more complex songs attract more males and get more food. The males benefit from feeding the best singing girlfriends because these are also the strongest birds with the most chicks in the nest.

Greater vasa parrots have the most complex sex life of any parrot so far studied. Scientists think most others are monogamous – real bastions of chastity in the avian world. So vasas have broken all the rules and are pillars of promiscuity instead. That's evolution in isolation for you. Like so much of Madagascar's wildlife, if you leave some normal, decent-living animals by themselves in the middle of the Indian Ocean for a few dozen million years they are bound to come up with something bizarre.

Jonathan Ekstrom did his PhD research on the greater vasa parrot. He now runs The Biodiversity Consultancy in London (www.thebiodiversityconsultancy.com).

NOSY BOENY (NOSY ANTSOHERIBORY) This is a small island, about a kilometre long, in Boina Bay, with some fascinating Antalaotra ruins dating from the 16th century. The ruins include several cemeteries, houses and mosques. The island is sacred to the local people so camping is prohibited – but day visits are allowed.

To reach the island, start from Katsepy and continue by road to the village of Boeny-Ampasy on the west side of the bay, where there are bungalows. A 1½-hour boat journey brings you to Nosy Boeny.

MAHAVAVY-KINKONY WETLAND COMPLEX With backing from the NGO BirdLife International (*www.birdlife.org*) and Asity (*www.asitymadagascar.org*) this wetland area received protected status in 2007. The two dozen interconnected lakes, river, delta, bays, marshland, mangroves, forest, savanna and caves included in the 268,236ha reserve form a haven for birders and other wildlife enthusiasts.

The wide variety of ecosystems here leads to extraordinary biodiversity, with plenty of fauna: nine species of lemur, including crowned and Decken's sifakas and the mongoose lemur, a similar number of bats, a host of reptiles and, of course, fish. But it is the birds that cause the most excitement: 143 species. And this is the only site where *all* of the Malagasy western waterfowl species may be seen. July to September are the best months for seeing breeding birds.

In the **Tsiombikibo Classified Forest**, near Mitsinjo, are several small beautiful ponds which are the refuge of white-backed ducks and African pygmy geese. Mitsinjo is the capital of the district but the gateway town is Namakia. It is a tough place to access independently. The port of Namakia may be reached in five to six hours by motorboat from Mahajanga but the sea is usually quite rough. Alternatively, from Katsepy it is three to four hours' drive, but the road beyond Mitsinjo is in poor condition and closed during the rainy season.

The town of **Mitsinjo** has some very basic accommodation and camping is possible too. The best option in **Namakia** is **La Cercle**, with budget and mid-range rooms. Contact Asity for the latest information on places to camp.

SOALALA AND BEYOND

SOALALA Only a handful of adventurous travellers come to Soalala, but this fascinating port is gaining importance as the gateway town to Tsingy de Namoroka and Baie de Baly national parks. John and Valerie Middleton report that 'there are several very large African baobabs and impressive pachypodiums. It was previously a French fort and at least two ancient cannons can be seen on the seafront. There are also many good eating places. Across the bay is a massive French shrimp farm.'

There is budget accommodation at **Chez la Mere de Nadia** (m *034 01 036 79/ 033 12 179 56;* e *lakana2005@yahoo.fr;* €€). The French owner, Maurice Bonafous, also provides a guide service and can organise all-in tours locally, including a 4x4 with air conditioning. Or you could camp in the quiet area near the beachfront.

Getting there Soalala has an airstrip served by Air Mad Twin Otter from Mahajanga or Tana about four times a week.

Taxi-brousses from Katsepy go to Soalala a few times week (12 hours/30,000Ar). By 4x4 it takes about nine hours, but the road is only passable from May to November.

Alternatively, the *boutres* (cargo boats) from Mahajanga frequently call at Soalala. It should cost around 10,000Ar for a passenger but it is not a trip for softies (see box on page 384). Other types of boats sometimes also make the trip, taking six to 12 hours. It is *fady* to take peanuts on this journey.

(**m** *033 11 968 89*; **e** *bbnrk.parks@gmail.com*) This relatively new national park is across the bay from Soalala, occupying the better part of the northwest peninsula and extending east across the bay to Cap Sada. It protects a variety of terrestrial and aquatic ecosystems: mangrove forests, coastal dunes, rivers, permanent lakes and dense dry semi-deciduous forests. The idyllic coastal villages surrounding the park offer visitors a glimpse into the Sakalava way of life. **Bemosary**, **Maroalika** and

MAHAJANGA TO MORONDAVA BY *BOUTRE*

Marko Petrovic

I and two Slovenian girls caught the *taxi-be de mer* from the sailing port in Mahajanga. It wasn't hard to find one going to Morondava and we quickly settled on a price of 60,000Ar each. These sailing ships which transport goods (and people) up and down the west coast vary in size but ours was average: 15m with two masts and a 30-tonne capacity. The boats have no motor, so departure is timed to coincide with the outgoing high tide. We left in the evening and at 02.00 the sailors hoisted the sails and a strong wind blew us southwards. Everybody except the helmsman (nine sailors and 15 paying passengers) slept on the deck.

The first day the wind was strong and the big waves made us sick. The boat sailed far from the coast which at times was barely visible. The sailors have nothing to help them navigate – not even a compass – yet at every moment they know where they are relative to the coast. At night they use the stars for navigation.

The second day there was neither wind nor waves and, with no shade, the heat was terrible. We took plenty of water with us and shared the rice which the other people cooked. With seasickness our appetites receded and we ate little, which wasn't a bad thing as there was no toilet on board. We stood in a queue in the bow...

Once some sharks paid us a visit and circled the boat. Somebody threw them some food which disappeared frighteningly quickly. Later we were approached by a motorboat with four dead turtles. One was transferred to our boat and a sailor immediately set about cutting up the beautiful animal. Pieces of fat from the carcass were hung up on the ropes and later eaten with the rice. The awful smell accompanied us for the rest of the voyage.

That night we experienced an incredible storm. The lightning flashes turned the sea an eerie greyish-white and the rain poured. The sailors set up a large (perforated) tarpaulin over the boom and everybody squeezed underneath for shelter. We were soaked, cold, and didn't sleep much.

At the end of the third day we finally reached our first port of call: Tamborano. The little town's harbour is reached via a river mouth – a risky business due to sand flats – so the onboard dugout canoe was sent out to guide us. When we finally set foot on dry land we swayed like drunks! This little town can only be reached by sea and air as the roads are impassable. There was no restaurant so one of the passengers we had befriended (the only French-speaker) took us to an Indian trader who kindly cooked us pasta. It was our first proper meal in four days.

The next day, thanks to a strong wind, we finally reached Maintirano, to offload our cargo of sugar and soap. It is as isolated as Tamborano, but this makes the people friendly and welcoming and we really grew to like this town.

A drunken sailor delayed the departure and the two girls decided to fly back to Tana. I, being stubborn and having enough time, decided to continue on the boat which, thanks to a very strong wind, reached Morondava in less than 24 hours. The sailors found it hilarious that I had been deserted by the girls but the drunken sailor was ashamed and avoided me!

Batainomby feature the most attractive white-sand beaches on the peninsula. Camping is permitted, but there are no facilities.

The two must-see inhabitants of the park are the ploughshare tortoise, endemic to the park, and the very rare Madagascar fish eagle. Baie de Baly also hosts a large community of migratory birds including the greater flamingo. Dolphins have also been known to trail the outgoing boat traffic.

GETTING THERE Whilst there is a park office in Soalala, you are best advised to visit the regional National Parks office in Mahajanga first to make arrangements. Transportation to and from the national park can be arranged here or through Maurice Bonafous (see *Soalala*, page 383).

TSINGY DE NAMOROKA NATIONAL PARK

Although protected since 1966, Tsingy de Namoroka only gained national park status in 2002. It is 164km southwest of Mahajanga and 50km south of Soalala. The park offers three distinct circuits (each taking 3 hours or more) showcasing the dense sub-humid forests of the west, crocodile caves, canyons and savanna – habitats for an impressive array of wildlife. Among them are 81 species of birds, including the endangered Madagascar teal (*Anas bernieri*) and the crested ibis. The 30 species of reptile include a black-and-yellow striped nocturnal snake (a species of *Stenophis*) endemic to Namoroka, and the locally endemic side-necked (or big-headed) turtle, *Erymnochelys madagascariensis*. Lemurs include Decken's sifaka, red-fronted brown lemur and western grey bamboo lemur, as well as nocturnal species.

Guide fees are 10,000Ar per circuit for groups of up to six. Many of the cave networks in Namoroka are unexplored and unmapped and should be entered only with a guide. Access arrangements are the same as for Baie de Baly (see above).

THE ROUTE NORTH

THE ROAD TO ANTSOHIHY From **Ambondromamy** (where RN6 meets RN4) parts of the road are not in great condition. Heading north, after about 1½–2 hours/84km, you reach **Mampikony** – the centre of onion production in Madagascar. The best hotel is the very basic **Cocotiers**.

The next section of road is the worst; it will take 2½–3 hours to travel the 82km to **Boriziny** (Port Bergé). Here onions give way to tobacco and cotton, and the best place to stay is **Le Monde**. Continuing to Antsohihy is a further 2–2½ hours/133km.

ANTSOHIHY This uninspiring town is a good base for exploration. It is also important for travellers, being at the crossroads of four important centres: southwest to Tana, north to **Ambanja**, northeast to **Bealanana** and southeast to **Befandriana** and **Mandritsara**. It's also possible to travel west by sea or (adventurously) by land.

Antsohihy is 3½–4 hours/217km from **Ambanja** on a good road.

Where to stay and eat

⌂ **Biaina** Thatched bungalows with en-suite bathrooms. By far the best accommodation in town. If you need help organising anything in the region, ask here for Philippe Robinet. €€

⌂ **Vona Vatolampy** (5 rooms) Clean, with mosquito nets. No restaurant but it is next to Biaina. €€

⌂ **Hôtel de France** Cheap rooms in the upper town, by the main square. €

⌂ **Plaisance** Opposite Hôtel de France. Reasonable cheap rooms with a bar downstairs. €

SEA EXCURSIONS FROM ANTSOHIHY Antsohihy is situated on a fjord-like arm of the sea which becomes the River Loza, along which taxi boats called *teftefs* operate. There is a regular boat service to **Analalava**, an isolated village accessible in the dry season by *taxi-brousse* (at least 4 hours) but otherwise only by boat (5 hours) or light aircraft. The best hotels in town are **Malibu**, on the seafront, and **Varatraza**.

Nosy Saba When I visited this island in the 1990s, I thought it was paradise, with coconut palms, curving bays of yellow sand, a densely forested section with clouds of fruit bats, coral and chameleons. This untouched Eden couldn't last, however, and a Frenchman has just built a luxury lodge here called **Nosy Saba Island Resort** (m *032 03 333 02/032 64 600 00;* e *contact@nosysaba.com; www.nosysaba.com;* 🍴) – with its own private airstrip and golf course! There are 27 villas in two sizes, each with direct access to the beach.

Nosy Lava The large island of Nosy Lava ('long island') lies temptingly off Analalava. Until 2004 it was a maximum-security prison, opened in 1911 by the French, housing up to 700 of the country's most vicious murderers and other criminals. Jolijn Geels reports that some of the ex-prisoners have chosen to stay and now act as guardians to the abandoned and decaying prison buildings of which they will give a guided tour on request.

Nosy Ifaho This tiny island off Analalava has a small patch of woodland with some trees of surprisingly large girth. This little sacred forest is home to many birds, flying foxes, and boas large enough to eat the baby goats that inhabit the island. Some fishermen live here too, but as it is *fady* to move fire or light (including torches) after dark, few people stay overnight.

MANDRITSARA

The road southeast from Antsohihy is in good condition. *Taxi-brousses* leave every morning, passing through **Befandriana Nord** where there is a basic hotel and continuing through beautiful mountain scenery to Mandritsara, the cultural centre of the Tsimihety people. The journey should take about five hours.

Mandritsara means 'peaceful' (literally 'lies down well') and was reportedly bestowed on the town by King Radama I during his campaigns. There are several hotels here including **Hôtel Pattes**, a nice little place with excellent food.

Mandritsara also, surprisingly, has one of the best hospitals in Madagascar: the **Baptist Missionary Hospital**. They have a regular turnover of medical students on their electives from all over the world; see box opposite.

BEALANANA

A good road with picturesque views runs 129km northeast from Antsohihy to Bealanana. The town is quite high (about 1,600m), and the climate with ample rainfall allows the cultivation of potatoes and a great variety of fruit.

Hotel Crête has simple but comfy rooms, some of which are en suite, and you can get a good meal at *hotely* **Faniry** just 200m away.

CONTINUING INLAND Heading further northeast you reach **Ambatoria** in less than 1½ hours along a beautiful stretch of road. This small lively town has many shops and is the last stop for the *taxi-brousse* and the last place you can buy petrol. Beyond Ambatoria you'll need a 4x4 and a guide. The next 25km to **Mangindrano** (no hotels) could take three hours, as there are several small rivers to ford.

Every year, thousands of clinical medical students head off to other countries to experience new cultures, practise their skills, and assist local health staff. Madagascar is one such destination and, having one of the lowest staff-to-population ratios and lacking access to essential services in many areas, offers a great insight into low-resource healthcare in contrast to the privileged developed world.

In the mission hospital in Mandritsara, a mix of local Christians, missionaries from Tana and European staff provide essential healthcare, surgical care and community public health services for a 200km radius.

Every patient has their own story. It's not often that doctors have time to listen to all the details, but as students we tend to ask more questions (often trivial or irrelevant to care) to build up a picture of how things have come about. In Mandritsara this led to some amazing stories from local people, both sad and joyful. There were babies with club feet, corrected over months by plaster casts; pregnant women who arrived just in the nick of time for an emergency caesarean section; men whose long-standing hernias strangulated, requiring immediate surgery; children whose pneumonia required fluids; premature twins who could finally go home after reaching a safe weight.

There are people I will never forget: the lone surgeon who got up in the middle of the night to deliver a dying baby (having first driven around the town to collect the theatre staff); the man who, blind for several years, left the hospital in joy without having to hold onto anyone's arm (he'd had a simple cataract removed); and the five-year-old who had a large head wound stitched up after being hit by one of the only cars in the entire region. Such courage both from staff (doing stitches with fishing line) and from patients (recovering from an operation with paracetamol). So many lessons learnt that will no doubt serve me well in the years to come... I hope to come back soon.

It's possible to visit the **Tsaratanana Massif** from here. Lefalle is an experienced guide who can organise porters. One of the great excursions in the area is to climb the highest mountain in Madagascar, **Maromokotro** (2,876m), but it takes at least a week to reach the peak (see box on page 346).

MAINTIRANO

The small western port of **Maintirano** is attractive for people who want to get well off the beaten track. In former days its laid-back, friendly attitude to visitors was largely a consequence of its isolation. The road from Tana is partly improved now, yet a *taxi-brousse* is still likely to take at least 24 hours to travel the 630km. Air Mad operates various Twin Otter routes via Maintirano, so there are flights most days. Boats leave for Mahajanga every new and full moon.

A reader points out that although it appears to be a seaside town on the map, 'it's as though the town has turned its back on the sea: virtually nothing overlooks the ocean'. On the edge of town opposite the shrimp factory is **Chalet du Rose** (✆ 65 022 52) which has mid-range suites and bungalows with air conditioning. **Voanio** is a good budget alternative.

A reasonable road runs from Maintirano to **Antsalova**, 119km away. This town, served by Air Mad's Twin Otter, is the northern entry point for the Tsingy de Bemaraha National Park. In theory there's a route through the park to Bekopaka.

TORTUES ILES BARREN (m *032 04 587 67; www.tortuesilesbarren.org*) This conservation initiative was launched in 2006 and is based on the Barren Islands some 50km from Maintirano. It is a WWF/Swiss-run project to study turtles and their exploitation. Contact them first if you're thinking of visiting.

TSINGY DE BEMARAHA NATIONAL PARK

(\ 22 013 96; e tsingy@simicro.mg or bemaraha@angap.mg; www.tsingy-madagascar.com) Protecting Madagascar's largest area of *tsingy*, this national park is one of the wonders of Madagascar and has rightly been recognised as a UNESCO World Heritage Site. The scenery rivals anything in the country and it's a treasure trove for botanists. At 152,000ha it is also one of Madagascar's largest protected areas.

The awe-inspiring grey forest of rock pinnacles is matched by the care with which walkways have been constructed to allow visitors to see this place in safety. Steps, boardwalks, steel ladders, cable ropes, and suspension bridges form a pathway allowing tourists to explore the *tsingy* in safety.

Amid all this grey are splashes of green from the pachypodiums and other strange succulents (see box opposite) which find footholds in the crevices. And there's plenty of wildlife too, including Decken's sifakas, red-fronted brown lemurs, chameleons and collared iguanids.

The River Manambolo marks the southern border of the park, cutting a spectacular gorge through the limestone. The main point of access is at **Bekopaka** on the north bank of the river. Here is the park entrance to the Petit Tsingy and the park office.

WHEN TO GO Access is currently impossible in the rainy season so you need to plan a visit between April/May and November/December. The heat can be oppressive from October to December; the best months are June and July, which are also good for river travel since the water is higher (but these are the least interesting months to see Kirindy, which is usually part of the package – you can't win!)

GETTING THERE By 4x4 Bekopaka is ten hours/187km from Morondava. Reaching Bekopaka by public transport is difficult, even in the dry season. Most of the hotels and campsites can provide the necessary transport to get to the trailheads. However, if you can afford it this is one place where it really does make sense to splash out on a car and driver from Morondava. But you will need a good vehicle; these are rough roads and stories of breakdowns abound. Most of the better hotels in Morondava organise tours to Bemaraha.

You can also access the park from the north via Antsalova, served by Twin Otter, or down the River Manambolo.

 WHERE TO STAY

🏠 **Orchidée du Bemaraha** (13 bungalows) m 032 07 596 58/032 50 898 79/032 05 714 14; e orchideedubemaraha@gmail.com; www.orchideedubemaraha.com. En-suite dbl, twin & family rooms. Superb food. €€€€

🏠 **Tsingy Lodge** (5 bungalows) m 033 11 507 56; e tsingy-lodge@yahoo.fr; www.tsingy-lodge.com. A recommended Malagasy-run lodge near the park office. Simple, clean bungalows. Run by an ex-guide. €€€€

🏠 **Relais de Tsingy** (6 bungalows) m 032 02 049 48; e relais.tsingy@yahoo.fr or renala.sabledor@moov.mg. A beautifully situated set of bungalows with en-suite bathrooms, overlooking the lake. €€€€

🏠 **Olympe du Bemaraha** (20 bungalows) \ 95 920 15/935 86; m 032 05 216 05; e olympedubemaraha@yahoo.fr; www.olympedubemaraha.com. On a hill overlooking Manambolo River & new rooms at the bottom of the hill. En-suite family bungalows with solar-heated shower & veranda. Restaurant with bar & panoramic view. €€€–€€€€

🏠 **Camp Croco** \ 22 630 86; f 22 344 20; e madcam@moov.mg; www.madcameleon.com. South side of the river. Safari-style tents with beds. Clean, shared toilets & showers. Bar & restaurant. Recommended. €€€

Tsingy is the Madagascar term for the razor sharp pinnacles produced by the surface erosion of limestone massifs by acidic rain. Over a prolonged period, caves have developed beneath the surface, and narrow canyons have been created by the cracking of the rock mass. There are numerous areas of *tsingy* in Madagascar but the Ankarana and Bemaraha national parks are most readily accessible to tourists.

Pandanus and *Dracaena* species are encountered in *tsingy* areas and are superficially similar, with tall thin stems and long thin dark green leaves. However, *Pandanus* tend to have thicker trunks, larger leaves, spikes on the trunk and serrated edges to the leaves compared with the slender smooth leaves of *Dracaena*. *Pandanus* often features a 'tripod-effect' produced by aerial roots.

Pachypodium lamerei, common throughout Bemaraha, is a spiny columnar plant when young but has a pale (almost white) smooth surface and bulbous base when older. Towering trees of *P. rutenbergianum* and *P. decaryi*, a small plant with a smooth globular base, are common in Ankarana. *P. ambongense* has a very localised habitat on the *tsingy* of Namoroka.

Euphorbia viguieri, thick green stems of up to 50cm tall with long whitish thorns and prominent red and green top-knots of floral parts, and numerous tree-like euphorbias with narrow green cylindrical stems, are common in both areas; whereas *E. ankarensis*, short sticks with attractive pale green cones of cyathophylls at the top, is confined to Ankarana where thousands of these plants occur. The low-growing species, *E. aureo-viridiflora*, *E. herman-schwarzii* and *E. neohumbertii*, and the larger species, *E. pachypodioides* and *E. tirucalli*, also occur in this area.

Commiphora spp, medium-sized trees, are common on the *tsingy* and are readily identified by the profuse scaling of bark, usually brown but sometimes with a greenish tinge. Eventually clumps of bark are shed to leave attractive pale-coloured plaques among the scaly bark. *Dalbergia* spp, *Cassias* (with pale green fine foliage appearing in October) and *Tamarindus indica* are huge trees common on the *tsingy*.

Adenia epigea (huge globular caudiciforms with a base up to 1m in diameter) and *A. lapiazicola* are common at Ankarana and *A. firingalavensis* occurs at Bemaraha. *A. firingalavensis* is easily identified by the dark dull green colour of the caudex which usually tapers upwards, but is occasionally spherical. It sometimes lacks a caudex when growing on soil, such as at Kirindy, suggesting that the harsh conditions of the *tsingy* may contribute to caudex formation as a survival mechanism.

Hildegardia erythrosiphon is a medium-sized tree with a buttressed base and masses of brilliant red flowers which are easily seen above the canopy in the deciduous forest. The bright yellow flowers with dark red or purple throat of *Uncarina* spp are also visible from a distance in the sparse forest. *U. ankaranensis* is confined to Ankarana, but *U. peltata* and *U. sakalava* are more widely distributed.

The dry deciduous forests in which the *tsingy* occur are characterised by very high local plant and animal endemism at the species, genera and family levels. While the adjacent grasslands are virtually sterile landscapes because of the ravages of comprehensive vegetation clearing and relentless slash-and-burn agriculture, the microenvironments on the *tsingy* have remained relatively intact and are among the most rewarding areas for plant enthusiasts visiting Madagascar.

🏠 **Tanankoay** (4 bungalows & tents) m 032 02 226 62; e rj_tony@yahoo.fr. Simple bungalows & campsite on the north side of the river. Only squat toilets for campers. €€€

🏠 **Auberge de Tsingy** Book via Morondava Beach (see page 395). Simple dbl bungalows with shared facilities. €

Ⓧ Camping Manambolo Main campsite on north shore of river; by park entrance. Very picturesque in shade of mango groves. Snack bar, shared bucket showers & squat toilets. Tent rental. €

EXCURSIONS IN THE PARK Although there are forested areas of the park with good wildlife, it is the *tsingy* that makes this place special. The park is divided broadly into the **Petit Tsingy** and **Grand Tsingy**, with circuits of widely varying difficulty. The easiest circuit is **Tantely** (2 hours), which gets you among the pinnacles of the Petit Tsingy. This can be combined with the **Andadoany** forest walk to make a four-hour circuit. However, for the most dramatic views you need to do the difficult **Ankeligoa** circuit in the Petit Tsingy and also visit the even more dramatic Grand Tsingy, a one hour/25km drive away. For both of these you need to be pretty fit and have no fear of heights. The best circuit in the Grand Tsingy, **Andamozavaky**, is a full day's excursion involving a lot of climbing and some caves (take a torch). The *tsingy* here is amazing, with pinnacles 50m high.

As a change from sweating in the *tsingy* you can take a pirogue up the Manambolo River to look for fish eagles and visit a cave with stalactites and stalagmites. There's also a lake near the park entrance with a resident pair of fish eagles and waterfowl such as white-faced whistling ducks, Humblot's herons and purple herons.

With the time and effort needed to get to Bemaraha, you should spend at least three days here so you can experience several different circuits. Note that it is *fady* in this region to point with your finger outstretched.

PERMITS AND GUIDES There may be a queue in the mornings at the park office (⊕ *07.00–16.00*). To make an early start, arrange your visit and get your permit the day before. See page 72 for permit prices. Guiding rates vary according to the length of the circuit and size of your group.

FITAMPOHA AND A MEETING WITH ROYALTY
Hilary Bradt

You don't expect to find a prince serving beer in a hot, dusty coastal town; nor to have an audience with a princess in a bar. But Belo-sur-Tsiribihina is the home of the Menabe (Sakalava) Royal Family, and even royals have to make a living, biding their time until the next *fitampoha*.

Every eight to ten years the royal family receives empowerment from the ancestors through this ceremony of washing the sacred relics. The relics are called *dady*, and comprise bones, and perhaps fingernails and teeth. They are stored in an iron box in a sacred house, *zomba*, which you can see in the southern part of the town, protected by a high fence of sharpened staves. In the old days the *dady* would be carried into battle to ensure victory.

Over a beer, Princess 'Georgette' told me about the ceremony, my guide acting as interpreter. She brought out a photo album from the last *fitampoha* in 2004 to illustrate her story. It takes place in August, on a Friday when there's a full moon. From Thursday midnight it is forbidden to wash in the river. Reeds must be collected at midday, from a special place an hour's walk from the town. The collecting and carrying of the reeds is accompanied by singing and dancing. Descendants of nobility wash the royal clothing and hang it on the reeds to dry. Friday is the sacred day, when the relics are washed in the river.

The princess, now 70, told us she was a direct descendant of King Toera, who fought the French in the war of independence, and chose death rather than surrender. The French agreed to educate his ten-year-old son who later became King Kamamy, governor of Menabe and the father of the princess sitting with me in that hot, dark bar. 'But there are descendants all over the world.'

BELO-SUR-TSIRIBIHINA

Where else can you find a royal family serving beer in a bar (see box opposite)? Belo is a pleasant town with several good restaurants and a lively Friday market. It is a natural stopping place *en route* to Bekopaka, and is also the finishing point for trips down the River Tsiribihina (see page 404), so sees quite a few visitors. Tsiribihina means 'where one must not dive' – supposedly because of crocodiles!

GETTING THERE Besides getting here by boat down the River Tsiribihina, Belo is accessible by road. Arriving from the north you have to cross the river by ferry to get to the *taxi-brousse* station for Morondava (30 minutes/8,000Ar).

There is also an airstrip serving twice-weekly Air Mad flights and charter planes.

WHERE TO STAY AND EAT
⌂ **Menabe** m 032 42 635 35/032 42 824 10. Opposite the Mad Zebu restaurant, this is the best hotel in town. €
⌂ **Suzanna, Tsiribihy & Hanida** all have basic cheap rooms. €
✕ **Mad Zebu** m 032 40 387 15/032 07 589 55. Despite its rather surprising name, this is the best restaurant in Belo. Excellent food served on a breezy patio.
✕ **Pacifique** Nr the market. Good food, especially the *crevettes*.

KIRINDY RESERVE

This is one of the most rewarding natural areas in Madagascar and is part of the 125,000ha Menabe protected area. It is not to be

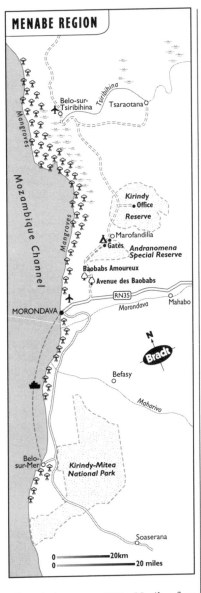

MENABE REGION

confused with the Kirindy-Mitea National Park (see page 399). Until a few years ago its sole purpose was the sustainable 'harvesting' of trees, but despite this selective logging, the wildlife here is abundant. It is one of the few places where you may see the giant jumping rat and the narrow-striped mongoose, and is also the best place in Madagascar to see the fossa. See box on page 392 for more on Kirindy's wildlife.

For a more exciting experience visit the park when the fossas are overcome with spring fever. Jonathan Ekstrom reports: 'They mate voraciously over four days between late October and late November. The timing is pot luck but you would be guaranteed good views. There are camera teams there every year to film it!'

Accommodation is pretty basic but even if you normally dislike roughing it, you should try to stay a night here. Day visitors see far less than those able to observe wildlife at the optimum time of dawn and dusk, and a night-time stroll is usually an exceptional wildlife experience with nocturnal lemurs and chameleons easily seen and – if you are really lucky – a giant jumping rat. On the other hand – if you're *unlucky* – you could have an experience such as readers Paul and Inbal Kolodziejski had on their honeymoon: 'An hour into the night walk our guide started to look nervous, walking back and forth. It turned out he'd lost the track. He started walking in circles and we could see he was beginning to panic – never a good sign from your guide in the middle of the night in a scary forest! After much frantic running around, he told us he must consult the spirit of his grandfather, so he crouched, covered his head, and rocked back and forth. We waited, having visions of sleeping in the forest. After he finished, he didn't look like he knew anything more than before, but at least he'd calmed down and we could talk to him!'

Eventually they stumbled across a numbered tree tag that allowed them to work out their location; perhaps grandfather had sent a signal after all.

KIRINDY: AN ISLAND WITHIN AN ISLAND
Lennart Pyritz

Madagascar is a separate world; an isolated island, home to countless unique species. Against this background, Kirindy is a superlative within a superlative. A number of species live nowhere else on earth but in this remnant of dry deciduous forest.

Monogamous pairs of giant jumping rats – Madagascar's largest rodents, which look like a peculiar kangaroo-rabbit crossbreed with a rat's tail – dig their burrows only in the soft, red soils of Kirindy. A second local endemic is the tiny Madame Berthe's mouse lemur, described less than a decade ago. Weighing just 30g, it is the world's smallest primate. Yet another special treat of Kirindy is the fossa, the island's largest carnivore. Incredibly elusive elsewhere in Madagascar, you cannot fail to see them around the campsite, always on the lookout for scraps. And if you visit in November, you may also witness their unique mating behaviour: a female spends many days in a tree copulating in turn with the several males queuing at the bottom.

Besides the fossa, jumping rats and eight lemur species (from the solitary, gnomish mouse lemurs to the troops of large sifakas), Kirindy is home to about 20 other mammals, including rodents, tenrecs, bats and the endangered narrow-striped mongoose. The majority of the lemurs are nocturnal, but they occur at exceptionally high densities, so you are guaranteed to see some. A night walk is a must! Kirindy is also a hotspot for ornithologists, with about 70 bird species, including the rare white-breasted mesite and crested ibis, vasa parrots, harrier hawks, kingfishers, sunbirds and vangas. Some 50 reptiles and 15 amphibians, as well as an innumerable variety of colourful insects, complete the zoological spectrum.

Kirindy's plants are equally notable, including three species of baobab and the endemic *hazomalany* tree. Several marked nature trails allow visitors to explore the forest vegetation.

Right next to the tourist camp, Prof Peter Kappeler and his team from the German Primate Center have been operating a research station since 1993, where an international group of field biologists studies the ecology and behaviour of Kirindy's fauna. Thus the tourist guides are constantly kept updated by the researchers, and eagerly pass on news of the very latest scientific discoveries to visitors.

Lennart Pyritz is a PhD student at the German Primate Center studying group coordination in red-fronted lemurs.

WHEN TO GO If you are seriously interested in the wildlife of Kirindy you should try to visit at the beginning of the rainy season (November to January). In addition to the fossa mating spectacle, these are the best months to see the giant jumping rat which is more active after the rain has softened the ground (but they tend to keep out of sight during a full moon).

Reptile viewing is excellent at this time of year too, especially collared iguanas and Madagascar hognose snakes. The iguanas seek open sandy spots to lay their clutches of eggs, while the snakes eagerly sniff out these freshly laid snacks, unearthing them with their snouts and swallowing the eggs whole.

Before the rains start at the beginning of December, the forest is dry. With no leaves on the trees, birds are easy to see. Climatically September and October are the best months. December to March is very hot and humid (and the road is often impassable), while in January and February there are terrible horseflies.

GETTING THERE AND AWAY Kirindy is about 65km/two to three hours northeast of Morondava, or 45km/1½ hours from Belo.

Package tours are offered by many Morondava hotels.

WHERE TO STAY AND EAT There are 12 bungalows, some with en-suite cold showers and shared flush toilets, or cheaper ones with shared showers and squat toilets. There is also some dormitory accommodation and camping is permitted for 10,000Ar. A small restaurant serves cold beer and simple meals.

Alternatively you could stay at Camp Amoureux, about 15 minutes south by vehicle (see page 397).

PERMITS AND GUIDES The entrance fee is 15,000Ar for three days; guides cost 4,000Ar per hour (up to five people), or 6,000Ar per hour on night walks.

MORONDAVA

The Morondava area was the centre of the Sakalava kingdom and their tombs (sadly now desecrated by souvenir hunters) bear witness to their power and creativity.

This was evidently a popular stopping-place for sailors in the past and they seem to have treated the natives generously. In 1833, Captain W F W Owen wrote of Morondava: 'Five boats came alongside and stunned us by vociferating for presents and beseeching us to anchor.'

Today Morondava is the centre of a prosperous rice-growing area – and has successfully introduced ostrich farming to Madagascar! For tourists it is best-known as a seaside resort with a laid-back atmosphere. Morondava is the southern gateway to many of the attractions of the western region and is the centre for visiting the western deciduous forest, the famous baobabs, Belo-sur-Mer and the Tsingy de Bemaraha National Park.

GETTING THERE AND AWAY Morondava is 701km from Tana and served by a decaying road that takes between 12 and 18 hours. The road is not bad until the 120km stretch between Miandrivazo and Malaimbandy, which can take six hours. The final stretch is also very poor but has its compensations: it's breathtakingly beautiful, with miles of rice paddies interspersed with grand baobabs picked out by the rays of the rising sun as you make your early morning arrival.

Morondava is also served by regular Air Mad flights and several boats including a twice-weekly ferry to Belo-sur-Mer (2½ hours).

For the route from Toliara, see page 221.

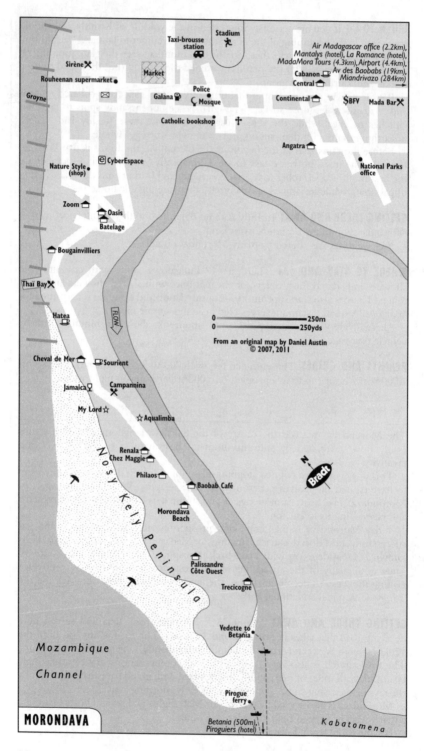

MORONDAVA

GETTING AROUND Baobab Café (see below) rents out quad bikes and the Mada Bar has motorbikes for hire.

WHERE TO STAY Most hotels are clustered along the beach on the peninsula known as Nosy Kely, which has suffered some major damage from erosion. There are more hotels in the downtown area.

Top end €€€€€
Palissandre Côte Ouest (29 bungalows) ⟍ 95 520 22; m 033 15 349 74; e palissandrecoteouest@gmail.com; www.palissandrecote-ouest.com. This swish new place promises the most upmarket accommodation in town. Dbl, twin & family bungalows with AC, TV, minibar, Wi-Fi, safe, hairdryer & en-suite bath. Boutique, pool & spa. All excursions organised; also fishing, boat trips, quad hire, kayaks, tennis & snorkelling gear. Credit cards accepted.

Upper range €€€€
Baobab Café (27 rooms) Nosy Kely; ⟍ 95 520 12; f 95 521 86; e baobabtours@blueline.mg; www.baobabcafe.net. The hotel backs onto the river on the east side of Nosy Kely (rooms overlooking the river can be smelly). AC rooms with en-suite facilities, minibar & TV. Good restaurant. Large swimming pool. Organises many tours & deep-sea fishing.

Chez Maggie (Masoandro) (12 bungalows) Nosy Kely; ⟍ 95 523 47; m 032 47 326 70; e info@chezmaggie.com; www.chezmaggie.com. Spacious bungalows & 2-storey chalets, all en suite with AC & hot water. Lovely garden setting, right on beach; small pool. Excellent restaurant. All local excursions organised & river trips (www.remoterivers.com). Owned by American Gary Lemmer. See ad on page 405.

Renala (13 bungalows & 6 rooms) Nosy Kely; ⟍ 95 520 89; m 032 04 976 88; e contact@renala.net; www.renala.net. Wooden bungalows, surrounded by gardens, with TV, Wi-Fi & en-suite facilities; most with AC. Trips organised; 4x4 hire. Very nice restaurant. Visa accepted.

Mid-range €€€
Mantalys Tsimahavaokely; ⟍ 95 928 47; m 032 42 048 77; e hotelmantalys@yahoo.fr. Just 2mins from airport, en-suite bungalows with lounge, TV & minibar. Swimming pool & internet; 4x4 hire.

Philaos (Filaos) (19 rooms) Nosy Kely; ⟍/f 95 520 81; m 032 05 621 02; e sica@moov.mg. Some rooms with AC & small kitchen; others much cheaper with fans. Very nice; secluded.

Morondava Beach (16 bungalows) ⟍ 95 523 18; m 032 40 213 99; e mbeach@blueline.mg; www.hgi-mbeach.com. A wide range of en-suite rooms at varying prices from fan & cold shower to hot water, minibar & AC. Full range of excursions.

ANT LIONS (KONONONO)

In the reserves of the south and west – or anywhere that trails are sandy rather than muddy – one of the most enjoyable pursuits for sadists is feeding the ant lions. Look for a small, conical pit in the sand, find an ant or other small insect, and drop it in. There'll be a flurry of activity at the bottom of the pit – grains of sand will be thrown up to smother the ant – and it will either be pulled dramatically down into the depths of the pit or manage to escape with its life.

The ant lion will metamorphose into a flying insect resembling a dragonfly. Children in the northwest of Madagascar have recognised the decorative potential of the larvae and call them kononono which means 'nipple badge'. Once you persuade one to grasp a soft piece of skin (such as a nipple) it will hang on for hours!

The name teaches you another Malagasy word: nono, which means 'nipple' or 'breast'. (Think of the sound of a baby sucking and you'll recognise the onomatopoeia.) And from this comes ronono, the Malagasy word for milk – literally 'sauce of the nipple'!

For more on ant lions see the box on page 48.

16

🛏 **Bougainvilliers** (8 bungalows & 12 rooms) Nosy Kely; \ 95 521 63/921 63; e bol_nd@yahoo.fr. Wide range of rooms/prices; some with AC; some en suite. Organises trips. Visa accepted.

🛏 **Continental** \ 95 521 52. Downtown 3-storey hotel with a variety of rooms: some budget & some with AC.

🛏 **Piroguiers** (4 bungalows) Betania; \ 95 526 19; e piroguiers@yahoo.fr. Fabulous bungalows on

stilts in a delightful Makoa fishing village across the river.

🛏 **La Romance** Namahora; \ 95 921 88; m 032 40 708 36; e laromance_restaurant@yahoo.fr. Situated 500m from main road. En-suite dbl & trpl bungalows with TV.

🛏 **Moramora Beach** e moramorabeach@ yahoo.com. At Kimona Beach, 4km up the coast from town. Simple bungalows.

Budget €€

🛏 **Batelage** (8 rooms) \ 95 527 32. A 4-storey hotel with en-suite rooms, half with AC.

🛏 **Trecicogne** (14 rooms) \ 95 520 69. Rooms with fans; some en suite. Good restaurant.

🛏 **Cheval de Mer** (6 rooms) m 032 04 703 91. Rooms are en suite with fan.

🛏 **Zoom** (9 rooms) \ 95 920 59; f 95 522 42. Good-value en-suite dbl rooms with fans & 2 with AC.

🛏 **Oasis** (4 bungalows) Rte de Batelage; \ 95 522 22; m 032 04 931 69; e vazahabe@dts.mad. Bungalows rather run-down but the bar & restaurant are great.

🛏 **Central** (8 rooms) m 032 05 621 02. On the main street. Simple en-suite rooms with fan.

✗ WHERE TO EAT

✗ **Sirène** Quality seafood at a reasonable price.

✗ **Thaï Bay** m 032 40 129 23. Restaurant & tapas bar in a lovely location.

✗ **Mada Bar** On the main street at the eastern end of town. Amazing ice cream & pizza. Kayaks & motorbikes for rent.

✗ **Oasis** Rte de Batelage; \ 95 522 22. Often has live music, drums & reggae performed by owner Jean La Rasta & local musicians. Bike hire.

✗ **Capannina** Malagasy/Italian-owned eatery with always-reliable food.

🍺 **Hatea** Nosy Kely. A small beachfront snack bar.

🍺 **Cabanon** Snack bar with recommended fries & homemade yoghurt.

🍺 **Sourient** Snack bar & 4x4 hire.

♀ **Jamaica** Watch the sunset over a homemade *punch coco*.

NIGHTLIFE There is a discotheque on Nosy Kely called **My Lord**. **Aqualimba** is a large open venue that sometimes hosts major musical events.

MONEY AND COMMUNICATIONS There's a branch of BFV on the main street with an ATM. The most popular cybercafé is **CyberEspace** (⌚ *Mon–Sat 07.00–19.00, Sun 07.00–12.00*), with a fairly fast connection for 70Ar/minute.

TOURIST INFORMATION, TOUR OPERATORS AND GUIDES

ℹ **Regional tourist office** m 032 04 923 50/032 40 766 82/032 04 687 60; www.baobab-madagascar.org

National Parks office Ni Havana bldg; \ 95 524 20; m 032 05 531 26; e ventyodile@yahoo.fr

MadaMora Tours m 032 02 361 20; e info@ mada-mora.com; www.mada-mora.com. Various excursions by truck.

Baobab Tours Based at Baobab Café. Large selection of vehicle & boat trips including deep-sea fishing. Pricey.

Remote River Expeditions e info@ remoterivers.com; www.remoterivers.com. Based at Chez Maggie. Vehicles & multilingual guides.

Catamaran, sailing, diving, birding & other specialist trips. See ad on page 406.

Francois Vahiako Head of the Morondava Guide Association. Based at Bougainvilliers.

Jean Michel Golfier Raherinirina \ 95 921 14; m 032 04 704 53; e hyerna2002@yahoo.fr. Recommended English-speaking guide.

Jean le Rasta Based at Oasis. Recommended by several travellers as efficient. Speaks good English & has a 4x4.

Yves Marohao \ 95 520 89; e codemena@ malagasy.com. English-speaking guide & tour organiser.

AVENUE DES BAOBABS (*www.alleedesbaobabs.org*) This cluster of towering Grandidier's baobabs is one of Madagascar's most famous views. In 2008 the Avenue (together with about 300 baobabs in the surrounding 1km) became an officially protected natural monument. There is now a car park and a fee to pay to visit. A new organisation called Fomba (Friends of Madagascar's Baobabs) is developing the area with a souvenir shop, information office, canopy walkway, campsite and tree nursery. You can support the projects by sponsoring a baobab via their website!

To get there turn left off RN35 about 13km from Morondava, and the baobabs are 5.5km further on. It takes about 40 minutes by car/taxi, or you can come by bike or quad. The best light for photography is just before sunset (it brings out the red hue in the bark) but sunrise is almost as good, and you're much more likely to have the place to yourself.

BAOBABS AMOUREUX These baobab 'lovers', so called because they are a romantically intertwined pair, have become almost as famous as Avenue des Baobabs itself. Turn left 3.5km beyond the Avenue and you will find them a further 3.5km down this track.

MAROFANDILIA If driving to or from Kirindy, do stop at this inspiring village. The **Boutique d'Art Sakalave** is a roadside shop 19km beyond the turning for the Baobabs Amoureux, and 28km from RN35. Begun as a Peace Corps project, the boutique is now a thriving independent business. The quality of the woodcarvings for sale is excellent and only wood from trees that are already dead and collected from community-managed forests is used. The prices are fair and the profits go directly to help the local community and to conserve the remaining forest. The boutique fosters a pride among the local Sakalava for their traditional craft and culture.

Nearby is **Camp Amoureux** (\ *22 636 61;* m *032 02 120 08/033 24 306 55;* e *m.ravaroson@fanamby.org.mg; www.fanamby.org.mg;* €€), with accommodation in the form of seven large sheltered tents, toilets, showers, and a restaurant area. The site was recently opened by FANAMBY and is a convenient base for exploring the area.

ANDRANOMENA SPECIAL RESERVE (*krm.parks@gmail.com*) This reserve just before Marofandilia protects 6,420ha of dense dry deciduous forest including three species of baobab. It is home to 11 species of reptile, 48 birds and seven lemurs including Verreaux's sifakas and red-fronted brown lemurs, both readily seen by day-time visitors. A further five species may be added if you go on a night walk. The giant jumping rat is also found here and there are several lakes with accompanying waterfowl.

Guides cost 5,000Ar per circuit of two to three hours. For permit prices see page 72. It takes about an hour to get here by car from Morondava (hotels and tour operators there can arrange a visit). If you are planning to visit independently, make arrangements at the National Parks office in Morondava first.

KIRINDY This reserve, some 60km from Morondava, is 18km beyond Marofandilia – so it is possible to see all of the above sites *en route* to or from Kirindy. The dry deciduous forests here are of great biological importance, protecting one of the most threatened forest types in the world. Kirindy is covered on page 391.

Jama Festival and marathon Each year, around the end of July, the Jama Festival celebrates the culture and environment of the Menabe region. Around the same time, the Vohitse Marathon is held – a race of over 200 international participants to promote environmental awareness.

MORONDAVA TO TOLIARA

BELO-SUR-MER Not to be confused with Belo-sur-Tsiribihina, this Vezo village and regional ship-building centre 70km south of Morondava is the gateway town to Kirindy-Mitea National Park.

The village itself is a collection of lagoon-side houses shrouded in palm trees; each family keeps a pig which is allowed to forage at night – Belo's mobile garbage disposals. Offshore, nine coral-fringed islands offer excellent snorkelling and diving. Little-known and seldom-visited, the reefs are in very good condition.

There are huge cargo vessels (*boutres*, gaffe-rigged *goelettes*) among the coconut palms at the lagoon, and these are still built by hand, mostly using exactly the same designs as the Bretons used centuries back (see box on page 384), taking some four to six years to complete each ship. Normally the lagoon presents a picturesque setting with *boutres* in all stages of construction, but Belo was hit by Cyclone Fanele in 2009, destroying or badly damaging many of the boats (not to mention the hospital, school and most houses), seriously impacting villagers' livelihoods.

Getting there and away Adventurers can go by pirogue, but it's easy to be overcharged for this uncomfortable trip. The normal price is 50,000–60,000Ar for a three- to four-day return trip. Under good winds it can take six to ten hours to sail to Belo from Morondava, but be prepared to camp overnight on the way. It's much easier to take the *taxi-be de mer* (see page 384), when it runs.

Overland by 4x4 is also an option from Morondava (4 hours) or Morombe (1½ days). Once the river levels drop the road is open – typically mid-June to mid-October. Air Mad has scheduled flights between Morondava and Toliara (sometimes via Morombe or Manja) twice a week each way.

 Where to stay and eat

🏠 **Marina** (8 bungalows & 1 suite) ✆ 95 249 50; m 032 02 803 68; e lamarinabelo@yahoo.fr. €€€€

🏠 **Ecolodge du Menabe** (9 bungalows) ✆ +871 763 963 816 (satellite phone); e info@menabelo.com; www.menabelo.com. Well-run hotel with dbl & twin rooms with solar power in nice garden. Diving, fishing & boat trips. €€€

🏠 **Dauphin** (6 bungalows) m 032 40 310 97. Spacious, clean bungalows with shared facilities. Excellent restaurant. €€

🏠 **Dorotel (Chez Dorothée)** (7 bungalows) m 033 01 863 54/032 04 703 54. Low-price simple seafront bungalows with shared toilet & basic shower. A range of land/sea excursions including transport to Morombe. €

🏠 **Chez Lova** m 033 16 114 43/032 40 192 49; e restolovabelo@yahoo.fr; http://lovabelo.voila.net. Much praised family-run business. Good food too & excursions. €

✗ **Bonne Bouffe** m 033 19 115 85; ① 12.00–20.30. Malagasy food including takeaway.

NOSY ANDRAVANO AND OTHER ISLANDS Belo is the base for visiting a cluster of nine interesting offshore islands, the largest of which is Nosy Andravano, but there are numerous islets. Those to the north are mere sandbanks, but the islands to the south have vegetative cover. Nomadic Vezo fishermen live on the northerly islands for six months of the year. There are shark carcasses and turtle shells left to dry on the sand, and fish and shark fins are salted in troughs. Each of the islands is fringed by coral reefs, although to view the healthy coral you may have to go up to 2km offshore. You can hire a pirogue in Belo to take you around the islands. Remember to bring enough water and food if you intend to camp.

CORAL BLEACHING
Alasdair Harris, Blue Ventures

Climate change, El Niño and the associated increases in sea surface temperatures have resulted in severe coral bleaching events in Madagascar in recent years and represent the greatest natural threat to these systems. Bleaching events are increasing in their frequency and severity and current estimates suggest it could become an annual event within 25–50 years. Dive operators in the tourist centres of Anakao and Ifaty have claimed almost 100% mortality of hard corals in shallow sites.

In addition to large-scale natural threats, local populations have significant effects on the health of Madagascar's coral reefs. Poor land-use practices are one of the primary anthropogenic threats to coastal biodiversity, and large areas of forest have been destroyed by rapid expansion of slash-and-burn agricultural systems. Wide-scale burning has exacerbated soil erosion, which now affects more than 80% of Madagascar's total land area. Raised levels of siltation on coral reefs, in particular in western Madagascar, have already been widely reported, most notably on near-shore reefs close to the mouths of rivers, such as the Onilahy and Fiherenana near Toliara.

There is now a critical need for better knowledge and understanding of Madagascar's marine and coastal ecosystem processes. It is essential to monitor the impacts of bleaching and the recovery rates of coral reefs, in order to incorporate resilience and resistance factors into the future selection and management of protected marine areas.

KIRINDY-MITEA NATIONAL PARK This national park is adjacent to Belo and protects a great variety of habitats, but sees only a few dozen visitors a year. It lies at the crossroads of two ecosystems: the west and the south, as well as coastal mangroves (comprising an astonishing seven tree species), dunes, lakes and beaches.

The two lakes, **Ambondro** and **Sirave**, are particularly interesting since they are *fady* to the local people so have been undisturbed for generations. Local legend tells of many beasts said to live in Kirindy-Mitea, including a half-horse half-zebu, a mangrove swamp monster called Bahisatsy, a wild man called Hako, and a Herculean man who once ripped a gigantic *nato* tree from its roots.

The less mythological wildlife more likely to be encountered by tourists includes most of the species of lemur that can be found in Kirindy or Andromena, as well as ring-tails (this is the northern limit of their territory). 'The park is a veritable kingdom of baobabs with three species and a density of these trees unparalleled elsewhere,' notes the WWF's Mark Fenn. 'The lakes near to Manahy have over 30 species of birds (many rare) and endangered waterfowl.'

The entrance to the park is at **Manahy**. There are two guides who speak English and cost 5,000Ar per two-hour circuit. See page 72 for permit prices. Organise your visit at the park office in Belo or Morondava.

MOROMBE This small, isolated town has reinvented itself for the 21st century. In the 1996 edition of this book Chris Balance wrote: 'Morombe clearly died when the French left, but 9,000 souls remain and they spend their time walking up and down the only street very slowly, shaking hands with each other and discussing the possibility that someone might build a proper road to them someday.' After the total eclipse of 2001, I wrote: 'The citizens now walk briskly up and down the street, shaking hands, and lamenting that the tourists have gone and there is still no decent road to their town.' In 2004, Alexander Elphinstone of Blue Ventures wrote: 'Contrary to Chris Balance, I feel that Morombe is a town that rocks every night of the week. It's the only Malagasy town I visited where the locals are partying

Monday through Sunday. Friendly people, for whom tourism is still a novelty. Beware the over-friendly local girls in bars; unfortunately I think Morombe is a place visited by old French men looking for such girls.'

There is still no decent road to Morombe, but it deserves a short visit. It's an unpretentious seaside town with a pleasant beach, active fishing village and mangroves. There are a few hotels, of which the mid-range **Baobab** (\ *22 427 01*), with beachfront bungalows, is probably the best.

If you continue south along the beach beyond the hotel, you will come to some nice mangroves where you can watch mudskippers. But please respect the local *fady* and refrain from approaching the tombs near here.

Getting there and away Morombe is usually accessible by road from Ifaty, either via the poor sandy road that hugs the coast (179km/10 hours) or the inland route through spiny forest (263km/12–24 hours). The former has breathtaking scenery but *taxi-brousses* only go as far as Salary; via the latter you can get to Morombe, Monja and beyond, but it can become impassable in the rainy season.

By sea, *boutres* or pirogues can be found in most villages.

Air Mad Twin Otter services land at the airstrip irregularly, coming either from Morondava or Toliara. There are no taxis at the airport and it's about a 20-minute walk into town.

'TO LIVE WITH THE SEA'   *Alasdair Harris, Blue Ventures*

The people of Madagascar's coastal villages are culturally, economically and spiritually tied to the sea. Villagers rely on marine resources for food, transport and trade, and often hold ceremonies and erect shrines thanking their ancestors for the bounty provided by the ocean. The Vezo people, located along the southwest coastal areas of Madagascar, are known as 'the people of the sea' because of their semi-nomadic seafaring culture (see page 403).

With some 3,000km of submerged coral reefs, Madagascar's coastal areas are among the most biologically diverse and yet least-studied ecosystems on earth. However, local demand for these resources is rising as a result of population growth and immigration from arid inland regions.

It has been estimated that at least half of all tourists arriving in Madagascar each year visit a coral reef area. Despite the biodiversity, economic importance and vulnerability of the country's coastal areas, Madagascar's coral reefs have been largely neglected from a conservation perspective, primarily because they do not harbour the same endemicity that is seen in 'biodiversity hotspot' terrestrial ecosystems. But the good news is that the people of Madagascar are now beginning to take steps to protect the marine resources they rely upon for survival.

Since 2003, the remote village of Andavadoaka has been the centre of an exciting new movement in coastal management in Madagascar. With the help of international marine conservation group Blue Ventures, Andavadoaka's fishing community has pioneered locally managed marine reserves and fisheries closures to improve the sustainability of the region's fisheries and protect the biodiversity underpinning the Vezo way of life. These pilot reserves have produced impressive results, improving fisheries catches and encouraging neighbouring villages to get involved.

Working together, these villages established **Velondriake**, the first community-managed marine protected area (MPA) in the country. Today, Velondriake (literally 'to live with the sea') is the largest locally managed marine reserve in the Indian Ocean, spanning over 800 square kilometres, and benefiting more than 10,000 people. The MPA incorporates 24 villages surrounding Andavadoaka, and protects coral reefs, mangroves, sea grass beds, baobab forests and other threatened habitats.

ANDAVADOAKA AND AMPASILAVA These two adjacent villages are on a truly fantastic beach 48km to the south of Morombe.

Andavadoaka has been described as the only coastal village in Madagascar whose setting rivals that of Taolagnaro. The area can boast the richest marine ecosystem on the southwest coast, and has therefore become the home for many migrating fishermen (see page 403), as well as a developing tourist resort. The diving is far superior to any that can be found at Anakao or Ifaty. Manta rays, whales, sharks and turtles are regularly seen and phenomenal megapods of up to 500 dolphins have also been sighted in recent years. The area also hosts the marine organisation Blue Ventures which is working on several impressive conservation projects.

Richard Nimmo of Blue Ventures writes: 'Andavadoaka is a remote village but tremendously rewarding as a result; a very different experience from the beach resorts like Ifaty and Anakao. It is a place where you can truly experience local culture and see the lives of fishermen unchanged for centuries. Andavadoaka is one of the largest fishing communities on the southwest coast and on a calm morning the fleet of outrigger canoes sailing out to fish at dawn is a magical sight.'

There are wonderful beaches as well as a rugged and striking arid landscape. And 3km from Andavadoaka are magnificent, stunted Grandidier's baobabs which attract enthusiasts from all over the world.

Ampasilava is 5km south of Andavadoaka.

Velondriake is governed through a *dina* – traditional village laws governing resource use that have been legalised by the state. Malagasy law gives strong enforcement and conflict resolution powers to the local communities, allowing them to levy fines for infractions of the *dina*.

Visitors can find out more at Velondriake's information centre at the southern end of Andavadoaka's beach, where arrangements can be made for visits into the MPA's diverse ecosystems, including guided tours to the baobab and mangrove forests, island visits, whale-watching, snorkelling and diving within marine reserves that protect some of the healthiest coral reefs in the country. Velondriake has a community-managed eco-lodge at the north end of Andavadoaka (see www.livewiththesea.org).

Since 2006, fisheries management models developed in Andavadoaka have inspired other villages to take control of their own fisheries, and locally managed reserves have since been established up and down the coast, with dozens of other villages replicating Velondriake's work over several hundred kilometres of coastline throughout the southwest. The effectiveness of Velondriake's reserves in increasing the size and catches of octopus – the region's most economically important fishery – also caught the attention of Madagascar's national government, which in 2005 passed legislation creating seasonal closures of the octopus fishery nationwide.

In 2009, Samba Roger, a former teacher from Andavadoaka and Velondriake's elected President, was awarded WWF's prestigious J Paul Getty Award for conservation. This highly respected award celebrates outstanding leadership in conservation and was given in recognition of Roger's inspirational role in Velondriake's success. He can be contacted through the Velondriake information centre.

The enormous accomplishments of Velondriake today are a testament to how local management of resources can be both successful and sustainable. Through creating a sense of ownership and pride of marine and coastal resources, as well as enabling communities to take lawful actions as necessary, Velondriake is achieving the primary goal of protecting marine and coastal biodiversity and traditional livelihoods in southwest Madagascar.

16

Getting there Ask around in Morombe to find a vehicle heading south. Hotel Baobab can sometimes assist, as the same family owns Coco Beach in Andavadoaka. The journey by road takes around two hours, or five hours by pirogue.

⌂ Where to stay and eat

⌂ **Laguna Blu Resort** Ampasilava; e lagunabluresort@lagunabluresort.com; www.lagunabluresort.com. Classy, expensive Italian-owned bungalows. Extremely comfy with hot running water. Transfers by 4x4 from Toliara (8hrs) or Morombe. Dive centre. ☸

⌂ **Manga Lodge** \ +881 631 554 454 (satellite phone; only on Sun/Tue/Thu 11.00–12.00). Just round the bay from Andavadoaka. Beachfront bungalows; beautiful view but quite isolated. Food excellent & copious. €€€

⌂ **Coco Beach** Charming Malagasy-owned rustic beach bungalows in a gorgeous setting. Book through the hotel Baobab in Morombe, or through Blue Ventures which is based here. €

⌂ **Chez Antoine** Very clean, multicoloured bungalows at the upper end of Andavadoaka. Some have en-suite shower (but shared toilets); others share bucket showers. €

MIANDRIVAZO

Said to be the hottest place in Madagascar, the town lies on the banks of the Mahajilo, a tributary of the Tsiribihina, and is the starting point for the descent of that river. Supposedly the name comes from when King Radama was waiting for his messenger to return with Rasalimo, the Sakalava princess of Malaimbandy with whom he had fallen in love. He fell into a pensive mood and, when asked if he was well, replied '*Miandry vazo aho*' ('I am waiting for a wife').

Getting there It's a ten-hour journey from Morondava by car or *taxi-brousse*, with one infamously bad stretch of road between Miandrivazo and Malaimbandy. The first 48km out of Morondava is as also quite bad. By *taxi-brousse* you'll be lucky to average 30kph on this stretch.

⌂ Where to stay and eat

⌂ **Pirogue (Lakana)** (6 bungalows & 6 rooms) Great views, but more than one reader has reported bad service & dirty rooms. €€

⌂ **Chez la Reine Rasalimo** Concrete bungalows on a hill overlooking the river. Dbl & trpl rooms with mosquito nets & fans; good food. €€

⌂ **Coin d'Or & le Gîte de Tsiribihina** A long name for a simple hotel with basic rooms. €

⌂ **Relais de Miandrivazo** On the main square. Comfortable basic rooms with mozzie nets. €

⌂ **Laizama** 'A simple but homely hotel (we often found ducks in the shower). Helpful management' (R Harris). €

DESCENDING THE TSIRIBIHINA RIVER This is a popular trip (see page 404) and can easily be set up from Miandrivazo. The guides have organised themselves into the Association Guide Piroguier Miandrivazo (AGPM) which seems very professional. Wherever you are staying, someone from AGPM will find you.

RIVER TRIPS

River trips offer an excellent way to access remote areas of Madagascar. Combining a river journey with standard overland, biking or trekking programmes can make an ideal adventure holiday. Several tour operators offer comfortable, well-catered river journeys and multi-activity itineraries suitable for all ages and interests.

The annual migration of Vezo fishermen from villages on Madagascar's southwest coast is, by many accounts, among the least understood human migrations of our time. It is a mass movement of fishermen and their families, who travel many hundreds of kilometres in search of fertile fishing grounds.

For many, the ultimate goal is the remote, off-shore Barren Island archipelago. There are no trees, no respite from the burning tropical sun, no vegetation at all – and no fresh water. It is easy to see how these fragmented sea-bound deserts, strung out in the vastness of the Mozambique Channel, got their name.

Yet, for as many as nine months of the year, small nomadic communities make this inhospitable land their home. Migrant families, who have sailed as far as 1,000km in dugout wooden pirogues to reach the islands, sleep under the sails of their boats. Their most important possessions are their fishing gear. Otherwise a few cooking pots, a plastic basin for washing and a drum for storing water suffice – they must bring everything onto the islands with them.

Following the seasonal movements of favoured fish species – those that fetch the highest price in local markets – some families will spend as much as two months at sea, making the long journey from their villages in the south.

The legacy of this complex human journey can be traced in the composition of the villages along the west coast. In all of these places, migrants of some kind or another – old and new – have settled. There are many migrations across the entire west and southwest coast of Madagascar. But the journeys from villages north of Toliara to the Barren Islands are among the longest and most dangerous routes.

The Vezo pirogues are battered by the force of oceanic southwesterly winds that charge up the Mozambique Channel. For vast stretches of the coastline there are very few places to come ashore to shelter from the high winds and huge swells.

Scattered safe landing places are hard to find, and days and nights can be spent at sea before it is possible to reach land. Every year there are casualties and deaths; fishermen that set sail in the morning and don't return, and divers who don't make it back to the surface alive. But while the dangers are great, the changing dynamics of this traditional migration make the risk worth taking for many Vezo.

What was once a largely subsistence-based movement to new fishing grounds, has become an increasingly commercialised temporary resettlement of fishermen. The demand on Asian markets for delicacies such as shark fin and sea cucumbers is pushing many of Madagascar's seafaring Vezo to the limits.

A devastating combination of climate change, and over-fishing caused by coastal population growth and industrial fishing, mean that Madagascar's fragile marine resources are in decline. The contest for what remains is tough. The Vezo now compete with mechanised trawlers – some fishing illegally in Malagasy waters.

What was once a way of relieving pressure on historic fishing grounds has become an intense and dangerous pursuit of the shark fin and sea cucumbers that are now the ocean's gold. As these resources dwindle, success for many of the younger migrants is short-lived. The sea has always provided for the Vezo, and money earned there is spent quickly on land, in the expectation that it can be earned again tomorrow. Yet many migrants now return home empty-handed – with only memories of an ocean in which sea life was once abundant and sharks so numerous that it was too dangerous to enter the water. For the Vezo, life is changing, and the very resources they depend upon for their existence are growing scarce.

Christina Corbett is a Madagascar-based radio and print journalist reporting for the BBC as well as various newspapers and magazines (e christina.corbett@gmail.com).

The West **RIVER TRIPS**

16

The most popular are floats on the lazy western rivers: Tsiribihina, Mangoky, Manambolo and Mahavavy. These trips can be done as organised tours or independently.

☞ **WARNINGS!** Some boats are quite shadeless, so take adequate sun protection and plenty of water. Pack your bags to protect sensitive items – one reader's rucksack got so hot in the sun that his camera film and tent both melted inside! If you need to use a sandbank as a toilet, make sure to bury your waste properly. And be certain to take all your trash away with you.

TOUR OPERATORS Most of the main operators listed in *Chapter 4* organise river trips on comfortable vessels with good food, camping equipment and experienced guides. The main specialists in the west are **Mad'Cameleon**, offering canoe trips on the Manambolo, and **Remote River Expeditions**, who take small groups on all the main rivers of Madagascar and have pioneered several new trips. Contact details for both are on page 86.

TSIRIBIHINA This is a three- to five-day trip, starting in Miandrivazo, and most people love it for the wildlife seen from the boat (mainly birdlife) as well as the glimpses of rural life on the riverbanks. In the dry season you will camp on sandbanks, but you will stay overnight in villages if you come in the rainy season.

Being the most popular river trip can mean that you will be camping alongside several other groups, however. Avoid this boat journey in June, July and August if the thought of seeing lots of other tourists *en route* depresses you.

In the dry season you would be well advised to book as early as possible to avoid getting an oversized boat (the lighter craft are snapped up early). Large heavy vessels have to be manually pushed around the sandbars when the water is low.

Most tour operators in Antsirabe (see page 178) can help arrange this trip.

MANAMBOLO On an organised tour the trip takes three days (though five allows for some rest and sightseeing), beginning at Ankavandra. This is a spectacular trip through the untouched homeland of the Sakalava. On the third day you pass through the dramatic Manambolo gorge between towering limestone cliffs, and through the Tsingy de Bemaraha Reserve. The chances of seeing the area's special wildlife, such as Decken's sifaka and the Madagascar fish eagle, are high.

It's rare for anyone to do the Manambolo independently, but Herman Snippe and Jolijn Geels achieved it in 1999. They took a variety of *taxi-brousses* from Tana to Tsiroanomandidy and on to Belobaka. From here they hired a guide to take them on foot to Ankavandra along the Route de Riz used by rice porters. This walk 'took three days and was wonderful' although they warn of a shortage of drinking water in the dry season. Ankavandra is pretty much owned and run by a M Nouradine, who owns the only hotel and river-worthy pirogues. The trip downriver cost Herman and Jolijn about €100, including two piroguiers and their food. In April, after rain, the two-and-a-half-day descent of the river was 'thrilling and spectacularly beautiful'.

MANGOKY The journey from Beroroha to Bevoay (approx 160km) runs through an isolated region in the southwest of the island, with no roads north or south of the river for more than 100km. This calm water stretch offers expansive beaches for camping and many yet-to-be-explored side canyons. The Mangoky passes through sections of dry deciduous forests which are dominated by perhaps the largest baobab forest on earth. There are three species, the most predominant being the huge *Adansonia grandidieri*.

However, this is no longer a pristine experience as large fires to the south in recent years have forced local populations to move closer to the river; small villages are appearing and the effects of their presence are bound to become more evident.

MAHAVAVY The Mahavavy was first explored in 1998, when the rafting team from Remote River Expeditions put in at Kandreho and ended in Mitsinjo. The area is extremely rich in both lemurs and birds (including fish eagles), with large expanses of beautiful forest. Lemur-viewing is far superior to the other western rivers, with plenty of Decken's and crowned sifakas and red-fronted brown lemurs – especially around the Kasijy forest and the riverine tamarind gallery forest between Bekipay and Ambinany.

WIN A FREE BRADT GUIDE
READER QUESTIONNAIRE

Send in your completed questionnaire and enter our monthly draw for the chance to win a Bradt guide of your choice.

To take up our special reader offer of 40% off, please visit our website at www.bradtguides.com/freeguide or answer the questions below and return to us with the order form overleaf.

(Forms may be posted or faxed to us.)

Have you used any other Bradt guides? If so, which titles? . . . .
. . . .

What other publishers' travel guides do you use regularly? . . . .
. . . .

Where did you buy this guidebook? . . . .

What was the main purpose of your trip to Madagascar (or for what other reason did you read our guide)? eg: holiday/business/charity . . . .
. . . .

How long did you travel for? (circle one)

weekend/long weekend   1–2 weeks   3–4 weeks   4 weeks plus

Which countries did you visit in connection with this trip? . . . .
. . . .

Did you travel with a tour operator?' If so, which one? . . . .
. . . .

What other destinations would you like to see covered by a Bradt guide?
. . . .

If you could make one improvement to this guide, what would it be?
. . . .

Age (circle relevant category) 16–25   26–45   46–60   60+

Male/Female (delete as appropriate)

Home country . . . .

Please send us any comments about this guide (or others on our list).
. . . .
. . . .
. . . .

Bradt Travel Guides
23 High Street, Chalfont St Peter, Bucks SL9 9QE, UK
✆ +44 (0)1753 893444 **f** +44 (0)1753 892333
e info@bradtguides.com
www.bradtguides.com

TAKE 40% OFF YOUR NEXT BRADT GUIDE!
Order Form

To take advantage of this special offer visit www.bradtguides.com/freeguide and enter our monthly giveaway, or fill in the order form below, complete the questionnaire overleaf and send it to Bradt Travel Guides by post or fax.

Please send me one copy of the following guide at 40% off the UK retail price

No	Title	Retail price	40% price
1	. . . .	. . . .	. . . .

Please send the following additional guides at full UK retail price

No	Title	Retail price	Total
. . .	. . . .	. . . .	. . . .
. . .	. . . .	. . . .	. . . .
. . .	. . . .	. . . .	. . . .

Sub total . . . .
Post & packing . . . .
(Free shipping UK, £1 per book Europe, £3 per book rest of world)
Total . . . .

Name . . . .

Address . . . .

Tel . . . .   Email . . . .

☐ I enclose a cheque for £ . . . . made payable to Bradt Travel Guides Ltd

☐ I would like to pay by credit card. Number: . . . .

   Expiry date: . . . / . . .   3-digit security code (on reverse of card) . . . . .

   Issue no (debit cards only) . . . . .

☐ Please sign me up to Bradt's monthly enewsletter, Bradtpackers' News.

☐ I would be happy for you to use my name and comments in Bradt marketing material.

Send your order on this form, with the completed questionnaire, to:

Bradt Travel Guides
23 High Street, Chalfont St Peter, Bucks SL9 9QE
☏ +44 (0)1753 893444   f +44 (0)1753 892333
e info@bradtguides.com   www.bradtguides.com

Ankarana Lodge

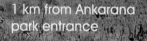
1 km from Ankarana
park entrance

info@ankarana-lodge.com
www.ankarana-lodge.com

Amarina Hotel...a world apart.
Nosy Be...differently.

Ambohiday - Nosy Be - Madagascar
BP 202 HELL Ville 207 / Tel : 261 20 86 921 28
Mail : reservation@amarinahotel.com / www.amarinahotel.com

Air Madagascar
Naturally !

London
Paris

Guangzhou
Bangkok

Nairobi
Moroni
Anjouan
Mayotte

Antananarivo
Mauritius
Reunion

Johannesburg

Coming to Madagascar? Let us introduce you to the warmth of Malagasy hospitality from the time you board your flight. Choose Air Madagascar to bring you to our unique country.

We fly nonstop from Paris Charles de Gaulle airport 4 times weekly, and can offer excellent flight connections for departures from London and many other UK cities. We look forward to flying you to the heart of Madagascar's nature.

Call your travel agent or tour operator for flights, or contact us for reservations and information:

✈ +44 (0)1293 596665

✈ +44 (0)1293 596668

✈ airmadagascar@aviareps-group.com

Air Madagascar
the natural choice

www.airmadagascar.com

You have chosen MADAGASCAR and look for *the best company!*

↣ Think about **MADAGASCAR EXPEDITION AGENCY** "**M.E.A**" to organize :

➢ Tailor – made itineraries (historical, cultural, wildlife in general)
➢ Specialized Tours: * Birding tour
                        * Mammals tour (lemurs…)
                        * Flora tour (orchids, baobabs …)
➢ Beach holidays
➢ Seminars, workshops,
➢ Honeymoon trip
➢ Sea kayaking expeditions
➢ Snorkeling
➢ River cruise expeditions
➢ Trekking and discovery trips

E-mail : mea@moov.mg
Tel/Fax : **+ 261 20 22 261 14**
Mobile : **+ 261 33 03 150 25**
www.tourmadagascar.com

ଓ *Winner of :*
- *International Tourism Trophy for 2006 & International Quality Service Trophy for 2007*

Two amazing places in Madagascar

www.princessebora.com
+261 20 57 04 003

PRINCESSE BORA LODGE & SPA
Sainte Marie

CAFE DE LA GARE
Antananarivo

www.cafetana.com
+261 20 22 611 12

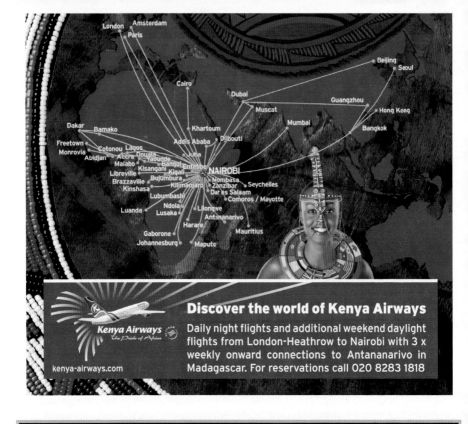

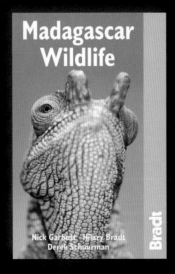

Appendix I

HISTORICAL CHRONOLOGY

AD 0	Approximate date for the first significant settlement of the island.
800–900	Dates of the first identifiable village sites in the north of the island. Penetration of the interior begins in the south.
1200	Establishment of Arab settlements. First mosques built.
1500	'Discovery' of Madagascar by the Portuguese Diego Dias. Unsuccessful attempts to establish permanent European bases on the island followed.
1650s	Emergence of Sakalava kingdoms.
Early 1700s	Eastern Madagascar is increasingly used as a base by pirates.
1716	Fénérive captured by Ratsimilaho. The beginnings of the Betsimisaraka confederacy.
1750	Death of Ratsimilaho.
1787	The future Andrianampoinimerina declared King of Ambohimanga.
1795/96	Andrianampoinimerina established his capital at Antananarivo.
1810–28	Reign of Radama I, Merina king.
1818	First mission school opened in Tamatave (Toamasina).
1820	First mission school opened in Antananarivo.
1828–61	Reign of Ranavalona I, Merina queen.
1835	Publication of the Bible in Malagasy, but profession of the Christian faith declared illegal.
1836	Most Europeans and missionaries leave the island.
1861–63	Reign of Radama II, Merina king.
1861	Missionaries re-admitted. Freedom of religion proclaimed.
1863–68	Queen Rasoherina succeeds after Radama II assassinated.
1868–83	Reign of Queen Ranavalona II.
1883	Coronation of Queen Ranavalona III.
1883–85	Franco-Malagasy War.
1895	Establishment of full French protectorate; Madagascar became a full colony the following year.
1897	Ranavalona III exiled first to Réunion and later to Algiers. Merina monarchy abolished.
1917	Death of Ranavalona III in exile.
1942	British troops occupy Madagascar.
1946	Madagascar becomes an Overseas Territory of France.
1947	Nationalist rebellion suppressed with thousands killed.
1958	Autonomy achieved within the French community.
1960	June 26. Madagascar achieves full independence with Philibert Tsiranana as president, following conservative, pro-French, anti-Communist policies.
1972	Tsiranana dissolves parliament and hands power to General Ramanantsoa who ends France's special position and establishes relations with Communist countries.

1975	Lieutenant-Commander Didier Ratsiraka is named head of state after a coup. The country is renamed the Democratic Republic of Madagascar and Ratsiraka is elected president for a seven-year term.
1976	Ratsiraka nationalises large parts of the economy and forms the AREMA party.
1980	The economy collapses and the IMF is called in. A market economy is gradually introduced.
1991	Demonstrations and strikes. Ratsiraka orders security forces to open fire on the crowds outside the presidential palace demanding his resignation. About 130 people are killed.
1992	Under pressure of demonstrations, Ratsiraka introduces democratic reforms replacing the socialist system, but is forced to resign.
1993	Albert Zafy elected president under a new parliamentary constitution. The birth of the Third Republic.
1996	Albert Zafy impeached.
1997	Didier Ratsiraka re-elected president.
2000	December. AREMA wins in most of the cities, apart from Antananarivo, in provincial elections. 70% of voters boycott the elections.
2001	May. Senate reopens after 29 years, completing the government framework provided for in the 1992 constitution.
2001	December. First round of presidential elections. Marc Ravalomanana claims the election was rigged and refuses to take part in a run-off. This leads to six months of turmoil with two parallel governments.
2002	July. *La Crise Politique* ends and Marc Ravalomanana becomes president.
2003	At the 5th World Parks Congress in Durban, South Africa, President Ravalomanana announces his intention to triple the protected areas of Madagascar by 2008.
2006	December. Marc Ravalomanana wins a second term in office. He announces the Madagascar Action Plan (MAP).
2009	March. Marc Ravalomanana toppled from power in a coup. Andry Rajoelina appoints himself President of the 'High Transitional Authority'.
2010	May. Andry Rajoelina announces plans to hold elections in November, later postponed until mid-2011.

THE ORDEAL OF TANGENA   *Hilary Bradt*

James Hastie, royal tutor in 1817, described one of the more barbaric tortures that King Radama I was using on his subjects: the Ordeal of Tangena. *Tangena* is a Malagasy shrub with a poisonous fruit. This poison was used to determine the guilt or innocence of a suspected criminal. A 'meal' consisting of three pieces of chicken skin, rice and the crushed *tangena* kernel was prepared. The suspect was then forced to drink large quantities of water to induce vomiting. If all three pieces of chicken skin reappeared the person was innocent (but often died anyway as a result of the poison). If the skin remained in the stomach the unfortunate suspect was killed, usually after limbs, or bits of limbs and other extremities, had been lopped off first.

One of the successes of Hastie's influence on the king was that the monarch agreed that, although the Ordeal of Tangena should continue, dogs could stand in for the accused. This decision was ignored by Queen Ranavalona who used it freely on the Christian martyrs she persecuted with such enthusiasm. Sir Mervyn Brown estimates that several thousand Malagasy met their deaths through the *tangena* shrub during Queen Ranavalona's long reign.

The Ordeal of Tangena was finally abolished by King Radama II in 1861.

Appendix 2

THE MALAGASY LANGUAGE

PRONUNCIATION The Malagasy alphabet is made up of just 21 letters (the English alphabet with C, Q, U, W and X omitted). Pronunciation is as follows:

a	as in 'hat'	j	as ds in 'pads'
e	as in 'bet'	s	between the s in 'sip' and the sh in
o	oo as in 'too'		'ship' but varies regionally
i/y	as ee in 'seen' but shorter	ai	like y in 'my'
g	as in 'get'	ao	like ow in 'cow'
h	almost silent	eo	pronounced ay-oo

STRESSED SYLLABLES Some syllables are stressed, others almost eliminated. This causes great problems for visitors and unfortunately – like in English – the basic rules are frequently broken. Generally, the stress is on the penultimate syllable, except in words ending in *-na*, *-ka* and *-tra* where stress shifts forward to the preceding syllable.

Occasionally a word may change its meaning depending on how it is stressed: *tánana* means 'hand', and *tanána* means 'town'. (This phenomenon is also common in English: *desért* means 'abandon', and *désert* means 'a hot dry place'.)

Malagasy words always end in a vowel. Usually this final vowel is virtually silent, except in the case of *-e* which is always stressed. That said, there is regional variation: for example, you will hear *azafady* ('please/pardon') pronounced both as 'azafad' and 'azafadee'.

GETTING STARTED The easiest way to begin to get a grip on Malagasy is to build on your knowledge of place names (you have to learn how to pronounce these in order to get around). As often noted throughout this book, most place names mean something so you have only to learn these meanings and – hey presto! – you have the elements of the language. Here are some bits of place names:

an-, am-, i-	at, the place where	*manga*	blue, good, mango
arivo	thousand	*maro*	many
be	big, plenty of	*mena*	red
fotsy, -potsy	white	*nosy, nosi-*	island
kely, keli-	small	*rano, -drano*	water
kily	tamarind	*tany, tani-*	land
mafana	hot	*tsara*	good
maha	which causes	*tsy, tsi-*	not, none
mainty, mainti-	black	*vato, -bato*	stone
maintso	green	*vohitra, vohi-, -bohi-*	hill, mountain

Thus Ambohitsara is 'the place of the good mountain': *am-bohi-tsara*.

VOCABULARY Stressed letters or phrases are underlined.

Social phrases

English	Malagasy	Phonetic pronunciation
Hello	*Manao ahoana*	*Mano oown*
	Salama	*Salam*
	Mbola tsara	*M'boola tsar*
	Manakory/Akory	*Manakoory/Akoory*
What news?	*Inona no vaovao?*	*Inoon vowvow?*
No news	*Tsy misy (vaovao)*	*Tsimeess (vowvow)*

The preferred word for 'hello' varies regionally, but *manao ahoana* will be understood wherever you go. These easy-to-learn phrases of ritualised greeting establish contact with people you pass on the road or meet in a village. For extra courtesy (important in Madagascar) add *tompoko*, pronounced 'toomp'k', at the end of each phrase.

Simple phrases for conversation

English	Malagasy	Phonetic pronunciation
What's your name?	*Iza no anaranao?*	*Eeza nanaranow*
My name is...	*Ny anarako...*	*Ny anarakoo*
Goodbye	*Veloma*	*Veloom*
See you again	*Mandra pihaona*	*Mandra pioon*
I don't understand	*Tsy azoko*	*Tsi azook*
I don't know	*Tsy haiko*	*Tsi haikoo*
Very good	*Tsara tokoa*	*Tsara t'koo*
Bad	*Ratsy*	*Rats*
Please/Excuse me	*Azafady*	*Azafad*
Thank you	*Misaotra*	*Misowtr*
Thank you very much	*Misaotra betsaka*	*Misowtr betsak*
Pardon (may I pass)	*Ombay lalana*	*M'bay lalan*
Let's go	*Andao andeha*	*Andow anday*
Cheers!	*Ho ela velona!*	*Wellavell*
I have nothing	*Tsy misy*	*Tsimeess*
I don't need it	*Fa tsy mila*	*Fatseemeel*
Go away!	*Mandehana!*	*Mandayhan*

Note: The words for yes (*eny*) and no (*tsia*) are hardly ever used in conversation. The Malagasy tend to say *yoh* for yes and *ah* for no, along with appropriate gestures.

Numbers

	Malagasy	Phonetic pronunciation
1	*iray/iraika*	*rai*
2	*roa*	*roo*
3	*telo*	*teloo*
4	*efatra*	*efatr*
5	*dimy*	*deem*
6	*enina*	*enna*
7	*fito*	*feetoo*
8	*valo*	*valoo*
9	*sivy*	*seev*
10	*folo*	*fooloo*
100	*zato*	*zatoo*
1,000	*arivo*	*areevoh*

Market phrases

English	Malagasy	Phonetic pronunciation
How much?	*Ohatrinona?*	*Ow<u>treen</u>*
Too expensive!	*Lafo be!*	*Laffbay*
No way!	*Tsy lasa!*	*Tseelass*

Basic needs

English	Malagasy	Phonetic pronunciation
Where is...?	*Aiza...?*	*<u>Ay</u>za*
Is it far?	*Lavitra ve izany?*	*<u>Lav</u>tra vay<u>zan</u>*
Is there any...?	*Misy ve...?*	*Mees vay*
I want...	*Mila... aho*	*Meel... aa*
I'm looking for...	*Mitady... aho*	*M'tadi... aa*
Is there a place to sleep?	*Misy toerana hatoriana ve?*	*Mees too <u>ay</u>ran atu<u>reen</u> vay*
Is it ready?	*Vita ve?*	*<u>Vee</u>ta vay*
I would like to buy some food	*Te hividy sakafo aho*	*Tayveed sak<u>aff</u> wah*
I'm hungry	*Noana aho*	*Noon<u>ah</u>*
I'm thirsty	*Mangetaheta aho*	*Mangataytah*
I'm tired	*Vizaka aho*	*Veesak<u>aa</u>*
Please help me!	*Mba ampio aho!*	*Bampeewhaa*

Useful words

English	Malagasy	Phonetic pronunciation
village	*vohitra*	*vooeetra*
house	*trano*	*tran*
road	*lalana*	*lalan*
town	*tanana*	*ta<u>nan</u>*
river	*ony*	*oon*
rivulet	*riaka*	*reek*
child/baby	*ankizy/zaza kely*	*ankeeze/zaza kail*
man/woman	*lehilahy/vehivavy*	*lay<u>laa</u>/vay<u>vaa</u>ve*
food/meal	*hanina/sakafo*	*anee/sak<u>aff</u>*
water	*rano*	*rahn*
rice	*vary*	*var*
eggs	*atody*	*atood*
chicken	*akoho*	*akoo*
bread	*mofo*	*moo<u>f</u>*
milk	*ronono*	*roonoon*
fish	*trondro*	*tr<u>oo</u>ndr*
meat	*hena*	*hen*
pig/pork	*kisoa*	*kisoo*
duck	*gana*	*gan*
zebu/beef	*omby*	*oomby*
sugar	*siramamy*	*seera<u>mam</u>*
tea	*dite*	*deetay*
coffee	*kafe*	*kafay*
salt	*sira*	*seer*
beer	*labiera*	*labee<u>air</u>*
butter	*dibera*	*diberr*
potato	*ovy*	*oov*
beans	*tsaramaso*	*tsaramass*

Note: In Malagasy the plural form of a noun is the same as the singular form.

Appendix 3

FURTHER INFORMATION

BOOKS Madagascar's historical links with Britain and the current interest in its natural history and culture have produced a century of excellent books written in English. This bibliography is a selection of my favourites in each category. Note that many are out of print but may be found second-hand.

General: history, the country, the people

Allen, P M & Covell M *Historical Dictionary of Madagascar* Scarecrow, US 2005 (2nd ed). A pricey (£59) but very comprehensive dictionary of important people and events in Madagascar's political, economic, social & cultural history from early times to present day.

Bradt, H *Madagascar* (World Bibliographical Series) Clio (UK); ABC (US) 1992. An annotated selection of nearly 400 titles on Madagascar, from the classic early works to those published in the early 1990s.

Brown, M A *History of Madagascar* D Tunnacliffe, UK 1996. The most accurate, comprehensive and readable of the histories, brought completely up to date by Britain's foremost expert on the subject.

Clifford, B *Return to Treasure Island and the Search for Captain Kidd* HarperCollins 2003. The story of Captain Kidd and the author's expedition to search for his ship, the *Adventure Galley*.

Covell, M *Madagascar: Politics, Economics and Society* (Marxist Regimes series) Frances Pinter, UK 1987. An interesting look at Madagascar's Marxist past.

Croft-Cooke, R *The Blood-Red Island* Staples, UK 1953. A racy and engaging account of a somewhat unconventional officer's adventures during British occupation in 1942.

Crook, S *Distant Shores: by Traditional Canoe from Asia to Madagascar* Impact Books, UK 1990. The story of the 4,000-mile Sarimanok Expedition by outrigger canoe from Bali to Madagascar. An interesting account of an eventful and historically important journey.

Dodwell, C *Madagascar Travels* Hodder & Stoughton, UK 1995. An account of a journey through Madagascar's most remote regions by one of Britain's leading travel writers.

Donenfeld, J Mankafy *Sakafo: Delicious Meals from Madagascar* iUniverse, USA 2007. The first English-language cookbook of Malagasy cuisine (the title means 'tasty food'). Some 70 recipes interspersed with endearing tales of the author's travels in Madagascar.

Drysdale, H *Dancing with the Dead: a Journey through Zanzibar and Madagascar* Hamish Hamilton, UK 1991. An account of Helena's journeys in search of her trading ancestor. Informative, entertaining and well written.

Ecott, T *Vanilla* Penguin, 2004. The UK and US editions are subtitled 'travels in search of the luscious substance' and 'travels in search of the ice cream orchid' respectively. Among other places, the author visits Madagascar, the world's biggest producer of this fragrant pod.

Ellis, W *Madagascar Revisited* John Murray, UK 1867. The Rev William Ellis of the London Missionary Society was one of the most observant and sympathetic of the missionary writers. His books are well worth the search for second-hand copies.

Eveleigh, M *Maverick in Madagascar* (Lonely Planet Journeys) Lonely Planet 2001. A well-written account of an exceptionally adventurous trip in the north of Madagascar.

Fox, L *Hainteny: the Traditional Poetry of Madagascar* Associated University Presses, UK & Canada 1990. Over 400 beautifully translated *hainteny* with an excellent introduction to the history and spiritual life of the Merina.

Grehan, J *The Forgotten Invasion: The Story of Britain's First Large-Scale Combined Operation, the Invasion of Madagascar 1942* Historic Military Press 2007. The first detailed account of a little-known aspect of Anglo-Malagasy history by a leading military historian.

Grunewald, O & Wolozan, D *Tsingy – Stone Forest, Madagascar* Editions Altus, France 2006. Stunning photography of Tsingy de Bemaraha. Available in UK from NHBS.

Laidler, K *Female Caligula: Ranavalona, the Mad Queen of Madagascar* John Wiley, UK 2005. The fascinating tale of Ranavalona's bizarre reign.

Lanting, F *Madagascar, a World out of Time* Robert Hale, UK 1991. A book of stunning, and somewhat surreal, photos of the landscape, people and wildlife. Text by renowned Madagascar experts John Mack and Alison Jolly.

McCaughrean, G *Plundering Paradise* Oxford University Press, UK 1996. Children's fiction (but good light reading for adults too) based on the story of pirate's son Ratsimilaho. An English brother and sister get caught up in real pirate adventures.

Murphy, D *Muddling through in Madagascar* John Murray, UK 1985. An entertaining account of a journey (by foot and truck) through the highlands and south.

Randrianja, S & Ellis, S *Madagascar: a short history* Hurst, UK 2009. A general history of the country presented chronologically.

Rasoloson, J *Malagasy-English/English-Malagasy Dictionary and Phrasebook* Hippocrene, US 2001. Handy local language guide for travellers.

Parker Pearson, Mike & Godden, Karen *In Search of the Red Slave* Sutton Publishing, UK 2002. An archaeological team goes in search of Robert Drury. An absorbing account which reads like a whodunit, but is equally interesting as a portrait of the Tandroy people.

Sibree, J *Madagascar Before the Conquest: the Island, the Country, and the People* T Fisher Unwin, UK 1896. Sibree (with William Ellis) was the main documenter of Madagascar during the days of the London Missionary Society. He wrote many excellent books on the island.

Spong, C *Madagascar: Rail and Mail* Indian Ocean Study Circle, 2003. Available from Keith Fitton (*50 Firlands, Weybridge, Surrey KT13 0HR*). £12 plus postage. A monograph detailing the country's philately and railways.

van den Boogaerde, P *Shipwrecks of Madagascar* Eloquent, USA 2009. An overview of around 100 notable shipwrecks off Malagasy shores.

Ethnography

Astuti, R *People of the sea: Identity and descent among the Vezo of Madagascar* Cambridge University Press, UK 1995. An academic exploration of what it means to be Vezo.

Bloch, M *From Blessing to Violence* Cambridge University Press, UK 1986. History and ideology of the circumcision ritual of the Merina people.

Ewins, E *Fihamy: a living legend* Blurb, USA 2005. An analysis of Malagasy oral tradition in a Masikoro village, centred on a banyan tree. Available from www.blurb.com

Haring, Lee *Verbal Arts in Madagascar: Performance in Historical Perspective* University of Pennsylvania Press, US 1992. Study of Malagasy folklore including more than 100 translated riddles, proverbs, *hainteny* and oratories.

Lambek, M *The Weight of the Past: Living with History in Mahajanga* Palgrave Macmillan, US 2002. The author looks at the role of history in the identity of the Sakalava.

Mack, J *Madagascar: Island of the Ancestors* British Museum, UK 1986. A scholarly and informative account of the ethnography of Madagascar.

Mack, J *Malagasy Textiles* Shire Publications, UK 1989.

Powe, E L *Lore of Madagascar* Dan Aiki (*530 W Johnson St, Apt 210, Madison, WI 53703*), US 1994. An immense work – over 700 pages and 260 colour photos – with a price to match. This is the only book to describe in detail and in a readable form all 39 ethnic groups in Madagascar.

Ruud, J *Taboo: a Study of Malagasy Customs and Beliefs* Oslo University Press/George Allen & Unwin, UK 1960. Written by a Norwegian Lutheran missionary who worked for 20 years in Madagascar. A detailed study of *fady*, *vintana* and other Malagasy beliefs.

Sharp, L A *The Possessed and the Dispossessed: Spirits, Identity and Power in a Madagascar Migrant Town* University of California Press, US 1993. Describes the daily life and the phenomenon of possession (*tromba*) in the town of Ambanja.

Sharp, L A *The Sacrificed Generation: Youth, History and the Colonized Mind in Madagascar* University of California Press, US 2002. An academic but very readable look at the role of the younger generation in Madagascar.

Wilson, P J *Freedom by a Hair's Breadth* University of Michigan, US 1993. An anthropological study of the Tsimihety people, written in a clear style and accessible to the general reader.

Natural history
Literature

Attenborough, D *Zoo Quest to Madagascar* Lutterworth, UK 1961. Still one of the best travel books ever written about Madagascar, with, of course, plenty of original wildlife observations. Out of print, but copies can be found; more readily available as part of the three-book compilation *Journeys to the Past* (1981).

Durrell, G *The Aye-aye and I* HarperCollins, UK 1992. The focal point is the collecting of aye-ayes for Jersey Zoo, written in the inimitable Durrell style with plenty of humour and travellers' tales.

Heying, H E *Antipode: Seasons with the Extraordinary Wildlife and Culture of Madagascar* St Martin's, USA 2002. Herpetologist Heather Heying recounts her experiences studying mantella frogs on Nosy Mangabe and presents her own view of the Malagasy.

Jolly, A *A World Like Our Own: Man and Nature in Madagascar* Yale University Press, 1980. The first and still the best look at the relationship between the natural history and people of the island. Highly readable.

Jolly, A *Lords and Lemurs* Houghton Mifflin, US 2004. The long-awaited sequel to *A World Like Our Own*. Alison Jolly knows Berenty better than anyone and writes about it better than anyone. This is a marvellous blend of scientific and anthropological fact in a book that reads like a novel. It's funny, engrossing and often surprising.

Pakenham, T *The Remarkable Baobab* Weidenfeld & Nicolson, UK 2004. A follow-up to *Remarkable Trees of the World* by the same author. This is the story of the baobab, six out of eight species of which live exclusively in Madagascar.

Preston-Mafham, K *Madagascar: A Natural History* Facts on File, UK & US 1991. The most enjoyable and useful book on the subject. Illustrated with superb colour photos (coffee-table format), it is as good for identifying strange invertebrates and unusual plants as in describing animal behaviour.

Quammen, D *The Song of the Dodo* Hutchinson, UK 1996. An interesting account of island biogeography and its implications for nature reserves.

Thompson, P *Madagascar: The Great Red Island* UK 2004. A self-published account of travels in Madagascar by a botanist, so of particular interest to plant-lovers. There's a useful appendix on plant names. Available from Amazon or the author (✆ *01588 672106*; e *peterthompson@burwaynet.com*).

Tyson, P *The Eighth Continent: Life, Death and Discovery in the Lost World of Madagascar* Perennial (HarperCollins), 2001. An American journalist's description of accompanying four scientific expeditions in Madagascar, with American, British and Malagasy scientists. Interspersed with extensive information on Madagascar's history, archaeology and natural history.

Weinberg, S *A Fish Caught in Time* Fourth Estate, UK 1999. The fascinating tale of the 1938 discovery of a live coelacanth – a fish previously believed extinct for millions of years – off Madagascar's shores.

Wilson, J *Lemurs of the Lost World: Exploring the Forests and Crocodile Caves of Madagascar* Revised 1995. An amusing and lively account of British scientific expeditions to Ankarana and subsequent travels in Madagascar.

Specialist literature and guides

Bradt, H; Schuurman, D & Garbutt, N *Madagascar Wildlife: A Visitor's Guide* Bradt Travel Guides (UK); Globe Pequot Press (US) 2008 (3rd edition). A photographic guide to the island's most interesting and appealing wildlife, including where best to see it.

Cribb, P & Hermans, J *Field Guide to the Orchids of Madagascar* Royal Botanic Gardens, Kew, UK 2007. Guide to Madagascar's extensive orchid flora; over 600 colour photos.

Dorr, L J *Plant Collectors in Madagascar and the Comoro Islands* Royal Botanic Gardens, Kew, UK 1997. Biographical and bibliographical information on over 1,000 individuals and groups.

Dransfield, J & Beentje, H *The Palms of Madagascar* Royal Botanic Gardens, Kew, UK 1996. A beautiful and much-needed book describing the many palm species of Madagascar.

Dransfield, J; Beentje, H; Britt, A; Ranarivelo, T & Razafitsalama, J *Field Guide to the Palms of Madagascar* Royal Botanic Gardens, Kew, UK 2006. A guide to more than 100 of the native palms with over 180 colour photo plus distribution maps for each species.

Garbutt, N *Mammals of Madagascar: A Complete Guide* A&C Black, UK 2007. This completely revised and updated guide contains photographs and distribution maps for all Malagasy mammals, including dozens of newly described species. Very comprehensive. Paperback; suitable for use as a field guide.

Glaw, F & Vences, M A *Field Guide to the Amphibians and Reptiles of Madagascar* 2007. The third edition of this thorough guide to the herpetofauna gives over 700 detailed species profiles and 1,500 colour photos. Available through NHBS. Also available in Malagasy.

Goodman, S & Benstead, J *The Natural History of Madagascar* Chicago University Press 2004. The most thorough and comprehensive account yet published. The island's geology, climate, human ecology and impact, marine ecosystems, plants, invertebrates, fish, amphibians, reptiles, birds, mammals and conservation written by no fewer than 281 authorities in their field. A hefty 1,709 pages.

Hermans, J; Hermans, C; Cribb, P; Bosser, J & Du Puy, D *Orchids of Madagascar* Royal Botanic Gardens, Kew, UK 2007. A checklist of all known Malagasy orchid species, with complete bibliography, superbly illustrated with colour photos. New edition; pricey (£75) but orchid enthusiasts will not care.

Hillerman, F E & Holst, A W *An Introduction to the Cultivated Angraecoid Orchids of Madagascar* Timber Press, US 1987. Includes a good section on climate and other plant life.

Jovanovic, O (*et al*) *Frogs of Madagascar: Genus Mantella* CI USA, 2008. Laminated pocket identification guide booklet.

Leuteritz, T (*et al*) *Turtles and Tortoises of Madagascar* CI USA, 2008. Laminated pocket identification guide booklet.

Martin, J *Masters of Disguise: A Natural History of Chameleons* Facts on File (US); Blandford (UK) 1992. Beautifully illustrated with photos by Art Wolfe; everything a chameleon aficionado could hope for.

Mittermeier, R (*et al*) *Lemurs of Madagascar* Conservation International 2010 (3rd edition). An extensively updated, illustrated field guide to all Madagascar's lemurs.

Mittermeier, R (*et al*) *Lemurs of Madagascar* CI USA, 2005. Laminated pocket identification guide booklet.

Mittermeier, R (*et al*) *Diurnal and Cathemeral Lemurs of Madagascar* CI USA, 2008. Laminated pocket identification guide booklet.

Mittermeier, R (*et al*) *Nocturnal Lemurs of Madagascar* CI USA, 2008. Laminated pocket identification guide booklet.

Morris, P & Hawkins, F *Birds of Madagascar: a Photographic Guide* Pica Press, UK 1999. I find this well-respected guide difficult to use in the field but it is the authoritative text and photos provide serious birders with the details they need for reliable identification.

Pedrono, M *The Tortoises and Turtles of Madagascar* Natural History Publications, Borneo 2008. Illustrated guide to Malagasy chelonians.

Rauh, W *Succulent and Xerophytic Plants of Madagascar* Strawberry Press, US 1995 & 1998. In two volumes. Expensive but detailed and comprehensive; lavishly illustrated with photos.

Rübel, A; Hatchwell, M & MacKinnon, J *Masoala: the Eye of the Forest* Theodor Gut Verlag, Switzerland 2003. A photographic book on the Masoala National Park available in English, French and German editions.

Sinclair, I & Langrand, O *Birds of the Indian Ocean Islands* Struik, South Africa 1999. The most user-friendly of the field guides to Madagascar's birds. Clear layout with a large number of excellent illustrations and distribution maps for quick reference on the trail. No photos but see next entry.

Sinclair, I; Langrand, O & Andriamialisoa *A Photographic Guide to the Birds of the Indian Ocean Islands* Struik, South Africa 2006. Similar to the above guide by the same authors, but with photos instead of illustrations and bilingual English/French text.

Where to buy books on Madagascar

Madagascar Library (Daniel Austin) www.madagascar-library.com. A detailed online catalogue of 2,000 books & articles. Photocopies of items from the library can be purchased (subject to copyright). The online bookstore (*www.madagascar-library.com/shop.html*) has more than 150 in-print book & CD titles for sale.

Discover Madagascar (Seraphine Tierney) 7 Hazledene Rd, Chiswick, London W4 3JB; ℡ 020 8995 3529; e discovermadagascar@yahoo.co.uk; www.discovermadagascar.co.uk. Seraphine puts out a catalogue of books on Madagascar which are in print but may be hard to find. She also sells Malagasy music CDs.

Mad Books (Rupert Parker) 151 Wilberforce Rd, London N4 2SX; ℡ 020 7226 4490; e rupert@madbooks.co.uk; www.madbooks.co.uk. Rupert specialises in old & rare (out-of-print) books on Madagascar & will send out his catalogue on request. He will also search for books.

Editions Karthala (France) 22–24 Bd Arago, 75013 Paris; www.karthala.com. This French publisher specialises in Madagascar, both for new titles & reprints.

Natural History Book Service (NHBS) 2 Wills Rd, Totnes, Devon TQ9 5XN; ℡ 01803 865913; f 01803 865280; www.nhbs.com

MAGAZINES
All available internationally by subscription unless otherwise stated.

Vintsy (bimonthly; mainly in French & Malagasy but always at least one article in English) www.vintsy.mg. WWF-Madagascar's conservation magazine.

Madagascar Magazine (quarterly; in French) www.madagascarmagazine.com. Latest news in economics, commerce, culture & tourism.

New Magazine Madagascar (monthly; in French) Malagasy music, fashion, art & events.

Enjeux (monthly; in French) e enjeux@netclub.mg. Business, tourism & economic analysis.

Revue de l'Océan Indien (monthly; in French) www.madatours.com/roi/. News & features from the Madagascar region.

Info Tourisme Madagascar (triannually in French) www.info-tourisme-madagascar.com. Official publication of the national tourist office. No subscription; available from ONTM in Tana.

MALAGASY PRESS

Madagascar Tribune (daily in French) www.madagascar-tribune.com

Midi Madagasikara (daily in French & Malagasy) www.midi-madagasikara.mg

L'Express (daily in French & Malagasy) www.lexpressmada.com

La Gazette de la Grande Ile (daily in French & Malagasy) www.lagazette-dgi.com

CONSERVATION BODIES

Madagascar National Parks Ambatobe, Antananarivo; ℡ 22 418 83/415 38; e contact@madagascar.national.parks.mg

Office National pour l'Environnement Antananarivo; ℡ 22 259 99; e one@pnae.mg; www.pnae.mg

WWF Madagascar Antananarivo; ℡ 22 348 85/88; e wwfrep@dts.mg

Wildlife Conservation Society (WCS) Madagascar Antananarivo; ℡ 22 528 79; e wcsmad@dts.mg

Institut Halieutique et des Sciences Marines (IHSM) Toliara; ℡ 94 435 52; e ihsm@syfed.refer.mg

Centre National de Recherche Océanographique (CNRO) Hell-Ville, Nosy Be

USEFUL WEBSITES
General
www.airmadagascar.com Domestic flight schedules.
www.sobika.com Online news and more.
www.madonline.com News, chat and general information.
www.annumada.com Malagasy telephone directory.
www.fco.gov.uk British Foreign Office advice on travel safety.
www.anglo-malagasysociety.co.uk Anglo-Malagasy Society.
www.malagasyworld.org Interactive Malagasy dictionary.
https://www.cia.gov/cia/publications/factbook/geos/ma.html CIA Factbook.
www.madagascar.gov.mg Malagasy government.
www.madagascar-library.com Detailed catalogue of books and articles on Madagascar.
www.wildmadagascar.org Madagascar's wildlife, parks, people and history by Rhett Butler.
www.frootsmag.com/content/madagascar/cdography Malagasy music on CD.

Natural history
www.savethelemur.com Madagascar Fauna Group.
www.durrell.org Durrell Wildlife Conservation Trust/Jersey Zoo.
www.wwf.mg World Wide Fund for Nature in Madagascar.
www.conservation.org Conservation International.
www.parcs-madagascar.com Madagascar National Parks.
www.lemur.duke.edu Duke University Primate Center.
www.sahonagasy.org Malagasy frog conservation project.
www.madagasikara-voakajy.org Malagasy bat conservation.
www.masoala.org Masoala National Park.
www.marojejy.com Marojejy National Park and Anjanaharibe-Sud Reserve.
www.masoala.ch Zoo Zürich's Masoala project.
www.mwc-info.net Madagascar Wildlife Conservation journal.
www.kew.org/science/directory/teams/Madagascar/ Kew Botanic Gardens.

A3

Index

Bold indicates main entries; *italic* indicates maps; NP = national park; SR = special reserve